THE SOCIOLOGY
OF THE CITY

The
Sociology
of the
City

Edited by

SANDOR HALEBSKY

Charles Scribner's Sons   NEW YORK

Copyright© 1973 Charles Scribner's Sons

This book published simultaneously in the
United States of America and in Canada–
Copyright under the Berne Convention

1 3 5 7 9 11 13 15 17 19 C/C 20 18 16 14 12 10 8 6 4 2

Printed in the United States of America
Library of Congress Catalog Card Number 72–1906
SBN 684–13192–7

Table of Contents

Preface

The reader may well approach another volume of selections on urban phenomena with some trepidation. In the last years there have been a plenitude of books offering edited collections of items on urban problems, crises, and protests. These items are a rather undisciplined array, broadly descriptive and with little theoretical content. The approach of this collection is quite different from previous efforts, even though reasonable amount of attention is given to contemporary urban dilemmas. This book, then, is an effort to meet the need for an effective, disciplined, and usable reader in urban sociology and other urban-related studies. It should be of interest to urban specialists, as well as the concerned layman.

This volume has been organized to provide an integrated, coherent, and theoretically sensitive review of many of the principal concerns of urban sociology. An effort has been made to develop a continuity between sections and to offer an evolving descriptive and theoretical statement. The selections and introductory essays provide a summary of the major elements in some of the main areas of urban sociology. Readings have been selected both for their individual quality and for their contribution to a cumulative and developing thematic presentation. The focus is on urban phenomena in advanced industrial society, particularly the United States. Constraints imposed in the attempt to provide a unified set of selections contained within a single volume have necessitated the exclusion of comparative material.

It is hoped that the rather extended introductory essays will serve a number of functions. They introduce the individual items, explain their significance, and help establish some integration or unity among them. They go beyond the few selections that can be reprinted here to provide a review of a number of the principal phenomena and issues in each major area. Through the use of fairly abundant bibliographic references cited in the introductory discussions, they also aide the student in pursuing additional readings. The considerable scope of each essay makes possible the use of the present volume as both a reader and text. The range of topics and literature introduced in our opening essays can also serve as jumping-off points for exploring further the various aspects of urban sociology otherwise not elaborated in the individual selections that are reprinted. The appendix at the end of the volume provides relevant demographic, economic, social, and other data crucial to any teaching and learning experience in the urban area.

A number of themes are present in this volume and have guided its preparation. Throughout, there is a stress on the multicausal and interrelated quality of the determinants of urban society. Urban growth and change, spatial forms, and the distribution of populations and facilities are interpreted as reflecting economic, social, cultural, political, and technological forces and their change. We thus stress an approach of a much broader character than the ecological one, the dominant perspective in urban studies. Cultural and social forms are perceived as maintaining a considerable viability independent of the physical and geographic properties of the metropolis. Another related theme suggests that the individual urban experience is mediated and shaped by the properties of the individual actor and his group. Thus, to a significant degree the urban environment is a construct of the individual's definition of that environment.

The position of the urban community in a far-ranging system of interdependencies is also stressed, and implicit is the need to comprehend urban society in open system terms. Moreover, the character of urban phenomena cannot be properly understood without a perception of the city or metropolitan community as integrated into, affected by, and dependent on, nationwide institutional structures. At a time of considerable metropolitan growth and apparent dominance, the urban community exhibits, somewhat anomalously, decreasing autonomy. These circumstances urge attention to the nature of patterns of national development in order to understand change and process at the local community level. They also suggest the possibility of changing patterns of societal, community, and individual integration. Thus, we urge that the notion of "urban problems" is a misnomer. So-called urban problems are a reflection of nationwide phenomena and derive from the functioning of nationwide institutions.

A collection of readings will inevitably fail to include even the principal properties of its area of substantive concentration. Unfortunately, this is especially true for a field such as urban sociology, whose integrity as a unified discipline or theoretical field cannot be clearly established. However, the scope of the present work and the character of the introductory essays may partly diminish the seriousness of such difficulties. Of relevance in this regard is the increasingly available material—essays, case studies, and readers—in the areas of urban problems, poverty, race relations, modernization, and comparative study, as well as on specific urban phenomena and issues.

All scholarly efforts must to some extent be a solitary undertaking. To a very high degree this has been true for the present volume. Acknowledgments are, however, due to Elisabeth Krabisch and Mary Edlow of Charles Scribner's Sons for their consideration and assistance. In her own way, my wife Ginny showed great patience and sympathetic indulgence as my involvements in this and other efforts seemed to continue without end.

Part I

THE ORIGIN AND
DEVELOPMENT OF
CITIES IN
HUMAN SOCIETY

THE APPEARANCE AND DEVELOPMENT OF CITIES WERE REFLECTIONS OF and stimuli to many changes in human society and man's relationship to his environment. Interpreting these changes requires attention to a complex causal network of interdependent technological, ecological, environmental, social, and cultural properties. Such an analysis suggests that the distinctiveness of cities cannot be perceived merely in terms of increased population, density, or man's altered relationship to his environment, important as these are. Even more notable was the altered character of social processes and institutions and their probable effect on the nature of human consciousness. It also suggests that urban growth and new social forms cannot be seen merely as a response to technological advances, but that such advances were partly called forth by the character of social institutions and that the application of technological skills was certainly initiated and mediated through social forms. It is also important to recognize that there were significant variations in the circumstances and patterns exhibited by the major instances of early urban growth (1, 4). While authorities differ on the relative emphasis to be given the various causal elements, the present discussion seeks a generally balanced, integrated view, with the stress being placed on the processional nature of urban development.

It will be useful to mention briefly some of the principal features in the complex process sometimes referred to as the "urban revolution" (1, 5, 9, 11). The well-known work of the distinguished archeologist V. Gordon Childe provides an engrossing account, especially in *Man Makes Himself* (6), of the role of technology and its interaction with social institutions. The author makes clear that man's increasing ability to master the environment, especially to domesticate animals and raise crops, signaled an immense, potential change in his circumstances. A wide array of burgeoning technical skills, however, and not merely farming and the domestication of animals, provided the potential for an increased food supply and its availability for large concentrated numbers. These technological changes supplied the basis for the creation and maintenance of larger urban communities.

Agricultural surplus and technological advance helped to free part of the population from agricultural subsistence pursuits. These developments laid the basis for a process of role differentiation and an increasingly diversified population. With an increasing concentration of population and continued technological advance, full-time craftsmen and strata appeared in early urban communities. Their activities and goals tended to engender further urban growth, and their skills nurtured the continuance and development of the new urban communities. The new technological advances and scientific knowledge of this period appeared in a wide variety of fields—transport, architecture, pottery, textiles, tools, metallurgy. These advances were the means to service a growing concentrated population, to transport needed goods, to clear the land more effectively, and to store commodities.

It is also necessary to note as Robert McC. Adams observes in his essay "The Origin of Cities" that

. . . the urban revolution was a decisive cultural and social change that was less directly linked to changes in the exploitation of the environment. To be sure, it rested ultimately on food surpluses. . . . But its essential element was a whole series of new institutions and the vastly greater size and complexity of the social unit, rather than basic innovations in subsistence. [3, p. 154]

While in an important sense the development of the ability to produce a food surplus was crucial for the appearance of cities, it was the needs of growing population concentrations that further stimulated advances in agriculture, as well as in transport, storage, etc. The ability to produce more food would mean little without the social and political structures that demanded such additional production and that could secure, concentrate, and distribute it.

Technological advances initiated or made possible certain social changes, such as the concentration of increased numbers, social differentiation, the appearance of complex organizational forms. Yet, these very social conditions also led to technological development as well as determining the uses of technology.

Thus, a crucial element in the appearance of the early cities was the change in social structure and organization. Changing structures of power and decision-making, as well as an increasingly complex and differentiated social structure and social organization, were vital prerequisites for the application and use of the skills and increasing resources of the Neolithic and later urban period. Characteristic of the city as well as necessary for its continuance was the appearance of new social organizational structures providing for the administration of complex political, economic, civil, and military tasks, and the requisite exercise of power. New economic structures incorporated an expanding system of trade and the distribution of an increasingly diverse array of products, the accumulation of resources, and the initiation of enterprise. Thus, the appearance and spread of cities both depended on, as well as furthered, far-reaching institutional change. Clearly, much of this was not a conscious process. Nor, was it a rapid one between clear-cut technological forces on the one hand and cities and the social, political, and economic forms therein on the other. Changes occurred slowly over time (though rapid in terms of earlier rates of change) as a step-by-step gradual alteration of social structures and technological expertise, though not in a uniformly predictable fashion (7).

Concomitant with the development of new social organizational forms, the process of social differentiation, and the appearance of diverse full-time special roles was, of course, an elaboration of the social structure of society. A much broader differentiation and inequality of power, status, and wealth was created. Religious, royal, military, scribe, artisan, and merchant-business classes began to appear and to alter the social and political shape of a previously more homogeneous nonurban society. Not only the uniformity of pursuits but also the integrative basis of community were shattered with urban society. What is especially important in understanding the rise of cities was that ascriptive, communal, corporate, and kin-based patterns of landowning and governance were significantly displaced by a hierarchical and increasingly autocratic social order where a small military–political–religious elite assumed a broad-ranging power that was exercised principally to advance the interests of this ruling elite (1).

The activities of this powerful elite class in stimulating and concentrating a surplus, however, was crucial for the appearance and growth of early urban societies. These dominant societal elements not only exacted tribute and taxes, but more generally ruled the society, oversaw the creation of the massive physical structures that characterized the urban community, supervised the clearing of land, effected tasks of irrigation, provided for defense, and engaged in military conflict. These functions were vital for the survival of the concentrated human settlements that constituted the early cities and were possible only through the creation in the early cities of administrative structures capable of a coordination, communication, and execution of large-scale tasks hitherto unknown. As a result these structures were capable of effectively concentrating and exercising a previously unparalleled amount of power.

The interaction process in which city growth is implicated is not exhausted, though, by the relationship between urban development and technological advances, a changing social structure, and new social organizational forms. Thus, Robert Adams has strongly stressed the close interchange that existed between the city and the broader ecological environment. He notes the need to "deal with city and countryside not only as opposed abstractions on an economic plane but as intimately interacting parts of an embracing cultural and ecological system" (2, p. 41). Adams stresses the existence of differing microenvironments, each exhibiting some divergence in subsistence products. In effect, such environments in the areas where cities first appeared constituted interdependent zones that led to a complementary exchange of products between, for instance, coastal and hinterland areas in Mesoamerica and in the Andean region (5, 14). Adams also suggests the impetus to possible social and scientific advances that such a trade may have engendered. Thus, the continuance, management, and growth of trade and exchange of commodities tended to stimulate the appearance of writing systems, greater administrative complexity. and centralized institutions—another illustration of the type of interdependent causal network among technology, economic activities, social structures and patterns, and structures of power that was suggested earlier.

The urban revolution also represented an immense change in the human condition and personal experience. While a sketch of its subjective character would be hazardous, a major component was probably a societal experience of alienation, in the sense of loss of an earlier pre-urban hunting or agrarian form of existence, including an estrangement from earlier forms of residential patterns, social structure and organization, and relationship to nature. Even in the worship of one's deities there is a condition of estrangement, as a developed priesthood, temple, and court serve more fully as intermediaries and barriers to direct communication with the gods.

Some of the other less subjective properties of change in the individual group circumstances may more easily be detailed. Note has already been made of the decline of a homogeneous communal order and the rise of considerably differentiated and hierarchical elite-dominated social, political, and economic structures. There was a movement, in effect, from mechanical to organic solidarity. Urbanization initiated the long-term historical process of detaching individuals from the comprehensive, familiar, shared networks of social interrelations imbedded in rural folk communities. Further, urban society is marked by a greater degree of functional interdependence. This holds both for the group in its relationship with populations and areas outside the immediate urban community, and for the individual in the sense of a loss of self-sufficiency in meeting individual needs through shared identical labor with others similarly circumstanced. The nature of these changes and new conditions suggest that urbanization and its associated social changes probably increased the problems of social instability, raised conditions of class interest and conflict, and began to lay the foundations for the appearance of new and competing ideologies. At the same time, the early cities began to reveal their historic function as a repository for, as well as initiator and propagator of, much of the advanced technical, scientific, and cultural knowledge and values of the society. The urban community thus becomes the principal source and means of change within the society and even beyond, in the wake of urban-initiated military, trade, and missionary activities.

Childe's essay "The Urban Revolution" (8) provides, among other considerations, a summary of the major distinctive properties of the early cities, properties which are partly explored in the preceding discussion. He also makes clear the considerable distance that human institutions, social structure, and knowledge have moved with the appearance of urban societies. The essay suggests the sharp contrasts that exist between agrarian and Neolithic or precivilized societies and the society and culture of the new urban communities. The new urban society is understood in the quality expressed by the composite of the traits that Childe enumerates, rather than any one or two particular traits. Thus, neither the absence of any property is crucial to defining the distinctive quality of urban civilization, nor conversely does the presence of any one or two traits in an otherwise agrarian society suggest an urban society.

The consideration by Adams and Childe of the conditions associated with the rise of cities is extended by the Sjobergs (17). Their selection provides an illuminating treatment of the importance and influence of power on the spread and decline of cities, thereby adding a vital factor to the causal complex already suggested. A developed power structure signifies not merely military strength, but also the political structure or apparatus to mobilize resources, initiate and carry out state power, and apply military might. Thus, power is important in helping to provide tribute, forced labor, physical security, and open trade routes, as well as for the more general exercise of political and economic rule.

The expansion of power or military control has generally meant a broadening of the economic base and resources of a society. Power was also vital, then as now, for the maintenance of the patterns of privilege and social structure that characterized early urban society. It is in such a context that the Sjobergs note that expansion of a group's domain or power, whether for the sake of conquest, tribute, trade, religious conversion, or other purposes, is a principal basis for the appearance of city life in rural or very lightly urbanized territories. They illustrate this process of the spread of cities from such diverse examples as the patterns exhibited by the Persian, Maurya, and Roman empires. Their discussion also briefly points out the importance of environmental circumstances and social values in the continuance, decline, or appearance of some cities.

Gideon Sjoberg's essay "The Preindustrial City" (15) extends the descriptive and procedural treatment developed to this point and introduces a major concern not yet treated. He continues the theme of the relationship between technological development and urban growth and offers a broad typological and developmental scheme for cities and their growth. Sjoberg's essay derives from his distinction between folk, feudal or preindustrial, and industrial society (16). These societies are distinguished in terms of technology, with each characterized by distinctive institutional and social structural patterns. He thus suggests a uniform set of responses and institutional forms in response to technological level. The folk society is defined by the absence of the production of a food surplus. It is marked by little specialization and is highly homogeneous. The preindustrial society and the cities in it are characterized by a technology based on animate sources of energy, and industrial society is characterized by the use of inanimate sources of energy. Thus, preindustrial cities, reflecting the technology of feudal society, are viewed as having in most instances broadly similar class, religious, familial, political, economic, and ecological structures, among other properties, regardless of distinctive cultural or historical time. Hence, the contention is made that there is a basic similarity between cities of such diverse places and periods as, for example, the cities of contemporary Asia and Africa, medieval Europe, and the cities of the ancient world.

Sjoberg's work is a broad-ranging classificatory and interpretive descriptive scheme that provides—especially in his more extended work (16)—a useful sketch of the major institutional structures and social patterns of preindustrial cities and their differences from modern industrial cities. Thus it helps to delineate the distinctive properties of modern urban centers and facilitates the initial analysis of a broad range of cities, indicating areas for study where deviations exist with his model. It calls attention again, though in perhaps too unmediated a fashion, to the importance of technology and some of the processes of change implicated in the process of industrialization.

Imaginative and broad-ranging as Sjoberg's effort is, the reader should be advised, however, of possible reservations to his work and of the complexity of the phenomena involved. Use of the term "feudal" is misleading. Most preindustrial societies are not feudal, as the concept is usually understood. In fact, the rise of cities in medieval Europe represents in important respects a break with and a disruption of feudal society. Further, as Cox (10) notes, the concept of industrialism does not refer to a social system as does the concept of feudalism. They are not parallel concepts. Sjoberg lacks appropriate attention to the role of mercantile and related economic factors in the development of cities, especially those of medieval Europe (12), as well as to the autonomy of such cities in regard to the larger society. Yet, as Weber (18) has contended, some preindustrial cities, most particularly those of medieval Europe, were distinctively characterized by such autonomy. It may be suggested that this carried some vital consequences for later societal growth. Where the preindustrial city involved a break with traditional society, societal evolution moved in the direction of the modern society. Where there was no such disjuncture or autonomy, such a societal change was in most instances considerably retarded. Finally, even if one grants a certain inherent determinate impetus in technological forms, the use and consequences of a given technology is dependent on the character of the prevailing values and social system. Thus, a more complete and processional analysis would have to modify Sjoberg's technological determinism to take account of the role of social and cultural factors, with a determination of the technological advances these encourage and discourage, and how they are applied and shaped. Discrepancy from Sjoberg's model might, in fact, be accounted for in this fashion.

The *Population Bulletin*'s essay (13) provides a broad descriptive and statistical overview of the growth of cities. It offers a useful sketch of the growth and decline of ancient empires and cities, urban growth in the industrial revolution, the experience of the United States, and the character of worldwide urbanization in the present century. It provides a sense of the general long-term trend toward an increase in the size, number, and distribution of cities. City growth is viewed partly as a response to population growth, often without the availability of sufficient resources and essential facilities and services for the growing urban populations. The growth of cities has generally been marked, the *Bulletin* suggests, by an increasing pressure on the productive capacity of the land, and with the strain on resources that growing population produces today, there is a threat of blight and deterioration. Noting the changing worldwide pattern of urban growth, it points out that urbanization is currently most marked in the underdeveloped nations. In fact, it may be added that these nations have a quite large proportion of the world's urban population, though only a small percentage of these societies are predominantly urban. Though not treated in the present selection, it should be noted that the recent pattern of urbanization in the underdeveloped nations contrasts with the earlier experience of western Europe. The cities of the underdeveloped nations have grown by the transfer of underemployed poor to the cities that have offered little more than the countryside in the way of economic opportunities. The European experience was more a phenomenon of urban growth reflecting a general pattern of industrial economic development, with the cities characterized by expanding economic opportunities. Much of the somewhat earlier urban growth of the underdeveloped societies was also less a product of internal economic development than a reflection of the relation of the underdeveloped society with the colonial power, the cities functioning as an administrative and economic center serving the needs of the imperial power.

The *Bulletin* does note, however, the tendency for the very disproportionate growth of the single large primary city in the underdeveloped society. Cities such as Santiago, Buenos Aires, Mexico City, and Accra provide striking evidence not only of how large a proportion of the urban population may reside in a single metropolitan area, but also of how significant a segment of the total national population the urban area may constitute.

REFERENCES

1. Adams, Robert McC., *The Evolution of Urban Society* (Chicago: Aldine Publishing Co., 1966).

2. _____, "Natural History of Urbanism," *The Fitness of Man's Environment,* Smithsonian Annual II (Washington, D.C.: Smithsonian Institution Press, 1967), pp. 41–55.

3. _____, "The Origin of Cities," *Scientific American* (September 1960), pp. 143–168.

4. Braidwood, Robert J., and Willey, Gordon R., eds., *Courses Toward Urban Life* (Chicago: Aldine Publishing Co., 1962).

5. _____, "Conclusions and Afterthoughts," *ibid.,* pp. 330–359.

6. Childe, V. Gordon, *Man Makes Himself* (New York: New American Library, 1951).

7. _____, *Social Evolution* (New York: Henry Schuman, 1951).

8. _____, "The Urban Revolution," *Town Planning Review,* 21 (April 1950), 3–17.

9. _____, *What Happened in History?* (Harmondsworth, England: Penguin Books, 1965).

10. Cox, Oliver Cromwell, "The Preindustrial City Reconsidered," *The Sociological Quarterly,* 5 (Spring 1964), 133–144.

11. Kraeling, Carl, and Adams, Robert McC., eds., *City Invincible: A Symposium on Urbanization and Cultural Development in the Ancient Near East* (Chicago: University of Chicago Press, 1960).

12. Pirenne, Henri, *Medieval Cities* (Garden City, N.Y.: Doubleday & Co., Inc., Anchor Books, 1956, originally appeared in 1925).

13. Population Reference Bureau, "The World's Great Cities: Evolution or Devolution?" *Population Bulletin,* 16 (September 1960), 109–130.

14. Sanders, W.T., "The Central Mexican Symbiotic Region: A Study in Prehistoric Settlement Patterns," in Gordon R. Willey, ed., *Prehistoric Settlement Patterns in the New World,* Viking Fund Publications in Anthropology No. 23 (N.Y.: Wenner-Gren Foundation for Anthropological Research, Inc., 1956), pp. 115–127.

15. Sjoberg, Gideon, "The Preindustrial City," *American Journal of Sociology,* 60 (March 1955), 438–445.

16. _____, *The Preindustrial City* (New York: The Free Press, 1960).

17. Sjoberg, Gideon, and Sjoberg, Andrée F., "Why Cities Have Developed, Spread and Declined," in *ibid.,* pp. 64–77, 79.

18. Weber, Max, *The City,* trans. and edited by Don Martindale and Gertrud Neuwirth (New York: The Free Press, 1958).

The Natural History of Urbanism
Robert McC. Adams

The underlying bond between cities and their hinterlands is that the existence of the former depends upon their capacity to mobilize and deploy the latters' agricultural surpluses. Perhaps this is a truism, but like all truisms it obscures a complex reality. Does it imply that major steps in urban development have depended upon prior improvements in agricultural productivity rather than vice versa? What meaning can be ascribed to the concept of an agricultural surplus that is independent of the social system in which it is voluntarily brought forward as offerings, forcibly extracted as taxes, or exchanged for other goods and services in an urban market? How much, in fact, of the whole range of interactions between city and countryside is accurately epitomized by a statement of their purely economic relationship?

Merely to ask these questions evokes a less constrictive approach. To understand the origins and evolution of urban centers, including the diversity of their institutional arrangements and physical forms, we must deal with city and countryside not only as opposed abstractions on an economic plane but as intimately interacting parts of an embracing cultural and ecological system.

Granting that such an undertaking may be of some historical or philosophical interest, what relevance does it have today as we grope for solutions to an unprecedented urban crisis? One argument, of course, is that the past continues to exercise a subtle but pervasive influence upon our perception of present realities. In this sense, as Benedetto Croce observed, all history is contemporary history. It must be studied if the patterns of thought and action we inherit are to be understood or even recognized and, in any case, these patterns cannot simply be excised at will from our present lives.

Equally important, the technological destruction of distance that characterizes our epoch is rapidly tending to fuse all of the metropolises of the world into instances of a single type. Hence some thought about earlier cities that were less closely in interaction with one another may help to clarify the basic attributes of cities generally. If we stress the positive and negative features of urbanism as a broad category of settlement and adaptation, features which in some cases have preserved an uneasy balance over millenniums, it may help us also to modify the sense of complete and wasteful novelty with which all too frequently current problems are regarded.

SOURCE: Robert McC. Adams, "The Natural History of Urbanism" in *The Fitness of Man's Environment*, Smithsonian Annual II, papers delivered at the Smithsonian Institute Annual Symposium, 1967 (Washington, D.C.: Smithsonian Institution Press, 1968), pp. 41–55. Reprinted by permission.

In long term evolutionary perspective, the growth of cities very closely followed the introduction of agriculture. No more than four to six millenniums seem to have separated the first reliance on domesticates—for even a minor proportion of the diet—from the emergence of settlements whose size and complexity unambiguously attest to their full urban status. In contrast to the many hundreds of millenniums of man's earlier biological and cultural development, this is a relatively insignificant interval. About the same interval, it might be noted, separated the Urban Revolution from the Industrial Revolution. Industrialism followed and was dependent upon certain concomitants of urban life: the accumulative growth of technology, the elaboration of economic systems permitting the support of craft specialists, and the appearance of a class of entrepreneurs able to mobilize capital for ends not previously sanctioned. It is hardly very useful, however, to say that the latter development was a *consequence* of the former. In the same way, the Food-Producing and the Urban Revolutions also must be distinguished from one another, even while we recognize that the order in which they occurred was a necessary and inevitable one.

What is more important about both agriculture and urbanism is that both originated independently in a number of widely separated centers in the Old and New Worlds rather than diffusing outward from a single source. This complicates the task of generalizing about their interrelationships, in that both similarities and differences between the separate instances need to be taken into account. On the other hand, the fact that there were essentially independent sequences of change culminating in roughly similar institutional arrangements highlights regularities in the processes of change and lends importance to the search for causal explanations of them. A systematic analysis of these regularities is severely limited, to be sure, by the narrowly specialized concerns and inherent obscurity of the early written sources. Prior to the advent of writing —generally, but not in all cases, closely associated with the onset of urban civilization itself—we are confronted with the still more severe shortcomings of a purely archeological record. Given such evidence, the fact that there were indisputable regularities is not as helpful as it might seem. Only an irrepressible optimist would assume that wide consensus and a real sense of closure are soon to be realized on even the basic processes involved.

Within the limitations of our data, conditions antecedent to the first appearance of urban centers can be quickly sketched. Although the beginnings of agriculture closely followed the end of the Pleistocene, they cannot be explained as merely the consequence of a new set of environmental conditions. To be sure, the introduction and spread of agricultural techniques was almost explosively far-reaching and rapid in comparison with the earlier, almost imperceptible, pace of increasing hunting-gathering efficiency and cultural complexity. Yet all the potential domesticates were confined to regions far removed from the marked climatic and life-zone changes associated with the advance and retreat of the glaciers. And such environmental changes as there were differed little from those that occurred repeatedly during earlier, warmer intervals of the Pleistocene. Having crossed some ill-defined threshold of complexity, what was apparently different some nine or ten thousand years ago was man's capacity to rapidly elaborate new responses to long preexisting environmental potentials.

Examples of this enhanced adaptive capacity can be found in many regions of both the Old and New Worlds. Perhaps the widest and most easily observed development was in the direction of increasing sedentism. Particularly favored were environmental niches in which different food resources complemented one another, permitting substantial enlargement of the local group through the full turn of seasons while at the same time reducing dependence upon migration. Technical innovations also played a part. While naturally there were differences from region to region, such improvements regularly included composite tools and weapons: the bow and arrow; ground stone utensils appropriate for carpentry, food preparation, and other uses; and new devices for transport with a potential importance by no means confined to the food quest.

The independent origins of agriculture in the Near East, Mesoamerica, and probably other regions can be thought of as manifestations of these widely occurring developments under circumstances in which the local biota included species of plants and animals that could be domesticated and utilized with the foraging, extractive, and culinary technology at hand. Retrospectively, the line between hunting or harvesting wild resources and consciously planting or breeding them appears to us as a Rubicon, but the portents of crossing it must not have been apparent to those who first did so. In the early post-Pleistocene milieu of increasingly assured manipulation and control of local food resources of all kinds, the elaboration of techniques we deem agricultural must have taken the form of intensified experimentation and a resultant sequence of small, locally variable improvements along already familiar lines.

The major initial effect of an agricultural mode of subsistence was the extension of the zones of settled life far beyond the restricted niches in which the potential domesticates originally were at home. Spreading outward from numerous local centers for particular species, such zones soon overlapped extensively. Agriculture was rendered more secure as a mode of subsistence through this increase in the varieties of domestic resources, and its seasonal cycle and requisite techniques were increasingly differentiated from those for hunting and gathering. The extent of the divergence between early agricultural economies and their precursors, however, should not be overestimated. Given still primitive techniques, the limited caloric value of many of the early cultigens, and almost uncounted natural hazards, the relative security and productiveness that we associate with agriculture was not within reach. As a way of life it was perhaps more continuously demanding than hunting and gathering, with the participation of all but the very young and very old being required in subsistence pursuits. Percentage calculations of dietary intake are possible only in rare instances, but the general pattern clearly was one of a necessary, continuing reliance on a broad spectrum of domesticates, weeds of cultivation, and naturally occurring foods.

With the establishment of a settled, agricultural, way of life, a new set of ecological processes can be discerned. To generalize from the Mesopotamian and Mesoamerican cases in which the data is most abundant, the regions of earliest urban growth were *not* identical with those in which agriculture had originated. One of the essential features of this geographical shift probably was the development of more intensive agricultural techniques for which previously marginal areas now became optimal, although we remain very poorly informed about the nature and timing of major innovations like irrigation, complementary planting of mixed crops to assure fertility, and the plow. Such innovations would permit the formation of greater food surpluses by individual agricultural producers. Perhaps more important, they also freed certain members of the community for at least part-time specialization and encouraged the accumulation of stores with which to meet periodic shortages.

On this basis a trend toward increasing population seems fairly certain. It is difficult, however, to confirm such a trend from the limited and indirect evidence of changing settlement patterns and the minuscule portions of archeological sites that generally are excavated. Thus, all that can be said with confidence is that the frontiers of agriculture continued to expand rapidly. And at the frontiers, of course, we must reckon not only with natural increases in population resulting from agriculture but also with the direct conversion to agriculture of former hunter-gatherers.

Perhaps the most reasonable demographic reconstruction at present is that, while there was some increase in population density generated by the shift to more intensive forms of cultivation, the scarce resource in early civilizations generally remained people rather than land. Accordingly, movement was relatively easy and there was little demographic inducement for the emergence of stable polities. Periodic reshufflings prevented the sharp polarization of society into small groups exercising a tight monopoly of productive resources and the resultant reduction of other groups to the permanent status of dependent retainers. If this is so, other factors must have been the primary motive forces behind the formation of early states: chronic inequalities in productivity between different regions; the selectively impoverishing effects of the numerous natural hazards to agricultural subsistence; the accumulative growth of redistributive institutions once they had passed beyond a certain critical threshold of size; and, perhaps, the military advantages conferred on those types of social organization best able to equip and mobilize large bodies of militia or professional soldiery.

Viewed from the standpoint not of labor productivity but of land productivity, the effects of agricultural intensification may have been equally significant. Means of transport remained primitive; in most of the New World only human portage was available, but even in the Near East the economic use of wheeled vehicles apparently followed the appearance of urban civilization only after a long interval. Hence, long-distance movements were confined to strategic raw materials and luxuries. Those agricultural hinterlands whose surpluses could be economically brought in to sustain the growth of population centers were of very limited radius. Techniques leading to increased output per unit area therefore directly permitted an increase in settlement size.

In short, increased size and density were perhaps the crucial characteristics of early urban centers. Numerous general treatises on cities notwithstanding, there is no evidence that the onset of urbanization was accompanied—much less caused—by rapid, significant changes in the prevailing division of labor. The overwhelming proportion of the population continued for some time to be engaged primarily in agricultural pursuits, as was still the case until very recently with many African cities. Congregated in large settlements, city dwellers were more easily subject to political control, taxation, military service, and corvee labor, but the contribution of specialized, urban crafts to the satisfaction of their primary needs remained extremely small. The small handfuls of craftsmen, scribes, and other specialists found in early cities were, for the most part, in the service of the major institutions and were employed primarily in the production of military equipment and ritual articles required for cult observances.

There was another feature of the newly emergent, intensive agricultural regimes which was central to the ensuing growth of urban societies. The areas in which independent civilizations originated seem to have been characterized by a series of specialized microenvironments for which different, equally specialized, subsistence pursuits were appropriate. Such was the case, for example, with the lateral succession of fishing, farming, and herding as one moved away from the major watercourses in the Near East, or with the replacement of one crop complex by another with increasing altitudes in the Mesoamerican and Andean highlands. The existence of interdependent zones of this type fostered the formation of "symbiotic regions" within which the complementary distribution of subsistence products could be effected. To deal with this new order of complexity, it is not surprising that writing systems were invented or independently elaborated, in turn permitting further increases in administrative complexity and lending formality and continuity to urban traditions. To the extent that these developments contributed to the formation of centralized institutions, the personnel and facilities of the latter could only contribute to the further growth of the principal settlements in which they were located.

The tempo and sequence of these ecological trends in relation to the onset of urban life still is largely obscure. There are at least a few well-documented cases to suggest that the initial growth of cities was generally rapid, sometimes even being the outcome of conscious policies applied within a single generation. Hence the achievement of the forms of civilized, urban life was relatively sudden; nevertheless, the fashioning and consolidation of the base that could support an urban superstructure may have been a much longer process. Almost certainly, for example, there were mechanisms of interzonal exchange and redistribution available and functioning on some level before new urban elites arose to redirect and administer them. To judge from comparable societies studied by recent ethnographers, somewhat similar purposes can be served by a variety of devices that do not presuppose the submission of scattered communities of agriculturalists to some paramount leadership. Bride-wealth payments linking exogamous, differently specialized communities are among such devices. So also are cycles of cult observances in shifting localities, which provide not only for the movement of religious ideas and pilgrims but also of goods.

In addition, there was undeniably at least some ordinary trade in items that were hardly luxuries long antedating the appearance of cities; obsidian for the manufacture of finely chipped stone tools is a widely occurring case in point. "Trade" in this sense, however, is a gross, essentially uninformative term that does nothing to clarify the relationship between the participating prehistoric communities or the manner in which such relationships were affected by the subsequent rise of urban centers. Fortunately, recent advances in archeological methodology suggest that we can soon move beyond the mere recognition of exotic materials to a quantitative analysis of some of the components of social behavior by which that material was circulated.

It may be useful at this point to restate the ecological role of early cities at the time of their origins. They seem fairly generally to have functioned as junction points or nodes in the appropriation and redistribution of agricultural surpluses. In addition, they provided a permanent base for the operation of new institutions that no longer merely mediated but, instead, authoritatively administered the interrelationships between specialized producers occupying adjacent econiches. Such institutions were embedded in realms of cultural meaning not confined to their primary ecological functions, including attempts on many levels to unify, symbolize, and stabilize the newly emergent, urban-dominated social patterns. Cities became focal points not merely for the safe storage of surpluses prior to their deployment, but for conspicuous expenditures for public building programs, for the maintenance of elites in luxurious surroundings, and for the enhancement of military power. With the concentration of wealth, early urban centers became both proponents of expansionism and powerful incentives for external attack. Massive fortifications accordingly became one of their dominant architectural forms.

A summary like the foregoing is necessarily abstract and generalized. It emphasizes recurrent features at the expense of known variations and lacunae in the evidence, hence perhaps seeming to imply that early cities everywhere were the outcome of a tightly interconnected, uniform set of causal processes. It may be taken to imply further that the superior adaptive potential of the city led in some direct fashion to its origin and contributed decisively to the spread of urbanism. What could be more advantageous, after all, than state-protected, rationally allocated stores of surpluses to compensate for year-to-year fluctuations in harvest? Or centralized investment in and control of irrigation canals and other facilities for intensive agriculture and the improvement of transport?

Although perhaps not incorrect at some fairly high level of abstraction, both implications are misleading. The subsequent growth and spread of cities cannot be understood as the irresistible sweep of a set of innovations which were obviously superior in socioeconomic terms. Instead, the process by which cities assumed the ecologically dominant role we now associate with them consisted of a shifting, complex, quite unstable, adjustment of environmental, economic, technological, political, and even ideological factors. Cumulatively, of course, the trend was irrevocably toward urbanism, but contained within this worldwide trend extending over millenniums were repeated advances and reverses at the local level. To understand this irregularity we must consider not just later increments in urbanism but also some of the attendant costs and dangers.

Perhaps the most informative single index of the subsequent evolution of cities is the increase in size. Early direct testimony on this is notoriously untrustworthy, so that historical demographers must depend on the convergence of secondary, approximate, probabilistic lines of reasoning. Even the order of magnitude of the population of particular cities often remains a matter of sharp debate, although there is broad agreement that older claims of immense size must be viewed with increasing skepticism. As a generalization for the Old World, probably no city was larger than several tens of thousands of inhabitants before the first millennium B.C., while by the Middle Ages cities of several hundreds of thousands occurred at intervals in the Mediterranean basin and across Asia to China. The picture is somewhat more obscure in the civilized areas of the aboriginal New World; the earlier stage certainly had been attained by not long after the time of Christ, while the onset of the second stage may have been close at hand when the independent sequence of development was ended by the Spanish Conquest.

Undoubtedly these parallel, decisive increases reflect improvements in the subsistence economy, but it is important to note that any such improvements rested on technical innovations only to a limited degree. In the aboriginal New World, in fact, crop complexes and methods of cultivation both seem to have remained remarkably stable. The Andean area offers partial exceptions, but at least in Mesoamerica there is no evidence for any significant advance in the technology or organization of agriculture from remote precivilized times until the flourishing urban societies so vividly described by the Spaniards.

To be sure, some new, specialized crops like sugar and silk were brought under cultivation in the Old World, many of them for the first time of a highly labor-intensive character suitable to increasing populations. With the exception of the westward spread of irrigated ricelands, however, few of the new items became subsistence staples. The harnessing of wind and water power for rotary movement was important in the spread of agriculture into arid areas and in reducing the costs of milling and similar operations, but its direct contribution to urban growth was hardly a major one.

The introduction of iron presents a somewhat more complicated case, although not a basically dissimilar one. With the rapidly spreading adoption of iron during the first millennium B.C., into the hands of agriculturalists came implements that were not only more durable than bronze but that could be produced much more cheaply and from more widely scattered bodies of ore. The availability of iron, however, led only very slowly to the development of more efficient tools and processing techniques. Probably its primary effects on urban life were associated instead with its low cost. Iron tools now became available to ordinary workmen deployed in large numbers on major public works directed toward the extension and improvement of agricultural lands. Partly as a consequence, the intensity of agriculture in the neighborhood of cities was increased through the formation of encircling "green belts" of irrigated, continuously cultivated orchards and truck gardens. Some areas of formerly limited agricultural potential also were transformed, including the Iranian plateau and parts of North Africa, with corresponding effects upon their political importance.

If the immediate hinterlands of cities were not converted by this process into metropolitan areas in the modern sense, they were nonetheless integrated into an urban-centered society to an unprecedented degree. To take only economic features for which the evidence is least ambiguous and most durable, there was a—not steady but, on the whole, cumulative—reduction in the self-sufficiency of even outlying peasant communities. To the eye of the reconnoitering archeologist, for example, a litter of iron, glazed pottery sherds, glass, and fired brick fragments, immediately distinguishes Near Eastern sites of all sizes occupied after roughly the time of Alexander from any earlier ones. All of these remains were the products of urban specialists which, after more than a millennium of having been largely restricted to official or luxury use, passed into general circulation with dramatic suddenness and irreversible effect. Coinage was perhaps the most important of the widely circulated new features, and it was also the only recent innovation among them. Its crucial significance lay not in any contribution to advancing technology but in the networks of economic interrelations that it facilitated: it was through these networks that other craft products reached wider, peasant markets.

As this suggests, the increase in urban size by a full order of magnitude was primarily a reflection of developments in political economy rather than in technology. The earlier, territorially consolidated unit was the city state, which either maintained itself as an island in a barbarian sea or else contended periodically with neighboring units of the same kind within a framework of regional rivalries and ephemeral alliances. In time, larger administrative units —of which the Third Dynasty of Ur and the Dynasty of Hammurabi in Babylon (and perhaps the Egyptian Old Kingdom, at an even earlier period) are good examples—began to make their appearance. Wider conquests were extended outward from a firmly pacified if not unified heartland, until, after a few generations, the thinness of the centralized administrative veneer became apparent. Then the old fissures reopened in the home territory and the assertions of hegemony over distant areas gradually were dropped.

By contrast, the great cities of classical and later times characteristically came into being as components of large, relatively long-lived, continental empires. Such cities were creatures of strong patrimonial regimes to a degree quite unmatched earlier. They directly depended on royal largesse for the support of the now predominant proportion of artisans, tradesmen, soldiers, and petty officials. Not infrequently, royal intervention was even more tangibly reflected in their planned, overall layouts.

As part of a wider spectrum of efforts to maintain or enlarge the central power and to prevent its devolution into the hands of a newly emergent landed nobility, these later cities were founded, manipulated, and (at times) even abandoned almost by royal whim. Behind numerous instances of capricious exercise of power, however, lay conscious policies of shifting populations to destroy parochial loyalties and of strengthening the administrative fabric over the whole realm. Unprecedented emphasis was attached to improvements in communications, with the development of "Royal Roads," post routes, and local garrisons and caravansaries to assure security of movement. With the relative success of these policies for long periods, warfare for the most part could be limited to distant frontiers with barbarians or to zones of contention with rival powers of like magnitude. This, in turn, permitted more intensive, long-range development of the vital central regions of empires, aided by the flow of refugees and captives inward from the frontiers.

Under circumstances like these, the ecology of cities no longer can be understood in terms of their immediate sustaining areas. By medieval times, many individual Old World cities were widely identified with particular specialized products—Damascus blades, Mosul muslins, Bokhara carpets, Venetian silks—confirming the existence of highly institutionalized, long-distance trade for which the stimulus and setting had become a genuinely international one. Rome in the first century A.D. was probably exceptional, in that a third of its wheat had to be shipped in from Egypt. To judge from studies of relatively recent examples of the same kind, virtually all of the necessary food supplies for most other preindustrial cities continued to be drawn from very limited, adjacent areas. But the raison d'être of all these imperial centers, as well as the explanation for the periodic rise and decline in their fortunes, lay in the policies and problems of patrimonial regimes which, like the cities themselves, had attained a new order of size.

We must return, however, to the price that had to be paid for these achievements. To begin with, for all but the most recent chapter of urban history, cities have not been sources of population growth but of severe population loss. It is uncertain whether preindustrial urban life was normally associated with lowered birth rates, but there is no doubt that urban mortality rates were much higher than rural ones prior to the very recent introduction of effective measures for public health. The increased density and aggregate size of settlement, in relation to primitive techniques of sanitation and other means of controlling vectors of disease, could only lead not just to greater periodic losses in epidemics but also to heightened mortality, particularly of infants and children, as a regularly prevailing feature. The growth of cities, and even their continuing existence, accordingly was always dependent on an inflow of population from rural districts and smaller towns.

The founding or expansion of cities that was repeatedly boasted of by strong rulers in antiquity could have been either an expression of the accelerated movement of urban immigrants in search of the prosperity that followed in the wake of conquest, or a consequence of the extension of more coercive forms of royal control over the countryside. Neither alternative substantially affected the urban-rural differences in mortality rates, except in the sense that exceptionally short-sighted and acquisitive regimes could compensate to a degree by substantially depressing the living standards of the rural peasantry. Attitudes of conscious and sustained encouragement for rural well-being on the whole are distinguished in historical records by their rarity, seldom occurring except at times of unusual political stability. Under most circumstances, there were practical difficulties in drawing off so large a surplus that the agricultural producers were reduced to or below a bare subsistence margin. But it is noteworthy that, at least in the Near East, general movement in time of famine was toward cities and not away from them. With absentee landlords and predatory officials, as well as with sustained high levels of banditry and periodic nomadic incursions, it would appear from this that reserves of food adequate to meet prolonged crises seldom could be accumulated in smaller settlements.

While the concentration of surpluses in urban centers brought some relative immunity from fluctuations in the harvest, this boon frequently was accompanied by an exposure to new perils. Traditions associated with urban institutions have a force and continuity of their own, limiting the mobility of city populations in response to disastrous changes in local environmental conditions. Any tendency toward increased full-time specialization in non-agricultural pursuits, of course, would have the same effect. Intensified urban pressure on agricultural resources can, and in some important cases evidently did, lead to soil exhaustion or, as a consequence of over-irrigation, to crippling increases in soil salinity. The substitution of monocrop cultivation for diversified agriculture, apparently as a dependent rural extension of urban, market-oriented economies, is widely known for its attendant impoverishment of both the land and the husbandman. Policies of excessive taxation made necessary by overextended urban establishments sometimes led to the abandonment of villages and farmlands, further accentuating the imbalance between rural capacities and urban demands.

There were drawbacks even where the positive contribution of the state seems most apparent. For example, the substitution of large-scale, state-run irrigation works for smaller, locally maintained systems enlarged the agricultural base on which cities could depend and placed new powers of control in the hands of their elites. However, because such systems were beyond the capacity of local agriculturalists to administer and maintain, they were dependent on the—altogether unlikely—permanent conjunction of urban economic strength, political stability, and favorable attitudes toward rural investment. Moreover, the truly large-scale systems of the last twenty-five hundred years or so, through the increased supplies of water they assured and their disruption of natural drainage patterns, vastly increased the dangers of salinization and consequent land abandonment.

What all of these processes have in common is the increased systemic fragility to which they led. Perhaps the clearest, most dismal reflection of that fragility was that both rural and urban population curves apparently were characterized by a succession of marked peaks and troughs, quite in contrast to the steady and rising curves of the last few centuries. The approach of an urban ecological climax, in other words, was only attained—prior to the Industrial Revolution—at the cost of a dangerous narrowing of ecological alternatives.

"Rural" and "urban" generally are employed as polar opposites, but the examples just cited suggest that from an ecological standpoint this is seriously misleading. Both categories represent a conflation of related and unrelated features, not all of which correspond neatly to the more or less assumed gross differences between the two. In fact, it would appear that the most essential characteristic of urban and rural adaptations was not their mutual isolation but their historic complementarity and interdependence. At best, they are somewhat arbitrarily defined components of a single, embracing, cultural-environmental system, each changing only in close response to changes in the other. The dichotomy between "rural" and "urban" which still persists in our thinking probably reflects an even deeper failure to understand that developments both in city politics and subsistence economics ultimately converge in their effects upon the success or failure of a society's whole pattern of adaptive responses to its environmental setting. Embodied in written traditions that formerly were largely limited to and inculcated by urban elites unfamiliar with agriculture, this misunderstanding continues to exert a negative influence on academic judgment and administrative policy.

*   *   *

The Urban Revolution

V. Gordon Childe

The concept of 'city' is notoriously hard to define. The aim of the present essay is to present the city historically—or rather prehistorically—as the resultant and symbol of a 'revolution' that initiated a new economic stage in the evolution of society. The word 'revolution' must not of course be taken as denoting a sudden violent catastrophe; it is here used for the culmination of a progressive change in the economic structure and social organization of communities

SOURCE: V. Gordon Childe, "The Urban Revolution," *Town Planning Review,* 21 (1950), 3–17. Reprinted by permission.

that caused, or was accompanied by, a dramatic increase in the population affected—an increase that would appear as an obvious bend in the population graph were vital statistics available. Just such a bend is observable at the time of the Industrial Revolution in England. Though not demonstrable statistically, comparable changes of direction must have occurred at two earlier points in the demographic history of Britain and other regions. Though perhaps less sharp and less durable, these too should indicate equally revolutionary changes in economy. They may then be regarded likewise as marking transitions between stages in economic and social development.

Sociologists and ethnographers last century classified existing pre-industrial societies in a hierarchy of three evolutionary stages, denominated respectively 'savagery,' 'barbarism' and 'civilization.' If they be defined by suitably selected criteria, the logical hierarchy of stages can be transformed into a temporal sequence of ages, proved archaeologically to follow one another in the same order wherever they occur. Savagery and barbarism are conveniently recognized and appropriately defined by the methods adopted for procuring food. Savages live exclusively on wild food obtained by collecting, hunting or fishing. Barbarians on the contrary at least supplement these natural resources by cultivating edible plants and—in the Old World north of the Tropics—also by breeding animals for food.

Throughout the Pleistocene Period—the Palaeolithic Age of archaeologists —all known human societies were savage in the foregoing sense, and a few savage tribes have survived in out of the way parts to the present day. In the archaeological record barbarism began less than ten thousand years ago with the Neolithic Age of archaeologists. It thus represents a later, as well as a higher, stage than savagery. Civilization cannot be defined in quite such simple terms. Etymologically the word is connected with 'city,' and sure enough life in cities begins with this stage. But 'city' is itself ambiguous so archaeologists like to use 'writing' as a criterion of civilization; it should be easily recognizable and proves to be a reliable index to more profound characters. Note, however, that, because a people is said to be civilized or literate, it does not follow that all its members can read and write, nor that they all lived in cities. Now there is no recorded instance of a community of savages civilizing themselves, adopting urban life or inventing a script. Wherever cities have been built, villages of preliterate farmers existed previously (save perhaps where an already civilized people have colonized uninhabited tracts). So civilization, wherever and whenever it arose, succeeded barbarism.

We have seen that a revolution as here defined should be reflected in the population statistics. In the case of the Urban Revolution the increase was mainly accounted for by the multiplication of the numbers of persons living together, i.e., in a single built-up area. The first cities represented settlement units of hitherto unprecedented size. Of course it was not just their size that constituted their distinctive character. We shall find that by modern standards they appeared ridiculously small and we might meet agglomerations of population today to which the name city would have to be refused. Yet a certain size of settlement and density of population is an essential feature of civilization.

Now the density of population is determined by the food supply which in turn is limited by natural resources, the techniques for their exploitation and the means of transport and food-preservation available. The last factors have proved to be variables in the course of human history, and the technique of obtaining food has already been used to distinguish the consecutive stages termed savagery and barbarism. Under the gathering economy of savagery population was always exceedingly sparse. In aboriginal America the carrying capacity of normal unimproved land seems to have been from .05 to .10 per square mile. Only under exceptionally favourable conditions did the fishing tribes of the Northwest Pacific coast attain densities of over one human to the square mile. As far as we can guess from the extant remains, population densities in palaeolithic and pre-neolithic Europe were less than the normal American. Moreover such hunters and collectors usually live in small roving bands. At best several bands may come together for quite brief periods on ceremonial occasions such as the Australian corroborrees. Only in exceptionally favoured regions can fishing tribes establish anything like villages. Some settlements on the Pacific coasts comprised thirty or so substantial and durable houses, accommodating groups of several hundred persons. But even these villages were only occupied during the winter; for the rest of the year their inhabitants dispersed in smaller groups. Nothing comparable has been found in pre-neolithic times in the Old World.

The Neolithic Revolution certainly allowed an expansion of population and enormously increased the carrying capacity of suitable land. On the Pacific Islands neolithic societies today attain a density of 30 or more persons to the square mile. In pre-Columbian North America, however, where the land is not obviously restricted by surrounding seas, the maximum density recorded is just under 2 to the square mile.

Neolithic farmers could of course, and certainly did, live together in permanent villages, though, owing to the extravagant rural economy generally practised, unless the crops were watered by irrigation, the villages had to be shifted at least every twenty years. But on the whole the growth of population was not reflected so much in the enlargement of the settlement unit as in a multiplication of settlements. In ethnography neolithic villages can boast only a few hundred inhabitants (a couple of 'pueblos' in New Mexico house over a thousand, but perhaps they cannot be regarded as neolithic). In prehistoric Europe the largest neolithic village yet known, Barkaer in Jutland, comprised 52 small, one-roomed dwellings, but 16 to 30 houses was a more normal figure; so the average local group in neolithic times would average 200 to 400 members.

These low figures are of course the result of technical limitations. In the absence of wheeled vehicles and roads for the transport of bulky crops men had to live within easy walking distance of their cultivations. At the same time the normal rural economy of the Neolithic Age, what is now termed slash-and-burnt or jhumming, condemns much more than half the arable land to lie fallow so that large areas were required. As soon as the population of a settlement rose above the numbers that could be supported from the accessible land, the excess had to hive off and found a new settlement.

The Neolithic Revolution had other consequences besides increasing the population, and their exploitation might in the end help to provide for the surplus increase. The new economy allowed, and indeed required, the farmer to produce every year more food than was needed to keep him and his family alive. In other words it made possible the regular production of a social surplus. Owing to the low efficiency of neolithic technique, the surplus produced was insignificant at first, but it could be increased till it demanded a reorganization of society.

Now in any Stone Age society, palaeolithic or neolithic, savage or barbarian, everybody can at least in theory make at home the few indispensible tools, the modest cloths and the simple ornaments everyone requires. But every member of the local community, not disqualified by age, must contribute actively to the communal food supply by personally collecting, hunting, fishing, gardening or herding. As long as this holds good, there can be no full-time specialists, no persons nor class of persons who depend for their livelihood on food produced by others and secured in exchange for material or immaterial goods or services.

We find indeed today among Stone Age barbarians and even savages expert craftsmen (for instance flint-knappers among the Ona of Tierra del Fuego), men who claim to be experts in magic, and even chiefs. In palaeolithic Europe too there is some evidence for magicians and indications of chieftainship in pre-neolithic times. But on closer observation we discover that today these experts are not full-time specialists. The Ona flintworker must spend most of his time hunting; he only adds to his diet and his prestige by making arrowheads for clients who reward him with presents. Similarly a pre-Columbian chief, though entitled to customary gifts and services from his followers, must still personally lead hunting and fishing expeditions and indeed could only maintain his authority by his industry and prowess in these pursuits. The same holds good of barbarian societies that are still in the neolithic stage, like the Polynesians where industry in gardening takes the place of prowess in hunting. The reason is that there simply will not be enough food to go round unless every member of the group contributes to the supply. The social surplus is not big enough to feed idle mouths.

Social division of labour, save those rudiments imposed by age and sex, is thus impossible. On the contrary community of employment, the common absorption in obtaining food by similar devices guarantees a certain solidarity to the group. For co-operation is essential to secure food and shelter and for defence against foes, human and subhuman. This identity of economic interests and pursuits is echoed and magnified by identity of language, custom and belief; rigid conformity is enforced as effectively as industry in the common quest for food. But conformity and industrious co-operation need no State organization to maintain them. The local group usually consists either of a

single clan (persons who believe themselves descended from a common ances-
tor or who have earned a mystical claim to such descent by ceremonial adoption) or a group of clans related by habitual intermarriage. And the sentiment
of kinship is reinforced or supplemented by common rites focussed on some
ancestral shrine or sacred place. Archaeology can provide no evidence for
kinship organization, but shrines occupied the central place in preliterate
villages in Mesopotamia, and the long barrow, a collective tomb that overlooks
the presumed site of most neolithic villages in Britain, may well have been also
the ancestral shrine on which converged the emotions and ceremonial activities
of the villagers below. However, the solidarity thus idealized and concretely
symbolized is really based on the same principles as that of a pack of wolves
or a herd of sheep; Durkheim has called it 'mechanical.'

Now among some advanced barbarians (for instance tattooers or wood-
carvers among the Maori) still technologically neolithic we find expert craftsmen tending towards the status of full-time professionals, but only at the cost
of breaking away from the local community. If no single village can produce
a surplus large enough to feed a full-time specialist all the year round, each
should produce enough to keep him a week or so. By going round from village
to village an expert might thus live entirely from his craft. Such itinerants will
lose their membership of the sedentary kinship group. They may in the end
form an analogous organization of their own—a craft clan, which, if it remain
hereditary, may become a caste, or, if it recruit its members mainly by adoption
(apprenticeship throughout Antiquity and the Middle Age was just temporary
adoption), may turn into a guild. But such specialists, by emancipation from
kinship ties, have also forfeited the protection of the kinship organization
which alone under barbarism, guaranteed to its members security of person
and property. Society must be reorganized to accommodate and protect them.

In pre-history specialization of labour presumably began with similar itinerant experts. Archaeological proof is hardly to be expected, but in ethnography metal-workers are nearly always full time specialists. And in Europe at
the beginning of the Bronze Age metal seems to have been worked and pur-
veyed by perambulating smiths who seem to have functioned like tinkers and
other itinerants of much more recent times. Though there is no such positive
evidence, the same probably happened in Asia at the beginning of metallurgy.
There must of course have been in addition other specialist craftsmen whom,
as the Polynesian example warns us, archaeologists could not recognize because they worked in perishable materials. One result of the Urban Revolution
will be to rescue such specialists from nomadism and to guarantee them
security in a new social organization.

About 5,000 years ago irrigation cultivation (combined with stock-breeding and fishing) in the valleys of the Nile, the Tigris-Euphrates and the Indus
had begun to yield a social surplus, large enough to support a number of
resident specialists who were released from food-production. Wa-
ter-transport, supplemented in Mesopotamia and the Indus valley by wheeled
vehicles and even in Egypt by pack animals, made it easy to gather food stuffs

at a few centres. At the same time dependence on river water for the irrigation of the crops restricted the cultivable areas while the necessity of canalizing the waters and protecting habitations against annual floods encouraged the aggregation of population. Thus arose the first cities—units of settlement ten times as great as any known neolithic village. It can be argued that all cities in the old world are offshoots of those of Egypt, Mesopotamia and the Indus basin. So the latter need not be taken into account if a minimum definition of civilization is to be inferred from a comparison of its independent manifestations.

But some three millennia later cities arose in Central America, and it is impossible to prove that the Mayas owed anything directly to the urban civilizations of the Old World. Their achievements must therefore be taken into account in our comparison, and their inclusion seriously complicates the task of defining the essential preconditions for the Urban Revolution. In the Old World the rural economy which yielded the surplus was based on the cultivation of cereals combined with stock-breeding. But this economy had been made more efficient as a result of the adoption of irrigation (allowing cultivation without prolonged fallow periods) and of important inventions and discoveries—metallurgy, the plough, the sailing boat and the wheel. None of these devices was known to the Mayas; they bred no animals for milk or meat; though they cultivated the cereal maize, they used the same sort of slash-and-burn method as neolithic farmers in prehistoric Europe or in the Pacific Islands today. Hence the minimum definition of a city, the greatest factor common to the Old World and the New, will be substantially reduced and impoverished by the inclusion of the Maya. Nevertheless ten rather abstract criteria, all deducible from archaeological data, serve to distinguish even the earliest cities from any older or contemporary village.

(1)   In point of size the first cities must have been more extensive and more densely populated than any previous settlements, although considerably smaller than many villages today. It is indeed only in Mesopotamia and India that the first urban populations can be estimated with any confidence or precision. There excavation has been sufficiently extensive and intensive to reveal both the total area and the density of building in sample quarters and in both respects has disclosed significant agreement with the less industrialized Oriental cities today. The population of Sumerian cities, thus calculated, ranged between 7,000 and 20,000; Harappa and Mohenjo-daro in the Indus valley must have approximated to the higher figure. We can only infer that Egyptian and Maya cities were of comparable magnitude from the scale of public works, presumably executed by urban populations.

(2)   In composition and function the urban population already differed from that of any village. Very likely indeed most citizens were still also peasants, harvesting the lands and waters adjacent to the city. But all cities must have accommodated in addition classes who did not themselves procure their own food by agriculture, stock-breeding, fishing or collecting—full-time specialist craftsmen, transport workers, merchants, officials and priests. All

these were of course supported by the surplus produced by the peasants living in the city and in dependent villages, but they did not secure their share directly by exchanging their products or services for grains or fish with individual peasants.

(3) Each primary producer paid over the tiny surplus he could wring from the soil with his still very limited technical equipment as tithe or tax to an imaginary deity or a divine king who thus concentrated the surplus. Without this concentration, owing to the low productivity of the rural economy, no effective capital would have been available.

(4) Truly monumental public buildings not only distinguish each known city from any village but also symbolize the concentration of the social surplus. Every Sumerian city was from the first dominated by one or more stately temples, centrally situated on a brick platform raised above the surrounding dwellings and usually connected with an artificial mountain, the staged tower or ziggurat. But attached to the temples were workshops and magazines, and an important appurtenance of each principal temple was a great granary. Harappa, in the Indus basin, was dominated by an artificial citadel, girt with a massive rampart of kiln-baked bricks, containing presumably a palace and immediately overlooking an enormous granary and the barracks of artisans. No early temples nor palaces have been excavated in Egypt, but the whole Nile valley was dominated by the gigantic tombs of the divine pharaohs while royal granaries are attested from the literary record. Finally the Maya cities are known almost exclusively from the temples and pyramids of sculptured stone round which they grew up.

Hence in Sumer the social surplus was first effectively concentrated in the hands of a god and stored in his granary. That was probably true in Central America while in Egypt the pharaoh (king) was himself a god. But of course the imaginary deities were served by quite real priests who, besides celebrating elaborate and often sanguinary rites in their honour, administered their divine masters' earthly estates. In Sumer indeed the god very soon, if not even before the revolution, shared his wealth and power with a mortal viceregent, the 'City-King,' who acted as civil ruler and leader in war. The divine pharaoh was naturally assisted by a whole hierarchy of officials.

(5) All those not engaged in food-production were of course supported in the first instance by the surplus accumulated in temple or royal granaries and were thus dependent on temple or court. But naturally priests, civil and military leaders and officials absorbed a major share of the concentrated surplus and thus formed a 'ruling class.' Unlike a palaeolithic magician or a neolithic chief, they were, as an Egyptian scribe actually put it, 'exempt from all manual tasks.' On the other hand, the lower classes were not only guaranteed peace and security, but were relieved from intellectual tasks which many find more irksome than any physical labour. Besides reassuring the masses that the sun was going to rise next day and the river would flood again next year (people who have not five thousand years of recorded experience of natural uniformities behind them are really worried about such matters!), the ruling

classes did confer substantial benefits upon their subjects in the way of planning and organization.

(6)   They were in fact compelled to invent systems of recording and exact, but practically useful, sciences. The mere administration of the vast revenues of a Sumerian temple or an Egyptian pharaoh by a perpetual corporation of priests or officials obliged its members to devise conventional methods of recording that should be intelligible to all their colleagues and successors, that is, to invent systems of writing and numeral notation. Writing is thus a significant, as well as a convenient, mark of civilization. But while writing is a trait common to Egypt, Mesopotamia, the Indus valley and Central America, the characters themselves were different in each region and so were the normal writing materials—papyrus in Egypt, clay in Mesopotamia. The engraved seals or stelae that provide the sole extant evidence for early Indus and Maya writing no more represent the normal vehicles for the scripts than do the comparable documents from Egypt and Sumer.

(7)   The invention of writing—or shall we say the inventions of scripts—enabled the leisured clerks to proceed to the elaboration of exact and predictive sciences—arithmetic, geometry and astronomy. Obviously beneficial and explicitly attested by the Egyptian and Maya documents was the correct determination of the tropic year and the creation of a calendar. For it enabled the rulers to regulate successfully the cycle of agricultural operations. But once more the Egyptian, Maya and Babylonian calendars were as different as any systems based on a single natural unit could be. Calendrical and mathematical sciences are common features of the earliest civilizations and they too are corollaries of the archaeologists' criterion, writing.

(8)   Other specialists, supported by the concentrated social surplus, gave a new direction to artistic expression. Savages even in palaeolithic times had tried, sometimes with astonishing success, to depict animals and even men as they saw them—concretely and naturalistically. Neolithic peasants never did that; they hardly ever tried to represent natural objects, but preferred to symbolize them by abstract geometrical patterns which at most may suggest by a few traits a fantastical man or beast or plant. But Egyptian, Sumerian, Indus and Maya artist-craftsmen—full-time sculptors, painters, or seal-engravers—began once more to carve, model or draw likenesses of persons or things, but no longer with the naive naturalism of the hunter, but according to conceptualized and sophisticated styles which differ in each of the four urban centres.

(9)   A further part of the concentrated social surplus was used to pay for the importation of raw materials, needed for industry or cult and not available locally. Regular 'foreign' trade over quite long distances was a feature of all early civilizations and, though common enough among barbarians later, is not certainly attested in the Old World before 3,000 B.C. nor in the New before the Maya 'empire.' Thereafter regular trade extended from Egypt at least as far as Byblos on the Syrian coast while Mesopotamia was related by commerce with the Indus valley. While the objects of international trade were at first

mainly 'luxuries,' they already included industrial materials, in the Old World notably metal, the place of which in the New was perhaps taken by obsidian. To this extent the first cities were dependent for vital materials on long distance trade as no neolithic village ever was.

(10) So in the city, specialist craftsmen were both provided with raw materials needed for the employment of their skill and also guaranteed security in a State organization based now on residence rather than kinship. Itinerancy was no longer obligatory. The city was a community to which a craftsman could belong politically as well as economically.

Yet in return for security they became dependent on temple or court and were relegated to the lower classes. The peasant masses gained even less material advantages; in Egypt for instance metal did not replace the old stone and wood tools for agricultural work. Yet, however imperfectly, even the earliest urban communities must have been held together by a sort of solidarity missing from any neolithic village. Peasants, craftsmen, priests and rulers form a community, not only by reason of identity of language and belief, but also because each performs mutually complementary functions, needed for the well-being (as redefined under civilization) of the whole. In fact the earliest cities illustrate a first approximation to an organic solidarity based upon a functional complementarity and interdependence between all its members such as subsist between the constituent cells of an organism. Of course this was only a very distant approximation. However necessary the concentration of the surplus really were with the existing forces of production, there seemed a glaring conflict on economic interests between the tiny ruling class, who annexed the bulk of the social surplus, and the vast majority who were left with a bare subsistence and effectively excluded from the spiritual benefits of civilization. So solidarity had still to be maintained by the ideological devices appropriate to the mechanical solidarity of barbarism as expressed in the pre-eminence of the temple or the sepulchral shrine, and now supplemented by the force of the new State organization. There could be no room for sceptics or sectaries in the oldest cities.

These ten traits exhaust the factors common to the oldest cities that archaeology, at best helped out with fragmentary and often ambiguous written sources, can detect. No specific elements of town planning for example can be proved characteristic of all such cities; for on the one hand the Egyptian and Maya cities have not yet been excavated; on the other neolithic villages were often walled, an elaborate system of sewers drained the Orcadian hamlet of Skara Brae; two-storeyed houses were built in pre-Columbian *pueblos,* and so on.

The common factors are quite abstract. Concretely Egyptian, Sumerian, Indus and Maya civilizations were as different as the plans of their temples, the signs of their scripts and their artistic conventions. In view of this divergence and because there is so far no evidence for a temporal priority of one Old World centre (for instance, Egypt) over the rest nor yet for contact between Central America and any other urban centre, the four revolutions just considered may be regarded as mutually independent. On the contrary, all later civilizations in the Old World may in a sense be regarded as lineal descendants of those of Egypt, Mesopotamia or the Indus.

But this was not a case of like producing like. The maritime civilizations of Bronze Age Crete or classical Greece for example, to say nothing of our own, differ more from their reputed ancestors than these did among themselves. But the urban revolutions that gave them birth did not start from scratch. They could and probably did draw upon the capital accumulated in the three allegedly primary centres. That is most obvious in the case of cultural capital. Even today we use the Egyptians' calendar and the Sumerians' divisions of the day and the hour. Our European ancestors did not have to invent for themselves these divisions of time nor repeat the observations on which they are based; they took over—and very slightly improved systems elaborated 5,000 years ago! But the same is in a sense true of material capital as well. The Egyptians, the Sumerians and the Indus people had accumulated vast reserves of surplus food. At the same time they had to import from abroad necessary raw materials like metals and building timber as well as 'luxuries.' Communities controlling these natural resources could in exchange claim a slice of the urban surplus. They could use it as capital to support full-time specialists—craftsmen or rulers—until the latters' achievement in technique and organization had so enriched barbarian economies that they too could produce a substantial surplus in their turn.

Why Cities Have Developed, Spread, and Declined
Gideon Sjoberg
and Andrée F. Sjoberg

*   *   *

Technology and social power, though not alone in stimulating urbanization, are the most crucial variables in accounting for the origin and proliferation of city life throughout the world. Just as technology had to progress before settlements could develop into true cities, so too it had to attain a still more advanced stage before cities could invade "remote" or "inhospitable" regions. In turn, of course, the spread of cities was a variable stimulating technological innovation, if in no other way than by providing mechanisms for increasing contacts among peoples with differing skills.

SOURCE: Gideon Sjoberg, from *The Preindustrial City* (New York: The Free Press, 1960), pp. 64–77, 79. Copyright © 1960 by The Free Press, a Corporation. Reprinted by permission of The Macmillan Company.

Unquestionably, for cities to expand and diffuse, the level of technology had to be such as to ensure the surplus of food and raw materials necessary to sustain non-agricultural specialists. But although the preindustrial technology advanced to the point that it permitted urban life to diffuse into many parts of the world, it also encountered barriers to city growth. Preindustrial cities, after all, have not inhabited the tundra or the broad desert regions where today industrial centers hold sway.

Technology. One of the technological achievements that opened the way for the proliferation of cities in the Old World was the shift from copper or bronze implements to those of iron, made possible by the invention of iron-working techniques apparently sometime around 1200 B.C. The increased efficiency and much greater cheapness and availability of iron tools augmented substantially the agricultural yield and the output of manufactures in already urbanized localities. Iron plows were far more durable than the earlier ones of bronze, stone, or wood. With iron, better wheeled vehicles became a reality, in turn facilitating the shipment of food and goods to the city's markets. And a variety of improved tools such as new types of drills, bits, specialized hammers, and effective axes appeared early in the iron age.[28]

In this era of improved technology, cities arose in environments formerly unsuited to urban settlement. Little wonder that Childe[29] observed that urbanization in the first five centuries of the iron age expanded at a greater rate than it had during the previous 15 centuries of the bronze age. Of course, the iron age began at different times in different regions. Childe was obviously referring to western Asia where, as noted, the iron age had its inception roughly about 1200 B.C.; iron-working techniques did not appear in China before about 600 B.C., were still later in Europe, and of course never were part of the pre-Columbian scene in the Americas. Moreover, in sectors of the Near East where political conditions were quite unstable at the beginning of the iron age, particularly in the Syropalestinian strip, urban centers actually declined for a time.[30] Granted that no one-to-one correspondence obtains between technology and urban development, the association is exceedingly high on a long-term basis.

But the term "iron age" connotes much more than the proliferation of iron implements. Associated with it, even in its early stages, were advances in modes of irrigation that consequently enhanced the agricultural yield and increased mechanization in the crafts as evidenced in such contrivances as pulleys and winches and new weaving techniques.[31] Not to be minimized as a technological innovation with far-reaching consequences was the apparently early iron-age development of coined money. Much more amenable to stan-

---

[28]H.H. Coghlan, "Metal Implements and Weapons," in Charles Singer *et al.* (eds.), *A History of Technology,* I (Oxford: Clarendon Press, 1954), 618.

[29]Gordon Childe, *What Happened in History* (New York: Penguin Books, 1946).

[30]Noth, *op. cit.,* p. 82.

[31]Charles Singer *et al.* (eds.), *A History of Technology,* II (Oxford: Clarendon Press, 1956), *passim.*

dardization than earlier forms of money, it promoted long-distance commerce and facilitated the marketing process within the city itself. Items of widely differing values could be exchanged with greater facility, as could goods and services. For example, persons engaged in service occupations could more easily exchange their economic product for the material goods they desired. Furthermore the use of coinage fostered economic enterprise involving investment, capital formation, etc.[32]

As a result of a variety of iron-age developments, communication improved markedly. Papyrus, an earlier bronze-age creation, was used more freely after the start of the iron age, and later centuries witnessed the development and spread of the alphabet, parchment, paper-making, and finally printing. An inevitable by-product of these more efficient media of communication was the increased extension of political empire and, concomitantly, urbanization.

Transportation was likewise affected by the technological advances of the early iron age. In addition to the better wheeled vehicles, there were now more efficient sailing ships that conveyed materials over long-distance sea routes. (While some of these vessels relied to a degree upon manpower for their propulsion, their use of sails to tap the available wind, an inanimate power source, constitutes—as with the later windmills and water-mills—a divergency in the preindustrial world from the usual dependence upon animate providers of energy.)

Technological developments had reached a sufficiently mature stage that by the time cities of later antiquity like Athens or Rome took shape, these could derive a portion of their sustenance from relatively distant places: the Greeks from North Africa, the eastern Mediterranean region, and north of the Black sea, and the Romans from all of these and western and central Europe as well. The dependence of cities upon long-distance transport for their sustenance now became an increasingly common pattern in preindustrial civilized societies.

Although in contrast to the present, technology in the preindustrial era advanced at a snail's pace, this period was by no means devoid of creativity; after all, it set the stage for the Industrial Revolution, the end result of many centuries of accumulated knowledge. Certainly the later preindustrial cities were larger, more complex, and in many ways more stable than the earlier ones. As noted, these more full-blown cities serve as the chief basis for our constructed type.

The Power Structure. But we can hardly comprehend urban growth simply in technological terms. Power operating through the social structure accounts for many urban developmental configurations.[33] Although the succeeding chapters treat in fuller detail the relationships of social power and city life,

[32]H. A. Innis, *Empire and Communications* (Oxford: Clarendon Press, 1950), p. 85.

[33]The relationship between social power and the rise and decline of cities has been discussed by Ibn Khaldûn, Giovanni Botero, and Ralph Turner. Although we owe a debt of gratitude to these scholars, our formulation seems to be an advance over their efforts.

documenting particularly the urban setting of the ruling group, we must, if we are to explain the growth, spread, and decline of cities, comment upon the city as a mechanism by which a society's rulers can consolidate and maintain their power and, more important, the essentiality of a well-developed power structure for the formation and perpetuation of urban centers.

As to the first point, a power group in the feudal society can sustain itself only if its members concentrate in the kinds of settlements we call urban. Often these are fortified places to protect the upper class against local marauders or invading armies. But invariably they are the focal points of transport and communication, enabling the ruling element not only to maintain surveillance over the countryside but to interact more readily with members of their own group in other cities as well as within a city. The congestion that defines the city maximizes personal, face-to-face communication therein, essential if the heads of the various bureaucratic structures—governmental, religious, and educational—are to sustain ties with one another. So too, craftsmen and merchants prosper in the urban milieu, whose density and occupational heterogeneity foster economic activity.

On the other hand, though the city helps to sustain the ruling elite, the latter's continuance, indeed the city's very growth and survival, *demand a well-developed power structure.* Without an effective political apparatus through which power can be exerted, cities could not derive sustenance from the hinterland. Peasant farmers, for example, rarely produce and relinquish a surplus willingly in feudal societies; thus tribute, taxation, and the like must be exacted if cities are to gain the wherewithal to support their populations. Through their control of the power structure the rulers obtain the largest share of the economic product and live in a style befitting what they consider their rightful heritage. Their dominant position within the society provides them with the means to import goods from abroad, and their urban residence makes such luxury items all the more accessible to them. However, the upper class is not the only segment of society to profit from a well-developed political organization. A stable power structure also enables merchants and artisans more effectively to pursue their supportive activities.

In light of the foregoing, we reason that social power is a prime variable in accounting for 1) the expansion of cities in both size and number, 2) their diffusion into previously non-urbanized or lightly urbanized areas, and 3) their decline (and occasional resurgence). We discuss each of these patterns in the order named, reinforcing our arguments with illustrative materials.

As to the first, our contention is that urban *growth* in societies is invariably highly correlated with the consolidation or extension of a political apparatus, be the result a kingdom or an empire. Of course, Innis,[34] among others, has shown that a society's ability to transform itself into an empire, or the latter's capacity to expand, is associated with the level of technological development attained therein, particularly in the sphere of communication.

[34]Innis, *op. cit., passim.*

The crux of our argument is that as a society broadens its political control it enlarges its economic base as well. City dwellers can then tap the resources of an ever-widening hinterland by draining off the agricultural surpluses of the peasantry and utilizing raw materials such as metal ores that the new domains might have to offer. And a stable political structure—e.g., by keeping trade routes open—permits an active economy. Without doubt, since cities first emerged, their fortunes have been functionally linked to military conquest and/or political stability.

It is hardly fortuitous that the great cities of the preindustrial world have been those within powerful kingdoms or in the heartland of an empire that has spread its tentacles into, and consolidated its domination over, a wide area. The city of Rome reached its apex at about the time the empire was at its peak. Likewise, in India the cities at the focus of the Maurya empire—especially Pataliputra—attained their greatest splendor at the height of imperial expansion, and the same can be said of Delhi, Fatehpore, and other leading urban centers of the Moghul empire in later India. Cambaluc and Hangchow in China were dazzling cities at the zenith of Mongol rule. In feudal Japan, cities reached their peak in the eighteenth century under the aegis of the powerful Tokugawa shogunate.

Not to be overlooked are the so-called city-states of medieval Europe— Venice, Genoa, Pisa, and others. Some were actually the centers of small discontinuous "empires" that included patches of territory in the eastern Mediterranean: colonies or trading depots that enabled them to dominate the sea-lanes between Europe and the Near East and without which they could not have aggrandized the urban homeland.[35] In like manner, a few of the Greek city-states functioned for a time as "empires." It follows that the denomination "city-state" is a deceptive one, for some of these social orders, say Athens, exercised dominion over a sizeable hinterland that included some far-flung cities.

Political control as a key variable in urbanization is confirmed by the capital city's pre-eminence in both size and over-all cultural influence in the feudal order. As site of the supreme ruler, the societal capital attracts to itself a disproportionately large share of the economic surplus that sustains the elite and those who serve this group—servants, artisans, and merchants, among others. And it is that segment of the ruling group centered in the capital that subsidizes the premier astrologers, artists, and musicians in the society. Men of belles-lettres find in the capital city support lacking elsewhere. In the end, the more imposing the power of the elite and the richer its domains, the more glittering the capital.

Having indicated that an elaborate power structure is associated with city growth, we move on to a related topic—the *dispersion,* or *diffusion,* of cities into previously non-urbanized, or very lightly urbanized, regions.

[35]Vasiliev, *op. cit.;* F. L. Ganshof, "The Middle Ages," in Ernest Barker *et al.* (eds.), *The European Inheritance,* I (Oxford: Clarendon Press, 1954), 311-511.

The extension of the power group's domain, notably through empire-building, is the primary mechanism for introducing city life into generally non-urbanized territories. Not only is urban living thereby fostered in the heart of the mother society, but it is carried ever outward upon the waves of conquest to the very borders of the empire, and perhaps beyond.

That the sphere of urbanization widens as the society extends its holdings should be little cause for wonder. Administrative and military centers are required to control the newly won lands; undoubtedly some of these have been established upon existing village sites. Around these settlements cluster artisans, merchants, and other assorted groups who function to sustain the non-agriculturists. Soon full-fledged cities develop. The military and other governmental administrators seek in urban living to maximize their contacts with one another and to take advantage of the communication and transportation ties with the societal capital; the small, isolated rural community cannot perform this function. Even when roads are built to outlying areas these connect only the most important cities. These urban outposts, moreover, are the channels through which is funnelled the economic surplus remitted to the heartland, there to satisfy the demands of the ruling elite.

The empirical evidence for these patterns is overwhelming. We indicated how the Persian empires of the seventh to fifth centuries B.C. introduced city life into western Central Asia. For example, Toprak-kala and Marakanda (part of whose site later was occupied by Samarkand) apparently became true cities at this time. In India, the first-known appearance of urban settlements in the central and southern zones—Ajanta and Kañchi, among others—was a by-product of the southward advance of the Maurya empire. Likewise in China the dispersal of cities over previously non-urban areas—particularly to the south and west—occurred under the Ch'in and the succeeding Han empire-builders. Now urban centers like Canton and Nanking first came into being, as well as a number along the Silk Road connecting China and the west of Asia.

The various Greek city-states set up colonies over much of the Mediterranean littoral. A few of these new cities were Cumae (whose colonists in turn built Neapolis, or Naples), Zancle (Messina), and Massalia (later Marseilles). Others included Olbia and Cherson on the Black sea. The Greeks, of course, established cities in previously urbanized regions as well—for example, in the late fourth century B.C. Alexander and his heirs were city-builders on a grand scale in the Near and Middle East.

The best-known instance of city-building in regions previously untouched by urban living is that which accompanied the spread of the Roman empire. Roman military conquests gave rise to cities in Gaul, Britain, northwestern and central Europe, and the Balkans, to say nothing of some previously urbanized regions like Spain, North Africa, and the Near East. Many of the cities of western Europe, particularly, seem to have grown up around military forts and were unquestionably administrative centers for the ruling clique.

Preindustrial-urban political systems not only diffuse city life outward as their domain expands, but, as mentioned earlier, they at times stimulate urbanization well beyond their formal political frontiers. This is likely to occur when emissaries like missionaries and, especially, merchants penetrate not-yet-urbanized societies under the aegis of a well-established power structure. Typically, an empire at its apogee contains an ever-growing body of urbanites and an upper class that has waxed more affluent and has increased its demands for a variety of goods. Merchants are thereby encouraged to extend their sphere of operation into more remote regions, with the result that entrepôts and emporia are set up which in turn may be transformed into small urban centers. Such an eventuality, of course, is largely dependent upon the degree of support and protection offered by the political base within the homeland. If nothing else, the far-flung trading centers require stable supply lines if they are to be maintained.

To illustrate this process, we cite the influx of Indian administrators, missionaries, and merchants into Southeast Asia, soon to be followed by the emergence of the first cities in this portion of the globe. So too, Chinese ventures into Japan triggered the earliest city development there. The Scandinavian and Baltic region owed its nascent urban centers to the activities of merchants and civil and clerical administrators who entered this area as representatives of the Hanseatic League ca. A.D. 1100. New cities have been stimulated by empires in already urbanized regions: Roman merchants (in reality members of minority groups in the Roman Empire, such as Syrians and Arabs), acting as emissaries of the Empire, built emporia in further Asia, which resulted, for example, in the development of Arikamedu (Pondicherry) in India out of a small indigenous village.[36]

Thus the political power variable explains urban growth and proliferation to the frontiers and beyond. It also accounts for some cities' *decline*—and occasional resurgence. Just as a city's capacity for growth is dependent in large part upon an elaborate political apparatus, so too, when this is withdrawn, the city will shrink or disappear. Especially is this true of societal capitals, the foci of power in the preindustrial civilized order and the chief target, on both military and symbolic grounds, of invading armies. Many cities therefore have been sacked, burned, and captured as their new rulers have burst upon the scene.

The sad decay that awaits some cities is dramatized by Babylon, Nineveh, and Anuradhapura, which lie today in ruins that only hint of a splendor long since passed. And the majestically carved remains at Angkor in Cambodia are mute testimony of a once-great urban complex. How many persons today have heard of Vijayanagar in India? Yet as capital of a Hindu empire in the thirteenth and fourteenth centuries it so impressed European travelers that they were to write of it in grandiloquent terms. Too, the waning of city life in western Europe after the eclipse of Roman power is evidence of the interrelationship between cities and societal power. These West European cities, inci-

[36]Mortimer Wheeler, *Rome Beyond the Imperial Frontiers* (London: G. Bell and Sons, 1954), p. 147, *passim.*

dentally, were to reappear after the ninth century in large part as a result of stimuli from the Byzantine and Arab empires, which seem then to have been near their apogee.[37]

Some may contend that we exaggerate the close tie between the submergence of an empire and the demise of its cities, perhaps citing Athens as a negative case. However, the history of Athens strongly supports our hypothesis. Athens did not decline sharply after the destruction of Greek power. Why? Because it was able to attach itself to another power constellation, the Roman empire, which adopted high Greek culture and subsidized Athens as a center of learning. But once Rome fell, the population and influence of Athens steadily dwindled; it was no longer underwritten by the succeeding empires in the region. Athens lay moldering during many centuries until that just past, when the community that perpetuates its name, tradition, and approximate site was made capital of modern Greece. On the other hand the Greek city-state of Byzantium followed a quite different course. Of minor import under Roman rule, with the demise of Rome it became capital of the Byzantine empire (under the name of Constantinople); still later it was the seat of Ottoman rule and, as Istanbul, it remains an important city to this day.

Thus, although cities usually flounder with the collapse of their political superstructure, some may be perpetuated under the new order—as was Athens and Greek cities of the Near East, like Alexandria or Antioch, under Roman rule. And others that experience a decline may undergo a renaissance when the political climate changes in their favor. Numerous urban centers—Jerusalem is an outstanding example—have been developed, destroyed, and rebuilt numerous times throughout their turbulent history, as a direct expression of shifting political tides.

The network of relationships among urban growth, spread, and decline can not be fully explored here. However, one highly significant pattern deserves special mention. This is that cities on the fringes of empire at times break away from the latter and become the bases of operation for the destruction of the mother cities. This process was at work in Europe—although it is rarely perceived by historians—when the so-called barbarians, actually groups like the Goths who had been partially urbanized and civilized by the Romans, rose up against and demolished Rome. Earlier, in Central Asia the Persians and Greeks, in the course of extending their imperial frontiers, had introduced urban living to indigenous people in the region, among whom were various Aryan and Turkic groups. These in turn assimilated within the urban milieu the techniques for driving out their conquerors and constructing empires of their own, including the Graeco-Bactrian, the Parthian, and the Kushanian.

---

[37]We remind ourselves that the Roman cities in Europe did not disappear completely during the so-called Dark Ages. While some sank to the status of small towns, or even villages, being resuscitated only in later centuries, others survived as small cities throughout this period.

A few writers are coming to define the larger feudal "manors" in Europe as small urban communities. We concur. Some of them did fulfil all our criteria for denomination as cities.

Moreover, scholars appear to ignore the fact that the "nomadic" Mongols had, before their accession to power, been in contact with urban centers—those established by the Chinese and the Turkic Uighurs. Then too, at least part of the Mongol officialdom, including a small literati, resided in cities like Karakorum and used these as their bases for the broad sweeps over Asia. Nomads completely lacking in the accoutrements of urban living could never have instilled fear in the hearts of civilized peoples to the extent the Mongols did.

Subject peoples, no matter how dissatisfied they may be, must acquire a high degree of knowledge of the use of weapons and military tactics, indeed of the administrative process itself, before they can rise up to smite the empire that nourished them. It is the conquerors themselves who, in the urban context, cultivate the skills and leadership capacities of their subjects, the more effectively to administer and exploit the resources of the region, and thereby sow the seeds of their own downfall. (An analogous process is occurring today as the industrial-urban apparatus is diffused from advanced societies to less developed ones; urbanites in the latter are reacting by rising up and "throwing off the yoke of colonialism.") Detailed analysis of the aforementioned and similar phenomena, as they affect the rise and decline of cities, must await a separate treatise.

Other Factors.   We have emphasized the role of technology and, particularly, political power as the prime variables in the development, proliferation, and downfall of cities, but we are not incognizant of the workings of other forces. The value system of a people may affect the fortunes of cities. Jerusalem undoubtedly has been perpetuated through time, despite its periodic destruction, because of its symbolic value for Christians, Muslims, and Jews alike. Yet we must be ever mindful that, without a series of power structures to support it, even Jerusalem could not have survived.

Environment, also, influences urbanization by imposing limits upon city growth. Likewise cities have vanished as a result of shifting environmental circumstances. Kish dies a peaceful death after the Euphrates River changed its course, leaving it cut off from its water supply, and Pompeii was obliterated in the eruption of Mt. Vesuvius. Nevertheless, on the whole, environment is more a dependent than an independent variable, being amenable in many respects to advances in technology and the prodigious impact of social power.

Turning to a more controversial issue, many readers familiar with the literature of city growth may wonder why we de-emphasize the link between commerce and urbanization. We do not deny that a commercial organization is necessary if a political system is to be maintained, but it is not as crucial for urbanization as most historians have contended; contrariwise, large-scale economic enterprise is highly dependent upon an effective power structure.

Our argument is grounded in a vast body of cross-cultural evidence. Nowhere do cities, even commercial ones, flourish without the direct or indirect support of a well-established state system. We can find no instance of significant city-building through commerce alone. The flowering of cities in western

Europe after the ninth century was the result of stimuli from the Byzantine and Arab empires, then at their apogee, which promoted the activities of merchants beyond their frontiers. Too many scholars writing of the Phoenician cities established around the western Mediterranean or the early commercial cities set down by the Muslims in Southeast Asia, such as Bantam and Malacca, have seen merely commercial, or economic, factors at work. They fail to recognize that the Phoenicians at the height of their commercial expansion were lords of the Mediterranean, or that the early port cities in Indonesia and Malaya were the foci of sultanates whose development paralleled the culmination of Islamic empire-construction to the west, e.g., in India, whence these cities derived their early support. Unquestionably, the factor of political power, much more than commerce, is the key to the rise and spread of urban centers throughout history.

The Preindustrial City
Gideon Sjoberg

In the past few decades social scientists have been conducting field studies in a number of relatively non-Westernized cities. Their recently acquired knowledge of North Africa and various parts of Asia, combined with what was already learned, clearly indicates that these cities are not like typical cities of the United States and other highly industrialized areas but are much more like those of medieval Europe. Such communities are termed herein "preindustrial," for they have arisen without stimulus from that form of production which we associate with the European industrial revolution.

Recently Foster, in a most informative article, took cognizance of the preindustrial city.[1] His primary emphasis was upon the peasantry (which he calls "folk"); but he recognized this to be part of a broader social structure which includes the preindustrial city. He noted certain similarities between the peasantry and the city's lower class. Likewise the present author sought to analyze the total society of which the peasantry and the preindustrial city are integral parts.[2] For want of a better term this was called "feudal." Like Redfield's folk (or "primitive") society, the feudal order is highly stable and sacred; in contrast, however, it has a complex social organization. It is charac-

---

[1]George M. Foster, "What Is Folk Culture?" *American Anthropologist,* LV (1953), 159-73.
[2]Gideon Sjoberg, "Folk and 'Feudal' Societies," *American Journal of Sociology,* LVIII (1952), 231-39.

SOURCE: Gideon Sjoberg, "The Preindustrial City," *American Journal of Sociology,* 60 (March 1955), 438-445. Copyright 1955 by the University of Chicago. Reprinted by permission of the author and the publisher, the University of Chicago Press.

terized by highly developed state and educational and/or religious institutions and by a rigid class structure.

Thus far no one has analyzed the preindustrial city per se, especially as it differs from the industrial-urban community, although Weber, Tönnies, and a few others perceived differences between the two. Yet such a survey is needed for the understanding of urban development in so-called underdeveloped countries and, for that matter, in parts of Europe. Such is the goal of this paper. The typological analysis should also serve as a guide to future research.

ECOLOGICAL ORGANIZATION

Preindustrial cities depend for their existence upon food and raw materials obtained from without; for this reason they are marketing centers. And they serve as centers for handicraft manufacturing. In addition, they fulfil important political, religious, and educational functions. Some cities have become specialized; for example, Benares in India and Karbala in Iraq are best known as religious communities, and Peiping in China as a locus for political and educational activities.

The proportion of urbanites relative to the peasant population is small, in some societies about 10 per cent, even though a few preindustrial cities have attained populations of 100,000 or more. Growth has been by slow accretion. These characteristics are due to the nonindustrial nature of the total social order. The amount of surplus food available to support an urban population has been limited by the unmechanized agriculture, transportation facilities utilizing primarily human or animal power, and inefficient methods of food preservation and storage.

The internal arrangement of the preindustrial city, in the nature of the case, is closely related to the city's economic and social structure.[3] Most streets are mere passageways for people and for animals used in transport. Buildings are low and crowded together. The congested conditions, combined with limited scientific knowledge, have fostered serious sanitation problems.

More significant is the rigid social segregation which typically has led to the formation of "quarters" or "wards." In some cities (e.g., Fez, Morocco, and Aleppo, Syria) these were sealed off from each other by walls, whose gates

[3]Sociologists have devoted almost no attention to the ecology of preindustrial centers. However, works of other social scientists do provide some valuable preliminary data. See, e.g., Marcel Clerget, *Le Caire: Étude de géographie urbaine et d'histoire économique* (2 vols.; Cairo: E. & R. Schindler, 1934); Robert E. Dickinson, *The West European City* (London: Routledge & Kegan Paul, 1951); Roger Le Tourneau, *Fès: Avant le protectorat* (Casablanca: Société Marocaine de Librairie et d'Édition, 1949); Edward W. Lane, *Cairo Fifty Years Ago* (London: John Murray, 1896); J. Sauvaget, *Alep* (Paris: Librairie Orientaliste Paul Geuthner, 1941); J. Weulersse, "Antioche: Essai de géographie urbaine," *Bulletin d'études orientales,* IV (1934), 27-79; Jean Kennedy, *Here Is India* (New York: Charles Scribner's Sons, 1945); and relevant articles in American geographical journals.

were locked at night. The quarters reflect the sharp local social divisions. Thus ethnic groups live in special sections. And the occupational groupings, some being at the same time ethnic in character, typically reside apart from one another. Often a special street or sector of the city is occupied almost exclusively by members of a particular trade; cities in such divergent cultures as medieval Europe and modern Afghanistan contain streets with names like "street of the goldsmiths." Lower-class and especially "outcaste" groups live on the city's periphery, at a distance from the primary centers of activity. Social segregation, the limited transportation facilities, the modicum of residential mobility, and the cramped living quarters have encouraged the development of well-defined neighborhoods which are almost primary groups.

Despite rigid segregation the evidence suggests no real specialization of land use such as functionally necessary in industrial-urban communities. In medieval Europe and in other areas city dwellings often serve as workshops, and religious structures are used as schools or marketing centers.[4]

Finally, the "business district" does not hold the position of dominance that it enjoys in the industrial-urban community. Thus, in the Middle East the principal mosque, or in medieval Europe the cathedral, is usually the focal point of community life. The center of Peiping is the Forbidden City.

ECONOMIC ORGANIZATION

The economy of the preindustrial city diverges sharply from that of the modern industrial center. The prime difference is the absence in the former of industrialism which may be defined as that system of production in which *inanimate* sources of power are used to multiply human effort. Preindustrial cities depend for the production of goods and services upon *animate* (human or animal) sources of energy—applied either directly or indirectly through such mechanical devices as hammers, pulleys, and wheels. The industrial-urban community, on the other hand, employs inanimate generators of power such as electricity and steam which greatly enhance the productive capacity of urbanites. This basically new form of energy production, one which requires for its development and survival a special kind of institutional complex, effects striking changes in the ecological, economic, and social organization of cities in which it has become dominant.

Other facets of the economy of the preindustrial city are associated with its particular system of production. There is little fragmentation or specialization of work. The handicraftsman participates in nearly every phase of the manufacture of an article, often carrying out the work in his own home or in a small shop near by and, within the limits of certain guild and community

[4]Dickinson, *op. cit.,* p. 27; O. H. K. Spate, *India and Pakistan* (London: Methuen & Co., 1954), p. 183.

regulations, maintaining direct control over conditions of work and methods of production.

In industrial cities, on the other hand, the complex division of labor requires a specialized managerial group, often extra-community in character, whose primary function is to direct and control others. And for the supervision and co-ordination of the activities of workers, a "factory system" has been developed, something typically lacking in preindustrial cities. (Occasionally centralized production is found in preindustrial cities—e.g., where the state organized slaves for large-scale construction projects.) Most commercial activities, also, are conducted in preindustrial cities by individuals without a highly formalized organization; for example, the craftsman has frequently been responsible for the marketing of his own products. With a few exceptions, the preindustrial community cannot support a large group of middlemen.

The various occupations are organized into what have been termed "guilds."[5] These strive to encompass all, except the elite, who are gainfully employed in some economic activity. Guilds have existed for merchants and handicraft workers (e.g., goldsmiths and weavers) as well as for servants, entertainers, and even beggars and thieves. Typically the guilds operate only within the local community, and there are no large-scale economic organizations such as those in industrial cities which link their members to their fellows in other communities.

Guild membership and apprenticeship are prerequisites to the practice of almost any occupation, a circumstance obviously leading to monopolization. To a degree these organizations regulate the work of their members and the price of their products and services. And the guilds recruit workers into specific occupations, typically selecting them according to such particularistic criteria as kinship rather than universalistic standards.

The guilds are integrated with still other elements of the city's social structure. They perform certain religious functions; for example, in medieval European, Chinese, and Middle Eastern cities each guild had its "patron saint" and held periodic festivals in his honor. And, by assisting members in time of trouble, the guilds serve as social security agencies.

The economic structure of the preindustrial city functions with little rationality, judged by industrial-urban standards. This is shown in the general nonstandardization of manufacturing methods as well as in the products and is even more evident in marketing. In preindustrial cities throughout the world

[5]For a discussion of guilds and other facets of the preindustrial city's economy, see, e.g. J. S. Burgess, *The Guilds of Peking* (New York: Columbia University Press, 1928); Edward T. Williams, *China, Yesterday and Today* (5th ed.; New York: Thomas Y. Crowell Co., 1932); T'ai-ch'u Liao, "The Apprentices in Chengtu during and after the War," *Yenching Journal of Social Studies,* IV (1948), 90-106; H. A. R. Gibb and Harold Bowen, *Islamic Society and the West* (London: Oxford University Press, 1950), Vol. I, Part I, chap. vi; Le Tourneau, *op. cit.;* Clerget, *op. cit.;* James W. Thompson and Edgar N. Johnson, *An Introduction to Medieval Europe* (New York: W. W. Norton Co., 1937) chap. xx; Sylvia L. Thrupp, "Medieval Guilds Reconsidered," *Journal of Economic History,* II (1942), 164-73.

a fixed price is rare; buyer and seller settle their bargain by haggling. (Of course, there are limits above which customers will not buy and below which merchants will not sell.) Often business is conducted in a leisurely manner, money not being the only desired end.

Furthermore, the sorting of goods according to size, weight, and quality is not common. Typical is the adulteration and spoilage of produce. And weights and measures are not standardized: variations exist not only between one city and the next but also within communities, for often different guilds employ their own systems. Within a single city there may be different kinds of currency, which, with the poorly developed accounting and credit systems, signalize a modicum of rationality in the whole of economic action in preindustrial cities.[6]

The economic system of the preindustrial city, based as it has been upon animate sources of power, articulates with a characteristic class structure and family, religious, educational, and governmental systems.

Of the class structure, the most striking component is a literate elite controlling and depending for its existence upon the mass of the populace, even in the traditional cities of India with their caste system. The elite is composed of individuals holding positions in the governmental, religious, and/or educational institutions of the larger society, although at times groups such as large absentee landlords have belonged to it. At the opposite pole are the masses, comprising such groups as handicraft workers whose goods and services are produced primarily for the elite's benefit.[7] Between the elite and the lower class is a rather sharp schism, but in both groups there are gradations in rank. The members of the elite belong to the "correct" families and enjoy power, property, and certain highly valued personal attributes. Their position, moreover, is legitimized by sacred writings.

Social mobility in this city is minimal; the only real threat to the elite comes from the outside—not from the city's lower classes. And a middle class—so typical of industrial-urban communities, where it can be considered the "dominant" class—is not known in the preindustrial city. The system of production in the larger society provides goods, including food, and services in sufficient amounts to support only a small group of leisured individuals; under these conditions an urban middle class, a semileisured group, cannot arise. Nor are

[6]For an extreme example of unstandardized currency cf. Robert Coltman, Jr., *The Chinese* (Philadelphia: E.A. Davis, 1801), p. 52. In some traditional societies (e.g., China) the state has sought to standardize economic action in the city by setting up standard systems of currency and/or weights and measures; these efforts, however, generally proved ineffective. Inconsistent policies in taxation, too, hinder the development of a "rational" economy.

[7]The status of the true merchant in the preindustrial city, ideally, has been low; in medieval Europe and China many merchants were considered "outcastes." However, in some preindustrial cities a few wealthy merchants have acquired considerable power even though their role has not been highly valued. Even then most of their prestige has come through participation in religious, governmental, or educational activities, which have been highly valued (see, e.g., Ping-ti Ho, "The Salt Merchants of Yang-Chou: A Study of Commercial Capitalism in Eighteenth-Century China," *Harvard Journal of Asiatic Studies,* XVII [1954], 130-68).

a middle class and extensive social mobility essential to the maintenance of the economic system.

Significant is the role of the marginal or "outcaste" groups (e.g., the Eta of Japan), which are not an integral part of the dominant social system. Typically they rank lower than the urban lower class, performing tasks considered especially degrading, such as burying the dead. Slaves, beggars, and the like are outcastes in most preindustrial cities. Even such groups as professional entertainers and itinerant merchants are often viewed as outcastes, for their rovings expose them to "foreign" ideas from which the dominant social group seeks to isolate itself. Actually many outcaste groups, including some of those mentioned above, are ethnic groups, a fact which further intensifies their isolation. (A few, like the Jews in the predominantly Muslim cities of North Africa, have their own small literate religious elite, which, however, enjoys no significant political power in the city as a whole.)

An assumption of many urban sociologists is that a small, unstable kinship group, notably the conjugal unit, is a necessary correlate of city life. But this premise does not hold for preindustrial cities.[8] At times sociologists and anthropologists, when generalizing about various traditional societies, have imputed to peasants typically urban kinship patterns. Actually, in these societies the ideal forms of kinship and family life are most closely approximated by members of the urban literate elite, who are best able to fulfil the exacting requirements of the sacred writings. Kinship and the ability to perpetuate one's lineage are accorded marked prestige in preindustrial cities. Children, especially sons, are highly valued, and polygamy or concubinage or adoption help to assure the attainment of large families. The pre-eminence of kinship is apparent even in those preindustrial cities where divorce is permitted. Thus, among the urban Muslims or urban Chinese divorce is not an index of disorganization; here, conjugal ties are loose and distinctly subordinate to the bonds of kinship, and each member of a dissolved conjugal unit typically is absorbed by his kin group. Marriage, a prerequisite to adult status in the preindustrial city, is entered upon at an early age and is arranged between families rather than romantically, by individuals.

The kinship and familial organization displays some rigid patterns of sex and age differentiation whose universality in preindustrial cities has generally been overlooked. A woman, especially of the upper class, ideally performs few

[8]For materials on the kinship system and age and sex differentiation, see, e.g., Le Tourneau, *op. cit.;* Edward W. Lane, *The Manners and Customs of the Modern Egyptians* (3d ed; New York: E. P. Dutton Co., 1923); C. Snouck Hurgronje, *Mekka in the Latter Part of the Nineteenth Century,* trans. J. H. Monahan (London: Luzac, 1931); Horace Miner, *The Primitive City of Timbuctoo* (Princeton: Princeton University Press, 1953); Alice M. Bacon, *Japanese Girls and Women* (rev. ed.; Boston: Houghton Mifflin Co., 1902); J. S. Burgess, "Community Organization in China," *Far Eastern Survey,* XIV (1945), 371-73; Morton H. Fried, *Fabric of Chinese Society* (New York: Frederick A. Praeger, 1953); Francis L. K. Hsu, *Under the Ancestors' Shadow* (New York: Columbia University Press, 1948); Cornelius Osgood, *The Koreans and Their Culture* (New York: Ronald Press, 1951), chap. viii; Jukichi Inouye, *Home Life in Tokyo* (2d ed.; Tokyo: Tokyo Printing Co., 1911).

significant functions outside the home. She is clearly subordinate to males, especially her father or husband. Recent evidence indicates that this is true even for such a city as Lhasa, Tibet, where women supposedly have had high status.[9] The isolation of women from public life has in some cases been extreme. In nineteenth-century Seoul, Korea, "respectable" women appeared on the streets only during certain hours of the night when men were supposed to stay at home.[10] Those women in preindustrial cities who evade some of the stricter requirements are members of certain marginal groups (e.g., entertainers) or of the lower class. The role of the urban lower-class woman typically resembles that of the peasant rather than the urban upper-class woman. Industrialization, by creating demands and opportunities for their employment outside the home, is causing significant changes in the status of women as well as in the whole of the kinship system in urban areas.

A formalized system of age grading is an effective mechanism of social control in preindustrial cities. Among siblings the eldest son is privileged. And children and youth are subordinate to parents and other adults. This, combined with early marriage, inhibits the development of a "youth culture." On the other hand, older persons hold considerable power and prestige, a fact contributing to the slow pace of change.

As noted above, kinship is functionally integrated with social class. It also reinforces and is reinforced by the economic organization: the occupations, through the guilds, select their members primarily on the basis of kinship, and much of the work is carried on in the home or immediate vicinity. Such conditions are not functional to the requirements of a highly industrialized society.

The kinship system in the preindustrial city also articulates with a special kind of religious system, whose formal organization reaches fullest development among members of the literate elite.[11] The city is the seat of the key religious functionaries whose actions set standards for the rest of society. The urban lower class, like the peasantry, does not possess the education or the means to maintain all the exacting norms prescribed by the sacred writings. Yet the religious system influences the city's entire social structure. (Typically, within the preindustrial city one religion is dominant; however, certain minority groups adhere to their own beliefs.) Unlike the situation in industrial cities, religious activity is not separate from other social action but permeates

[9]Tsung-Lien Shen and Shen-Chi Liu, *Tibet and the Tibetans* (Stanford: Stanford University Press, 1953), pp. 143-44.

[10]Osgood, *op. cit.,* p. 146.

[11]For information on various aspects of religious behavior see, e.g., Le Tourneau, *op. cit.;* Miner, *op. cit.;* Lane, *Manners and Customs;* Hurgronje, *op. cit.;* André Chouraqui, *Les Juifs d'Afrique du Nord* (Paris: Presses Universitaires de France, 1952); Justus Doolittle, *Social Life of the Chinese* (London: Sampson Low, 1868); John K. Shryock, *The Temples of Anking and Their Cults* (Paris: Privately printed, 1931); Derk Bodde (ed.), *Annual Customs and Festivals in Peking* (Peiping: Henri Vetch, 1936); Edwin Benson, *Life in a Medieval City* (New York: Macmillan Co., 1920); Hsu, *op. cit.*

family, economic, governmental, and other activities. Daily life is pervaded with religious significance. Especially important are periodic public festivals and ceremonies like Ramadan in Muslim cities. Even distinctly ethnic outcaste groups can through their own religious festivals maintain solidarity.

Magic, too, is interwoven with economic, familial, and other social activities. Divination is commonly employed for determining the "correct" action on critical occasions; for example, in traditional Japanese and Chinese cities, the selection of marriage partners. And nonscientific procedures are widely employed to treat illness among all elements of the population of the preindustrial city.

Formal education typically is restricted to the male elite, its purpose being to train individuals for positions in the governmental, educational, or religious hierarchies. The economy of preindustrial cities does not require mass literacy, nor, in fact, does the system of production provide the leisure so necessary for the acquisition of formal education. Considerable time is needed merely to learn the written language, which often is quite different from that spoken. The teacher occupies a position of honor, primarily because of the prestige of all learning and especially of knowledge of the sacred literature, and learning is traditional and characteristically based upon sacred writings.[12] Students are expected to memorize rather than evaluate and initiate, even in institutions of higher learning.

Since preindustrial cities have no agencies of mass communication, they are relatively isolated from one another. Moreover, the masses within a city are isolated from the elite. The former must rely upon verbal communication, which is formalized in special groups such as storytellers or their counterparts. Through verse and song these transmit upper-class tradition to nonliterate individuals.

The formal government of the preindustrial city is the province of the elite and is closely integrated with the educational and religious systems. It performs two principal functions: exacting tribute from the city's masses to support the activities of the elite and maintaining law and order through a "police force" (at times a branch of the army) and a court system. The police force exists primarily for the control of "outsiders," and the courts support custom and the rule of the sacred literature, a code of enacted legislation typically being absent.

In actual practice little reliance is placed upon formal machinery for regulating social life.[13] Much more significant are the informal controls exerted by the kinship, guild, and religious systems, and here, of course, personal standing is decisive. Status distinctions are visibly correlated with personal attributes, chiefly speech, dress, and personal mannerisms which proclaim ethnic group,

[12]Le Tourneau, *op. cit.,* Part VI; Lane, *Manners and Customs,* chap. ii; Charles Bell, *The People of Tibet* (Oxford: Clarendon Press, 1928), chap. xix; O. Olufsen, *The Emir of Bokhara and His Country* (London: William Heinemann, 1911), chap. ix; Doolittle, *op. cit.*

[13]Carleton Coon, *Caravan: The Story of the Middle East* (New York: Henry Holt & Co., 1951), p. 259; George W. Gilmore, *Korea from Its Capital* (Philadelphia: Presbyterian Board of Publication, 1892), pp. 51–52.

occupation, age, sex, and social class. In nineteenth-century Seoul, not only did the upper-class mode of dress differ considerably from that of the masses, but speech varied according to social class, the verb forms and pronouns depending upon whether the speaker ranked higher or lower or was the equal of the person being addressed.[14] Obviously, then, escape from one's role is difficult, even in the street crowds. The individual is ever conscious of his specific rights and duties. All these things conserve the social order in the preindustrial city despite its heterogeneity.

CONCLUSIONS

Throughout this paper there is the assumption that certain structural elements are universal for all urban centers. This study's hypothesis is that their form in the preindustrial city is fundamentally distinct from that in the industrial-urban community. A considerable body of data not only from medieval Europe, which is somewhat atypical,[15] but from a variety of cultures supports this point of view. Emphasis has been upon the static features of preindustrial city life. But even those preindustrial cities which have undergone considerable change approach the ideal type. For one thing, social change is of such a nature that it is not usually perceived by the general populace.

Most cities of the preindustrial type have been located in Europe or Asia. Even though Athens and Rome and the large commercial centers of Europe prior to the industrial revolution displayed certain unique features, they fit the preindustrial type quite well.[16] And many traditional Latin-American cities are quite like it, although deviations exist, for, excluding pre-Columbian cities, these were affected to some degree by the industrial revolution soon after their establishment.

It is postulated that industrialization is a key variable accounting for the distinctions between preindustrial and industrial cities. The type of social structure required to develop and maintain a form of production utilizing inanimate sources of power is quite unlike that in the preindustrial city.[17] At the very least, extensive industrialization requires a rational, centralized, extra-community economic organization in which recruitment is based more upon

[14]Osgood, *op cit.*, chap. viii; Gilmore, *op. cit.*, chap. iv.

[15]Henri Pirenne, in *Medieval Cities* (Princeton: Princeton University Press, 1925), and others have noted that European cities grew up in opposition to and were separate from the greater society. But this thesis has been overstated for medieval Europe. Most preindustrial cities are integral parts of broader social structures.

[16]Some of these cities made extensive use of water power, which possibly fostered deviations from the type.

[17]For a discussion of the institutional prerequisites of industrialization, see, e.g., Bert F. Hoselitz, "Social Structure and Economic Growth," *Economia internazionale,* VI (1953), 52–77, and Marion J. Levy, "Some Sources of the Vulnerability of the Structures of Relatively Non-industrialized Societies to Those of Highly Industrialized Societies," in Bert F. Hoselitz (ed.), *The Progress of Underdeveloped Areas* (Chicago: University of Chicago Press, 1952), pp. 114 ff.

universalism than on particularism, a class system which stresses achievement rather than ascription, a small and flexible kinship system, a system of mass education which emphasizes universalistic rather than particularistic criteria, and mass communication. Modification in any one of these elements affects the others and induces changes in other systems such as those of religion and social control as well. Industrialization, moreover, not only requires a special kind of social structure within the urban community but provides the means necessary for its establishment.

Anthropologists and sociologists will in the future devote increased attention to the study of cities throughout the world. They must therefore recognize that the particular kind of social structure found in cities in the United States is not typical of all societies. Miner's recent study of Timbuctoo,[18] which contains much excellent data, points to the need for recognition of the preindustrial city. His emphasis upon the folk-urban continuum diverted him from an equally significant problem: How does Timbuctoo differ from modern industrial cities in its ecological, economic, and social structure? Society there seems even more sacred and organized than Miner admits.[19] For example, he used divorce as an index of disorganization, but in Muslim society divorce within certain rules is justified by the sacred literature. The studies of Hsu and Fried would have considerably more significance had the authors perceived the generality of their findings. And, once the general structure of the preindustrial city is understood, the specific cultural deviations become more meaningful.

Beals notes the importance of the city as a center of acculturation.[20] But an understanding of this process is impossible without some knowledge of the preindustrial city's social structure. Although industrialization is clearly advancing throughout most of the world, the social structure of preindustrial civilizations is conservative, often resisting the introduction of numerous industrial forms. Certainly many cities of Europe (e.g., in France or Spain) are not so fully industrialized as some presume; a number of preindustrial patterns remain. The persistence of preindustrial elements is also evident in cities of North Africa and many parts of Asia; for example, in India and Japan,[21] even though great social change is currently taking place. And the Latin-American city of Merida, which Redfield studied, had many preindustrial traits.[22] A

---

[18] *Op. cit.*

[19] This point seems to have been perceived also by Asael T. Hansen in his review of Horace Miner's "The Primitive City of Timbuctoo," *American Journal of Sociology,* LIX (1954), 501–2.

[20] Ralph L. Beals, "Urbanism, Urbanization and Acculturation," *American Anthropologist,* LIII (1951), 1–10.

[21] See, e.g., D. R. Gadgil, *Poona: A Socio-economic Survey* (Poona: Gokhale Institute of Politics and Economics, 1952), Part II; N. V. Sovani, *Social Survey of Kolhapur City* (Poona: Gokhale Institute of Politics and Economics, 1951), Vol. II; Noel P. Gist, "Caste Differentials in South India," *American Sociological Review,* XIX (1954), 126–37; John Campbell Pelzel, "Social Stratification in Japanese Urban Economic Life" (unpublished Ph.D. dissertation, Harvard University, Department of Social Relations, 1950).

[22] Robert Redfield, *The Folk Culture of Yucatan* (Chicago: University of Chicago Press, 1941).

conscious awareness of the ecological, economic, and social structure of the preindustrial city should do much to further the development of comparative urban community studies.

The World's Great Cities: Evolution or Devolution?
Population Reference Bureau, Inc.

A major side-effect of the unprecedented speed-up in world population growth today is the ever-increasing concentration of people in cities the world over.

The rate of city growth will continue to vary in different areas of the world, decelerating in the older, industrial countries and accelerating in the agrarian, underdeveloped countries which hold two thirds of the world's people.

Urbanization is a vastly different process in those countries than it was in the West where the Industrial Revolution generated the capital needed to build the economies which could provide for the growing populations. Jobs were plentiful in the industrial cities of the West, and this provided the "pull" for the countless millions who migrated, and still do, from country to city.

The situation is often the reverse in the underdeveloped countries today. There, the "push" is the gross overcrowding of the rural population living at or near the bare subsistence level. More often than not, the migrant goes to an even more precarious urban situation where he cannot find work readily and must spend his limited savings. From the socio-economic and humanitarian points of view, the trek to the cities in the underdeveloped countries will continue to be more of a curse than a blessing as it absorbs limited capital and generates tension.

Today, there are 61 cities with a million people or more in the world, compared with only ten in 1900.

Now two people out of every ten live in cities of 20,000 or more population. If the present trend continues—and there is every indication that it will for some time—almost half the world's population will live in cities that size by 2000; and by 2050, nine people out of every ten.

The giant of all time, the New York-northeastern New Jersey metropolitan agglomeration, has a population of over 14.5 million, according to preliminary tabulations from the 1960 census. That is more than the combined population of Australia and New Zealand; and it is almost half the entire population of Mexico!

SOURCE: Population Reference Bureau, from "The World's Greatest Cities: Evolution or Devolution?," *Population Bulletin*, 16 (September 1960), 109–124, 129–130. Reprinted with the permission of the Population Reference Bureau, Inc.

New York's borough of Manhattan shows a 15 percent decline in population since the 1950 census. But with 1.7 million people Manhattan's population density is 75,900 per square mile.

On the other side of the world, Calcutta's population of 5.7 million is small in comparison. But projections based on current trends would give Calcutta a population of between 35 and 66 million by the year 2000! At Manhattan's density, Calcutta would sprawl over an area about as large as Rhode Island.

Obviously, such a projection is merely a *reductio ad absurdum.* The problems of food distribution and sanitation in the absence of very rapid economic development are only two of many factors which would cause death rates to rise and check such multiplication of people long before standing-room-only develops.

Few people seem to understand that the pattern of tomorrow's city is being formed by today's rapid population growth. Will the city remain the traditional center of culture or will it degenerate into a socio-economic sinkhole for mankind?

Can the sprawling shantytowns which make up the cities of Asia, Africa and Latin America evolve into habitable places which provide adequate services so necessary to urban life?

Will the shabby, decaying, smog-ridden central cities of the industrial West be cleansed of the blight which has been accumulating since the Industrial Revolution began? Or, will the deteriorating central cities continue to sprawl out at an even faster rate, consuming untold acres of prime farm land with their insatiable appetite for space? Will these cities be able to win back the fleeing, more prosperous residents and the industries whose tax revenue is essential to their financial stability?

As man increasingly becomes a city-born and city-bred creature, the problems of city living and city organization will intensify in complexity and embrace the planet. Drift and improvisation cannot solve them. Dynamic global action is essential now if the cities of tomorrow are to have a true, not imagined, relationship to the needs and enduring values of the people who will live in them.

FROM THE BEGINNING

Today's cities trace their origin to the villages of pre-history where a few hundred people lived and walked each day to their fields to produce the food necessary for survival. As animal domestication and the development of agriculture increased the efficiency of food production, those people who were no longer needed to tend the land became potters, spinners, weavers and other artisans.

The great cities of ancient time rose in India's rich alluvial Indus valley, in the lands adjacent to the Mediterranean, the Red Sea, and the Persian Gulf and in China. They were relatively small places covering a few square miles.

Little is known about the size of the population of these ancient cities. Obviously, that was controlled by the agricultural economies which supported them, and the agricultural surpluses which made urban societies possible were never very large. Until about 1000 B.C., it is believed that no more than 1 or 2 percent of the world's population were city dwellers, and that these prehistoric metropolises did not exceed 100,000 people. Until very recently, urban communities have been dangerous places to live because, with primitive amenities, and no knowledge of the cause and control of disease, even low degrees of congestion invited epidemics. Brutally high death rates appear to have held life expectancy at birth to no more than about 20 years.

With the growth of population, the city grew in size. As its population pressed ever-more severely on the food supply, the city had to absorb more land. According to Harrison Brown, Professor of Geochemistry, California Institute of Technology, land seizure and the right to water were frequent causes of war; and many wars were started by "half-starved barbarians who cast envious eyes upon urban wealth and decided to attempt to take it for their own." Often they succeeded. Discussing the rise and fall of those early cities, Dr. Brown states:

> The populations of the ancient oriental empires were eventually limited by deaths resulting from starvation, disease, and war, and, to a lesser extent, by conscious control of conception, by abortion, and by infanticide. Sanitation measures were seldom taken, except in the homes of the higher classes. Famine surged over the ancient lands at frequent intervals. As the crowded conditions, the filth, and the food situation in the ancient cities worsened, contagious diseases, and with them high rates of infant mortality, prevailed.

> *   *   *

> Thus increased mortality and, to a lesser extent, conscious family limitation continuously lowered the rate of population growth in the ancient oriental empires. But in the new regions where urban culture was surging upward, populations grew rapidly. The changes resulted in the destruction of old civilizations and the creation of new ones.

The fascinating history of the world's great cities cannot be told in limited space. Only the briefest discussion of the urbanization of Europe is possible here.

Many of the world's ancient cities were already in ruins by the time the Greco-Roman civilization (600 B.C. to 400 A.D.) arose and created the first great cities of the west. New civilizations in the Orient were also building proud and beautiful new cities, and many of these flourished along the great trade routes of Europe and Asia.

Athens and Rome were among the first great cities on the European continent. Rome, Alexandria and Byzantium (Constantinople, and now called Istanbul) became the giants of the period, with estimated peak populations of

350,000, 216,000 and 190,000, respectively. Some historians allege that Rome had over a million people at her zenith. Athens, Syracuse and Carthage had populations of 120,000 to 200,000.

During the early days of the Greek and Roman Empires, population growth remained in balance with the food supply. But the rapid growth of the cities soon put heavy pressure on the productive capacity of the land. Unfortunately, Greek civilization evolved in a region where only 20 percent of the land area could be cultivated, and this placed severe limits on food production. As the cities grew, their populations became increasingly dependent upon imports of grain from outlying districts and provinces. As the demand for food grew, hills and mountains were laid bare of their forests. Few of those areas have recovered from the exploitative land practices prevalent during the golden years of the Greek Empire.

The Roman Empire repeated this pattern but destruction extended over a vastly greater area. The insatiable appetite of the rapidly growing population denuded Italy's hills and mountains and made deserts of untold millions of acres along the Mediterranean. Again, as the population of the Italian peninsula grew rapidly, grain imports from adjacent regions and then from Africa became necessary to feed the multitudes. As the center of the empire continued to pile up population, the desperate need for food spurred Roman conquest. According to the historian, V. G. Simkovitch:

> Province after province was turned by Rome into a desert, for Rome's exactions naturally compelled greater exploitation of the conquered soil and its more rapid exhaustion. Province after province was conquered by Rome to feed the growing proletariat with its corn and enrich the prosperous with its loot. The only exception was Egypt, because of the overflow of the Nile . . . Latium, Campania, Sardinia, Sicily, Spain, Northern Africa, as Roman granaries, were successively reduced to exhaustion. Abandoned land in Latium and Campania turned into swamps, in Northern Africa into a desert. The forest-clad hills were denuded.

With the fall of the Roman Empire, Europe entered a period of population ebb which lasted from about 450 to 950 A.D. Italy, Gaul, Iberia, North Africa, Greece and Egypt were especially affected, and so were their cities. It has been estimated that Rome had about 350,000 people at the time of Augustus, 241,000 around 200 A.D., 172,600 about 350 A.D., 36,000–48,000 and 500 A.D., and only 30,000 in the 10th century. Cities of fairly considerable size had grown up elsewhere. Baghdad with an estimated population of 300,000 was the capital of the Caliphate Empire. Cordoba with 90,000, and Seville with 52,000 had risen in Moorish Spain, Constantinople with its 160,000 to 200,000 inhabitants was the pride of the Byzantine Empire.

Usually new cities of the period arose around an old Roman armed camp, at a crossing of a river, around a church, an abbey or a fortified chateau. Frequent wars made high places desirable locations for cities of the Middle Ages because they were easily defended. Many of these cities had two settle-

an any other was made by the British physician, Edward Jenner, whose
 accination against smallpox was introduced in 1792. This initial step in man's
ability to defer death opened the way for controlling the diseases and epidemics
which had flourished in villages and cities since the beginning of time. To
asteur and an army of microbe and virus hunters who have followed Jenner
oes the credit for making the city a relatively safe place in which to live.

HE INDUSTRIAL-URBAN REVOLUTION, 1800–1900

Throughout history, cities have often experienced rapid spurts of growth,
ut the tremendous growth potential they now display could not have devel-
oed without the techniques of modern medicine, public health and sanitation.
hese made cities safe havens for the rapidly increasing working class of the
Industrial Revolution. In England, the death rate began to fall about 1730 and
continued a leisurely downward trend for more than two centuries. The slow
ace of that decline allowed another important phenomenon to develop—a
ow decline in the birth rate. This appears to have occurred first in France
out the middle of the 17th century, in Ireland during the 1820's, in the
nited States after 1830 and in England during the 1870's.

TABLE I. TOTAL WORLD POPULATION AND WORLD URBAN POPULATION: 1800–950

	World population	Population (in millions) living in localities of:			Percent of world population living in localities of:		
Year		20,000 to 100,000	100,000 and over	Total	20,000 to 100,000	100,000 and over	Total
1800	906	6.1	15.6	21.7	0.7	1.7	2.4
1850	1,171	22.9	27.5	50.4	2.0	2.3	4.3
1900	1,608	59.3	88.6	147.9	3.7	5.5	9.2
1950	2,400	188.5	313.7	502.2	7.8	13.1	20.9

SOURCE: United Nations, *Report on the World Social Situation,* New York, 1957, p. 114.
(Based on data from Kingsley Davis and Hilda Hertz.)

In 1798, Thomas Robert Malthus, a 32-year-old curate who was astounded
' the rabbit-like proliferation of the working people living in misery and
qualor, published his famous critical analysis on the problem of poverty in
ngland. He insisted that to effect a cure of the "unspeakable ills of society"
' would be necessary to get to the root of the matter. As Malthus viewed the
roblem, "the poverty and misery arising from a too rapid increase of popula-
on had been distinctly seen, and the most violent remedies proposed, so long

ments, one on the heights and another nearby on a plain which
and fields for cultivation. A relatively small population lived '
area, and as population grew the walls were extended.

When Europe's population began to increase again durin;
tury, cities began to grow and the number of villages also
period of growth came to an abrupt halt in 1348 when the
swept across Europe. It has been estimated that 20 to 25 perce:
died in two disastrous years, and that by 1400 this and other
reduced the continent's population to about 60 percent of the p

FROM THE RENAISSANCE TO THE INDUSTRIAL REVOLU
1400–1800

Population grew slowly during the first part of the Rena
celerated toward the end of the period. City population follo\
pattern. In Italy, the cradle of the Renaissance, the populat:
shifted up and down while that of Venice and Rome about (

Two of the giants of modern times, London and Paris, w(
growth during this period. Estimates of the population of Pari
from 130,000 to 500,000.

The impact of technology on population growth was even n
demonstrated during the period 1600–1800. Technological ad
portation gave great impetus to commerce and exploration.
northern Europe began the colonization of the New World, ar
off some of the surplus population. Cities were established al(
coast of North America and many maritime cities of Europe g
the empty lands of America were filled up by the descendant
from Europe, the frontier pushed westward.

The vast breadbaskets of North America made food m
Europe. Prior to the American Revolution, Edmund Burke
gland's annual import of grain from America exceeded a m
value. The population of the North American continent grew
20 to 30 percent a decade after the initial settlement, but not a
was due to natural increase. Immigration had been an import
population growth of the United States from 1620 until Wo

During the 17th and 18th centuries, the foundations wei
of the great European fortunes which later supplied the capital
the Industrial Revolution. In England, technological adva
manufacturing and agriculture were setting the stage for that i
ushered in the most rapid population growth the world and i
had ever known. The conversion of two million acres of wast·
to farming during the 18th century greatly increased agricultı
and the food surplus available for the urban population.

The discovery which possibly had a greater impact on pc

ago as the times of Plato and Aristotle." Malthus defined the problem in these terms: *How to provide for those who are in want in such a manner as to prevent a continual increase in their numbers and of the proportion which they bear to the whole society.*

Malthus was followed by a succession of "pamphleteers"—one was Francis Place, a working man himself—who denounced the congestion and miserable living conditions and urged the working people to have fewer children. Finally, in 1876, the right to discuss fertility control was established in the British Isles when the government lost the case of "Regina *vs* Charles Bradlaugh and Annie Besant." This decision established the right to distribute a pamphlet concerning birth control which had been widely circulated throughout England for 40 years and it opened the way to free dissemination of fertility control information.

Kingsley Davis, one of this country's leading students of urbanization, points to several factors which helped the cities of western Europe achieve a much higher degree of urbanization than the ancient cities:

> Yet it was precisely in western Europe, where cities and urbanization had reached a nadir during the Dark Ages, that the limitations that had characterized the ancient world were finally to be overcome. The cities of Mesopotamia, India, and Egypt, of Persia, Greece, and Rome, had all been tied to an economy that was primarily agricultural, where handicraft played at best a secondary role and where the city was still attempting to supplement its economic weakness with military strength, to command its sustenance rather than to buy it honestly. In western Europe, starting at the zero point, the development of cities not only reached the stage that the ancient world had achieved but kept going after that. It kept going on the basis of improvements in agriculture and transport, the opening of new lands and new trade routes, and, above all, the rise in productive activity, first in highly organized handicraft and eventually in a revolutionary new form of production—the factory run by machinery and fossil fuel. The transformation thus achieved in the nineteenth century was the true urban revolution, for it meant not only the rise of a few scattered towns and cities but the appearance of genuine urbanization, in the sense that a substantial portion of the population lived in towns and cities.

England, the world's most highly urbanized country today, is the classical example of the processes of industrialization and urbanization because she led the world in both. By 1801, 26 percent of the population of England and Wales lived in cities of 5,000 or more; and 21 percent in cities of 10,000 or more. The United States did not reach this degree of urbanization until 1880 when 25 percent of the population lived in cities of 5,000 or more. In contrast, only about 20 percent of India's population live in cities of that size today.

By 1861, 55 percent of the total population of England lived in urban areas; and by 1891, 72 percent, with only 1.3 percent of the population living in urban districts smaller than 3,000 population. Until 1861, the rural population suffered a relative decline in numbers as cities grew more rapidly. The numerical peak of the rural population, 9.1 million, was reached in 1861. It declined 11 percent, to 8.1 million by 1891.

London, a mud flat on the banks of the Thames when Caesar arrived, grew from 864,800 to 4,232,000 between 1801 and 1891—an increase of almost 400 percent. In 1891, Greater London with 5.6 million people, three fourths of whom lived in the city proper and the remainder in the "outer-ring," had the distinction of being the world's largest city. It covered an area of 690 square miles and included every parish of which any part was within 12 miles of Charing Cross. Today, it has an area of 722 square miles, and includes the Administrative County of London (London AC) also Middlesex County, and parts of Surrey, Hertfordshire, Essex and Kent Counties. The population of Greater London is slightly over 8.2 million. London AC which includes the City of London and 28 metropolitan boroughs is identical with the 1891 area. It comprises 117 square miles and has a population of 3.2 million that represents a 28 percent decline from its 1901 peak.

Between 1811 and 1891, England's large cities with 100,000 population increased from 1.2 million to more than 9.2 million. Although London absorbed a lesser share of this growth, 14.6 percent of Britain's population lived in the capital city of 1891 and 17.3 percent lived in the other large cities. In terms of the aggregate urban population, 44 percent resided in London and the 23 large cities.

USA DURING THE 1800's

The first census was taken in 1790, soon after the Republic was born. It reported a population of 3,929,214. Only 5 percent lived in the 24 "urban" places of 2,500 population or more. Obviously, the rural-urban distinction was not clear-cut, and most of the people lived under essentially rural conditions. The largest cities were port cities: Philadelphia, New York, Boston, Charleston and Baltimore. According to Conrad and Irene B. Taeuber who are leading authorities on the growth of population in the United States:

> The clustering of settlers in small compact groupings began early, but the leading places of the colonial period were small. Boston, the largest place in the American colonies, had about 4,500 inhabitants in 1680. Ten years later the number had climbed to 7,000, but it required nearly 50 years to double this number. A decline of some 1,500 persons in the 10 years after 1740 is attributed to smallpox and war. Before recovery to the 1740 figure had occurred, the Revolutionary War had begun, and with it came a further reduction. The estimates for 1780 place Boston's numbers at only 10,000. After that war, the city recovered rapidly, and by the time of the first census in 1790, its total population was reported as 18,000. But by then both Philadelphia and New York had overtaken Boston, with Philadelphia in the lead. In 1790, the leading cities were Philadelphia, New York, Boston, Charleston (South Carolina), and Baltimore.

As in the Old World, urban growth in the United States was stimulated by the rapid rate of population growth and the accelerating pace of technology. The abundance of fertile land could sustain an ever-growing urban population. Land was easy to own. People married early, had children early and had many of them.

The port cities were the first to grow, then as traffic on rivers and canals pushed industrialization beyond the coastal areas, new cities began to rise. After 1840, the railroads became the most important single factor in the formation of new cities and their growth.

Every decade since the first census in 1790, with the exception of that of 1870, urban population grew faster than rural. The decade of 1840 recorded the most rapid urban growth when the population in urban places almost doubled. But the urban increase was not numerically larger than the rural until the Civil War. Since 1860, with the single exception of the 1870's, every decade has shown greater urban than rural numerical growth. From 1880 until 1940, urban growth has accounted for from 60 to 90 percent of total growth. Between 1940 and 1950, United States population increased by 19 million, rural population declined 3 million while urban population grew by 22 million!

By 1900, the nation's population had grown to nearly 76 million. Almost 40 percent lived in urban areas—ten times as many people as in 1800. The number of urban areas with 2,500 population or more had increased to 1,737 by 1900. There were 38 places of 100,000 or more in the United States and, collectively, they claimed 19 percent of the country's population.

The first great city of over 100,000, New York, reached that mark in 1820. In 1790, New York City had only 33,131 people. By 1960, it had over 7.7 million, and that represents a 23,172 percent increase in 170 years.

The total population of the five largest cities has grown from 7.6 million in 1900 to 17.3 million in 1960. Now, one out of every ten United States citizens lives in these five cities.

While urban agglomeration and the growth of suburbs were well advanced by 1900, the nation had experienced nothing comparable to the rapid urban growth which was to take place during the next 60 years. By 1900, there were already 50 urban areas which would have qualified as "principal standard metropolitan areas" under the 1950 census definition, i.e., having a population of 100,000 or over. These contained 24 million people, almost one third of the total U. S. population.

WORLD-WIDE URBANIZATION 1900–1960

World population is growing at an unprecedented rate today. The world still is far from a city world, even though it has been moving in that direction at an ever-accelerating rate since 1800. However, urbanization will continue to spread for some time to come as the underdeveloped areas strive for economic development.

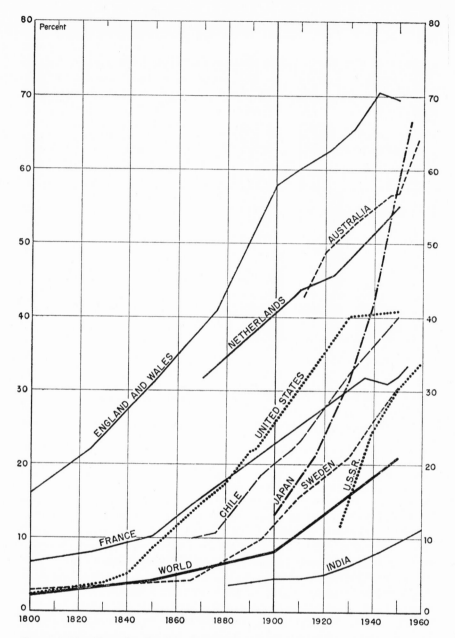

Figure 1: The Growth of Urban Populations Since 1800

Here is shown the percent of the total population of various countries living in localities of 20,000 or more. (The unit is 25 or more for the United States and Sweden.) For the world as a whole the proportion of dwellers in medium-size and large cities has quadrupled, from under 5 percent to over 20 percent. In the United States the proportion has increased tenfold as the nation has shifted from predominantly rural to one of the most highly urbanized countries. (Data from United Nations *Report on the World Social Situation* and other sources.)

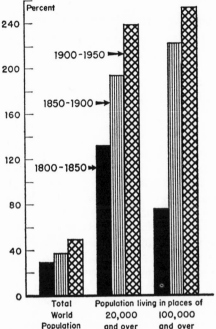

Figure 2: The Increase in World and Urban Population

This graph shows the percentage increase in the total population of the world and of the population living in medium-size and large cities since the early part of the Industrial Revolution. During this time, world population increased at a rate unprecedented in previous history, but the movement into cities was far more rapid. In these explosive growing urban areas will be found some of the most serious political, social and economic problems in the next fifty years.

Today, over 20 percent of the world's people, or more than 500 million, live in urban areas of 20,000 or more, compared with only about 2 percent in 1800. Over three fifths of today's urbanites live in large cities of 100,000 or more, and they represent 13 percent of total world population.

In 1900, there were ten cities with one million or more population in the world: five in Europe, three in North America and only one in Asia and in Russia. In 1955, there were 61 cities of that size. Of the 28 in Asia, nine were in China and six in India. Europe had 16 cities of a million or more and the United States had five.

Urban growth rates reached their peak in Europe and America during the latter part of the 19th century and tapered off after that. They have been most rapid in Asia and Africa during the first half of the 20th century. The United Nations *Report on the World Social Situation*, published in 1957, carried a detailed discussion of world urbanization which included chapters on "Social

Problems of Urbanization in Economically Underdeveloped Areas," "Urbanization in Africa South of the Sahara" and "Urbanization in Latin America." The Report utilizes the research of many leading students of urbanization, and its tables and graphs summarize historical and present growth trends. This issue of the *Bulletin* draws heavily on that important document.

The speed-up in population growth in the economically underdeveloped areas of the world is accompanied by the traditional acceleration in the growth of cities in those areas. Discussing present and future trends, the Report states:

> A major factor in the present and the anticipated future acceleration is the sudden spurt of urban growth in economically under-developed countries. Between 1900 and 1950, the population living in cities of 100,000 or more in Asia mounted from an estimated 19.4 million to 105.6 million (a gain of 444 percent), and in Africa from 1.4 million to 10.2 million (a gain of 629 percent).
>
> . . . the large-city population of Asia and Africa has increased much more rapidly during the twentieth century than it did during the nineteenth century while in Europe and America, urban growth reached its peak in the latter part of the nineteenth century and slowed down thereafter. These shifting rates of growth have meant that Asia, which contained nearly two-thirds of the world's population in large cities in 1800, had less than a fourth by 1900; but then the trend started to reverse, and by 1950 Asia had one-third of the world's large-city population.

The Report compares the difference between the present trend of urban growth and urbanization in Asia and Africa with the trends in Europe during the first half of this century:

> In spite of rapid urban growth, the increase in degree of urbanization in Asia and Africa still did not equal the increase in Europe during 1900–1950. The reason for this paradox lies in the distinction . . . between urban growth and urbanization. While the population of Asia living in cities of 100,000 or more increased prodigiously from 19.4 million in 1900 to 105.6 million in 1950, the percentage of the total population living in such cities increased only from 2.1 per cent to 7.5 per cent; in other words, there was only a 5.4 per cent shift in the structure of the total population, while in Europe there was an 8 per cent shift in the same period. Because the urban population still represents only a small proportion of the total population in Asia (and other less developed regions), a small change in the degree of urbanization will produce a large amount of urban growth; or conversely stated, a large amount of urban growth is required to make a significant impact upon the population structure.
>
> In the majority of the less developed countries, the rural population has continued to grow along with the urban population, although at a slower pace, but in many of the developed countries the absolute size of the rural population has remained constant or even declined in recent decades, so that the national population increase has been absorbed by the already heavy urban population.

Noting that there are important differences in the levels and trends of urbanization among the industrially more advanced countries and among the less deveolped countries, the Report states:

> . . . Several of the economically less-developed countries, particularly in Latin America, have higher levels of urbanization—as measured by this particular criterion—than certain European countries.

TABLE II.   POPULATION IN LARGE CITIES (100,000 AND OVER) BY MAJOR CONTINENTAL REGIONS

Area	*Population (in millions) in large cities*				*As percent of total population*			
	1800	1850	1900	1950	1800	1850	1900	1950
World	15.6	27.5	88.6	313.7	1.7	2.3	5.5	13.1
Asia	9.8	12.2	19.4	105.6	1.6	1.7	2.1	7.5
Europe*	5.4	13.2	48.0	118.2	2.9	4.9	11.9	19.9
Africa	0.30	0.25	1.4	10.2	0.3	0.2	1.1	5.2
America	0.13	1.8	18.6	74.6	0.4	3.0	12.8	22.6
Oceania	—	—	1.3	5.1	—	—	21.7	39.2

*Including USSR.

SOURCE: United Nations, *Report on the World Social Situation,* New York, 1957, p. 114. (Based on data from Kingsley Davis and Hilda Hertz.)

> . . . Some of the more urbanized and industrialized countries experienced a marked slowing-down of their urbanization rate during the period between 1930 and 1950 . . . France, the United States and (between 1940 and 1950) Japan; England and Wales actually experienced a slight drop between 1941 and 1951. Such a slowing-down or regression may be due to several possible factors: the reaching or approaching of a natural limit of urbanization, depending upon the economy of the country; the effects of the depression of the 1930's and of the Second World War; a shift from city growth to suburban growth—with the improvement of transportation and the overcrowding of cities, suburban localities are growing much more rapidly than cities proper in a number of countries (the United States is an outstanding example). The relative weight of these different factors is not know.
>
> Other countries have shown a remarkable increase in degree of urbanization since 1930. This includes Puerto Rico and the USSR. In the latter country, between 1926 and 1955, while the total population increased only 34 per cent, the population in cities of 100,000 or more increased more than four times.
>
> . . . Ceylon, on the other hand, is remaining relatively stable at a low level of urbanization.

DIFFERENCES IN THE PATTERN OF URBANIZATION

In 1950, the world's major regions of industrial urban settlement were Australasia, Northwestern Europe, Northern America, Northeast Asia and Southern South America. These areas included about 25 percent of total world population, but 52 percent living in cities of 100,000 or more. By major world areas, Africa was the least urbanized, with only 9 percent of the population in cities of 20,000 or more. Australasia was the most heavily urbanized, with 47 percent in cities of that size.

During the past 25 years, the two largest countries of the communist world, USSR and China, have experienced very rapid urbanization. In the USSR in 1959, 48 percent of the total population was living in cities, compared with only 32 percent in 1939. In 20 years, the urban population grew by almost 40 million, an increase of two thirds. In 1959, 23 percent of the total population and almost 50 percent of the urban population lived in cities of 100,000 or more. Since 1939, many new cities have risen in the USSR. The seven largest are: Kaliningrad, 202,000; Angarsk, 134,000; Klaypeda, 89,000; Yuzhno-Sakhalinsk, 86,000; Volzhskiy, 67,000; Vorkuta, 65,000; Oktyabrskiy, 65,000.

It has been estimated that 20 million Chinese migrated from rural to urban areas between 1949 and 1956. This almost equals the total population of the three Benelux countries and "undoubtedly constitutes one of history's largest population shifts in so short a time . . ." China's inland cities have experienced fantastic growth. Estimates indicate that in the western provinces alone, Lanchow grew from 200,000 in 1950 to 680,000 in 1956; Paotow from 90,000 in 1949 to 430,000 in 1957; Kalgan from 270,000 in 1949 to over 630,000 in 1958; Sian from less than one-half million in 1949 to 1,050,000 in 1957.

Furthermore, there is a heavy concentration of China's urban population in her large cities. In 1953, 103 cities of 100,000 or more accounted for 49 million people, or 63 percent of the total urban population. However, only 13 percent of the total population lived in cities. In contrast, about 46 percent of the United States urban population lived in cities of 100,000 or more in 1950, and 64 percent of our total population lived in urban localities.

The growth rate of the urban population of the USSR between 1950 and 1959 was 4 percent per annum. In China between 1949 and 1956 the urban growth rate appears to have been at the rate of 6.5 percent per annum.

Within countries, there are great variations in extent and rate of urbanization. For example, in 1950, the northeastern part of the United States had one quarter of the total population and one third of its urban population. Within this region, Vermont has the lowest degree of urbanization (36 percent), while New Jersey had the highest (87 percent).

In some regions of the world, a single large city—usually the capital city —contains a high proportion of a nation's total population and its urban population. In many countries, well over 50 percent of all the urban population is concentrated in the capital city. This is especially true of several Latin

TABLE III. ESTIMATED POPULATION OF WORLD'S 20 GREATEST METROPOLITAN AGGLOMERATIONS

Metropolitan Area	Year	Population (in thousands)	Principal City	Year	Population (in thousands)
New York—Northeastern New Jersey	1960*	14,577	New York City	1960*	7,710
Tokyo—Yokohama	1955	11,349	Tokyo	1955	6,969
London	1956	10,491	London	1956	3,273
Moscow	1956	7,300	Moscow	1959	5,032
Paris	1954	6,737	Paris	1954	2,850
Osaka—Kobe	1955	6,405	Osaka	1955	2,547
Shanghai	1953		Shanghai	1953	6,204
Chicago—Northwestern Indiana	1960*	6,726	Chicago	1960*	3,493
Buenos Aires	1955	5,750	Buenos Aires	1955	3,575
Calcutta	1955	5,700	Calcutta	1955	2,750
Los Angeles—Long Beach	1960*	6,690	Los Angeles	1960*	2,448
Essen—Dortmund—Duisburg (Inner Ruhr)	1955	5,353	Essen	1955	691
Bombay	1955	4,400	Bombay	1955	3,600
East & West Berlin	1955	4,245	East Berlin	1955	1,140
			West Berlin	1955	2,195
Philadelphia—New Jersey	1960*	4,289	Philadelphia	1960*	1,960
Mexico City	1955	3,900	Mexico City	1955	2,800
Rio de Janeiro	1955	3,750	Rio de Janeiro	1955	2,900
Detroit	1960*	3,761	Detroit	1960*	1,672
Leningrad	1955	3,500	Leningrad	1959†	2,888
Sao Paulo	1955	3,300	Sao Paulo	1955	2,600

*U. S. Bureau of the Census; 1960 data are preliminary.
†USSR All-Union Population Census of 1959.

SOURCE: International Urban Research, *The World's Metropolitan Areas,* Berkeley, University of California Press, 1959, unless otherwise indicated.

American countries, and the trend there was discussed in an earlier *Population Bulletin,* August 1958:

> The unique feature in Latin America's urbanization is the high concentration of people in relatively few metropolitan areas, usually the national capitals. Except in Brazil and Colombia, the largest city has more inhabitants than all the other cities of 100,000 and more combined. In 13 of the 20 countries, at least 10 percent of the people live in the largest city or metropolitan area, usually the capital city. In six of these countries the largest city contains one-fifth or more of the national

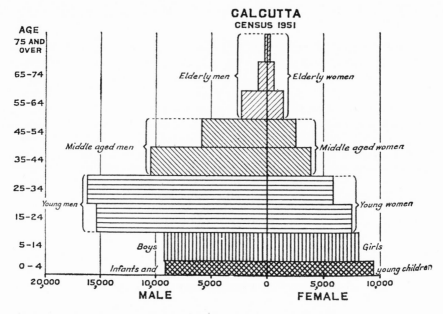

Figure 4: Age-Sex Distribution of the Population of Calcutta

This graph from the 1951 census of India shows the enormous preponderance of males between 20 and 40 in a great Asian city. The excess of males is found in all ages except among those under five and 75 and over. Multitudes of men in the prime of life, separated from their families and living under primitive conditions, pose a most serious problem of urban adjustment in the underdeveloped countries.

population: 33 percent in Uruguay, 29 percent in Argentina, 23 percent in Chile and Panama and 21 percent in Cuba and Costa Rica. One out of six Venezuelans lives in Caracas.

If 20 percent of the United States' population lived in the capital city, Washington, D. C. would have 34 million people!

In 1955, the world had 1,107 metropolitan areas of 100,000 or more. Asia contained almost one third of these or 341 and Europe over one fourth or 279. Northern America had 202, Latin America 78 and Oceania only 11. The nations with the largest number were the United States, 189; USSR, 148; and China, 103. Of the world's 108 metropolitan areas with one million or more, 34 were in Europe, excluding USSR, 32 were in Asia, and 26 were in North America.

The four largest metropolitan areas in the world have a total population of almost 44 million people. The Tokyo-Yokohama urban agglomeration with 11.3 million people in 1955 (almost 7 million of them in Tokyo) by now may be almost as large as the New York-New Jersey metropolitan area (over 14 million people in 1960). London's metropolitan area had 10.5 million people in 1956, 3.2 million of them in London proper. Suburbia has not reached the USSR, for in 1955, Moscow's metropolitan area, although the fourth largest in the world, was considerably smaller than the three other giants. It had 7.3 million people; and slightly over 5 million of them lived in Moscow itself.

New York City's five boroughs have a population of 7.7 million. The borough of Manhattan with 1.7 million in 1960 records a decline of 15 percent from the 1950 census. Its population density is 75,900 people per square mile!

Japan, with 92 million people and a land area about the size of Montana, is one of the most highly urbanized nations. She has 64 cities of 100,000 population or more, and their combined total is over 21.3 million. That is about a fourth of Japan's total population and about 7 percent of all the people in the world who reside in cities of that size.

CONTRASTS IN CITY LIFE

Despite the ever-accelerating rate of urbanization since 1800, modern man continues to be tied to the land. Four out of every five people in the world still live in the country. However, the trek to cities will accelerate during the decades ahead as the economically underdeveloped countries strive to become industrial societies.

But the speed-up in the rate of social change makes the urbanization process a very different one today in those countries than it was in the Western world. Since the Industrial Revolution began, the continuous migration in the West from country to city has been a flight from low-paid rural jobs to more lucrative jobs and greater opportunities in urban areas. But in underdeveloped countries today the movement to cities is more of a shift from unproductive rural situations to even less productive urban situations with no income gain and with grievous drain on limited savings due to higher living costs.

*　　*　　*

THE CITY OF TOMORROW

When the city of antiquity first began to emerge, transportation was by foot, communication by word of mouth, and space—that playground of 20th-century man—was thought to be an inverted bowl with holes punched in it. In the field of transportation and communication, invention and technology have moved farther in one century than in the preceding two thousand centuries.

Generations of scientific research and highly sophisticated planning have brought man to the stage where he can bounce messages off a balloon orbiting in space. By jet plane he can reach any spot on the planet in less than a day. But in the area of social invention man's approach to many urgent problems, among them population control and city planning, still smacks of the Dark Ages rather than the technological age of invention and creative improvization. A do-nothing, know-nothing approach or a Micawberish hope that "something will turn up" does not resolve crises.

It is very likely that in the city man first will have to face the fact that space is the finite factor in the multiplication of people. In all probability, projections which indicate that a century hence Calcutta's population could increase by 35 to 66 million, or that New York City could be half or two thirds that size will never materialize. However, they serve to warn of nightmares to come unless man begins to apply his foresight and his great inventive skills to check his unprecedented population growth and to solve the problems which that growth has created.

Part II

URBAN PROCESS,
GROWTH, AND
INTERDEPENDENCE

THE ECOLOGICAL PERSPECTIVE ON URBAN GROWTH AND INTERDEPENDENCE will be the major theme in this section. The ecological dimension represents two possible major concerns. One is the description of the distribution and interrelationship of facilities, services, and populations and the nature of their change. In addition, the ecological perspective may also be taken to represent a distinctive theoretical orientation to understanding urban structure. All students of the city must perforce be attentive to the former concerns. Fewer, however, are persuaded that ecological theory provides an adequate interpretation of the spatial patterning of urban life and institutions. The present section attends principally to the ecology of the city in descriptive terms, though some consideration is given in the readings and in these introductory comments to the nature of ecological theory. An effort is made, however, to go beyond a distinctive ecological theoretical perspective and to suggest some of the additional factors that determine spatial patterning and, more broadly, urban organization.

Some Urban Processes and Forms: The Ecological Dimension

Ecological theory is an explanatory scheme that interprets urban structure and change in terms of an unconscious, presocial, largely economic-based competitive adjustment between diverse populations and facilities striving for optimum spatial location under conditions of dominance within a given environment. The competing parties distribute themselves spatially as a result of resolving contending forces, such as those between relative resources on the one hand and the urgency of maximizing factors of convenience, accessibility, environmental attractiveness, and cost on the other. The role of social and political institutions, purposes, human values, and subjectivity is denied[1] (90, 127). While recent neoclassical ecologists presumably incorporate social organization as one of their explanatory variables, it is suggested here that it is essentially applied in a rigid fashion, without attention to the role of volition, choice, and the wide range of optional responses and demands that inhere in social organization. The mediating role of social organization for non-social ecological elements is not elaborated.[2]

[1]For a number of summary descriptions of different schools of ecological thought and some representative readings see the collection edited by George Theodorson, *Studies in Human Ecology* (115), and his section introductions.

[2]Some recent ecologists led by Leo Schnore and Otis Dudley Duncan have sought to develop a distinctive ecological approach in terms of the determinate role of the four causal variables of social organization and the less social factors of population, environment, and technology in accounting for urban structure, change, and interdependence. See 24, 25, 27, 97, 98.

Earlier ecological theory and models of urban structure and growth find brief summary expression in the useful essay by Harris and Ullman, "The Nature of Cities" (56). While the three models of internal urban structure described by the authors— Burgess' concentric zone theory, Hoyt's sector theory, and the multiple nuclei conception—differ in a number of important regards, the implicit explanatory scheme underlying these conceptions is clearly an ecological one. Thus, environmental, transport, economic, and nonsocial factors are stressed as determining location within a competitive framework. Urban structure is perceived in terms of the operation of the principle of dominance. Dominance is essentially a condition wherein population and facilities are spatially ordered in regard to, integrated in terms of, and to an important extent controlled by, the functions of a strategic unit located at some point. The urban area is also perceived as exhibiting districts or natural areas characterized by distinctive populations, facilities, or social properties that are interpreted as a product of a competitive process that leads to a grouping or segregation of similar populations and functions. A significant and enduring feature of these theories is that they are formulated in terms of processes of growth and change, and are not static models of urban areal structure.

Some of the insufficiencies in the ecological perspective are suggested in the selections by Firey, Form, and Willhelm (30, 34, 127). A principal thrust of their criticisms is the lack of attention to the influence of social and cultural factors in urban structure; thus, their role in constraining and shaping the outcome of more exclusively ecological variables. Walter Firey's noted study of Boston (32) points out that land use was discrepant with what could be expected from a purely ecological model where the emphasis is on the role of market forces. He stresses the vital role played by cultural values and sentiments in the determination of land use. He shows how the symbolic quality and sentiments associated with certain central yet historical landmark, park, and low-density areas in Boston have continued to be important determining elements of urban structure. Such sentiments and cultural values are neither ecological variables nor are they derivable from ecological elements. In fact, their impact on urban structure has gone counter to that predictable from the essentially competitive economic analysis of the ecologists. Nor are Firey's observations unique. The existence of enclaves, land reserved for special uses—religious, political, recreational, or aesthetic—even in the heart of the city, is not unusual. This clearly contradicts other more economic uses.

The role of cultural and social values in determining residential settlement and movement has been elaborated in a number of studies. Jonassen (62) has pointed to the importance of sociocultural factors in explaining why Norwegian immigrants settled in particular areas of New York City and why they made the later moves they did. He notes that "*the movement of these people must be referred to factors that are volitional, purposeful, and personal and that these factors may not be considered as mere accidental and incidental features of biotic processes and impersonal competition"* (62, p. 38). Kosa's study (64) of the settlement pattern of Hungarian immigrants in Canada and the United States in this century shows that it was significantly influenced by a distinctive set of cultural values, among which a stress on economic success and the acquisition of property were especially important.

In a somewhat different direction Theodore Caplow's summary discussion (16) of his own observations and that of other students on the structure of French cities notes a number of significant findings. For example, he points to the absence of sharp disparities in land values and hence their lack of dominance over site-determination. Thus, the distribution of facilities, populations, and patterns of daily movement do not accord with the usual expectations of ecological theory.[3]

William Form observes, in "The Place of Social Structure in the Determination of Land Use" (34), that the land market is principally dominated by four interacting groupings—real-estate building groups, industry and business, homeowners, and local governmental agencies concerned with land usage. Of course, their relative influence is not equal, and the policies of some, realtors and builders, for example, pose important constraints on the other groups, especially homeowners. In effect, however, their actions represent the impact of several powerful social forces, distinctive group purposes and perspectives, and peculiar historic circumstances that are all significantly determinate of the nature of land usage. These elements differ from the competitive forces of the ecological model. One of Form's major concerns is the considerable influence of power often, but not always, economically based and only at times in accord with the direction predictable from a purely ecological model. Form points out that ". . . the image of a free and unorganized market in which individuals compete impersonally for land must be abandoned" (34, p. 317). His selection also provides a useful account of the interactions between these different groups and the kinds of factors that influence their purposes and relative effectiveness.

Sidney Willhelm's essay (127) provides a wide-ranging critique of the ecological perspective. Incorporating points similar to those raised in the preceding, he also notes that the neoclassical ecologist's attempt to remedy earlier shortcomings in ecological theory through including the concept of social organization as one of the four ecological variables does not meet the type of criticisms that have been developed here.[4] Social organization is used as a given rather than as an approximation of the normative and behavioral properties associated with a particular dimension of the social system —political, economic, or occupational. More explicitly, no given response can be assumed in any particular institutional area or value complex. A condition of choice prevails. Hence, the nature of land usage or population movement, for example,

---

[3]A collection of items stressing the social and cultural influences on land usage may be found in Theodorson, especially in Part II, Section C, and to some extent in Part III. The Jonassen, Kosa, and Caplow selections are reprinted there, among others.

[4]The reader will recall that the other three variables in the ecological complex are population, environment and technology.

cannot be successfully determined without an analysis of the choice potentials, the values, sentiments, historical circumstances, social structural constraints, and the distribution and purposes of relevant economic, social, and political power that bear on the social organization in question. Significantly, even the competitive process itself reflects a distinct cultural value complex (128). This kind of analysis, however, does not inhere in and is not attempted in what Willhelm defines as the neoclassical materialist school of ecology, a prestigious and influential area of contemporary ecological thought. The reader can, of course, turn to the essay itself for a number of other far-ranging criticisms which the present discussion and other selections have not considered.

The present comments have not referred to what Willhelm has labeled the voluntaristic and Theodorson, the sociocultural approach. The essays by Form and Firey, for instance, could be interpreted as illustrative of the orientation represented by this school of ecologists. The type of criticisms developed in the preceding pages do not apply to this approach. However, to perceive ecology as broadly as the scope of factors evidenced in the sociocultural perspective is to begin to lose any distinctive theoretical, though not descriptive, focus for ecology. In effect, this approach makes ecology identical in a number of major particulars with more general nonecological sociological analysis. It leaves unresolved the major problem of elaborating a theoretical scheme that would integrate both material, nonsocial, impersonal causal factors and the social, cultural, political, and historical elements that are the concern of traditional sociological analysis.

With the relatively recent developments in social area analysis and other multivariate factorial efforts to describe and conceptualize urban social structure, significant advance has been made over earlier, more narrowly spatial-centered, ecological efforts. The extract from the monograph by Shevky and Bell (104) provides some of the major properties of social area analysis. This is an approach partly characterized by the effort to understand urban social structure (not its spatial structure) in a society characterized by increasing social differentiations and extension of scale. Social area analysis proposes that three unidimensional indices—social rank, urbanization, and segregation[5]—can serve to differentiate urban populations. Another theoretical property of this scheme is the perspective that it contains for interpreting the nature of the urban order. Stressed in Peter Orleans' essay (82) and elaborated by Scott Greer in his *The Emerging City* (46), it urges the need for increased attention to the disassociation of spheres of contemporary life as well as the integrative role of shared interests and organizational ties. It is an approach that provides a beginning toward understanding the conditions for societal integration and personal sustenance in contemporary

[5]These have also been referred to in some writings as economic status, familism, or family status or life style, and ethnic status. See Bell, "Economic, Family, and Ethnic Status" (3).

society, conditions perhaps markedly different than in earlier more homogeneous and less socially differentiated societies. Yet, this is still an interpretation open to question: witness the still vigorous mass society critiques of the social order and texture of life.

Social area analysis has perhaps found its most extensive application and widest acceptance on a more descriptive level. It was successfully used, for instance, by Anderson and Egeland (2) in their attempt to reconcile Burgess' "concentric zone" and Hoyt's "sector" theory of residential structure. They showed that Burgess' concentric zone model tends to apply to the urbanism or familistic dimension, but Hoyt's sector, or radial, theory of growth was descriptive of the distribution of population by social rank, although not in terms of familistic properties. Its ability to provide a more refined and convenient approach to the description, identification, and systematic classification of sections of the city also aids in the selection of populations and areas for more intensive research. A notable feature here—followed and further developed by more recent elaborate factorial analysis of urban populations—is that social area analysis starts to comprehend population differences within the city by first constructing summary descriptive indices, only then attempting to map the distribution of population (1, p. 200). Thus, social areas are not spatially determined but are first derived in terms of certain specific social properties, which are then located in space.[6]

In research it is a scheme that has been effective in relating both the response of populations to the area or neighborhood in which they reside and the social patterns present in such an area to the social properties of the population in that particular neighborhood (4, 6, 7, 47, 48). It has also provided a convenient means of carrying out comparative urban analysis, and this has lent support to the effort to relate social area analysis theory to conceptions of increasing scale and social differentiation. More interesting, however, are the cultural and social factors that have constrained the theory[7] (2, 72, 73), a circumstance not initially recognized.

While social area analysis has been of considerable value in both descriptive and theoretical terms, its usefulness is restricted by a number of factors. Theoretical and empirical problems exist in the attempt to translate increasing scale and differentiation, perceived as societal level phenomena, to the level of subunits within the society (8, 58, 112, 120). It has also been noted that the applicability of social area analysis is limited by such cultural and social factors that preserve the independence of the three major dimensions of economic, familial, and ethnic status (1) and produce an urban

[6]The use of census tracts, however, to organize social distributions may well pose problems, especially where a tract is not socially homogeneous.

[7]Abu-Lughed (1) provides a useful bibliography of various social area analysis studies. A more diverse bibliography may also be found in Duncan W. G. Timms, *The Urban Mosaic, Towards a Theory of Residential Differentiation* (116).

population where these dimensions serve to characterize and distinguish among populations.[8] Difficulties in these regards have encouraged a factorial, multivariate analysis of various census tract data in order to derive basic analytic dimensions descriptive of the population rather than assuming them beforehand (79, 86, 92, 111, 112).

Urbanization and Metropolitan Growth

One of the most significant properties of recent American society is the increasing urbanization of society, particularly the growth of metropolitan areas. While it was not until 1920 that at least half of the American population resided in nonrural communities, the most rapid period of urban growth was in the last portion of the nineteenth century. In the middle of the last century only slightly more than one-seventh of the country's population was classified as urban. By the turn of the century 40 percent of the nation lived in urban areas. Today more than 73 percent of the population are urban residents. However, urban growth before the present century significantly followed traditional patterns. Growth was principally that of compact, dense, and well-defined urban cores, though some evidence of suburban growth does stretch back to as early as the last third of the eighteenth century. The significant feature of more recent growth is not only the increasing decline of the rural population, but also the growth of metropolitan areas. The sharp distinction between city and countryside disappears as population and facilities are diffused over a much wider area, as urban densities drop and as there is increased decentralization even while an increasing proportion of society become urban residents. Thus, the proportion of the national population in metropolitan regions has increased from 31.8 percent in 1900 to nearly 69 percent at the latest census. However, this growth has been occurring increasingly in the suburban areas. In the years between 1950 and 1970, for instance, the metropolitan area population outside the central cities increased at a rate approximately four times that of the central cities, so that somewhat less than 55 percent of the metropolitan population is now outside the central cities, compared to a little more than 38 percent in 1940. The distinguished planner Hans Blumenfeld has, in fact, suggested that the metropolis is a revolutionary stage in urban growth, "a basically new form of human settlement" (10, p. 51). Yet, much of our thinking, he suggests, is still in terms of older and now archaic conceptions of city structure and the "nature" of the city and the countryside.

Urban growth in America, including the development of metropolitanism reflects

[8]This therefore qualifies the earlier attempts by Bell (3) and Maurice Van Arsdel, Jr., Santo Carmilleri, and Calvin Schmid (119) to establish the original contributions of social area analysis theory.

the effect of a number of phenomena. One has been the continuing increase in agricultural productivity and the tremendous decline in the size of the agrarian labor force, under conditions of increasingly large-scale farming and a lack of employment opportunities in rural areas. The early concentration of industry in the cities in a rapidly developing nation, the advances in transportation, means of distribution, communication networks, as well as large-scale foreign immigration, all contributed to the growth of urban centers. The marked transformation in recent decades of the cities into metropolitan areas continued to reflect technological developments—especially in the area of new transportation innovations, the economics of industrial diffusion out of the central cities, the economic and market advantages of suburban location, the physical decay of the older cities, increasing affluence, and the force of both personal values and governmental policy.

Philip Hauser's summary statement (57) provides a useful review of some of the major characteristics and data on metropolitan growth in the United States. He also discusses some of the major forces changing land-use patterns in the metropolis—urban renewal, the increasing industrialization of suburban areas, and family use of the metropolitan area in terms of changing requirements of the life cycle. Attention is given to the importat role and pattern of foreign immigration and internal migration in urban and metropolitan growth. He also notes, as Burgess did earlier (15), the exceedingly rapid rate of growth of cities in America, a rate that in a relatively brief period of time converted once outlying attractive areas into the inner zone of the city and a generally low income deteriorating area. With an increasing fixity of urban boundaries such inner zones represent a considerable portion of the central city.

Hauser considers briefly what some students of the city interpret as the third stage of urbanization, after the growth of cities and metropolitan areas—the appearance of huge urban complexes called "supercity," "strip city," "conurbations," or "megalopolis" (named after a city planned by the ancient Greeks in the fourth century B.C.). In this recent manifestation of urban sprawl a continuous extension of principally urban residents develops, though rural communities will be included as they are engulfed. The megalopolis encompasses several major and some minor cities joined by strips of generally urban settlement, though extensive nonurban land usage is present. Although fragmented politically and administratively, and often crossing several state, provincial, or regional boundaries, the megalopolis exhibits considerable economic and social cohesion and exchange. In *Megalopolis—The Urbanized Northeastern Seaboard of the United States*, French geographer Jean Gottman (43) has provided the most extensive available study of the megalopolis,[9] which he interprets as an

[9]For a sprightly summary of Gottman's lengthy study the reader can consult Wolf Von Eckardt, *The Challenge of Megalopolis* (124). A series of papers related to the phenomenon of megalopolis have been edited by Jean Gottman and Robert A. Harper, eds., *Metropolis on the Move, Geographers Look at Urban Sprawl* (44). Also see the essay by Christopher Tunnard, "America's Super-Cities," *Harper's Magazine* (117).

irreversible phenomenon. Not a phenomenon limited to the United States, the megalopolis has begun to appear in the more industrially advanced and heavily populated nations such as Germany, England, the lowland countries, and Japan.

Some elaboration of Hauser's discussion of patterns of immigrant settlement and acceptance is pertinent to an understanding of ethnic and racial residence patterns. The rate of accommodation into American society and the extent to which ethnic and racial ghettos have declined has significantly depended on the language, religious, cultural, and racial background of immigrants and migrants and on the time of their arrival, although racial factors have been most influential. Immigrants from areas that have greatly contributed to American cultural patterns, such as western and northern Europe, have been accepted most readily, particularly when Protestant and English-speaking. Those from southern and eastern Europe, who in addition were often either Catholic, Jewish, or Greek Orthodox, and of course, non-English-speaking, were less readily accepted and have dispersed more slowly in American society.

This preponderant importance of racial factors is evidenced by the experience of black, yellow, and other non-white populations. The time of arrival is also important. The earlier generation of western and northern European immigrants obviously had more time in which to find a secure place in American society, and they also came to the United States while land on the frontier was still available and the rapid industrial growth of the United States to some extent provided economic opportunities that demanded few special skills or extensive schooling. However, such opportunities declined toward the close of the nineteenth century when the immigrants arrived from southern and eastern Europe. The opportunities have been even more sharply lacking in recent years as the Puerto Rican and black populations streamed into the urban centers (13, 22, 29, 41, 76, 80, 83, 109, 124). A more specific analytic scheme than that implied by the preceding would also have to take into account the level of the stratification system at which the migrant entered.[10] These comments are not to deny the very great difficulties the early migrants and their descendants experienced in achieving occupational and personal success, or, more recently, the improvement over time in the circumstances of contemporary black and Puerto Rican urban migrants (36).[11]

Internal migration, both of whites and blacks, has in recent decades been an important factor in urban growth. From 1920 to 1960 25 million people left the farms

[10]Though addressed to circumstances somewhat different than the United States case in regard to migration, see the article by Stanley Lieberson, "A Societal Theory of Race and Ethnic Relations" (69).

[11]The reader will find that there is an extensive and varied literature on immigration, migration, assimilation, and acculturation. It ranges from considering the response accorded diverse immigrant populations, the experience of settlement in particular urban centers and at different periods of time, to theoretical models of the dynamics and patterns of migration, settlement, and assimilation (14, 35, 38, 40, 41, 42, 52, 55, 61, 71, 75, 106).

for the cities. Part of the impetus for this movement is revealed by the fact that from 1940 alone agricultural productivity has increased 400 percent. Black movement, almost all in and from the South, constituted a significant though minor portion of this internal migration. The pattern of black migration began to be revealed clearly as far back as the end of the last century, but became especially vigorous during World War I. The movement has increased in recent years with approximately 1.8 million blacks in each of the last two decades leaving the rural areas of the South for urban centers in both the South and the North. The net migration of blacks during this period— almost exclusively into urban centers—was nearly 3 million. And by the census of 1960 they showed a greater degree of urban residency than whites, 73.2 percent to 69.6 percent, a sharp change from the beginning of the twentieth century when the ratio was close to one to two (29, 80). Blacks now constitute more than 20 percent of the population in the central cities, more in the larger cities. From 1960 to 1970 there was a net increase of 3.2 million blacks in the central cities, with a net loss of 600,000 whites. On the other hand, suburban white population increased 28 percent.

One social consequence of suburban growth has been the increasing separation between large portions of the poor and minority groups, on the one hand, and the better advantaged, dominant groups in American society. Similarly, one striking feature of urban residential patterns has been their segregated character (50, 70, 114). While earlier immigrant ghettos significantly declined over time, present black ghettos, for instance, are growing. As the Taeubers have shown by detailed analysis, whatever the region or type of community "white and Negro households are highly segregated. . . . In fact, Negroes are by far the most residentially segregated urban minority group in recent American history" (114, p. 2), even more so than Chicanos, Puerto Ricans, and Orientals. Patterns of segregation are continued and sharpened by black movement into the city, white migration to the suburbs and the process of black succession in formerly white areas, as well as by segregated patterns of new home construction (101). These partly reflect, of course, past historical experience, societal and group values, and various institutional practices.

It should be pointed out that racial residential segregation cannot in most instances be accounted for by economic factors. Thus, many low and modest income areas both within the central city and the suburbs lack almost any black representation. Similarly, many predominantly black areas contain a significant number with means sufficient to meet rental and purchase prices in various all-white neighborhoods. Nor has the improvement in the socioeconomic status of black populations necessarily led to any alteration in the degree of segregation. The Taeubers have concluded, on the basis of careful empirical analysis in their *Negroes in Cities*, that "the net effect of economic factors in explaining segregation is slight" (114, p. 94, 113). A significant import of such findings is that even if income levels improve there is little hope for a lowering of residential segregation, if past practices and experiences are a guide.

The differential location of minority group residence and the response to minority group movement is predominantly determined by the nature of American values, prejudices, and group strains. One aspect of this broader area, the question of the effect on housing values of black movement into a previously all or very predominantly white area, is charged with considerable emotion and great misunderstanding. There is the widespread myth that the value of housing drops with black movement into a white residence area. Yet, there is a considerable literature that effectively refutes such a proposition. McEntire (74) summarizes one of the major studies on the effects of racial change on property values, Luigi Laurenti's *Property Values and Race* (68). He also briefly considers Rapkin and Grigsby's analysis of racial movement (89) on the character of housing demand in the area affected. Such work, as well as the findings reported earlier by Laurenti for San Francisco (67), Ladd's analysis of property values in Ann Arbor (66), Palmore and Howe's New Haven Study (84), Hunt's study of Kalamazoo (60), and Northwood and Barth's study in Seattle (81), reveals that the movement of black families into essentially middle-class, single-family, white residence areas, whether occurring in merely one or two instances or in much larger numbers does not lower property values; if anything, prices go up. This would appear to hold true as long as a demand for homes continues either by blacks or whites or both, as in fact appears to be the case. Where prices drop it is usually the result of panic selling where a large number of homes are hastily pushed onto the market. Even here, however, prices will after a time regain or exceed previous levels.

In addition to providing further evidence on the stability of housing prices, McEntire's review of Rapkin and Grigsby's study of interracial neighborhoods in Philadelphia suggests that even in a zone of racial transition, white buyers are present in substantial numbers. However, they account for a distinct minority of home sales and will be most evident in areas of good homes and slow change. Further, the white home purchasers try to locate farther away rather than closer to already resident black families. Yet, the fact remains, an important one McEntire stresses, that a significant number of white families did choose to buy homes in an area of transition. Further, neither in background characteristics nor in attitudes did this white population appear distinctive. In a related vein it has been shown that even in communities witnessing a fairly marked change from white to increasing black occupancy, it cannot be assumed that there has been a flight of whites from the community. Merely the normal rate of residential change under circumstances where blacks face residential restrictions in other neighborhoods may—given the character of realty sale practices or the increased reluctance of nonresident whites to move into a changing neighborhood—lead to succession of population as blacks occupy those vacancies that normally appear over time in a neighborhood (77).[12]

[12]For a review of instances of interracial housing the reader can consult George Grier and Eunice Grier, *Privately Developed Interracial Housing: An Analysis of Experience* (49). The Grier book studies housing projects that were integrated from their initiation.

With the selection from Raymond Vernon's *Metropolis 1985* (122), our attention
shifts to the characteristics of differential class concentration in the metropolitan area
and in combination with the remaining two selections, to some of the major properties
and processes of suburban growth and change in intrametropolitan relationships.
Vernon served as the director of the three-year study of the New York metropolitan
region carried out by Harvard University's Graduate School of Public Administration
in the latter part of the 1950s. His own volume is "an interpretation of the principal
findings" of the study that appeared in the other eight volumes. The present selection
includes at the beginning a suggestive model of change. However, it focuses principally on some of the major features of the movement and distribution of population
and facilities in the New York metropolitan region.[13] It notes the decline of population
(or stability at best) in the urban core, with the movement out to suburban areas. It
considers the factors that are important in determining where populations will locate
in the region, stressing the role of family income, job location, life-cycle, and, somewhat more indirectly, that of race. These factors are influential within an overall effort
by the individual to balance desires for greater space against maximizing access to
central city employment and services.[14] Most generally, there is a pattern of increased
income levels being farther removed from Manhattan, though high income groups are
also significantly present in Manhattan itself.

Vernon's selection does not describe the reasons that account for the large movement of population to the suburbs in the past twenty-five years. A growing body of
research, however, has suggested the importance of quite pragmatic considerations.
Work by Gans and Bell and others (5, 19, 39) has indicated that the greater ease at
satisfying home and family-oriented concerns is of particular importance, with com-
munity- and neighborhood-related purposes also of some significance. These findings
contrast with the earlier emphasis in some writings of the 1950s on status striving, the
changing nature of American values with emphasis on consumptive styles, and the
response to the presumed disquietude and stresses of modern industrial and rationalized society (91, 103, 126).

A balanced view must recognize the very great importance of the pragmatic
concerns cited by such writers as Gans and Bell. Yet, it is reasonable to suggest that

[13]The region comprises twenty-two counties in three states. The core of the region consists
of all the New York City boroughs except Richmond, plus Hudson County in New Jersey, an
inner ring of the Jersey counties of Bergen, Passaic, Essex, and Union, plus the borough of
Richmond, and the New York State counties of Westchester and Nassau. The outer ring contains
the more outlying New York State counties of Rockland, Orange, Putnam, and Dutchess counties
and Suffolk County east of Nassau, plus Fairfield County in Connecticut, and the New Jersey
counties of Morris, Somerset, Middlesex, and Monmouth.
[14]The interested reader will find this process and the role of these factors more fully treated
in the first volume of the study by Edgar Hoover and Raymond Vernon, *Anatomy of a Metropolis*
(59), especially in chapter 6, "Spacious Living vs. Easy Access" and chapter 7, "Who Lives
Where and Why."

such purposes are also present among some of those who do not move and perhaps this differential response may be partly accounted for by the influence on migrants of those less easily understood and verbalized pressures suggested in earlier writings about suburbs. It is also plausible to suggest that some of those who do move are probably more likely than those who remain to be responding to the values implicated historically in America's denigration of cities as compared to the rural or small-town community. Movement also appears to depend on the nature of physical facilities and the unavailability of housing within the central cities, both pragmatic concerns. In a more indirect fashion, as far as individual motivation is concerned, movement depends on population density, rate of metropolitan growth, the character of urban spatial configurations, and a number of technological factors (23, 51, 87, 93, 94, 98). However, these can only offer a partial explanation, though they may be especially appropriate for interpreting differences in historical or comparative rates of growth.

Vernon elaborates on the nature of business movement out of the central city and into the suburbs. While treating this as principally a movement of retail business, especially department stores, he notes that there is a more general though not as strong a movement of other consumer-oriented activities, such as banking, insurance, real estate, and various professions. In effect, "consumer activities have followed the shift of residences" (59, p. 162). The reader should be aware, however, that what is involved here in many instances is not the movement of individual businesses (or industry) but the disproportionate establishment of new concerns, businesses, or the branches of older central city businesses in the suburbs as compared with those remaining in the urban core. Businesses most likely to stay predominantly within the metropolitan centers are those that have a specialized and limited appeal and those that deal in unstandardized items, such as art galleries, quality furniture, and apparel stores. A central location maximizes the market and provides an opportunity for comparative shopping. Though not covered in the present selection, it is also the case that a considerable portion of central office-based clerical operations are still strongly attracted by the central business district.

Business activities of an industrial nature, however, have tended to move out. This is especially true for heavy industry, with its need for considerable and economical space, minimal zoning restrictions, and the increased availability of a suburban labor force. Though less marked, the growth of light industry has also tended to occur outside of the older urban cores. These patterns of population and institutional location and change have produced some alteration in the patterns of daily population movements. While a large number of people still enter the downtown business, entertainment, and cultural areas every day, there has been a considerable increase in intrasuburban travel for work, shopping, and other activities (9, 18, 78). There is also a pattern of reverse commuting as low and semiskilled labor travels from the center city to employment opportunities in the contiguous communities, communities where exclusionary practices, high land costs, and the insufficiencies of the home construction industry have minimized the availability of moderately priced homes for minority group members and less affluent whites.

With the selection from Alvin Boskoff's text on urban sociology, we move to a description of the character of the urban area that lies outside the central city and the nature of some of the interdependencies within it. In addition to the metropolitan center, the major components of the urban region (similar in many respects to the metropolitan area concept) include the suburbs, urban fringe, satellite cities, and exurbia. Boskoff provides an illuminating account of the area outside of the central city, a region often referred to as the suburbs, or the inner and outer rings, but which Boskoff's discussion makes clear is marked by a diverse array of communities, populations, and land usage. His essay also begins to suggest the quite different functions that these areas and communities serve and some of the consequences they bring for the overall urban region and its change and growth over time. Underlying Boskoff's account is a sense of the interrelations between different areas and communities; the broader urban region is interpreted as a functional entity dominated by the central city.[15] Some of the relationships and processes that are present here receive elaboration in later discussion and in the concluding items of this section.

With the striking expansion of metropolitan populations outside the central urban core since the conclusion of World War II, there has been considerable effort to understand the pattern of this urban growth and the factors accounting for it and to clarify the major differences between suburban and metropolitan populations. The selection by the eminent demographer Leo Schnore, "The Socio-Economic Status of Cities and Suburbs" (98), is principally addressed to the latter question. Schnore's paper has helped stimulate a considerable body of research and discussion developing and modifying Schnore's major thesis on suburban selectivity. Discussed in his essay and more fully elaborated in his own later work and that of his students (100, 102) is a theory of the nature of the evolution of the city. Implicit also are some notions on possible motivations for suburban population movement.

Schnore's essay suggests that the higher socioeconomic status (in terms of income, education, and occupation) of the suburbs, as compared with that of the central cities, is not a uniform phenomenon.[16] Essentially this condition holds for the larger and

[15]For an elaboration and discussion of some of the distinctions and processes treated in Boskoff, see 31, 33, 65, 96.

[16]What Schnore contrasts are the central cities of urbanized areas with the remainder of such areas, referred to as suburbs. By using urbanized areas rather than the SMSA, he excluded areas of a lower density and more rural character. At the same time, however, he included under suburbs both incorporated communities and the urban fringe in urbanized areas. However, see Schnore's later essay, "Measuring City-Suburban Status Differences" (101). Some later investigators were to stress the importance of a tripartite distinction between central cities, suburbs and urban fringe rather than a dichotomized comparison. See Joel Smith, "Another Look at Socioeconomic Status Distributions in Urbanized Areas" (108).

older metropolitan areas, age being the more important condition. The rate of annexa-tion of contiguous territory by the central city is a related and also an important factor. Thus, the younger, usually smaller, territorially growing cities progressively reverse the more familiar notion of the suburbs as having a higher socioeconomic status.[17] The evolutionary model referred to in the present essay, more fully sketched the following year in Schnore's "Urban Structure and Suburban Selectivity" (100) and considered further in his 1969 paper with Joy Jones (102), essentially posits a movement of upper socioeconomic status populations out of the central city only over time, with lower status groups, initially at the periphery, found increasingly at the center. Thus, the suburban population changes from a disproportionately lower socioeconomic status to a predominantly middle- and finally disproportionately middle- and upper-class status. The analyses of Schnore and his associates reinforce the proposition that through time the population of suburbs and their metropolitan core grows increasingly dissimilar. The two latter papers also stress the character of population movement to the suburbs as a function of urban structure. The aspects of urban structure considered by Schnore include the interdependent influence of the location, size, age, annexation history, housing circumstances, and color composition of urbanized areas.

While the general analysis of suburban selectivity made by Schnore and his associates appears reasonable, it also seems true that as suburbs grow they tend to maintain the character of their earlier socioeconomic level. There is a persistence or stability of socioeconomic properties (28). This circumstance suggests the value of extending the discussion of suburban selectivity by taking into account the influence of a number of important factors. These include the variations between different urban areas in regard to the socioeconomic levels of earlier suburban communities in such areas, their relative size vis-à-vis the urban core, and the relative population distribu-tion among the suburban communities. It is not unreasonable to suggest that there exist patterned differences between urban areas in terms of the age, size, and location of the urban areas.

In a somewhat different vein there is the recent analysis of Joel Smith (108), which confirms Schnore's broader findings, but extends and somewhat modifies the analyses of Schnore and his students. Smith elaborates on the need, acknowledged earlier by Schnore, to differentiate urbanized areas into cities, suburbs, and fringe areas in recognition of suburban complexity. His analysis also shows the importance of in-come in determining suburban movement, suggesting the need for a more careful and fuller consideration of the various aspects of socioeconomic status. Smith also points

[17]The findings reported by Schnore and others usually do not distinguish possible difference in residential patterns as between white and nonwhite populations. However, differences do seem to exist with higher status nonwhites more usually resident in the central cities, even in the smaller metropolitan areas. More extensive analysis on the location of different type population groups, however, seems clearly needed. See Mary G. Powers, "Class, Ethnicity, and Residence in Metropolitan America" (88).

out that the population of metropolitan centers with a higher socioeconomic status than that of their suburbs are only a fraction of the population of those urban centers where this condition is reversed. He further helps to establish some sense of balance by pointing out that the range of socioeconomic status differences within the urbanized areas outside the central city is as great, sometimes even greater, than the range between this suburban ring and the metropolitan center. In effect, a wide range of socioeconomic levels is found in all parts of the metropolitan community, though individual subcommunities will tend to exhibit a somewhat distinctive socioeconomic level. Smith continues the effort of showing that a broad array of factors account for and specify the process of suburban selectivity. And he makes the fundamental theoretical point that ". . . the total process of metropolitan area population differentiation is part of a response to a larger societal process of organization and differentiation" (108, p. 449).

Systemic Forms and Interdependence

Warren and Greer provide a more explicit consideration of points inherent in some of the preceding material. They are responding to the fact that the contemporary community, especially in an industrially advanced society, is deeply involved in a far-ranging system of interdependencies. These extend to all areas of institutional or community life. In the broadest terms such interdependence is expressed along two dimensions. That which is most frequently treated in the scholarly literature is the functional relationship between communities under varying conditions of dominance. However, of increasing importance also is the relationship and dependence of all communities and spheres of community activity on nationwide structures of authority and power, in effect, on centralized institutions, not communities. The thrust of the brief selections from Warren and Greer are essentially in this direction.

For example, Scott Greer, writing in the context of the theoretical perspective sketched by the initiators of the social area analysis school, reflects a popular scholarly view that a major trend of modern society is the long-term process of social differentiation, with a consequent extensive division of labor and specialization. This is a perspective joined to a stress on a related process of change, the development of large-scale, rationalized, formal organizations (105, 107, 110). Such changes have significantly underlain the appearance of nationwide economic, cultural, media, political, and other institutional structures within which communities, local institutions, and populations are increasingly implicated. In effect, these structures are increasingly subject to nationwide hierarchical structures of authority and power, seriously reducing local distinctiveness, autonomy, and efficacy. This occurrence has posed such diverse scholarly and practical problems as trying to determine what constitutes phenomena distinct to the community—in effect, what are community-level phenomena; in what terms can the contemporary individual find identity, meaning, and expressiveness; how and to what extent can communities, local institutions, and individuals influence and control their circumstances effectively; what type of patterns of relationship do communities develop vis-à-vis each other; and further, to what extent and in what direction must the conception of the urban community as the locus of distinct urban phenomena be redefined.

Clearly, the two brief selections by Warren and Greer can only begin to indicate the direction in which a few of the concerns presented here may be conceptualized. Some further suggestions are noted in the following section and the discussion of relevant issues is continued. Yet, a more extensive discussion than that possible here would be necessary for any kind of adequate treatment of the relevant questions and processes.

Both Warren and Greer should be read therefore as part of an attempt to understand the social system of the community and the relationship of the community to other entities and as a reflection of the broad, long-range, historical changes in society. Warren outlines the terms in which the community and units within it are related to other subsystems existing within the community, and those other systems existing significantly outside the community, though extending into the community as well. These are structural and functional relationships conceptualized in terms of horizontal and vertical patterns. The determinants of the pattern within which a community subsystem is implicated are clearly not given inherent properties of the subsystem, but arise from the type of relationship in which it is involved. Thus, some community units may have relationships both of a vertical and horizontal character, or, put differently, be implicated in both horizontal and vertical patterns. Community subsystems implicated in a horizontal pattern of relationship are characterized by activities directed toward continuance of interorganization and interpersonal relationships, or maintenance activities. Those implicated in vertical patterns are involved in task-oriented activities. That is, they seek to control and utilize the environment so as to maximize the attainment of particular goals. Several other general points are made by Warren. He notes the "pulsating interchange" between the task performance and maintenance activities. He also suggests that the focus of community social system concerns are shifting from horizontal to vertical relationships. While Warren perceives the community as a distinct social system, it is also understood as constituted of various subsystems. It is such subsystems, not the community as such, which are related to extracommunity systems.

Writing more explicitly of the long-term historical process of social differentiation and increasingly far-ranging forms of communication and transportation, Greer stresses society's increase in scale. In effect, he is referring to the increasing existence of an extensive interdependent network of specialized, yet coordinated or integrated, populations and activities. The growth of cities and their continued vitality is dependent upon their role as "control centers" within such a network. This has meant that communities and individuals in their diverse activities, and in the social organizational expression of these activities, are implicated in a greater range and intensity of inter-dependence and, hence, of communication and control. Failures in executing functions of communication and control will limit the increase of scale, and consequently the growth of cities and social organizations. Moreover, the inability by the individual or the community to fit into or adapt to such nationwide networks may seriously prejudice the viability of the community or the satisfaction of individual needs.

The prominence of large-scale, non-areal based social organizations or bureaucracies is a major feature of the society of increasing scale, and frequently a more consequential membership for the individual than his locality of residence. In one sense to be urban is to be implicated in such a network. Hence, the notion follows of a society as essentially an urban society and "urbanism reflects the acculturation of sub-groups to a society-wide normative structure" (46, p. 49). This treatment suggests, as does Warren's discussion, the consequences of the above for the appearance of conditions of powerlessness, loss of autonomy, decline of the vitality of the local community through the loss of meaningful functions for the individual and his membership groups, and the precariousness of maintaining a distinctive local normative order.

The Warren and Greer selections point to phenomena of increasing importance in contemporary American society—the sharp decline of the autonomy, control, and distinctiveness possessed by communities. We would suggest that even the viability of the horizontal pattern of urban subsystem relationships of which Warren writes is increasingly threatened by the growing scope and dominance of the vertical patterns. These circumstances reflect the broad-ranging processes of social differentiation, vertical integration, and rationalization, and the concomitant development of nation-wide systems of transportation, communication, political control, and economic enterprise to which reference has been made. Vidich and Bensman's searching account, *Small Town in Mass Society* (123), powerfully describes this circumstance for a small rural community. However, the vital fact is that this is a phenomenon in which all communities are deeply involved. In a related context, one expression of the bankruptcy of contemporary ideology, particularly though not exclusively at the common man level, is the continuance of a set of beliefs on local control and governance that ignores the reality of the dependence of the individual community on broader institutional structures and decisions (123).

Implicated in the foregoing discussion is the anomalous situation that while the population of the cities has grown over time and the nation has become increasingly urbanized, and while control centers and dominant elites of government and corporate enterprise have been urban-based, the autonomy and ability of the cities to control their own circumstances has significantly declined. This has followed from the development of significantly centralized nationwide structures of power and authority and the increased reliance of cities on external agents. Circumstances such as these underlay the earlier suggestion that the dimension of principal importance in urban interdependencies was not that which focused on the interrelationship of urban centers.

While the present discussion has focused on institutional and social system changes, in these are implicated far-reaching consequences for the nature of the community and the personal lives of individuals. The changing nature of the community was partly confronted in earlier references to social area analysis. It becomes important to recognize that community may have to be increasingly, though not exclusively, defined in terms of nonlocale-based interest associations. Problems in individual lives of meaningfulness, identity, responsiveness, and unity are the other face of many of the changes sketched and the changing nature of community.

There is an extensive and elaborate literature that discusses the interdependence between communities, dominance gradients within which communities are implicated, variations in differentiation within metropolitan areas, and differential functions and their consequences that cities exhibit. Building on earlier efforts (20, 21, 45, 75), the influential study by Donald Bogue, *The Structure of the Metropolitan Community: A Study of Dominance and Subdominance*[18] (11), elaborated the internal spatial structure of the broader metropolitan centers and hinterland cities, and the activities located therein, with the gradient of dominance expressed in terms of the related integration, influence and determination of institutional functioning for interdependent cities. These efforts have been extended by Kish (63), Vance and Sutker (121), Galle (37), Pappenfort (85), O.D. Duncan and his colleagues (26), and others.[19] Such work has described a much wider system of hierarchical and dominance relationships between metropolitan centers themselves, rather than merely with their hinterlands. Further, it has been necessary to go beyond a focus on distinct metropolitan centers and to conceptualize a broader ecological field determinate of intercommunity relationships, a more inclusive system of relationships whose breadth may even be as wide as the whole of the society. The particular functions in question determine whether the "urban hierarchy" is explicable in regional, or broader national terms. The lack of a self-contained set of interrelationships between communities and hinterland has meant that it has become increasingly inappropriate to conceive of a set of interurban relationships as existing within a closed system. It becomes necessary to interpret contemporary interurban patterns in open system terms. In other words, it is important, as Schnore has remarked (100) to move beyond a self-contained

[18]A number of sociological regional studies, including excerpts from Bogue (11), Dickenson (20), and Gras (45), are reprinted in part V, "Regional Studies" of Theodorson (115). Also see Robert Carroll (17) for a somewhat different view.

[19]See the review essay by Schnore (100).

conceptualization of the metropolitan community and to perceive its intercommunity relationships as existing within, shaped by, related to, and part of a broader social system, without which neither the community nor its interrelationship can be adequately sketched. As a practical matter, however, it is often necessary to pursue particular empirical investigation within a more constrained focus.

REFERENCES

1. Abu-Lughed, Janet L., "Testing the Theory of Social Area Analysis: The Ecology of Cairo, Egypt," *American Sociological Review,* 34 (April 1969), 198–212.

2. Anderson, Theodore R., and Egeland, Janice A., "Spatial Aspects of Social Area Analysis," *American Sociological Review,* 26 (June 1961), 392–398.

3. Bell, Wendell, "Economic, Family, and Ethnic Status," *American Sociological Review,* 20 (January 1955), 45–52.

4. _____, "Social Areas: Typology of Urban Neighborhoods," *Community Structure and Analysis,* Marvin Sussman, ed., (New York: Thomas Y. Crowell, 1959), pp. 61–92.

5. _____, "The City, the Suburb, and a Theory of Social Choice," *The New Urbanization,* Scott Greer, *et al.*, eds., (New York: St. Martin's Press, 1968), pp. 132–168.

6. _____, and Boat, Marion D., "Urban Neighborhoods and Informal Social Relations," *American Journal of Sociology,* 62 (January 1957), 391–398.

7. _____, and Force, Maryanne, "Urban Neighborhood Types and Participation in Formal Associations," *American Sociological Review,* 21 (February 1956), 25–34.

8. _____, and Moskos, Charles C., Jr., "A Comment on Udry's 'Increasing Scale and Spatial Differentiation,' " *Social Forces,* 42 (May 1964), 414–417.

9. Berry, Brian J. L., *Commercial Structure and Commercial Blight* (Chicago: University of Chicago, Department of Geography, Research Paper No. 85, 1963).

10. Blumenfeld, Hans, "The Modern Metropolis," in *Cities,* A Scientific American Book (New York: Alfred A. Knopf, 1967), pp. 41–57.

11. Bogue, Donald J., *The Structure of the Metropolitan Community: A Study of Dominance and Subdominance* (Ann Arbor: Horace Rackham Graduate School, University of Michigan, 1949).

12. Boskoff, Alvin, "Emergence and Structure of the Urban Region: Suburb, Satellite, and Fringe," *The Sociology of the Urban Region,* 2nd ed. (New York: Appleton-Century-Crofts, 1970), pp. 106–130, selected pages.

13. Bracey, John H., Jr., Meier, August, and Rudwick, Elliot, eds., *The Rise of the Ghetto* (Belmont, California: Wadsworth Publishing Co., 1971, paper).

14. Brody, Eugene B., ed., *Behavior in New Environments, Adaptation of Migrant Populations* (Beverly Hills, California: Sage Publications, 1970).

15. Burgess, Ernest W., "The Growth of the City: An Introduction to a Research Project," in Park, Robert F., Burgess, Ernest W., and McKenzie, R.D., *The City* (Chicago: University of Chicago Press, 1925), pp. 47–62.

16. Caplow, Theodore, "Urban Structure in France," *American Sociological Review*, 18 (October 1952), 544–570.

17. Carroll, Robert L., "The Metropolitan Influence on the 168 Standard Metropolitan Area Central Cities," *Social Forces*, 42 (December 1963), 166–173.

18. Chinitz, Benjamin, "Introduction - City and Suburb," in Benjamin Chinitz, ed., *City and Suburb* (Englewood Cliffs, N.J.: Prentice-Hall, Inc., 1964, paper), pp. 3–50.

19. Clark, S. D., *The Suburban Society* (Toronto: University of Toronto Press, 1966).

20. Dickenson, Robert F., "Metropolitan Regions of the United States," *Geographical Review*, 24 (April 1934), 278–286.

21. _____, *City, Region, and Regionalism* (London: Deegan Paul, 1947).

22. Drake, St. Clair, and Cayton, Horace, *Black Metropolis: A Study of Negro Life in a Northern City* (New York: Harcourt, Brace, 1945).

23. Duncan, Beverley, et al., "Patterns of City Growth," *American Journal of Sociology*, 67 (January 1962), 18–29.

24. Duncan, Otis D., "Human Ecology and Population Studies," in Hauser, Philip M., and Duncan, Otis D., eds., *The Study of Population* (Chicago: The University of Chicago Press, 1959), pp. 678–716.

25. _____, "From Social System to Ecosystem," *Sociological Inquiry*, 31 (Spring 1961), 140–149

26. _____, et al., *Metropolis and Region* (Baltimore: The Johns Hopkins Press, 1960).

27. _____, and Schnore, Leo F., "Cultural, Behavioral, and Ecological Perspectives in the Study of Social Organization," *American Journal of Sociology*, 65 (September 1959), 132–153.

28. Farley, Reynolds P., "Suburban Persistence," *American Sociological Review*, 29 (February 1964), 38–47.

29. _____, "The Urbanization of Negroes in the United States," *Journal of Social History*, I (Spring 1968), 241–258.

30. Firey, Walter, "Sentiment and Symbolism as Ecological Variables," *American Sociological Review*, 10 (April 1945), 140–148.

31. _____, "Ecological Considerations in Planning for Urban Fringes," *American Sociological Review*, 11 (August 1946), 411–421.

32. _____, *Land Use in Central Boston* (Cambridge: Harvard University Press, 1947).

33. _____, et al., "The Fusion of Urban and Rural," in Labutut, J., and Lane, W. J., eds., *Highways in Our National Life* (Princeton, N.J.: Princeton University Press, 1950).

34. Form, William, "The Place of Social Structure in the Determination of Land Use," *Social Forces*, 32 (May 1954), 317–323.

35. Freedman, Ronald, *Recent Migration to Chicago* (Chicago: University of Chicago, 1950).

36. Fried, Marc, "Deprivation and Migration: Dilemmas of Causal Interpretation," *Behavior in New Environments*, Brody, Eugene B., ed., (Beverly Hills, California: Sage Publications, 1970), pp. 23–71.

37. Galle, Omer R., "Occupational Composition and Metropolitan Hierarchy: The Inter- and Intra-metropolitan Division of Labor," *American Journal of Sociology*, 69 (November 1963), 260–269.

38. _____, and Taeuber, Karl F., "Metropolitan Migration and Intervening Opportunities," *American Sociological Review*, 31 (February 1966), 5–13.

39. Gans, Herbert J., *The Levittowners: How People Live and Politic in Suburbia* (New York: Pantheon Books, 1967).

40. Germani, Gino, "Migration Acculturation," *Handbook for Social Research in Urban Areas*, Hauser, Philip M., ed. (Paris: UNESCO, 1966), pp. 159–178.

41. Glazer, Nathan, and Moynihan, Daniel B., *Beyond the Melting Pot: The Negroes, Puerto Ricans, Jews, Italians, and Irish in New York City* (Cambridge: Harvard University Press, 1963).

42. Gordon, Milton M., *Assimilation in American Life* (New York: Oxford University Press, 1964).

43. Gottman, Jean, *Megalopolis - The Urbanized Northeastern Seaboard of the United States* (Cambridge: M.I.T., 1961).

44. _____, and Harper, Robert A., eds., *Metropolis on the Move, Geographers Look at Urban Sprawl* (New York: John Wiley, 1967, paper).

45. Gras, N. S. B., *An Introduction to Economic History* (New York: Harper and Row, Publishers, 1922).

46. Greer, Scott, *The Emerging City, Myth and Reality* (New York: The Free Press, 1962).

47. _____, "Urbanism Reconsidered: A Comparative Study of Local Areas in a Metropolis," *American Sociological Review,* 21 (February 1956), 19–25.

48. _____, and Kube, Ella, "Urbanism and Social Structure: A Los Angeles Study," in Sussman, Marvin, ed., *Community Structure and Analysis* (New York: Thomas Y. Crowell, 1959), pp. 61–92.

49. Grier, George, and Grier, Eunice, *Privately Developed Interracial Housing: An Analysis of Experience* (Berkeley: University of California Press, 1960)

50. Grodzins, Morton, *The Metropolis as a Racial Problem* (Pittsburgh: University of Pittsburgh Press, 1958).

51. Gross, Edward, "The Role of Density as a Factor in Metropolitan Growth in the United States of America," *Population Studies,* 8 (November 1954), 113–120.

52. Gulick, John, Bowerman, Charles F., and Back, Kurt W., "Newcomer, Enculturation in the City, Attitudes and Participation," in Chapin, F. Stuart, Jr., and Weiss, Shirley F., eds., *Urban Growth Dynamics in a Regional Cluster of Cities* (New York: John Wiley, 1962), pp. 315–358.

53. _____, *The Uprooted* (Boston: Little, Brown & Co., 1952).

54. Handlin, Oscar, *Boston's Immigrants: A Story in Acculturation* (Cambridge: Harvard University Press, 1959).

55. _____, *The Newcomers* (Cambridge: Harvard University Press, 1959).

56. Harris, Chauncy D., and Ullman, Edward L., "The Nature of Cities," *The Annals of the American Academy of Political and Social Science,* 242 (November 1945), 7–17.

57. Hauser, Philip M., "The Growth of Metropolitan Areas in the United States," from *Population Perspectives* (New Brunswick, N.J.: Rutgers University Press, 1960), pp. 96–98, 100–129.

58. Hawley, Amos, and Duncan, Otis D., "Social Area Analysis: A Critical Appraisal," *Land Economics,* 33 (November 1957), pp. 337–348.

59. Hoover, Edgar, and Vernon, Raymond, *Anatomy of a Metropolis* (Cambridge: Harvard University Press, 1959).

60. Hunt, Chester L., "Private Integrated Housing in a Medium Size Northern City," *Social Problems,* 7 (Winter 1960), 196–209.

61. Jackson, J. A., ed., *Migration* (London: Cambridge University Press, 1969).

62. Jonassen, Christen T., "Cultural Variables in the Ecology of an Ethnic Group," *American Sociological Review,* 14 (February 1949), 32–41.

63. Kish, Leslie, "Differentiation in Metropolitan Areas," *American Sociological Review,* 19 (August 1954), 388–398.

64. Kosa, John, "Hungarian Immigrants in North America: Their Residential Mobility and Ecology," *Canadian Journal of Economics and Political Science,* 22 (August 1956), 358–370.

65. Kurtz, Richard A., and Ficher, Leanne B., "Fringe and Suburb: A Confusion of Concepts," *Social Forces,* 37 (October 1958), 32–37.

66. Ladd, William M., "Effect of Integration on Property Values," *American Economic Review* (September 1962), 801–808.

67. Laurenti, Luigi M., "Effects of Non-white Purchases on Market Prices of Residence," *The Appraisal Journal* (July 1952), 314–329.

68. _____, *Property Values and Race* (Berkeley: University of California Press, 1960).

69. Lieberson, Stanley, "A Societal Theory of Race and Ethnic Relations," *American Sociological Review,* 26 (December 1961), 902–910.

70. _____, *Ethnic Patterns in America* (New York: The Free Press, 1963).

71. Lowry, I. S., *Migration and Metropolitan Growth: Two Analytic Models* (San Francisco: Chandler Publishing Co., 1966).

72. McElrath, Dennis, "The Social Areas of Rome: A Comparative Analysis," *American Sociological Review,* 27 (June 1962), 376–391.

73. _____, "Social Differentiation and Societal Scale," in Scott Greer, et al., eds., *The New Urbanization* (New York: St. Martin's Press, 1968).

74. McEntire, Davis, "The Housing Market in Racially Mixed Areas," from *Residence and Race* (Berkeley: University of California Press, 1960), pp. 157–171.

75. McKenzie, Roderick D., *The Metropolitan Community* (New York: McGraw-Hill Book Co., Inc., 1933).

76. Mills, C. Wright, Senior, Clarence, and Goldsen, Rose K., *The Puerto Rican Journey* (New York: Russell, 1950).

77. Molotch, Harvey, "Racial Change in a Stable Community," *American Journal of Sociology,* 75 (September 1969), 226–238.

78. Moses, Leon, and Williamson, Harold W., "Location of Economic Activities in Cities," *The American Economic Review,* 57 (1966), 211–222.

79. Murdie, Robert A., *The Factorial Ecology of Metropolitan Toronto, 1951–1961: An Essay on the Social Geography of the City,* Department of Geography Research Paper No. 116 (Chicago: University of Chicago Press, 1968).

80. Newman, Dorothy K., "The Negro's Journey to the City Part I," *Monthly Labor Review,* 88 (May 1965), 502–507.

81. Northwood, Lawrence K., and Barth, Ernest A. T., *Urban Desegregation* (Seattle: University Press, 1965).

82. Orleans, Peter, "Robert Park and Social Area Analysis: A Convergence in Urban Sociology, *Urban Affairs Quarterly,* 9 (June 1966), 5–19.

83. Osofsky, Gilbert, *Harlem: The Making of a Ghetto* (New York: Harper and Row, Publishers, 1968, paperback).

84. Palmore, Ferdman, and Howe, John, "Residential Integration and Property Values," *Social Problems,* 10 (Summer 1962), 52–55.

85. Pappenfort, Donnell M., "The Ecological Field and the Metropolitan Community," from Hirsch, Werner Z., ed., *Urban Life and Form* (New York: Holt, Rinehart and Winston, Inc., 1963).

86. Pedersen, Paul O., Modeller for *Befolkningsstruktur og Befolkningsudvikling i Storbyomrader Specielt med Henblik pa Storkebenhavn* (Copenhagen: State Planning Institute, 1967, Danish text with English summary).

87. Powers, Mary G., "Age and Space Aspects of City and Suburban Housing," *Land Economics,* 40 (November 1964), 380–387.

88. _____, "Class, Ethnicity, and Residence in Metropolitan America," *Demography,* 5 (1968), 443–448.

89. Rapkin, Chester, and Grigsby, William, *The Demand for Housing in Racially Mixed Areas* (Berkeley: University of California Press, 1960)

90. Reisman, Leonard, "The Ecologists: Analysts of Urban Patterns," *The Urban Process* (New York: The Free Press, 1964), pp. 93–121.

91. Riesman, David, "The Suburban Dislocation," *The Annals of the American Academy of Political and Social Science,* 314 (Fall 1957), 123–146.

92. Robson, B. T., *Urban Analysis, A Study of City Structure* (Cambridge: Cambridge University Press, 1969).

93. Schnore, Leo F., "The Growth of Metropolitan Suburbs," *American Sociological Review,* 22 (April 1957), 165–173.

94. _____, "Metropolitan Growth and Decentralization," *American Journal of Sociology,* 63 (September 1957), 171–180.

95. _____, "Satellites and Suburbs," *Social Forces,* 36 (December 1957), 121–127.

96. _____, "Social Morphology and Human Ecology," *American Journal of Sociology,* 63 (May 1958), 620–634.

97. _____, "The Myth of Human Ecology," *Sociological Inquiry,* 31 (Spring 1961), 128–131.

98. _____, "The Socio-Economic Status of Cities and Suburbs," *American Sociological Review,* 28 (February 1963), 76–85.

99. _____, "Urban Form: The Case of the Metropolitan Community," *Urban Life and Form,* Werner A. Hirsch, ed. (New York: Holt, Rinehart and Winston, Inc., 1963), pp. 169–197.

100. _____, "Urban Structure and Suburban Selectivity," *Demography,* 1 (1964), 164–176.

101. _____, "Measuring City-Suburban Status Differences," *Urban Affairs Quarterly,* 3 (September 1967), 95–108.

102. _____, and Jones, Joy K. O., "The Evolution of City-Suburban Types in the Course of a Decade," *Urban Affairs Quarterly,* 4 (June 1969), 421–442.

103. Seeley, John, Sim, R. Alexander, and Loosley, Elizabeth W., *Crestwood Heights* (New York: Basic Books, 1956).

104. Shevky, Eshref, and Bell, Wendell, *Social Area Analysis* (Stanford: Stanford University Press, 1955).

105. Shils, Edward, "The Theory of Mass Society," in Olson, Philip, ed., *America as a Mass Society* (New York: The Free Press, 1963), pp. 30–47.

106. Slotkin, James S., *From Field to Factory* (Glencoe: The Free Press, 1960).

107. Smelser, Neil J., "Toward a Theory of Modernization," in Etzioni, Amitai and Eva, eds., *Social Change* (New York: Basic Books, Inc., 1964), pp. 258–274.

108. Smith, Joel, "Another Look at Socioeconomic Status Distributions in Urbanized Areas," *Urban Affairs Quarterly,* 5 (June 1970), 423–453.

109. Spear, Allan H., *Black Chicago, The Making of a Negro Ghetto, 1890–1920* (Chicago: University of Chicago Press, 1967).

110. Stein, Maurice R., *The Eclipse of Community* (Princeton: Princeton University Press, 1960).

111. Sweetser, Frank L., Jr. "Factor Structure as Ecological Structure in Helsinki and Boston," *Acta Sociologica,* 8 (Fasc. 3, 1965), 205–225.

112. _____, "Factorial Ecology: Helsinki, 1960," *Demography,* 2 (1965), 372–386.

113. Taeuber, Karl F., "The Effect of Income Redistribution on Racial Residential Segregation," *Urban Affairs Quarterly,* 4 (September 1968), 5–14.

114. _____, and Taeuber, Alma F., *Negroes in Cities* (Chicago: Aldine Publishing Co., 1965).

115. Theodorson, George, ed. *Studies in Human Ecology* (New York: Harper and Row, 1961).

116. Timms, Duncan W. G., *The Urban Mosaic, Towards a Theory of Residential Differentiation* (London: Cambridge University Press, 1971).

117. Tunnard, Christopher, "America's Super-Cities," *Harper's Magazine,* 217 (August 1958), 59–65.

118. Udry, J. Richard, "Increasing Scale and Spatial Differentiation: New Tests of Two Theories from Shevky and Bell," *Social Forces,* 42 (May 1964), 403–413.

119. Van Arsdel, Maurice, Jr., Carmilleri, Santo M., and Schmid, Calvin F., "The Generality of Urban Social Area Indexes," *American Sociological Review,* 23 (June 1958), 277–284.

120. _____, "An Investigation of the Utility of Urban Typology," *Pacific Sociological Review,* 4 (Spring 1961), 26–32.

121. Vance, Rupert B., and Sutker, Sara Smith, "Metropolitan Dominance and Integration," in Vance, Rupert B., and Demerath, N. J., eds., *The Urban South* (Chapel Hill, N.C.: The University of North Carolina Press, 1954), pp. 114–134.

122. Vernon, Raymond, "From Tenement to Split Level," *Metropolis 1985* (Cambridge: Harvard University Press, 1960), pp. 135–165.

123. Vidich, Arthur J., and Bensman, Joseph, *Small Town in Mass Society* (Princeton: Princeton University Press, 1958).

124. Von Eckardt, Wolf, *The Challenge of Megalopolis* (New York: Macmillan, 1964).

125. Weaver, Robert, *The Negro Ghetto* (Chicago: University of Chicago Press, 1948).

126. Whyte, William H., Jr., *The Organization Man* (New York: Simon and Schuster, 1956).

127. Willhelm, Sidney, "The Concept of the 'Ecological Complex': A Critique," *American Journal of Economics and Sociology,* 23 (July 1964), 241–248.

128. _____, and Sjoberg, Gideon, "Economic vs Protective Values in Urban Land Use Change," *The American Journal of Economics and Sociology,* 19 (January 1960), 151–160.

A SOME URBAN PROCESSES AND FORMS: THE ECOLOGICAL DIMENSION

The Nature of Cities

Chauncy D. Harris
and Edward L. Ullman

Cities are the focal points in the occupation and utilization of the earth by man. Both a product of and an influence on surrounding regions, they develop in definite patterns in response to economic and social needs.

Cities are also paradoxes. Their rapid growth and large size testify to their superiority as a technique for the exploitation of the earth, yet by their very success and consequent large size they often provide a poor local environment for man. The problem is to build the future city in such a manner that the advantages of urban concentration can be preserved for the benefit of man and the disadvantages minimized.

Each city is unique in detail but resembles others in function and pattern. What is learned about one helps in studying another. Location types and internal structure are repeated so often that broad and suggestive generalizations are valid, especially if limited to cities of similar size, function, and regional setting. This paper will be limited to a discussion of two basic aspects of the nature of cities—their support and their internal structure. Such impor-

SOURCE: Chauncy D. Harris and Edward L. Ullman, "The Nature of Cities," *The Annals of the American Academy of Political and Social Sciences,* 242 (November 1945), 7–17. Reprinted by permission.

tant topics as the rise and extent of urbanism, urban sites, culture of cities, social and economic characteristics of the urban population, and critical problems will receive only passing mention.

THE SUPPORT OF CITIES

As one approaches a city and notices its tall buildings rising above the surrounding land and as one continues into the city and observes the crowds of people hurrying to and fro past stores, theaters, banks, and other establishments, one naturally is struck by the contrast with the rural countryside. What supports this phenomenon? What do the people of the city do for a living?

The support of a city depends on the services it performs not for itself but for a tributary area. Many activities serve merely the population of the city itself. Barbers, dry cleaners, shoe repairers, grocerymen, bakers, and movie operators serve others who are engaged in the principal activity of the city, which may be mining, manufacturing, trade, or some other activity.

The service by which the city earns its livelihood depends on the nature of the economy and of the hinterland. Cities are small or rare in areas either of primitive, self-sufficient economy or of meager resources. As Adam Smith stated, the land must produce a surplus in order to support cities. This does not mean that all cities must be surrounded by productive land, since strategic location with reference to cheap ocean highways may enable a city to support itself on the specialized surplus of distant lands. Nor does it mean that cities are parasites living off the land. Modern mechanization, transport, and a complex interdependent economy enable much of the economic activity of mankind to be centered in cities. Many of the people engaged even in food production are actually in cities in the manufacture of agricultural machinery.

The support of cities as suppliers of urban services for the earth can be summarized in three categories, each of which presents a factor of urban causation:[1]

1. Cities as central places performing comprehensive services for a surrounding area. Such cities tend to be evenly spaced throughout productive territory (Fig. 1). For the moment this may be considered the "norm," subject to variation primarily in response to the ensuing factors.
2. Transport cities performing break-of-bulk and allied services along transport routes, supported by areas which may be remote in distance but close in connection because of the city's strategic location on transport channels. Such cities tend to be arranged in linear patterns along rail lines or at coasts (Fig. 2).
3. Specialized-function cities performing one service such as mining, manu-

---

[1]For references see Edward Ullman, "A Theory of Location for Cities," *American Journal of Sociology,* Vol. 46, No. 6 (May 1941), pp. 853–64.

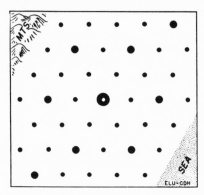

Fig. 1.—Theoretical distribution of central places. In a homogeneous land, settlements are evenly spaced; largest city in center surrounded by 6 medium-size centers which in turn are surrounded by 6 small centers. Tributary areas are hexagons, the closest geometrical shapes to circles which completely fill area with no unserved spaces.

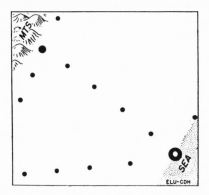

Fig. 2.—Transport centers, aligned along railroads or at coast. Large center is port; next largest is railroad junction and engine-changing point where mountain and plain meet. Small centers perform break of bulk principally between rail and roads.

Fig. 3.—Specialized-function settlements. Large city is manufacturing and mining center surrounded by a cluster of smaller settlements located on a mineral deposit. Small centers on ocean and at edge of mountains are resorts.

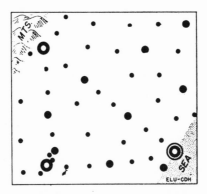

Fig. 4.—Theoretical composite grouping. Port becomes the metropolis and, although off center, serves as central place for whole area. Manufacturing-mining and junction centers are next largest. Railroad alignment of many towns evident. Railroad route in upper left of Fig. 2 has been diverted to pass through manufacturing and mining cluster. Distribution of settlements in upper right follows central-place arrangement.

facturing, or recreation for large areas, including the general tributary areas of hosts of other cities. Since the principal localizing factor is often a particular resource such as coal, water power, or a beach, such cities may occur singly or in clusters (Fig. 3).

Most cities represent a combination of the three factors, the relative importance of each varying from city to city (Fig. 4).

Cities as Central Places

Cities as central places serve as trade and social centers for a tributary area. If the land base is homogeneous these centers are uniformly spaced, as in many parts of the agricultural Middle West (Fig. 1). In areas of uneven resource distribution, the distribution of cities is uneven. The centers are of varying sizes, ranging from small hamlets closely spaced with one or two stores serving a local tributary area, through larger villages, towns, and cities more widely spaced with more special services for larger tributary areas, up to the great metropolis such as New York or Chicago offering many specialized services for a large tributary area composed of a whole hierarchy of tributary areas of smaller places. Such a net of tributary areas and centers forms a pattern somewhat like a fish net spread over a beach, the network regular and symmetrical where the sand is smooth, but warped and distorted where the net is caught in rocks.

The central-place type of city or town is widespread throughout the world, particularly in nonindustrial regions. In the United States it is best represented by the numerous retail and wholesale trade centers of the agricultural Middle West, Southwest, and West. Such cities have imposing shopping centers or wholesale districts in proportion to their size; the stores are supported by the trade of the surrounding area. This contrasts with many cities of the industrial

East, where the centers are so close together that each has little trade support beyond its own population.

Not only trade but social and religious functions may support central places. In some instances these other functions may be the main support of the town. In parts of Latin America, for example, where there is little trade, settlements are scattered at relatively uniform intervals through the land as social and religious centers. In contrast to most cities, their busiest day is Sunday, when the surrounding populace attend church and engage in holiday recreation, thus giving rise to the name "Sunday town."

Most large central cities and towns are also political centers. The county seat is an example. London and Paris are the political as well as trade centers of their countries. In the United States, however, Washington and many state capitals are specialized political centers. In many of these cases the political capital was initially chosen as a centrally located point in the political area and was deliberately separated from the major urban center.

Cities as Transport Foci and Break-of-Bulk Points

All cities are dependent on transportation in order to utilize the surplus of the land for their support. This dependence on transportation destroys the symmetry of the central-place arrangement, inasmuch as cities develop at foci or breaks of transportation, and transport routes are distributed unevenly over the land because of relief or other limitations (Fig. 2). City organizations recognize the importance of efficient transportation, as witness their constant concern with freight-rate regulation and with the construction of new highways, port facilities, airfields, and the like.

Mere focusing of transport routes does not produce a city, but according to Cooley, if break of bulk occurs, the focus becomes a good place to process goods. Where the form of transport changes, as transferring from water to rail, break of bulk is inevitable. Ports originating merely to transship cargo tend to develop auxiliary services such as repackaging, storing, and sorting. An example of simple break-of-bulk and storage ports is Port Arthur-Fort William, the twin port and wheat-storage cities at the head of Lake Superior; surrounded by unproductive land, they have arisen at the break-of-bulk points on the cheapest route from the wheat-producing Prairie Provinces to the markets of the East. Some ports develop as entrepôts, such as Hong Kong and Copenhagen, supported by transshipment of goods from small to large boats or vice versa. Servicing points or minor changes in transport tend to encourage growth of cities as establishment of division points for changing locomotives on American railroads.

Transport centers can be centrally located places or can serve as gateways between contrasting regions with contrasting needs. Kansas City, Omaha, and Minneapolis-St. Paul serve as gateways to the West, as well as central places for productive agricultural regions, and are important wholesale centers. The ports of New Orleans, Mobile, Savannah, Charleston, Norfolk, and others served as traditional gateways to the Cotton Belt with its specialized production. Likewise, northern border metropolises such as Baltimore, Washington, Cincinnati, and Louisville served as gateways to the South, with St. Louis a gateway to the Southwest. In recent years the South has been developing its own central places, supplanting some of the monopoly once held by the border gateways. Atlanta, Memphis, and Dallas are examples of the new southern central places and transport foci.

Changes in transportation are reflected in the pattern of city distribution. Thus the development of railroads resulted in a railroad alignment of cities which still persists. The rapid growth of automobiles and widespread development of highways in recent decades, however, has changed the trend toward a more even distribution of towns. Studies in such diverse localities as New York and Louisiana have shown a shift of centers away from exclusive alignment along rail routes. Airways may reinforce this trend or stimulate still different patterns of distribution for the future city.

Cities as Concentration Points for Specialized Services

A specialized city or cluster of cities performing a specialized function for a large area may develop at a highly localized resource (Fig. 3). The resort city of Miami, for example, developed in response to a favorable climate and beach. Scranton, Wilkes-Barre, and dozens of nearby towns are specialized coal-mining centers developed on anthracite coal deposits to serve a large segment of the northeastern United States. Pittsburgh and its suburbs and satellites form a nationally significant iron-and-steel manufacturing cluster favored by good location for the assembly of coal and iron ore and for the sale of steel to industries on the coal fields.

Equally important with physical resources in many cities are the advantages of mass production and ancillary services. Once started, a specialized city acts as a nucleus for similar or related activities, and functions tend to pyramid, whether the city is a seaside resort such as Miami or Atlantic City, or, more important, a manufacturing center such as Pittsburgh or Detroit. Concentration of industry in a city means that there will be a concentration of satellite services and industries—supply houses, machine shops, expert consultants, other industries using local industrial by-products or waste, still other industries making specialized parts for other plants in the city, marketing channels, specialized transport facilities, skilled labor, and a host of other facilities; either directly or indirectly, these benefit industry and cause it to expand in size and numbers in a concentrated place or district. Local personnel with the know-how in a given industry also may decide to start a new plant producing similar or like products in the same city. Furthermore, the advantages of mass production itself often tend to concentrate production in a few large factories and cities. Examples of localization of specific manufacturing industries are clothing in New York City, furniture in Grand Rapids, automobiles in the Detroit area, pottery in Stoke-on-Trent in England, and even such a speciality as tennis rackets in Pawtucket, Rhode Island.

Such concentration continues until opposing forces of high labor costs and congestion balance the concentrating forces. Labor costs may be lower in small towns and in industrially new districts; thus some factories are moving from the great metropolises to small towns; much of the cotton textile industry has moved from the old industrial areas of New England to the newer areas of the Carolinas in the South. The tremendous concentration of population and structures in large cities exacts a high cost in the form of congestion, high land costs, high taxes, and restrictive legislation.

Not all industries tend to concentrate in specialized industrial cities; many types of manufacturing partake more of central-place characteristics. These types are those that are tied to the market because the manufacturing process results in an increase in bulk or perishability. Bakeries, ice cream establishments, ice houses, breweries, soft-drink plants, and various types of assembly plants are examples. Even such industries, however, tend to be more developed in the manufacturing belt because the density of population and hence the market is greater there.

The greatest concentration of industrial cities in America is in the manufacturing belt of northeastern United States and contiguous Canada, north of the Ohio and east of the Mississippi. Some factors in this concentration are: large reserves of fuel and power (particularly coal), raw materials such as iron ore via the Great Lakes, cheap ocean transportation on the eastern seaboard, productive agriculture (particularly in the west), early settlement, later immigration concentrated in its cities, and an early start with consequent development of skilled labor, industrial know-how, transportation facilities, and prestige.

The interdependent nature of most of the industries acts as a powerful force to maintain this area as the primary home of industrial cities in the United States. Before the war, the typical industrial city outside the main manufacturing belt had only a single industry of the raw-material type, such as lumber mills, food canneries, or smelters (Longview, Washington; San Jose, California; Anaconda, Montana). Because of the need for producing huge quantities of ships and airplanes for a two-ocean war, however, many cities along the Gulf and Pacific coasts have grown rapidly during recent years as centers of industry.

Application of the Three Types of Urban Support

Although examples can be cited illustrating each of the three types of urban support, most American cities partake in varying proportions of all three types. New York City, for example, as the greatest American port is a break-of-bulk point; as the principal center of wholesaling and retailing it is a central-place type; and as the major American center of manufacturing it is a specialized type. The actual distribution and functional classification of cities in the United States, more complex than the simple sum of the three types (Fig. 4), has been mapped and described elsewhere in different terms.[2]

[2]Chauncy D. Harris, "A Functional Classification of Cities in the United States," *The Geographical Review,* Vol. 33, No. 1 (Jan. 1943), 85–99.

The three basic types therefore should not be considered as a rigid framework excluding all accidental establishment, although even fortuitous development of a city becomes part of the general urban-supporting environment. Nor should the urban setting be regarded as static; cities are constantly changing, and exhibit characteristic lag in adjusting to new conditions.

Ample opportunity exists for use of initiative in strengthening the supporting base of the future city, particularly if account is taken of the basic factors of urban support. Thus a city should examine: (1) its surrounding area to take advantage of changes such as newly discovered resources or crops, (2) its transport in order to adjust properly to new or changed facilities, and (3) its industries in order to benefit from technological advances.

INTERNAL STRUCTURE OF CITIES

Any effective plans for the improvement or rearrangement of the future city must take account of the present pattern of land use within the city, of the factors which have produced this pattern, and of the facilities required by activities localized within particular districts.

Although the internal pattern of each city is unique in its particular combination of details, most American cities have business, industrial, and residential districts. The forces underlying the pattern of land use can be appreciated if attention is focused on three generalizations of arrangement—by concentric zones, sectors, and multiple nuclei.

Concentric Zones

According to the concentric-zone theory, the pattern of growth of the city can best be understood in terms of five concentric zones[3] (Fig. 5).

1. *The Central Business District.* This is the focus of commercial, social, and civic life, and of transportation. In it is the downtown retail district with its department stores, smart shops, office buildings, clubs, banks, hotels, theaters, museums, and organization headquarters. Encircling the downtown retail district is the wholesale business district.

2. *The Zone in Transition.* Encircling the downtown area is a zone of residential deterioration. Business and light manufacturing encroach on residential areas characterized particularly by rooming houses. In this zone are the principal slums, with their submerged regions of poverty, degradation, and disease, and their underworlds of vice. In many American cities it has been inhabited largely by colonies of recent immigrants.

[3]Ernest W. Burgess, "The Growth of the City," in *The City,* ed. by Robert E. Park, Ernest W. Burgess, and Roderick D. McKenzie (Chicago: University of Chicago Press, 1925), pp. 47–62; and Ernest W. Burgess, "Urban Areas," in *Chicago, an Experiment in Social Science Research,* ed. by T. V. Smith and Leonard D. White (Chicago: University of Chicago Press, 1929), pp. 113–138.

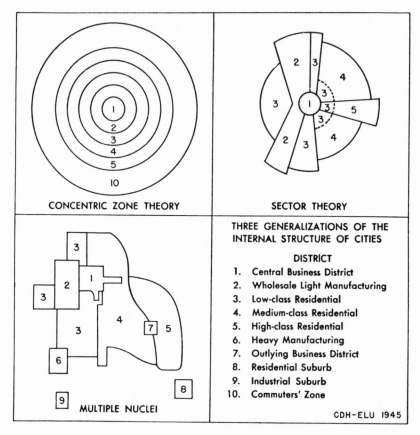

CONCENTRIC ZONE THEORY

SECTOR THEORY

MULTIPLE NUCLEI

THREE GENERALIZATIONS OF THE
INTERNAL STRUCTURE OF CITIES

DISTRICT
1. Central Business District
2. Wholesale Light Manufacturing
3. Low-class Residential
4. Medium-class Residential
5. High-class Residential
6. Heavy Manufacturing
7. Outlying Business District
8. Residential Suburb
9. Industrial Suburb
10. Commuters' Zone

CDH–ELU 1945

Fig. 5.—Generalizations of internal structure of cities. The concentric-zone theory is a generalization for all cities. The arrangement of the sectors in the sector theory varies from city to city. The diagram for multiple nuclei represents one possible pattern among innumerable variations.

3. *The Zone of Independent Workingmen's Homes.*   This is inhabited by industrial workers who have escaped from the zone in transition but who desire to live within easy access of their work. In many American cities second-generation immigrants are important segments of the population in this area.

4. *The Zone of Better Residences.*   This is made up of single-family dwellings, of exclusive "restricted districts," and of high-class apartment buildings.

5. *The Commuters' Zone.*   Often beyond the city limits in suburban areas or in satellite cities, this is a zone of spotty development of high-class residences along lines of rapid travel.

Sectors

The theory of axial development, according to which growth takes place along main transportation routes or along lines of least resistance to form a star-shaped city, is refined by Homer Hoyt in his sector theory, which states that growth along a particular axis of transportation usually consists of similar types of land use[4] (Fig. 5). The entire city is considered as a circle and the various areas as sectors radiating out from the center of that circle; similar types of land use originate near the center of the circle and migrate outward toward the periphery. Thus a high-rent residential area in the eastern quadrant of the city would tend to migrate outward, keeping always in the eastern quadrant. A low-quality housing area, if located in the southern quadrant, would tend to extend outward to the very margin of the city in that sector. The migration of high-class residential areas outward along established lines of travel is particularly pronounced on high ground, toward open country, to homes of community leaders, along lines of fastest transportation, and to existing nuclei of buildings or trading centers.

Multiple Nuclei

In many cities the land-use pattern is built not around a single center but around several discrete nuclei (Fig. 5). In some cities these nuclei have existed from the very origins of the city; in others they have developed as the growth of the city stimulated migration and specialization. An example of the first type is Metropolitan London, in which "The City" and Westminster originated as separate points separated by open country, one as the center of finance and commerce, the other as the center of political life. An example of the second type is Chicago, in which heavy industry, at first localized along the Chicago River in the heart of the city, migrated to the Calumet District, where it acted as a nucleus for extensive new urban development.

The initial nucleus of the city may be the retail district in a central-place city, the port or rail facilities in a break-of-bulk city, or the factory, mine, or beach in a specialized-function city.

The rise of separate nuclei and differentiated districts reflects a combination of the following four factors:

1. Certain activities require specialized facilities. The retail district, for example, is attached to the point of greatest intracity accessibility, the port district to suitable water front, manufacturing districts to large blocks of land and water on rail connection, and so on.

[4]Homer Hoyt, "City Growth and Mortgage Risk," *Insured Mortgage Portfolio,* Vol. 1, Nos. 6–10 (Dec. 1936–April 1937), *passim;* and U. S. Federal Housing Administration, *The Structure and Growth of Residential Neighborhoods in American Cities* by Homer Hoyt (Washington: Government Printing Office, 1939), *passim.*

2. Certain like activities group together because they profit from cohesion.[5] The clustering of industrial cities has already been noted above under "Cities as concentration points for specialized services." Retail districts benefit from grouping, which increases the concentration of potential customers and makes possible comparison shopping. Financial and office-building districts depend upon facility of communication among offices within the district. The Merchandise Mart of Chicago is an example of wholesale clustering.

3. Certain unlike activities are detrimental to each other. The antagonism between factory development and high-class residential development is well known. The heavy concentrations of pedestrians, automobiles, and streetcars in the retail district are antagonistic both to the railroad facilities and the street loading required in the wholesale district and to the rail facilities and space needed by large industrial districts, and vice versa.

4. Certain activities are unable to afford the high rents of the most desirable sites. This factor works in conjunction with the foregoing. Examples are bulk wholesaling and storage activities requiring much room, or low-class housing unable to afford the luxury of high land with a view.

The number of nuclei which result from historical development and the operation of localization forces varies greatly from city to city. The larger the city, the more numerous and specialized are the nuclei. The following districts, however, have developed around nuclei in most large American cities.

The Central Business District.   This district is at the focus of intracity transportation facilities by sidewalk, private car, bus, streetcar, subway, and elevated. Because of asymmetrical growth of most large cities, it is generally not now in the areal center of the city but actually near one edge, as in the case of lake-front, riverside, or even inland cities; examples are Chicago, St. Louis and Salt Lake City. Because established internal transportation lines converge on it, however, it is the point of most convenient access from all parts of the city, and the point of highest land values. The retail district, at the point of maximum accessibility, is attached to the sidewalk; only pedestrian or mass-transportation movement can concentrate the large numbers of customers necessary to support department stores, variety stores, and clothing shops, which are characteristic of the district. In small cities financial institutions and office buildings are intermingled with retail shops, but in large cities the financial district is separate, near but not at the point of greatest intracity facility. Its point of attachment is the elevator, which permits three-dimensional access among offices, whose most important locational factor is accessibility to other offices rather than to the city as a whole. Government buildings also are commonly near but not in the center of the retail district. In most cities a separate "automobile row" has arisen on the edge of the central business

---

[5]Exceptions are service-type establishments such as some grocery stores, dry cleaners, and gasoline stations.

district, in cheaper rent areas along one or more major highways; its attachment is to the highway itself.

The Wholesale and Light-Manufacturing District. This district is conveniently within the city but near the focus of extra city transportation facilities. Wholesale houses, while deriving some support from the city itself, serve principally a tributary region reached by railroad and motor truck. They are, therefore, concentrated along railroad lines, usually adjacent to (but not surrounding) the central business district. Many types of light manufacturing which do not require specialized buildings are attracted by the facilities of this district or similar districts: good rail and road transportation, available loft buildings, and proximity to the markets and labor of the city itself.

The Heavy Industrial District. This is near the present or former outer edge of the city. Heavy industries require large tracts of space, often beyond any available in sections already subdivided into blocks and streets. They also require good transportation, either rail or water. With the development of belt lines and switching yards, sites on the edge of the city may have better transportation service than those near the center. In Chicago about a hundred industries are in a belt three miles long, adjacent to the Clearing freight yards on the southwestern edge of the city. Furthermore, the noise of boiler works, the odors of stockyards, the waste disposal problems of smelters and iron and steel mills, the fire hazards of petroleum refineries, and the space and transportation needs which interrupt streets and accessibility—all these favor the growth of heavy industry away from the main center of the large city. The Calumet District of Chicago, the New Jersey marshes near New York City, the Lea marshes near London, and the St. Denis district of Paris are examples of such districts. The stockyards of Chicago, in spite of their odors and size, have been engulfed by urban growth and are now far from the edge of the city. They form a nucleus of heavy industry within the city but not near the center, which has blighted the adjacent residential area, the "back-of-the-yards" district.

The Residential District. In general, high-class districts are likely to be on well-drained, high land and away from nuisances such as noise, odors, smoke, and railroad lines. Low-class districts are likely to arise near factories and railroad districts, wherever located in the city. Because of the obsolescence of structures, the older inner margins of residential districts are fertile fields for invasion by groups unable to pay high rents. Residential neighborhoods have some measure of cohesiveness. Extreme cases are the ethnically segregated groups which cluster together, although including members in many economic groups; Harlem is an example.

Minor Nuclei. These include cultural centers, parks, outlying business districts, and small industrial centers. A university may form a nucleus for a quasi-independent community; examples are the University of Chicago, the University of California, and Harvard University. Parks and recreation areas occupying former wasteland too rugged or wet for housing may form nuclei for high-class residential areas; examples are Rock Creek Park in Washington and Hyde Park in London. Outlying business districts may in time become major centers. Many small institutions and individual light manufacturing plants, such as bakeries, dispersed throughout the city may never become nuclei of differentiated districts.

Suburb and Satellite.   Suburbs, either residential or industrial, are characteristic of most of the larger American cities.[6] The rise of the automobile and the improvement of certain suburban commuter rail lines in a few of the largest cities have stimulated suburbanization. Satellites differ from suburbs in that they are separated from the central city by many miles and in general have little daily commuting to or from the central city, although economic activities of the satellite are closely geared to those of the central city. Thus Gary may be considered a suburb but Elgin and Joliet are satellites of Chicago.

Appraisal of Land-Use Patterns

Most cities exhibit not only a combination of the three types of urban support, but also aspects of the three generalizations of the land-use pattern. An understanding of both is useful in appraising the future prospects of the whole city and the arrangement of its parts.

As a general picture subject to modification because of topography, transportation, and previous land use, the concentric-zone aspect has merit. It is not a rigid pattern, inasmuch as growth or arrangement often reflects expansion within sectors or development around separate nuclei.

The sector aspect has been applied particularly to the outward movement of residential districts. Both the concentric-zone theory and the sector theory emphasize the general tendency of central residential areas to decline in value as new construction takes place on the outer edges; the sector theory is, however, more discriminating in its analysis of that movement.

Both the concentric zone, as a general pattern, and the sector aspect, as applied primarily to residential patterns, assume (although not explicitly) that there is but a single urban core around which land use is arranged symmetrically in either concentric or radial patterns. In broad theoretical terms such an assumption may be valid, inasmuch as the handicap of distance alone would favor as much concentration as possible in a small central core. Because of the actual physical impossibility of such concentration and the existence of separating factors, however, separate nuclei arise. The specific separating factors are not only high rent in the core, which can be afforded by few activities, but also the natural attachment of certain activities to extra-urban transport, space, or other facilities, and the advantages of the separation of unlike activities and the concentration of like functions.

The constantly changing pattern of land use poses many problems. Near the core, land is kept vacant or retained in antisocial slum structures in anticipation of expansion of higher-rent activities. The hidden costs of slums

[6]Chauncy D. Harris, "Suburbs," *American Journal of Sociology,* Vol. 49, No. 1 (July 1943), p. 6.

to the city in poor environment for future citizens and excessive police, fire, and sanitary protection underlie the argument for a subsidy to remove the blight. The transition zone is not everywhere a zone of deterioration with slums, however, as witness the rise of high-class apartment developments near the urban core in the Gold Coast of Chicago or Park Avenue in New York City. On the fringe of the city, over ambitious subdividing results in unused land to be crossed by urban services such as sewers and transportation. Separate political status of many suburbs results in a lack of civic responsibility for the problems and expenses of the city in which the suburbanites work.

Sentiment and Symbolism as Ecological Variables
Walter Firey

Systematization of ecological theory has thus far proceeded on two main premises regarding the character of space and the nature of locational activities. The first premise postulates that the sole relation of space to locational activities is an impeditive and cost-imposing one. The second premise assumes that locational activities are primarily economizing, "fiscal" agents.[1] On the basis of these two premises the only possible relationship that locational activities may bear to space is an economic one. In such a relationship each activity will seek to so locate as to minimize the obstruction put upon its functions by spatial distance. Since the supply of the desired locations is limited it follows that not all activities can be favored with choice sites. Consequently a competitive process ensues in which the scarce desirable locations are preempted by those locational activities which can so exploit advantageous location as to produce the greatest surplus of income over expenditure. Less desirable locations devolve to correspondingly less economizing land uses. The result is a pattern of land use that is presumed to be most efficient for both the individual locational activity and for the community.[2]

Given the contractualistic milieu within which the modern city has arisen and acquires its functions, such an "economic ecology" has had a certain

[1] See Everett C. Hughes, "The Ecological Aspect of Institutions," *American Sociological Review.* I:180-9, April, 1936.

[2] This assumption of a correspondence between the maximum utility of a private association and that of the community may be questioned within the very framework of marginal utility analysis. See particularly A. C. Pigou, *The Economics of Welfare.* Second Edition, London: 1924, Part II, ch. 8. For a clear presentation of the typical position, see Robert Murray Haig, "Towards an Understanding of the Metropolis—the Assignment of Activities to Areas in Urban Regions," *Quarterly Journal of Economics.* 40:402-34, May, 1926.

SOURCE: Walter Firey, "Sentiment and Symbolism as Ecological Variables," *American Sociological Review,* 10 (April 1945), 140-148. Reprinted by permission.

explanatory adequacy in describing urban spatial structure and dynamics. However, as any theory matures and approaches a logical closure of its generalizations, it inevitably encounters facts which remain unassimilable to the theoretical scheme. In this paper it will be our purpose to describe certain ecological processes which apparently cannot be embraced in a strictly economic analysis. Our hypothesis is that the data to be presented, while in no way startling or unfamiliar to the research ecologist, do suggest an alteration of the basic premises of ecology. This alteration would consist, first, of ascribing to space not only an impeditive quality but also an additional property, viz., that of being at times a symbol for certain cultural values that have become associated with a certain spatial area. Second, it would involve a recognition that locational activities are not only economizing agents but may also bear sentiments which can significantly influence the locational process.[3]

A test case for this twofold hypothesis is afforded by certain features of land use in central Boston. In common with many of the older American cities Boston has inherited from the past certain spatial patterns and landmarks which have had a remarkable persistence and even recuperative power despite challenges from other more economic land uses. The persistence of these spatial patterns can only be understood in terms of the group values that they have come to symbolize. We shall describe three types of such patterns: first, an in-town upper class residential neighborhood known as Beacon Hill; second, certain "sacred sites," notably the Boston Common and the colonial burying-grounds; and third, a lower class Italian neighborhood known as the North End. In each of these land uses we shall find certain locational processes which seem to defy a strictly economic analysis.

The first of the areas, Beacon Hill, is located some five minutes' walking distance from the retail center of Boston. This neighborhood has for fully a century and a half maintained its character as a preferred upper class residential district, despite its contiguity to a low rent tenement area, the West End. During its long history Beacon Hill has become the symbol for a number of sentimental associations which constitute a genuine attractive force to certain old families of Boston. Some idea of the nature of these sentiments may be had from statements in the innumerable pamphlets and articles written by residents of the Hill. References to "this sacred eminence,"[4] "stately old-time appearance,"[5] and "age-old quaintness and charm,"[6] give an insight into the attitudes attaching to the area. One resident reveals rather clearly the spatial referability of these sentiments when she writes of the Hill:

[3]Georg Simmel, "Der Raum und die räumlichen Ordnungen der Gesellschaft," *Soziologie.* Munich: 1923, pp. 518-22; cf. Hughes, *op. cit.*

[4]John R. Shultz, *Beacon Hill and the Carol Singers.* Boston: 1923, p. 11.

[5]*Bulletin of the Society for the Preservation of New England Antiquities.* 4:3, August, 1913.

[6]Josephine Samson, *Celebrities of Louisburg Square.* Greenfield, Mass.: 1924.

It has a tradition all its own, that begins in the hospitality of a book-lover, and has never lost that flavor. Yes, our streets are inconvenient, steep, and slippery. The corners are abrupt, the contours perverse. . . . It may well be that the gibes of our envious neighbors have a foundation and that these dear crooked lanes of ours were indeed traced in ancestral mud by absent-minded kine.[7]

Behind such expressions of sentiment are a number of historical associations connected with the area. Literary traditions are among the strongest of these; indeed, the whole literary legend of Boston has its focus at Beacon Hill. Many of America's most distinguished literati have occupied homes on the Hill. Present day occupants of these houses derive a genuine satisfaction from the individual histories of their dwellings.[8] One lady whose home had had a distinguished pedigree remarked:

I like living here for I like to think that a great deal of historic interest has happened here in this room.

Not a few families are able to trace a continuity of residence on the Hill for several generations, some as far back as 1800 when the Hill was first developed as an upper class neighborhood. It is a point of pride to a Beacon Hill resident if he can say that he was born on the Hill or was at least raised there; a second best boast is to point out that his forebears once lived on the Hill.

Thus a wide range of sentiments—aesthetic, historical, and familial—have acquired a spatial articulation in Beacon Hill. The bearing of these sentiments upon locational processes is a tangible one and assumes three forms: retentive, attractive, and resistive. Let us consider each of these in order. To measure the retentive influence that spatially-referred sentiments may exert upon locational activities we have tabulated by place of residence all the families listed in the Boston *Social Register* for the years 1894, 1905, 1914, 1929, and 1943. This should afford a reasonably accurate picture of the distribution of upper class families by neighborhoods within Boston and in suburban towns. In Table I we have presented the tabulations for the three in-town concentrations of upper class families (Beacon Hill, Back Bay, and Jamaica Plain) and for the five main suburban concentrations (Brookline, Newton, Cambridge, Milton, and Dedham). Figure I portrays these trends in graphic form. The most apparent feature of these data is, of course, the consistent increase of upper class families in the suburban towns and the marked decrease (since 1905) in two of the in-town upper class areas, Back Bay and Jamaica Plain. Although both of these neighborhoods remain fashionable residential districts their prestige is waning rapidly. Back Bay in particular, though still surpassing in

[7]Abbie Farwell Brown, *The Lights of Beacon Hill.* Boston, 1922, p. 4.
[8]*Cf.* W. Lloyd Warner and Paul S. Lunt, *The Social Life of a Modern Community*, New Haven, 1941, p. 107, on this pattern.

TABLE I. NUMBER OF UPPER CLASS FAMILIES IN BOSTON, BY DISTRICTS OF CONCENTRATION, AND IN MAIN SUBURBAN TOWNS, FOR CERTAIN YEARS

	1894	1905	1914	1929	1943
Within Boston					
Beacon Hill	280	242	279	362	335
Back Bay	867	1166	1102	880	556
Jamaica Plain	56	66	64	36	30
Other districts	316	161	114	86	41
Suburban Towns					
Brookline	137	300	348	355	372
Newton	38	89	90	164	247
Cambridge	77	142	147	223	257
Milton	37	71	106	131	202
Dedham	8	29	48	69	99
Other towns	106	176	310	403	816
Total in Boston	1519	1635	1559	1364	962
Total in Suburbs	403	807	1049	1345	1993
Totals	1922	2442	2608	2709	2955

Tabulated from : *Social Register, Boston*

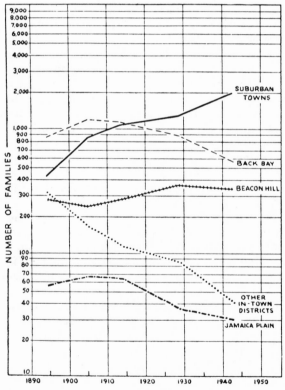

Figure I. Number of Upper Class Families in Boston, by Districts of Concentration, and in Suburbs, for Certain Years.

numbers any other single neighborhood, has undergone a steady invasion of apartment buildings, rooming houses, and business establishments which are destroying its prestige value. The trend of Beacon Hill has been different. Today it has a larger number of upper class families than it had in 1894. Where it ranked second among fasionable neighborhoods in 1894 it ranks third today, being but slightly outranked in numbers by the suburban city of Brookline and by the Back Bay. Beacon Hill is the only in-town district that has consistently retained its preferred character and has held to itself a considerable proportion of Boston's old families.

There is, however, another aspect to the spatial dynamics of Beacon Hill, one that pertains to the "attractive" locational role of spatially referred sentiments. From 1894 to 1905 the district underwent a slight drop, subsequently experiencing a steady rise for 24 years, and most recently undergoing another slight decline. These variations are significant, and they bring out rather clearly the dynamic ecological role of spatial symbolism. The initial drop is attributable to the development of the then new Back Bay. Hundreds of acres there had been reclaimed from marshland and had been built up with palatial dwellings. Fashion now pointed to this as the select area of the city and in response to its dictates a number of families abandoned Beacon Hill to take up more pretentious Back Bay quarters. Property values on the Hill began to depreciate, old dwellings became rooming houses, and businesses began to invade some of the streets. But many of the old families remained on the Hill and a few of them made efforts to halt the gradual deterioration of the district. Under the aegis of a realtor, an architect, and a few close friends there was launched a program of purchasing old houses, modernizing the interiors and leaving the colonial exteriors intact, and then selling the dwellings to individual families for occupancy. Frequently adjoining neighbors would collaborate in planning their improvements so as to achieve an architectural consonance. The results of this program may be seen in the drift of upper class families back to the Hill. From 1905 to 1929 the number of *Social Register* families in the district increased by 120. Assessed valuations showed a corresponding increase: from 1919 to 1924 there was a rise of 24 percent; from 1924 to 1929 the rise was 25 percent.[9] The nature of the Hill's appeal, and the kind of persons attracted, may be gathered from the following popular write-up:

> To salvage the quaint charm of Colonial Architecture on Beacon Hill, Boston, is the object of a well-defined movement among writers and professional folk that promises the most delightful opportunities for the home seeker of moderate means and conservative tastes. Because men of discernment were able to visualize the possibilities presented by these architectural landmarks, and have undertaken the gracious task of restoring them to their former glory, this historic quarter of old Boston, once the centre of literary culture, is coming into its own.[10]

[9] *The Boston Transcript.* April 12, 1930.
[10] Harriet Sisson Gillespie, "Reclaiming Colonial Landmarks," *The House Beautiful.* 58:-239–41, September, 1925.

The independent variable in this "attractive" locational process seems to have been the symbolic quality of the Hill, by which it constituted a referent for certain strong sentiments of upper class Bostonians.

While this revival was progressing there remained a constant menace to the character of Beacon Hill, in the form of business encroachments and apartment-hotel developments. Recurrent threats from this source finally prompted residents of the Hill to organize themselves into the Beacon Hill Association. Formed in 1922, the declared object of this organization was "to keep undesirable business and living conditions from affecting the hill district."[11] At the time the city was engaged in preparing a comprehensive zoning program and the occasion was propitious to secure for Beacon Hill suitable protective measures. A systematic set of recommendations was drawn up by the Association regarding a uniform 65-foot height limit for the entire Hill, the exclusion of business from all but two streets, and the restriction of apartment house bulk.[12] It succeeded in gaining only a partial recognition of this program in the 1924 zoning ordinance. But the Association continued its fight against inimical land uses year after year. In 1927 it successfully fought a petition brought before the Board of Zoning Adjustment to alter the height limits in one area so as to permit the construction of a four million dollar apartment-hotel 155 feet high. Residents of the Hill went to the hearing en masse. In spite of the prospect of an additional twenty million dollars worth of exclusive apartment hotels that were promised if the zoning restrictions were withheld the petition was rejected, having been opposed by 214 of the 220 persons present at the hearing.[13] In 1930 the Association gained an actual reduction in height limits on most of Beacon street and certain adjoining streets, though its leader was denounced by opponents as "a rank sentimentalist who desired to keep Boston a village."[14] One year later the Association defeated a petition to rezone Beacon street for business purposes.[15] In other campaigns the Association successfully pressed for the rezoning of a business street back to purely residential purposes, for the lowering of height limits on the remainder of Beacon street, and for several lesser matters of local interest. Since 1929, owing partly to excess assessed valuations of Boston real estate and partly to the effects of the depression upon families living on securities, Beacon Hill has lost some of its older families, though its decline is nowhere near so precipitous as that of the Back Bay.

Thus for a span of one and a half centuries there have existed on Beacon Hill certain locational processes that largely escape economic analysis. It is the symbolic quality of the Hill, not its impeditive or cost-imposing character, that most tangibly correlates with the retentive, attractive, and resistive trends that

[11] *The Boston Transcript.* December 6, 1922.
[12] *The Boston Transcript.* March 18, 1933.
[13] *The Boston Transcript.* January 29, 1927.
[14] *The Boston Transcript.* April 12, 1930.
[15] *The Boston Transcript.* January 10, January 29, 1931.

we have observed. And it is the dynamic force of spatially referred sentiments, rather than considerations of rent, which explains why certain families have chosen to live on Beacon Hill in preference to other in-town districts having equally accessible location and even superior housing conditions. There is thus a non-economic aspect to land use on Beacon Hill, one which is in some respects actually dis-economic in its consequences. Certainly the large apart-ment-hotels and specialty shops that have sought in vain to locate on the Hill would have represented a fuller capitalization on potential property values than do residences. In all likelihood the attending increase in real estate prices would not only have benefited individual property holders but would have so enhanced the value of adjoining properties as to compensate for whatever depreciation other portions of the Hill might have experienced.

If we turn to another type of land use pattern in Boston, that comprised by the Boston Common and the old burying grounds, we encounter another instance of spatial symbolism which has exerted a marked influence upon the ecological organization of the rest of the city. The Boston Common is a survival from colonial days when every New England town allotted a portion of its land to common use as a cow pasture and militia field. Over the course of three centuries Boston has grown entirely around the Common so that today we find a 48-acre tract of land wedged directly into the heart of the business district. On three of its five sides are women's apparel shops, department stores, theaters and other high-rent locational activities. On the fourth side is Beacon street, extending alongside Beacon Hill. Only the activities of Hill residents have prevented business from invading this side. The fifth side is occupied by the Public Garden. A land value map portrays a strip of highest values pressing upon two sides of the Common, on Tremont and Boylston streets, taking the form of a long, narrow band.

Before considering the ecological consequences of this configuration let us see what attitudes have come to be associated with the Common. There is an extensive local literature about the Common and in it we find interesting sentiments expressed. One citizen speaks of:

> . . . the great principle exemplified in the preservation of the Common. Thank Heaven, the tide of money making must break and go around that.[16]

Elsewhere we read:

> Here, in short, are all our accumulated memories, intimate, public, private.[17]
> Boston Common was, is, and ever will be a source of tradition and inspiration from which the New Englanders may renew their faith, recover their moral force, and strengthen their ability to grow and achieve.[18]

[16]Speech of William Everett, quoted in *The Boston Transcript.* March 7, 1903.
[17]T. R. Sullivan, *Boston New and Old.* Boston: 1912, pp. 45–6
[18]Joshua H. Jones, Jr., "Happenings on Boston Common," *Our Boston.* 2:9–15, January, 1927.

The Common has thus become a "sacred" object, articulating and symbolizing genuine historical sentiments of a certain portion of the community. Like all such objects its sacredness derives, not from any intrinsic spatial attributes, but rather from its representation in peoples' minds as a symbol for collective sentiments.[19]

Such has been the force of these sentiments that the Common has become buttressed up by a number of legal guarantees. The city charter forbids Boston in perpetuity to dispose of the Common or any portion of it. The city is further prohibited by state legislation from building upon the Common, except within rigid limits, or from laying out roads or tracks across it.[20] By accepting the bequest of one George F. Parkman, in 1908, amounting to over five million dollars, the city is further bound to maintain the Common, and certain other parks, "for the benefit and enjoyment of its citizens."[21]

What all this has meant for the spatial development of Boston's retail center is clear from the present character of that district. Few cities of comparable size have so small a retail district in point of area. Unlike the spacious department stores of most cities, those in Boston are frequently compressed within narrow confines and have had to extend in devious patterns through rear and adjoining buildings. Traffic in downtown Boston has literally reached the saturation point, owing partly to the narrow one-way streets but mainly to the lack of adequate arterials leading into and out of the Hub. The American Road Builders Association has estimated that there is a loss of $81,000 per day in Boston as a result of traffic delay. Trucking in Boston is extremely expensive. These losses ramify out to merchants, manufacturers, commuters, and many other interests.[22] Many proposals have been made to extend a through arterial across the Common, thus relieving the extreme congestion on Tremont and Beacon streets, the two arterials bordering the park.[23] Earlier suggestions, prior to the construction of the subway, called for street car tracks across the Common. But "the controlling sentiment of the citizens of Boston, and of large numbers throughout the State, is distinctly opposed to allowing any such use of the Common."[24] Boston has long suffered from land shortage and unusually high real estate values as a result both of the narrow confines of the peninsula comprising the city center and as a result of the exclusion from income-yielding uses of so large a tract as the Common.[25] A further difficulty has arisen from the rapid southwesterly extension of the business district in the past two decades. With the Common lying directly in the path of this extension the

[19] *Cf.* Emile Durkheim, *The Elementary Forms of the Religious Life.* London: 1915, p. 345.
[20] St. 1859, c. 210, paragraph 3; Pub sts. c 54, paragraph 13.
[21] M. A. De Wolfe Howe, *Boston Common.* Cambridge: 1910, p. 79.
[22] Elisabeth M. Herlihy, Ed., *Fifty Years of Boston.* Boston: 1932, pp. 53–4.
[23] See, for example, letter to editor, *The Boston Herald.* November 16, 1930.
[24] *First Annual Report of the Boston Transit Commission.* Boston: 1895, p. 9.
[25] John C. Kiley, "Changes in Realty Values in the Nineteenth and Twentieth Centuries," *Bulletin of the Business Historical Society.* 15, June, 1941, p. 36; Frank Chouteau Brown, "Boston: More Growing Pains," *Our Boston.* 3, February, 1927, p. 8.

business district has had to stretch around it in an elongated fashion, with obvious inconvenience to shoppers and consequent loss to businesses.

The Common is not the only obstacle to the city's business expansion. No less than three colonial burying-grounds, two of them adjoined by ancient church buildings, occupy downtown Boston. The contrast that is presented by 9-story office buildings reared up beside quiet cemeteries affords visible evidence of the conflict between "sacred" and "profane" that operates in Boston's ecological pattern. The dis-economic consequences of commercially valuable land being thus devoted to non-utilitarian purposes goes even further than the removal from business uses of a given amount of space. For it is a standard principle of real estate that business property derives added value if adjoining properties are occupied by other businesses.[26] Just as a single vacancy will depreciate the value of a whole block of business frontage, so a break in the continuity of stores by a cemetery damages the commercial value of surrounding properties. But, even more than the Common, the colonial burying-grounds of Boston have become invested with a moral significance which renders them almost inviolable. Not only is there the usual sanctity which attaches to all cemeteries, but in those of Boston there is an added sacredness growing out of the age of the grounds and the fact that the forebears of many of New England's most distinguished families as well as a number of colonial and Revolutionary leaders lie buried in these cemeteries. There is thus a manifold symbolism to these old bury-grounds, pertaining to family lineage, early nationhood, civic origins, and the like, all of which have strong sentimental associations. What has been said of the old bury-grounds applies with equal force to a number of other venerable landmarks in central Boston. Such buildings as the Old South Meeting-House, the Park Street Church, King's Chapel, and the Old State House—all foci of historical associations—occupy commercially valuable land and interrupt the continuity of business frontage on their streets. Nearly all of these landmarks have been challenged at various times by real estate and commercial interests which sought to have them replaced by more profitable uses. In every case community sentiments have resisted such threats.

In all these examples we find a symbol-sentiment relationship which has exerted a significant influence upon land use. Nor should it be thought that such phenomena are mere ecological "sports." Many other older American cities present similar locational characteristics. Delancey street in Philadelphia represents a striking parallel to Beacon Hill, and certain in-town districts of Chicago, New York, and Detroit, recently revived as fashionable apartment areas, bear resemblances to the Beacon Hill revival. The role of traditionalism in rigidifying the ecological patterns of New Orleans has been demonstrated in a recent study.[27] Further studies of this sort should clarify even further the

[26]Richard M. Hurd, *Principles of City Land Values.* New York: 1903, pp. 93–4.

[27]H. W. Gilmore, "The Old New Orleans and the New: A Case for Ecology," *American Sociological Review.* 9:385–94, August, 1944.

true scope of sentiment and symbolism in urban spatial structure and dynamics.

As a third line of evidence for our hypothesis we have chosen a rather different type of area from those so far considered. It is a well known fact that immigrant ghettoes, along with other slum districts, have become areas of declining population in most American cities. A point not so well established is that this decline tends to be selective in its incidence upon residents and that this selectivity may manifest varying degrees of identification with immigrant values. For residence within a ghetto is more than a matter of spatial placement; it generally signifies acceptance of immigrant values and participation in immigrant institutions. Some light on this process is afforded by data from the North End of Boston. This neighborhood, almost wholly Italian in population, has long been known as "Boston's classic land of poverty."[28] Eighteen percent of the dwellings are eighty or more years old, and sixty percent are forty or more years old.[29] Indicative of the dilapidated character of many buildings is the recent sale of a 20-room apartment building for only $500. It is not surprising then to learn that the area has declined in population from 21,111 in 1930 to 17,598 in 1940.[30] To look for spatially referable sentiments here would seem futile. And yet, examination of certain emigration differentials in the North End reveals a congruence between Italian social structure and locational processes. To get at these differentials recourse was had to the estimation of emigration, by age groups and by nativity, through the use of life tables. The procedure consists of comparing the actual 1940 population with the residue of the 1930 population which probably survived to 1940 according to survival rates for Massachusetts. Whatever deficit the actual 1940 population may show from the estimated 1940 population is a measure of "effective emigration." It is not a measure of the actual volume of emigration, since no calculation is made of immigration *into* the district between 1930 and 1940.[31] Effective emigration simply indicates the extent of population decline which is attributable to emigration rather than to death. Computations thus made for emigration differentials by nativity show the following: (Table II.) Thus the second generation, comprising but 59.46 percent of the 1930 population, con-

[28]Robert A. Woods, Ed., *Americans in Process*. Boston, 1903, p. 5.

[29]Finance Commission of the City of Boston, *A Study of Certain of the Effects of Decentralization on Boston and Some Neighboring Cities and Towns*. Boston: 1941, p. 11.

[30]Aggregate population of census tracts F1, F2, F4, F5: *Census Tract Data, 1930 Census,* unpublished material from 15th Census of the United States, 1930, compiled by Boston Health Department, table 1; *Population and Housing—Statistics for Census Tracts, Boston.* 16th Census of the United States, 1940, table 2.

[31]By use of *Police Lists* for two different years a count was made of immigration into a sample precinct of the North End. The figure (61) reveals so small a volume of immigration that any use of it to compute actual emigration by age groups would have introduced statistical unreliability into the estimates. Survival rates for Massachusetts were computed from state life tables in: National Resources Committee, *Population Statistics, 2. State Data.* Washington: 1937, Part C, p. 38. The technique is outlined in C. Warren Thornthwaite, *Internal Migration in the United States.* Philadelphia: 1934, pp. 19–21.

TABLE II. EFFECTIVE EMIGRATION FROM THE NORTH END, BOSTON, 1930 TO 1940, BY NATIVITY

Nativity	1930 Population	Per cent of 1930 Pop. in each Nativity Group	Effective Emigration 1930– 1940	Per cent of Emigration accounted for by each Nativity Group
American-born (second generation)	12553	59.46	3399	76.42
Italian-born (first generation)	8557	40.54	1049	23.58
Totals	21110	100.00	4448	100.00

Calculated from: census tract data and survival rates

tributed 76.42 percent of the effective emigration from the North End, whereas the first generation accounted for much less than its "due" share of the emigration. Another calculation shows that where the effective emigration of second generation Italians represents 27.08 percent of their number in 1930, that of the first generation represents only 12.26 percent of their number in 1930.

Equally clear differentials appear in effective emigration by age groups. If we compare the difference between the percentage which each age group as of 1930 contributes to the effective emigration, and the percentage which each age group comprised of the 1930 population, we find that the age groups 15–24 account for much more than their share of effective emigration; the age groups 35–64 account for much less than their share.[32] In Table III the figures preceded by a plus sign indicate "excess" emigration, those preceded by a minus sign indicate "deficit" emigration. In brief, the North End is losing its young people to a much greater extent than its older people.

These differentials are in no way startling; what is interesting, however, is their congruence with basic Italian values, which find their fullest institutionalized expression in the North End. Emigration from the district may be viewed as both a cause and a symbol of alienation from these values. At the core of the Italian value system are those sentiments which pertain to the family and

[32]Obviously most of the emigrants in the 15–24 age group in 1930 migrated while in the age group 20–29; likewise the emigrants in the 35–64 age group migrated while in the 40–69 age group.

the *paesani.* Both of these put a high premium upon maintenance of residence in the North End.

Paesani, or people from the same village of origin, show considerable tendency to live near one another, sometimes occupying much of a single street or court.[33] Such proximity, or at least common residence in the North End, greatly facilitates participation in the *paesani* functions which are so important

TABLE III.   DIFFERENCE BETWEEN PERCENTAGE CONTRIBUTED BY EACH AGE GROUP
TO EFFECTIVE EMIGRATION AND PERCENTAGE IT COMPRISED OF 1930 POPULATION

Age Groups as of 1930	Differences between Percentages	
	Male	Female
under 5	−1.70	−0.33
5–9	+0.38	+0.04
10–14	+0.21	+2.66
15–19	+4.18	+3.01
20–24	+2.04	+2.35
25–34	−0.97	−0.07
35–44	−2.31	−1.09
45–54	−1.43	−1.17
55–64	−2.29	−1.19
65–74	−1.13	−0.59
75 and over	uncalculable	

Calculated from: census tract data and survival rates

to the first generation Italian. Moreover, it is in the North End that the *festas,* anniversaries, and other old world occasions are held, and such is their frequency that residence in the district is almost indispensable to regular participation. The social relationships comprised by these groupings, as well as the benefit orders, secret societies, and religious organizations, are thus strongly localistic in character. One second generation Italian, when asked if his immigrant parents ever contemplated leaving their North End tenement replied:

> No, because all their friends are there, their relatives. They know everyone around there.

It is for this reason that the first generation Italian is so much less inclined to leave the North End than the American born Italian.

Equally significant is the localistic character of the Italian family. So great is its solidarity that it is not uncommon to find a tenement entirely occupied

[33]William Foote Whyte, *Street Corner Society.* Chicago: 1943, p. xix.

by a single extended family: grandparents, matured children with their mates, and grandchildren. There are instances where such a family has overflowed one tenement and has expanded into an adjoining one, breaking out the partitions for doorways. These are ecological expressions, in part, of the expected concern which an Italian mother has for the welfare of her newly married daughter. The ideal pattern is for the daughter to continue living in her mother's house, with she and her husband being assigned certain rooms which they are supposed to furnish themselves. Over the course of time the young couple is expected to accumulate savings and buy their own home, preferably not far away. Preferential renting, by which an Italian who owns a tenement will let apartments to his relatives at a lower rental, is another manifestation of the localizing effects of Italian kinship values.

Departure from the North End generally signifies some degree of repudiation of the community's values. One Italian writes of an emigrant from the North End:

> I still remember with regret the vain smile of superiority that appeared on his face when I told him that I lived at the North End of Boston. *"Io non vado fra quella plebaglia."* (I do not go among those plebeians.)[34]

As a rule the older Italian is unwilling to make this break, if indeed he could. It is the younger adults, American-born and educated, who are capable of making the transition to another value system with radically different values and goals.

Residence in the North End seems therefore to be a spatial corollary to integration with Italian values. Likewise emigration from the district signifies assimilation into American values, and is so construed by the people themselves. Thus, while the area is not the conscious object of sentimental attachment, as are Beacon Hill and the Common, it has nonetheless become a symbol for Italian ethnic solidarity. By virtue of this symbolic quality the area has a certain retentive power over those residents who most fully share the values which prevail there.

It is reasonable to suggest, then, that the slum is much more than "an area of minimum choice."[35] Beneath the surface phenomenon of declining population there may be differential rates of decline which require positive formulation in a systematic ecological theory. Such processes are apparently refractory to analysis in terms of competition for least impeditive location. A different order of concepts, corresponding to the valuative, meaningful aspect of spatial adaptation, must supplement the prevailing economic concepts of ecology.

---

[34]Enrico C. Sartorio, *Social and Religious Life of Italians in America*. Boston: 1918, pp. 43–4.

[35]R. D. McKenzie, "The Scope of Human Ecology," in Ernest W. Burgess, Ed., *The Urban Community*. Chicago: 1926, p. 180.

The Place of Social Structure in the Determination of Land Use: Some Implications for a Theory of Urban Ecology*

William H. Form

Deriving a satisfactory theory of land use change is a pressing problem for both ecologists and urban sociologists.[1] Most of the current thinking on this subject revolves around the so-called ecological processes. A brief inspection of the literature reveals, however, a lamentable lack of agreement on the definition, number, and importance of the ecological processes.[2] It is apparent that the economic model of classical economists from which these processes are derived must be discarded in favor of models which consider social realities.

In studying land use change, this paper proposes that ecology abandon its sub-social non-organization orientations and use the frame of reference of general sociology. Even though the focus of attention of ecology may remain in the economic realm, a sociological analysis of economic behavior is called for. This means that most of the current ecological premises must be converted into research questions capable of sociological verification.

The first step is to analyze the social forces operating in the land market. Obviously the image of a free and unorganized market in which individuals compete impersonally for land must be abandoned. The reason for this is that the land market is highly organized and dominated by a number of interacting organizations. Most of the latter are formally organized, highly self-conscious,

---

*Adapted from the presidential address delivered before the Ohio Valley Sociological Society, April 25, 1952. I am indebted to Gregory P. Stone for a critical reading of the manuscript.

[1] For purposes of simplification this paper will limit itself to a consideration of land use change in middle-size, growing, industrial cities of the United States. Historical analysis of land use change is not within the province of this paper because of the methodological difficulties in reconstructing the ecological processes.

[2] One reason for this confusion centers on the controversy whether human ecology should be related to or divorced from biological ecology. Amos H. Hawley claims that the difficulties of human ecology arise from its isolation from the mainstream of ecological thought in biology; see his "Ecology and Human Ecology," *Social Forces,* 22 (May 1944), pp. 399–405. Warner E. Gettys is of the opinion that human ecology should free itself from its primary dependence on organic ecology; see his "Human Ecology and Social Theory," *Social Forces,* 18 (May 1940), pp. 469–476.

SOURCE: William H. Form, "The Place of Social Structure in the Determination of Land Use: Some Implications for a Theory of Urban Ecology," *Social Forces,* 32 (May 1954), pp. 317–323. Reprinted by Permission of the University of North Carolina press.

and purposeful in character. Although at times their values and interests are conflicting, they are often overlapping and harmonious. That is, their relationships tend to become structured over a period of time. From a study of this emerging structure one obtains a picture of the parameters of ecological behavior, the patterns of land use change, and the institutional pressures which maintain the ecological order.

FOUR ORGANIZATIONAL CONGERIES IN THE LAND MARKET

The interacting groups, associations, and relationships which comprise this emerging structure may be identified by asking such questions as: (a) Who are the largest consumers of land? (b) Which organizations specialize in dealing with land? and (c) Which associations mediate the conflicts of land use? Preliminary research suggests that, among the many associations and interests in American society, four types of social congeries or organizational complexes dominate the land market and determine indirectly the use to which land is put.

The first and perhaps most important of these congeries is the real estate and building business.[3] Since they know more about the land market of the city than comparable groups, it is suggested that the study of the real estate-building groups (along the lines of occupational-industrial sociology) would provide more insight into the dynamics of land use change then present studies which are based on the sub-social ecological processes. The analysis of real estate organizations is an especially good starting point to build a sociological ecology because these organizations interact with all of the other urban interests which are concerned with land use.[4]

The second social congeries which functions in the land market are the larger industries, businesses, and utilities. While they may not consume the greatest quantities of land, they do purchase the largest and most strategic parcels. Unknowingly their locational decisions tend to set the pattern of land use for other economic and non-economic organizations. Most of the land use decisions of these central industries and businesses are a response to peculiar historic circumstances in the community. Therefore it would seem fruitless to describe *a priori* the geometric shape of the city as a series of rings, sectors, or diamonds.

The third social constellation in the land market is composed of individual

[3]It appears that an interpenetration of organization and interests of these two groups is increasing so rapidly in American cities that for many purposes they may be conceived as one interest group.

[4]This is strongly suggested by strikingly parallel studies in two different types of cities. Cf. Everett C. Hughes, A Study of a Secular Institution: The Chicago Real Estate Board (unpublished Ph.D. dissertation, University of Chicago, 1928); Donald H. Bouma, An Analysis of the Social Power Position of the Real Estate Board in Grand Rapids, Michigan (unpublished Ph.D. dissertation, Michigan State College, 1952).

home owners and other small consumers of land. In a sense their position is tangential to the structure or important only under rather unusual circumstances. Most of their decisions on where to buy, when to buy, and what land to buy are fitted into an administered land market and are not, as many would assume, individual, discrete, free, and unrelated. The social characteristics of the consumers, their economic power, degree of organization, and relations to other segments of the community help explain the role they play in the market of land decisions.

The fourth organizational complex is comprised of the many local governmental agencies which deal with land, such as the zoning boards, planning commissions, school boards, traffic commissions, and other agencies. This organizational complex is loosely knit internally, for its segments often function at cross purposes. Their relations to other groups in the community vary with political currents. Unlike other organizations, these governmental agencies are both consumers of land and mediators of conflicting land use interests. Thus political agencies not only acquire land to placate private and public pressures, they are also called upon to resolve conflicts between different types of land consumers. Moreover, some of these governmental agencies try to fulfill a city plan which sets the expected pattern of the ecological development of the city.

These four organizational complexes[5]—real estate, big business, residents, and government—do not comprise all of the organizational entities which participate in land use decisions. However, they are the main ones. Once identified, the problem is to find the nature of the social relationships among these organizational complexes. Is a stable pattern discernible? How does the pattern manifest itself in physical space? In what direction is the pattern emerging as a response to inter-institutional trends in the broader society? To answer these questions, an analytical model is needed to appraise the social relations among the four organizational congeries identified above.

ELEMENTS IN THE ANALYTICAL MODEL

Sociologists have not yet derived completely satisfactory schema to analyze inter-organizational relations, either in their structural or dynamic dimensions. However, ecologists are dependent on such general schema as have already been worked out. Some of the basic elements in the analytical scheme to appraise the relations among the four land consuming groups are described below.

[5]Each organizational complex is comprised of groups, associations, aggregations, social categories, and other types of social nucleations. To facilitate communication, the term "grouping" will be used to refer to this organizational complex. I am indebted to Professor Read Bain for pointing to the need for terminological clarification in matters dealing with interaction of different types of social nucleations.

1. The first element in the model is the amount and types of economic resources which each "grouping" has to buttress its land use decisions. Obviously the resources of the four "groupings" differ considerably. Thus, industry has property and capital which are somewhat greater and more mobile than those of the real estate industry. In addition to their tax resources, governmental agencies have the power to expropriate land in their own name or in the name of any interest which can control them. The individual home owner and the small businessman, on the other hand, not only have the smallest but the least organized economic resources. The economic resources of each group must be carefully gauged in each community where there is a contest to control particular parcels of land. However, economic resources comprise only one cell in the paradigm needed to analyze the structural setting of land use changes.

2. The second factors which merit consideration are the manifest and latent functions of each "grouping" in the land market. Thus, the functions of the real estate industry include, in addition to maximizing its earnings, bringing knowledge of available land to different segments of the community. Moreover it tries to organize the land market and control land values to assure itself stability and continuity of income.[6] In the process of so doing, the realtors come into contact with political, citizen, and business agencies.[7] The land interests of big business, on the other hand, are much more specific and spasmodic than those of the real estate business. The desire of businessmen to have large stretches of land under one title, to obtain land additions close to present plant operations, and to dominate the landscape of the community, often leads them to make diseconomic decisions which are in conflict with those of other groups.

Government agencies have quite different and sometimes conflicting functions to perform. Among these are: protecting present tax values, acquiring parcels of land for specific public or quasi-public uses, altering certain land use patterns to conform to the plan of the "city beautiful," acting as a clearing house and communication channel for those who need land use data. Most important, they mediate conflicts in land use and exercise their legitimate authority for groups which curry their favor.

Individual residents and small businessmen are mostly concerned with preventing changes in land use. They tend to be defensive-minded and sentimentally attached to their neighborhoods and to fight to prevent the encroachment of usages which would threaten present economic and social investments. In general, resident groupings do not play dynamic roles in changing urban land usages.

[6]See Everett C. Hughes, "Personality Types and the Division of Labor," in Ernest W. Burgess (ed.), *Personality and the Social Group* (Chicago: University of Chicago Press, 1929), especially pp. 91–94.

[7]*Ibid.* Hughes indicates that the real estate industry is a loose federation of different types of businessmen. Each type plays a different role to correspond to its clientele and market.

3. The internal organization of these four groupings differs considerably. Knowledge of this factor is important to assess the degree to which they may be mobilized to fight for control over desired lands. Often small, unified, and organized groups with meagre economic resources can dominate larger, richer, and more loosely knit groups in a land struggle. These four "groupings" differ in their internal structure and external relations. There is an urgent need for research to study the cleavages, cliques, alliances, and arrangements found within and among these groupings. However, certain trends may now be noted.

The real estate industry is slowly emerging from a haphazard aggregation of local agents to a tightly organized professional or fraternal society which seeks to establish control over the land market.[8] Big business and industry, on the other hand, have typically bureaucratic structures capable of marshalling tremendous resources in the community for or against other land-interested groups. Municipal agencies, though individually powerful, are often unaware of each other's activities. Therefore they tend to comprise a loosely knit set of bureaus which often function at cross purposes. Since many governmental agencies are tied into the fabric of private associations, they are united to common action only under unusual external pressures. Individual residents and small businesses are the most loosely organized.[9] In fact, they tend to remain unorganized except under "crisis" conditions.

4. Each grouping has an accountability pattern differing in its consequences for action. Each has different kinds of pressures and influences to which it must respond. For example, the real estate organizations are primarily accountable to themselves and sometimes to their largest customers, the building industry and utilities. On the other hand, the local managers of larger corporations tend to be accountable to other managers, stockholders, and board members who may not reside in the community. Thus, local managers may have to respond in their land decisions to pressures generated outside of the community. Municipal agencies are formally accountable to the local citizens who are, according to the issues, realtors, individual landlords, businessmen, educational, political, or any other organized interest.

Each of the four social congeries being considered is organized differently as a pressure group interested in land use policies. Each, in a sense, lives in a power situation which consists of its relation to the other three. Different kinds of alliances are made among them and among their segments, depending on the issues. The types of collective bargaining situations which arise among them must be studied in a larger context in order to understand the sociology of land use decisions. For example, businessmen who are sometimes appointed as members of city planning commissions may be constrained to play roles

---

[8] *Ibid.*

[9] Higher status areas of the city are usually more formally organized to protect land uses than are lower status areas. The formation of neighborhood "improvement and betterment" associations stabilizes land use and resists the invasion of other land uses.

incongruous with their business roles. As members of residential and recreational organizations they may be forced to make decisions which may seem contradictory to their economic interests.

5. In land decisions involving the whole city, the image which each grouping has of the city must be appraised. The realtors are usually the most enthusiastic boosters of the city. They envision an expanding city with an ever-growing land market, for this assures them income and security. Consequently, they exert pressure on the municipal agencies to join them in their plans for the "expansive city."

However, municipal officials do not conceive of the city primarily as a market. They see it as the downtown civic center, the city beautiful, and the planned community. Although desiring an expanding city, they are equally concerned with the politics and aesthetics of locating parks, avenues, schools, and other services. At times their aesthetic-political plans conflict with the boom ideology of the realtors and the industry-oriented plans of businessmen. Indeed this is almost inevitable in some situations, for politicians must secure votes to remain in office. Plans for different areas of the city must be weighed in terms of how they affect votes.[10]

The industrialists conception of the community tends to be more partial than that of any other group. Since industries often have allegiances to non-community enterprises, they are not necessarily enamoured by the vision of the expansive city or the city beautiful. They are inclined to view the city primarily as their work plant and residence. They usually regard the existence of their enterprises as economic "contributions" to the city. Therefore they feel that any land decisions they desire as businessmen, golfers, or residents are "reasonable and proper" in view of their "contribution" to the locality. When their demands are not met, they can threaten to remove the industry to more favorable communities.

The citizen's view of the city is also segmental. He tends to envision it as his neighborhood, his work plant, and "downtown." These are the areas he wants to see protected, beautified, and serviced. Since residents do not comprise a homogeneous group, obviously their community images differ. The nature of the intersection of the segmentalized city images of these four social congeries provides one of the parameters for studying their interaction. Needless to say, other non-ecological images that these groups have of themselves and of each other have a bearing on their relations. However, since the problems of this paper are more structural than social psychological, this area will not be expanded.

6. Other factors in the analytical scheme may be derived which point to the different orientations and relationships existing among these groups. For example, their primary value orientations differ. For government, community "service" is ostensibly the chief value; for real estate, it is an assured land

---

[10]For an illuminating case history of this, see William Foote Whyte, *Street Corner Society* (Chicago: University of Chicago Press, 1947), pp. 245–252.

market; for business, it is profitable operations; for the resident, it is protection. Another distinction may be in terms of the amount and type of land interests of the groups. Whereas real estate is interested in communal lands, and industry is concerned with its private land use. The future task of sociologists will be to select the most important interactional areas of these groups to locate the forces responsible for land use patterns and changes.

LAND USE CHANGES IN A ZONING CONTEXT

Following the selection of some of the important dimensions in the paradigm, the task is to characterize briefly the pattern of the relationships among the four "groupings." In the broadest sense, the model to be followed is that used in analyzing the collective bargaining structure and process.[11] An excellent place to begin observing the "collective bargaining" relations among these groupings is in the zoning process of cities. Zoning is recommended because the methodological problems of studying it are minimal, and yet the kinds of intergroup relations found there are not unlike those in non-zoning relations.

Since almost every city of any consequence in the United States is zoned, any significant deviation in a pattern of land use necessarily involves a change in zoning. It would appear then that sociologists and ecologists should study the relations of land-interested agencies to municipal agencies.[12] Most zoning commissions tend to freeze an already existing pattern of land use. If they formulate plans for city growth, these plans tend to correspond to a sector image of expanding areas of ongoing land use. This results in a rather rigid ecological structure which inevitably generates pressures for changes. Since such changes involve obtaining the consent of municipal agencies, a political dimension insists itself in the study of ecological processes.

Traditional ecologists may object to this social structural and political approach to problems of land use change. They may suggest that the ecological concept of "dominance" provides the answer to the question of which group will determine land use or land use change. An examination of this concept in the ecological literature reveals a basic shortcoming. Ecological dominance refers to economic control in the symbiotic sense; it provides no analytical cues to appraise the relations among organizations which comprise the structure dealing with land use changes.[13]

[11]Herbert Blumer, "Sociological Theory in Industrial Relations," *American Sociological Review,* 12 (June 1947), pp. 271–278. See also the articles in Richard A. Lester and Joseph Shister (eds.), *Insights into Labor Issues* (New York: The Macmillan Company, 1948); William Foote Whyte, *Pattern for Industrial Peace* (New York: Harper and Brothers, 1951); H. D. Lasswell, *Politics* (New York: McGraw-Hill, 1936).

[12]Richard Dewey, "The Neighborhood, Urban Ecology, and City Planners," *American Sociological Review,* 15 (August 1950), pp. 502–507.

[13]See R. D. McKenzie, *The Metropolitan Community* (New York: McGraw-Hill, 1933), pp. 81–313; Don J. Bogue, *The Structure of the Metropolitan Community* (Horace J. Rackham School of Graduate Studies, University of Michigan, 1949), pp. 10–13.

Traditional ecologists may object that the proposal to study the relations of the four land "groupings" in a political context is merely a methodological innovation, in that the *results* of such a study would point to the same pattern of land use change available by recourse to the traditional ecological processes. They may reason that determination of land use after all is an economic struggle or process, in which the most powerful economic interests determine to what use land will be put. While it is true, they may agree, that this process is not as simple and as impersonal as hitherto believed, the end result is very much the same.[14]

The writer has recently been gathering cases of zoning changes that have occurred in Lansing, its fringe, and in the outlying areas. In addition, cases have been observed where attempts to institute zoning changes have failed. In both types of changes the questions were asked: (a) Did naked economic power dictate the decision to change or not to change the zoning? (b) Could the outcome of these cases be predicted by using a cultural ecology frame of reference? A brief analysis of the cases revealed that no simple economic or cultural analysis could account for success or failure of zoning changes. The actual outcome could be better analyzed on the basis of the paradigm suggested above. Four cases will be briefly summarized to suggest typical kinds of alliances found in attempts to change land use.

In Lansing, the zoning commission may recommend changes in zoning but the City Council must approve of them. This means that all changes in land use must occur in a political context. In 1951, a local metal fabricating plant asked the Council to rezone some of its property from a residential to a commercial classification so that an office building could be erected on it. The residents of the area, who are mostly Negroes, appeared before the Council urging it to refuse the request on the ground that the company had not lived up to legal responsibilities to control obnoxious smoke, fly-ash, traffic, and so on. In addition, they contended that space for Negro housing was limited and rezoning would deprive them of needed space. Moreover, they hinted that the company's request came indirectly from a large corporation which would eventually obtain the property. In short, they urged rejection of the request not on its own merits but on the basis that the company had not lived up to its community responsibilities. Company spokesmen denied any deals, promised to control air pollution, and got labor union spokesmen to urge rezoning. The Council complied. Four months later all of the properties of the company, including the rezoned area, were sold to the large corporation in question.

Here is a clear case of economically powerful interests consciously manipulating land uses for their purposes. The question arises: why did not the large corporation itself ask for rezoning? Apparently, it realized that greater resis-

---

[14]In this respect the position of ecologists is not significantly different from the Marxist analysis of land use changes. This may explain the appeal of the ecological approach to some otherwise sophisticated sociologists. I am indebted to G. P. Stone for the elaboration of this idea.

tance would have been met. The local company is a medium-sized, old, home-owned enterprise which has had rather warm relations with its employees. The large corporation, on the other hand, is a large, impersonal, absentee-owned corporation that has at times alienated local people.[15] Therefore, its chances of getting this property without fanfare were increased by the use of an intermediary.

Yet business does not always win. In another case, a respectable undertaker established a funeral parlor in a low income residential area. The local residents objected strenuously to the presence of the business. The legal aspects of the case remained obscure for a time, because the undertaker insisted he did not embalm bodies in the establishment. In a preliminary hearing he appeared to have won a victory. The aroused residents called upon the Republican ward leader who promised to talk to the "authorities." Just before a rehearing of the case, the undertaker decided to leave the area, for he was reliably informed that the decision would go against him.

Struggles between businessmen and government do not always work out in favor of the former. Currently, the organized businessmen of East Lansing are fighting an order of the State Highway Commission which has passed a no parking ordinance to apply to the town's main thoroughfare. The retailers are fearful that they will lose business if the order holds. Since business will not be able to expand in the same direction if the order holds, pressure to rezone residential areas in the community for commercial and parking purposes will be forthcoming. In a community where residents are a strong, vocal, upper middle status group majority, such pressure may be resisted strongly. Clearly a power struggle involving the State, local businessmen, local government, and the residents will determine the ecological pattern of the city.[16] A knowledge of their relationships is needed to predict the outcome of the struggle and the future ecological changes in the community.

S. T. Kimball has documented a case where the failure to inaugurate zoning involved the same kind of social structural analysis of group relations as suggested above. Kimball studied a suburban rural township where the upper middle status groups failed in a referendum to obtain zoning in the face of an industrial invasion of the area. An analysis of the case showed that the issue would be misunderstood if studied as a struggle of economic interests. In fact, the industrial interests were not an important variable in the case. The failure of the referendum was accounted for by analysis of five types of relationships: (a) those among the suburbanites, (b) those within the township board, (c) those between the supervisor and his constituents, (d) those between the

---

[15] For example, workers insist that during the depression the company recruited Southerners rather than local labor.

[16] My colleague, G. P. Stone, suggests that it begins to appear that the State's position will force a very unusual ecological phenomenon: a business district turning its back to the main highway and reorienting itself to the "backyards," as it were.

farmers and suburbanites, and (e) those between the supervisor and the informal "leaders" in the community.[17]

CONCLUSIONS

This paper has proposed the need to consider social structure in addition to ecological and cultural factors in the study of changes in land use. The traditional ecological processes are no longer adequate tools to analyze changes in land use. These processes, like most ecological concepts, are based on models of eighteenth century free enterprise economics. Yet fundamental changes in the structure of the economy call for new economic models which in turn call for a recasting of general ecological theory. The new vital trend of cultural ecology does not do this adequately, for it considers the structural realities of urban society only indirectly.

This paper proposes that ecological change be studied by first isolating the important and powerful land-interested groupings in the city. Certain elements in an analytical scheme have been proposed to study the collective bargaining relationships among these groupings. The *forces* that operate in land use change may well be studied in the socio-political struggles that are presently occurring in the area of zoning. A brief survey of some changes in urban zoning points to the greater adequacy of the sociological over the traditional ecological analysis for understanding and predicting land use changes.

[17]Solon T. Kimball, "A Case Study of Township Zoning," *Michigan Agricultural Experiment Station Quarterly Bulletin,* 28 (May 1946), p.4.

The Concept of the 'Ecological Complex': A Critique*
Sidney M. Willhelm

I

The writings dealing with human ecology reflect two schools of thought. There is what we can refer to as the materialistic orientation on the one hand and the voluntaristic approach on the other.

Materialistic writers seek explanation for ecological developments in nonsocial conditions by arguing that specific forces determine ecological

*Presented at the annual meetings of the American Sociological Association, Washington, D.C., August, 1962.

SOURCE: Sidney Willhelm, "The Concept of the 'Ecological Complex': A Critique," *American Journal of Economics and Sociology,* 23 (1964), 241-248. Reprinted by permission.

phenomena apart from man's efforts to intervene through the imposition of social choice. In defending their case, materialists implicitly or specifically deny the relevance of social values and/or culture. A schism, however, prevails among materialistic ecologists: one group holds to a biotic interpretation of ecological developments, while another advocates a physical viewpoint. We shall label the biotic positon "traditional materialism" and the physical orientation "neoclassical materialism."

The biotic ecological approach of traditional materialists, stemming out of Social Darwinism, generally defines man's distribution over space resulting from biotic competition as the subject matter for human ecology. Traditional materialists then proceed to study biotic competition as a subsocial process through such concepts as dominance, succession, invasion, natural areas, concentric zones, sectors, etc. Sociologists such as Robert Park, Ernest Burgess, Roderick McKenzie, Robert Faris, among others, founded the now passé biotic perspective.[1]

In 1938, the biotic framework came under severe criticism with the publication of Milla Aissa Alihan's critique, *Social Ecology*, and Warner Gettys' significant article.[2] In 1947, two other works questioning traditional materialism appeared: Walter Firey's *Land Use in Central Boston* and an article by A. B. Hollingshead.[3] These writers launched a new perspective for human ecology which we can call the "voluntaristic" approach. Writers voicing the voluntaristic orientation vigorously attack as unrealistic the biological premises of traditional materialism and demand instead that ecologists seek explanation solely in man's social organization. We might also mention the names of William Form, Christen Jonassen and Gideon Sjoberg, who, among others, persist in writing as voluntarists.[4]

However, for purposes of this paper, we shall focus our attention upon the most recent ecological argument, namely, the "neoclassical" materialistic position. We may identify writers of this type by their reliance upon *physical* factors. The neoclassical ecologists, while relinquishing the biotic inclinations of their materialistic predecessors, nonetheless hold to impersonal notions to

[1]Robert E. Park, *Human Communities: The City and Human Ecology* (Glencoe, Ill.: Free Press, 1952); Ernest W. Burgess, *The Urban Community* (Chicago: University of Chicago Press, 1926); R. D. McKenzie, *The Metropolitan Community* (New York: McGraw-Hill, 1933); Robert E. L. Faris, "Ecological Factors in Human Behavior," in J. McV. Hunt (ed.), *Personality and the Behavior Disorder* (New York: Ronald Press Co., 1944), pp. 736-57.

[2]Milla Aissa Alihan, *Social Ecology* (New York: Columbia University Press, 1938); Warner E. Gettys, "Human Ecology and Social Theory," *Social Forces,* 18 (May, 1940), pp. 469-76.

[3]Walter Firey, *Land Use in Central Boston* (Cambridge: Harvard University Press, 1947); A. B. Hollingshead, "A Re-Examination of Ecological Theory," *Sociology and Social Research,* 31 (January-February, 1947), pp. 194-204.

[4]William Form, "The Place of Social Structure in the Determination of Land Use: Some Implications for a Theory of Urban Ecology," *Social Forces,* 32 (May, 1954), pp. 317-23; Christen Jonassen, "Cultural Variables in the Ecology of an Ethnic Group," *American Sociological Review,* 19 (February, 1954), pp. 3-10; Gideon Sjoberg, *The Preindustrial City* (Glencoe, Ill.: Free Press, 1960), Chap. IV.

justify the "neoclassical" label. The most outstanding representatives of neo-classical materialism are Amos Hawley, Otis Duncan, Leo Schnore, Jack Gibbs and Walter Martin.[5]

Neoclassical materialists generally define the responses of man's suste-nance and/or social organization[6] to certain "objectified" elements as the domain for ecological investigation; they firmly reject notions of subjectivity. These writers examine what is commonly called the "ecological complex"—consisting of population, social organization, environment and technology.

These four factors, according to neoclassical materialists, are external, physical—hence impersonal—conditions that absolutely determine ecological phenomena regardless of cultural or social efforts to interject direction and choice. Man's behavior—irrespective of his culture and social values and his social activities and irrespective of volition—must comply with certain imper-sonal physical conditions to be ecologically relevant from this materialistic perspective.

II

A methodological evaluation of the neoclassical argument indicates, how-ever, that, like its biotic predecessors, this contemporary attempt to establish the field of human ecology on an impersonal basis simply cannot be sustained. The non-social contentions of neoclassical materialism fail to meet valid stand-ards of performance owing to the several errors arising from the attention ecological materialists give to false analytical premises.

First, materialists resort to tautological reasoning when they lay claim to the ecological complex in formulating a problem for investigation. According to this orientation, ecologists should examine "the precise technological, demographic, and environmental conditions under which various urban forms of organization may be expected to appear."[7] Hawley, Duncan, Schnore, Gibbs and Martin, among others, insist, then, that they seek to investigate the interre-lationships between the variables constituting the ecological complex. After positing data relevant only to the ecological complex as "analytically distin-guishable elements,"[8] neoclassical materialists then proceed to explain their

---

[5] Amos Hawley, *Human Ecology* (New York: Ronald Press, 1950); Otis Dudley Duncan and Leo Schnore, "Cultural, Behavioral, and Ecological Perspectives in the Study of Social Organiza-tion," *American Journal of Sociology,* 65 (September, 1959), pp. 132-49; Leo F. Schnore, "Social Morphology and Human Ecology," *American Journal of Sociology,* 63 (May, 1958), pp. 620-34; Jack P. Gibbs and Walter T. Martin, "Toward a Theoretical System of Human Ecology," *Pacific Sociological Review,* 2 (Spring, 1959), pp. 29-36.

[6] For purposes of our summary and analysis of the writings by neoclassical materialists, we shall equate "sustenance activities" and "social organization."

[7] Duncan and Schnore, *op. cit.,* p. 138.

[8] Otis Dudley Duncan, "Human Ecology and Population Studies," in Philip M. Hauser and Otis Dudley Duncan (eds.), *The Study of Population* (Chicago: University of Chicago Press, 1959), pp. 683-84.

ecological data by the identical "ecological complex." Thereby they become tautological.

In short, the neoclassical materialist relies upon the ecological complex not only to furnish his data but also to analyze his data. Thus the subject matter and explanation are identical for the neoclassical materialist: population, organization, environment and technology provide the data for analysis in terms of population, organization, environment and technology.[9] Because it remains to be demonstrated that a tautological proposition can be empirically tested, the neoclassical orientation offers little in the way of scientific comprehension.

A second error committed by neoclassical materialists results from the mixed order of data that resides in the ecological complex. In this complex, we find the neoclassical materialists indiscriminately blending the non-material element of social organization with the material components of technology, geography and population. While these writers define all ecological variables external to the acting individuals, this cannot provide a rational basis for their insistence that material elements, such as the environment, determine the modes and/or content of social organizations. In no instance do we find an ecological materialist offering a *common* basis for the possibility of *interaction* between physical and social data. In short, where is the level of analysis that includes both orders of data? Stuart Chase, among others, notes the lack of logical premises for this type of neoclassical argument by exclaiming:

> The scientific method demands that when facts are compared, they must be of the same order. Do not add cabbages to electrons and expect to get a total which means anything.[10]

Sorokin's many works reflect his insistence that the two orders cannot be mixed in such a way that analyses "derive the conclusion that the material variable . . . determines the immaterial variable."[11] On the basis of similar reasoning, it can be shown that the neoclassical's "ecosystem"[12] has no empirical referent and hence cannot prevail even on a conceptual level.

A third shortcoming in this position stems from its firm belief that social values are psychological and therefore must be excluded from an ecological inquiry. The justification for this neoclassical statement rests upon the contention that ecologists must assume a collective perspective rather than an individualistic framework supposedly intrinsic to the social-value concept. This

---

[9]Substantiation for this contention can be found in the many articles in which the neoclassical concept is applied. For example: Leo F. Schnore, "Social Problems in the Underdeveloped Areas: An Ecological View," *Social Problems,* 8 (Winter, 1961), pp. 182-201; Otis Dudley Duncan, "From Social System to Ecosystem," *Sociological Inquiry,* 31 (Spring, 1961), pp. 140-9.

[10]Stuart Chase, *The Proper Study of Mankind* (New York: Harper, 1948), p. 21.

[11]Pitirim A. Sorokin, *Sociocultural Causality, Space, Time* (Durham: Duke University Press, 1943), p. 61.

[12]Duncan, "From Social System to Ecosystem," *op. cit.*

logic, however, necessitates the omission of problems that simply cannot be separated by analytical finesse. Furthermore, we shall note that the neoclassical materialist fails to present a collective perspective since he relies upon data that are entirely individualistic. But let us first consider the error of data-omission that results from the attempt by neoclassical ecologists to separate the inseparable.

III

Complete trust in external determinants precludes the possibility of choice. Yet there are many instances of choice situations within the very subjects presented by neoclassical materialists. Duncan, for example, deals with the smog situation in Los Angeles as though a population *automatically* reflects the changing physical setting through a social organization's implementation of technological devices in a *unidirectional* fashion, when in fact serious alternative responses have been and are now being discussed by governmental agencies as well as other social organizations.[13] Disputes involving *populations* with regard to establishing the form and/or content of *social organizations* within Los Angeles for *technological* control of the *environmental* smog are taking place. But Duncan presents his analysis as though a social organization merely mirrors environmental alterations in a rigor mortis fashion.

Schnore continually acknowledges the possibility of choice in dealing with social problems of underdeveloped countries from an ecological perspective— *e.g.*, the on-and-off-again birth-control policy in Communist China, the alternatives of capitalism and Marxism for industrialization, the possibility of choosing the "correct" course of action in contradistinction to "failure."[14] He goes so far as to claim: "The harsh truth is that there are *alternative* forms of government, and the main organizational question facing us is which of the various directions will be taken by the new nations of the world."[15]

Yet such writers do not introduce concepts in their ecological framework to deal with choice situations. Instead, they perceive fixed relationships between the forces composing the ecological complex which operate outside any individual and which dictate the course of ecological developments.[16] Neoclassical materialists insist that the social structure, population, technology and environment *preordain* the course of ecological events. Even in their analyses of social organization they perceive external determinism by relying solely upon what we might call the "normative argument"—the implicit contention that the mere presence of a norm and recognition of it by actors result in

[13] *Ibid.*
[14] Schnore, "Social Problems in the Underdeveloped Areas," *op. cit.*
[15] *Ibid.*, p. 191. Emphasis in the original.
[16] The ecological studies by other neoclassical writers also contain this fixation notion. For example: Jack P. Gibbs and Walter T. Martin, "Urbanization and Natural Resources: A Study in Organizational Ecology," *American Sociological Review*, 23 (June, 1958), pp. 266-77.

conformity to the requirements of the norm. If this proposition be true, rather than social action we have reflex in human behavior; rather than decision-making processes, we have structural edict; rather than actors choosing between alternatives, we have the structure "making" decisions. Social action becomes irrelevant and is, at most, a mere revelation of social structure rather than the establishment of a social structure.

But the normative argument fails to account for social behavior and an existing social organization because it cannot explain (1) the selection from alternative normative courses of action and (2) conformity or non-conformity to the normative pattern itself.[17] To insist that a social structure chooses from its own alternative structural possibilities and that it is the very nature of a social structure to generate conformity or non-conformity to its own structural features as implied by neoclassical ecologists—all this is only to argue from a tautological perspective of structure determining structure. There can be no empirical testing of this tautological position.

The elimination of the concept of social values by neoclassical materialists inadvertently leaves only a theory that makes both social action and social organization preordained, inevitable and unalterable; man himself is only a passive creature manipulated by forces of change that the neoclassical ecologists define as "external," "physical" conditions; man is simply a physical particle performing in limbo to the dictates of the ecological complex.

The concept of social values is not, as claimed by neoclassical ecologists, a psychological analytical tool; the concept is as sociologically relevant as the notion of social organization. Social values involve the conceptual characteristics of any other sociological construct in that they have references to aspects of social life that are shared, acquired, transmitted from one generation to another as well as from one society to another, etc.

The rejection of the social-value concept, however, has not meant that the neoclassical materialists have rid themselves of individualistic notions in favor of a collective emphasis. The overwhelming preference for employing census material as a basic source for ecological data[18] commits the neoclassical ecologists not to a collective orientation at all, but rather to the notion that the mere summation of discrete units yields the whole. Census data do not form a collective representation; such information is strictly individualistic and is collected from that point of view to contradict the neoclassical collective perspective. Moreover, neoclassical materialists do not fully appreciate the apparent fact that census data represent the collection of characteristics selected according to specific governmental requirements which are not neces-

---

[17] The normative argument is suggested by Emile Durkheim's observation that the very existence of norms infers that social behavior is or could be contrary to normative stipulations.

[18] For example: Hawley, *op. cit.,* Part II; Otis Dudley Duncan, "Population Distribution and Community Structure," *Cold Spring Harbor Symposia on Quantitative Biology,* 22 (1957), pp. 357-71. The strongest statement on this facet of neoclassical materialism has been expressed by Leo Schnore in a paper delivered at the national meetings of the American Sociological Association, St. Louis, September, 1961.

sarily conducive to proper scientific inquiry.[19] To permit a formal agency the opportunity to gather data according to the needs of a certain organization rather than by the scientist for scientific investigation prevents the intrusion of data which could be relevant for ecology. In short, the ecologist must not come to rely, as do the neoclassical ones, upon others for data that involve obvious non-scientific criteria for collection.

IV

A final aspect concerning values includes both traditonal and neoclassical ecology. In each perspective we find a rejection of the social value concept on the ground that explanations must be established in terms of non-social and impersonal forces. By stressing biotic and physical factors that "demand" compliance, ecological materialism offers a positivistic approach which denies the relevance of volition. However, materialism is not value-free simply because there is ample empirical evidence to demonstrate that it merely expresses a particular value system existing within the American culture at the present time. Several studies of zoning activities clearly sustain this contention.[20] The empirical data reveal that the theoretical approach of ecological materialism reflects that has been called the "economic-value orientation"—a social-value perspective voiced by certain decision-makers who contribute to the zoning process.[21] Both materialists and economically oriented decision-makers perceive identical physical conditions as determining the forms of social organization in the adaptation to space.

The competitive process which ecological materialists contend takes place in accordance with efficiency[22] is merely a reflection of the profit-motive orientation of some decision-makers in the zoning process and, more broadly, of many individuals in the American culture. The zoning data show that man's efforts to accommodate to cost[23] simply express a desire on the part of certain individuals to adjust in this manner. The facts of existing land usages and

[19]See Henry S. Shryock, Jr., "The Natural History of Standard Metropolitan Areas," *American Journal of Sociology*, 63 (September, 1957), pp. 163-70.

[20]Sidney Willhelm and Gideon Sjoberg, "Economic vs. Protective Values in Urban Land Use Change," *American Journal of Economics and Sociology*, 19 (January, 1960), pp. 151-60; Form, *op. cit.* An extensive discussion of this point is to be found in Sidney M. Willhelm, *Urban Zoning and Land-Use Theory* (New York: Free Press of Glencoe, 1962), Chap. VII.

[21]Willhelm and Sjoberg, *op. cit.*

[22]For example: George Kingsley Zipf, *Human Behavior and the Principle of Least Effort* (Cambridge: Addison-Wesley Press, 1949), p. 350; Robert E. L. Faris, *op. cit.*, p. 373; and Amos Hawley, *op. cit.*, pp. 278 and 215.

[23]Robert Murray Haig, "Toward an Understanding of the Metropolis," *Quarterly Journal of Economics*, 40 (May, 1926), pp. 420-4; Richard U. Ratcliff, "Efficiency and the Location of Urban Activities," in Robert Moore Fisher (ed.), *The Metropolis in Modern Life* (New York: Doubleday, 1955), pp. 125-48; Richard U. Ratcliff, *Real Estate Analysis* (New York: McGraw-Hill, 1961), p. 36.

geographical conditions which ecological materialists label "impersonal" forces dictating the distribution of ecological phenomena[24] are essential aspects of the economic-value orientation to be found in the zoning process. And, finally, the notion of "functional organization"[25] in terms of an "ecological complex," espoused by certain ecological materialists, restricts ecological investigation to those very aspects of social life considered to be the *only* relevant data by the persons in the community who advocate the economic-value orientation in the zoning of property.

Consequently, in the light of empirical testing, it is most difficult for materialists to argue a value-free exposition when in fact they voice a prevailing American value system.

A final limiting consideration of neoclassical materialism is the inability of the orientation to delineate a field of study. That is, the ecological complex simply does not specify the subject matter for the human ecologist in a discriminating fashion. If human ecology is the study of data involved in the ecological complex advanced by the neoclassical proponents, then there is no aspect of modern society that lies beyond the ecological orbit. In other words, there are no sociological phenomena aside from ecological considerations in coping with industrialized societies. What social activity, for example, can take place within the American society that does not involve a population, an environment, an organization and a technology? The ecological complex presents a distinction without a difference.

In sum, the ecological position now so much in vogue cannot persist without basic modification. The tautological reasoning, the physical orientation, the mixed order of data, the indifference toward the social-value concept, the reliance upon individualistic census data in lieu of a collective approach, and a non-delineated subject are outstanding fallacies inherent in the present neoclassical position. An ecological perspective that contains these limitations cannot lead to a fruitful examination of sociological or ecological phenomena.

---

[24] McKenzie, *op. cit.,* p. 247; Hawley, *op. cit.,* p. 385; Duncan and Schnore, *op. cit.,* p. 144; Duncan, "Human Ecology and Population Studies," *op. cit.,* p. 683.
[25] Duncan and Schnore, *op. cit.,* p. 145 .

Social Area Analysis

Eshref Shevky and Wendell Bell

CONSTRUCT FORMATION AND THE FRAMEWORK OF SOCIAL TRENDS

An Overview

The urban typology of *The Social Areas of Los Angeles* (1949) is a classificatory schema designed to categorize census tract populations in terms of three basic factors—social rank, urbanization, and segregation. Each census tract population was given three scores, one for each of the indexes of the factors; and then the tract populations with similar configurations of scores on the three indexes were grouped together into larger units called social areas. We begin the restatement of our theoretical orientation by sketching out the reasoning which led to the development of the constructs of social rank, urbanization, and segregation as basic factors in the social differentiation and stratification of the contemporary city. Although an elaboration follows in the remainder of Chapter II, the chief elements of our argument have been laid out in schematic form in Table II–1. The arrows in the table indicate the direction of our reasoning. These trends, of course, are interrelated, but their interconnections are not indicated in the table.

We conceive of the city as a product of the complex whole of modern society; thus the social forms of urban life are to be understood within the context of the changing character of the larger containing society. In Column 1 of Table II–1 we have given some statements descriptive of modern society as compared with traditional societies, or of a particular modern society compared at two points in time. These we call "postulates concerning industrial society" and they each are aspects of the increasing scale of modern society. As descriptive statements, or broad postulates, their analytic utility is not very great. Their utility increases, however, to the extent that we can identify the modes of organization associated with them.

In Column 2 of Table II–1 we make such an identification. Three broad sets of interrelated trends are specified: these are changes in (1) the distribution of skills, (2) the organization of productive activity, and (3) the composition

SOURCE: Eshref Shevky and Wendell Bell, from *Social Area Analysis: Theory, Illustrative Application and Computational Procedures* (Stanford, Calif.: Stanford University Press, 1955), pp. 3-5, 17-22, 59. Reprinted with the permission of the publisher, Stanford University Press. Copyright 1955 by the Board of Trustees of Leland Stanford Junior University.

of the population. These three trends appear to be most descriptive of the changing character of modern society. At particular points in time, given social systems can be conceived as standing in differential relationships to these three major trends. As illustrative of these trends, three sets of changes are given in Column 3 of Table II–1. These are changes in the arrangement of occupations, changes in the ways of living, and redistribution of the population in space. The trends are here seen as specific changes in the structure of a given social system.

However, subpopulations in a particular society at a given point in time also can be conceived as standing in differential relationships to these three sets of structural changes. In Column 4 of Table II–1 the three sets of structural changes in a given social system (Column 3) have been redefined as *structural reflections* of change to serve as descriptive and analytic concepts for the study of modern social structure. Thus, from certain broad postulates concerning modern society and from the analysis of temporal trends, we have selected three structural reflections of change which can be used as factors for the study of social differentiation and stratification at a particular time in modern society. These factors are social rank, urbanization, and segregation.

The next step in the construction of the urban typology is to select indexes of the three factors. Sample statistics related to the constructs and available for urban analysis are listed in Column 5 of Table II–1. These categories represent those given in the 1940 census bulletins for population and housing statistics by census tracts. With the constructs designated and the elements of each of the three major social trends specified, it was a simple matter to group the census variables into three groups according to the constructs to which they were most related. Certain of these census variables are more direct measures of the constructs than the others and are more useful as measures of the three factors. The variables selected to compose the indexes of social rank, urbanization, and segregation are indicated on Column 6 of Table II–1. These derived measures indicate aspects of urban population which are most clearly indicative of the changing distribution of skills, the changing organization of productive activity (especially the changing structure of the family), and the changing composition of the population.

*   *   *

THE CONSTRUCTS AND THE INDEXES

Social Rank. The construct of social rank is specified from the changing distribution of skills in the development of modern society as a significant differentiating factor among individuals and subpopulations in modern society at one point in time. Individuals and groups are seen at this point in time as being significantly differentiated with respect to one of the long-term trends

TABLE II-1 STEPS IN CONSTRUCT FORMATION AND INDEX CONSTRUCTION

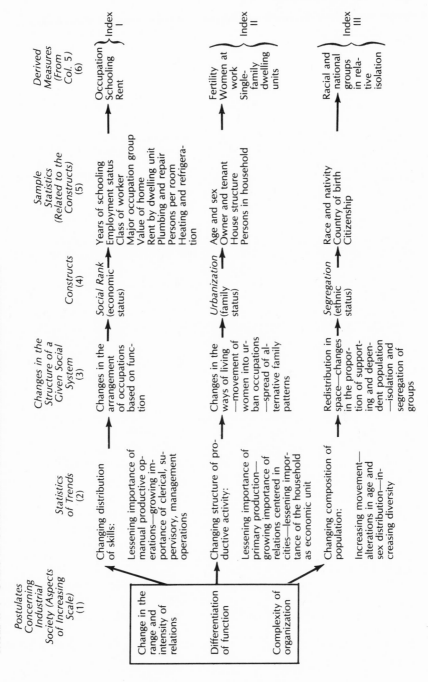

Postulates Concerning Industrial Society (Aspects of Increasing Scale) (1)	Statistics of Trends (2)	Changes in the Structure of a Given Social System (3)	Constructs (4)	Sample Statistics (Related to the Constructs) (5)	Derived Measures (From Col. 5) (6)
Change in the range and intensity of relations **Differentiation of function** **Complexity of organization**	Changing distribution of skills: Lessening importance of manual productive operations—growing importance of clerical, supervisory, management operations	Changes in the arrangement of occupations based on function	*Social Rank* (economic status)	Years of schooling Employment status Class of worker Major occupation group Value of home Rent by dwelling unit Plumbing and repair Persons per room Heating and refrigeration	Occupation Schooling ⎱ Index I Rent ⎰
	Changing structure of productive activity: Lessening importance of primary production—growing importance of relations centered in cities—lessening importance of the household as economic unit	Changes in the ways of living —movement of women into urban occupations —spread of alternative family patterns	*Urbanization* (family status)	Age and sex Owner and tenant House structure Persons in household	Fertility Women at work ⎱ Index II Single-family dwelling units ⎰
	Changing composition of population: Increasing movement—alterations in age and sex distribution—increasing diversity	Redistribution in space—changes in the proportion of supporting and dependent population —isolation and segregation of groups	*Segregation* (ethnic status)	Race and nativity Country of birth Citizenship	Racial and national groups in relative isolation ⎱ Index III

which has been important in the development of the character of modern society.

An index of social rank can be constructed from a grouping of the available census variables which are evident elements of the changing distribution of skills. We select measures of occupation, education, and rent to compose an index of social rank from among the possible measures because of their greater central importance in the changes in distribution of skills. Occupation, of course, is the key variable.

Urbanization. In like manner a second factor, urbanization, is constructed which also is hypothesized to be a basic differentiating dimension for individuals and groups in modern society at a given point in time. This current differentiating factor is derived from the changing structure of productive activity, the second major trend in the development of modern society. Two components of this major trend are measured by an index of urbanization composed of a measure of fertility, which reflects changes in the relation of the population to the economy and changes in the function and structure of the family, and measures of house type and women in the labor force, which reflect changes in the function and structure of the family.

The third component of the changing structure of productive activity, change in the ranges of relations centered in cities, an extremely important facet of the idea of urbanization, is only indirectly measured with our index of urbanization. We hypothesize a relation between the variable, women in the labor force, and the range of relations centered in the city, but the development of an adequate index will largely depend on the possibility of the construction of a regional typology for the United States as a whole. That is, the range of relations centered in cities cannot be measured on the basis of one metropolitan area, or a selected sample of cities for which we happen to have small area statistics.

Segregation. Finally, another construct, segregation, is derived which is hypothesized to be a third basic factor significantly differentiating modern society. Again a dimension for the analysis of the differentiation of modern society at a given point in time is selected because it reflects in structural terms a major trend which has significantly determined the present character of that society. This trend is composed of changes in the composition of the population which are manifested by redistribution of the population in space, alteration in the age and sex composition, and the isolation of groups.

Variables composing the index of segregation measure differences in individuals and groups which reflect this trend. For a subpopulation the relative concentration of specified ethnic groups, i.e., members of the "new" migration and nonwhites, is the index of segregation. The variables of foreign-born from certain countries available in the census bulletins are selected to approximate a measure of the members of the "new" migration.

Urban Typology. From our analysis of social trends we identify three constructs—social rank, urbanization, and segregation—which we hypothesize are basic factors of urban differentiation and stratification. Census tract populations are grouped into types on the basis of similar configurations of scores on the indexes of the three factors. Employing the concept of attribute space, a three-dimensional space is constructed with the indexes of social rank, urbanization, and segregation as the three axes. Tracts near to one another in this social attribute space have similar patterns of scores on the three indexes and are grouped into a type. Thus, the typological analysis, which is described in detail in Chapter V, is a logically demonstrable reflection of those major changes which have produced modern, urban society.

Verification. Two hypotheses implicit in the formulation of this social area typology have been tested for the Los Angeles Area and the San Francisco Bay Region as of 1940. The first hypothesis is that the three basic elements in the typology—social rank, urbanization, and segregation—are three factors necessary to account for the observed social differentiation between urban subpopulations; and the second hypothesis is that the indexes constructed to measure the three factors are unidimensional measuring instruments. Both of these hypotheses were tested by Bell (1952) with the use of factor analysis. The results of the factor analysis in each of the urban areas supported the hypotheses, and it was concluded that the findings represented a partial validation of the entire method of typological analysis.

From the factorial analyses described above it was possible to conclude only that the three factors are necessary to account for the observed social variation between census tract populations. There is some evidence, however, to conclude that these factors are *adequate* as well as necessary to account for most of the observed variation between tract populations which can be extracted from the population and housing data given in the census tract bulletins. Working independently, Professor Robert C. Tryon, University of California, Berkeley, has located in the Bay Region as of 1940 three principal clusters which are comparable to social rank, urbanization, and segregation. These three clusters almost completely account for the variation between tract populations with respect to census variables. Thus, a description of the tract populations based on social rank, urbanization, and segregation captures most of the significant variation between tract populations which is revealed by census categories.

*   *   *

POSSIBLE USES OF THIS METHOD OF ANALYSIS

We will attempt to indicate here some of the possible uses of this approach to social phenomena.

Various Units of Analysis. To date all of the published work utilizing this method has dealt with the census tract as the unit of analysis. In both *The Social Areas of Los Angeles* (1949) and the study of the Bay Region presented in Chapter V the census tract is the unit of analysis, and the major focus of interest is the internal differentiation of a particular urban area. There is no reason, however, why a typology based on the three social dimensions—social rank, urbanization, and segregation—could not be utilized, with different specific measures in the indexes if necessary, for the study of cities with the city as the unit of analysis, for the study of regions, or even for the study of countries. The construction of a regional typology, perhaps based on the county as the unit of analysis, could represent one of the next steps in the development of the typology and a logical extension of the recent work of Hagood (1943), Bogue (1951), and others. Also, certain other populations for which information is desired might be selected as a unit of analysis. Most of the possible uses of the typology which are briefly stated in the remainder of this chapter can be accomplished at any of these levels of analysis.

The Delineation of Subareas. At the various levels of analysis the typology can be used to define systematically and rigorously subareas having similar configurations of scores on the three social dimensions. Using the census tract as the unit of analysis, for example, the city can be subdivided into the mosaic of social worlds about which Wirth (1938) writes. Our term "social area" reveals the manner in which we group one set of units into larger units on the basis of their similarity with respect to their social characteristics. The concepts of "natural area" and "subculture" are not unrelated to our concept "social area" for we view a social area as containing persons with similar social positions in larger society. The social area, however, is not bounded by the geographical frame of reference as is the natural area, nor by implications concerning the degree of interaction between persons in the local community as is the subculture. We do claim, however, that the social area generally contains persons having the same level of living, the same way of life, and the same ethnic background; and we hypothesize that persons living in a particular type of social area would systematically differ with respect to characteristic attitudes and behaviors from persons living in another type of social area.

The mere delineation of these subareas for a city, and the precision with which it is accomplished by this method, should be of descriptive value to the social scientist and city planner alike. The method presented here offers a more parsimonious and more general description of the subareas of the city than do the "community fact books."

Comparative Studies at One Point in Time. This method might be used to compare the social differentiation of one country with another, one region with another, or one city with another. For example, there are 12,633 census tracts in the sixty-nine urban areas tracted in 1950. As formulated here, this method allows the description of the internal social differentiation of each of the sixty-nine urban areas in a comparative framework. The census tracts falling in a particular social area are similar with respect to social rank, urbanization, and segregation whether the tracts are in Los Angeles, San Francisco, Detroit, Duluth, Rochester, or any of the other tracted urban areas. It is hypothesized, however, that the pattern of internal social differentiation

—that is, the way the tracts are distributed with respect to social rank, urbanization, and segregation—would vary from one city to another, but that certain types or particular recurrent space-time-value patterns could be determined. Some of the many questions which might be answered by such a comparative study are: Do Negroes in Western cities live in the same, higher, or lower social rank areas than Negroes in cities in the South, or the Northeast, or the Midwest? Is the difference between high social rank areas and low social rank areas greater in Southern cities or in cities in the West, Northeast, Midwest, etc.? Are subareas of high urbanization (low family status) in Northeastern cities more typically of low social rank or high social rank when compared with cities in other regions? Are there areas within Western cities which have unique configurations with respect to social rank, urbanization, and segregation, or do cities in all regions have all of the possible social area types even though they may have more or fewer of a particular type? More generally, we are led to ask to what extent the observed orderly character of intra-urban forms in the metropolitan areas of the West Coast are universal properties not only of large American cities, but cities in general of the Western world and of contemporary urban life everywhere.

Similar types of questions can be raised concerning the social area distribution of census tract populations in cities of different sizes—large cities compared to medium-sized cities, and compared to smaller cities. Also, characteristic patterns of internal social differentiation can be determined for cities which have different dominant functions. The recreational city can be compared to the commercial city, or the industrial city, or the mixed city. What different types of social differentiation can be located within cities performing different functions? The questions are endless, but it is our task here merely to indicate the type of problem which might be approached by the application of this typology in a comparative framework.

Similar questions can be raised at other levels of analysis. The application of the typology to the 3,103 counties for which 1950 census data are available, for example, offers an even more comprehensive and complete comparison of regional differences in social differentiation.

Comparative Studies at Two Points in Time.   As a parsimonious method for the description of changes in the social differentiation of a city, or a region, or a country, the typology can be used to test hypotheses concerning the conditions of change. The application of the typology to the 1940 and 1950 census data for the San Francisco Bay Region presented in this report represents the beginning step in such a sociological study. Our purpose in this report is to illustrate the application of the procedures in a comparative framework and to demonstrate just exactly what type of information the typology alone yields. The next and more important question, however, is what has brought about these observed changes in the social differentiation of the Bay Region? To answer this question we must examine data other than those given in the census tract statistics. We must look to data external to our typology, e.g., movements of industry and commerce, shifts in the location of government agencies, as well as changes in the *national* economy, migration trends, and the like.

In this type of study the changes in the social differentiation of a population described by the application of the typology are considered to be dependent variables and the conditions for change are searched out and systematically related to the broader social structural changes.

A Framework for the Execution of Other Types of Research.   While correlations based upon census tract averages must be used with caution, the typological analysis for a particular city offers an efficient method for studying the attitudes and behaviors of individuals living in the various types of neighborhoods in the city. Again the geographical distribution of a particular attitude or behavior would not be of primary interest. Rather, the relationship between the attitude or behavior and type of community as to social rank, urbanization, and segregation would be of primary importance. For example, Aubrey Wendling (1954) has related suicide rates in San Francisco census tracts to the social rank, urbanization, and segregation scores of the tracts. A considerable amount of the variation in suicide rates can be explained by these three factors. Other variables which might be studied for which data are readily available are number of registered voters, people's choices of candidates as measured by voting behavior, mental disorders, crime rates, etc. In each case the particular behavior would be related to the social character of the tract population as measured by the three factors: social rank, urbanization, and segregation.

In addition to its use as a frame for the manipulation of available statistics such as crime rates, suicide rates, and others, the typology can be used as a frame for the design and execution of field studies. It is our belief that detailed field investigations of subareas within the city can profit from this typological analysis in at least two ways. First, the typological analysis will aid in the location of the kind of subarea which is to be studied. The problem to be investigated may require that a particular type of subarea be singled out for study. A census tract's scores on social rank, urbanization, and segregation define important aspects of the social character of the tract population. In this operation the social area analysis is used as a sampling device during the design of the study. Second, the typological analysis provides a generality to field investigations of urban subareas often lacking in discrete studies of some specific aspect of urban life. This typology offers to such intensive studies articulation and integration with a larger mass of ordered data. Two studies now nearing completion, one in Los Angeles and one in San Francisco, were designed, in part, to test the utility of this typology as a frame for the execution of intensive studies of urban sub-areas.

*   *   *

CONCLUSION

*   *   *

We believe that the formulation of social trends in relation to current differentiating factors, including the typology based on these factors, in its present form has sufficient coherence, internal consistency, and specificity for us to make these further claims for it:

a) It is simple in statement.
b) It serves as an organizing principle.
c) It is theory-linked; it permits the derivation of testable propositions.
d) It is precise in its specifications; it permits observer agreement.
e) It represents a continuity with similar formulations which it aims to replace.

Robert Park and Social Area Analysis: A Convergence of Traditions in Urban Sociology
Peter Orleans

In 1915, Robert Park published "The City: Suggestions for the Investigation of Human Behavior in the Urban Environment."[1] That essay served as a prolegomena for the research which occupied students of the Chicago school of urban studies for more than a quarter of a century. Thirty-four years later, in 1949, Eshref Shevky introduced an alternative approach to the study of urban phenomena in his volume on the social areas of Los Angeles.[2] Following

[1] Robert Park, "The City: Suggestions for the Investigation of Human Behavior in the Urban Environment," originally published in the *American Journal of Sociology*, XX (March, 1916), pp. 577–613; reprinted with the corpus of his work in urban sociology in Robert Park, *Human Communities: The City and Human Ecology* (New York: The Free Press, 1952).

[2] Eshref Shevky and Marilyn Williams, *The Social Areas of Los Angeles* (Berkeley and Los Angeles: The University of California Press, 1949). This publication was followed in 1955 by the publication of Eshref Shevky and Wendell Bell, *Social Area Analysis Theory, Illustrative Application and Computational Procedures* (Stanford: Stanford University Press, 1955). Further amplification of the approach is to be found in Wendell Bell, "Social Areas: Typology of Neighborhoods," and an example of research in this tradition is to be found in Scott Greer and Ella Kube, "Urbanism and Social Structure: A Los Angeles Study." Both of these papers were originally published as Chapters 3 and 4 in Marvin Sussman (ed.), *Community Structure and Analysis* (New York: Thomas Y. Crowell, 1959).

SOURCE: Peter Orleans, "Robert Park and Social Area Analysis: A Convergence of Traditions in Urban Sociology," *Urban Affairs Quarterly*, 1 (June 1966), 5–19. Reprinted by permission of the publisher, Sage Publications, Inc.

in the tradition encompassed by social area analysis, Scott Greer, in 1962 with the publication of *The Emerging City: Myth and Reality,* addressed himself to questions similar to those broached by Park.[3] This paper will examine several aspects of the work represented by these two approaches in American urban sociology in an attempt to indicate the contributions each has made and can make to the elaboration of a coherent theory of urban life.

The study of urban life has been concerned with the analysis of ecological space and social differentiation, the interaction of both, and the bearing of each upon the development and maintenance of order within the urban milieu. The apparent discrepancy between the two traditions of urban study to be examined in this paper stems in large measure from the extent to which they emphasize one of these concerns (ecological space or social differentiation) to the relative exclusion of the other. It will be argued that this difference in emphasis is based on different views of the structure and quality of urban life. Each, in turn, has influenced the way in which the problem of order in the urban milieu has been stated and treated.

A preliminary note of caution is required. The discussion to follow is concerned largely with the work of three scholars. It is not the writer's intention to deprecate or to caricature the work of any of them. Park is unquestionably a seminal figure in the field of urban sociology and his essay, "The City," has had a considerable impact on the direction and organization of urban studies in the United States over the last half-century. It cannot and should not be lightly dismissed; but it must be considered in the light of parallel as well as subsequent developments if advances in the field of urban studies are to be made and are to be cumulative.

It is clear that the work of Shevky and his students has been informed by Park's contributions, even though it represents both a departure from and an extension of Park's work. Only time and newly accumulated research can determine its significance. But a comparison of the two approaches—a comparison which delineates the points of contrast and emphasizes the areas of convergence, and a comparison which attempts to analyze the reasons for both —might assist in furthering the art.

ECOLOGICAL SPACE AND SOCIAL DIFFERENTIATION

Although Park's analysis of urban life emphasized the significance of ecological factors, his work clearly indicates a recognition of the importance of social differentiation. This communality with social area analysis is often overlooked by students working in both traditions. Social area analysis has been criticized for its inadequate conceptualization of ecological factors and

---

[3]Scott Greer, *The Emerging City: Myth and Reality* (New York: The Free Press, 1962), especially Chapters 2 and 3.

its almost exclusive concern with social differentiation. The discrepant aspects of these two approaches, as well as the areas of convergence between them, the reasons for both, and the implications of each will be explored below.

In the portion of his essay entitled "Industrialization and the Moral Order," Park notes that the disposition to barter or exchange goods and services gives rise to the division of labor and that the proliferation of tasks is a function of the extent of the market. "The outcome of this process is to break down or modify the older economic and social organization of society, which was based on family ties, local associations, on culture, caste, and status, and to substitute for it an organization based on occupational and vocational interests."[4] The result is the development of occupational types and vocationally oriented interest-based organizations.

Here, then, Park focuses on the conditions which produce the communality of interests that give rise to association. In recognizing these conditions, he shares a common concern with students in the social area analysis tradition, notably Greer.[5] However, whereas social area analysts are concerned with explicating the significance of the occupational form of differentiation (as well as others) for the development of a normative order, Park devalues the role played by occupationally based secondary organizations in generating and sustaining the moral order.

> The effect of the vocations and the division of labor is to produce . . . not social groups but vocational types: the actor, the plumber and the lumber-jack. The organizations like the trade and labor unions which men of the same trade or profession form are based on common interests. In this respect they differ from forms of association like the neighborhood which are based on contiguity, personal association, and the common ties of humanity . . . The effects of the division of labor as a discipline, i.e., as a means of molding character, may therefore be best studied in the vocational types produced.[6]

Accordingly, Park chooses to emphasize individual predilections, attitudes, natural abilities, and the like and to focus on recruitment and mobility within and between occupations instead of the changing structure of occupations and its implications for the organization of occupationally based secondary associations in the urban community.

That Park does not see interest-based associations as generators of a moral order is, perhaps, due to the fact that he relies on spatial contiguity for this purpose. This is made clear by his discussion in the section of his essay entitled "The City Plan and Local Organization." His thesis is that natural geographic advantages and disadvantages determine in advance the outline of the urban plan, the location, and the character of the city's constructions. Eventually,

[4]Robert Park, *op. cit.,* p. 24.
[5]Scott Greer, *op. cit.,* passim.
[6]Robert Park, *op. cit.,* p. 24.

however, subtler influences of rivalry and economic necessity tend to control the distribution of the population.

> Within the limitations prescribed . . . personal tastes and conveniences, vocational and economic interests, infallibly tend to classify the population of big cities. In this way the city acquires an organization and distribution of the population which is neither designed nor controlled.[7]

Each section of the city takes on the character and the quality of its inhabitants, its differentiated and relatively segregated populations. Thus, what was initially a mere geographic expression is transformed into a congeries of neighborhoods with sentiments, traditions, and local histories, and the past imposes itself upon the present in each of these semiautonomous areas—that mosaic of social worlds that touch but do not interpenetrate.

In this view the geographic contiguity of people serves as a basis for social contact and association out of which a normative order eventually develops. Thus, in this portion of his essay, Park indicates a concern for *both* the spatial distribution and the social differentiation of the population, the implications of each for the other, and of both for the total urban complex. Natural forces are seen as responsible for the initial distribution, concentration, and segregation of urban populations. Social organization derives after the fact from proximity and neighborly contact as well as the relative homogeneity of the spatially contiguous populations. "Local interests and associations breed local sentiment, and under a system which makes residence the basis for participation in government, the neighborhood becomes the basis for political control."[8] In other words, neighborhood provides the site for a developing normative order.

It is Park's recognition of the important role played by spatial contiguity in the development of normative order that leads him to pose the following kinds of questions:

> What are the outstanding "natural" areas, i.e., areas of population segregation?

> How is the distribution of population within the city affected by (a) economic interests, i.e., land values? (b) sentimental interest, race? vocation, etc?

> What are the elements of which (neighborhoods) are composed? To what extent are (neighborhoods) the product of a selective process?

> What are the relative permanence and stability of (neighborhood) populations?

> What about the age, sex, and social condition of the people?[9]

[7]Robert Park, *ibid.,* p. 16.
[8]Robert Park, *ibid.,* p. 18.
[9]Robert Park, *ibid.,* pp. 18, 22.

In effect, Park is asking what characteristics of a population distributed in distinctive spatial enclaves have what kinds of effect on the development of the normative order. The strong implication is that the organization of urban populations is largely a function of the interaction of the differentiated attributes of such populations and their spatial distribution (concentration and segregation).

In short, as he sought to delineate appropriate research topics in the sections of his essay discussed above, Park relied on conceptions of a naturalistic ecology and *laissez faire* economics (both of which emphasize the fortuitous and problematic organization and the normative dislocation of the population) to adduce two aspects of urban society. According to one view, the basis of association rests with the congruence of occupational and/or economic interests. According to the other view, the basis of association rests with the exigencies of the spatial configuration of distinct populations. Each of the two bases of association discussed by Park may be seen as establishing preconditions for a normative order.

Park's conceptualization of the problem is distinguished from that of the social area analysts by its emphasis on the ecological community (the "natural" area) and its concern with the spatial basis of association rather than association growing out of a communality of interest. The implications of this difference for the formulation and treatment of the problem of order in the urban milieu will be considered below. First, however, it is necessary to examine the social area analysis approach offered by Shevky and his students.

In contrast to Park, Shevky neglects ecological space and focuses almost entirely upon social differentiation. His work has often been treated as though it represented a revision or extension of the traditional ecological approach to urban studies; but such an interpretation derives, in this writer's estimation, from a misreading of his efforts.[10] Shevky has never purported to have offered an ecological analysis. Rather he emphasized the significance of what he refers to as *social space.*

Social space refers to an attribute space representing a conceptual typology of positional differences which are denoted by measures of a series of characteristics of population aggregates. While there is no denying that these population aggregates are located in ecological space and that their location may have consequences for their internal organization as well as their interdependence with the encompassing milieu, the aggregated characteristics of such populations are seen by Shevky and his students as more significant than their spatial *location.* Hence, social area analysts are led to a formulation in which ecological space *per se* is of minor importance.[11]

[10]A. Hawley and O. D. Duncan, "Social Area Analysis: A Critical Appraisal," *Land Economics,* 1957, 33, 337–345. See also George Theodorson (ed.), *Studies in Human Ecology* (New York: Harper and Row, 1961), especially the introduction to Part II, pp. 129–134.

[11]Such a position should not seem strange to sociologists who have a long and revered tradition of attributing behavioral variation to variables such as class and race, etc., treated as though they are ecologically unbounded.

A weakness of the social area analysis formulation has not been its disregard of ecological factors but rather its lack of any systematic specification of the relationship that social space bears to physical space. It is undoubtedly the failure to delineate this relationship that has elicited much of the confusion over its status *vis-à-vis* ecological theory and research.

Shevky's neglect of ecological space constitutes a radical departure from the Chicago school of urban studies as represented in the work of Park and his students. Social area analysis facilitates the study of forms of social differentiation apart from considerations of spatial location. The assumption upon which this mode of analysis rests is that positional similarity, with respect to a limited number of significant social attributes (e.g., skills, ethnicity, life style, migrant status), reflects common situations. For example, the specific attributes of population aggregates, which denote various forms of social differentiation, are presumed to indicate differences in access to limited sets of opportunities as well as subjugation to particular sets of constraints. Accordingly, positional similarity is considered to be indicative of a communality of interests. This, in turn, provides a basis for the social contact and association which generate and support a normative order.[12]

Approaching the analysis of urban life through the study of significant forms of social differentiation permits one to locate and examine normative orders independent of spatial considerations. Some forms of differentiation, such as life style or ethnicity, may locate spatially distinct enclaves—the fertile valleys or suburbia or the ethnic ghettos in the central city. Others, such as skill or migration distinctions, may locate spatially unbounded communities of interest—occupational communities or regional associations.

Under most circumstances, the nexus of several forms of differentiation will locate ecologically undefined population aggregates (social spaces or social areas). These exhibit varying propensities to become engaged in different kinds of spatially unbounded communities of interest often represented in secondary organizations (e.g., the League of Women Voters, industrial and craft unions, religious cults, athletic associations, professional societies, philanthropic clubs).

Each secondary organization, with its own distinctive normative order, may generate primary ties which do not depend upon spatial contiguity for their sustenance. These primary ties may provide a satisfactory alternative to the amenities generally associated with spatially contained communities and ecologically distinct natural areas. In general, social area analysts are concerned initially with locating organizationally distinctive, but ecologically indeterminate, communities of interest, and ultimately with exploring their implications for the normative organization of diverse populations in the urban environment.

[12]Scott Greer and Peter Orleans, "The Mass Society and the Para-Political Structure," *American Sociological Review,* 27 (October, 1962), pp. 634–646. A similar thesis is advanced by James Beshers in his book *Urban Social Structure* (New York: The Free Press, 1962).

To recapitulate briefly what has been stated above, both Park and Shevky in their efforts to develop an approach to the study of urban life have emphasized the importance of various forms of social differentiation and their potential consequences for the development of a normative order. Park was much more explicit in his recognition of the role played by spatial contiguity in the development of such a normative order, tending to neglect the essentially nonspatial alternative of normative orders deriving from communities of interest. Shevky, by contrast, neglected the effects of ecological space and thereby failed to specify the significance of spatial contiguity for the development of a normative order.

In the absence of an explicit recognition and acknowledgment of the significance of ecological space, Shevky is restricted to a consideration of communities of interest alone as the generators of a normative order. For Shevky, spatial contiguity is, in effect, an unexplicated concept. Of the students in the social area analysis tradition, Greer alone has attempted to deal with the role played by ecological space in setting the conditions for the development of a normative order. Accordingly, Greer's extension of Shevky's formulation (as it is presented in his book *The Emerging City: Myth and Reality*) serves as a basis for the discussion of the social area analysis formulation in the balance of this paper.[13]

THE ANTIURBAN BIAS AND THE PROBLEM OF ORDER

It is one thing to suggest that two schools of thought differ in the emphasis they ascribe to different mechanisms—association based on spatial contiguity as opposed to association predicated on a communality of interests—seen to be generators and maintainers of normative order. It is something else to attempt to understand the reasoning which underlies and supports the differing emphases and to recognize the implications that these alternative conceptualizations bear to the statement and treatment of the problem of order in the urban milieu. Our contention here is that the romantic attachment to the preurban community is largely responsible for the ecologically and pathologically oriented studies of urban life, and further that the concern with the pathological conditions of life in the city grew out of the assumption that the normative efficacy of the spatially inclusive community declined in proportion to the urbanization of society.[14]

Prior to the advent of the extreme aggregation of populations at fixed locations and the accompanying proliferation of specialized tasks required to

[13]For an attempt to relate gross variations in population type to a theory of spatially based social organization, see Scott Greer, "The Social Structure and Political Process of Suburbia," *American Sociological Review,* 25 (August, 1960), pp. 514–526.

[14]The antiurban bias in American letters and science has been aptly described by Morton and Lucia White in their book, *The Intellectual Versus the City* (Cambridge: Harvard University Press and the M.I.T. Press, 1962). Chapter 10, which takes up Park's work, is especially relevant.

coordinate and control human activities under such circumstances, there existed neither the need for nor the possibility of developing and sustaining interaction patterns contingent upon the communalities of differentiated interests. However, the urban-industrial revolution made possible—indeed required—the development of new forms of association growing out of newly created and elaborated types of collectivities, which may have supplemented rather than replaced their predecessors.

The radical transformation of the human condition brought about by the urban-industrial revolution was initially disruptive of traditional values and institutions. And it was not uncommon for perceptive analysts to decry the loss of the significance of the spatially inclusive community—the traditional ecological community—that had been so familiar. But, in our view, the theoretical bankruptcy of much contemporary urban analysis is attributable largely to the failure to overcome traditional biases and to replace outmoded notions about the conditions which sustain and nurture a normative order with conceptions which are more appropriate to current conditions.

Both Park and Greer emphasize the contrast between the urban milieu and preurban or nonurban settlements. Because the urban community is different, it poses new problems with respect to the maintenance of order. Accordingly, both men are centrally concerned with the problem of order. But the concern of each is affected by his assumptions regarding how and why the urban community differs from other kinds of settlements.

Most students of urban life assume, at least implicitly, that urbanization entails change. However, they differ in their assessment of the implications of this change. To a large extent the difference is a function of the extent to which the change is seen as evolutionary in character (i.e., from a noncomplex to a complex communal form; from a spatially inclusive locality group to a community consisting of spatially indistinct exclusive membership groups).

Some students, including Shevky and Greer, assume that urbanization involves an organizational transformation. Others, Park among them, assume that urbanization involves an organizational disruption or dislocation. The difference in these assumptions is critical because it ultimately affects the kinds of theoretical issues addressed—the kind of urban theory to be constructed.

The pathological view of urban life that has dominated American urban sociology stems largely from the conception that the evolutionary development of the communal form involves a dislocation of traditional and valued institutions and that this has deleterious effects on the individuals involved. The characterization of the urban community as seen from this perspective is usually based on the enumeration of interactional qualities which are presumed to be distinctive. Simmel's view that urban life is abstracted, segmentalized, pecuniary, sophisticated, predatory, and impersonal is a case in point.[15]

[15]Georg Simmel, "The Metropolis and Mental Life," in Kurt Wolff (trans.), *The Sociology of Georg Simmel* (New York: The Free Press, 1950).

To the extent that Park, a student of Simmel's, accepted such a characterization of urban life, his concern with the problem of order in the urban community came to be focused on the study of the personal consequences of and
reactions to life in a socially disruptive and disorganized environment—an
environment in which the opportunities and constraints circumscribed by the
spatially inclusive community are devalued, modified, or replaced.

If Park attempts to draw attention to the changing conditions of an urban-
izing economic organization in his discussion of "Industrialization and the
Moral Order," he also discusses some of the implications of such changes for
the maintenance of order in the urban community. The last two sections of his
essay, which deal with "Secondary Relations and Social Control" and "Temperament and the Urban Environment," constitute an elaboration of this
concern. It is in these two sections of the essay that Park betrays, or portrays,
his ambivalence about urbanism as a way of life.

In these sections of the essay, Park reiterates a point made earlier—that
changes in the economic organization of the city ultimately require a modification of the mechanisms of social control. The reasoning here is that changes
in the economic order, because they are destructive of the traditional spatially
inclusive community, modify the nature of social relations and therefore alter
interpersonal expectations and obligations. He suggests that:

> The interactions which take place among the members of (the urban community)
> are immediate and unreflecting. Intercourse is carried on largely within the region
> of instinct and feeling. Social control arises, for the most part spontaneously, in
> direct response to personal influences and public sentiment. It is the result of a
> personal accommodation, rather than the formulation of a rational and abstract
> principle.[16]

Given such a world view it is possible to invoke value judgments in developing comparative appraisals of the urban and the non-urban community. And
given the difficult adjustments required of individual men under the conditions
of rapid change associated with the urbanization of society, as well as the
existence of pervasive traditional values which are likely to be in conflict with
those that support and sustain urban life, it is not surprising that the study of
pathology becomes a focal point for the analyses of urban life.

Accordingly, Park devotes his attention to the "disintegrating influences
of city life" attributable in large measure to the proliferation of secondary
relations which have affected and presumably infected "most of our traditional
institutions, the church, the school, and the family." Along these lines, he
chooses to pose the following kinds of questions in outlining appropriate lines
of research for the urban sociologist:

[16]Robert Park, *op. cit.*, p. 33.

To what extent are the moral qualities of individuals based on native character? To what extent are they conventionalized habits imposed upon them or taken over by them from the group?

What are the native qualities and characteristics upon which the moral and immoral character accepted and conventionalized by the group are based?

What connection or what divorce appears to exist between mental and moral qualities in the groups and in the individuals composing them?

What are the external facts in regard to the life in Bohemia, the half-world, the red-light district, and other "moral regions" less pronounced in character?

To what extent are the regions referred to the product of the license; to what extent are they due to the restrictions imposed by city life on the natural man?[17]

For the most part American urban sociology, responding to the Parkian heritage and abetted by the enigmatic nature of the complex urban environment, has attended to the collective behavior, institutional dislocation, and psychodynamic aspects of urban life.

In contrast to this approach, Greer's attention to the problem of order in the urban community has focused on newly innovated mechanisms of social control or on the revision of old mechanisms of social control. This orientation stems from a position that takes as its point of departure the idea that the city represents a different communal form from that to be found in the nonurban settlement because it constitutes a distinctive set of problems related to the coordination and control of human activities.

While he does not deny that individuals may confront difficult problems of personal adjustment and that they vary in the extent of their involvement in the urban community, Greer is more concerned with the organizational aspects of life in the metropolis. Accordingly, the significance of the pathology of the urban condition, at least at the individual level, is minimized and muted in his analyses. Greer's concern with pathology is generally restricted to the organizational problems of urban life engendered by the diversity of values to be found in various segments of the metropolitan population.[18]

Greer succeeds in extricating himself from the ecological considerations which held Park in check. Influenced by Shevky's concern with the positional implications of various social attributes and using the social area analysis schema to locate urban populations which share distinctive qualities along several dimensions of social differentiation, Greer is able to emphasize the normative significance of spatially unrestricted communities of interest which derive from the elaboration of functional activities in the urban setting. This

---

[17]Robert Park, *op. cit.,* pp. 48, 50.

[18]For an example of his treatment of an organizational problem of urban life, see Scott Greer, "Traffic, Transportation, and the Problems of the Metropolis," in Robert Merton and Robert Nisbet (eds.), *Contemporary Social Problems* (New York: Harcourt, Brace & World, 1961).

is indicated by his statement that "the highly differentiated set of activities necessary for [the persistence of the city] requires complex and effective integrative mechanisms in order to produce predictability and structural stability through time."[19] The city, as an organizational unit, displays massive uniformities, orderly change, remarkable stability. Accordingly, "much of the behavior of the urban population can be understood and predicted through a knowledge of the group structures that absorb the energy of individuals and coordinate their behavior in time."[20]

To give substance to this assertion Greer relies on two mechanisms that bear a remarkable resemblance to the forms of association based on space and specialty described by Park in the first two sections of his essay. He develops the notions of the inclusive locality group and the exclusive membership group.[21] The latter can be broader in content than the occupational community; but it is definitely a collectivity, nonspatially defined, based upon a communality of interests and the generator of a normative order. The former is analogous to the traditional ecological community, the natural area, the neighborhood.

These two types of collectivities cross-cut one another and between them they account, in large measure, for the development and the maintenance of normative order in the urban setting. And, they amount to an attempt, on Greer's part, to interrelate as well as to distinguish between spatially distinct and spatially unbounded forms of association—an attempt to tie Shevky's notion of social space to what in the social area analysis schema is the unexplicated concept of ecological space.

There are undoubtedly spatially distinct and socially differentiated population aggregates in the urban milieu which fail to generate either associations based upon spatial contiguity or associations predicated upon communalities of interest. Although such segments of the urban population are undoubtedly not representative of the urban condition, they represent a significant social (or, perhaps more correctly, asocial) form. For such populations, Park's concern with the problem of order is critical. But, it would be a serious error to focus attention primarily upon such populations, considering them representative of urban conditions as a whole, and thereby obscuring a conception of urban social organization.

The point to be stressed, then, is essentially this: Diversity and complexity are not necessarily productive of social disorganization. To restrict one's concerns to the pathology of urban life is to leave unaccounted for the most distinctive, if more subtle, fact of urbanism as a way of life, indeed of all collective life, namely, its organization.

The main thrust of the argument in this paper has been to urge that students of urban life consider the existence and importance of inclusive local-

---

[19]Scott Greer, *op. cit.,* p. 54.
[20]Scott Greer, *op. cit.,* p. 56.
[21]Scott Greer, *op. cit.,* Chapter 2.

ity groups in the city to be problematic, and further to recognize that the lack of a spatially based normative order may be supplanted or supplemented by the kind of spatially unrestricted normative order generally associated with exclusive membership groups. Moreover, it has been suggested that the rudiments of each are embodied in the two approaches to the sutdy of urban life offered by Park and the social area analysts. This represents a significant point of convergence between these two traditions in urban sociology. Once this convergence has been recognized, the next step is to explicitly and systematically make the conceptual connection between the socially differentiated community and the spatially distinct community and to begin to determine empirically the relationship spatially unrestricted communities of interest bear to those communities in which association is a function of spatial contiguity.

B URBANIZATION AND METROPOLITAN GROWTH

The Growth of Metropolitan Areas in the United States
Philip M. Hauser

*   *   *

II

Even more dramatic than the national resurgence in total population growth in the United States is the explosive increase in the urban and particularly in the metropolitan area population. Throughout the history of this nation, population has become increasingly concentrated in urban and metropolitan places.

When our first census was taken in 1790 there were only 24 urban places in this country—places having 2500 or more persons. They contained only 5 per cent of the nation's population, some 200,000 out of almost 4 million. Only two of these places had more than 25,000 persons—New York and Philadelphia. By 1950, there were over 4700 such urban places, including almost two-thirds of the national population—nearly 100 million persons (Table 16). In 1960, about 122 million persons lived in urban places—some 68 per cent of the total population.

The tendency of the American population to become increasingly concen-

SOURCE: Philip M. Hauser, from "The Growth of Metropolitan Areas in the United States," *Population Perspectives* (New Brunswick, N.J.: Rutgers University Press, 1960), pp. 96–98, 100–129. Reprinted by permission.

TABLE 16. URBAN AND RURAL POPULATION FOR THE UNITED STATES, 1790 TO 1950, ESTIMATED FOR 1960 AND PROJECTED TO 1980.

Selected dates	Population (thousands)			
	Total	Urban	Rural	Per cent urban
1790	3,929	202	3,728	5.1
1800	5,308	322	4,986	6.1
1850	23,192	3,544	19,648	15.3
1900	75,995	30,160	45,835	39.7
1920	105,711	54,158	51,552	51.2
1950*				
Old def. urban	150,697	88,927	61,770	59.0
New def. urban	150,697	96,468	54,230	64.0
1960	180,000	122,000	58,000	68.0
1970	214,000	150,000	64,000	70.0
1980	260,000	190,000	70,000	73.0

*New definition, in general, includes places having 2500 or more persons whether incorporated or unincorporated in contrast with old definition which included only incorporated places of this size.

SOURCE: Data for 1790 to 1940: Bureau of the Census, *Historical Statistics of the United States,* Government Printing Office. Washington, D.C., 1949, p. 25.
Data for 1950: Bureau of the Census, *Statistical Abstract of the United States, 1959,* Government Printing Office, Washington, D.C., 1959, p. 17.
Data for 1960 to 1980: Percent urban drawn from estimates by Bogue and applied to total population projections of U.S. Bureau of the Census, assuming continuation of postwar birth rate (see Chapter 2), Donald J. Bogue, *The Population of the United States* (Glencoe, Illinois: Free Press, 1959), p. 784.

trated in large clumpings is even more manifest in the growth of metropolitan areas, the nucleus of which is the city of 50,000 or more.[4] In 1900, areas which would have qualified as Standard Metropolitan Areas in 1950 contained about a third of the total population, about 24 million persons (Table 17). Between 1900 and 1950, while the population of the country doubled, that outside the metropolitan areas increased by only 50 per cent; and that in metropolitan areas more than tripled. In consequence, by 1950 some 57 per cent of the population lived in 168 Standard Metropolitan Areas—about 85 million persons.[5] In 1960, about 63 per cent of the total population, about 112

[4]The Standard Metropolitan Area was defined by the federal government in 1950, as, in general, one or more central cities of 50,000 or more inhabitants, the county in which the central city (or cities) were located, and such contiguous counties as by various social and economic criteria were oriented to the central city (or cities). For details of the definition, see Bureau of the Census, *County and City Data Book, 1956* (Washington, D.C.: Government Printing Office, 1957).
[5]Donald J. Bogue, *Population Growth in Standard Metropolitan Areas, 1900–1950* (Housing and Home Finance Agency) (Washington, D.C.: Government Printing Office, 1953), p. 13; and United States Bureau of the Census, *Census of Population: 1950,* Vol. I, pp. 1–3 and 1–69.

**TABLE 17.   POPULATION OF METROPOLITAN AREAS OF THE UNITED STATES, 1900
TO 1960 AND PROJECTED TO 1980.**

Date	Number of SMA's	Population (millions)	Per cent of U.S. pop.	Per cent in ring
	Estimates for Principal Standard Metropolitan Areas			
1900	52	24.1	31.9	38.1
1910	71	34.5	37.6	35.9
1920	94	46.1	43.7	34.7
1930	115	61.0	49.8	36.4
1940	125	67.1	51.1	38.2
1950	147	84.3	56.0	42.4
	Standard Metropolitan Areas			
1950	168	84.5	56.1	41.5
	Standard Metropolitan Statistical Areas			
1960	211	111.7	62.8	48.7
	Projections			
1970	—	139*	65*	54*
1980	—	174*	67*	58*

*See notes 9 and 12.

SOURCES: U.S. Bureau of the Census and Donald J. Bogue, except as noted above—see Notes
5 and 6.

million persons, resided in 211 "Standard Metropolitan Statistical Areas," the
nomenclature adopted by the federal government in 1959.[6]

III

*   *   *

In the United States, urbanization during the nineteenth century and met-
ropolitanization during the twentieth may be regarded as a continuation of
changes in aggregative living resulting from improved technology and evolving
economic and social organization. A larger proportion of the population became concentrated in urban and metropolitan places because clumpings of
people and economic activities constituted relatively efficient producer and
consumer units and helped to bring about the ever rising level of living of the
people of the United States. Urban and metropolitan agglomerations of population and economic activities were in part the cause and in part the effect of
increased division of labor, specialization, economies of scale, and external
economies. They permitted minimization of the frictions of space and com-

[6]United States Department of Commerce, Bureau of the Census, *1960 Census of Population,* "Preliminary Reports," PC(P3)–4, pp. 2 and 19.

munication in making a living and in the performance of social and political functions.[8]

The postwar upsurge in the rate of population growth, in combination with the continuing play of these technological, economic, and social forces, has served to accelerate the rate of urban and metropolitan growth. During the first half of the century, urban places absorbed about 79 per cent and metropolitan areas 73 per cent of the increase in the total population of the United States (Table 18). Under the impact of mobilization for war, urban areas absorbed 76 per cent and metropolitan areas over 80 per cent of the total national population gain between 1940 and 1950. Between 1950 and 1960 both urban and metropolitan places absorbed over 80 per cent of the total population increase of the nation. Should the observed trends continue it is possible that by 1970 some 70 per cent of the population, or 150 million, and by 1980 some 73 per cent, or 190 million people, will be living in urban places (Table 16). By 1970 some 65 per cent of the population, or about 137 million persons, and by 1980 some 67 per cent, or over 174 million persons, may be resident in metropolitan areas[9] (Table 17).

TABLE 18.   PER CENT OF TOTAL U.S. POPULATION INCREASE IN STANDARD METROPOLITAN AREAS BY CENTRAL CITY AND RING 1900–1950.

		Per cent of U.S. increase				
Date	U.S. increase	Standard metropolitan area	Central cities	Rings	Urban	Rural
1950–60*	100.0	81	16	65	86 †	14 †
1940–50	100.0	80.6	31.6	49.0	76.2	23.8
1930–40	100.0	61.6	24.8	36.8	61.5	38.5
1920–30	100.0	80.9	46.4	34.5	86.7	13.3
1910–20	100.0	75.0	52.5	22.6	88.5	11.5
1900–10	100.0	61.6	43.7	· 17.9	74.1	25.9
1900–50	100.0	73.2	40.6	32.7	78.7	21.3

*From preliminary census release—see Note 6.
†Estimated from Table 16.

SOURCE: See Note 5 except for 1950–60.

[8]Raymond Vernon, *The Changing Economic Function of the Central City* (New York: CED, January 1959); O. D. Duncan *et al.*, *Metropolis and Region* (Baltimore: Johns Hopkins, 1960), Chap. 2.

[9]Projections of metropolitan area population based on percentages estimated by Cuzzort applied to census population projections (assuming continuation of postwar fertility). Percentages in Ray P. Cuzzort, "The Size and Distribution of Metropolitan Areas in 1975," in *Applications of Demography, The Population Situation in the U.S. in 1975,* ed. D. J. Bogue, pp. 62 ff.

IV

Throughout the course of this century, while population was becoming
increasingly metropolitanized, it was also becoming more decentralized within
metropolitan areas (Fig. 15). Between 1900 and 1950, suburban populations
grew at a rate about one and one third times that of the central city populations
(Table 19). Between 1940 and 1950, the last decade of this period, suburban
population growth was two and one half times that of central cities. Between
1950 and 1960, metropolitan areas manifested even greater rates of decentralization, with suburban populations growing about five times as fast as central
cities—48 per cent as compared with 9 per cent.

Figure 15

GROWTH OF POPULATION OF METROPOLITAN AREAS BY CENTRAL
CITY AND RING COMPARED WITH GROWTH OF UNITED STATES,
1900–1980

NOTE: DRAWN ON LOGARITHMIC SCALE SO THAT SLOPE
OF LINE INDICATES RATE OF INCREASE

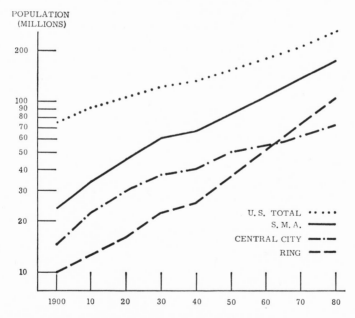

SOURCE: U.S. Bureau of the Census and Projections—see text.

Suburbia, then, has been absorbing increasingly larger proportions of total
metropolitan growth. Between 1900 and 1950, suburbia accounted for 45 per
cent of the total gain in metropolitan areas. During the last decade of this

TABLE 19. PER CENT POPULATION INCREASE IN STANDARD METROPOLITAN AREA BY CENTRAL CITIES AND RINGS, AND URBAN AND RURAL POPULATION FOR THE U.S. 1900 TO 1960.

		Per cent increase				
Date	U.S. population	Standard metro-politan areas	Central cities	Rings	Urban	Rural
1950–60*	17.5	25.3	9.4	47.7	†	†
1940–50	14.5	21.8	13.9	34.7	19.5‡	7.9‡
1930–40	7.2	8.5	5.4	13.9	7.9	6.4
1920–30	16.1	27.1	23.8	33.2	27.3	4.4
1910–20	14.9	25.4	27.7	21.3	29.0	3.2
1900–10	21.0	32.0	36.6	24.3	39.3	9.0
1900–1950	98.3	177.8	159.2	208.1	295	125

*From preliminary census release—see Note 6.
†1960 census data not yet available when table prepared.
‡Old definition—see Table 16.

SOURCE: See Note 5 except for 1950–60.

period, 1940 to 1950, the suburbs contributed 61 per cent of the total metropolitan growth, and during the fifties, about 80 per cent.

As the result of these growth differentials, the relative size of central city and suburb has, of course, been affected. In 1900, 38 per cent of the population of metropolitan areas was in suburbia (Table 17). By 1950, the proportion had risen to 42 per cent. In 1960, suburban population constituted 49 per cent of metropolitan area population.

In recent years there has been much interest in this trend toward decentralization of population within metropolitan areas. It has been widely referred to as the "flight to the suburbs." To the extent that this expression indicates that central cities are being denuded of population by persons streaming into suburbia, it is only a half-truth. For although it is true that throughout the history of our cities populations have ever moved outward from the center, in the process of "radial expansion"[10] through which cities grew, it is also true that this movement has simultaneously been offset by an inflow of newcomers to the center.

There are two basic reasons for the increased decentralization of population within the Standard Metropolitan Areas. Since these will continue to operate in the coming years, it is well to set them forth. The first and more

[10]Robert E. Park and Ernest W. Burgess, *The City* (Chicago: University of Chicago, 1925), pp. 50 ff.

fundamental reason is to be found in the shift from nineteenth to twentieth century technology. Nineteenth century technology was symbolized by the steam engine, the belt and pulley, and the horse-drawn vehicle. This technology created centripetal forces which produced dense population agglomerations around the factory. In contrast, twentieth century technology is symbolized by electric power, by the automotive complex—the auto, the truck, and the highway—and by the telephone. Twentieth century technology generates centrifugal rather than centripetal forces, making possible greater dispersion of both industry and population within metropolitan areas. Perhaps a better way to put it is to say that twentieth century technology made possible larger clumpings of people and economic activities than did that of the nineteenth century.

The second factor contributive to decentralization of population within metropolitan areas is so simple that it tends frequently to be overlooked. Metropolitan suburban rings are growing more rapidly than central cities in the United States because central cities since about 1920, on the average, have been filled up.[11] The population of our metropolitan areas has continued to grow with the expansion of the economic base. Central cities have relatively fixed boundaries set forth in a state charter. Because economic reality does not stop at arbitrary city limits, continued population growth necessarily transcended city political boundary lines. The continued growth of metropolitan areas has necessarily meant increasing proportions of growth beyond city limits.

These forces accounting for differentials in the growth of suburbs and central cities are still operating. The trend, therefore, may be expected to continue during the decades which lie ahead. Between 1960 and 1970, with a gain of perhaps 27 million persons in metropolitan areas, about 7 million are likely to augment the population of the city and over 20 million will move into suburbia. By 1970, of perhaps 139 million persons in metropolitan areas, 75 million may be in suburbs, and only 64 million in central cities. Between 1950 and 1980, with a possible increase of 90 million persons in Standard Metropolitan Areas, only 23 million would be added to the population of central cities, and the remaining 67 million would settle in the suburbs.[12] Thus, by 1970, 54 per cent, and by 1980, 58 per cent, of metropolitan population would be resident in suburbia (Table 17).

Although metropolitan United States as a whole is experiencing rapid growth, some areas are actually losing population, and the explosive growth is confined mainly to the suburbs. Of the 211 Standard Metropolitan Statistical Areas, 9 lost population between 1950 and 1960; and of 256 central cities in metropolitan areas, 73 lost population.[13]

[11]Donald J. Bogue, *op. cit.* (1957), p. 18; Amos H. Hawley, *The Changing Shape of Metropolitan America: Deconcentration Since 1920* (Glencoe, Illinois: Free Press, 1956).
[12]Based on percentage projected by Ray P. Cuzzort, *op. cit.*
[13]See Note 6.

Individual metropolitan areas, and especially the smaller ones, are subject to population losses by reason of the changing economy, relatively large industrial shifts, or the denudation of resources on which local industries may depend. Central cities, on the whole, and especially the older and larger ones, have reached a point of relative stability in size. Apart from annexations, they will probably experience relatively small gains or losses from now on, depending largely on how changing land use patterns may increase or decrease population densities within their boundaries.

It should also be noted that the non-metropolitan population, and especially the rural-farm population, is not experiencing explosive growth. Over the first half of this century population in non-metropolitan areas increased by only 50 per cent while metropolitan populations more than tripled. Between 1950 and 1960, non-metropolitan population increased by only 7 per cent, as compared with a metropolitan increase of over 25 per cent.

Rural-farm population has actually decreased over the period in which it has been counted in this country—that is, since 1910. From a level of about 32 million it declined to about 30 million by 1930, despite great total population gains. During the depression thirties farm population rose again, but with improved economic conditions at the end of the decade farm out-migration increased, and by 1940 farm population had again declined to about its 1930 level. During World War II farm population decreased rapidly and although there was some increase with demobilization it had declined to about 25 million by 1950. In 1960, farm population numbered about 17 million. Should the trend continue farm population may have shrunk to about 12 million by 1980, despite explosive national growth.[14] The decline in rural-farm population reflects the increased mechanization and productivity of American agriculture. Acreage under cultivation throughout the period of decline of farm population has changed relatively little, whereas productivity per acre has, of course, continued to increase greatly.

V

Basic changes in land use patterns and the structure of the metropolitan area have accompanied metropolitan area explosive population growth and decentralization. Further changes may be anticipated with the tremendous population expansion which is projected.

Present patterns of land use in our metropolitan districts reflect the origin and growth of the area's economic base and the process of peopling. Urban and metropolitan places had their origin at a point or points which encompassed their first economic functions. Such a point was frequently a break in means of transportation. In Chicago, for example, the major point of origin was the point of junction of the Chicago River and Lake Michigan. From this

[14]Donald J. Bogue, op. cit. (1959), p. 785.

point the city developed and expanded. It grew to the South, to the North, and
to the West, but, for obvious reasons, not so much to the East.

Residential land use patterns were a function of the geometry of urban
growth and the play of market forces. Since the city necessarily grew away
from its point of origin, the newer residential areas were always farthest from
the center. These outlying areas were more desirable places to live, partly
because they were newer and partly because, with rapid technological advance,
they incorporated the benefits of improved technology. Consider, for example,
the changes in kinds of residential lighting. The earliest structures in many of
our cities were illuminated by the kerosene lamp. With advances in technology,
the kerosene lamp gave way to gas illumination, which in turn was displaced
by electric lighting, with wiring originally pulled through gas light fixtures.
This improved illumination was in turn outmoded by superior electric lighting
installed independently of gas fixtures. Moreover, homes so illuminated were
generally improved in other respects such as in plumbing, appliances, and
picture windows.

It has been noted that the tempo of United States urban and metropolitan
growth was an exceedingly rapid one. Our cities grew not structure by structure but by subdivision, neighborhood, and community. To draw upon
Chicago again as an illustration, it may be recalled that that city was first
reported in a census of the United States in 1840, at which time it had a
population of 4,470. Two decades later, in 1860, Chicago was a city of over
100,000; by 1870, a city of over 250,000; by 1880, a city of over half a million;
and by 1890, Chicago contained more than 1 million inhabitants. Chicago
became a city of over a million within a period of fifty years!

Partly as the result of technological advances but partly too because of
explosive rates of growth requiring tremendous additions to the city's physical
plant, the inner and older zones of our cities became obsolescent and, eventually, blighted and decayed. Our urban plant decayed as it had developed, at
fabulous rates, not structure by structure but by entire neighborhoods at a
time.

The processes by which city neighborhoods developed, flourished, became
obsolescent, and decayed tended to follow uniform patterns throughout the
land. The histories of the inner and older areas of our cities have been, on the
whole, remarkably uniform. Present inner and older areas were, at their origin,
outlying suburbs containing the residences of the fashionably elite. With the
continued growth of the city they became, more and more, inner zones, and
followed similar patterns of changes in their residential occupancy. They
housed first the middle class, then workingmen's families and finally, in many
cases, they were turned over to rooming houses and slums. The present inner
zones of our cities and metropolitan areas had a natural history of continuous
decline in occupancy, from higher to lower income groupings of the population. With the exceedingly rapid growth of our metropolitan areas, the outlying better residential neighborhoods of one generation became the inner, older,
and less desirable neighborhoods of the next.

Explosive urban and metropolitan growth, together with the play of market forces, determined both the patterns of land use and the distribution of the population in space. Place of residence in metropolitan areas was determined by social and economic status, with the lower income groups living in the center of the city and the higher income groups toward the periphery (Fig. 16 . . .). Rapid growth and the play of market forces produced for the American people the highest mass level of living ever achieved by any nation in the history of man. But they also produced the slum, which became a matter of national and international disgrace and, in recent years, an issue in national politics as well.

As the metropolitan area agglomeration grew in size with twentieth century technology, the size of inner and older zones also increased. Because city boundary lines have tended to remain relatively fixed while metropolitan clumpings of people and economic activities expanded, larger and larger proportions of the total central city land area have become inner and older zones of the entire metropolitan area and have been taken over by lower income groups; and increasing proportions of the higher income groups in the entire metropolitan area have become residents of suburbia.

The urban residential land use patterns which we have inherited will probably be greatly modified during the coming decade by forces which are already at work to change them.

VI

Among those forces which must change the patterns of land use in our metropolitan areas are urban renewal programs in central cities, the explosive growth and increasing industrialization of suburban areas, and the discernible tendency for the family to use the metropolitan areas in accordance with the changing requirements of the family cycle.

The urban renewal program is the culmination of a long series of efforts to deal with the problem of urban obsolescence and decay. It is a concerted and systematic attempt on the part of the federal government, in cooperation with city governments, to raze and rebuild the decayed inner core of our central cities, to rehabilitate aging neighborhoods not yet completely decayed, and to conserve the remainder of the residential plant. Thus, its purpose is to alter drastically the natural history of city neighborhoods described above. Urban renewal is an effort, at mid-twentieth century, to clean up the obsolete and decayed parts of the urban plant—the mess produced as a by-product of our remarkable and explosive economic and population growth.

The impact of urban renewal is increasingly visible throughout the land. Urban renewal programs are bulldozing and rebuilding the inner zones of our cities in much the same manner as they grew and decayed—not by individual structures but by entire neighborhoods at a time.[15]

[15] *Urban Redevelopment: Problems and Practices,* ed. Coleman Woodbury; also *The Future of Cities and Urban Redevelopment* (Chicago: University of Chicago, 1953); Julia Abrahamson, *A Neighborhood Finds Itself* (New York: Harper, 1959).

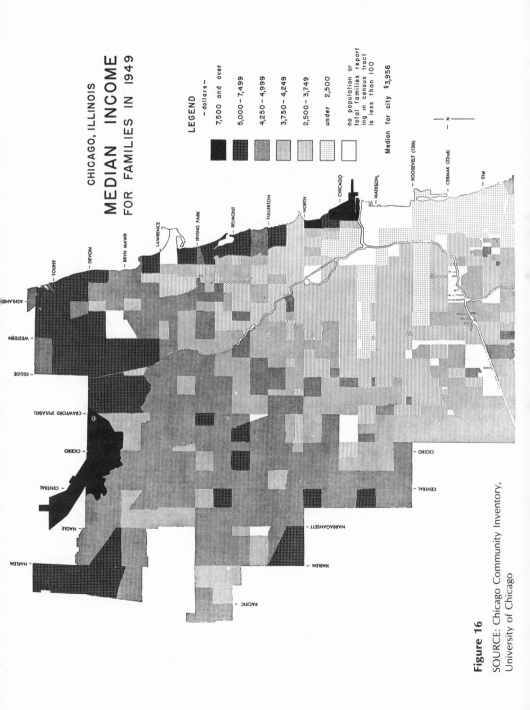

CHICAGO, ILLINOIS

MEDIAN INCOME

FOR FAMILIES IN 1949

LEGEND

— dollars —

7,500 and over

5,000 – 7,499

4,250 – 4,999

3,750 – 4,249

2,500 – 3,749

under 2,500

no population or
total families report-
ing in census tract
is less than 100

Median for city $3,956

Figure 16

SOURCE: Chicago Community Inventory,
University of Chicago

The rate at which urban renewal will proceed will vary with the fortunes of the major political parties and the course of the business cycle. Expenditures for the program are likely to be greater in Democratic than Republican administrations, and in recession or depression than in times of business prosperity. But it may be taken for granted that the urban renewal program has become part of the United States political scene and is here to stay.

As we have seen, our suburban areas are going through the same kind of rapid growth as did central cities during the nineteenth and early twentieth centuries. There is increasing evidence that parts of the suburbs are now faced with the same concomitants of explosively rapid growth—rapid obsolescence and decay.

A factor contributing to the residential downgrading of suburban areas is the decentralization of industry. Industry, like population, is decentralizing within some metropolitan areas because the central city is filled up for many industrial purposes.[16] Industrial concentrations in suburbia are accompanied by housing developments designed for relatively low income workers. Such realty developments have, on the whole, not maintained the standards of housing which have characterized suburban areas in the past—in fact, a good part of what is being built in suburbia, "urban sprawl," is virtually slum even before the concrete is dry.[17] Many of the newer developments have inadequate provisions for drainage, sanitation, and water supply, not to mention recreation, educational facilities, and transportation facilities. Some suburban developments have been deliberately located to escape central city or other municipal zoning and code provisions.

As a consequence of both obsolescence and the new developments in suburbia, newcomers to metropolitan areas are beginning to have available a wider choice than before of cheap and sub-standard housing in which to settle. In-migrants to metropolitan areas are finding ports of entry in suburbia as well as in the inner and older zones of the city, so that suburban areas are no longer developing entirely through the process of radial expansion. A major source for the growth of outlying parts of many metropolitan areas is direct in-migration, rather than radial expansion. A major source for the growth of outlying parts of many metropolitan areas is direct in-migration, rather than radial expansion. Analysis of in-migration to metropolitan rings between 1940 and 1950 shows that of over 7 million net in-migrants to suburbia, about half represented direct migration to the suburbs from places other than the central cities.[18] This process has undoubtedly continued since 1950.

The combination of urban renewal in the inner zones of central cities and

---

[16]For analysis of suburbanization of industry, see E. M. Kitagawa and D. J. Bogue, *Suburbanization of Manufacturing Activity Within Standard Metropolitan Areas* (Oxford, Ohio: Scripps Foundation, 1955).

[17]The Editors of *Fortune, The Exploding Metropolis* (New York: Doubleday, 1958), Chap. 5.

[18]Donald J. Bogue, *Components of Population Change, 1940–1950: . . .* (Oxford, Ohio: Scripps Foundation, 1957), Chap. 3.

blight and urban sprawl in the suburbs is tending to disrupt the pattern of population distribution which has placed the higher income groups farthest out from the center of the city. Should these trends continue, the residential land use pattern in metropolitan areas would be turned inside out, with the newer and more desirable areas located in the rebuilt inner city zones as well as in the most distant parts of suburbia.

Another factor tending to destroy historical and present patterns of residential land use in metropolitan areas is the increasing tendency for the family use of the metropolitan area to change in accordance with its varying requirements during the course of the "family cycle."[19] That is, newly married couples tend both to work and to live in the central city, relatively close to the central business or central manufacturing district which affords them employment. With the coming of children, in keeping with an old American dream, the couple tends to move to outlying areas for fresh air, green grass, and relatively open spaces in which to rear their families. But when the children leave the family for college or marriage, there is a growing tendency for parents with an "empty nest" to gravitate back toward central city residence. In fact, there is some evidence that some such couples are drifting toward high rise, efficiency type accommodations built in urban renewal areas in central cities. Such a reverse movement makes good sense when it is borne in mind that no one is left at home to cut the grass, and that closing a house down is more complicated than leaving an apartment when there is an opportunity to visit Florida or California in the winter, or to baby-sit with grandchildren. The elderly couple without children constitutes an increasingly important source for the recentralization of central city population.

This type of cyclical use of the metropolitan area is by no means yet the modal one, but considerations which may not be readily apparent strongly suggest that the pattern is there. In 1890, for example, when the last child left the family for marriage, the average wife in the United States had become a widow. By 1950, as the result of decreased age at marriage, decreased birth rate, increased concentration of child bearing under age 30, and decreased death rate accompanied by increased longevity, this was no longer the situation. By 1950, when the last child left home for marriage the average wife still had a husband, and the couple had the prospect of an additional fourteen years of life together. The difference between zero years of marital existence after the children had left home in 1890, and an average of fourteen such years in 1950,[20] is translatable into literally millions and millions of husband-and-wife years of life together without children in the later years. In the aggregate, this change in less than two human generations has created a demand for a new type of housing and land use which will inevitably affect residential land use patterns.

[19]Paul C. Glick, "The Life Cycle of the Family," *Marriage and Family Living,* XVII, No. 1 (February, 1955); see also Paul C. Glick, *American Families* (New York: John Wiley & Sons, 1957), Chaps. 3, 4, 5.
[20]*Ibid.,* p. 68.

Finally, any consideration of the modification of land use patterns and the structure of our metropolitan areas must include reference to emergent "megalopolis."[21] Tremendous growth of the kind in prospect necessarily means the spilling of population into the open country areas of our metropolitan ring —into exurbia and interurbia. It means that inter-metropolitan area space will be inundated and metropolitan areas, therefore, will tend to coalesce.

The merging of metropolitan areas into "megalopolis" is already in evidence. On the Northeastern seaboard, for example, the area from Boston to Washington constitutes perhaps the farthest advanced and largest of our emergent megalopolises, one that might be termed "Atlantic-opolis" (Fig. 17). In the Middle West several megalopolises are in evidence. One, stretching from Milwaukee to Chicago to South Bend, may form the anchor of a future "Lake Michigan-opolis." Another from Chicago to Peoria to St. Louis may constitute a "Seaway-opolis." Detroit, Toledo, and Cincinnati offer still another possibility as "Erie-opolis." Moreover, it may be noted that the Chicago-Detroit areas could be linked into a super "Great Lake-opolis," which might also include the area from Toledo to Cleveland to Pittsburgh.

On the West Coast a "Pacific-opolis" is emerging from San Francisco to Sacramento to the North and West, and from San Francisco to Fresno to Los Angeles to San Diego to the South. In the North Pacific areas "Puget-opolis" is visible in the developments from Everett, Seattle, and Tacoma in Washington, down through Portland and Salem in Oregon. Other such developments are visible in at least potential outline form as follows:

Jacksonville to Orlando to Miami on the Eastern Coast of Florida; and Jacksonville to Orlando to Ft. Myers on the Western Coast—a potential "Florid-opolis";

Buffalo to Utica to Albany as a "Canal-opolis" linking with "Atlantic-opolis";

Knoxville to Chattanooga to Birmingham as "South Appalachian-opolis";

Denver to Pueblo as a "Rocky-opolis";

Salt Lake City and surrounding area as "Salt Lake-opolis";

Dallas to Houston to Galveston to Fort Worth to San Antonio as a saddle-shaped "Texas-opolis";

Durham to Atlanta as "Piedmont-opolis";

New Orleans to Mobile to Tallahassee as "Gulf-opolis."

With the interplay of the forces described we may be entering a new cycle of development in metropolitan area residential land use patterns—a cycle undoubtedly accelerated by rapid growth. It is almost certain that the present

[21]The term "megalopolis" was proposed by Jean Gottmann, *Virginia at Mid-Century* (New York: Henry Holt & Co., 1955), pp. 41, 174, 472–79. Other terms to designate essentially the same phenomenon include "connurbation," Patrick Geddes, *Cities in Evolution* (London: 1915), p. 168; "metropolitan region" (series of eight articles reprinted from *New York Times,* January 27 to February 3, 1957); "strip cities" (*U.S. News & World Report,* April 5, 1957. See Fig. 17).

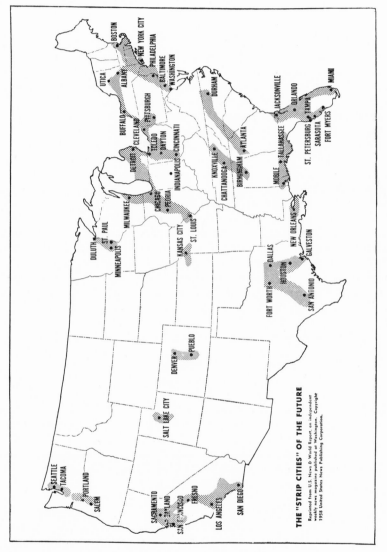

THE "STRIP CITIES" OF THE FUTURE

Reprinted from U.S. News & World Report, an independent
weekly news magazine published at Washington. Copyright
1958 United States News Publishing Corporation.

Figure 17

residential stratification of population by social and economic status will change in the metropolitan area in the future. It may be anticipated that there will be both good and bad neighborhoods in the inner and older zones of the city, throughout the city, and throughout the suburbs. Whether a neighborhood will be good or bad will depend much less on the accident of its history, its proximity to the point of origin of the city, and the play of the market mechanism, than on various forms of government interventionism—on city planning, urban renewal and related programs, zoning, codes, and the changing requirements of the population itself as evidenced by rapidly changing age structure, family formation, and changes in the family cycle. We can expect the overflowing population to inundate exurbia and interurbia, and to produce new forms of metropolitan structure in emergent megalopolis.

VII

Urban and metropolitan areas in the United States have been peopled largely by flows of population from the outside. Up to World War I these included a relatively large volume of immigration in addition to internal migratory flows from rural and especially rural-farm areas. Since World War I, and particularly since World War II, internal migratory streams have been the predominant source of "outside" population.

The nation as a whole was, like the urban areas, peopled in large measure through immigration from abroad. Between 1820 and 1960 about 42 million immigrants that the federal government managed to count came to the United States.[22] They came in large waves during the nineteenth and early twentieth centuries. In mid-nineteenth century, streams of Irish and German immigrants followed the potato famine and economic difficulties in Ireland and the abortive revolutionary attempt of 1848 in Germany. Toward the end of the nineteenth century, crop failures and general economic depression set in motion relatively large volumes of Scandinavian immigrants. During the early part of the twentieth century, sources of immigration to the United States shifted from Northern and Western to Southern and Eastern Europe—to Russians and Poles, including the Jewish groups, to Italians, Greeks, and other peoples from Eastern European nations, who left their homelands for the new opportunities beckoning in the rapidly developing United States.

The processes by which newcomers to urban and metropolitan areas made their entry, achieved a place of residence, and found a niche in the economy and status in the social order, were strikingly uniform. Adapting themselves to the land use patterns described above, the newcomers almost invariably found their ports of entry in the inner, older, and less desirable zones of the city. They worked at the most menial and poorest paid occupations. They were the lowest in social status in the community.

[22]Bureau of the Census, *Statistical Abstract of the United States* (1959), p. 23.

Each wave of newcomers was greeted in the same fashion by those who had preceded them and who had already settled in the community—that is, by attitudes ranging from suspicion and distrust to outright hostility, prejudice, and discriminatory practices. Each group of newcomers was awarded some pithy designation implying inferior status. During the nineteenth century, for example, the new arrivals were greeted as "krautheads," "micks," and "dumb swedes." During the twentieth century we admitted "polacks," "sheenies," "wops," "bohunks," and the like. There were no mass exceptions to this rule.

With the passage of time, each wave of newcomers climbed the socio-economic ladder as measured by place of residence, education, occupation, income, and general acceptability. It is a striking fact that even today there is a high correlation between the place of residence of immigrant stock and the length of time they have lived in the community. The censuses of the United States reveal a pattern which undoubtedly will be evident for some time to come (Figs. 18 and 19). The longer the immigrant group has been in the community, the farther out from the center of the city is their median location point and the more dispersed or "integrated" is their residential pattern. The shorter the time the immigrant group has been in the community, the closer to the center of the city is their average location point and the more concentrated or "segregated" tends to be their residential distribution. Moreover, the longer the length of residence of the group, the higher tends to be its economic status as measured by type of occupation pursued and income and its social status as measured by educational achievement, broader access to the social and cultural life of the community, and increased general acceptability.[23]

It is not an over-generalization to state that segregated living in the decayed and blighted areas of the city, menial occupation and low income, hostility, prejudice, and discriminatory practices have not been reserved for any one or two minority newcomer groups in the history of this nation. On the contrary, they have been democratically available to all new arrivals without regard to race, religion, or origin.

The processes by which waves of immigrants entered into the American scene are popularly known as "Americanization." To the sociologist and anthropologist they are the processes of acculturation—accommodation and assimilation. Although the "melting pot" theme has probably been overstated in the sense that many of our immigrant groups continue to retain their national, cultural, linguistic, or religious identification, it is clear that the relatively open and competitive social and economic order in the United States has, on the whole, afforded opportunity for successive waves of immigrants to

[23]Oscar Handlin, *The Uprooted* (Boston: Little, Brown & Co., 1951), and *The Newcomers* (Cambridge, Mass.: Harvard University Press, 1959); O. D. and Beverly Duncan, *The Negro Population of Chicago* (Chicago: University of Chicago Press, 1957); Stanley Lieberson and O. D. Duncan, "Ethnic Segregation and Assimilation," *American Journal of Sociology*, 64 (January, 1959), pp. 364–74; Karl E. Taeuber, "Residential Segregation of Urban Non-Whites" (Ph.D. dissertation, Harvard University, 1960); Stanley Lieberson, "Comparative Segregation and Assimilation of Ethnic Groups" (Ph.D. dissertation, University of Chicago, 1960).

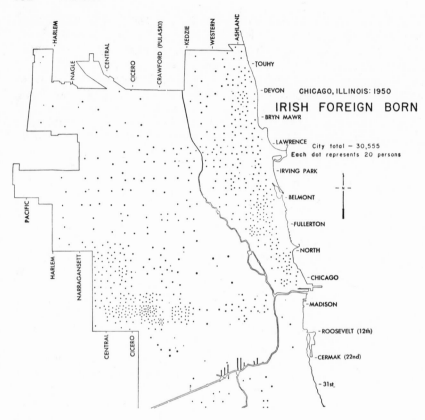

Figure 18
SOURCE: Chicago Community Inventory, University of Chicago

achieve varying degrees of integration into the economic, social, and political orders.

It is not generally recognized that the rapidity of our population growth and relative youth of this nation make the United States one of the more heterogeneous nations on the face of the earth, one which, in large measure, has yet to achieve unification or integration. As recently as 1950, for example, over a fifth of the population of the United States was either foreign-born or native of foreign or mixed parentage; and over a tenth were of nonwhite race.[24] That is, only two-thirds of the population of the United States, as recently as 1950, was native white of native parents. As recently as 1900, little more than half of the population of the United States was native white. Moreover, as recently as 1950, in four of our five largest cities, native white population of

[24]United States Bureau of the Census, *op. cit.* (1959), p. 28.

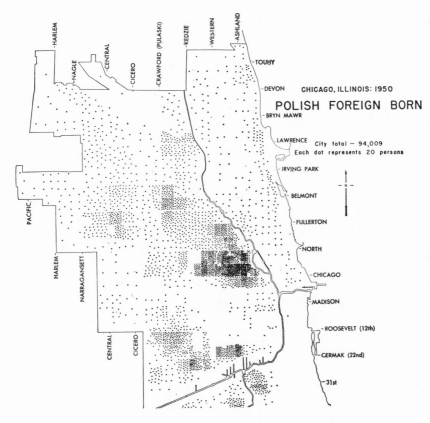

CHICAGO, ILLINOIS: 1950

POLISH FOREIGN BORN

City total — 94,009

Each dot represents 20 persons

Figure 19

SOURCE: Chicago Community Inventory, University of Chicago

native parentage constituted less than half of the total. In New York in 1950, only 34 per cent of the population as native white of native parentage; in Chicago, only 41 per cent; in Philadelphia, only 46 per cent; and in Detroit, only 42 per cent. Los Angeles was the only city among the five largest in the United States in which the native white population of native parentage was greater than half, and even there it was only 55 per cent. The first generation in which virtually all the people of the United States share a common nativity is yet to come.

The most recent newcomers to urban and metropolitan United States are in-migrants rather than immigrants. The visible Negro and less visible rural white, especially Southern rural white, in-migrant has replaced the waves of immigrants as a major source of new metropolitan manpower. These in-migrants are, of course, supplemented by flows of Puerto Ricans and Mexicans. Let us focus on the Negro in-migrant to urban and metropolitan areas, for whom the census data permit some analysis.

For purposes of perspective, it is well to note the historical internal distribution of Negroes. The Census of 1860 reported that 92 per cent of all Negroes in the country lived in the South. A half-century later the Census of 1910 disclosed that the concentration of Negroes in the South had decreased by only 3 percentage points, that is, it had declined to 89 per cent.

The first large internal migratory movement of Negroes began during World War I. These migratory streams were the product of a number of forces, chief of which was undoubtedly the need for labor to man industries, and especially war industries in the North, as the United States served as the arsenal for the Allied Powers. Successful U-Boat warfare almost swept Allied shipping from the high seas, and by thus greatly restricting immigration created economic opportunity for the Negro. Moreover, the changing economy in the South was beginning to free the Negro from the soil.

The passage of the Immigration Exclusion Acts during the 1920's greatly curtailed the flow of immigrants. Despite special provisions to admit refugee groups from time to time, immigration has since been a relatively negligible source of growth of United States population. The continuation of internal migratory movements of Negroes from the rural South to urban areas in the North and West, and also to urban places in the South, took the place of the streams of immigrants that could no longer come to man the expanding urban and industrial economy. The exodus of Negroes from the rural South, dampened during the depression thirties, was greatly accelerated by the manpower requirements of World War II. By 1950 only 68 per cent of the Negroes in the United States were left in the South, and by 1960 only about 60 per cent.

Continuation of the present trend could produce a break-even point in the distribution of the Negro between the North and the South by 1970.[25] That is, it is possible that by 1970 there will be as many Negroes in the North and West as remain in the South.

Streams of Negro migrants not only moved from the South to the North and West, but also from predominantly rural to predominantly urban areas. In 1910, only 27 per cent of the Negroes in this nation lived in urban places as defined by the Census, that is in places having 2500 or more persons. By 1950, about 60 per cent of the Negro population was urban, and by 1960 the proportion of Negroes living in cities approximated two-thirds. The trend could easily make this about three-fourths by 1970.[26]

In 1950, over 90 per cent of the Negroes in the North and in the West, and about 48 per cent of the Negroes in the South, lived in urban places. By 1950, nonwhite population in metropolitan areas numbered 8.3 million. This number reflected a fourfold increase since the beginning of the century and an increase

[25]Projections by Population Research and Training Center, University of Chicago, for Commission on Race and Housing. On file.
[26]*Ibid.*

of over two-fifths (44.3 per cent) between 1940 and 1950.[27] Thus the Negro, in a little more than a human generation and a half, has been drawn from rural existence under relatively primitive conditions in the South to urbanism as a way of life. Many of the frictions and problems of adjustment in inter-group relations which create hardships both for the Negro in-migrant and the communities of origin and destination may be viewed as products of the exceedingly high rates of population growth and rapid changes in population distribution.

In streaming to metropolitan areas, the in-migrant Negro has generally found the same port of entry as preceding waves of white immigrants. His area of first settlement has been the inner, older, and blighted zones of the metropolitan area,[28] although it should be noted that, because of the increasing industrialization of suburbia, the Negro is also finding industrial areas in suburbia a port of entry to the metropolitan area.[29] Analysis of population movement within metropolitan areas shows the older resident white population following the traditional pattern by moving outward as the latest newcomer, the Negro, enters. This is the pattern of radial expansion described above, but a new development is that in the postwar period the pattern has meant that white populations moved outward beyond the limits of the city as the Negro entered. Thus, the Negro became an increasingly larger proportion of the central city population. By reason of the relatively fixed city boundaries and the process of radial expansion, central city population is becoming decreasingly white and increasingly Negro.

Between 1940 and 1950, as my colleague Professor Bogue has shown, a net total of 6 million persons migrated to Standard Metropolitan Areas. Of this number 4.4 million were white, and 1.6 million nonwhite, migrants. Of the 1.6 million nonwhite migrants, 1.3 million entered central cities and a little over 300,000 the metropolitan rings. The net migration of 4.4 million white persons to Standard Metropolitan Areas, however, was made up of a net in-migration of 6.9 million white persons to suburbia, and a net out-migration of 2.5 million white persons from central cities.[30] This process has undoubtedly continued during the fifties and may well persist for some time to come.

---

[27]Taeuber and Taeuber, *op. cit.*, p. 140; Bogue, *op. cit.* (1959), p. 149.
[28]Duncan and Duncan, *op. cit.*, Chap. 5.
[29]Bogue, *op. cit.* (1957), p. 111.
[30]*Ibid.*, p. 37.

The Housing Market in Racially Mixed Areas
Davis McEntire

Two studies undertaken for the Commission on Race and Housing deal specifically with the impact of racial mingling in residence areas on local housing markets. One is an inquiry into the effects on residential property values of nonwhite entry into formerly all-white neighborhoods.[1] The second study is an analysis of demand for housing in racially mixed areas of one large city.[2]

PROPERTY VALUES AND RACE

According to traditional and widespread opinion, Negroes, and other minorities as well, are dangerous to property values when they seek housing, as they must, outside established minority residence areas. Underlying this belief are two basic propositions: first, that whites will not live in areas entered by nonwhites, and second, that nonwhite demand for housing is not sufficient to replace the vanished white demand and hence, prices must fall.

To many, these propositions seem self-evident, but in recent years both have been challenged. Not only have proponents of racial equality endeavored to demonstrate the error of the "property values myth," but in the real estate appraisal profession, increasing doubts have been expressed about the validity of the traditional doctrines under present-day conditions.

The importance of the problem needs no emphasis. Fear of financial loss gives every property owner in white neighborhoods a direct personal stake in excluding minorities, at least up to a point. Convictions that racial mingling injures property values influence business decisions to build, finance, and sell in ways that restrict the opportunities of nonwhites to acquire housing and limit them to certain districts. In acting on the assumption that values in an area are going to fall, the housing industry and property owners may help to bring about the anticipated result. If major lenders act together to reduce their loans in an area, they may be not merely recognizing but making a shift to lower prices, by eliminating a part of the demand. Similarly, when homeown-

---

[1]Luigi Laurenti, *Property Values and Race: Studies in Seven Cities.*

[2]Chester Rapkin and William G. Grigsby, *The Demand for Housing in Racially Mixed Areas: A Study of the Nature of Neighborhood Change.*

SOURCE: David McEntire, from *Residence and Race* (Berkeley: University of California Press, 1960), pp. 157–171. Originaly published by the University of California Press; reprinted by permission of the Regents of the University of California.

ers in an affected area hasten to sell before the expected price decline occurs, the resulting oversupply of houses may push down their selling prices.[3]

The motive, moreover, of preserving capital, an eminently respectable purpose, often provides moral justification for racial discrimination. People may consider themselves not merely justified but even obligated to exclude minorities for the sake of maintaining values. The real estate board in one large city took this ground in a public statement of policy:

> It is a matter of fact and experience that when a Negro or Chinese or Japanese or Filipino moves into a white district, the house values drop. . . . *We don't look at this as a social problem. For us this is an economic problem.* Looking at it this way, the Board has asked that its members not introduce into a residential district any occupancy or race which will have the effect of lowering values.[4]

In similar vein, a savings and loan association executive said in interview: "There are lots of things we would like to do personally, such as treating everybody equally, . . . but we are responsible for millions of dollars. . . . We will lend on properties up to three blocks away from colored areas but not closer. . . ."

Twenty years and more ago, real estate authorities asserted the adverse effect of nonwhite occupancy on values straightforwardly and with few qualifications. Fisher (1923), McMichael and Bingham (1923), Babcock (1932), Hoyt (1933, 1939), and other authors of standard texts and treatises pronounced a common judgment, accepted apparently without dissent.[5] Property appraisal standards of the Federal Housing Administration incorporated the accepted doctrine.

Since World War II, differing theories have been advanced by professional appraisers and others. According to one contemporary theory, the price depression associated with nonwhite entry is only temporary. House prices weaken in areas anticipating a racial change and may continue depressed during the early stages of transition, but after transition, prices rise again.[6] Myrdal espoused this view in the *American Dilemma* (1944).[7] More recently Charles A. Benson, chief appraiser of a leading mortgage-finance institution, reporting on a study of price changes in two Chicago areas—one all-white and one in racial transition—concludes:

[3] This type of collective behavior, akin to panics, bank runs, and hoarding sprees, has been termed by Merton, the "self-fulfilling prophecy." Robert K. Merton, "The Self-Fulfilling Prophecy."

[4] Statement on behalf of the San Francisco Real Estate Board, reported in "The Negro in San Francisco," *San Francisco Chronicle,* November 6, 1950. Italics supplied.

[5] The relevant professional writings are reviewed in Laurenti, *Property Values and Race,* chap. ii.

[6] George W. Beehler, Jr., "Colored Occupancy Raises Values," *The Review of the Society of Residential Appraisers,* XI, no. 9 (September, 1945). See also Stanley L. McMichael, *McMichael's Appraising Manual,* p. 169.

[7] Gunnar Myrdal, *An American Dilemma,* p. 623.

... prices of residences are depressed from 30 percent to 55 percent when an area is threatened by transition. As soon as transition becomes a fact, prices tend to rise. ... After transition has been accomplished, prices in the then Negro area compare favorably with prices in the city as a whole and are controlled by supply and demand.[8]

Some appraisers hold that nonwhite occupancy may actually enhance real estate values in certain conditions. According to the authorities just mentioned, active movement of nonwhites into an area is better for values than the continued threat of entry. Thurston Ross writes that "in poor and slum sections racial encroachment sometimes raises the economic standards of the neighborhood." He reports "instances where obsolescence has been arrested and additional years of useful life given a neighborhood by racial encroachment, particularly when older people are displaced by younger groups of the encroaching race."[9]

The newer theories differ from the old in recognizing a variety of conditions under which nonwhite movement into an area can take place, and consequently a range of possible effects on values. Weaver especially emphasizes variation. Reviewing the evidence available in 1948, he wrote:

> The effect of Negro occupancy upon property values varies from one section of the city to another and from one time to another. ... The arrival of a few Negroes may be the signal for a great decline in selling prices or it may lead to an appreciable increase. Much depends upon the state of the total housing market and the manner in which colored people enter an area. ... *There is no one universal effect of Negro occupancy upon property values.*[10]

Weaver's view is reiterated by Abrams, who finds a complex of factors at work and "no fixed rules as to when minority neighbors raise or lower values."[11]

Appraisal policies of the Federal Housing Administration reflect the change in appraisal thinking. Where once the FHA flatly asserted the value-destroying tendency of mixed neighborhoods, in successive editions of the *Underwriting Manual* provisions touching race and property values have become steadily more qualified. References to "social and racial classes" have been deleted in favor of the more neutral "user groups," and the *Manual* now states,

> If a mixture of user groups is found to exist it must be determined whether the mixture will render the neighborhood less desirable to present and prospective occupants. If the occupancy of the neighborhood is changing from one user group

[8]Charles A. Benson, "A Test of Transition Theories," *The Residential Appraiser,* Vol. 24, no. 8 (August, 1958), 8. Quoted with permission of the Society of Residential Appraisers.
[9]Thurston H. Ross, "Market Significance of Declining Neighborhoods."
[10]Robert G. Weaver, *The Negro Ghetto,* p. 293. Italics in original.
[11]Charles Abrams, *Forbidden Neighbors,* pp. 286, 292.

to another, . . . any degree of risk is reflected in the rating. . . . Additional risk is not necessarily involved in such change.[12]

These judgments of real estate and housing authorities have been based mainly on professional experience and observation rather than on research, for few factual studies have been made of what actually happens to house prices when nonwhites move into new areas. Difficult problems of method confront the study of this question. Merely to observe the course of prices in a neighborhood experiencing racial change tells little, for the movements observed might well be caused by factors other than the racial change. The measurement of racial influence on values is especially complicated by the tendency of minority groups to concentrate in slum and deteriorating sections affected by various adverse influences. To attribute the lower rents and prices in such areas solely to the presence of nonwhites would be obviously misleading.

To isolate the price effects of racial mixture, the price performance of racially mixed areas must be compared with some standard that is free of the racial influence being investigated. Laurenti's research for the Commission on Race and Housing attempts to do this. Twenty neighborhoods, recently become racially mixed, in San Francisco, Oakland, and Philadelphia were chosen for study. Each neighborhood, called a "test area," was matched with a "control" neighborhood which had remained all white. Each pair of neighborhoods was chosen according to criteria to ensure that the two would closely resemble each other in major factors affecting house prices. Criteria for matching included the age, type, and market value of houses, topography, location, land-use pattern, income and broad occupational class of residents, and the character of neighborhood development. A large number of areas were sifted in the search for matching pairs. Comparability of the paired neighborhoods was checked with local real estate brokers, appraisers, lenders, and assessors familiar with the histories of the areas. Informed local judgments were followed in fixing the area boundaries, usually marked by topographic features, arterial streets, or subdivision limits. All areas chosen were away from the central city districts and built up largely with single-unit, owner-occupied houses in the middle-value range. This collection of neighborhoods, therefore, represents the residences of the home-owning middle class in the cities studied. Within this category and subject to the limitations of matching, neighborhoods were selected to give as much diversity as possible in price class and degree of nonwhite occupancy.

The data consist of prices paid for houses in test and control neighborhoods during a period beginning before the entry of nonwhites into the test area and ending in the latter part of 1955. In most of the test areas the first nonwhite buyers arrived during the early postwar years. Sources of price data were the multiple listing services in San Francisco and Oakland, information from real

[12]Housing and Home Finance Agency, Federal Housing Administration, *Underwriting Manual,* Rev. April, 1958, sec. 1320.

estate brokers, and a real estate directory in Philadelphia, generally considered a reliable source of data for real estate transactions. Approximately ten thousand sales prices were collected, representing about half of all transactions in the San Francisco-Oakland areas and total sales in the Philadelphia areas during the periods studied.

For each neighborhood the collected prices were averaged by quarter years. In some areas with a wide range of prices, ratios of selling price to assessed valuation were computed and averaged by quarters. Using these quarterly averages, the movement of house prices in the neighborhoods entered by nonwhites was compared with price movements in matching all-white neighborhoods. Some of the twenty test areas were sufficiently similar to more than one control area to permit multiple comparisons. In all, thirty-four paired comparisons were made. Analysis yielded the following principal findings:

1. In fourteen of the thirty-four comparisons (41 percent), test prices stayed within 5 percent, plus or minus, of control prices during the observation period. This is considered to mean no significant difference in price behavior.
2. In fifteen comparisons (44 percent), test prices ended relatively higher than control prices, by margins of more than 5 to 26 percent.
3. In the remaining five comparisons (15 percent), test prices ended the observation period relatively lower than control prices, by margins of 5 to 9 percent.
4. From the date of first nonwhite entry to the end of the observation period, twenty of the thirty-four comparisons showed larger percent increases each quarter for test prices than for control prices.

At the end of the observation period (fall, 1955) the proportion of nonwhite residents in the twenty test areas varied from less than 2 percent to more than 70 percent. The data were examined to determine whether the extent of nonwhite entry affected the comparative performance of test and control area prices, with results given in table 27.

As shown in the table, test areas in all ranges of nonwhite occupancy manifested both superior and inferior price performance as compared with control areas, but in every category, the majority of significant differences favored the test areas.

Distribution of test areas by percent of population nonwhite corresponds approximately to their distribution by average house value. The three neighborhoods with very limited nonwhite entry are of the exclusive type with houses considerably more expensive than any of the other areas. It is most unlikely that these neighborhoods can become all or mainly nonwhite within the foreseeable future, in contrast to the eight areas at the other end of the scale which were well on their way toward complete racial transition. It is significant, therefore, that in both classes of neighborhoods, nonwhite entry was more often associated with strengthening than with weakening house prices.

TABLE 27. PAIRED COMPARISONS OF TEST AND CONTROL AREA PRICES BY PERCENT OF NONWHITES IN TEST AREA POPULATIONS

Test areas by percent of population nonwhite, 1955	Total	Paired comparisons of price movements		
		No significant difference*	Test area higher	Control area higher
30 to 75 percent				
8 areas	16	10	5	1
14 to 28 percent				
6 areas	9	3	4	2
6 to 7 percent				
3 areas	5	. . .	4	1
3 percent or less				
3 areas	4	1	2	1

*Differences less than 5 percent.

SOURCE: Luigi Laurenti, *Property Values and Race,* Special Research Report to the Commission on Race and Housing (Berkeley and Los Angeles: University of California Press, 1960), chaps. vi, vii, and viii.

The facts of this study contradict the theory that nonwhite entry into a neighborhood must produce a fall in property values. The findings are consistent with newer theories emphasizing a diversity of price outcomes according to circumstances; however, for the areas and time periods studied, the entry of nonwhites into previously all-white neighborhoods was more often associated with price improvement or stability than with price declines.

In assessing the significance of these findings, several factors must be borne in mind. The time period—end of the war through 1955—was one of unprecedented Negro demand for housing generated by large population movements to northern and western cities, by the new economic position of Negroes, and by the increasing availability of mortgage credit. A great backlog of Negro demand had accumulated, and the persistence of exclusion barriers through most of the better housing supply served to concentrate this pent-up demand on the areas open to Negroes.

In the neighborhoods studied, the behavior of white residents seemed to be quite different from the traditional response of whites to nonwhite entry. Although some of the areas showed considerable disturbance, there was almost complete absence of the panic flight of whites which in the past has characterized many zones of racial transition. In many of the neighborhoods, the white residents were anxious to sell but waited until they could get adequate prices from incoming buyers. Under the existing conditions, the nonwhite market offered sufficient demand to move the properties without price weakening—

in fact, at prices generally somewhat higher than prevailed in comparable areas not affected by racial change.

These considerations may account for the maintenance of an orderly market and stable or rising prices in those areas heavily entered by nonwhites and evidently destined for complete racial transition. They do not explain the favorable price movements in the neighborhoods with low nonwhite proportions, for these depended upon continuing demand from whites. The conclusion must be that in these relatively expensive and desirable neighborhoods, a sparse scatter of nonwhites, almost imperceptible to most residents or prospective residents, did not noticeably affect the attractiveness of the areas in the white market.

HOUSING DEMAND IN RACIALLY MIXED AREAS

The second study to be considered goes behind the facts of price movements to analyze the components of demand for housing in areas undergoing racial transition. This study analyzed all house sales recorded during 1955 in four areas of Philadelphia. Two of the areas contained relatively good housing, and in two the housing was mainly poor. Each quality pair further consisted of one area undergoing rapid racial transition and one where the Negro population was growing slowly. In all four areas, Negroes occupied 20 to 30 percent of the dwelling units.

A racial transition zone is commonly pictured as one where whites are leaving and nonwhites coming in. The Philadelphia study found the process to be considerably more complex. Among some two thousand home buyers, 443 or more than one-fifth were whites. Although outnumbered more than three to one by Negroes, the presence of white buyers in substantial numbers is, nevertheless, a significant fact from several points of view. It refutes the notion that whites will not buy in an area once entered by Negroes, and calls for inquiry into the conditions under which whites will continue to buy in such areas. As discussed previously (chap. iv), whether any area can maintain a racially mixed composition depends, of course, on its ability to attract new white residents.

Investigation of the trend of house prices in one area (good housing, rapid transition) revealed a substantial price advance from 1948 through 1955, of approximately the same magnitude as occurred in the city as a whole. The rise appeared most pronounced in the sections of heavy Negro entry and rapid departure of whites. This is further evidence that racial change is not necessarily associated with depressed prices.

Mortgage lenders often take a dubious view of racially mixed areas, but this was not true in Philadelphia. Financing was liberal and played a key role in sustaining demand and prices. Ninety percent of the white buyers and practically all the Negroes depended on mortgage financing to acquire their homes. The loans came almost entirely from established institutional sources. Negroes obtained mortgage terms more liberal than those advanced to whites. A third of the Negro buyers borrowed the entire purchase price and another third received 90 percent or more financing. Only 43 percent of the whites received 90 percent loans or better. Negro borrowers also received more favorable interest rates. Four-fifths of them paid less than 5½ percent, as compared with three-quarters of the whites. The superior terms obtained by Negroes are explained by the higher percentage of VA and FHA loans made to this group. In addition to interest, "points" were generally charged, especially on VA loans, the typical charge being 5 percent. Point charges were usually paid by the seller but, in the judgment of informed observers, passed on to the buyer in the form of higher prices permitted by liberal VA appraisals. The role of easy financing in supporting the price rise is thus doubly apparent. Down payments of 10 percent to zero enabled large numbers of Negroes to buy who could not have met the down payment requirements of conventional loans.

The liberal policies of Philadelphia lending institutions toward these mixed-occupancy areas are a departure from the general practice of mortgage lenders. It should be noted that the loans were both safe and profitable. Nearly all were government insured or guaranteed. The willingness of sellers to pay point charges permitted lenders to combine the safety of guaranteed loans with the higher interest rates associated with conventional mortgage loans. Lenders were also influenced, undoubtedly, by the abundance of mortgage funds available in 1955. Whether they would take the same view of transition-area risks in a period of credit stringency is problematic.

Negro and white buyers paid virtually identical average prices for the homes they acquired except in the one area of poor housing and rapid transition, where Negroes paid substantially more than whites, on the average, and presumably acquired better dwellings. Negroes and whites received about the same value for their housing dollar, paying substantially the same prices for similar houses.

Analysis of the spatial distribution of Negro and white purchases reveals a marked tendency toward racial separation. Among the study areas, the ratio of Negro to white buyers was three to one in the area of good housing and rapid change, but twenty-seven to one in the area characterized by poor housing and fast change. In a third area, where the housing is good but change slow, Negroes were outnumbered by white buyers two to one.

Within the areas some blocks have become wholly Negro occupied, others are mixed, still others have not yet received a Negro resident. In the two areas accounting for the great majority of white purchases, about a third of the blocks were white, but they were the location of the large majority of all purchases by white families.

To measure more strictly the spatial relationship of Negro and white purchases, two calculations were made including the proportion of white purchases made in a mixed block or adjacent to a mixed block,[13] and the

[13]The unit of measurement consisted of five contiguous blocks in the shape of a cross in which the house acquired by the white purchaser was in the central block. If any of the five blocks was mixed in occupancy, the whole unit was classified as mixed.

percent of white families who purchased homes on the same street front or directly across the street from Negro residents. The second measure, obviously, is a more critical test of residential proximity, since residents in the same street between intersections are likely to encounter each other frequently in the course of ordinary comings and goings. In the study areas, moreover, the predominant row-type single-family houses are highly homogeneous on any given street, allowing no symbolism of status differences among the residents.

The two measures yielded a striking result. Nearly three-fourths of the white purchases were found in a mixed block or adjacent to a mixed block, that is, within a maximum of three linear blocks from a Negro resident. But only 27 percent of the white buyers acquired homes on the same street front or facing a street front on which Negro families lived, whereas the remainder purchased on all-white street fronts and facing street fronts. Thus, it seems that the closer the proximity of Negroes, the smaller will be the proportion of white purchasers in any mixed area. This result was, of course, not unexpected. However, the significant finding may not lie in the sharp drop-off in proportion of white purchasers, but in the fact that 119 white families chose to buy homes on mixed streets. The other white families, moreover, by purchasing in an area of transition, exposed themselves to the likelihood of having near Negro neighbors in the not distant future.

White families who choose to buy homes in the same areas with nonwhites, because they go against a behavior norm, may be thought to have some unusual characteristics or motivations which account for their actions. The present study searched for such characteristics but was unable to find any which significantly differentiated the group from the white home-buying population at large. In many ways the white purchasers resembled the resident white population in the areas into which they bought.[14]

As in the general home-buying population, a large proportion of these purchasers were young families. Two-thirds of the family heads were less than forty-five years old. Three-fourths had children less than eighteen and half had children of school age—percentages somewhat higher than among all home purchasers in Philadelphia during 1955 and 1956.[15] About half of the purchasers had attended high school; their educational attainment was similar to that of the resident population of the study areas in 1950. Occupationally, the purchaser family heads showed no unusual concentration in professional or other groups which might be associated with special views on race. Their family incomes, from available scanty evidence, were somewhat lower than those of all recent Philadelphia home purchasers, but averaged about the same as white family incomes in the city as a whole. Two-thirds of the purchaser

[14]Data for this phase of the study were obtained by interviews with 194 white families who purchased homes during 1955 in mixed blocks or adjacent to a mixed block, 100 white renter families in mixed blocks, and 196 Negro home purchasers in the study areas.
[15]U. S. Bureau of the Census, *1956 National Housing Inventory,* Philadelphia Supplement (unpublished).

families were Catholic, a proportion somewhat higher than in the Philadelphia white population but similar to the composition of the study areas.

The Negro purchaser group was quite similar to the white buyers, only somewhat younger, with fewer children, slightly lower family incomes, and a smaller representation in the white-collar and skilled-craftsman occupations.

The white purchasers did not have unique or impelling motives for buying in the mixed areas. Most, in interview, gave commonplace reasons for their choice, mentioning such factors as convenience to work, school, friends and relatives, suitability of the house, or simply, "I'm accustomed to the neighborhood and I like to live here." Familiarity with the neighborhood and attachment to it evidently played an important role in the housing choices of these purchasers, for more than 60 percent of them had lived in the area before buying their homes.

As to racial attitudes, the fact that this group of home purchasers decided to buy in mixed areas implies that they were at least comparatively receptive to the presence of Negroes. However, in interviews, they did not express attitudes of unusual tolerance. If any were motivated by a desire to give a personal example of racial democracy, they were few in number. More than a third of those interviewed expressed varying degrees of dissatisfaction with the presence of Negroes, but strongly negative sentiments were rare. Attitudes of acceptance or rejection were markedly correlated with the degree of hypothetical proximity. Sixty percent of the respondents expressed approval or indifference to the residence of Negroes in the neighborhood; 40 percent to residence on the same block; and 31 percent to residence in an adjacent house. Only 4 percent of the respondents voiced strong disapproval of Negro residence in the neighborhood, but 31 percent were strongly negative toward having Negro neighbors next door.

The racial attitudes expressed by these white home purchasers are fairly consistent with their observed behavior in choosing locations. All of them bought in a general area of mixed occupancy. But as the proximity of Negroes increased, in passing from area to zone to block to street, the proportion of white purchasers contracted.

CONCLUSIONS

During the time period covered by the present studies, surging Negro demand, supported by growing availability of mortgage credit and concentrated at certain points, was sufficient to maintain and to strengthen house prices in many areas of racial transition. Market stability was helped by the apparently changing attitudes of white property owners which led them generally to refrain from flooding the market with houses on the appearance of Negroes. To an appreciable extent, whites continued to buy into some racially mixed areas, and this too, of course, helped to keep prices up.

In the future, it is certain that Negroes and other minorities will continue to enter many neighborhoods that are now all-white. But some of the conditions which in the recent past generated strong Negro demand for housing in transitional areas are disappearing. Consequently, predictions from recent experience for the future must be heavily qualified. The pent-up housing demand of Negroes which accumulated during the war and early postwar years has by now been satisfied in large part. The increasing market freedom which minorities are gaining, together with the growing social differentiation of the groups, means undoubtedly that their housing demand will be more dispersed and more varied in the future than in the past. Nonwhites are apt to enter more areas than the nonwhite population can fill, and for some areas complete racial transition will be impossible. As noted, this is already true in some higher-priced neighborhoods. Hence there is likely to be an increasing number of neighborhoods where the maintenance of a sufficient market for houses will require white as well as nonwhite buyers in adequate numbers.

The Philadelphia study found white buyers in numbers which may be thought impressive yet were not sufficient to maintain for long the mixed-occupancy pattern. Where four-fifths of the purchasers in a particular area are nonwhite and only one-fifth white, the outcome is plain. The one area where only a third of the purchasers were Negro does have the prospect of a stable interracial balance, if the present ratio is maintained.

The Philadelphia white buyers did not come from any special group in the population nor were they characterized by unusually favorable attitudes toward Negroes. Their motivations for purchase were those of home buyers generally. Similar findings concerning white purchasers in new interracial housing developments are reported in chapter xii. This absence of distinctive traits coupled with the acknowledged general lessening of racial prejudice in the white population during the past twenty years suggests the existence of considerable potential demand by white families for housing in racially mixed areas.

At present, most mixed neighborhoods compare unfavorably with all-white areas in quality of housing, community facilities, or social conditions. But as minority groups gain more freedom in the housing market, an increasing number of good-quality residence areas will be brought into the mixed category. Urban renewal programs may continue to rehabilitate some of the existing deteriorated mixed areas.

The critical racial factors limiting the number of both prejudiced and unprejudiced white buyers who will purchase in mixed areas are the actual or expected number and proportion of non-whites in the mixed community, and the spatial distribution of nonwhite residences in relation to the homes which white buyers contemplate acquiring. The two factors are related; however, the Philadelphia data show white purchasers to be more accepting of Negroes a short distance away than in the immediate vicinity. An increasing proportion of Negroes in a mixed area is reflected in a shrinkage of white demand, but the behavior of white buyers seems to be related more to the anticipated than to the actual proportion of Negroes.

The level of white demand and consequently the prospects for achieving *both* a stable racial mixture and stable or rising prices in an area depend primarily, therefore, on the expectations of white buyers. In the past, it has been the most common expectation that a neighborhood once entered by nonwhites would become wholly occupied by them, and in most cases events have justified this anticipation. The present outlook, however, is for an increasing number of neighborhoods where this expectation cannot be fulfilled. What this implies for demand and prices in those areas is problematic. If white demand for housing in a given area shrinks in anticipation of racial transition, but Negro buyers do not appear in the expected numbers, the prices of residences may well decline. But present trends may lead to a revision of expectations of white buyers, and to the extent that this occurs, race will tend to lose its importance in the housing market.

From Tenement to Split Level
Raymond Vernon

*   *   *

THE CHANGING NEIGHBORHOODS

Few neighborhoods of the New York Metropolitan Region have remained stable in population for very long. In periods as brief as a decade or two, some have experienced explosive increases in population, some significant declines. Numerous forces have contributed to these population changes. Typically, increases have gone hand in hand with building booms; but they also have occurred through widespread "conversions" of old structures, through the doubling-up of families and the opening of rooming houses. Neighborhood declines have sometimes come about through the wholesale wrecking of old structures or the encroachment of business uses; but more commonly the population has simply "thinned out" in the existing structures, leaving smaller family groups in the same old dwelling units.

*   *   *

The fact that populations could decline in some neighborhoods of old cities is hardly news. Manhattan's East Side had begun to register declines by 1910,

SOURCE: Raymond Vernon, from *Metropolis 1985* (Cambridge: Harvard University Press, 1960), pp. 135–165. Copyright 1960 by Regional Plan Association, Inc. Reprinted by permission of the publisher, Harvard University Press.

and the island as a whole had begun decreasing in population by 1920. In one decade or another after 1920, Jersey City, Newark, and Paterson also registered net population declines. But the extensiveness of the declines occurring in some neighborhoods of these old city areas was obscured by the fact that growth was taking place in other neighborhoods at the same time; the city totals, therefore, often showed a bland stability, compounded from growth in some areas and decline in others.

By 1957, however, population declines had become endemic to large portions of the old cities, areas so large as to dominate the city totals. For the four principal boroughs of New York City, the pervasiveness of the decline can be seen in Chart 14. All Statistical Districts in Manhattan, almost all of them in Brooklyn, most of the Bronx, and portions of Queens show a drop in population.

So much for first impressions. What lay behind these changes in population totals? Considerable light is shed on the shifts by getting down into the neighborhoods of the Region and observing the various phases through which they have passed. This kind of analysis involves a lot of risks, of course, mostly risks of oversimplification and over-easy generalization. No two neighborhoods are exactly alike; no two mature and decay in quite the same way. Still, we are not altogether foreclosed from generalization: there are common stages in the evolution of many neighborhoods, stages whose existence seems to explain what we see in the population trends.

Stage 1 in the evolution is the transformation from undeveloped rural land to residential neighborhood. Thirty or forty years ago, during the building boom of the 1920's, that change was taking place in a great arc not very far from Manhattan and in lesser arcs on the outer edges of Newark and the other old cities of the Region. In portions of Essex and Bergen Counties, and in wide areas of the Bronx, Queens, southern Westchester, and western Nassau, one can still recognize the neighborhoods created in that period. The housing there was responsive to the wants of that era—high-rise apartments crowding small sites near mass transit facilities; two-family houses shoulder to shoulder on shaded streets, sometimes with their single-car garages, sometimes without; more elaborate suburban dwellings in a few neighborhoods, on sites spacious by the standards of the 1920's but undersized by those of persons with analogous income status today.

Depression and war slowed down the growth of new neighborhoods for fifteen years or so after 1929. When building was resumed in the late 1940's, the arc of swiftest growth had shifted farther outward from the old city centers. Now one could see the new neighborhoods springing up just beyond the earlier ring. Bergen and Essex Counties still were growing swiftly, but they were growing at points farther from the Core and on a style different from that of the 1920's—with more spacious use of the land and with much less regard for the location of suburban railroad lines, trolleys, and buses. The Bronx and Queens still had their growing edges, but the swiftest changes were to be found farther out, in middle Westchester, middle and eastern Nassau, and Rockland.

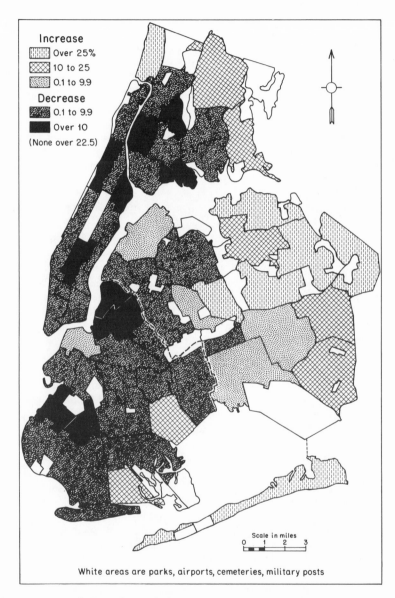

**Chart 14.   Population Change in Four Boroughs of New York City, by Statistical
Districts, 1950–1957**

By the late 1950's the arc of swiftest growth had moved still farther outward touching Monmouth, Middlesex, Somerset, and Morris Counties, swinging through undeveloped parts of Rockland and northern Westchester Counties, and biting a big portion out of Suffolk County on Long Island.

In the last few years, the pattern of development characterizing Stage 1 has changed further. Stage 1 is now almost exclusively a stage of single-family construction. In fact, in the counties of the Region now passing through that stage, such as Suffolk and Monmouth, over 95 per cent of the new dwelling units are in single-family houses. What is more, development now is more diffused; colonies of homes have been rising in cow pastures and potato fields, with considerable open space between colonies. Inside the colonies, too, land is being used with a more profligate hand. In Passaic County, for instance, though the average lot in new subdivisions had been only a little more than one-quarter of an acre in 1950, it rose to nearly half an acre by 1957. In Westchester County, roughly the same sort of increase took place during the same period.

Some neighborhoods, after arriving at Stage 1, have settled back to a long period of quiescence. Others, however, have not allowed many years to pass before beginning to show signs of Stage 2. In this phase, another rash of building takes place—only this time apartment houses dominate more than before. In the 1950's, this pattern was appearing very strongly on the outermost edges of some of the Core counties, in a few sizable Inner Ring cities (Elizabeth and Paterson), and in some commuter settlements with exceptionally good access to New York City, such as the commuter stops on the Hudson Division of the New York Central and on the Long Island Railroad.

The increased emphasis on apartment houses during this second stage is not hard to understand. The cost of land sites acquired in the course of Stage 2 is usually much too high for single-family development. Some of the sites acquired in Stage 2 are patches of open space, by-passed in the first building wave because of the pitch of the land or because of rocky outcroppings, or simply because they were not for sale at a reasonable price. Other sites are developed in Stage 2 by buying up and demolishing the oldest single-family structures in the neighborhood. In any of these circumstances, the cost of acquiring and preparing the site for building has been high.

Some years after the completion of Stage 2, the neighborhood is sometimes ripe for Stage 3—for down-grading and conversion. At this juncture, there is little new construction but there is population and density growth through the crowding of the existing structures. In some neighborhoods, Stage 3 may never happen or may be delayed so long that its theoretical possibility does not matter. The stretch of Fifth Avenue facing Central Park, for instance, went through Stage 2 some fifty years ago, but still clings to its high-income character. The Riverdale area in the northwest corner of the Bronx, more recently converted to apartment structures, promises to hold its quality for some time to come.

But much of Manhattan's upper West Side, sections of the middle Bronx and Brooklyn, and neighborhoods in New Jersey's older cities have lately seen the shift. It is in Stage 3 that the old structures in the aging neighborhoods begin to be offered to the newest inmigrants in the Region—today to Puerto Ricans and Negroes, yesterday to the Italians and Jews, before that to the Germans and Irish. Ignorant of the housing market, strapped by lack of income, anxious to be part of a large labor pool, these groups take what they can get in the crowded central areas of the Region; and what they can get is usually the structures just giving up the ghost as middle-income habitation. For the most part, the newcomers are young—at the time of life at which they are building a family. Shortly after settling into their new quarters, therefore, they are likely to add further to the population of the newly "invaded" neighborhoods.

After the in-migrant couples have settled down, however, the pattern is ready for change again. Now we come to Stage 4, the "thinning-out" stage characteristic of slum areas a few decades after they have been turned over to slum use. This is the stage at which, today, we find large areas of Manhattan, including Harlem and the lower West Side, and considerable portions of the Bronx and Brooklyn, as well as the inner sections of Jersey City, Newark, and Paterson.

There is a temptation to suppose that this thinning-out process comes about because families enveloped by these unsavory surroundings flee the slum areas as soon as they can, leaving unfilled vacancies or boarded-up structures in their wake. Without doubt, this sometimes occurs. But more of the population decline is accounted for by another process. Families in the run-down neighborhoods of the Region move infrequently, less often than those in the newer neighborhoods. The 1950 Census showed, for instance, that only about 8 per cent of the population of the Bronx, Brooklyn, and Hudson County had moved in a prior twelve-month period, whereas the proportion in counties like Richmond, Passaic, and Fairfield was between 13 and 16 per cent. Once settled, the heads of families tend to stay put; it is their children and their boarders who move out, for the most part, leaving their elders behind to enjoy more space in their deteriorating structures. So it is that some neighborhoods in the lower East Side today are heavily dominated by aging immigrants, remnants of the wave of Jewish migration of the early twentieth century and of the early Puerto Rican wave of the 1920's.

We come at last to Stage 5, the renewal stage. This stage is no more inevitable than the ones that preceded. Where Stage 5 occurs, it usually takes two contrasting forms.

One of these is luxury apartments, either built on the sites of decayed tenements painstakingly assembled by private developers, or created by the expensive remodeling of old brownstones and other structures of felicitous design. So far, this kind of renewal has been confined to only a few areas in the Region. The East Side in Manhattan is laced through with renewals of this sort. Greenwich Village has begun to show a good deal of such activity. And here and there, in cities of the Inner Ring, one sees a high-priced apartment structure that could be said to represent the private recapture of slum-blighted sites.

The other type of neighborhood renewal is much more dependent upon the action of public authorities and the availability of public funds. Sometimes there are subsidies to private developers, aimed at bringing down the site costs or reducing the cost of borrowed money to levels at which medium-priced rentals can be charged; and sometimes there are continuing operating subsidies to bring rentals within reach of low-income families.

In New York City itself, renewal projects of heroic proportions have been developed during the past twenty years, involving public funds in various ways. The programs have affected a considerable number of people; over 85,000 dwelling units were built between 1946 and 1957, and nearly 500,000 people are housed in these structures. Yet, all told, the effects of these programs on land use in the City have been astonishingly small. The land area these projects occupy is not much over two square miles. In Manhattan, Brooklyn, and the Bronx, where renewal has made the greatest progress, only 1.4 per cent of the total land area has been involved. Even when we add private building to public renewal, we find that in these three boroughs, in the twelve years from 1946 to 1957 inclusive, only a fraction of 1 per cent of the dwellings were replaced per year.

THE UNDERLYING FORCES

The ferment of the Region's neighborhoods has produced a distribution of the Region's populations clearly responsive to a few basic demands. One way to detect these demands is to trace the residential patterns of groups of breadwinners at different levels of the income ladder.

Consider those at the top. Such people are drawn, to a disproportionate extent, from managerial and professional occupations. Therefore, if access to the job were the only consideration in selecting a residence, this group would be expected to have a considerable affinity for the center of the Region—mostly for Manhattan and secondarily for Newark. At the same time, however, the income level of this group gives its members considerable freedom to choose a home wherever their desires lead. If they prefer a short trip to the office and spur-of-the-moment access to the bright lights and cultural diversions of Manhattan, the high cost of tolerable living quarters in Manhattan need not act as a bar. Contrariwise, if they prefer spacious country living, even though it involves two or three cars for the family and an expensive commuting bill, they are in a position to pay the price.

In point of fact, this group has exercised its freedom of choice by selecting every combination of access and spaciousness. Some have settled in a fifty-block stretch of Manhattan's East Side where a three-and-a-half room "cooperative" apartment can be had with an initial payment of $15,000 or so, and something like $175 monthly as maintenance charges. Others have preferred a little less access and a little less congestion, choosing equally costly housing in attractive and convenient areas like Riverdale and Brooklyn Heights. Still others have clung to old, relatively exclusive inner-suburban communities that grew up around rail commuter stations in the days when only the well-to-do commuted from such distances at all: Westchester communities like White Plains, Scarsdale, Bronxville, and Pelham Manor, and New Jersey suburbs like Short Hills.

But these communities, though they have managed to retain some of their pristine exclusiveness by restrictive zoning, still have not satisfied the wants of some of the higher-income group for spaciousness and semi-isolated luxury. So another segment with jobs in Manhattan and Newark has accepted the long and expensive daily trip from remote places like Pound Ridge, New York; Wilton, Connecticut; and Red Bank, New Jersey. As a result of this variety of choices, we find professional workers making up a disproportionately large part of the population of Rockland, Morris, Nassau, and Westchester Counties, as well as of Manhattan; and the managerial group shows up strongly in Nassau and Westchester. (Notice the omission of such counties as Bronx, Brooklyn, Queens, and Essex; we shall return to them later.)

Wherever they have settled in suburban areas, the upper-income groups have bought comparative spaciousness—that is to say, they have tended to select communities where living densities were low, as compared with other communities having a similar degree of access to Manhattan. This tendency can be seen in Table 17, which presents some figures based upon a survey of 200-odd communities in the Region as of the mid-1950's; the communities are located in a belt made up of five whole counties and parts of two others, a belt predominantly suburban in character and predominantly in the Inner Ring. In this table, the municipalities are classified by family income and also by access zones according to the length of commuting time to midtown Manhattan; access zone 1 is closest, access zone 2 is fifteen minutes beyond, and so on. Here, we see that in any given access zone the communities whose families had the highest median incomes were also communities with comparatively low residential densities. Other things equal (such as access), it is evident that people in the New York Metropolitan Region who can afford it will use their income to buy spacious living.

As we descend the income scale, the pattern changes. One major reason for the change is that building costs, coupled with zoning regulations and building codes, rule out the choice of new construction for a substantial portion of the Region's population.

A major group, therefore, is limited in its choice of housing to the existing stock or to subsidized housing, wherever the housing may be. Just how each segment among the users of second-hand dwellings has made its choice is described in one of the underlying reports in this series. Here, it will be enough to look at two or three segments of particular interest.

One is the group defined by the Census as clerical workers. In terms of income, these workers rank below the professionals and the managers but well above the laborers and service workers. As we saw in earlier chapters, the main job market of the clerical workers is Manhattan, with a lesser concentration in Newark. The principal concentrations of their homes are in the boroughs just outside Manhattan—in Brooklyn, the Bronx, Queens, Richmond, and Hudson County. These, therefore, make up a considerable proportion of the subway riders who daily fill the trains into Manhattan's central business district. Given their inability to command precious high-priced space in the lower half of Manhattan and their unwillingness to occupy slum space in that area, their compromise between access and spaciousness is found in the "bedroomy" boroughs just beyond Manhattan, lending a solid middle-class stamp to these areas.

TABLE 17.   DWELLING UNITS PER ACRE OF RESIDENTIALLY DEVELOPED LAND[a] IN SELECTED MUNICIPALITIES CLASSIFIED BY MEDIAN INCOME AND BY ACCESS TO MANHATTAN

Ranking of municipality based on median income per family[b]	Access Zone				
	1	2	3	4	5
Top fifth	—	3.82	3.86	3.26	—
2nd fifth	—	5.69	5.29	4.05	3.21
3rd fifth	—	8.90	6.22	6.52	3.28
4th fifth	7.80	9.61	8.48	5.39	4.31
Bottom fifth	27.79	7.86	9.29	2.23	3.83

[a] In 1954–55.
[b] In 1949.

SOURCE: Edgar M. Hoover and Raymond Vernon, *Anatomy of a Metropolis* (Cambridge: Harvard University Press, 1959), p. 170. Income data were from U. S. *Census of Population.*

Further down on the income ladder, we come to the least affluent of the Region's inhabitants, most of them confined to the oldest and most obsolescent structures of the Region (and, of course, to the low-cost public housing units). For many of these people, it is not income alone that confines them to the oldest housing of the Region, but also color or ethnic origin. Negroes and Puerto Ricans—but especially Negroes—still encounter difficulty in breaking out of the oldest neighborhoods. This problem is becoming less acute in the Region, but it is still one of considerable importance in shaping residential patterns.

The lowest income groups in the Region, therefore, are largely confined to Manhattan and Hudson County, to large portions of Brooklyn and the Bronx, to parts of Queens, and to the more central districts of cities like Newark, Paterson, Passaic, Elizabeth, and Bridgeport—districts which were fully built up long ago. Some low-income families, too, are found in small dilapidated enclaves in well-to-do suburban neighborhoods; still others are found in shanty towns in the Ramapo Mountains and other "rural slums" scattered through the Region's outer reaches; but these groups outside of the old cities are not important numerically.

For the bulk of the lowest income groups, the run-down housing in the Region's oldest areas provides reasonably good access to the major job markets. For their livelihood, these groups rely heavily on unskilled service and factory jobs and goods-handling jobs. Various sources help us to pinpoint the counties where these types of jobs are most commonly found. As best we can tell, the jobs of "laborers" are found in greatest number in the Region's heavy industrial belts: one on the New Jersey side of the Hudson River from the Amboys up to Weehawken; another on the New York side from Hunts Point and Long Island City down to Brooklyn's Red Hook. The jobs of "service workers"—a mixture of occupations, including such callings as barbers, domestics, watchmen, and elevator operators—are strongly concentrated in Manhattan. But the importance of domestic help in high-income counties of the Inner and Outer Rings, such as Westchester and Suffolk, gives "service workers" some importance in the mix of occupations in those areas.

Though the job market and the residential areas of the lowest income groups coincide reasonably well, they are a little out of kilter in one respect. On the whole, the residences are more tightly confined to the center of the Region than the jobs. These groups, therefore, account for a considerable part of the "reverse commuting" that goes on every day in the Region—commuting outward from the center each morning, rather than the other way around. As a matter of fact, some streams of "reverse commuting" represent the fastest-growing elements in the changing commuting pattern. Groups of Negro and Puerto Rican men, traveling by car pool from Harlem and the Bronx to the New Jersey industrial belt each morning, have swelled the daily outbound flow over the George Washington Bridge. Groups of Negro women, traveling daily from upper Manhattan and the Bronx to Westchester communities, also contribute heavily to the reverse flow. This is a factor to be reckoned with in projecting the future distribution of population in the Region.

When the whole picture of residential location in the Region is totted up, it confirms some very old saws. As Chart 15 shows, Manhattan proves indeed to be a borough of the very poor and the very rich. In the Core counties surrounding Manhattan, though pockets of low-rent housing are important and growing more so, the general pattern is of a heavy commitment to the middle-income groups. Beyond these counties, in the Inner Ring, the high-income professionals and managers place their dominant stamp on the income distribution. And in the remote counties of the Outer Ring, the net impact of wealthy exurbanities, middle-income craftsmen and factory workers, and low-income domestics is to produce an income distribution little different from that of the Region as a whole.

Apart from job access and income, however, there is another characteristic

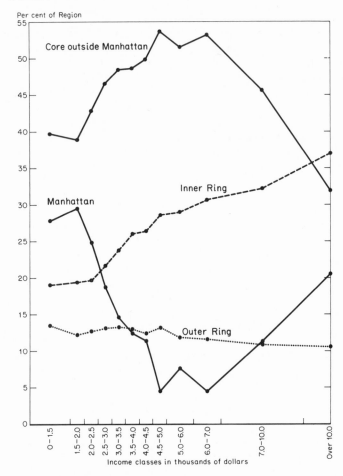

Chart 15.   Geographic Distribution of Income Recipients by Income Classes, New York Metropolitan Region, 1949

NOTE: "Income recipients" means families and unrelated individuals reporting income.

SOURCE: U. S. *1950 Census of Population.*

that accounts for the Region's population distribution; this is the prevalence of children in the family. The higher the proportion of children in the household, the stronger is the incentive for a family to seek lower-density single-family housing with agreeable neighborhood conditions and good schools. This drive seems to permeate every income level and every racial group in the Region. All appear to have an eye to the advantages of an

environment which will boost the children's chances, educationally and socially. But each family has to satisfy that drive within the limitations imposed
by its income level and by its general preference for living among people of
its own kind.

The results of these preferences are seen in Table 18, which presents an
analysis based on the 200-odd Inner Ring communities previously covered in
Table 17. Though the table looks complicated on first glance, it makes a
number of simple points. In each of the five income classes shown, the communities with a low proportion of children tend to be those in which there is
good access to Manhattan but high living densities; and where the proportion
of children is high, the access-density position is reversed. What is more, the
communities with a low proportion of children are those with more mul-
tifamily dwellings and with little building activity.

This preference of all income groups to find less congested living whenever
children are involved, at least to the extent that their means allow, is seen in
the distribution of age groups in different parts of the Region. Though 22 per
cent of the Region's population was under 15 years in 1950, the comparable
ratio in Manhattan was only 16.7 per cent. In the other Core counties it was
22.1 per cent; in the Inner Ring, 23.7 per cent; and in the Outer Ring, 23.4
per cent.

There is a method, therefore, in the evolving patterns of the Region's
neighborhoods—a method which reflects the choice between job access and
spacious living for each income level and which mirrors the preference of each
for more spaciousness as children appear on the scene. But the location of jobs
has been changing, and so have the modes of travel to and from jobs. Income
levels also have been changing, and so have the age make-up and family
composition of the Region. All these changes must be taken into account when
one projects the Region's future.

THE FORCES IN MOTION

The largest single force leading to the redistribution of the Region's populations is the changing location of the Region's jobs. As we have seen, jobs are
not located in the Region altogether independently of where the work force
lives. Some manufacturing plants are obliged to settle close to low-income
neighborhoods in order to recruit workers at rock-bottom wages. Large research laboratories are prepared to indulge the suburban preferences of their
scientific work force by locating outside the central areas of the Region. And
of course the location of most jobs in the retail trades and many in commercial
banking faithfully reacts to shifts in the Region's population. Nonetheless,
most jobs in manufacturing and wholesaling, and jobs in some lines of office
work, can shift and have shifted their location from one part of the Region to
another without much need to consider how the population itself was shifting.

Given the importance of job access and given the relative independence of

**TABLE 18. CHARACTERISTICS OF SELECTED MUNICIPALITIES IN THE REGION, AC-
CORDING TO INCOME AND PROPORTION OF CHILDREN** [a]

Ranking of municipality based on median income per family, 1949	Dwelling units per acre of residentially developed land, 1954–55	Per cent of dwelling units in multifamily structures, 1950	Average access rating [b]	Per cent increase in dwelling units 1950–1954
MUNICIPALITIES WITH LOW PROPORTION OF POPULATION UNDER 15 (LESS THAN 22.5%)				
Total	11.9	32%	2.12	6.2%
Top fifth	6.8	40	2.25	11.5
2nd fifth	5.6	19	2.00	10.4
3rd fifth	10.6	33	2.25	4.9
4th fifth	8.8	30	2.22	6.6
Bottom fifth	16.0	39	2.00	5.7
MUNICIPALITIES WITH MEDIUM PROPORTION OF POPULATION UNDER 15 (22.5 TO 24.5%)				
Total	7.8	18%	3.03	11.8%
Top fifth	3.4	11	3.33	17.3
2nd fifth	4.4	18	3.40	18.5
3rd fifth	8.0	18	2.70	14.7
4th fifth	7.8	23	3.09	11.2
Bottom fifth	16.2	26	2.83	6.8
MUNICIPALITIES WITH HIGH PROPORTION OF POPULATION UNDER 15 (OVER 24.5%)				
Total	4.6	12%	3.19	19.0%
Top fifth	3.5	10	2.94	21.9
2nd fifth	5.1	12	3.24	18.4
3rd fifth	5.2	6	3.09	21.8
4th fifth	8.7	16	3.40	5.0
Bottom fifth	4.1	21	3.80	23.5

[a] Age data from U. S. *1950 Census of Population.*
[b] Average of access zone numbers as in Table 17.

SOURCE: Edgar M. Hoover and Raymond Vernon, *Anatomy of a Metropolis* (Cambridge:
Harvard University Press, 1959), p. 180.

so many establishments in locating their plants in the Region, the residences
can be expected to follow the jobs more than the other way around. It is not
enough, however, to speak of all jobs as if they were a homogeneous mass.
Office jobs, we observed—elite office jobs in particular—were holding up in the
central business district of Manhattan better than other types. Even though
Manhattan's growth in office jobs was comparatively slow, it *was* growth, not
decline. And since this absolute growth is likely to continue, the need of

high-income people for access to the central business district will almost certainly increase.

This possibility has to be considered alongside another. Spacious suburban living—living which combines exclusiveness with at least tolerable access—will be more and more difficult to attain as the years go by. The upper income groups, fleeing from contact with the outward spread of the speculator's subdivision, are already having to settle in areas which strain the limits of the commuter's endurance. Unless there is a greatly accelerated growth in the use of helicopters, the upper income groups may be forced to resort rather more to luxury apartment living in the City. The numbers involved cannot be large, of course; the price of space for luxury apartments is too high for more than a tiny minority of those who work in the central business district. But their total demand could make a measurable impact on the use of land in and close by the central business district.

Changes in the distribution of jobs inside the New York Metropolitan Region in the decades just ahead are also likely to affect the residential preferences of the lowest income groups, to the extent that they can exercise any choice in the matter. The lowest-income jobs are concentrated in manufacturing, wholesaling, and personal services. Manufacturing and wholesaling activities are showing declines in employment in Manhattan and are evidencing only slight growing power in the Core counties. The service jobs may still grow a little in the central business district of Manhattan, but the prospect in the areas just beyond that district is one of decline—until one reaches the newer suburbs of the Inner Ring and beyond, where rapid growth is likely. Accordingly, on balance, the need for job access is likely to pull the low income groups outward from New York City toward the Inner Ring.

This likelihood is enhanced by various factors. One is that the Puerto Rican, by any yardstick that can be found, seems to be following the same patterns of adjustment as those of other immigrant groups before him. Allowing for the fact that no two such groups have experienced exactly the same adjustment process, the Puerto Rican's adjustment seems very much like those of groups with somewhat similar cultures in the past—a little like the pattern of the Southern Italian, for instance. In general, field studies show that his job skills have increased, his job opportunities have expanded, and his aspirations or those of his children have risen. The trek of the German from the East Side to Yorkville and Brooklyn, and of the Jew from Rivington Street to the Bronx and White Plains, promises to be repeated once again by the Puerto Rican.

The position of the Negro, too, is showing signs of change, though at another pace. The social and contractual bars which have excluded the Negro from suburban neighborhoods in the Region, even when he was in a position to pay for space in those neighborhoods, seem to be weakening a little. It is hard to demonstrate this sort of conclusion by objective means. But there are various straws in the wind. The recent rate of increase in the Negro populations of Inner Ring cities has been phenomenal. In Newark, the "nonwhite" population rose 109 per cent between 1950 and 1958. In Mount Vernon, New

Rochelle, East Orange, Montclair, and Englewood, the rise appears to have taken place at about the same rate. And all this at a time when populations in Harlem have been declining. True, most of these increases were simply due to the development of new black ghettoes in suburban areas, but some represented the diffusion of the Negro's living patterns.

The Negro's desire for less congested living is a force which will continue to push him outward from the Region's center. An analysis of contemporary Negro periodicals suggests that there has been a rapid adoption by the Negro of all the status symbols and aspirations of the whites, including the aspiration for spacious living. A study of some 82 Negro families which had moved from a privately owned housing project in Harlem between 1952 and 1956 pointed in the same direction. Questioned about their move, 72 named "desire to own a home'" as one of their reasons for moving, just as any white group would do. The same study suggests the extent to which Negroes now get help in finding new quarters. Among this group, 35 were led to their new quarters by real estate agents and 33 by friends already in the area. The fact that so many could arrange to buy a house means, of course, that they were not among the lowest income groups in the Region. But their willingness to leave the Negro ghetto and their ability to find homes outside of Harlem through real estate agents and friends point the way which other Negroes will follow to the extent that their means allow.

With their job opportunities moving outward, the chances are very strong that low income groups will grow in the suburban areas as speedily as housing opportunities permit. Large-scale public housing projects in New York City may slow down the move, but it is doubtful that such projects could stem or reverse the flow.

Will housing opportunities in the Region exist to accommodate the flow? The housing which will become obsolescent and ripe for down-grading over the next twenty years will be drawn largely from stock built between 1910 and 1930, during a period when the Region's population increased by about 4,000,000. Much of this housing will be turned over for low-income use; and much of it is located in outlying parts of the Core counties and in the Inner Ring. The obsolescence rate of the block of housing built before 1930 promises to be especially high because most of it was built without much regard for the existence of the automobile. At the same time, no projection which we would consider realistic contemplates an increase in the demand for such housing in the Region anywhere near as great as the prospective increase in supply. The net result, therefore, is likely to be a continued—perhaps an accelerated—thinning out of populations in existing slum housing in the Region. The pressures which generate doubling-up, conversions, and crowded rooming houses in the "new" slums may well be reduced. It is certain that the densities generated in the newly down-graded neighborhoods will be lower than those in the old slums, extending a trend toward declining slum densities which has been apparent in the Region for thirty or forty years.

Developments in passenger transportation facilities in the Region—not only in subways and suburban commuting systems but also in roads, river crossings, and parking facilities—can condition the responses of all groups in the Region to future changes in the location of their jobs. No complex analysis is needed to understand what has been happening in the Region in the interplay between passenger facilities and population shifts. The urge for outward movement came from forces which were partly independent of the passenger facilities. But the speed and extent of this outward movement depended critically on the kind of passenger facilities laid down. New York City's construction of a subway system capable of the speedy mass movement of commuters improved the opportunities for the development of the Manhattan central business district and helped lay an economic basis for cramming nearly 8,000,000 people within its five boroughs. The lower traffic potentials of the transportation system provided by the New Jersey municipalities were a factor in the more diffused growth of that part of the Region.

The overriding force in transportation in recent decades, of course, has been the automobile. Some of its effects have been almost too obvious for comment: it has dispersed population by opening up new territory far from the subway lines and suburban trains; and it has made possible a more lavish use of the land by adding so much to the urban supply. Some of the automobile's effects have been subtle and devious. For example, it has lapped off the cream of the subways' and suburban railways' business by taking over much of their off-peak and week-end volume. Just in the brief period between 1948 and 1956, the number of subway passengers entering the Manhattan central business district outside the hours of 7 to 10 in the morning fell by 20.8 per cent, though the number during those peak hours fell only 11.7 per cent. The impact of the new competition on the subways and the suburban lines, therefore, has been double-barreled: the competition has meant not only a loss of business but a loss of the kind of business which the rails could service without adding much to their capacity and their costs. In the circumstances, the pressure for rate increases on the mass transit lines was inevitable. But to achieve a rate increase was only to be mired a little deeper; for with each rate increase, the off-peak travelers and the commuters—but especially the off-peak travelers—shifted even more strongly to the use of the automobile.

The figures in Table 19 mirror the shift from mass transit to the automobile in trips to the central business district. The thirty-year growth of automobile and taxi travel into the Manhattan central business district is phenomenal; and so is the dip in the use of rapid transit and suburban railroad after 1948.

Figures from another source disclose added aspects of the shifting patterns of travel inside the Region. An analysis of Hudson River crossings, made by the Port of New York Authority, shows some striking changes between 1948 and 1958. Trips from New Jersey homes to Manhattan's central business district declined considerably—the net consequence of a big drop in rail and ferry travel, off-set in part by a rise in auto and bus travel. The big growth in river crossings (other than truck crossings) has come from two sources: from New Jerseyites bound for New York locations *outside* of Manhattan's central

TABLE 19. NUMBER OF PERSONS ENTERING MANHATTAN CENTRAL BUSINESS DISTRICT[a] IN VEHICLES ON A TYPICAL BUSINESS DAY, BY MODE OF TRAVEL, SELECTED YEARS, 1924–1956

	Thousands of persons					Percentage of total number				
	1924	1932	1940	1948	1956	1924	1932	1940	1948	1956
Total	2,343	2,697	3,271	3,691	3,316	100.0	100.0	100.0	100.0	100.0
Auto and taxi	249	430	503	577	736	10.6	15.9	15.4	15.7	22.2
Bus	—	40	150	290	246	—	1.5	4.6	7.8	7.4
Truck	82	86	116	80	92	3.5	3.2	3.5	2.2	2.8
Trolley	161	88	59	24	3	6.9	3.2	1.8	0.6	0.1
Rapid transit	1,531	1,752	2,169	2,389	1,970	65.3	65.0	66.3	64.8	59.4
Railroad (commuter)	217	216	206	283	233	9.3	8.0	6.3	7.6	7.0
Ferry (pedestrians)[b]	103	85	68	48	36	4.4	3.2	2.1	1.3	1.1

[a]Here defined as Manhattan south of 61st Street.
[b]Pedestrians are not counted unless they entered by ferry.

SOURCE: Regional Plan Association, Bulletin 91, Hub-Bound Travel in the Tri-State Metropolitan Region: Persons and Vehicles Entering Manhattan South of 61st Street, 1924–1956 (New York, 1959).

business district; and from New Yorkers headed for New Jersey points, most of these no doubt being the "reverse commuters" to whom we referred earlier. All told, therefore, the figures confirm the general picture of a dispersion in commuter travel: a breaking up of the simple old pattern of convergence in the central business district; and a shift from rails to rubber.

In view of the way in which jobs and residences seem to be redistributing themselves in the Region, some new difficulties seem in store for the mass transit facilities. Our projections imply that the number of commuters demanding daily access to the central business district, whether by automobile, bus, or suburban train, will show a considerable increase over the next few decades, the increase being due principally to the rise of office work. At the same time, as manufacturing and wholesale jobs decline in the central business district, the short-haul business of the subways will further decline. The aspiration for the split-level-with-garage in the suburbs which permeates all income levels except perhaps the very highest (where it has already been realized to the extent desired), will surely continue to redistribute the remaining subway riders outward from the center of the Region. Many former subway riders will move beyond the subway's range. Some of them will continue to use the subway for the final stage of the inbound trip to the office; others will make the whole trip by suburban railroad, at the very time when some of the railroad companies will be bending every effort to avoid expanding their facilities to supply a service which they consider profitless; and still others will travel exclusively on rubber tires.

Public subsidies will probably slow the deterioration in the quantity and quality of suburban rail service, but not enough, we suspect, to stem some continued shift from railroads to the automobile. Accordingly, we project an increased use of the automobile for commuting. The bottleneck to the growth of the central business district, therefore, may prove to be the facilities afforded to the automobile commuter—not only the approach roads but the parking areas as well. This is a generalization which applies even more patently to the downtown financial district of Manhattan than to the midtown area.

Outside the central business district, the impact of the automobile promises to be more of what it already has been. The high-speed expressways lacing their way through the Region are continually opening up new stretches of undeveloped territory. Shortly, new roads extending westward from the Hudson River will open up stretches of Morris County and even bring Sussex County, lying just outside the limits of the Region, within commuting range of Manhattan. New circumferential links, such as the Cross Westchester Expressway and Route 287 . . . , will tie the expressways together in a complex which will accommodate travel from one point on the periphery of the Region to another. The pattern will loosen the ties of the residential suburbs to the Region's cities even further, and will give an added impetus for the leapfrogging of residential developments into localities far removed from Manhattan and Newark.

If one adds rising incomes explicitly to the list of variables affecting residential shifts, as we have already done implicitly in our earlier discussion of the

Puerto Rican and the Negro, the addition only serves to reinforce the generalizations broached earlier. In 1939, Manhattan residents recorded the highest per capita income of all the counties of the Region, fully 63 per cent above the Region average. At that time, some of the counties which were destined soon thereafter to grow with particular rapidity were reporting a comparatively low per capita income: Bergen and Union were each 15 per cent below the Region average, Queens 21 per cent below, Nassau 26 per cent below, and even Westchester 7 per cent below. By 1956, however, Manhattan's per capita income no longer was the highest in the Region and the fast-growing counties mentioned above had all swung from levels below the Region average to levels above; by that date the Manhattan figure was only 14 per cent above the Region, while Bergen and Union were each 9 per cent above, Queens 6 per cent above, Nassau 25 per cent above, and Westchester 24 per cent above.

What was happening seems apparent enough. In the redistribution of populations in the Region, families at the upper end of the income scale were shifting outward faster than the others. This was the overriding tendency notwithstanding the fact that Negroes and Puerto Ricans—most of them with comparatively low incomes—seem to have had a part in the outward move, and notwithstanding the fact that the demand for high-rent luxury apartments grew considerably in Manhattan. Despite these eddies in the current, one could still describe the current itself as an outward movement of those who could best afford it. And there is little to suggest that the future will differ in this respect from the past.

One other factor needs close examination for its future implications, namely, the changing age distribution and household composition of the Region's populations. It takes no special act of clairvoyance to project, with fair precision, the number of adults, by age groups, likely to be residing in the Region in the next two or three decades; most of these prospective residents are already present in the Region. Our best estimates indicate that between now and 1985, the fraction over 65 years of age will expand the fastest. The group between ages 35 and 64 will be very slow to increase in number, partly because the new arrivals in this group will include the lean crop of depression babies and partly because there will be continued out-migration by those of more advanced years within the group. But the increase in the group aged 15 to 34 will be very rapid.

This pattern would seem to imply, among other things, another upsurge in family formation and another wave of construction in single-family suburban developments, with the emphasis on economy appropriate to the age of the young parents. The increase in the number of older inhabitants may also suggest a rise in the demand for small-household housing, conveniently located. But a "convenient" location for this group need not be the central city. For every one in the group whose income and social ties suggest a central-city location, there are likely to be several whose income or social preferences will rule out such a choice. To the extent that these persons give up their single-family homes in the suburbs, they are likely to settle for apartment-house living in the same neighborhoods, close to friends, children, and other social ties.

These comments add up to a comparatively simple picture. Close by the central business district, we shall see more demand for high-income housing. Just beyond, for miles in every direction, we are likely to see a continued thinning out and aging of populations—a thinning out which may be modified but surely will not be reversed by public housing programs; and a similar trend will probably prevail in the old cities of the Region's outlying counties. Everywhere else in the Region there will be population increase. Some of it will arise from the added building of multiple dwellings. But most of it will be single-family housing, spread out spottily on the landscape, eating up land at new high rates.

PURSUING THE CONSUMER

We have reached the stage in our analysis of the Region's changing structure in which an earlier promise can be redeemed. In the last chapter we said that the locations of employees who are engaged in serving the consumer could best be discussed in conjunction with population trends.

The obvious point that retail trade and consumer services tend to grow in close parallel with population and income was already made in Chapter 6. The related point that the ascendancy of suburban living has changed the "mix" of these consumer activities also was discussed. Our problem here, however, is one of identifying the shifts inside the Region in the location of this changing group of consumer activities.

The dominant fact, of course, is that as residences have redistributed themselves outward from the Region's center, the trades and services which cater to the consumer have followed close in their wake. Chart 16 shows the main trends in retail trade (the selling of goods rather than services). As population grew faster in the Inner and Outer Rings than in the Core, employment in the retail trades did likewise. Retail sales were redistributed outward even faster than population, probably because the personal income of the Region also was shifting faster than population. If we divide the Region up along different lines from those in the Chart, comparing the old cities of the Region with all the rest, the pattern so familiar in other contexts appears once more. Retail trade was growing much more slowly in the old cities than in the rest of the Region. In fact, measured by employment, retail trade was actually declining in those cities in the period from 1948 to 1954, and there are various indications that the decline has continued since.

But there is more to the story. If consumer activities have followed the shift of residences, it is also true that some kinds of retail trade and consumer services have followed residences more faithfully than others. Specifically, some lines have clung more tenaciously to the central shopping areas in the

Chart 16. Retail Trade and Population Trends in Main Zones of New York Metropolitan Region, 1929–1954

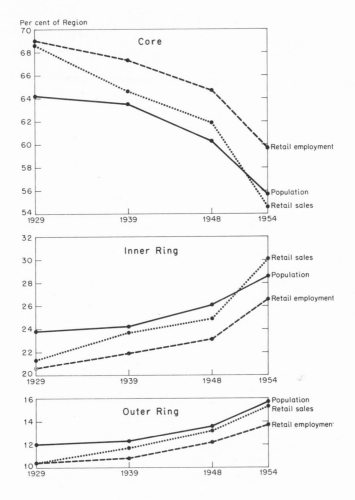

SOURCE: Population estimates are our own, based on U. S. *Census of Population*. Other data based on U. S. *Census of Business* for years shown.

hearts of Manhattan, Newark, and Brooklyn. By and large, these have been activities which were more highly concentrated in the central shopping areas in the first place: jewelry stores, apparel and accessory shops, eating and drinking places, hotels, and movie theatres. And, if hard figures could be had, they would also show that art galleries, museums, and a number of other "consumer" activities have tended to cling to their central locations in the Region.

The reasons for the heavy initial concentration of these activities in the central shopping areas and for their continuing disposition to cling to these areas go back to concepts that are by now familiar. Some activities which serve the consumer are spread through every neighborhood; others are not. When the product or service involved is comparatively standardized—when the consumer can get approximately the same product or service at approximately the same price from one outlet to the next—his disposition is to buy from the nearest outlet and thereby to minimize the time and costs involved in shopping. Accordingly, highly standardized products or services for which there is a heavy demand are marketed in every neighborhood, as close as possible to the consumer's doorstep.

If the demand for a product or service is fairly thin, however, the tendency of the seller is to seek a location which taps a sufficiently large market to support his existence. The purveyor of pianos and the exhibitor of first-run movies, therefore, are more likely to be found at a major transportation hub than elsewhere. And where the nature of the product or service is highly unstandardized, as in the case of "style" goods, its purveyors are likely to gravitate to a common point where the consumer's demand for comparative shopping can be satisfied. This is what accounts for the centralized locational pattern of apparel stores, jewelry stores, and art galleries. And some of the unstandardized lines are centralized for still another reason: they serve not only a local market but also a market of out-of-towners brought to the metropolis by business or pleasure.

Table 20 illustrates the shift in sales between the three main central shopping areas of the Region and the rest of the Region for the center-oriented lines from 1948 to 1954. Of the individual trades and services shown in the table, only department stores exhibit a pronounced tendency to shift outward from the central shopping areas. The trek of department stores toward the suburbs has been in evidence for several decades, and especially in the years after World War II. Some of the old "downtown" stores have gone out of business; others, like Macy's and Gimbel's, have opened branches in the suburbs. The shift in the period since World War II, however, has been more rapid than concurrent population changes and more rapid, in our view, than one might have reason to expect in the future. Department stores, unlike retail lines organized in smaller units, probably make their adjustments to population shifts by fits and starts, not as a gradual or continuous process. These stores are so large in scale that it takes a considerable move in population to engender a locational shift. When the shift occurs, however, a move by any one store has a substantial impact, not only because each store is so large but also because of the response of competitors in trying to match the move. The postwar shifts appear to us to represent a catching-up operation, a massive adjustment to a shift in population which has been going on for some time.

Outside of the three counties in the Region containing major central shopping areas, most consumer trade and service activities have mirrored the shift in employment and jobs from one county to the next with astonishing consistency. In each consumer line covered by the federal Census of Business, a simple formula is capable of expressing with considerable precision the relation between the population or jobs of the county in any year and the number of employees engaged in the particular line. For counties without major central shopping areas, therefore, once we know where the population and other jobs are likely to be, we can predict with a certain assurance the likely location of consumer-serving jobs.

TABLE 20.   SALES IN CENTRAL SHOPPING AREAS [a] OF MANHATTAN, NEWARK, AND BROOKLYN AS PERCENTAGE OF SALES IN NEW YORK METROPOLITAN REGION, BY SELECTED CONSUMER TRADES AND SERVICES, 1948 AND 1954

	1948	1954
All retail trade, plus hotels, motels, movie theatres	21.1	17.4
Retail trade		
Department stores	71.5	61.9
Furniture, furnishings, appliances	19.3	18.4
Jewelry stores	47.1	44.8
Apparel and accessories	38.6	36.9
Eating, drinking places	25.8	24.8
All other retail trade [b]	8.2	6.3
Consumer services		
Hotels and motels	65.0	63.9
Movie theatres	26.6	29.2

[a]"Central business districts" as defined by U. S. Census Bureau. For Manhattan, this is an area much smaller than the central business district as referred to elsewhere in this volume; the smaller Census area falls approximately between Third and Tenth Avenues and between Central Park and Canal Street.
[b]For example, food stores, atuo dealers, gasoline stations, and liquor stores.

SOURCES: U. S. *1954 Census of Business,* series on "Retail Trade," "Selected Services," and "Central Business District Statistics," supplemented by our estimates.

The close tie to population or job changes appears not only in the activities bearing the Census designations "retail trade" and "consumer services" but also in a variety of other activities whose patronage comes from consumers close to their homes or places of business. Commercial banking services are one such activity. Though one tends to think of the banks in the New York area as national institutions, a major part of their jobs is related to such local activities as consumer loans. Besides, the national function is confined to only a few major banks in New York City, most of the others being geared to serve a local clientele. The same can be said for numerous other activities, including life insurance field offices, with their eye to the selling and servicing of local customers; neighborhood real estate offices, managing and selling local properties; local government offices; and most lawyers, doctors, and accountants.

These pursuits—these consumer-oriented segments of banking, law, insurance, and the like—are not distributed in the Region exactly in proportion to residences. They tend to centralize somewhat because of the need to be near clients at their places at work as well as near their residences, and the need for communication with others—lawyers with accountants and with other lawyers, insurance agents with real estate brokers, all of them with government officials, and so on. Hence they compromise between a thoroughly centralized location in the Region and a thoroughly diffused one. But there is not much doubt that the shift of populations has been pulling these consumer-oriented services outward. This is why Nassau and Suffolk counties saw a 132 per cent increase in commercial bank employment between 1947 and 1956, and why such counties saw spectacular increases in pursuits like life insurance, law offices, and real estate.

As one surveys the outward shift of the populations in the New York Metropolitan Region and of the consumer activities tied to them, the forces behind the shift seem near-inexorable. Basic technological developments in transportation and deep-seated changes in consumer wants appear to lie behind the phenomenon. Here and there one sees evidence of preferences which breast the main tide; the occasional reappearance of a disillusioned exurbanite in his former city haunts, the gradual growth of apartments-in-the-city for the very rich—these are phenomena whose impact cannot be overlooked. The bigger risk, however, is that their implications for the future will be exaggerated rather than overlooked. Short of some fundamental alteration in consumer outlook or in urban environment, the trends for the future seem likely to represent a continuation—even a speed-up—of the dispersive tendencies of the past.

Emergence and Structure of the Urban Region: Suburb, Satellite, and Fringe

Alvin Boskoff

The urban region, which is a continuously evolving entity, is slowly gaining serious recognition as the most important and strategic unit in modern society.

* * *

1. Historically, suburbs have been a major mechanism of urban growth through specialization. Suburban quarters usually contained specialized occupational groups (merchants, artisans, religious practitioners) who were initially necessary but socially unassimilable in the city structure.[6] It is interesting to note that before the 18th century, suburbanites were principally workers and marginal merchants;[7] only in the modern era in western nations have suburbs attained desirable status for secure and economically successful categories. In non-Western nations, however, suburbs remain as reservoirs of the marginal and impecunious, particularly those who have migrated from tribal or rural village communities.

2. It should be recalled that central cities themselves are resultants of long-term annexation of suburban settlements. Indeed, in some cities the modern core area was originally a suburb.[8] In earlier generations, extension of municipal boundaries was not fiercely contested; identity was then not as important as the advantages of suburban inclusion. Currently, in the Netherlands, suburbs are planned by city officials and are annexed before population

[6]W. G. Hoskins, *Local History in England* (London, Longmans, Green, 1959), pp. 82–89; H. J. Dyos, *Victorian Suburb* (Leicester, Leicester University Press, 1961), pp. 36–38; Pierre Francastel, ed., *Les Origines des villes polonaises* (Paris, Mouton, 1960), pp. 33–36.

[7]Edgard Kant, "Suburbanization, Urban Sprawl, and Commutation," in David Hannerberg *et al.*, eds., *Migration in Sweden: A Symposium* (Lund, C. W. K. Gleerup, 1957), p. 245.

[8]Francastel, *op. cit.*, pp. 36, 198; Sam B. Warner, Jr., *Streetcar Suburbs* (Cambridge, Harvard University Press, 1962), pp. 57–127.

SOURCE: Alvin Boskoff, from *The Sociology of Urban Regions,* 2nd ed. (New York: Appleton-Century-Crofts, 1970), pp. 106, 107, 110–116, 118–128. Copyright © 1970 by Meredith Corporation. Reprinted by permission of Appleton-Century-Crofts, Educational Division, Meredith Corporation.

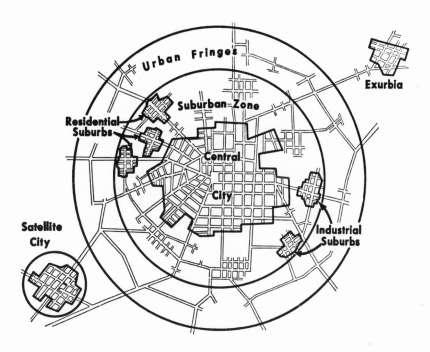

Figure 1. A Simplified Ecological Diagram of the Urban Region

growth and development attain problematic status.[9] Therefore, much of suburban history reveals collaboration in municipal growth, in establishing the modern contours of cities. Only when central cities and their services become firmly based and extensive (i.e., important facilities and services are easily exportable) can suburban areas seek and maintain their apparent independence.

3. Contemporary suburban migrants are not unformed wanderers, empty vessels awaiting the distinctive contents of their new location. They are socialized representatives of family, occupational, religious, and status categories—though they may differ in some respects from their status peers in premigration communities. Suburbanites select suburbs for one or more of several definite personal and cultural reasons, and appear to evaluate suburban residence in terms of those reasons or motives. No study has yet documented a clear-cut "conversion effect" on suburban migrants (e.g., a change in values, birth

[9]Joseph F. Mangiamele, "How Europeans Mold Their Cities," in Goodwin F. Berquist, Jr., ed., *The Wisconsin Academy Looks at Urbanism* (Milwaukee; Wisconsin Academy of Sciences, Arts and Letters, May, 1963), p. 49.

patterns, political orientation). As Ktsanes and Reissman aptly and accurately phrase it, suburbia is "new houses for old values."[10]

4. But suburban areas exhibit significant changes in a very visible way: the diversification of family and status categories over time. Though the pattern is not equally clear in all types of suburbs in the U.S. and Western nations, the following seems to be a basic sequence in suburban development.

(a) First to locate in the area are "pioneer" residents from established middle or upper status categories, who can afford the relatively scarce housing facilities and the cost of commuting.[11] The major exceptions to this pattern have occurred since World War II and derive from two sources. One variation can be explained by suburban or fringe relocation of industry, such as in California, Sydney, Long Island.[12] Migrants, therefore, tend to be primarily skilled workers and their families. But a second variation derives from large scale planned suburban areas (public or private), which are designed specifically for lower class or modest middle class families. The Levittowns in Long Island, Pennsylvania, and New Jersey are notable examples, while English and Scotch housing estates illustrate the public form of this variation.[13]

(b) As more homes are built and as public facilities are made available (roads, schools, shopping areas), younger families in lower middle and lower status categories constitute a contrapuntal migrant stream, if restrictive zoning is absent. Normally, the second stream locates at the edges of the older suburb, where land costs are lower or where enterprising subdividers provide housing developments at moderate cost and with palpably inaccurate though picturesque names.

(c) On the heels of this second suburban invasion come marginal families who are primarily small proprietors, unskilled workers, and semi-skilled clerical employees. These are marginal not only in terms of income but also in their

[10]S. D. Clark, *The Suburban Society* (Toronto, University of Toronto Press, 1966), pp. 48–97; Herbert J. Gans, *The Levittowners* (New York, Pantheon Books, 1967), pp. 24, 224–239; Bennett M. Berger, *Working-Class Suburb* (Berkeley, University of California Press, 1960), Chap. 6; Robert C. Wood, *Suburbia: Its People and Their Politics* (Boston, Houghton Mifflin, 1959); Carl Werthman *et al., Planning and the Purchase Decision: Why People Buy in Planned Communities* (Berkeley, Center for Planning and Development Research, University of California, July, 1965, mimeo), pp. 12–14, 166–167; Thomas Ktsanes and Leonard Reissman, "Suburbia—New Homes for Old Values," *Social Problems,* 7 (Winter, 1959–1960), pp. 187–195.

[11]Warner, *op. cit.*

[12]Berger, *op. cit.;* T. Brennan, "Urban Communities," in A. F. Davies and S. Encel, eds., *Australian Society: A Sociological Introduction* (New York, Atherton Press, 1965), p. 299.

[13]William M. Dobriner, *Class in Suburbia* (Englewood Cliffs, N.J., Prentice-Hall, 1963), Chap. 4; Gans, *op. cit.;* E. I. Black and T. S. Simey, eds., *Neighbourhood and Community* (Liverpool, University Press of Liverpool, 1954), Part I (The Liverpool Estate), Part II (The Sheffield Estate); John Spencer, *Stress and Release in an Urban Estate* (London, Tavistock Publications, 1964); Ruth Durant, *Watling: A Survey of Social Life on a New Housing Estate* (London, P. S. King, 1939); Michael Young and Peter Willmott, *Family and Kinship in East London* (London, Routledge and Kegan Paul, 1957), pp. 97–135; Peter Willmott and Michael Young, *Family and Class in a London Suburb* (London, Routledge and Kegan Paul, 1960); Ronald Frankenberg, *Communities in Britain* (Baltimore, Penguin Books, 1966), Chaps. 7, 8.

expressed uncertainties about objectives and residence in the area. Obviously, this category directly refutes the alleged "middle-classness" of suburbs.[14] But, in a sense, middle class suburbanites unwittingly establish the bases for such a paradoxical migrant category. Of course, some of these marginal families simply are old residents of areas that have been infiltrated by movements summarized in *(a)* and *(b)*.[15]

(d) In suburban areas or zones where commercial and/or industrial developments have *followed* the population trends just described, a second wave of professional, managerial, and technically proficient occupational categories tends to augment the pattern of diversification. At this point, the scarcity of suburban land arrests the prodigal subdivision of one-family homes on one- to four-acre lots. Instead, we find the increasing resort to high-rise apartments and most recently, a more economic use of land in town houses, whose high cost often represents a triumph of fashion over spaciousness.[16]

5. The formerly dominant concept of dormitory suburbs, once quite accurate, is much less applicable during the past 20 years in the U.S. and Western Europe. Only in the peripheral slums of Latin America and Africa is the traditional journey to work to the central city still pervasive. But this involves commuting by unskilled, marginal suburbanites, rather than the voluntary daily hegira of the natty middle class professional, executive, or white collar worker. In recent years, suburban job opportunities for managerial, professional, and skilled persons have greatly expanded, encouraging urbanites to locate in convenient suburban areas and also motivating suburbanites to become long-term settlers in suburban zones[17] (unlike the stereotype of the restless suburbanite, who allegedly uses the suburb as a way-station in his relentless ascent on the social ladder).

6. Most important, however, are the cultural and organizational consequences of the developed suburb. Contrary to the institutional aridity of the dormitory suburb and its "suburban sadness," more suburbs are developing local sources of recreation, uplift, education, desired retail services, banking, and voluntary or formal associations. In short, to an extent that is not generally recognized, suburbs tend to become indistinguishable in operation (rather than location) from portions of the central city.[18]

7. Consequently, whatever distinctive features suburbs may possess initially (relative homogeneity, commuting patterns, spaciousness, low taxes) these seem to be transitional. Functionally, suburbs begin as spatial additions

[14]Alvin Boskoff, "Social and Cultural Patterns in a Suburban Area: Their Significance for Social Change in the South," *Journal of Social Issues,* 22 (January, 1966), pp. 85–94.

[15]Nelson N. Foote et al., eds., *Housing Choices and Housing Constraints* (New York, McGraw-Hill, 1960), p. 164.

[16]Anshel Melamed, "High-Rent Apartments in the Suburbs," *Urban Land,* 20 (October, 1961), pp. 1–6.

[17]Lowdon Wingo, Jr., ed., *Cities and Space* (Baltimore, Johns Hopkins Press, 1963), p. 90; Sidney Goldstein and Kurt B. Mayer, *Residential Mobility, Migration, and Commuting in Rhode Island* (Providence, Rhode Island Development Council, September, 1963), p. 18; Brennan, *op. cit.,* p. 299.

[18]Clark, *op. cit.,* pp. 12–14; Gans, *op. cit.,* pp. 288, 409.

to urban cores. Increasingly, they tend to become distant subcenters of urban populations and activities. The only remaining distinction of any meaning seems to be political independence through incorporation.

SUBURBAN TYPES

Since suburbs are products of varied motives, pressures, and facilities, and likewise exhibit historical development or change in population, it does not seem satisfactory to use the prevailing distinction between residential and industrial or employing suburbs.[19] Instead, we may begin with this distinction (direct vs. indirect relation to the central city) and further subdivide each in terms of two important dimensions: dominant motives or goals of residents; and dominant social class patterning of an area. The resulting 12 types are presented in Figure 2, primarily as a conceptual map for organizing available data, but also as a base for future investigation of suburban phenomena.

As yet only six of these suburban types can be identified empirically, though other "cells" may be found to be appropriate to areas familiar to other students of urbanism. With unavoidable oversimplification, let us try to focus on the special features of each type.

Figure 2.   A Suggested Classification of Suburbs

DOMINANT CLASS STRUCTURE	DIRECT RELATION TO CITY		INDIRECT RELATION TO CITY	
	Escape Motives	*Positive Motives*	*Escape Motives*	*Positive Motives*
Upper	1 Traditional suburb	4	7	10
Middle and mixed	2 Identity conscious suburb	5 Stable suburb (Levittown)	8	11 Stable suburb (DeKalb County, Ga.)
Lower	3	6 Housing estate Suburban slum	9	12 Industrial suburb

[19]Leo F. Schnore, "Satellites and Suburbs," *Social Forces, 36* (December, 1957), pp. 121–129. Cf. Charles S. Liebman, "Functional Differentiation and Political Characteristics of Suburbs," *American Journal of Sociology, 66* (March, 1961), pp. 485–490.

1. Traditional Upper-Class Suburb

This type, so ably dissected by Cleveland Amory,[20] is numerically small and increasingly untypical of recent trends in suburban development. Essentially, this type is marked by a preponderance of long established, high-status families, comparatively little turnover in population, location near towns or villages that have extensive, independent histories, and an understandable concentration in the Northeast (e.g., near Boston, New York City, and Philadelphia).

2. The Identity-Conscious Suburb

This is a highly obtrusive and controversial type of suburb—and a continuing object of fictional and journalistic diagnosis. Most of these suburbs were carved out of fringe areas following World War II, while some were developed as recently as a decade ago. The major feature or tone seems to be one of recently acquired or desired upward mobility, which is connected with a pervasive distaste for the central city in its spatial, political, and demographic aspects. Most families in this suburban type are commuters who appear to identify their personal independence with the political isolation of their community. In general, residents are in professional and managerial occupations and tend to be in the late 30s and 40s age categories. The residential character of the area and the maintenance of relative status homogeneity are prime consideration.[21]

3. The Mass-Produced Suburb

This is perhaps the most representative and numerous of contemporary suburban forms. Its residents are predominantly interested in good, reasonably priced housing, which is unobtainable in their respective central cities. Indeed, they retain some attachment to the city beyond the necessity of commuting to offices and shops in the city. For many, this dual allegiance involves some strain, as reflected in considerable interest in local social participation (civic organizations, etc.) and in campaigns for obtaining local urban facilities from limited tax funds or voluntary contributions.[22] The typical resident (usually in the salaried professions, lesser administrative posts, or in moderately successful businesses) plans to settle in the suburb, rather than to seek higher status by frequent moves. However, the major problem—and challenge—seems to be the newness of such developments, with a resultant inadequacy in varied cultural facilities. Good examples may be found in Levittown, New Jersey, and several British housing estates near London, Liverpool, and Sheffield.

[20]Cleveland Amory, *The Proper Bostonians* (New York, E. P. Dutton, 1947).

[21]Good examples of this type are discussed in John R. Seeley *et al., Crestwood Heights* (New York, Basic Books, 1956); Alvin H. Scaff, "The Effect of Commuting on Participation in Community Organizations," *American Sociological Review,* 17 (April, 1952), pp. 215–220; William H. Whyte, Jr., "The Transients," *Fortune* (May-August, 1953); William H. Whyte, Jr., *The Organization Man* (New York, Simon and Schuster, 1956), Part 7.

[22]See references in note 13.

4. The Suburban Slum

The foremost illustration of this type is the Latin American favela or barriada and the bidonville of African urban concentrations. Such areas are marked by makeshift, unimaginably crowded housing for impoverished Negro or Indian migrants from rural areas. These suburbanites, unable to afford urban apartments, live with or near relatives or acquaintances from home communities and participate in informal networks of aid and recreation with neighbors and kinsmen. Work opportunities tend to be largely in unskilled jobs in the city, with the journey to work a noisy and uncomfortable experience by ancient bus or train.[23] Clearly, the expected amenities of suburban living are simply not available. More important, these suburbs seem to show neither improvement nor development, only continued cramming of more migrants.

5. The Stable Variegated Suburb

Apparently this type of suburb has developed without much notice, proba- bly during the last ten years. It seems to have derived either from the identity- conscious or mass-produced type because of one or more local attractions (e.g., considerable space for expansion, quality of local education, scenic features, or presence of a high status facility such as a university, prestige hospital, etc.). Whatever the specific reasons, the original settlers discourage the rapid addi- tion of new subdivisions from nearby vacant lots and farms. The more recent migrants represent a wide span of professional and white collar occupations and have previous experience in suburban or city living.

Perhaps the crucial element in this suburban type is the increasing location of appropriate jobs within the suburb or in adjacent suburban areas. While daily commuting to the city persists, an appreciable proportion of suburbanites come to reside near their jobs. Consequently, a reciprocal interest in the character of the suburb tends to develop in suburban employers and suburban residents. Both emphasize the necessity of local facilities (schools, shopping, civic organizations, the arts) as a means of encouraging continued residence and community stability. But with increasing facilities, the more attractive this suburb becomes for different social categories, from both city and fringe areas. Thus, the basis for a considerable population mix (largely excluding non- whites) is firmly established.

*   *   *

As suburban areas become more populated, existing suburbs may be ex- pected to develop toward the stable variegated type. Unfortunately, specific suburbs have not been studied over long periods of time, so that we might identify processes of suburban change. Yet we may hypothesize that economic

---

[23]Philip M. Hauser, ed., *Urbanization in Latin America* (New York, Columbia University Press, 1961), Chaps. 6, 8, 9.

and industrial relocation into suburban areas will be followed by increasing diversification of status levels and family types within the same suburban area or zone. In that case, suburbs tend to re-create the structure of the central city and can no longer be viewed as ecologically or functionally distinct.

6. The Industrial Suburb

It is quite apparent that the industrial or employing suburb has been relatively ignored in recent years as an object of urban studies, in favor of the residential or dormitory type. Perhaps two features of the industrial suburb, however, can be considered well established. *(a)* Understandably, the occupational and social class distributions of industrial suburbs are weighted toward the skilled and semiskilled categories, and likewise toward lower and lower middle status groups. *(b)* In recent years, the relative population growth of industrial suburbs has been significantly smaller than that of residential suburbs. This is true for all sections of the nation, for all sizes of central city and suburb, and for all distances from the central city. Perhaps these comparative trends reflect an approximation to saturation in growth of industrial suburbs, particularly of the larger and older suburbs. The rate of growth is lowest, for example, in the Northeast and highest in the newer industrial suburbs of the West and South.[25] Suburban growth in general seems to depend on expansion of residential areas, rather than on employment opportunities in industrial suburbs.

THE ROLES OF SUBURBAN FORMS

The social and cultural differentiation in suburban areas should curb the over-confident comparisons and distinctions between city and suburban entities. Indeed, such comparisons—based on census data—are really between central cities and rings (i.e., noncity portions of given Standard Metropolitan Areas), so that suburbs are unfortunately lumped with fringe areas and villages. However, if we make use of available data with some caution, the following overall differences between city and ring can be identified (though it may be presumed that these are decreasingly valid patterns).

1. Population increase is decidedly greater in ring areas as a consequence both of migration from central city and migration from fringe and small town areas (outside the SMA) to the suburbs. In 1950, ring areas accounted for over 21 percent of metropolitan population, while the most recent estimate is almost 30 percent. Central cities have generally had net population

[25]Leo F. Schnore, "The Growth of Metropolitan Suburbs," *op. cit.,* pp. 29–34. A recent study of an industrial suburb in California is Bennett M. Berger, *Working-Class Suburb* (Berkeley, University of California Press, 1960); Robert E. Dickinson, *The West European City* (London, Routledge and Kegan Paul, 1951), pp. 85, 229–231.

losses, or very slight increases. Even great population losses have been masked by annexation of suburban fringe areas since 1950.[26]

2. Sex ratios are somewhat higher in ring areas, particularly in comparison with commercial central cities. This is related to the characteristics below.

3. Marriage rates tend to be higher in ring areas, probably as a consequence of selective migration of family units to such areas.

4. Age distribution is somewhat more skewed toward younger age categories in ring areas.

5. Income and occupational distributions show larger concentrations in higher or more prestigeful categories in ring areas.

6. Educational levels in ring areas for those 25 years and over are higher than in cities. Nonwhites in ring areas, however, have in the past had lower educational levels than these city counterparts, perhaps indicating selective migration of skilled and semi-skilled nonwhites to industrial suburbs.

In view of suburban variety and the diminishing differences between central city and suburb, what can we conclude about the contributions of suburbs to modern urban regions? Perhaps the basic consideration is a distinction between early and developed phases of urbanization and the related notion of differential significance of suburbs according to phase of urbanization.

In earlier urban waves, and in the first phases of urban development during the past 150 years, suburbs seem to have operated as specialized outposts of the city, as potential or actual substitutes for activities or facilities the city could not conveniently provide. For example, industrial suburbs enabled the core to serve its commercial and administrative-governmental needs without the encroachment of factories. Likewise, early suburban forms enabled higher status categories to experiment with the fruits of their achievement in ways that were impossible in the built-up portions of the city. One consequence, of course, was the heightening of status distinctions, and also the implicit provision of tangible goals or vehicles or urban achievement and social mobility. However, the epiphenomenal or auxiliary character of these suburbs largely prevented serious concern for a local range of urban services and facilities. They could not function as communities in the full sense of the term, which perhaps accounts for the long-standing criticism of suburbia.

More recently, the previously analyzed suburbs have been supplemented by developed suburban forms, which seem to function in a different manner. It is quite likely that the stable, variegated suburb provides an alternative and more satisfactory setting for family living and child rearing in terms of more space, more and newer facilities, better public education, and more flexibility. It is by no means utopia, but it may represent a resurgence of satisfying family life for many acquainted with the urban frustrations of the Great Depression.

[26]Duncan and Reiss, op. cit., pp. 119–123; Leo F. Schnore, "Municipal Annexations and the Growth of Metropolitan Suburbs, 1950–60," American Journal of Sociology, 67 (January, 1967), pp. 406–417.

Perhaps the suburban birth rate and the emphasis on activities for children and youths reflect a collective appreciation of the "new suburbia."

In addition, the variegated suburbs permit or encourage the broadening of middle social categories in the urban region by providing space for various segments of middle life-styles, and allowing for direct and indirect communication and participation among these categories. Perhaps this explains the immense popularity of suburban PTAs and similar groups, in which are mixed such emphases as concern for children, participation in family units, identification with the local area, and civic rather than class or status responsibility. Furthermore, though there are some signs of change, the central city has been generally perceived as uncongenial to middle class ideals. Consequently, migration from central cities (or from suburb to suburb) can be interpreted, not as antiurban, but as a search for a substitute for the city. Such a quest can only be satisfied in the variegated suburb and thus we would predict the largest suburban population increase in Western nations in this type of suburb.

Finally, to the extent that these functions are successfully performed, the developed suburbs may be interpreted as the prime socializer of the professional, managerial, and technical personnel required for the continued and expanding operation of metropolitan entities. As cities progressively increase their demand for tertiary occupational categories, the dependence of cities on such suburbs will likewise grow, simply because cities have not been consciously or consistently designed for retaining ambitious and capable families.

Taken as a whole, suburban variety reflects the typical urban opportunity for experimentation, specialization, flexibility, and change. Urban regions develop largely through the mechanisms of suburbanization, often without control or understanding of these processes. The immediate effects of suburbanization on the central city are either added costs for provision of services, or reduced revenues (which instead flow to county or other non-municipal units). However, urban economists are not agreed on the actual long-term financial burden which suburban growth imposes on city governments.[27] In any case, urban and suburban populations are both directly and indirectly dependent on one another. Suburban growth eases population pressure on the central city, thereby providing opportunities for alert cities to replace slum areas and substandard housing, as well as to plan for the future availability of desired services and facilities. Suburbs, on the other hand, are the beneficiaries of preexisting urban concentrations of capital, skills, and expensive facilities.

If earlier suburbs, with their specialized facilities, formalized their interdependence through annexation by the metropolis, the more balanced suburbs

[27]Amos H. Hawley, "Metropolitan Population and Municipal Government Expenditures in Central Cities," *Journal of Social Issues*, 7 (1951), pp. 101–108; Ruth L. Mace, *Municipal Cost-Revenue Research in the United States* (Chapel Hill, Institute of Government, University of North Carolina, 1961); Harvey E. Brazer, *City Expenditures in the United States* (New York, National Bureau of Economic Research, 1959), Occasional Paper #66, p. 58.

of the current era face the same issue: does spatial separation justify autonomy or does the continued attractiveness of suburbia depend on joint financing and planning of regional networks of facilities and resources?

THE URBAN FRINGE

It is to be expected that the nature of the urban region becomes increasingly difficult to identify and analyze as one moves from the city proper to the region's periphery. At the present time, the urban fringe (and closely related labels for this type of area) is therefore understandably vague, or so variably defined that its characteristics do not form a coherent whole. But there is enough valid information to conclude that the fringe is not chaotic, but a meaningful entity in the urban regional complex.

If we recall the imputed nature of the urban region as a system in continuous operation, involving the basic processes of growth, differentiation, and coordination, then the fringe can be initially approached as that part of the region most immediately relevant to regional expansion and therefore least subject to the process of regional coordination. From a purely geographic standpoint, most of the fringe area thus defined is peripheral. But, as many urban land inventories have shown, there are fringe areas or islands in the suburban zone, and even within the city limits.[28]

Since suburban areas develop from previously fringe territories, it is clearly necessary to distinguish these two regional parts from one another. The fringe possesses several identifying features.

1. Its general location is beyond the suburban zone or cluster, but normally near main highways or watercourses.
2. The land use pattern of the fringe is a crescive, uncoordinated accumulation of residential, commercial, manufacturing, and special service (private hospitals, cemeteries, etc.) types, with considerable amounts of vacant land.
3. The residential facilities of the fringe tend toward lower levels of attractiveness and physical repair (e.g., tourist cabins, trailer homes).
4. The employed population tends to be drawn from lower status categories than are found in the residential suburb.
5. Since the fringe as an urban appendage is relatively new, or in early stages of development, it normally lacks both urban services (e.g., pressurized gas for cooking and heating, adequate water systems, paved streets, etc.) and

[28]See Richard B. Andrews, "Elements in the Urban Fringe Pattern," *Journal of Land and Public Utility Economics,* 18 (May, 1942), pp. 169–183; George S. Wehrwein, "The Rural-Urban Fringe," *Urban Geography,* 18 (July, 1942), pp. 217–228; Walter Firey, "Ecological Considerations in Planning for Urban Fringes," *American Sociological Review,* 11 (August, 1946), pp. 411–421.

local social organization, such as its own government, school system, police and fire protection, and churches. Firey and Wehrwein have therefore called the fringe "an institutional desert."[29]

6. The outer rim of the fringe, also called the extended fringe, is adjacent to, or intermixed with, more or less active agricultural areas.

7. Because of the encroachment of more settled suburban areas, the fringe is in constant change with respect to boundary lines. In general, however, fringe areas and fringe population are declining.

The Role of the Fringe

The importance of the fringe is considerable, though comparatively little definitive data are available. Essentially, the urban fringe has been a major source of urban expansion, from which have eventually emerged the residential and industrial suburbs. In addition, the fringe provides an interesting but still unexplored locus of social and cultural contacts between urban and rural families, since population movements to the fringe involve families from farms and villages, as well as from the central city.[30] On the other hand, the absence of effective social controls (either from the city, county, or local area) tends to make the fringe attractive to irresponsible land developers, criminals, gamblers, and nuisance activities (roadhouses, dumping areas)—all of which may interfere with the orderly expansion of the urban region and with the search for adequate residential accommodations.

SATELLITE CITIES

At the outer edge of the fringe, but often in a segment of the fringe of the largest cities, are located one or more satellite communities whose status and functional importance to the urban region are somewhat unique. Known variously as independent cities (i.e., not within census-defined regions), employing satellites, hinterland cities, and subdominant communities, the satellite city is in some respects a miniature version of the central city.[31] However, the satellite should be distinguished both from the central city and the industrial suburb (with which it has sometimes been confused). For simplicity, it may be helpful to classify satellite cities into two categories—*large:* 100,000 population or over; and *small:* 10,000 to 100,000 population—thus enabling us to note gross variations in characteristics related to size whenever the data permit.

[29]Wehrwein, *op. cit.,* p. 223; Walter Firey, *Social Aspects of Land Use Planning in the Country-City Fringe* (East Lansing, Michigan State College Agricultural Experiment Station, June, 1946).

[30]Myles W. Rodehaver, "Fringe Settlement as a Two-Dimensional Movement," *Rural Sociology,* 12 (March, 1947), pp. 49–57.

[31]Donald J. Bogue, *Population Growth in Standard Metropolitan Areas 1900–1950* (Washington, Housing and Home Finance Agency, December, 1953), pp. 40–45.

In general, satellite cities appear to have their origin prior to and therefore independent of the rise of central cities. Many satellites once had pretensions to urban grandeur, but newer and more favorably situated cities (both geographically and politically) have come to overshadow their older, less fortunate competitors. Thus, the satellite, as the name implies, operates in a functionally restricted manner in the regional complex. This is substantially true for both size categories.

Unlike most suburbs but in line with central cities, satellite cities are politically independent, formally organized communities. They generally supply their residents with the normal range of community services—often with distinct quality in the larger satellites—but are rarely able to afford such urban accomplishments as art museums, symphony orchestras, etc.

The relative location of smaller satellite cities is normally beyond the fringe and frequently at points roughly intermediate to contiguous urban regions. Consequently, the satellite tends to have an exposed or marginal location, in contrast to the relatively shorter distance between the suburb and central city. In some instances (i.e., the larger satellites), the satellite is almost adjacent to its central city—across a river or bay (e.g., Council Bluffs, Iowa and Omaha, Nebraska; Jersey City and New York City; Camden, N.J. and Philadelphia).

By comparison with either residential or industrial suburbs, the satellite tends to have a larger average population size. This results from the greater life span of the satellite, but more significantly from the greater range of activities and services.

The satellite city, unlike the residential but somewhat similar to the industrial suburb and the central city, is a predominantly employing area of the urban region, as measured by the proportion of residents who work in the community as against those who commute to the central city for employment. Recent studies indicate that satellites specialize both in manufacturing and various types of retail trade, with a preponderance of manufacturing in northern and midwestern satellites, and diversified retail trade in the south. As Schnore points out, satellites provide few employment opportunities in transportation, resort and recreational functions, or wholesale activities.[32] Consequently, while the satellite resembles the central city as a source of jobs, it functions as a supplement, rather than a competitor, to the metropolitan center.

There is some evidence that satellite communities possess distinctive population characteristics, which seem to be intermediate to those of the central city and suburban areas. On the basis of incomplete data, the satellites seem to lie between the city and suburb on such features as percent of nonwhites, sex ratio, proportion of married males, and proportion of younger persons. Other studies

[32]Schnore, "Satellites and Suburbs," loc cit.; Grace M. Kneedler, "Functional Types of Cities," in Paul K. Hatt and Albert J. Reiss, Jr., eds., Reader in Urban Sociology (New York, The Free Press of Glencoe, 1951), pp. 49–53; Clarence F. Ridley et al., eds., The Municipal Year Book 1953 (Chicago, International City Managers Association, 1953), pp. 54–56.

point to the comparatively lower status levels of satellite populations, as measured by median rentals and property values.[33]

In general, satellite communities show an average population increase considerably below that of suburbs, though comparable to or higher than that of central cities. The relative stability of satellites probably indicates a continuing specialization in a few economic functions, with a consequent de-emphasis on residential expansion (which is currently the greatest source of population increase).

The role of the satellite city in urban regions has been well described as "subdominant."[34] It is important as a specialized though unofficial agent of the central city which aids in furnishing services and organization to the distant subareas of the region. This function is neither planned nor voluntary, but it is probably the major basis for survival of satellite communities. The unintended result is a strengthening of the invisible bonds which maintain a regional identity. Not only does the satellite flourish under this division of labor, but the central city is thereby relieved of some of its staggering responsibilities in providing facilities for urbanites beyond municipal limits. It should be recalled that a substantial proportion of the population in the urban fringe (as defined by the Census Bureau)—20 percent—resides in incorporated areas each having 2,500 population or over.[35] These areas are often what we have referred to as satellite communities.

EXURBIA

The farthest thrust of the urban region is both relatively recent and somewhat rare.[36] Only the very largest cities—New York City, Chicago, and Los Angeles—seem to develop one or more exurban outposts, which are located well beyond the fringe in what were originally rural or village communities. The exurban area may or may not be geographically continuous with the more familiar segments of the urban region. But it is nevertheless closely linked with the central city.

Exurbia is generically similar to suburbia, although the exurbanite often refuses to consider himself in the same universe with the suburbanite. Both types represent a basic ambivalence toward the big city; both wish to escape —but not too far (either physically or psychologically) from the cultural magnetism of the metropolis. Exurbia and suburbia differ, however, in their opportunities to express this ambivalence and in the means used to implement it.

[33]Duncan and Reiss, *op. cit.*, pp. 171–175; Schnore, "Satellites and Suburbs," *loc. cit.*

[34]Donald J. Bogue, *The Structure of the Metropolitan Community* (Ann Arbor, Mich., Horace H. Rackham School of Graduate Studies, University of Michigan, 1949), pp. 18–20, 61–62.

[35]Bogue, *Population Growth in Standard Metropolitan Areas,* p. 43.

[36]The following discussion is primarily based on A. C. Spectorsky, *The Exurbanites* (Philadelphia, J. B. Lippincott, 1955).

The exurbanite, by virtue of his occupation, has superior opportunities for escape. He (or she) is typically in the creative branches of the vast urban communications industry—advertising, commercial art, radio, television, films, magazines, and playwriting. From an ecological standpoint, given the desire to escape, these occupations are significant in that they do not require daily attendance at a downtown office or studio. In addition, they yield comparatively large salaries—$20,000 and up, with an average probably around $50,000. Consequently, the exurbanite can easily arrange to live at a considerable distance from the central city, unlike the typical suburbanite.

If exurbia is therefore both residence and workshop, how are specific locations selected? Escape involves physical distance, of course, but also physical contrast with the city and some link with previous marks of successful escape. These conditions are satisfied by rural and semirural areas where artists and writers of the recent past lived and worked—e.g., Bucks County, Pennsylvania and Fairfield County, Connecticut.[37] Exurbia is therefore a specialized, modernized, financially successful version of the artists' colony, located 40–50 miles from the commercial center with which it maintains a sustained symbiotic relationship.

It is difficult to appraise the role of exurbia in the urban region. However, some relevant inferences can be made from the fragmentary information now available. Exurbanites, far out of proportion to their numbers, control (or at least significantly channel) the tastes and underlying ideals of urbanites in general. This is inherent in their occupational role, though many exurbanites would rather be "artistic" than merely expert tools of persuasion and amusement. In addition, as a special status group (based on their "glamorous" occupations, high incomes, and semibohemian living), exurbanites are among the pacesetters of urban fashion. The foreign car as a status item (rather than a more economical form of transportation), for example, was first adopted by exurbanites. Finally, exurban populations seem to be unwitting agents of a restrictive urban regionalism, while trying to retain the low density and high social status of "snob zoning" (such as requiring a minimum of four acres and $30,000 homes).[38]

THE URBAN REGION AS A FUNCTIONAL ENTITY

Throughout the preceding analyses of specialized parts in the urban region, it was difficult to ignore linkages between parts, and also the interrelations between specific parts and the central city. Indeed, the development and special character of each type of regional part could only be understood as a cumulative set of adjustments to some aspect (or aspects) of the central city.

[37] Boston seems to have acquired an exurban area in Hillsborough and Rockingham Counties of New Hampshire. See *The New York Times,* February 5, 1961.
[38] *The New York Times,* November 11 and December 16, 1956.

However, urban sociologists regard the central city as the dominant unit, not only with respect to influence on any one type of subdominant community, but as the subtle integrator of interrelations in the entire regional complex. In other words, the urban region is approached as a functional unity based on a territorial-social division of labor more or less influenced by the operation of the central city; and on recognizable patterns of coordination among the parts, which are directly or indirectly imposed by ongoing processes (social, cultural, and ecological) within the central city. Since this coordination and regional organization are highly complex, at present we can only try to indicate their essential character through research evidence that is illustrative and inferential, rather than conclusive.

Dominant Ecological Patterns

With some variations by region and size of central city, the basic dominance of the metropolis is most clearly evident in the familiar constellation of specialized zones or rings around the central city (see Fig. 1). This remarkably consistent pattern of differentiation is usually interpreted as a consequence of attempts (conscious or unintended) to accommodate to the centralized economic and political influence of the metropolis.

It has been suggested, furthermore, that specialized zones closest to the central city should therefore show greater internal specialization (i.e., sharper differences between community units) than that of more distant zones. This is based on the theory that the power of an organizing center decreases with distance, and that its power over dependent units is reflected in varying degrees of specialization (which is viewed as an adjustive mechanism) within such units. Recently, some evidence has been presented which supports this theory for a sample of 24 SMAs.[39] Suburban communities closest to the central city were found to exhibit greater variations among themselves than were discovered in outer suburban areas in such relevant factors as occupational distribution (particularly in percent of professionals and operatives), average monthly rental and physical condition of dwellings, concentration of non-whites, and voting behavior. Perhaps these differences can be explained as a consequence of the urban emphasis on status distinctions, which presumably diminishes as urbanization decreases.

Patterns of Population Distribution

Theoretically, metropolitan dominance should be indirectly expressed in the overall pattern of population density and distribution in the urban region. More specifically, the various areal parts of the region should exhibit predictably different population features as a consequence of their respective relations with the central city. For example, we would expect the urban fringe to have a lower density of population than the residential and industrial suburbs and

---

[39]Leslie Kish, "Differentiation in Metropolitan Areas," *American Sociological Review,* 19 (August, 1954), pp. 388–398.

a greater prevalence of urban population features in areas most accessible to the central city.

In general, these expectations have been fairly well substantiated by Bogue in studies of 67 of the largest urban regions of the U.S.[40] Not only does population density tend to decrease with distance from the metropolis, but the larger the metropolis (and therefore the greater the presumed influence) the greater the relative density. As expected, Bogue also demonstrates a relative concentration of persons with urban features in areas closest to central cities. A special analysis of sectors radiating from the metropolis to the regional periphery further shows that population density is considerably higher in sectors containing highways to other major cities and in those marked by the presence of satellite cities than in sectors which had neither feature. Central cities, therefore, seem to operate as latent regulators of regional population patterns, a situation that perhaps facilitates the economic dominance of the metropolis.

Economic Dominance

A growing fund of investigations concerned with metropolitan dominance emphasizes the direct and indirect economic dependence of the so-called hinterland on the central city. The pioneer formulations of this approach were made by Gras, McKenzie, and several urban geographers, but it is only recently that economic control has been verified by Bogue and others.[41] In the decade 1940–1950, central cities tended to provide disproportionately higher amounts of wholesale, retail, and diversified services (e.g., repairs, warehousing facilities) than other components of the urban region. Bogue found that population groupings within a 35-mile radius of the metropolis were specially dependent on the latter for retail commodities and diversified services, while dependence on wholesale services was even more marked for a 65-mile radius from the city. Beyond a 65-mile radius, in sectors containing either intermetropolitan highways or satellite cities, this dependence of the hinterland gradually declined. As summarized by McKenzie and Bogue, these economic patterns indicate that satellite cities, suburbs, and the fringe specialize in activities which do not directly compete with the superior resources of the metropolis.

*   *   *

[40] Bogue, *The Structure of the Metropolitan Community,* pp. 31–54.

[41] N. S. B. Gras, *An Introduction to Economic History* (New York, Harper and Brothers, 1922), Chaps. V, VI; McKenzie, *op. cit.,* pp. 70–84, 313; Eugene Van Cleef, *Trade Centers and Trade Routes* (New York, Appleton-Century-Crofts, 1937); Harold M. Mayer and Clyde F. Kohn, eds., *Readings in Urban Geography* (Chicago, University of Chicago Press, 1959), Sections 7, 10; Bogue, *The Structure of the Metropolitan Community,* pp. 38–40, 54–60; Melvin E. DeFleur and John Crosby, "Analyzing Metropolitan Dominance," *Social Forces,* 35 (October, 1956), pp. 68–75.

The Socio-Economic Status of Cities and Suburbs*

Leo F. Schnore

Students of urbanization in the United States seem to take it as axiomatic that the socio-economic status of "suburbia" is higher than that of the city. At least since the first statement of the Burgess zonal hypothesis in 1924, it has been generally assumed that such measures as income, education and occupational standing will ordinarily tend to exhibit an upward-sloping gradient with increasing distance away from the center of the urban agglomeration.[1] The Burgess scheme, taken in all its detail, has been subjected to considerable critical debate over the years. It has been attacked and defended with great vigor.[2] Despite the lack of consensus concerning the concentric zonal model as an adequate description of cities in general, the existence of broad status differences in favor of American suburbs seems to be an accepted part of our thinking. Hauser has provided a succinct account, and one to which most students of the subject would probably subscribe:

> Residential land use patterns were a function of the geometry of urban growth and the play of market forces. Since the city necessarily grew away from its point

*This study was supported by the research phase of the University of Wisconsin Urban Program, under the terms of a grant from the Ford Foundation. I am also grateful for assistance and technical facilities provided by the Social Systems Research Institute and the Numerical Analysis Laboratory, University of Wisconsin. The aid of four of my colleagues in the Institute —Arthur S. Goldberger, Verona Hofer, Roger F. Miller, and Norman B. Ryder—is especially appreciated.

[1] It will be recalled that the Burgess zones were originally described largely in terms of socio-economic status. Thus outside the CBD and the "zone in transition" (containing "first-settlement immigrant colonies, rooming-house districts, and homelessmen areas") were Zone III, "The Zone of Independent Workingmen's Homes," Zone IV, "The Zone of Better Residences," and Zone V, "The Commuter's Zone." See Ernest W. Burgess, "The Growth of the City: An Introduction to a Research Project," *Publications of the American Sociological Society,* 18 (1924), pp. 85–97; reprinted in Robert E. Park, Ernest W. Burgess, and Roderick D. McKenzie, *The City,* Chicago: University of Chicago Press, 1925, pp. 47–62.

[2] For criticisms, see Milla A. Alihan, *Social Ecology: A Critical Analysis,* New York: Columbia University Press, 1938; Maurice R. Davie, "The Pattern of Urban Growth," in George Peter Murdock, editor, *Studies in the Science of Society,* New Haven: Yale University Press, 1937, pp. 133–161; Walter Firey, *Land Use in Central Boston,* Cambridge: Harvard University Press, 1947. For a defense, see James A. Quinn, "The Burgess Zonal Hypothesis and Its Critics," *American Sociological Review,* 5 (April, 1940), pp. 210–218.

SOURCE: Leo F. Schnore, "The Socio-Economic Status of Cities and Suburbs," *American Sociological Review,* 28 (February 1963), 76–85. Reprinted by permission.

of origin, the newer residential areas were always farthest away from the center. . . .

The histories of the inner and older areas of our cities have been, on the whole, remarkably uniform. Present inner and older areas were, at their origin, outlying suburbs containing the residences of the fashionably elite. With the continued growth of the city they became, more and more, inner zones, and followed similar patterns of changes in their residential occupancy. They housed first the middle class, then workingmen's families and finally, in many cases, they were turned over to rooming houses and slums. . . .

Explosive urban and metropolitan growth, together with the play of market forces, determined both the patterns of land use and the distribution of population in space. Place of residence in metropolitan areas was determined by social and economic status, with the lower income groups living in the center of the city and the higher income groups toward the periphery. . . .

Because city boundary lines have tended to remain relatively fixed while metropolitan clumpings of people and economic activities expanded, larger and larger proportions of the total central city land area have become inner and older zones of the entire metropolitan area and have been taken over by lower income groups; and increasing proportions of the higher income groups in the entire metropolitan area have become residents of suburbia.[3]

While this passage would not be accepted as a "universal" account, applicable to cities around the world,[4] it sums up the prevalent view with respect to the development of current differences in socio-economic status between cities and suburbs in the United States.

Even the most familiar notions, however, are deserving of reexamination from time to time. In this instance, there are a number of reasons for reopening the question. First, the results of inquiries in other parts of the world, and in other historical periods, might lead us to question some of our cherished generalizations.[5] Second, generalizations about American cities and suburbs

[3]Philip M. Hauser, *Population Perspectives,* New Brunswick, New Jersey: Rutgers University Press, 1960, pp. 110–112. In subsequent sections, Hauser goes on to suggest some ways in which the future patterns of American cities may differ from the historical sequence described in the quotation.

[4]Referring especially to a series of studies in Latin America, Gist has observed that there is "ample evidence that ecological theory based on the study of [North] American cities is not necessarily applicable to cities in other parts of the world." Noel P. Gist, "The Urban Community," in Joseph B. Gittler, editor, *Review of Sociology: Analysis of a Decade,* New York: John Wiley and Sons, Inc., 1957, p. 170.

[5]With respect to the residential location of socio-economic strata in "preindustrial" cities, Sjoberg reports as follows: "The preindustrial city's central area is notable also as the chief residence of the elite. . . . The disadvantaged members of the city fan out toward the periphery, with the very poorest and the outcastes living in the suburbs, the farthest removed from the center." He reports that archeological and historical evidence, together with accounts of the residential structure of contemporary cities in all major world regions, "all confirm the universality of this land use pattern in the non-industrial civilized world." See Gideon Sjoberg, *The Preindustrial City: Past and Present,* Glencoe, Ill.: The Free Press, 1960, pp. 97–98.

tend to be based upon highly aggregated statistics for all "metropolitan areas" taken together, with contrasts between "central cities" and outlying "rings" emphasized; the hazard here is that the experience of the very largest metropolitan areas will unduly influence the results by sheer weight of numbers. Third, "suburbs" lacking the characteristics commonly attributed to them can be found in all parts of the United States. Many of them are quite low on all the common measures of socio-economic status.[6] Moreover, even the most vigorous defenders of the Burgess hypothesis have seen fit to limit its scope rather sharply.[7] Finally, an exploratory study of income differentials between larger American cities and suburbs in 1950 has suggested that city-fringe income differentials are not so clearly and uniformly in favor of outlying areas as commonly supposed.[8]

UNITS, DATA AND PROCEDURES

The availability of new 1960 census materials permits some simple tests of the hypothesis that suburban fringe populations possess, on the average, higher socio-economic status than the populations of central cities. Rather than using materials for metropolitan areas, where the rings frequently contain rural and agricultural populations, we have selected the "urbanized area" as the basic unit. The U.S. Bureau of the Census delineated 213 such areas in conjunction with the 1960 census. According to an official description.

> An urbanized area contains at least one city of 50,000 inhabitants or more in 1960, as well as the surrounding closely settled incorporated places and unincorporated areas. . . . *An urbanized area may be thought of as divided into the central city, or cities, and the remainder of the area, or the urban fringe.* . . .
>
> Arrangements were made to include within the urbanized area those enumeration districts meeting specified criteria of population density as well as adjacent incorporated places. Since the urbanized area outside of incorporated places was defined in terms of enumeration districts, the boundaries of the urbanized area for the most part follow such features as roads, streets, railroads, streams, and other clearly defined lines which may be easily identified by census enumerators in the field and often do not conform to the boundaries of political units.[9]

---

[6]See Bennett M. Berger, *Working-Class Suburb,* Berkeley and Los Angeles: University of California Press, 1960. In addition to residential suburbs inhabited by blue-collar workers, there are many industrial satellites characterized by low income. See Leo F. Schnore, "Satellites and Suburbs," *Social Forces,* 36 (December, 1957), pp. 121–127.

[7]See James A. Quinn, *Human Ecology,* New York: Prentice-Hall, Inc., 1950, Chapter VI.

[8]Leo F. Schnore, "City-Suburban Income Differentials in Metropolitan Areas," *American Sociological Review,* 27 (April, 1962), pp. 252–255.

[9]U.S. Bureau of the Census, *U.S. Census of the Population: 1960,* Volume I, *Characteristics of the Population,* Part A, "Number of Inhabitants," Washington, D.C.: U.S. Government Printing Office, 1961, pp. xviii–xx; italics added. See also Richard A. Kurtz and Joanne B. Eicher, "Fringe and Suburb: A Confusion of Concepts," *Social Forces,* 37 (October, 1958), pp. 32–37.

Although the U.S. Bureau of the Census has carefully avoided using the term "suburb" in describing the outlying portion of the urbanized area, such a usage is somewhat preferable to calling this area the "urban fringe," for the latter term has been commonly employed to refer to an area of mixed rural and urban land use. With Duncan and Reiss, we prefer to conceive the outlying (non-central city) portion of the urbanized area as consisting of *two* areal components—suburbs *and* the urban fringe—but we will use the term "suburb" as a matter of convenience.[10]

Our procedure was extremely simple. Comparisons of central cities and suburbs were possible in 200 urbanized areas.[11] We have tabulated the number of areas in which the values on certain socio-economic status variables were higher in one or the other of these two areas—city or suburb. The three measures of socio-economic status employed here were: (1) median family income, (2) the per cent of the population aged 25 years or over with four years of high school or more, and (3) the proportion of the total employed labor force in white-collar occupations. In short, we have used measures of income, education, and occupation—the three traditional variables employed in sociological analyses of stratification.

FINDINGS: CITY-SUBURBAN STATUS DIFFERENTIALS BY SIZE

Table 1 contains a comparison of the socio-economic status of central cities and suburban fringes in areas categorized by population size. While none of the cities in the two largest size classes exceeds its suburbs in income, increasing proportions do so as one moves down the size range to the very smallest areas. The same general results are seen in the second column, where a measure of educational achievement is employed. Again, the two largest size classes (38 areas) fail to show a single instance in which cities outstrip their suburbs. Moving down the full range of sizes, however, one finds that many small cities rank higher in educational status than their suburbs. Finally, the third column reveals the same general picture, although there are differences in detail. While there are few very large central cities containing higher proportions of white-collar workers than their respective suburbs, they are not nearly so numerous—absolutely or relatively—as in the smaller size classes. In the

[10]Otis Dudley Duncan and Albert J. Reiss, Jr., *Social Characteristics of Urban and Rural Communities, 1950,* New York: John Wiley and Sons, Inc., 1956, Chapter 11; see especially footnote 3, p. 118.

[11]The thirteen urbanized areas for which city-suburban comparisons could not be made include Meriden, Connecticut; Topeka, Kansas; Lewiston-Auburn, Maine; Raleigh, North Carolina; Lawton, Oklahoma; and the following eight areas in Texas: Amarillo, Beaumont, El Paso, Laredo, Lubbock, San Angelo, Tyler and Wichita Falls. All of the data were taken from the U.S. Bureau of the Census, *General Social and Economic Characteristics,* "Advance Reports," Series PC(A3), Tables 32 and 33. Individual reports for states were issued between July 14, 1961 and April 27, 1962.

TABLE 1. CITY-SUBURBAN DIFFERENTIALS IN SOCIO-ECONOMIC STATUS, BY SIZE OF
URBANIZED AREA, 1960

Size of Urbanized Area, 1960	Per Cent of Urbanized Areas with Suburban Values Higher in:			
	Median Family Income	Per Cent Completing High School	Per Cent White Collar	Number of Areas
1,000,000 and over	100.0	100.0	87.5	16
500,000–1,000,000	100.0	100.0	86.4	22
250,000–500,000	79.3	75.9	55.2	29
150,000–250,000	72.1	62.8	48.8	43
100,000–150,000	70.3	64.9	40.5	37
50,000–100,000	56.6	49.1	30.2	53
All areas	74.0	68.5	50.5	200

smaller areas, in fact, clear majorities show higher values for central cities.

In sum, the popular view of city-suburban differentials in socio-economic status is derived mainly from the experience of the larger areas. Since the averages for all areas taken together are inevitably weighted by the situation in the largest areas, they can be very misleading as a description of individual areas.[12] In smaller areas (those between 50,000 and 100,000), the city itself is more likely to contain populations that are—on the average—higher in status than those found in the suburban fringe. Whether one measures socio-economic status by income, education, or occupation, the results are the same:

[12]The following differences appeared between cities and suburbs in the 157 urbanized areas delineated in conjunction with the 1950 census:

	Cities	Suburbs
Median school years completed	9.9	11.1
Per cent in white collar occupations	45.2	46.9
Median personal income (dollars)	2,249	2,449

SOURCE: Duncan and Reiss, op. cit., pp. 127–130; city-suburban differentials were also shown according to sex and color.

In 1960, the 213 urbanized areas showed the following aggregate differences:

	Cities	Suburbs
Median school years completed	10.7	12.0
Per cent in white collar occupations	40.6	50.3
Median family income (dollars)	5,945	7,114

SOURCE: "Advance Reports," Series PC(A3)-1, Table 100.

The status differentials again favor the suburbs. The 38 urbanized areas of 500,000 or more contained more than 70 per cent of the total population in urbanized areas (almost 96 million persons), and the above averages are heavily weighted by the experience of these large areas. The popular generalizations regarding city-suburban differences are accurate as descriptions of *individuals according to place of residence,* but they are misleading statements about *areas of habitation.*

there is a marked association between size and the direction of city-suburban differentials.

What are the factors that lie behind the differences that can be observed among size classes? One line of interpretation involves sheer *age of settlement.* Cities vary in age, and a well-known association exists between age and size; in the 213 urbanized areas of 1960, for example, the correlation between size of central city and age is +.478, and that between size of urbanized area and age is +.502.[13] Nevertheless the correlation is not very high, and it might be expected that areas of the same size, but differing in age, will differ in residential structure. But first let us examine the extent to which age itself is associated with city-suburban differentials in socio-economic status.

FINDINGS: CITY-SUBURBAN STATUS DIFFERENTIALS BY AGE

We have measured the "ages" of these 200 urbanized areas by counting the number of decades that have passed since their central cities first contained 50,000 inhabitants. Table 2 shows the city-suburban comparisons on our three measures of socio-economic status according to age. The first column reveals that suburban fringes consistently register higher median family incomes in the older areas; none of the 31 cities reaching a size of 50,000 in 1880 or earlier has a higher average income than its suburbs. In contrast, the newer urbanized areas tend consistently to show larger and larger proportions of central cities with higher incomes. When the measure of educational status is employed, as in the second column, the results are generally the same. The proportion of persons completing at least a high school education is consistently higher in the suburbs of older cities, while newer cities tend to show the opposite pattern. Similarly, the occupational measure suggests that age is clearly associated with city-suburban differentials in socio-economic status. Examining the third column, we find that none of the 31 oldest cities exceeds its suburban fringe in the proportion of white-collar workers. At the other extreme, three out of every four of the newest cities contain higher proportions of white-collar workers than their adjacent suburbs.

As with size, then, we have found another series of marked associations between age and the direction of city-suburban differentials in socio-economic status. The common conception—that higher status people live in the suburbs —tends to be true of the very oldest areas, but it is progressively less true of newer areas. In cities that have only reached substantial size (50,000 inhabi-

---

[13]The measure of "age" is the number of decades that have passed since the central city (or cities) first contained 50,000 inhabitants. Bogue and Harris reported a correlation of +.596 between age (as measured here) and size of 125 metropolitan areas in 1940; see Donald J. Bogue and Dorothy L. Harris, *Comparative Population and Urban Research via Multiple Regression and Covariance Analysis,* Oxford, Ohio and Chicago: Scripps Foundation for Research in Population Problems, Miami University, and Population Research and Training Center, University of Chicago, 1954, Appendix Table II, p. 75.

tants) in recent decades, cities themselves contain populations that are higher in status than those in their own adjacent suburbs. Not only is the popular generalization concerning city-suburban status differentials inadequate as a description of all urbanized areas, but it is also directly contrary to the facts in the newest areas.

TABLE 2. CITY-SUBURBAN DIFFERENTIALS IN SOCIO-ECONOMIC STATUS, BY AGE OF CENTRAL CITY

Census Year in Which Central City (or Cities) First Reached 50,000	Per Cent of Urbanized Areas with Suburban Values Higher in:			
	Median Family Income	Per Cent Completing High School	Per Cent White Collar	Number of Areas
1800–1860	100.0	100.0	100.0	14
1870–1880	100.0	100.0	100.0	17
1890–1900	86.1	75.0	58.3	36
1910–1920	75.0	75.0	54.2	48
1930–1940	71.9	56.3	31.3	32
1950–1960	50.9	47.2	24.5	53
All areas	74.0	68.5	50.5	200

FURTHER ANALYSIS: A MULTIVARIATE APPROACH

The preceding comparisons of cities and their suburbs by socio-economic status have demonstrated that higher status groups tend to occupy the periphery of *older* and *larger* urban areas. But age and size are themselves correlated. The next analytical problem became one of assessing the relative "weight" to be assigned to age and size as predictors of city-suburban differentials in socio-economic status. In view of the marked correlation between the independent variables and the limited number of cases for analysis (200 urbanized areas), we were obliged to turn to partial correlation techniques.

Our procedure was again extremely simple. For each of the three separate measures of socio-economic status for each urbanized area, we assigned arbitrary numerical values—a "0" if the central city was higher, and a "1" if the suburban fringe was higher.[14] We then computed zero-order and partial correlation coefficients between each of the three dependent variables (education,

[14]See Daniel B. Suits, "The Use of Dummy Variables in Regression Equations," *Journal of the American Statistical Association,* 52 (December, 1957), pp. 548–551; for an illustrative usage, see John B. Lansing and Dwight M. Blood, "A Cross-Section Analysis of Non-Business Air Travel," *Journal of the American Statistical Association,* 53 (December, 1958), pp. 923–947.

occupation, and income) and the independent variables. We then repeated the analysis using suburb-city ratios, i.e., dividing the suburb's value on each of the three measures by the city's respective value.

Besides age and size, however, we took care to add a third "independent" variable. *This variable was the percentage of the total urbanized area's 1960 population found within the central city or cities.* The rationale for its inclusion in this phase of the analysis was as follows: (a) The 200 urbanized areas under study differ considerably in this proportion, ranging from a low of 27.2 per cent in Wilkes-Barre, Pennsylvania, to a high of 99.7 per cent in Austin, Texas. (b) Inspection of the data for the 200 urbanized areas indicated that this proportion was negatively associated with all three of the dependent variables, the measures of socio-economic status differentials, and with both of the independent variables whose predictive ability we wished to assess. In other words, urbanized areas with a high proportion of population in central cities tended to show higher city values on income, education, and occupation, and they also tended to be smaller and newer. (c) This proportion seemed to us a rough but useful measure of the extent to which a city has been successful in extending its official boundaries to keep up with the physical spread of urban development within its immediate vicinity. Some large cities are surrounded by "iron rings" of established incorporated suburbs or other political units which are extremely resistant to absorption by annexation, while other cities are free—whether by virtue of facilitating legal arrangements or by possession of powers of one kind or another—to annex outlying territory with relative ease.[15] In any event, we wished to eliminate the statistical effect of this "confounding variable," the extent to which the politically defined city is coextensive with the physically defined urbanized area. For ease of expression, we shall refer to this factor as the "annexation" variable throughout the balance of the discussion.

[15]State laws are extremely variable in this respect. Texas statutes apparently grant the municipality the greatest freedom to annex nearby territory, and it is noteworthy that all of the Texas cities in this study expanded their limits between 1950 and 1960. Law is apparently not the only critical factor, however, for some cities are reputed to use their control over the water supply or vital municipal services as a means of coercing outlying populations into joining the city. As for the ability of the measure used here to serve as a "proxy variable," representing annexation success, the following tabulation suggests that it is reasonably adequate:

Per Cent of Urbanized Area Population in City, 1960	Number of Urbanized Areas	Per Cent with Annexations by Central City, 1950–60
90.0 or more	39	89.7
80.0–89.9	36	83.3
70.0–79.9	33	78.8
60.0–69.9	36	75.0
50.0–59.9	29	72.4
Less than 50.0	27	55.6
All areas	200	77.0

Table 3 shows the zero-order correlations between each of the six variables and every other variable included in the analysis. The two bases of scoring cities and suburbs are shown above and below the diagonal. Except for the negative associations between the "annexation" factor and all the others, the coefficients are positive. Note the especially high correlations among the dependent variables when ratios are employed. The latter intercorrelations, although of interest, are of no immediate consequence for our analysis, since we wished to use these three variables as separate tests or assessments of the relative predictive ability of size and age, holding constant the confounding "annexation" factor.

TABLE 3.   ZERO-ORDER CORRELATION COEFFICIENTS*

	Independent Variables			Dependent Variables		
	Size	Annexation	Age	Education	Occupation	Income
Size	—	—.2341	.5006	.1789	.1825	.1574
Annexation	—.2341	—	—.3457	—.2982	—.2733	—.2883
Age	.5006	—.3457	—	.3753	.4781	.3701
Education	.1975	—.3943	.4861	—	.6204	.7023
Occupation	.1730	—.4246	.4590	.9478	—	.5759
Income	.1730	—.3660	.4135	.8393	.8538	—

*Above diagonal, correlations based on scoring cities and suburbs (0 and 1) as "dummy variables." Below diagonal, suburb-city ratios.

The results of these three assessments are reported in Tables 4 and 5, summaries of the two partial correlation analyses. Besides the multiple and partial correlation coefficients, we show the *beta* coefficients—the partial regression coefficients in standard form—and t statistics. The three separate analyses of educational, occupational, and income differentials on two different bases yield highly similar results. Both tables show that the predictive ability of population size is substantially reduced when the other two variables—age and annexation—are taken into account. In fact, the signs of the coefficients are reversed in all three instances in both tables, shifting from positive in the zero-order correlations to negative in the partials, and falling below the level of statistical significance. By contrast, age continues to serve as a highly significant predictor of city-suburban differentials in socio-economic status; when size and annexation are held constant, age continues to exert a large and measurable influence upon the direction of the differences between cities and suburbs.

TABLE 4. SUMMARY OF FIRST PARTIAL CORRELATION ANALYSIS, WITH CITIES AND SUBURBS SCORED AS "DUMMY VARIABLES"

Dependent variable	Education			Occupation			Income		
Multiple correlation coefficient	.4012			.4857			.3943		
Independent variable	Size	Annexation	Age	Size	Annexation	Age	Size	Annexation	Age
Controlled variables	Annexation Age	Size Age	Size Annexation	Annexation Age	Size Age	Size Annexation	Annexation Age	Size Age	Size Annexation
Partial correlation coefficients	−.0263	−.1951	.2833	−.0856	−.1375	.4164	−.0494	−.1872	.2903
Beta coefficients	−.0277	−.1932	.3223	−.0863	−.1287	.4768	−.0523	−.1857	.3320
t statistics	−0.037	−2.785	4.136	−1.202	−1.944	6.411	−0.693	−2.668	4.246

TABLE 5. SUMMMARY OF SECOND PARTIAL CORRELATION ANALYSIS, WITH SUBURBAN-CITY RATIOS

Dependent variable	Education			Occupation			Income		
Multiple correlation coefficient	.5374			.5366			.4680		
Independent variable	Size	Annexation	Age	Size	Annexation	Age	Size	Annexation	Age
Controlled variables	Annexation Age	Size Age	Size Annexation	Annexation Age	Size Age	Size Annexation	Annexation Age	Size Age	Size Annexation
Partial correlation coefficients	−.0849	−.2818	.3986	−.1036	−.3264	.3720	−.0653	−.2653	.3217
Beta coefficients	−.0826	−.2627	.4366	−.1010	−.3090	.4028	−.0665	−.2580	.3576
t statistics	−1.192	−4.111	6.085	−1.458	−4.834	5.610	−0.916	−3.853	4.756

CONCLUSIONS

Sheer age of settlement has emerged as the best predictor of the direction of city-suburban differences in socio-economic status. Older urbanized areas tend strongly to possess peripheral populations of higher socio-economic standing than found in the central cities themselves. In contrast, newer cities tend to contain populations ranking higher on education, occupation, and income than their respective suburbs. To some extent, these differences are also revealed when urbanized areas are classified by size, but control of the latter factor does not eliminate the apparent importance of age as a factor in residential structure.

What is it about sheer age of settlement that might account for the observed differences? The first thing the student of the American city might consider is the fact that the housing stock of older areas of occupancy is obsolescent. These areas, concentrated near the center of the political city, are filled with older structures in such disrepair that enormous efforts have recently been directed toward slum clearance and renewal, and toward renovation of "blighted" areas which are fast becoming slums. These are the areas which have come to be occupied by groups at the bottom of the socio-economic ladder—groups which have strictly limited housing choices. In the older urbanized areas, new additions to the available housing stock have tended over the years to be added at the physical margins of the built-up area. New housing developments, in other words, have been concentrated in outlying zones, where they have come to be occupied by those who can afford the costs of home ownership and the added transportation charges that go with peripheral residence.[16]

In newer urbanized areas, the housing stock of the central city itself is neither so old nor so run-down as to be unattractive to potential home-owners of the expanding "middle class." At the same time, the pressures exerted by the competition of alternative (non-residential) land uses on inner zones now appear to be less intense in these newer cities than they were in older cities at comparable stages in the past; with the availability of the automobile and the truck, industrial and commercial land uses are less likely to be thrusting out inexorably from the heart of the city, and more likely to be "leap-frogging" the interior residential zones for new shopping centers and industrial parks at

[16]We say that the more favored classes will ordinarily pre-empt the newer and more desirable housing areas, and that with the expansion of the built-up territory, these areas have been typically located at the periphery in American cities. We simply assume a high degree of locational freedom on the part of the wealthy, who may occupy practically any area, as compared with the lower classes, who are much more severely restricted with respect to residential choices. Thus the wealthy may live very near the center if they are willing to pay the high costs involved in competing with non-residential land uses. Most American cities reveal such elite enclaves very near the downtown area; consider only Beacon Hill in Boston, as described by Firey, and Chicago's Gold Coast, shown in the original Burgess map as a deviant case. From one perspective, these areas represent "survivals" of an earlier pattern of land use, but there is nothing mysterious about the mechanism that produces them.

the outer periphery. As a consequence, central residential zones in newer cities may be less likely to undergo the "succession" or "sequent occupance" of progressively lower status groups experienced by neighborhoods in the older cities.

As for the older cities, a fascinating question is raised by these materials: *Have they evolved in a predictable direction?* Burgess conceived his zonal hypothesis as a "growth model," or a statement couched entirely in terms of process, and not as a static or cross-sectional representation of urban spatial structure. The very title of his original essay—"The Growth of the City"— indicated his intentions. In referring to the stylized map of Chicago that accompanied his original statement of the zonal hypothesis, Burgess remarked that "This chart represents an ideal construction of the tendencies of any town or city to expand radially from its central business district. . . . This chart brings out clearly the main fact of expansion, namely, the tendency of each inner zone to extend its area by the invasion of the next outer zone."[17]

As to the location of the "elite," in fact, Burgess noted that "the present boundaries of the area of deterioration were not many years ago those of the zone now inhabited by independent wage-earners, and within the memories of thousands of Chicagoans contained the residences of the 'best families.' "[18] Or consider the testimony of Homer Hoyt. Two sets of maps showing "high-grade," "intermediate," and "low-grade" residential areas for Chicago in 1857, 1873, 1899, and 1930 reveal that the "high-grade" areas were very near the center in 1857 and that they shifted toward the periphery over the years.[19] But Chicago is only one case. Consider Heberle's account of developments in the American South:

> It seems to be characteristic for the older, smaller, cities in the South that the homes of the socially prominent families were to be found just outside the central —and only—business district. . . . As the city grew and as wealth increased, the "old" families tended to move towards the periphery. . . . The old homes are then coverted into rooming houses and "tourist homes." This in itself is nothing peculiar to the South. However, it so happens that in the kind of city under consideration, the poorer people usually lived at the edge of town. This was particularly the case with Negroes. It happens, therefore, quite frequently that white people infiltrate into suburban areas occupied by Negroes, buying their property or cancelling their leases.[20]

[17]Burgess, "The Growth of the City," in *The City, op. cit.,* p. 50.

[18]*Ibid.,* pp. 50–51.

[19]Homer Hoyt, *The Structure and Growth of Residential Neighborhoods in American Cities,* Washington, D.C.: Federal Housing Administration, 1939, Figure 29, p. 83, and Figure 31, p. 166. This shift is described in detail in Homer Hoyt, *One Hundred Years of Land Values in Chicago,* Chicago: University of Chicago Press, 1933, Chapter VI.

[20]Rudolf Heberle, "Social Consequences of the Industrialization of Southern Cities," *Social Forces,* 27 (October, 1948), pp. 34–35.

In sum, we might outline a rough "evolutionary model" to describe the changes in older urban areas. With growth and expansion of the center, and with radical improvements in transportation and communication technology, the upper strata have shifted from central to peripheral residence, and the lower classes have increasingly taken up occupancy in the central areas abandoned by the elite. Despite mounting land values occasioned by the competition of alternative (non-residential) land uses, the lower strata have been able to occupy valuable central land in tenements, subdivided dwellings originally intended for single families, and other high-density "slum" arrangements.

The evolutionary sequence roughly sketched here is far from complete. For one thing, it requires more attention to what Burgess called "the survival of an earlier use of a district." A case in point is the persistence of elite areas near the centers of many cities, a deviation from the general pattern to which we have already alluded. More generally, it requires elaboration of the role of "historical residues," such as the significance of a city's development in a particular transportation era. For example, casual observation suggests a whole series of differences between pre- and post-automobile cities in the United States—differences in street patterns, land uses, and residential densities. Unfortunately, precise historical data are rather difficult to obtain and to evaluate, and the problem of attributing current significance to "survivals" from an earlier epoch always remains.[21]

Nothing in the preceding account is intended to suggest that a fixed and immutable "final stage" has been achieved in older American cities. Concerning the future implications of current developments, Hauser has observed:

> The combination of urban renewal in the inner zones of central cities and blight and urban sprawl in the suburbs is tending to disrupt the pattern of population distribution which has placed the higher income groups farthest out from the center of the city. Should these trends continue, the residential land use pattern in metropolitan areas would be turned inside out, with the newer and more desirable areas located in the rebuilt inner city zones as well as in the most distant parts of suburbia.[22]

In conclusion, we must emphasize that our own efforts to reconstruct the past development of urban residential structure are speculative. They are based on a thin line of evidence derived from cross-sectional observations of broad status groups in cities of different age. One hesitates to assert on the basis of these materials that a determinate "evolutionary sequence" occurs with the maturation of urban areas. Longitudinal inferences cannot be readily derived

[21]A suggestive treatment of the evolution of residential neighborhoods is contained in Edgar M. Hoover and Raymond Vernon, *Anatomy of a Metropolis,* Cambridge: Harvard University Press, 1959, pp. 190–207. See also Raymond Vernon, "The Economics and Finances of the Large Metropolis," *Daedalus,* 90 (Winter, 1961), pp. 31–47.

[22]Hauser, *op. cit.,* p. 115.

from cross-sectional observations. Nothing presented here denies the existence of an historical series of outward shifts of higher status groups from the center to the periphery, but proof of such a sequence is not established in this study.

Further research must undertake just such historical reconstructions of the major shifts in location of socio-economic strata in cities as they have grown and matured. The availability of census tract data for 30 years in a number of urban areas opens up one line of analytical possibilities. Certainly the finer observational grain afforded by tract analyses is preferable to the kind of gross city-suburban comparisons set out in this paper. Models for comparative research of this kind already exist in the literature.[23] Perhaps a more pressing need is that for models which will predict the future growth and structure of newer cities. It is already apparent that their development will differ in numerous respects from the patterns displayed by older cities. A revival of urban research effort, focussed on certain "classic" problems in ecological analysis, and using modern research techniques in a comparative framework, should yield rich returns in the way of understanding the growth and changing spatial structure of the American city.

[23]Beverly Duncan, Georges Sabagh, and Maurice D. Van Arsdol, Jr., "Patterns of City Growth," *American Journal of Sociology,* 67 (January, 1962), pp. 418–429; Otis Dudley Duncan and Beverly Duncan, "Residential Distribution and Occupational Stratification," *American Journal of Sociology,* 60 (March, 1955), pp. 495–503; Otis Dudley Duncan and Stanley Lieberson, "Ethnic Segregation and Assimilation," *American Journal of Sociology,* 64 (January, 1959), pp. 364–374; Stanley Lieberson, "Suburbs and Ethnic Residential Patterns," *American Journal of Sociology,* 67 (May, 1962), pp. 673–681. The only related topic that has received detailed historical treatment is the outward dispersion of various immigrant groups over the years; see Paul F. Cressey, "Population Succession in Chicago: 1898–1930," *American Journal of Sociology,* 44 (July, 1938), pp. 59–69; Richard G. Ford, "Population Succession in Chicago," *American Journal of Sociology,* 56 (September, 1950), pp. 156–160; and Stanley Lieberson, "The Impact of Residential Segregation on Ethnic Assimilation," *Social Forces,* 40 (October, 1961), pp. 52–57.

C SYSTEMIC FORMS AND INTERDEPENDENCE

The American Community as a Social System: The System's Vertical and Horizontal Patterns
Roland L. Warren

THE SYSTEM'S VERTICAL AND HORIZONTAL PATTERNS

To the present writer, a type of analysis which seems much more applicable and useful than the external-internal concepts in the consideration of communities as social systems is one which distinguishes between a community's vertical pattern and its horizontal pattern. In describing this distinction, we will be considering the final question which we posed for our consideration of the extent to which communities could be treated as social systems: *What is the relation of community social system units to other social systems?*

As a start, let us remind ourselves that community subsystems are often, though not always, parts of social systems which extend beyond the community. Examples are chain stores, branch banks, branch offices or plants of a national company, local offices of state or federal governmental agencies, and so on. Still other community units, like churches, schools, and local government, stand in a definite though less clearly defined relationship to extracom-

SOURCE: Roland L. Warren, from *The Community in America* (Chicago: Rand McNally & Company, 1963), pp. 161–166. © 1963 by Rand McNally & Company, Chicago. Reprinted by permission.

munity systems. We shall define a community's *vertical* pattern as the structural and functional relation of its various social units and subsystems to extracommunity systems. The term vertical is used to reflect the fact that such relationships often involve different hierarchical levels within the extracommunity system's structure of authority and power. The relationships are typically those of a system unit to the system's headquarters, although several intervening levels may occur. Thus, our community's bank was also the central office for a whole system of branches located in other communities. The vertical relationship between the local unit and the other units of the system was downward. Often the relation is upward, from a church to a denominational headquarters, from a local chain store to the district office, from the local branch plant to the national headquarters, from a local health association chapter to the national association.

The term *vertical pattern* is used to indicate that we are not referring primarily to a particular type of unit (though some local units may be clearly more relevant than others) but to a type of relationship shared to a greater or lesser extent by all local units, some very emphatically through clear systemic relationships to extracommunity systems, others less strongly bound in systemic ties to extracommunity systems, others bound not so much to extracommunity social systems as to cultural patterns in the surrounding culture. An example of this last is an individual nuclear family whose systemic kinship ties extending outside the community are minimal, let us assume, but whose structure and function are nevertheless closely related to regional and national culture patterns extending far beyond the community.

At the same time, there is a relationship *across* the many different units and subsystems which operate on the community level. We shall define a community's *horizontal pattern* as the structural and functional relation of its various social units and subsystems to each other. The term "horizontal" is used to indicate that, roughly speaking, the community units, *insofar as they have relevance to the community system,* tend to be on approximately the same hierarchical level (a community unit level, as opposed to a state, regional, national, or international level of authority, administration, decision-making, and so on). We use the term "pattern" to describe this relationship to indicate that we are not referring primarily to one type of community unit as opposed to another, but rather to a type of relationship into which all community units come in some of their aspects, a relationship which poses a different set of goals, organizational demands, norms, and so on, from that involved in the vertical pattern.

The vertical-horizontal distinction corresponds roughly, though not completely, to Homans' distinction between the external and internal systems.[1] As we shall see, the community functions in relation to its environment as it performs tasks which relate it increasingly to the surrounding geographic environment, indeed, to ever larger and larger environments. The specific subsystems which perform these functions tend to have strong formal organi-

[1]George C. Homans, *The Human Group* (New York: Harcourt, Brace, 1950).

zation dictated by the necessity of getting the job done and also by the patterns laid down by the extracommunity systems of which they may be a part. Thus the vertical pattern tends to be similar to Homans' external system.

As the community functions, however, relations spring up which are based on sentiment and not dictated by the environment. Although these relations correspond to what Homans called the internal system, they are only part of what is meant by the community's horizontal pattern. The other part is the formal organization of the coordinating function. The formal aspects of the organization through which the member units of a system are related to each other are placed by Homans in the external system. We shall nevertheless consider them part of the horizontal pattern, and here is the crux of the matter. For purposes of community analysis, the division into the relation of local subsystems to extracommunity systems (vertical pattern) and the relation of the subsystems to each other (horizontal pattern) seems more fruitful as a basis for analysis than does the difference between relations dictated by environment or based on spontaneous sentiment which Homans singled out for special emphasis in his external-internal distinction.

Turning now to the task-maintenance distinction, we once again find a fruitful analytical tool of great usefulness, but not exactly the same as the vertical-horizontal pattern distinction. The similarity is in the fact that task performance often relates community subsystems to extracommunity systems in a vertical pattern, while maintenance activities have to do more with the relation of different subsystems to each other on the local level. For all practical purposes, the two sets of terms correspond—giving us, incidentally, the opportunity to borrow liberally from theory and hypotheses relating to the task-maintenance dichotomy in our analysis of the community as a system.

They do not correspond precisely, however. An example of lack of correspondence would be a chamber of commerce which carries on a program of improving the appearance of the community's main street. Here is a specific task which brings diverse subsystems together in a common undertaking at the community level. As such, the horizontal pattern, not the vertical pattern, is principally involved. Yet it is a task operation. The vertical pattern is involved, incidentally, in the relationship of the local chamber of commerce to the national Chamber of Commerce.

By and large, however, we can note that task performance by the community's constituent subsystems—schools, churches, factories, voluntary associations—tends to orient them toward extracommunity systems. On the other hand, maintenance functions tend to be carried on across the subsystems of the community, involving the horizontal pattern of relationships among these local units.

We are now in a position to raise and answer a question regarding the manner in which the community as a social system operates to preserve or restore equilibrium. Homans, in a brief but incisive analysis of the disintegration of a New England community, Hilltown, emphasized the relationship between equilibrium and social control, . . . He wrote:

What we can see is that interaction, activity, sentiment, and norms in Hilltown, unlike some other groups we have studied, were not working together to maintain the *status quo* or to achieve further integration of the group. Instead the relationships between the elements of behavior were such as to lead, in time, toward the condition Durkheim called *anomie*, a lack of contact between the members of a group, and a loss of control by the group over individual behavior.[2]

Thus, equilibrium involves the community's ability to exercise sufficient social control to achieve adequate conformity to community norms and to minimize change impacts.

It is interesting to note, also, that viewed as a social system, the community does display behavior analogous to the pulsating interchange between instrumental activity, as indicated in goal-attainment and adaptational behavior, and expressive activity, as indicated in integrative and tension-management behavior. One sees this pulsation, described by Parsons and Bales as applying to social system behavior in the small group, manifesting itself in the community as various community units carry on activities, often in relation to extracommunity systems, which have the effect of accomplishing certain tasks, such as the development of a new cancer clinic or the organization of a local chapter of a national voluntary association. The performance of such tasks often places a strain on existing relationships among the various community units, and maintenance activities must be performed if a new equilibrium is to be achieved. In a sense, the pulsation is symbolized in the existence of vertically oriented health associations and the horizontally oriented community welfare councils.

The performance of intrumental functions, largely by the community's vertical pattern, and expressive functions, largely by the horizontal pattern, was described earlier by the author as follows:

> Thus we begin to see the community as a social system which undergoes stresses and strains but whose overall longtime process is one of increasing differentiation of function and structure, and whose chief orientation of interest and association is shifting from the horizontal to the vertical. . . . We also begin to get a picture of the dynamics of induced community change, in which the problem-area specialist and his vertically-oriented interest group achieve accomplishments which in turn make for greater differentiation of function and also create tensions within the community. Complementing this function is that of the permissive community organizer with his horizontal focus of interest and his typical leadership functions of tension reduction and co-ordination among the parts of the system.[3]

[2] *Ibid.,* p. 367.

[3] Roland L. Warren, "Toward A Reformulation of Community Theory," *Human Organization,* XV, No. 2 (Summer, 1956), 11, reprinted in *Community Development Review,* vol. IX (June, 1958). See also "Local Autonomy and Community Development," *Autonomous Groups,* vol. XV, No. 102 (Fall and Winter, 1959), and "Community Patterns and Community Development" . . . .

Thus, in the question of equilibrium, as in the other questions raised regarding the applicability of system analysis to the community, we find that the community passes muster. We have found the major dimensions of social system analysis to be applicable to the community in a degree sufficient to give us reassurance that further exploration along these lines is worth while.

But before going on, let us consider some of the special characteristics of the community and decide how we shall proceed with them. Looking back now at Moe's three ways in which communities are different from other social systems,[4] we recall observing that the fact that the community is a "system of systems" should give us little difficulty, for so is a formal organization. He also indicated that the community as a social system is implicit in nature as compared with the explicitness of a formal organization. This is true, but then so is a small informal friendship group, such as that described by Whyte in *Street Corner Society*.[5] Such informal groups, although not explicit in the sense of a formal organization, are widely recognized as social systems.

Moe's second point, however, is more crucial: The community is not structurally and functionally centralized in the same sense as a formal organization. This is true. It is, of course, also true of small informal groups. In the case of small groups, however, the internal pattern is much more readily discernible and gives a much greater impression of a coherent, identifiable group than do most communities. We have noted that communities as such do not have formal structures, though their constituent subsystems may have. We have also noted that such community subsystems may be integrally related to extracommunity systems, but that the community itself is not.

These are characteristics which we should observe and take due account of as we proceed with our analysis. One additional difficulty remains, the major one yet to be confronted. This is the relative strength of the vertical systemic ties linking community units to extracommunity systems, as compared with the relative weakness of the horizontal ties linking local community units with each other. Recognizing the strong relation of the local post office to the United States postal system, acknowledging that its operation and its policies are not determined within the community but are merely implementations of a national system, we are confronted with a choice. We can either say that the post office, not being a community phenomenon, will therefore not be included in our definition of the community system, and will be ignored in our analysis; or we can recognize that the post office and numerous other community-based units have stronger ties to extracommunity systems than they do to other units within the community, but treat them much as we treat any other community subsystem, in terms of input-output relations with the rest of the community. The local post office, for example, performs certain services related to mail for

[4]Edward O. Moe, "Consulting with a Community System: A Case Study," *Journal of Social Issues*, XV, No. 2 (1959).

[5]William F. Whyte, *Street Corner Society: The Social Structure of an Italian Slum* (Chicago: University of Chicago Press, 1943).

other community subsystems. It also provides a source of employment in the production-exchange-consumption function; brings money into the community from the federal government in the form of wages and local expenditures for equipment, heat, light, rent; takes money out of the community in the form of postage charges, and so on. We shall follow this course, which is facilitated by our insistence on defining the community in terms of specified locality-relevant functions and on differentiating between input-output relations of the community's subsystems and of the community itself as a social system.

In following this course, preferring to accept and incorporate into our analysis those community subsystems which are strongly related to extracommunity systems, we shall necessarily give more attention to the nature of these extracommunity systems than we otherwise would. Thus, though the task may be more demanding, we shall have come to grips with the problem of the increasing vertical orientation of local community subsystems. In Chapter 3 it was pointed out that the "great change" was operating in the direction of strengthening the ties of community subsystems to extracommunity systems and of weakening community coherence and autonomy. We pointed out elsewhere that this has occurred to such an extent that some students of the community suggest that the term should be completely abandoned. We prefer to paraphrase Mark Twain by saying that the report of the community's death is greatly exaggerated, and to note and to analyze carefully the structural and functional change occurring in American communities as they adapt and change in response to change impacts—particularly the seven aspects of the "great change" which have already been considered in detail.

*　　*　　*

The Dynamics of Increase in Scale
Scott Greer

*　　*　　*

The dynamics of metropolitan society are implicit in the basic structure presented; if we wish to understand the important changes going on in the metropolis, we must look to the societal changes in the geographical division of labor and in the processes of integration. Doing so, we find concurrent trends in both, mutually dependent, their interaction producing very rapid shifts in the carrying society and in its relations with the city.

SOURCE: Scott Greer, from *The Emerging City* (New York: The Free Press, 1962), pp. 41–54. Copyright © 1962 by The Free Press of Glencoe, a Division of The Macmillan Company. Reprinted with permission of The Macmillan Company.

If we take, as a beginning, American industry in the mid-nineteenth century, the most striking changes since have been (1) the increasing use of nonhuman sources of energy, translated through machines into human values; (2) the increasing span of the organizational networks in which men and machines are integrated for productive and distributive purposes; and (3) a resulting increase in the amount of productivity for each human participant.

The increasing rate of energy transformation includes greatly improved transportation and communication media; the consequences may be summarized in one statement—the space-time ratio (or cost in time for traveling a given distance) has greatly decreased. This is apparent in the transportation of persons and goods (including energy, such as electricity) and in the transmission of messages. The implications of these changes are that space, for all practical purposes, is no longer fixed. It is a barrier to the extension of activities, but as the mechanisms of extension improve it becomes simply a channel for integration. Thus, the shrinking space-time ratio allows the use of human actors who are increasingly widely separated but whose activities can be just as closely coordinated as before.[11]

This makes possible the increased span of organizational networks that coordinate behavior. Geographical division of labor includes intensive agricultural specialization, with an increased emphasis upon the national market and decline of the subsistence aspect of farming, and a similar development of industrial and service specialization. Recreation is increasingly a function centered in two cities, with the entire nation dependent upon them—just as it depends upon the Texas gas deposits for heat, the Florida and California groves for morning citrus. Such extreme specialization can only be coordinated through giant organizations, rapid transport, and a national market where information is exchanged at the speed of electric currents or radio waves.

The increased use of nonhuman energy and machinery, however, has also produced a rapid shift in the distribution of the labor force. Agricultural and other extractive industries demand a smaller proportion of the total; manufacturing also demands only a small proportion (though production increases rapidly) and the proportion in the professional, clerical, and service occupations increases steadily. Complex machinery using nonhuman energy increases the proliferation of occupational classes. There are greater demands for highly skilled labor as the unskilled laborer ceases to be the base for the industrial pyramid (his place taken by the machine). At the same time, the growth of the large-scale control systems, the bureaucracies of business and government, increases the proportion of workers whose job is in the making, processing, and

[11]The consequences of a shifting space-time ratio for societies and cities are discussed at considerable length in "Traffic, Transportation, and the Problems of the Metropolis," Scott Greer, in *Contemporary Social Problems,* Robert K. Merton and Robert A. Nisbet (eds.), New York: Harcourt, Brace and Company, 1961. For a careful analysis of societal consequences, see George R. Taylor, *The Transportation Revolution: 1815–1860,* in the "Rinehart Economic History of America Series," New York: Holt, Rinehart, and Winston, 1951.

distribution of messages—that is, order and control. Thus, the primary orientation of many workers is toward either complex symbolic problems or people, and this in turn leads to higher formal educational qualifications. Finally, changes in the organization of work cause an increase in productivity per person, and a steady upward movement of the average rewards.

Thus, as the society increases in scale, only a small and dwindling proportion remain rural, and there is a general upward movement of the entire population with respect to occupational level, educational level, and income level. Occupations require more learning of the society's symbolic store and more individual discrimination; they yield more rewards in the form of leisure, access to goods and services, and (with higher education) access to meaning, or "culture." Altogether, the societal surplus in man-hours, money, and symbols, spells a very wide latitude of choice for the average individual, compared with any previous historical epoch.[12]

INCREASE IN SCALE: THE NATIONAL SYSTEM

The process of increase in societal scale is a vast, complex, and completely interdependent process. The consequences of the process are revolutionary for human life; they change the nature of the human home in society to a form it has never before manifested. While material technologies have been crucial in this development, our chief focus of interest will be upon the equally crucial organizational technologies, those developing forms that have made possible the rational coordination of human activities over vast areas of space and time.

By society we mean the bounded network of interdependence resulting in mutual control of behavior; as the scale of an organizational network increases, so does the meaningfully defined "society." Increase in scale, however, includes both an extension of the society and a transformation of the internal order. The extension of the control system may be initiated by either military force or trade, resulting in the dominance of either the governmental or the economic system, but they tend eventually to coincide in scale, for the two kinds of order are complementary. Government sets the rules within which economic exchange can develop, while economic exchange demands such rules. However originated, the process knits together diverse populations into a single network of interdependence; through migration toward the centers of surplus, through amalgamation into a larger governmental and economic unit, the constituent populations are conjoined. Their ethnic histories differentiate them one from another, but their dependence, their communication and their

[12]The shifts in occupational distribution are spelled out in Colin Clark, *op. cit.* Florence, *op. cit.,* shows in detail the causes and consequences of increasing scale of economic enterprise, and its effects upon occupational distribution. For a general discussion of societies as energy-transformation systems, see Fred Cottrell's brilliant study, *Energy and Society,* New York: The McGraw-Hill Book Co., Inc., 1955. The argument of this chapter relies heavily upon his analyses, as well as those previously cited by Wilson and Wilson and by Shevky and Bell.

tasks subject them to the influence of the "moving total" that makes up the society of increasing scale.

At the societal level, looking from the center of the organizational network, the extension of the control systems has three aspects of major importance: (1) the widening of the radii of interdependence, (2) the increasing range of the communications flow, and (3) the widening span of control and compliance.

1. *The Widening of the Radii of Interdependence Means That, Whether Men Know It or Not, They Become Mutual Means to Individual Ends.* As mutual dependence is translated into social relations and these become organizations, control centers arise for the purpose of relating the various activities of each extended organization and, equally important, the relationships among various organizations. Historically, such control centers have been in cities, whether the control is economic, political, or ecclesiastical. The importance of the city for the surrounding society is then necessarily a function of the extensiveness and the intensity of interdependence. We have spoken of the transformation of the internal order of a society with increase in scale; this transformation results, in part, from the increasing number of necessary societal tasks that are delegated to large, specialized organizational networks. As the basic tasks so ordered increase in number, the *intensity of interdependence* increases. The society of the tenth century in Europe moved toward large-scale integration of religious control, but this was not accompanied by political and economic control. Consequently, the control centers, the "cities" of the bishoprics, were of comparatively small account in ordering the entire range of the behavior of the European population. Their growth into the cities of contemporary Europe reflects, as Pirenne makes clear, the increase in the intensity of interdependence, or, as Shevky and Bell phrase it, "the increase in the range of activities centered in cities."[13]

Thus the growth of cities is a direct result (and a reinforcing mechanism) of the increase in scale of carrying societies. Though specific societies manifest varying causal sequences, and the city or the state may have been at a given point a "prime mover" toward the next stage of expansion, cities are dependent for their existence upon their role as control centers in the large-scale market, government, ecclesia, or some combination of such structures. Typically, contemporary cities are headquarters or subsidiary centers of the national market and the nation state.

2. *As a Concomitant of the Widening Radii of Interdependence, Increasing Scale Produces an Increasing Range and Content of the Communications Flow.* That is, communication from a given center goes further and affects more

---

[13]Henri Pirenne, *The History of Europe,* New York: Doubleday Co. (Anchor Edition), 1959. Shevky and Bell, *op. cit.,* p. 10. For an excellent study relating function to urban settlement see Jack P. Gibbs and Walter T. Martin, "Urbanization and Natural Resources: A Study in Organizational Ecology," *American Sociological Review,* 23, p. 140. For a recent work on the relationship between function and location of metropolitan complexes in the United States see *Metropolis and Region* by Otis Dudley Duncan, W. Richard Scott, Stanley Lieberson, Beverly D. Duncan, and Hal H. Winsborough, Baltimore: Johns Hopkins Press, 1960.

people in more ways. Communication is a vital part of the organizational structures that integrate action; as interdependence increases in scope, then, increased communication is a necessary condition for handling the problems it poses. Inadequate communications (whether of persons, goods, or messages) will, in fact, prevent the translation of interdependence into organization (thus the media of communication severely limited the possible scale of the early empires.)[14] The tendency toward increase in scale may be accelerated by improved communication. It may also be checked or reversed through communications failures, for the vital structural members, the extended organizations to which are delegated basic societal tasks, may be unable to perform at a minimal level.

The large-scale organizational networks are instrumental in carrying the communications flow of the larger society. The corporation, state bureaucracy, or bureaucracies of church, labor union and voluntary organizations, are basically oriented to their own survival and housekeeping needs. But they also carry a diverse content of messages and symbols through the relevant populations, by-products irrelevant to the carrying organization, from jokes to propaganda. And, at the same time, communication becomes itself a specialized network of formal organizations, for it becomes a social product with exchange value at the marketplace. The mass-media industries arise, allowing a form of direct communication with a very large proportion of the total population that bypasses organizational structures.

The centers of the communications networks—whether of the formal organizational systems or of the mass media themselves—are typically situated in cities. They carry messages that are delivered from the point of view of those who sit on a high place and see far, those who live at the center among the "peak organizations" of modern man. They become impregnated with urban norms they then diffuse, directly and indirectly, to the total society. In this sense the city is a prime mover—not because it is a large, dense, heterogeneous collection of nonagricultural persons—but because it is at the control and communications center of the total society. It "acculturates" the total society to a new point of view. Much of what we have called urbanism is subsumed under this point of view, but when it becomes diffused throughout a society, what shall we call it? It implies wider horizons, larger scale, a frame of reference that is societal rather than local. It is, essentially, cosmopolitanism, the way of life in the great polity.

3. *The Increase in Scale Results in a Widening Span of Compliance and Control with Given Social Organizations.* The necessities of persistence, when interdependence is so widespread, lead to a constant increase in the size and functions of specific organized groups. Corporations, labor unions, govern-

---

[14]See, for example, Ralph Turner, *The Great Cultural Traditions,* New York: The McGraw-Hill Book Co., Inc., 1941, especially Chapter XX, Vol. 2, "Structure and Process in Cultural Development." Gilmore also has some useful observations on the relationships between organization and transport, *Transportation and the Growth of Cities, op. cit.*

mental bureaus, churches, whose members become private (or semipublic) governments are, with their dependents, major proportions of the total population. Such organizations are relatively free of a given locality; they are exclusive membership groups that span cities, counties, and states, but that control only their immediate members and publics.

These organizations manifest certain structural similarities, due to the necessary conditions of specialization and integration. They are, first of all, enormous systems within which the key actors are employees. They manifest a complex division of labor, a proliferation of roles and formalized norms of interaction. They are hierarchically organized, with great variations in the power and the rewards available to actors in the different scalar roles. They emphasize particularly the importance of technical and organizational specialists: those who control symbols and people are their elites. They are, in short, bureaucracies.

The salience of such large-scale organizations in the society, their nationwide span of control, and the similarity of their division of labor and rewards, tend to develop a stratification system cutting across widely varying geographical and cultural subregions of the society. The system is based upon function, translated into occupational classification and the associated rewards. It is indifferent to, if not antithetical to, older stratification systems based upon origin—"social class" in Warner's sense, or "race."[15] Such role systems are oriented toward a national organization, a nation-wide industry, a nation-wide profession, rather than the conventions of the particular *locale* in which they find themselves. Though the members may reside in the hinterland, their true home is still the organizational networks, their hallowed ground the headquarters city. They are representatives of a corporate society, like the member of the Society of Jesus or the colonial officer in the jungle.

They are national citizens.

INCREASE IN SCALE: THE LOCALITY GROUP

From the point of view of the analyst concerned with organizational systems, the process of increase in scale is one that involves scattered and distinctive subgroups in a larger order. Within this expanding order they either assume corporate roles or disintegrate, their actors being assigned roles in the larger system. In either case, the local group becomes dependent upon, then interdependent with, the expanding network of activity. This is accompanied by an increase in the amount of communication flow and its range, and results

[15]Hughes has presented a case study of the conflict of norms between small-scale agrarian society and large-scale corporate enterprise, in *French Canada in Transition,* Chicago: University of Chicago Press, 1943. The conflict arising when norms based upon family and ethnic identity confront norms of bureaucracy (and some rationalizations arising therefrom) is analyzed in "Queries Concerning Industry and Society Growing Out of the Study of Ethnic Relations and Industry," *American Sociological Review,* 14, 211–220.

in the acculturation of the interdependent populations to a normative structure that assumes and implements the larger system. With increasing compliance of the locality group's members, an ordering of behavior results that is nationwide in scope. Much of what is called "urbanization" (the concentration of population in cities) may be interpreted as increasing interdependence; that which is termed "urbanism" reflects the acculturation of subgroups to a society-wide normative structure; the phenomena sometimes referred to as "conformism" or "uniformity" (or "loss of individualism") may be interpreted as compliance with the norms of large scale organizations, spanning the society.

When one turns his attention to any specific subgroups within the total society (locality group, village, ethnic enclave, or colony) the process is reciprocated in (1) loss of autonomy, (2) exposure to conflicting norms, and (3) fragmentation of the total social order.[16]

1. *The Loss of Autonomy* is inevitable, for as the local group is integrated in a larger order the price is loss of economic and governmental self-sufficiency. The extended but exclusive membership organizations become crucial to the ongoing of the local area (providing resources, protection, transportation, and the like) yet their control centers are far away. These organizations are specialized and do not include all of the spatially defined group; at the same time they include members from many scattered localities. As functions are transferred to such organizations, people become less dependent on the near at hand, and the local group's *raison d'être* in autonomy is considerably weakened.

2. *Exposure to Conflicting Norms* from afar, through the organizational networks or the mass media, is a major result. Members are exposed, outside the surveillance and control of the local community, to wider horizons, to norms and models not immediately given in their social environment. The loss of cultural *apartheid* would be, in any case, a problem for the existing local normative order. Since the new messages are brought through the channels of the larger, dominant society, however, they are a direct threat to the unique norms and values evolved in the local group.

3. *Fragmentation of the Local Normative Order* is a predictable consequence; some of the members of the local group must conform to patterns from afar, since they are dependent upon the large, extended organization for their livelihood. Others take advantage of the local group's loss of coercive power to exploit added degrees of freedom; they experiment with new means to old ends, they try new ends, they exercise freedom of choice. Others, still, are dependent upon the local order for social position and rewards; their life is controlled by its norms, but with the attrition of dependence (and therefore

---

[16]Arthur J. Vidich and Joe Bensman have recently documented these consequences for a small town in New York State in *Small Town in Mass Society,* Princeton: Princeton University Press, 1959. They emphasize both the consequences of disappearing autonomy and the ideological responses to them. Nisbet has treated the matter with an emphasis upon the usurpation of local autonomy by arms of the nation state, in *The Quest for Community: A Study in the Ethics of Order and Freedom,* New York: Oxford University Press, 1953, especially Part Two, "The State and Community."

the basis for order), they find it impossible to communicate or to enforce compliance. (The cutting edge of the sanctions depended, after all, upon the interdependence of the local group.) When individuals become committed to groups centering outside the locality, the new dependence brings a measure of independence from their neighbors.

Thus the local group loses its integrity and approaches amalgamation in the large-scale society. The behavior of its members in many crucial areas of activity cannot be understood, save as a part of the role system in the nation-wide corporation, labor union, political party, or governmental bureau. *Social amalgamation* is evident in the dominance of local action by the extended organization. Acculturation is equally obvious, as the ends and means, the "blueprints for living," are changed in the direction of the "urbane"—the society-wide culture.

INCREASE IN SCALE: AUTONOMY AND CENTRALIZATION

The argument thus far leads to the conclusion that when a society increases in scale it experiences an initial increase in differentiation, becoming in many matters polyglot and conflict ridden, a "mosiac of worlds that touch but do not interpenetrate." However, as the process continues, the society moves toward cultural homogeneity and conformity to the larger order: "urbanism" eventually accompanies compliance. The argument, pushed to its logical conclusion, may result in images of "the mass society" leading, in turn, to robot citizens and the totalitarian state. It certainly indicates a diminution of the variety and color derived from ethnic inheritance (whether the origin was in migration, as commonly occurred in the United States, or in peasant societies of the hinterland, as was the case in Europe); it also indicates a decline in the resisting power of the local units.[17]

The decline of the ethnically distinct, organizationally autonomous locality group does not, however, indicate that such a centralized society is apt to occur. The locality group, village, or metropolis, is an inescapable social form with powerful bases in interdependence. We have noted earlier, in analyzing the structure of the city, the major consequences of the organization's immediate environment. Spatial collocation produces problems of order and a need for common facilities, strengthening the local role system and resulting in a coercive power over the actions of each exclusive membership group. The

---

[17]Rudolph Heberle in "Observations on the Sociology of Social Movements," *American Sociological Review,* 14, 354–355, has made the observation that much of the sectionalism of American society, its variation in culture by region, is in some degree an optical illusion, for the changing configuration of economic enterprise is the key variable between regions. As it shifts and is integrated in larger networks of control, regionalism gives way to national categories. Samuel Lubell has applied the same distinction between region and class in his *Future of American Politics, op. cit.* He predicts the emergence of truly national parties, based on nation-wide class interviews, in his final chapter, "The Nation State."

corporation or state bureaucracy must come to earth in order to work, and wherever it does it finds neighbors.

It also tends to take root. We have emphasized the functional basis of the large-scale bureaucracies in the *social product:* they provide sustenance, protection, social honor—products instrumental to the various ends of their members. We must remember that a given group may also have, as its functional basis, the *social process*—or interaction as a valued end in itself. The social process is very apt to emerge in any group; once present, it affects the strength of the group, for it increases interdependence, extends and enriches the normative structure and the role system, and makes possible a very rigorous control over the behavior of the constituent members.

The social process is the basis for that aspect of social structure that Cooley calls the "primary group."[18] Such is its power that some analysts have equated it with necessary conditions for personality organization and security; certainly it humanizes the environment, calling out many bases for loyalty and devotion other than the overt function of the group—the social product. It is most apt to arise in face-to-face interaction, among small aggregates that, for whatever reason, interact repeatedly and often. Therefore, the local setting of the organization has a strong tendency to foster local commitments. In friendship pairs, cliques, and fraternities (and sometimes even a "community" including all members of the spatially defined group) the social process results in commitments to the normative structure of the spatially inclusive group, vulnerability to its sanctions and compliance with its rules.

For these reasons the local "branches" of large-scale organizations are not immune to the normative order of the locality group. Their tasks force them to take account of the neighbors, and their involvement in primary group relations leads to a two-way traffic in influence. Another consequence of the primary dimension, one that has been often noted (though chiefly as a problem internal to the large-scale bureaucracy) is the likelihood that the local group in the organization will itself develop a powerful primary dimension—one separating "this branch" from the remainder of "the organization." Such localism, when accompanied by tendencies toward variations in norms and roles (the inevitable result of specific application from general rules), may result in a distinct subculture within the firm or agency—and this subculture is apt to persist because of its organizational base. Such a subculture will often incorporate many of the norms of the locality group within which the branch is located. This is especially likely if members are recruited from local boys, but, even with recruitment from distant localities, primary relationships with

[18]Arthur Ross has discussed the common framework of discourse between union and management representatives implied in collective bargaining situations in *Trade Union Determinants of Industrial Wage Policy,* Berkeley and Los Angeles: University of California Press, 1949. The translation of interorganizational relationships into role requirements of leaders is explored in *Last Man In: Racial Access to Union Power,* by Scott Greer, New York: The Free Press of Glencoe, 1959.

necessary associates make the exclusive organization permeable to its cultural and its organizational surroundings.

As a result, there is a general tension between the large-scale, segmentally defined, formal organization on one hand, and the small-scale nuclear groups that make up its task forces. The latter must commit themselves, in some degree, to the normative order of the locality group—they are dependent upon it in carrying out the very tasks assigned by the larger system. Furthermore, spatial separation from the larger structure and spatial segregation (along with members of many other groups) in a given locale tend to produce in some matters greater differences *between* spatially separated groups than *within* each group considered separately. The increasing acculturation of the society to metropolitan scale does not, then, result only in a tendency toward standardization. Differentiation is created anew, by the ancient mechanisms of *relative isolation* and *differential association* among those in a given spatial area as compared with those scattered afar.

Part III

URBAN SOCIETY:
SOCIAL AND POLITICAL
PROCESS AND FORMS

THE NATURE OF URBAN LIFE AND EXPERIENCE HAS LONG HELD A FASCINA-
tion for the student of the city. One of the major perspectives in the study of the city
has conceptualized urban society as a mass society, lacking personal ties and a sense
of community. To a considerable extent the present discussion and selections are
involved in a critical dialogue with this orientation. In the first section, some of the
principal perspectives implicit in such a dialogue are discussed in broad theoretical
terms. The later material then sketches some of the major properties of urban social
structure. Issues of a related but somewhat different character are introduced by
Norton Long's essay and the last few articles. To some extent Part II has already
introduced a number of points pertinent to our present discussion.

Theoretical Perspectives

A number of major themes are presented in the first set of essays. These include
the interpretation of urban society as a mass society, fragmented and impersonal, with
the disappearance of neighborhoods as a basis for association. However, the contrasting view that personal ties, satisfaction, and local-based relations do continue for
many types of groups is also presented. There is also a concern with the changed bases
of personal order or integration and the altered nature of social relationships. The
changes in urban society are interpreted, from the ecological point of view, as accounted for by properties of size, density, and heterogeneity and from a broader
perspective as reflecting an increasing divison of labor, industrialization, and growth
of rationalized bureaucratic organizational structures. Often the differing views in
interpreting urban society significantly reflect disagreement over the extent to which
the consequences of these properties are present, or, where present, the extent to
which they are tempered by particular properties of the population involved. In some
discussions reference is also made to the role of societal values in shaping the nature
of the urban social system and personal experiences within it. A consideration of the
urban political process and integration in broad social system terms concludes the
initial theoretical essays.

Louis Wirth's essay, "Urbanism as a Way of Life," (122) is a classic statement of
a major tradition (the Chicago school) in the study of the city and urban life. It
particularly reflects the writings of Robert Park (79) with their stress on the competitive, heterogeneous, and fragmented personal properties of the contemporary city and
complements Simmel's earlier essay (97) on the nature of urban consciousness and
the consequences of the urban milieu for individual personality. Wirth's essay is also
in accord with a popular theme in sociological and anthropological thought elaborating a rural- or folk-urban continuum (47, 63, 87). Such a continuum seems implicit
in Wirth's essay, given its reliance on ecological properties of size, density, and
heterogeneity.

Wirth seeks a distinctive sociological definition and theory of the city. He defines a city in terms of the ecological variables of large size, density, and heterogeneity. He succinctly traces the consequences of these properties for a distinctively urban social structure and way of life. Thus, he develops a series of propositions relating the basic physical properties of the city to the appearance of such characteristics as segmented social contacts, superficiality, anonymity, transitory relationships, the predominance of secondary associations, specialization, and the rise of formal contacts. These circumstances are viewed as undermining common bonds of sentiment and intimacy, as well as the vitality of the neighborhood as a basis for satisfying personal relationships; they are also perceived as productive of distinctive personality properties. Urbanization and urbanism is represented for Wirth not only by the physical properties of a city but also by the social characteristics that follow from it. Thus, starting with a limited number of discrete physical properties he has deduced social and social psychological properties that identify a distinctive urban way of life and establish a peculiarly sociological model of the city.

While Wirth's essay is a powerful statement and has stimulated a great deal of further research and theoretical elaboration, other findings suggest the need for serious qualifications. Thus, it is essential to distinguish between urbanization and urbanism. The former refers to the development of the ecological properties distinctive to the city—large size, density, and heterogeneity. Urbanism, however, may be used more specifically as a referent for a distinctive set of cultural and social properties—for instance, those that Wirth details. It then becomes possible to consider the extent to which these occur together or may vary independently. Thus, there may be urbanized communities with or without the properties of urbanism, and vice versa.[1] Alternate theoretical formulations and existing empirical material both point to a considerable degree of independence between the properties of urbanization (increased size, density, and heterogeneity) and the social structural forms and processes of the city. This suggests that urbanism, or the presumably distinctive social and cultural properties that Wirth identified with the city, may be more a product of the peculiar cultural, social, and industrial elements of American society than the ecological and demographic factors that he had stressed.

A sizable body of anthropological and sociological literature has significantly qualified the type of account provided by scholars such as Wirth, Simmel, and Park. Tax's studies of Guatemalan Indian villages (107, 108) has shown that some of Wirth's "urban" properties are present in small, low-density, homogeneous communities. Concentrating on the urban centers of the underdeveloped nations of Asia and ad-

---

[1]David Popenoe (83), in this regard, outlines a three-fold distinction, adding a third condition that he refers to as the urban process—i.e., social organizational processes of increasing division of labor, greater interdependence, and greater complexity. And, in fact, he interprets the condition of urbanism as more likely following from the urban process than urbanization, though all may appear independently of each other.

dressing himself to the appropriateness of the broader rural-urban dichotomy, Philip
Hauser (47) has reported that such cities frequently do not exhibit the properties
expected to arise under conditions of large size, density, and heteregeneity, and that
conversely, the properties viewed as distinctive to folk or rural societies are nonetheless present in these urban centers. Albert Reiss' comparison of differences in interpersonal contacts between rural and urban American populations (88) shows little distinctive residential differences in this regard.

A considerable body of research has examined neighborhood interdependence,
familial, and organizational relationships in American and British communities. Relevant here are findings of studies in the social area analysis tradition (10, 11, 43); of
ethnic and neighborhood social patterns and relationships (34, 43, 64, 106, 110, 111,
116, 126); on the continuance of primary kinship ties and aid, especially, though by
no means only, among working class populations[2] (1, 15, 23, 27, 37, 59, 91, 102,
104); and on broader personal involvements in the urban setting (4, 23, 53, 60, 98,
110, 117). These studies suggest a wide diversity of urban experiences and personal
and social circumstances, the continuance of the neighborhood in some respects as
a basis of association and the presence of noninstrumental personal contact, and
supportive relationships at variance with Wirth's and Simmel's expectations. Stressing
the continued importance of primary groups in the urban setting, R. N. Morris in his
review of Wirth's theory has suggested that "a further theory of urban life . . . needs
to recognize that primary groups are an integral part of urban society and perform
significant functions: they are not merely remnants of rural life, but intrinsic elements
in all known societies" (75, p. 25). Morris does suggest, however, that the data is
mixed on some important aspects of Wirth's urban model, so that in some particulars
it is not without support.

A fundamental point that has to be made is that the presumed inherent dynamics
of any institutional structures, urban social properties, or ecological factors such as
those that Wirth and others deal with are defined, in part, by the individual himself
and are mediated through and constrained by a diversity of conditions. These include
the cultural properties of the group and society; the degree and nature of communal
membership; the stage of the individual life cycle; individual attitudes and personal
resources, including type of occupation and class membership; nature of nationwide
patterns of communication, institutional and value structures and the character of
individual participation therein; degree of technological development and its characteristics; and distinctive patterns of development of major institutions, among other
considerations. This is the underlying theme implicit in the diverse empirical material
referred to above. Various scholars have made this theoretical issue and analytic
postulate clear. William Kolb (61), pointing to the cultural and time-bound character

---

[2]The Sussman and Burchinal (104) essay is a useful review of some of the major findings
on continuance of family relationships.

of Wirth's theory, stresses the importance of a society's values, particularly the emphasis on universalistic and achievement value orientations, if the conditions of large size, density, and heterogeneity are to lead to the type of social and personal properties that Wirth details and associates with urbanism. In a still different direction, Peter Mann, in his book *An Approach to Urban Sociology* (71), develops the diverse uses of neighborhoods at different stages in the life of an individual. This is one of the points, among others, that is developed in Herbert Gans' noted essay, "Urbanism and Suburbanism as Ways of Life: A Reevaluation of Definitions" (33).

A balanced assessment of Wirth's theory, however, would seem to require some recognition of a distinctive, though considerably qualified, influence of size, density, and heterogeneity on personal and social forms, particularly in American society with its distinctive cultural complex and institutional forms. The present writer would suggest the reasonableness of an analysis such as Richard Dewey's (22) which offers a highly qualified acceptance of the consequentiality of ecological factors and recognizes the increased probability of impersonality, anonymity, and social contacts.[3] A close reading of much of the research on kinship, organizational, and neighborhood relationships that is offered to refute the Wirth model suggests that the scope, quality, amount, and meaningfulness of such relationships is often not very considerable, though that which is present confounds the urban models of Wirth, Simmel, and Park. While a conclusive evaluation is not possible without rural or nonurban comparative material, it could be contended that the urban environment at least tends toward some of the social and personal circumstances that Wirth, Simmel, and Park noted. Even here, though, the "meaning" or consequentiality of such circumstances is dependent on the background, resources, and expectations of the individual and may not run in the direction envisioned by Wirth and his precursors, or in the writings of mass society theorists.

Herbert Gans' frequently cited essay, "Urbanism and Suburbanism as Ways of Life: A Reevaluation of Definitions" (33), elaborates a perspective at variance with that of Wirth. He suggests that Wirth was implicitly contrasting the city to folk society and was thus led to stress properties absent in the latter circumstance—size, density, and heterogeneity. Gans stresses the role of social and cultural factors in determining response to the city and the patterns of life found there. Given the wide range of social and cultural properties exhibited by urban populations, Gans is readily led to stress the diversity of ways of life in the urban setting and between cities and suburbs. In effect, Gans suggests that Wirth's conception of the nature of urban life cannot be assumed to represent the totality of urban life. Rather, it is merely one of the diverse

[3]In a qualified acceptance of some elements of Wirth's analysis, Dewey suggests the need to conceive of sociocultural phenomenon and rural-urban change as two separate continua, properties of the former being present or absent irrespective to the "urban" properties of size and density. He does recognize, however, some minimal structural and social properties that follow from size and density.

ways of life that coexist in the metropolis, and that portion of the community to which
it applies can be accounted for by social and cultural factors without attention to
ecological variables. Thus, Gans is also skeptical of the concept of a distinctively urban
way of life.

The determining factors that Gans stresses are life-cycle stage, economic class
characteristics, cultural properties—especially ethnic group membership—the degree
of residential stability of an area, and the degree of residential choice that an individual
possesses. Though not elaborated, it would appear that these are consequential in
determining urban life patterns because of a number of conditions that inhere in them.
Thus, implicated in any particular stage of the life-cycle, in a specific class position,
or, in a particular cultural pattern are distinct expectations and needs, individual
interests, group memberships and associated social patterns, including the extent of
personal ties, and distinct personal and economic resources. These would significantly
shape the experience and properties of urban life for the individual.

Gans distinguishes between the inner and outer city, and the suburbs, suggesting
that only within the first area does the pattern of life referred to by Wirth appear and
then only as one of several possible life styles. The reader will note that Gans concludes his discussion by pointing to the influence of national policies and national
economic, social, and cultural properties on many of the factors that serve to determine urban life style and options, as well as on the social and cultural factors that
distinguish the population groupings and behavior that Gans develops in his essay.

In some respects both the Gans and Wirth essays relate to our earlier discussion
and papers on the ecological and social area analysis perspectives which expressed
a concern about which properties to use in terms of characterizing and contrasting
urban populations. Gans also relates to the issue raised earlier concerning the nature
and source of urban-suburban difference.

The selection by Elwin Powell, "The Evolution of the American City and the
Emergence of Anomie" (84), carries forward some of the questions already raised and
also relates to the theoretical criticisms of the ecological perspective previously
sketched. His treatment resembles, as he recognizes, Firey's analysis in *Land Use in
Central Boston* (26). Firey pointed out that the decline of close group bonds, attributed to life in the city, can be explained more appropriately by the effect of the
contemporary American economic system. Powell's contribution is of especial interest because it conceptualizes city properties in terms of a historical dimension and
processes of change. He thereby lays the basis for perceiving some properties of the
city as peculiar to certain specific conditions and time periods, and not others. Essentially, he considers a possible condition of urban life, anomie—or the estrangement
of its inhabitants from each other—not as a reflection of distinctive demographic
ecological properties, but as a result of a type of industrial economic order, laissez-
faire capitalism, and its associated values (especially that of individualism, competition, and materialism). Thus, it is the social and cultural properties of a particular urban

society and not the inexorable effects of either ecological properties or an urban way of life that produce a divided community and personal circumstances of isolation, meaninglessness, or disorganization. He states,

> . . . in the evolution of Buffalo from a cohesive community to an atomized society it is not the process of urbanization but the development of the economic institution which is the decisive factor. The social character of the American city—the anomie of the urban way of life—is a product of the spirit of capitalism [84, p. 166].

A valuable analytic point in Powell's essay is its recognition that it is the combination of the institutional forms with a distinctive set of values expressive of laissez-faire capitalism, and not merely the institutional forms alone, that are determinate of anomie.

As the careful readers will recognize, Powell's essay is a broad and suggestive analysis that contributes to the theoretical perspective developed in the present volume. It is not intended, however, as a definitive study. Its determination of the circumstances of the diverse populations in Buffalo and of their interrelationships is quite brief and not established. Nor does it discuss the possible existence or absence of conditions intervening between laissez-faire capitalism with its associated values and a condition of anomie. Thus, the extent to which the former leads to the circumstances noted may be variable, depending on the presence or lack of group communal forms and membership, interest group organization, and political responsiveness.[4] A more specific definition of the concept of anomie would also have been helpful.[5]

In the last of the introductory theoretical essays, "The Local Community as an Ecology of Games" (68), Norton Long has addressed himself to the problem of societal integration in the highly differentiated American community. In consequence, he has also described one of the distinctive properties of the urban political system. In the former concern he continues the discussion of a problem raised in the preceding unit, though the earlier treatment was more in terms of the basis of cohesion among the urban inhabitants than between different institutional areas. In effect, Long starts with a basic observation that an "inclusive over-all organization for many general purposes is weak or non-existent" (68, p. 252) in the urban community. Yet, he suggests, a

---

[4] Of course, in most instances such intervening conditions are either lacking or of questionable efficacy, given the institutional and value complex associated with a free-market, unfettered capitalism.

[5] Professor Powell is apparently using anomie to refer to two types of conditions, though this is not made clear. One use is in reference to the character of the relationships between the peoples of Buffalo (partially comprehended by the concept of community integration), while the other—and more usual application of the concept—is in reference to the nature of individual circumstance and the relationship of the individual to the broader society.

considerable degree of institutional integration does arise from the striving by individual groups in society for their own ends. Long uses an analogy of a set of games for the diverse institutional areas in the community, each with distinctive and known purposes, strategies, roles, that can be known and forecast by others. This provides an overall order for the urban polity. There is not, however, an agency clearly charged with or effectively functioning in terms of the broader common good or public interest.

Long's is an insightful and felicitious presentation. Yet, a couple of serious questions are slighted. One is the extent to which a few of the major interests or institutional areas or "games" tend to significantly shape the "games" played by other institutional sectors and populations, particularly in regard to the ability to meet particular group needs, as well as broader, community-wide purposes. In other words, actors, groups, and institutions are not equal in power and in the extent to which they shape the rules and outcome of the interactions within the urban polity. In this respect some may be much more significant than others.

Thus, for instance, a distinctive patterning and direction of the broader polity and urban social system appear to be established by the functioning of the private corporate sector, realtors, the construction industry, banks, and the automobile industry, some of which extend significantly beyond community boundaries. Further, the very complex of values associated with unfettered competitive profit-oriented enterprise that such groups and activities perpetuate in the community will influence how the "games" are played, the relative strength of contending parties, and the extent to which a broader, community-wide agency takes shape and uses the power at its disposal. Thus, the urban polity may exhibit much more of a distinctive patterning, direction, and type of policy (or lack of policy) than is suggested by Long's commentary. This may also result, of course, from the consequences of population movement and distribution, the character of transportation networks, and the viability of the national economy, etc. Yet, these possibilities are not random either in the type of consequences and issues they pose. In part, they reflect the nature of specific decisions and policies established by the public and private sector, and could be altered by governmental action.

Long does not make clear the extent to which he believes that the process he describes furthers the community good. One could effectively contend, in fact, that there are increasingly severe dysfunctions from a polity organized and functioning in the terms described. Most succinctly, as is partly suggested in the essay, broader community-wide purposes—the public interest—is not served. Such concerns, for example, as environmental preservation and enhancement, recreational and cultural opportunities, ease of transportation or movement, and equality of opportunity and treatment, are not concerns or needs distinctive to any one group. They cut across all community sectors. Though there are some organized interest groups, and "games" in these regards, their scope is miniscule compared to the breadth of population and depth of needs in such areas. A polity functioning merely or even predominantly in terms of self-centered, narrow, pluralistic, interest-group collectivities fails, often grievously, in meeting broader community or public concerns. While the system so effectively described by Long serves to more or less meet some group needs and maintain a generally ongoing integrated institutional complex, it is seriously ineffective in a whole range of basic areas of vital concern to urban citizens as individuals and as members of a shared community.

Social Patterns and Process

While the major themes presented in the essays describing urban social patterns and processes have already been noted in a general way, the following comments indicate some of the specific elaborations made by the authors. The present discussion also notes a number of additional aspects of social structure and process that significantly extend the scope of the description provided so far.

The study by Bell and Force (12) of some important properties of formal organizational membership further elaborates the character of the urban social system. Their analysis of four census tract neighborhoods in San Francisco distinguished on dimensions developed by social area analysis presents a number of significant findings. With the neighborhoods essentially uniform on ethnicity, but differing in regard to some major socioeconomic and familistic properties, Bell and Force relate extent of male (the population studied) organization membership, attendance, and officeholding to both the properties of individuals and presumably to the distinctive properties of the neighborhoods in which the individuals are resident. One general finding is that in all areas, isolation, at least in terms of ties to formal organizations, is not extensive, though this appears to require important reservations in strong blue-collar and low-skilled areas where perfunctory trade union membership may hide the degree to which there is a lack of ties. Even in terms of multiple memberships and frequency of attendance all neighborhoods, especially high-income areas, have either a majority or significant minority involved organizationally. Education, income, and occupation categories relate to organizational membership in the expected directions. An interesting finding, though somewhat difficult to interpret, is that familistic and urban areas containing populations with similar education, occupation, or income levels will nevertheless exhibit differing degrees of organizational involvement. The authors suggest that this may be accounted for by the possible influence of the neighborhood on individual behavior. Its elaboration in further research would be valuable, though it is possible that little more may be involved in this regard than the differing availability of organizational membership in areas of high and low involvement. The notion of an individual's self-image, noted by Bell and Force, as being a possible causal element is somewhat vague, and its importance is probably slight.

A related and more likely factor is that there are processes of differential selection in neighborhood settlement patterns, with different neighborhoods having a recognized character, life style, locational conveniences, and type of population. Given the variations in life style and city interests, even within similar income, occupation, educational categories, and differences between neighborhoods, such differential selectivity is not too surprising. And it need not involve, though it may, any discrepancies between an individual's objective class position and individual self-image. Thus, it could be contended that distinctive neighborhood patterns or membership may reflect the characteristics of the individual inhabitants, rather than the properties of the neighborhood as a unit. The authors also note a number of other interesting relationships between neighborhood, individual properties, and organizational membership.

There is a quite extensive literature on both formal and informal social relationships in the urban context, though significantly limited unfortunately in the scope of the phenomena examined and problems pursued.[6] Essentially, this work shows that formal and informal social participation is at least moderately extensive for all socioeconomic levels, though the quality and scope of such participation may be significantly qualified for some. The degree of formal organizational membership, however, varies directly with class level. Concomitantly, the lower socioeconomic strata will exhibit a proportionately greater degree of informal relationships (4, 11, 12, 29, 30, 39, 46, 62, 90, 94, 125). Also, the type of organizations joined tends to vary between strata, with community- and service-oriented associations being more prominent among middle-class and upper-class populations, and "special stratum interest" organizations, in Bell and Force's terminology (11), and strictly socially nurturant organizations more frequently attracting the working-class population (12, 19, 48, 51, 72). Voluntary associations serve various purposes for their members. They may aid the adjustment of migrants to a strange city and urban milieux, provide fraternal and welfare aid, offer a setting for personal experience and responsiveness, provide a means of maintaining or seeking specific group interests, make possible advancing distinctive individual interests, or provide a means for status striving.

In informal associations urbanites, and rural residents even more so, find a source of extensive interpersonal relationships. Bell and Boat's "Urban Neighborhoods and Informal Social Relations" (10), drawing on the same study as that reported in Bell and Force (12), presents findings similar to those reported by various other students. They report the presence of a fairly extensive, overall degree of informal social contacts by males, being most extensive with relatives and friends and less with coworkers and neighbors. Many will lack association with one or more of these populations, but have quite close contacts with one or two others. They also show variation in amount and type of contacts by neighborhood life-style and economic level. High familistic areas,

[6]For a useful summary treatment, see Marshall (72).

for instance, exhibit distinctly greater contacts with kin than low familistic areas. Life style, however, is a less effective determinant of overall social relationships in higher income areas. While the degree of formal organizational participation varies with class strata, this is less likely to be the case with informal contacts. Where differences occur in the latter, it is principally in terms of the type of informal associations in which different class individuals are involved.

Some of the material dealing with social participation has a direct bearing on the character of community and neighborhood in the metropolis. This is found especially in the studies in the social area analysis tradition. However, there are also various general treatments of the urban neighborhood and studies of specific neighborhoods, class, or ethnic populations that considerably elaborate the social system forms present on the local level.[7] In the social area analysis tradition the material by Greer (39), Greer and Orleans (44), and Greer and Kube (43) indicates considerable variation in patterns of local community involvement and commitment among urban neighborhoods and the inappropriateness of the mass society model for much local-level urban life. Yet, on the whole, they note the limited nature of the local community. In their focus on various types of neighborhood-level personal contacts both Greer (39) and Greer and Kube's studies of Los Angeles (43) reveal a moderate level of local-based involvement, yet also considerable variation between neighborhoods.

> In summary, these sharp variations in localism indicate that the disappearance of the 'local community' and neighborhood in the city is far from complete. It is most nearly true in the highly urban area, but in those neighborhoods characterized by familism there is considerable vitality in local associations. This is evident in neighboring, local organization and church participation, readership of the local community press, and ability to name local leaders. It is accompanied by an attitude of commitment to the area as 'home'—a place from which one does not want or expect to move. In participation and in felt permanence, the highly urban areas had a much weaker hold on their residents [39, p. 106].

As a general statement it is possible to say, Greer suggests, that concern with and involvement in urban neighborhoods is present for many, but to a limited degree. Thus, he elaborates on Janowitz' concept of the "community of limited liability." Because the local community is involved in and dependent on nonareal institutions, because its social life and nearly all significant political activities are located elsewhere, and because it offers a fair amount of mobility, the local community secures only very partial loyalty and commitment and offers only a weak network of interaction and, therefore, cannot create a strong, local normative order. Yet, for many, especially those with a familistic life pattern (children, single-family homes, and with wives

[7]See page 271 for citations to a number of appropriate references.

at home) "the local residential community still encompasses some very crucial structures . . ." (41, p. 108). It is the site for considerable interfamily communication and
sociability, absorbs much of the time, energy, and money of the family, and where
a somewhat larger residential area is considered, it presents a number of common
concerns and conditions of interdependence[8] (41, chap. 4).

The urban neighborhood community has been the subject of a number of relatively detailed analyses, especially in studies of ethnic and working-class areas. Results
are of a rather mixed character. Where there are developed cultural bonds and
patterns in a distinct ethnic area, especially where there are kinship ties among
long-time residents, one may expect to find strong neighborhood attachments and
considerable supportive social relationships, and the local neighborhood or community may be considered quite viable (34, 121). A long-settled, economically stable,
working-class area may exhibit, to a lesser extent, similar properties. Though the
interpersonal relationships here may be of a constricted character and the quality of
involvement thin, conditions of friendly contact, a sense of companionship, and at
least moderate satisfaction appear to prevail (15, 58, 73, 126). However, where
cultural bonds are weaker, residential mobility usually higher, and economic stress
greater, or settlement patterns such as to disrupt a sense of a distinctive ongoing
community, the attainment of a viable and satisfying local neighborhood is more
difficult, community cooperation is low, suspicion is high, and community institutions
are weak (70, 96). Yet, even in the latter circumstances certain age and sex groups,
particularly teen-age youths and young adult males, may develop a fairly active and
extensive set of social relationships (64, 106).

The discussion by Marc Fried and Peggy Gleicher, "Some Sources of Satisfaction
in the Urban Slum" (32), provides some sense of the kind of importance that the local
urban neighborhood may hold for ethnic, moderately low-income, working-class
populations. It also indicates some of the major neighborhood social patterns. Their
study reveals a strong identification and high satisfaction within the community,
extensive kin and other social relationships, and an apparent focus on and familiarity
with the West End area to the exclusion of the rest of the city. This suggests the viability
of community within the urban context for these "urban villagers," in contrast to the
expectations of a mass society model. It makes clear the importance of understanding
the urban neighborhood in terms of the meaning of the residential neighborhood
experience to the individual inhabitant. Localism, or the existence of a specific identity
with the area of residence, is also identified as helpful in understanding the residential
patterns of such a population. They also note that this includes the focusing of one's

---

[8]There is a considerable controversy over the place of neighborhood or community within
a "desirable" or future urban order. This is not considered in the present volume, but some
relevant discussions include Jane Jacobs (55), Reginald Issacs (54), Mumford (77), Nisbet (78),
and Young and Willmott (126), among others; also, see the more general review by Suzanne
Keller (57).

social relations within such an area, as well as a distinctive organization of and response to physical space and objects.

The latter involves a spatial sense that minimizes distinctions or differences within any physical area. This contrasts with the spatial conceptualizations that they attribute to the middle class. The latter is perceived as having a much more selective and differentiated perception of physical space with considerably less permeability of the boundaries between residential structures and environs. Their discussion in these regards highlights their observation that the effects of residential movement and settlement will vary with the kind of population involved. In effect, the response to and results of residential movement are influenced by the extent of an individual's spacial identity and the degree and nature of the orientation to local-based, social relationships, physical objects, and individual spacial location.

While Fried and Gleicher's discussion provides an illuminating treatment, as a descriptive account its conclusions are significantly qualified by the fact that the population studied is a strongly ethnic-based one (Italian-American), as well as one that has been resident for a long time in the area and has had considerable family-based relationships in the West End. Thus, the positive image that may tend to be conveyed of slum living would appear to reflect not slums generally, but lower-income, socially stable areas possessing strong and distinctive cultural and social properties. Wolf and Lebeaux (123) have pointed out that such properties and the circumstances of positive community attitudes are more frequently lacking in low-income slum areas. In a different direction, Fried and Gleicher's discussion of the relationship of middle-class populations to area of residence may require some slight reservation in terms of taking account of differences in life-style, even within a given class strata.

Their selection also contributes to an understanding of some of the concerns in the two concluding sections of the present volume. It treats of one type of disadvantaged population, touches on the destruction of their area by urban renewal policies and bureaucratic agencies over which they had very little control, and carries a number of implications for urban programs of change.

Neighborhood and community relationships and ties are only one aspect of the broader urban social patterns in which the individual is involved and in terms of which urban social structure can be characterized. The institution of the family also encompasses a distinctive set of relationships. We focus here on two concerns—family and kin ties in urban society as another source of interpersonal relationships and the properties and consequences of kinship systems in an industrially advanced urban society. The Litwak selection, "Geographic Mobility and Extended Family Cohesion" (66), is primarily concerned with the latter, though it does suggest the presence of a greater degree of family contacts than the mass model.

The Litwak essay and a great deal of the material already cited describing family patterns in contemporary industrial urban society offer an account significantly at variance with the view of more "classical" urban theory, such as that expressed by Wirth, as well as the perspectives presented in many earlier texts on the family[9] and by functional theorists such as Talcott Parsons (80, 81). In its interpretation of the development of Western society, functional theory stressed a close functional interdependence between industrial and urban change, a developing market-exchange economy, and a concomitant form of social organization, the small nuclear family. The latter is seen as developing in terms of the constraints and needs presumably arising from the other broad institutional changes. The isolated nuclear family is thus perceived as "functional" for an industrial urban society. The possibility that this implicit causal relationship may be absent or that a range of family forms may accord with urban industrial society is not developed (37).

The Litwak essay, as well as the research and commentaries to which reference has been made, describe some major properties of the contemporary family, especially that of social relationships, in both the industrial urbanized societies and those that are still underdeveloped. While these suggest that on the whole there has been a weakening of bonds and contacts between members of the extended family, the nuclear family is still not socially isolated from kinship ties and interpersonal exchange. The presence of mutual assistance is noted below, but there is also the continuance of some family visiting and ordinary socializing, group activities, and somewhat ritualized and regular family reunions which appear bilaterally and along generational lines. These are facilitated by modern means of transportation and communication, encouraged by a sense of obligation, the benefits of mutual aid that families provide, and the difficulty, at times, of establishing close supportive ties with others.

Some of the characteristics of primary relationships in the family are specified in Bert Adams' study *Kinship in an Urban Setting* (1). He suggests that these characteristics are greatest between children and parents. Contact among children occurs predominantly when there are home visits and on family ritual occasions, otherwise most usually by mail or phone. The presence of older parents leads, however, to a greater degree of contact among siblings. Family patterns also appear to exhibit some class differences, with middle-class families maintaining greater family contact among geographically scattered kin than among the working class. Adams finds greater family interaction among the working class than the middle class, though such differences are not especially borne out by some of the social area analysis research cited previously. Litwak notes, however, that most studies of working-class and ethnic family patterns are, in effect, dealing "with vestiges of the 'classical extended' family" (66, p. 12). A significant shift from earlier extended family relationships would appear to be the rather limited degree of contact with secondary kin, though ethnic and ghetto communities may at times still exhibit the earlier patterns.

Litwak (66, 67) elaborates an alternate formulation of family structure and func-

[9]See the citations in Sussman and Burchinal (104).

tioning to the classical extended-family, isolated nuclear-family dichotomy that appears in the work of Parsons, Linton, and Wirth. Litwak accepts the proposition that the classical extended family has declined and is dysfunctional for mobility but does not accept the isolated nuclear family as the only meaningful alternative. He persuasively urges the recognition of the presence of a third alternate form—the modified extended family where family relationships can be maintained in an industrial, bureaucratized society (in light of improvements in communication), even under conditions of·geographic mobility. In contrast to the contention that it is only the nuclear family that fits in with the mobility demands and needs of industrial society, he plausibly contends that it can be shown that modern extended families "have far greater facilities than the isolated nuclear family for encouraging spatial movement" (67, p. 386). His findings show that orientation to extended family will encourage movement when individuals are in the upswing of their career. The extended family, he suggests, has not lost its function nor does the practice of family aid lead to occupational nepotism, as earlier theory has maintained. In addition, while face-to-face contact is reduced by mobility, orientation to family is retained. Litwak's research provides support to the proposition that extended family relations are viable both in social terms and for the encouragement and aid that they offer for geographic and occupational mobility in contemporary industrial society.[10]

There have been some major changes, however, in the nature of the family, family relationships, and the functions performed by the family. The diffuse range of tasks handled predominantly by the family has declined: procreation, personal sustenance and socialization remain as its major functions. Its role in terms of status placement is still of some importance, though reduced. Educational training and occupational placement are principally attained elsewhere, as has increasingly been the case with the provision of avenues for cultural and leisure pursuits, political participation, and financial and welfare aid. On the whole this would appear to hold as well, but less strongly and uniformly in the industrial urban sectors of non-Western societies. Litwak also notes, in a somewhat different direction, the decline of geographic propinquity and the absence of strict authority relations. It may also be suggested that the individual in Western society is generally less constrained by extended family obligations, pressures, and influence, and has a greater emotional investment in his immediate than in his extended family.

With the selection from Duncan Timms' study of residential differentiation (109), material of a somewhat different order is introduced into the present discussion of

[10]In a more historical and transactional social-psychological analysis dealing with the properties and consequences of family structure, Richard Sennett's (95) insightful analysis of middle-class Chicago families during the period of heavy industrial growth in the latter part of the nineteenth century extends the present analysis through suggesting the impediments that the small, inwardly focused, nuclear family offered to successful adaptation to industrial and urban change.

urban sociological patterns and processes. In the opening chapter of his study Timms summarizes some of the theoretical and empirical material dealing with a number of significant behavioral phenomena and processes perceived in the context of the urban neighborhood. Reprinted here is his discussion of the relationship between friendship and propinquity and between neighborhood properties and "deviant" behavior, especially juvenile delinquency and mental illness. Brief mention is also made of the community context of education. While a portion of this material relates to our previous concern with the nature of the neighborhood in the urban context, much of Timms' discussion introduces material otherwise not treated here.

A number of major points are presented in Timms' account. He considers the influence of location on the development of contacts and friendships and the development of distinctive group properties, personal circumstances, and individual feeling tone. Ecological structure is thus perceived as influencing sociocultural structure with the important qualification that this circumstance pertains only to populations which are highly homogeneous in several important regards, and which also share common, distinctive, and clearly bounded residential circumstances.

Still, these are properties that urban neighborhoods do at times exhibit. Timms also considers the phenomenon of the continuance of similar behavioral patterns over time, especially juvenile delinquency, even though the residential population changes. This is suggestive of the role of distinctive neighborhood properties on influencing behavior. A major type of neighborhood community property stressed in his review of the relevant literature is the type of normative inconsistencies, traditions or cultures existing and perpetuated, either in some form of cultural transmission over time or in the process of different groups facing similar conditions. His account describes several explanations of what some of these conditions may be, such as the internal structuring of social relations in the neighborhood, differential association, and differential illegitimate opportunities. Timms notes the general paucity of efforts to relate other nondelinquency forms of "deviant" behavior to the neighborhood setting.

He does describe, however, some efforts to relate some psychiatric disorders and suicide, especially mental disorder, to characteristics of the community. Timms' discussion thus illumines one of the vital properties in conceptualizing the social patterns and structure of a community—the distinctive properties of different urban neighborhoods, and how some of these cultural and social differences underlie some of the differential behavior patterns present in the city. It shows the importance of Louis Wirth's aphorism of the city as a "mosaic of social worlds."

Zald's study (127) points toward a dimension of community structure and process frequently ignored. He considers the influence of a community's demographic, ecological, and social properties, which he refers to as "urban ecology," upon organizational functioning and effectiveness. One has here an effort to link important elements of the social process within a community with certain community properties. The community setting within which organizations function may be perceived as the neighborhood or some other subcommunity area, or for some organizations, the community as a whole, though only the former circumstance is considered here. Organizational effectiveness is related to community properties in terms of the needs of social organizations for securing support or resources from the community, and the differing ability and willingness of communities to provide support. Such support may be quite variable and could include funds, citizen participation, favorable legislation, and involvement of prestigious community figures. While Zald focuses on a voluntary service organization, the type of organization is unlimited in principle and could include business, church, health, cultural, or other spheres of activity[11] (13, 25).

He uses urban differentiation to refer to the variable distribution of community properties and, hence, the potentially different degrees of support and resources available to neighborhood or subcommunity-located organizations. Urban differentiation is not important here in its own terms, but because of the properties associated with it, principally socioeconomic differences. In the circumstance under analysis variation between local areas is encompassed by four, principally demographic, characteristics; the support or resources offered are essentially judged in terms of the provision of "board members with organization-enhancing characteristics"; and the organizations studied are local YMCAs. Zald concludes that poor areas have greater difficulty recruiting board members residing within the area, and that the status of board members varies with subcommunity income and employment properties (in effect, with the processes of urban differentiation). The more effective departments possess higher-status boards and are larger departments, both these properties being related to effectiveness.

The limited quality of Zald's data—the very narrow index of board effectiveness; the possible bias on rater evaluation of board strength due to properties of its members rather than performance; lack of information on the inability to control other organizational and community determinants of variations in board and department effectiveness than those studied in the research; and the absence of any processional or case analysis that might further test the relationships implicated in the study or illumine why they have the influence imputed to them—make this analysis only a suggestive one. Yet, it is an original theoretical and empirical work that effectively points to the

[11]The reader may be interested in a paper developing a somewhat related theoretical point. In an earlier study Hawley (49) has interpreted a community's ability to establish a successful urban renewal effort in terms of certain fundamental social system properties—the extent of power concentration. This, rather than the properties, performance, or interrelationships of individual leaders or key actors, is conceptualized as the determinate element. Here, of course, effectiveness is considered in terms of community, rather than organizational performance, and community rather than subcommunity properties are considered. These are social rather than demographic properties, but the theoretical point involved is similar to that implicit in Zald's study. The social system rather than individual actor focus of both Zald and Hawley's work readily lends itself to comparative community analysis.

importance of the community context of organizational functioning. Thus, it reminds us that a significant component of the process and pattern of metropolitan society involves the functioning of social organizations and that organizational activities and performance are in turn reflective of community properties. Not a fully researched area, its study should provide important illumination on the structure and functioning of the metropolis.

Urban Political Process

It should be apparent to even the casual observer that the urban political process covers a wide range of concerns. The present selections can elaborate just a few fundamental ones.[12] Reflecting a theme variously expressed in the present volume, is the considerable constraint and influence of external political forces and bureaucratic structures on urban political decision making and policy options. The decisions and policies, for instance, of the departments of Defense, Housing, and Urban Development and of the Federal Bureau of Public Roads; federal urban renewal decisions; the actions of state highway departments; state and federal education policies; federal legislation and policy on welfare, schools, and integration—all carry significant consequences for the local community, political and otherwise. Even policies concerning nonurban areas of American society, such as agriculture, produce a significant range of consequences for the cities. This is also true for the policies of private corporate business, especially programs on plant and office location. Yet, both in the private and public sector the ability of the city to influence the character of decisions and policy development by external institutions is slight. Conversely, many of the programs that are developed within the urban centers are "initiated from without the system (that is, by federal or state sources), or by highly mobilized elite groups successful in separating their activities from the urban, political process . . ." (124, p. 206).

The citizen of the urban polity is often apathetic and possesses little knowledge of local affairs. Consequently, there is minimal threat to established political and private power. Another significant property of urban politics is the great difficulty of securing action on the public needs that exist in the cities. The reasons are various and include political fragmentation, lack of resources, and public apathy. However, also important is the distinctive property of the urban community that was implicit in Norton Long's essay (68) cited earlier, the predominance of narrow distinct interest groups, principally in the business-economic area, while the organization of the broader public is slight. Rather than reflecting public needs, policy—either by action

[12]A number of volumes have reprinted items surveying the field of urban politics. Original studies and discussions are also numerous. Several items include 5, 6, 7, 18, 10, 21, 24, 36, 42, 69, 86, 92, 124.

or failure to act—reflects the pressures of organized, specific, limited-interest groups.[13] The fragmented and ineffectual character of urban political structures complements the ineffectiveness of action on public needs. Metropolitan areas as well as individual urban centers are characterized by a multitude of independent, poorly coordinated special authorities, districts, and local governments. The authority of centrally elected officials, such as the mayor, are generally sharply limited. Hence, the potential for effective action by municipal government is quite weak. This is compounded, of course, by limited financial resources, especially as more affluent population sectors and business enterprise has moved beyond the city boundaries.

The distinguished urbanologist Robert Wood has pointedly noted that the urban political system "functions only minimally to 'solve problems' except the most routine ones." It is characterized, among other properties, by "the use of institutions to raise issues rather than to settle them; the creation of new power centers across the metropolitan terrain faster than the merger or regularizing of relations among old ones; [and] an increasing disposition of the system's output to be a function of stimuli from outside of its own boundaries. In short, compared to criteria which suggest that government normally possesses qualities of purposefulness, rationality, regularized processes, and the power for the deliberate resolution of issues and conflicts, urban politics is devoid of most of the properties of a manageable enterprise" (120, p. 206).

The readings selected for the present volume do not attempt to survey the range of properties and processes characteristic of urban political structures. They stress the narrower yet very crucial concerns of achieving an effective change and exercise of power as previously underrepresented minority populations secured political control; some of the characteristics and difficulties in extending the range of community participation in governing; and the influence of extracommunity relationships on the distribution of community power.

Edward Greer's description of Gary, Indiana, and Richard Hacker's mayoralty succinctly covers a very wide range of topics (38). One of the major elements in his report is a vigorous and disturbing account of the complex of factors that constrain an effective assumption of municipal power by a previously unrepresented black constituency and a reform-minded mayor. One of the basic problems posed is the inability to govern without use of existing bureaucratic and administrative personnel, many of whom are hostile to change. This has meant, among other consequences, that certain policy and administrative priorities could not be effectively implemented and the lack of participation in governance by the new constituency weakened popular support and the opportunity for politically educating the citizenry. On a wider level, the inability to function without reliance on external elements has meant, Scott

---

[13]This is also true, of course, on the national scene, and achieving policy more responsive to public needs is a serious problem. However, there are a number of important differences in the national arena that can result in more public responsive legislation.

Greer suggests, being significantly coopted by and contained within the national political system, with "the liberating process of the struggle for office . . . aborted" (40). Unfortunately, Greer fails to develop or sustain this somewhat questionable assertion.[14]

Greer's essay, however, goes considerably beyond the preceding points. His is a damning description of the moral corruption and even lawlessness of major institutions in American society as they are sometimes found at the local municipal level. The large corporation, the small business, the trade unions, and the mass media are indicted for seriously retarding effective and honest governance, and the development of an unbiased and informed citizenry. Additional constraints on effective governance in Gary were various. Severe financial inadequacy was a major one, seriously aggravated by the gross underassessment of the United States Steel Corporation. Yet, the city faced rising needs and costs. Other impediments to innovative, or even merely effective, government included the fragmentation of city government, governmental corruption, working-class hostility and racism. Racism was also evident in the practices of both the local government and United States Steel. Local government was characterized as a sterile enterprise, little motivated or able to improve the general welfare or initiate social change. One function of the city administration was the supervision and protection of organized crime.

While the circumstances of Gary were unique in some respects, Greer's essay makes clear the obstacles that may be placed in the way of a black assumption of effective local power. He indicates some of the difficulties in securing change even when municipal power is achieved and points to the dependence on external forces, the depth and manifold expressions of racism—even among so-called respectable elements—and some of the impediments to effective local government. Additional comparative studies, however, would be valuable in evaluating the Gary phenomenon in a broader context. Efforts at theoretical and empirical analysis pointed toward illuminating the type of national and local policies; and individual and group stratagems that would maximize the probability of the effective exercise of power by reform movements and minority populations would also be extremely useful for social change and social welfare at the local level.

[14]Greer appears to exaggerate the "neocolonial" process to which he refers, and the existence of other theoretical options. It could be contended that much of the reliance on national-based elements and the federal government is the universal property of communities given the nature of urbanization in contemporary American society. This reflects the long-term process of vertical integration and the existence of a complex nation-wide system of interdependence. The city is part of nation-wide institutions and affected by decisions made elsewhere and needs access to external resources. The ability of a city to opt out of this circumstance appears nil at present, without drastically far-reaching institutional change—if then. This is not a situation that can, in many instances, be accounted for through the malevolence or planned actions of any group.

The Van Tils (112) are concerned with an issue generating acrimonious contention in the sphere of forms of government. The issue is that of greater citizen participation in determining both the functioning of those institutions in which the citizen is involved and the public policies and programs of those institutions. Clearly, this is an issue that in many instances transcends the boundaries of the local community. Its origin would appear to arise significantly from a growing concern over the estrangement of many from existing institutional and governmental functioning, a desire to increase the responsiveness of decision makers and to mold policy in accord with a group's interpretation of its needs, the hope of increasing the effectiveness of community-based programs and of institutional functioning, the development of an increased democratic ethic in some quarters, and the attempt in some instances to develop a more politically conscious and effective population.

A host of empirical and theoretical questions are suggested by the phenomena of citizen or community participation, and current work has only begun their exploration. The selection by the Van Tils is a conceptual analysis of the principle of citizen or community participation; it also describes the evolution and response to types of citizen participation in the application of established national programs on the local, community, and neighborhood level. As such it gives no attention to the related and at least equally relevant question of forms of government within local-based institutions (such as the schools and police). Thus, it focuses essentially on community response to what are, in effect, externally established goals and programs, a setting possibly much less auspicious for successful instances of citizen participation than might be true in regard to locally based, ongoing institutions.

In the broadest terms, however, their paper offers two important contributions. Their model of types of citizen participation provides a theoretical contribution to an understanding of the concept of community or citizen participation, and their elaboration of the controversy and consequences engendered by the practice of citizen participation illumines some of the group interests and political dynamics that are involved. Thus, they provide an indication of how difficult it is to democratize forms of governance in the face of already organized and often entrenched political and other interest groups. The attention that the Van Tils give to the response to the effort at instituting citizen participation and to its changing forms relates, of course, to the problems of governing and the democratizing of political institutions that were introduced more broadly in the Greer essay.

The Van Tils develop a number of other points of considerable importance. Their article stresses the great difficulty in maintaining those forms of citizen participation that involve an exercise of the predominant decision-making power by those affected. The precariousness of such a situation arises from the opposition of interests already entrenched in power. They also point to the consequences for policy as the character of citizen participation varies. Thus, where only leadership elements are considered, the interests of those most affected are ignored. Conversely, where the citizens who are affected by an externally contrived program, such as urban renewal, do have conclusive determination of political and administrative concerns, their stance is likely to be negative, and the envisioned program blocked. Where there is movement away from effective citizen involvement, especially on political concerns, the program becomes a provision of services run by the middle class. They also note that where administrative concerns are separate from political access and decision making, and the effort is to run a depoliticized program, it becomes very difficult to maintain an effective program and to continue local citizen interest and involvement. The article also points to the widespread pessimism about the feasibility and wisdom of the theory and practice of citizen participation, stemming not only from political obstacles but also from presumed citizen ignorance, lack of interest, general negativism, and disunion. The response of the authors themselves, however, is not a defeatist one. They urge—significantly—the need for "new institutional forms" that can serve to enhance the input of population needs and interests to the political system, and within which, presumably, the poor (or the citizenry generally, we might add) can play a decision-making role.

Walton's essay and Warren's thoughtful response is an effort of two perceptive students of the American community to provide an original theoretical perspective in explaining the variation in power structures found among communities. Walton's analysis is a response to a very extensive body of empirical material on community power structure that appeared since Hunter's classic 1953 study of Atlanta, *Community Power Structure* (52). A number of major concerns has characterized the work in this area,[15] including the meaning of power and power structure, and how it shall be studied (whether principally by locating those involved in community decisions or by establishing who have the reputation for preponderant influence); the description of the structure of community power and in what groups or actors power is predominantly located, if any; and, somewhat more recently, what community properties underlie different power configurations and decision-making processes and outcomes.[16] One of the major issues has been whether community power structure is concentrated or pluralistic. To what extent, in other words, is preponderant power in regard to the diverse areas of community life concentrated within the hands of a small number of key individuals. Or, can it best be understood as diffused among a fairly large number, none of whom has the ability to determine or block action in more than one or two community spheres.[17] An aspect of this controversy is the extent to which

[15]The following readers contain much of the major items in the field: Aiken and Mott (3), Bonjean, et al. (14), Clark (17), and Hawley and Wirt (50). Two landmark studies are Hunter (52), and Dahl (20). The volumes by Agger, et al. (2), Freeman (31), and Presthus (85) will also be of especial interest, as is Polsby's (82) earlier critical review of the field.

[16]The latter is an especially fruitful direction for continued work, and includes such reviews and contributions as Rossi (93), Clark (16), Gilbert (33), Walton (110), and Mott (76).

[17]The reader will recall that a major import of Long's essay was in the latter direction. We suggested, however, that underlying an apparently diffuse structure of power, community power and decisions might still exhibit a distinct patterning.

business interests and leadership is determinate of community decisions. Walton suggests that the issue here can best be put not in terms of what is *the* power structure of American cities, but rather what circumstances account for a pluralist distribution of power in some communities and its concentration in others. His essay is an attempt to further an answer. Thus, he is not concerned with the question of who has power and in what areas.

Essentially, Walton concludes from an earlier survey (114) of the relationship of community properties and the characteristics of the distribution of community power that whether power is monolithic or diffused will be significantly determined by the extent to which spheres of community activity are connected with extra community systems. He uses Warren's distinction here between the vertical and horizontal dimensions of community organization that we introduced earlier. He reasons that where there is an increasing interdependence with external community institutions, power in the community will more likely be dispersed and community leadership competitive. The reasoning is that with external involvements the local normative order and consensus supportive of the existing power structure will be disrupted, as well as possibly new interests and involvements introduced. Very little, however, is said of the latter. These will create "circumstances conducive to the emergence of competing power centers."

Walton's stress on the importance of extracommunity involvements and their influence on community is a significant contribution. However, as Warren (115) makes clear it is questionable whether this can be accounted for by the concept of a changing community "normative order." It may simply be that increased vertical integration broadens the economic, organizational, and political resources and external constraints available at the local community level to different populations. This can account for an alteration in the distribution and exercise of power at the local level without resort to the notion of a fragmented normative order. It could, in fact, be contended that community consensus might be no higher in some instances of concentrated community power than where power is dispersed, except that in the latter circumstance the means for organizing and expressing contrary perspectives and interests are more readily available.

A useful area for research would be an elaboration of a typology of possible types of vertical integration, both in terms of high and low integration as well as in regard to different institutional areas. One could then more readily attempt a determination of what properties of such interdependence have what consequences on community power structure. A Walton points out, even multipower structures do not necessarily mean a truly competitive system (113, note 22). This kind of effort would require attention to and further an understanding, as well, of the properties (socioeconomic status of the local population, degree of organizational expertise and resources, nature of group consciousness, and prevailing political culture norms, for example) that would influence power distribution and its effectiveness.

Interesting as much of the work in the community power and decision-making field is, a fundamental determination of community decisions is obscured where the focus is on which actors make what decisions or which have a reputation for the ability to make or influence community decisions. Yet, such is the concern in almost all community power studies and it tends to inhere in Walton's discussion (109, 110). What does not receive consideration is the degree of influence exercised by the institutional, political, and cultural properties of a community or society on the decisions made, options pursued, or possibilities raised. Spinrad, for instance, in his review and assessment of community power studies has pointed out that:

> Those who are powerful in specific crucial institutional areas of community life may neither possess the appropriate reputations not participate in many significant community-relevant decisions. Their power comes from the functions of their institutions. The decisions they make within their apparently limited sphere may be so consequential for the rest of the community or society that they are inherently "powerful," as long as the positions of their groups are maintained.
> This is particularly true of "business" in a "business society." [99, p. 344]

It can also be maintained that the power of different groups and individuals and, hence, community decisions will roughly reflect the degree of correspondence between the properties and needs of given populations and the predominant social and political values of the society. Thus, for instance, the dominance of a laissez-faire, competitive ideology of minimal governmental initiative, cautious at best in its humanity and derogating poverty and personal failure at achieving material success, provides a very favorable atmosphere for certain types of policies, as it discourages others. Concomitantly, this means the effectiveness of groups will be differentially influenced. Some may never even have to assert themselves, as particular threatening policies may never even appear as an issue, lacking as they do an acceptive value complex (6).

REFERENCES

1. Adams, Bert N., *Kinship in an Urban Setting* (Chicago: Markham Publishing Co., 1968, paper).

2. Agger, Robert, Goldrich, Daniel, and Swanson, Bert F., *The Rules and the Ruled: Political Power and Impotence in American Communities* (New York: John Wiley & Sons, 1964).

3. Aiken, Michael, and Mott, Paul E., eds., *The Structure of Community Power* (New York: Random House, 1970).

4. Axelrod, Morris, "Urban Structure and Social Participation," *American Sociological Review,* 21 (February 1956), 13–19.

5. Bachrach, Peter, and Baratz, Morton S., "Two Faces of Power," *American Political Science Review,* 56 (December 1962), 947–952.

6. _____, "Decisions and Nondecisions: An Analytical Framework," *American Political Science Review,* 57 (September 1963), 632–642.

7. Banfield, Edward C., *Political Influence* (Glencoe, Illinois: Free Press, 1960).

8. _____, ed., *Urban Government,* rev. ed. (New York: The Free Press, 1969).

9. _____, and Wilson, James Q., *City Politics* (Cambridge: Harvard University Press and MIT Press, 1963).

10. Bell, Wendell, and Boat, Marion, "Urban Neighborhoods and Informal Social Relations," *American Journal of Sociology,* 62 (January 1957), 391–398.

11. Bell, Wendell, and Force, Maryanne, "Social Structure and Participation in Different Types of Formal Associations," *Social Forces,* 35 (May 1956), 345–350.

12. _____, "Urban Neighborhood Types and Participation in Formal Associations," *American Sociological Review,* 21 (February 1956), 25–34.

13. Blankenship, L. Vaughn, and Elling, Ray, "Organizational Support and Community Power Structure: The Hospital," *Journal of Health and Human Behavior,* 3 (Winter 1962), 257–268.

14. Bonjean, Charles M., Clark, Terry N., and Linberry, Robert L., eds., *Community Politics* (New York: Free Press, 1971, paper).

15. Bott, Elizabeth, *Family and Social Networks* (London: Tavistock Publications, Ltd., 1957).

16. Clark, Terry N., "Power and Community Structure: Who Governs, Where and When?" *The Sociological Quarterly,* 8 (Summer 1967), 291–316.

17. _____, ed., *Community Structure and Decision-making: Comparative Analysis* (San Francisco: Chandler Publishing Co., 1968).

18. Coutler, Philip B., ed., *Politics of Metropolitan Areas* (New York: Thomas Y. Crowell Co., 1967, paper).

19. Curtis, Russell L., Jr., and Zurcher, Louis A., Jr., "Voluntary Associations and the Social Integration of the Poor," *Social Problems,* 18 (Winter 1971), 339–357.

20. Dahl, Robert A., *Who Governs?* (New Haven: Yale University Press, 1961).

21. Danielson, Michael N., ed., *Metropolitan Politics* (Boston: Little, Brown and Co., 1966, paper).

22. Dewey, Richard, "The Rural-Urban Continuum: Real but Relatively Unimportant," *American Journal of Sociology,* 66 (July 1960), 60–66.

23. Dotson, Floyd, "Voluntary Associations Among Urban Working Class Families," *American Sociological Association,* 16 (October 1951), 687–693.

24. Dye, Thomas R., and Hawkins, Brett, eds., *Politics in the Metropolis* (Columbus, Ohio: Charles E. Merrill Books, Inc., 1967, paper).

25. Elling, Ray, and Halebsky, Sandor, "Organizational Differentiation and Support: A Conceptual Framework," *Administrative Science Quarterly,* 6 (September 1961), 185–209.

26. Firey, Walter I., *Land Use in Central Boston* (Cambridge: Harvard University Press, 1947).

27. Firth, Raymond, ed., *Two Studies of Kinship in London* (London: London School of Economics Monographs on Social Anthropology, Number 15, 1956).

28. _____, "Family and Kinship in Industrial Society," *The Development of Industrial Societies,* Paul Halmos, ed. *The Sociological Review* Monograph No. 8 (Keele: University of Keele, 1964), 65–87.

29. Foskett, John M., "Social Structure and Social Participation," *American Sociological Review,* 20 (August 1955), 433–436.

30. Freeman, Howard E., Novak, Edwin, and Reeder, Leo C., "Correlates of Membership in Voluntary Associations," *American Sociological Review,* 22 (October 1957), 528–533.

31. Freeman, Linton C., *Local Community Leadership* (Syracuse: University College, 1960).

32. Fried, Marc, and Gleicher, Peggy, "Some Sources of Satisfaction in the Urban Slum," *Journal of the American Institute of Planners,* 27 (November 1961), 305–315.

33. Gans, Herbert, "Urbanism and Suburbanism as Ways of Life: A Reevaluation of Definitions," *Human Behavior and Social Process,* Arnold M. Rose, ed. (Boston: Houghton Mifflin Company, 1962), 625–648.

34. _____, *The Urban Villagers* (New York: The Free Press, 1962).

35. Gilbert, Claire W., "Community Power and Decision-Making: A Quantitative Examination of Previous Research," in Terry N. Clark, ed., *Community Structure and Decisionmaking: Comparative Analysis,* pp. 139–156.

36. Goodman, Jay S., ed., *Perspectives on Urban Politics* (Boston: Allyn and Bacon, Inc., 1970, paper).

37. Greenfield, Sidney M., "Industrialization and the Family in Sociological Theory," *American Journal of Sociology,* 67 (November 1961), 312–322.

38. Greer, Edward, "The 'Liberation' of Gary, Indiana," *Trans-action,* 8 (January 1971), 30–39, 63.

39. Greer, Scott, "Urbanism Reconsidered: A Comparative Study of Local Areas in a Metropolis," *American Sociological Review,* 21 (February 1956), 19–25.

40. _____, *Governing the Metropolis* (New York: John Wiley & Sons, 1962).

41. _____, *The Emerging City, Myth and Reality* (New York: The Free Press, 1962).

42. _____, *Metropolitics, A Study of Political Culture* (New York: John Wiley & Sons, 1963).

43. _____, and Kube, Ella, "Urbanism and Social Structure: A Los Angeles Study," *Community Structure and Analysis,* Marvin Sussman, ed. (New York: Thomas Y. Crowell Co., 1959), 93–112.

44. _____, and Orleans, Peter, "The Mass Society and the Parapolitical Structure," *American Sociological Review,* 27 (October 1962), 634–646.

45. Guterman, Stanley S., "In Defense of Wirth's 'Urbanism as a Way of Life,'" *American Journal of Sociology,* 74 (March 1969), 492–499.

46. Hagedorn, Robert, and Labovitz, Sanford, "Participation in Community Associations by Occupation: A Test of Three Theories," *American Sociological Review,* 33 (April 1968), 272–283.

47. Hauser, Philip M., "Observations on the Urban-Folk and Urban-Rural Dichotomies as Forms of Western Ethnocentrism," *The Study of Urbanization,* Philip M. Hauser and Leo F. Schnore, eds. (New York: John Wiley and Sons, Inc., 1965), 503–517.

48. Hauskneckt, Murray, *The Joiners* (New Jersey: The Bedminister Press, 1962).

49. Hawley, Amos, "Community Power and Urban Renewal Success," *American Journal of Sociology,* 68 (January 1963), 422–431.

50. Hawley, Willis D., and Wirt, Frederick M., eds., *The Search for Community Power* (Englewood Cliffs, N.J.: Prentice-Hall, Inc., 1968, paper).

51. Hodges, Harold M., Jr. "Peninsula People: Social Stratification in a Metropolitan Complex," *Education and Society,* W. Warren Kallenback and Harold M. Hodges, Jr., eds. (Columbus, Ohio: Charles E. Merrill Books, Inc.), 389–420.

52. Hunter, Floyd, *Community Power Structure: A Study of Decision Makers* (Chapel Hill: University of North Carolina, 1953).

53. Innis, Philip H., "The Social Structure of Communication Systems: A Theoretical Proposal," *Studies in Public Communication,* No. 3 (Summer 1961), 12–44.

54. Isaacs, Reginald, "The Neighborhood Theory," *Journal of the American Institute of Planners,* 14 (Spring 1948), 15–23.

55. Jacobs, Jane, *The Death and Life of Great American Cities* (New York: Random House, 1961).

56. Janowitz, Morris, *The Community Press* (Glencoe, Illinois: The Free Press, 1952).

57. Keller, Suzanne, *The Urban Neighborhood: A Sociological Perspective* (New York: Random House, 1968, paper).

58. Kerr, Madeline, *The People of Ship Street* (London: Routledge and Kegan Paul, 1958).

59. Key, William H., "Rural-Urban Differences and the Family," *Sociological Quarterly,* 2 (January 1961), 49–56.

60. _____, "Urbanism and Neighboring," *Sociological Quarterly,* 6 (Autumn 1965), 379–385.

61. Kolb, William, "The Social Structure and Function of Cities," *Economic Development and Cultural Change* (October 1954), 30–46.

62. Komarovsky, Mirra, "The Voluntary Associations of an Urban Dweller," *American Sociological Review,* 11 (December 1946), 686–698.

63. Lewis, Oscar, "Further Observations on the Folk-Urban Continuum and Urbanization with Special Reference to Mexico City," Philip M. Hauser and Leo F. Schnore, eds., *The Study of Urbanization,* pp. 491–503.

64. Liebow, Elliot, *Tally's Corner, A Study of Negro Streetcorner Men* (Boston: Little, Brown and Co., 1967, paper).

65. Linton, Ralph, "The Natural History of the Family," in Ruth Nanda Anshen, ed., *The Family: Its Function and Destiny* (New York: Harper and Brothers, Publishers, 1949), 30–52.

66. Litwak, Eugene, "Geographic Mobility and Extended Family Cohesion," *American Sociological Review,* 25 (June 1960), 385–394.

67. _____, "Occupational Mobility and Extended Family Cohesion," *American Sociological Review,* 25 (February 1960), 9–21.

68. Long, Norton E., "The Local Community as an Ecology of Games," *American Journal of Sociology,* 64 (November 1958), 251–261.

69. _____, *The Polity* (Chicago: Rand McNally & Co., 1962).

70. Lyford, Joseph P., *The Airtight Cage* (New York: Harper & Row, 1966).

71. Mann, Peter H., *An Approach to Urban Sociology* (London: Routledge & Kegan Paul, 1965).

72. Marshall, Dale Rogers, "Who Participates in What? A Bibliographic Essay on Individual Participation in Urban Areas," *Urban Affairs Quarterly,* 4 (December 1968), 201–223.

73. Mogey, John M., *Family and Neighborhood: Two Studies in Oxford* (London: Oxford University Press, 1956).

74. _____, "Family and Community in Urban-Industrial Societies," *Handbook of Marriage and the Family,* Harold T. Christensen, ed. (Chicago: Rand McNally and Company, 1964), 501–529.

75. Morris, R. N., *Urban Sociology* (New York: Frederick A. Praeger, Publishers, 1968).

76. Mott, Paul F., "Power, Authority, and Influence," *The Structure of Community Power,* Michael Aiken and Paul F. Mott, eds. (New York: Random House, 1970), 3–16.

77. Mumford, Lewis, "The Neighborhood and the Neighborhood Unit," *Town Planning Review,* 24 (January 1954), 256–270.

78. Nisbet, Robert A., *Community and Power* (New York: Oxford University Press, 1962, paper).

79. Park, Robert E., *Human Communities, the City and Human Ecology* (Glencoe, Illinois: Free Press, 1952).

80. Parsons, Talcott, "The Social Structure of the Family," *The Family: Its Function and Destiny,* Ruth Nanda Anshen, ed. (New York: Harper and Brothers, Publishers, 1949), 241–274.

81. _____, "Revised Analytical Approach to the Theory of Social Stratification," *Class, Status, and Power: A Reader in Social Stratification,* Reinhart Bendix and Seymour M. Lipset, eds. (Glencoe, Illinois: The Free Press, 1953), 92–128.

82. Polsby, Nelson W., *Community Power and Political Theory* (New Haven: Yale University Press, 1963).

83. Popenoe, David, "On the Meaning of Urban in Urban Studies," *Urban Affairs Quarterly* (September 1965), 17–33.

84. Powell, Elwin H., "The Evolution of the American City and the Emergence of Anomie: A Culture Case Study of Buffalo, New York: 1810–1910," *British Journal of Sociology,* 13 (June 1962), 156–169.

85. Presthus, Robert, *Men at the Top: A Study in Community Power* (New York: Oxford University Press, 1964).

86. Rabinovitz, Francine F., *City Politics and Planning* (New York: Atherton Press, 1969).

87. Redfield, Robert, "The Folk Society," *American Journal of Sociology,* 41 (January 1947), 293–308.

88. Reiss, Albert J., Jr., "Rural-Urban and Status Differences in Interpersonal Contacts," *American Journal of Sociology,* 65 (September 1959), 182–195.

89. Reiss, Paul J., "The Extended Kinship System: Correlates of and Attitudes on Frequency of Interaction," *Marriage and Family Living,* 24 (November 1962), 333–339.

90. Reissman, Leonard, "Class Leisure and Social Participation," *American Sociological Review,* 19 (February 1954), 76–84.

91. Robins, Lee N., and Tomanec, Miroda, "Closeness of Blood Relatives Outside the Immediate Family," *Marriage and Family Living,* 24 (November 1962), 340–346.

92. Rogers, David, *The Management of Big Cities* (Beverly Hills, California: Sage Publications, 1971).

93. Rossi, Peter H., "Power and Community Structure," *Midwest Journal of Political Science,* 4 (November 1960), 39–401.

94. Scott, John C., Jr., "Membership and Participation in Voluntary Associations," *American Sociological Review,* 22 (June 1957), 315–326.

95. Sennett, Richard, *Families Against the City, Middle Class Homes of Industrial Chicago, 1872–1890* (Cambridge: Harvard University Press, 1970).

96. Sexton, Patricia Gayo, *Spanish Harlem, Anatomy of Poverty* (New York: Harper & Row, Publishers, 1965).

97. Simmel, Georg, "The Metropolis and Mental Life," *The Sociology of Georg Simmel,* Kurt H. Wolff, trans. & ed. (Glencoe, Illinois: Free Press, 1950).

98. Smith, Joel, Form, William H., and Stone, Gregory P., "Local Intimacy in a Middle-Sized City," *American Journal of Sociology,* 60 (November 1954), 276–284.

99. Spinrad, William, "Power in Local Communities," *Social Problems,* 12 (Winter 1965), 335–356.

100. Streib, Gordon F., "Family Patterns in Retirement," *The Journal of Social Issues,* 14 (May 1958), 46–60.

101. Sussman, Marvin, "The Help Pattern in the Middle Class Family," *American Sociological Review,* 18 (February 1953), 22–28.

102. _____, "The Isolated Nuclear Family: Fact or Fiction," *Social Problems,* 6 (Spring 1959), 333–340.

103. _____, and Burchinal, Lee, "Kin Family Network: Unheralded Structure in Current Conceptualizations of Family Functioning," *Marriage and Family Living,* 24 (August 1962), 231–240.

104. Sussman, Marvin, and Burchinal, Lee, "Parental Aid to Married Children: Implications for Family Functioning," *Marriage and the Family,* 24 (November 1962), 320–339.

105. Sutcliffe, John P., and Crabbe, B. D., "Incidence and Degrees of Friendship in Urban and Rural Areas," *Social Forces,* 62 (October 1963), 60–67.

106. Suttles, Gerald D., *The Social Order of the Slum, Ethnicity and Territory in the Inner City* (Chicago: University of Chicago Press, 1968).

107. Tax, Sol, "Culture and Civilization in Guatemalan Societies," *Scientific Monthly* (May 1939).

108. _____, "World View and Social Relations in Guatemala," *American Anthropologist,* 43 (January 1941), 27–42.

109. Timms, Duncan W. G., "The City as a Mosaic of Social Worlds - The Neighborhood and Behavior," *The Urban Mosaic* (New York: Cambridge University Press), 9–15, 16–27, 34–35.

110. Tomeh, Aida K., "Informal Participation in a Metropolitan Community," *Sociological Quarterly,* 8 (Winter 1967), 85–102.

111. Townsend, Peter, *The Family Life of Old People* (London: Routledge and Kegan Paul, 1957).

112. Van Til, Jon, and Van Til, Sally Bould, "Citizen Participation in Social Policy, The End of the Cycle?" *Social Problems,* 17 (Winter 1970), 312–323.

113. Walton, John, "The Vertical Axis of Community Organization and the Structure of Power," *Social Science Quarterly,* 48 (December 1967), 353–368.

114. _____, "A Systematic Survey of Community Power Research," *The Structure of Community Power,* Michael Aiken and Paul E. Mott, eds. (New York: Random House, 1970), 443–464.

115. Warren, Roland L., "A Note on Walton's Analysis of Power Structure and Vertical Ties," *Social Science Quarterly,* 48 (December 1967), 369–372.

116. Whyte, William F., Jr., *Street Corner Society* (Chicago: University of Chicago Press, 1943).

117. Wilensky, Harold L., "Orderly Careers and Social Participation: The Impact of Work History on Social Integration in the Middle Class," *American Sociological Review,* 26 (August 1961), 521–539.

118. _____, and Lebeaux, Charles N., *Industrial Society and Social Welfare* (New York: Free Press, 1965, paper).

119. Williams, Oliver, *Metropolitan Political Analysis* (New York: Free Press, 1971).

120. _____, and Press, Charles, eds., *Democracy in Urban America,* 2nd ed. (Chicago: Rand McNally and Co., 1969).

121. Wirth, Louis, *The Ghetto* (Chicago, Ill., University of Chicago Press, 1928).

122. _____, "Urbanism as a Way of Life," *American Journal of Sociology,* 44 (July 1938), 1–24.

123. Wolf, Eleanor P., and Lebeaux, Charles N., "On the Destruction of Poor Neighborhoods by Urban Renewal," *Social Problems,* 15 (Summer 1967), 3–8.

124. Wood, Robert, *1400 Governments* (Cambridge: Harvard University Press, 1961).

125. Wright, Charles R., and Hyman, Herbert, "Voluntary Association Memberships of American Adults," *American Sociological Review,* 22 (June 1958), 284–294.

126. Young, Michael, and Willmott, Peter, *Family and Kinship in East London* (New York: Free Press, 1957).

127. Zald, Mayer, "Urban Differentiation, Characteristics of Boards of Directors and Organizational Effectiveness, *American Journal of Sociology,* 73 (November 1969), 261–272.

A THEORETICAL PERSPECTIVES

Urbanism as a Way of Life
Louis Wirth

I. THE CITY AND CONTEMPORARY CIVILIZATION

Just as the beginning of Western civilization is marked by the permanent settlement of formerly nomadic peoples in the Mediterranean basin, so the beginning of what is distinctively modern in our civilization is best signalized by the growth of great cities. Nowhere has mankind been farther removed from organic nature than under the conditions of life characteristic of great cities. The contemporary world no longer presents a picture of small isolated groups of human beings scattered over a vast territory, as Sumner described primitive society.[1] The distinctive feature of the mode of living of man in the modern age is his concentration into gigantic aggregations around which cluster lesser centers and from which radiate the ideas and practices that we call civilization.

The degree to which the contemporary world may be said to be "urban" is not fully or accurately measured by the proportion of the total population living in cities. The influences which cities exert upon the social life of man

[1] William Graham Sumner, *Folkways* (Boston, 1906), p. 12.

SOURCE: Louis Wirth, "Urbanism as a way of Life," *American Journal of Sociology,* 44 (July 1938), 1–24. Copyright 1938 by the University of Chicago. Reprinted by permission of the publisher, the University of Chicago Press.

are greater than the ratio of the urban population would indicate, for the city is not only in ever larger degrees the dwelling place and the workshop of modern man, but it is the initiating and controlling center of economic, political, and cultural life that has drawn the most remote parts of the world into its orbit and woven diverse areas, peoples, and activities into a cosmos.

The growth of cities and the urbanization of the world is one of the most impressive facts of modern times. Although it is impossible to state precisely what proportion of the estimated total world-population of approximately 1,800,000,000 is urban, 69.2 per cent of the total population of those countries that do distinguish between urban and rural areas is urban.[2] Considering the fact, moreover, that the world's population is very unevenly distributed and that the growth of cities is not very far advanced in some of the countries that have only recently been touched by industrialism, this average understates the extent to which urban concentration has proceeded in those countries where the impact of the industrial revolution has been more forceful and of less recent date. This shift from a rural to a predominantly urban society, which has taken place within the span of a single generation in such industrialized areas as the United States and Japan, has been accompanied by profound changes in virtually every phase of social life. It is these changes and their ramifications that invite the attention of the sociologist to the study of the differences between the rural and the urban mode of living. The pursuit of this interest is an indispensable prerequisite for the comprehension and possible mastery of some of the most crucial contemporary problems of social life since it is likely to furnish one of the most revealing perspectives for the understanding of the ongoing changes in human nature and the social order.[3]

Since the city is the product of growth rather than of instantaneous creation, it is to be expected that the influences which it exerts upon the modes of life should not be able to wipe out completely the previously dominant modes of human association. To a greater or lesser degree, therefore, our social life bears the imprint of an earlier folk society, the characteristic modes of settlement of which were the farm, the manor, and the village. This historic influence is reinforced by the circumstance that the population of the city itself is in large measure recruited from the countryside, where a mode of life reminiscent of this earlier form of existence persists. Hence we should not expect to find abrupt and discontinuous variation between urban and rural types of personality. The city and the country may be regarded as two poles in reference to one or the other of which all human settlements tend to arrange

[2]S. V. Pearson, *The Growth and Distribution of Population* (New York, 1935), p. 211.

[3]Whereas rural life in the United States has for a long time been a subject of considerable interest on the part of governmental bureaus, the most notable case of a comprehensive report being that submitted by the Country Life Commission to President Theodore Roosevelt in 1909, it is worthy of note that no equally comprehensive official inquiry into urban life was undertaken until the establishment of a Research Committee on Urbanism of the National Resources Committee. (Cf. *Our Cities: Their Role in the National Economy* [Washington: Government Printing Office, 1937].)

themselves. In viewing urban-industrial and rural-folk society as ideal types of communities, we may obtain a perspective for the analysis of the basic models of human association as they appear in contemporary civilization.

II. A SOCIOLOGICAL DEFINITION OF THE CITY

Despite the preponderant significance of the city in our civilization, however, our knowledge of the nature of urbanism and the process of urbanization is meager. Many attempts have indeed been made to isolate the distinguishing characteristics of urban life. Geographers, historians, economists, and political scientists have incorporated the points of view of their respective disciplines into diverse definitions of the city. While in no sense intended to supersede these, the formulation of a sociological approach to the city may incidentally serve to call attention to the interrelations between them by emphasizing the peculiar characteristics of the city as a particular form of human association. A sociologically significant definition of the city seeks to select those elements of urbanism which mark it as a distinctive mode of human group life.

The characterization of a community as urban on the basis of size alone is obviously arbitrary. It is difficult to defend the present census definition which designates a community of 2,500 and above as urban and all others as rural. The situation would be the same if the criterion were 4,000, 8,000, 10,000, 25,000, or 100,000 population, for although in the latter case we might feel that we were more nearly dealing with an urban aggregate than would be the case in communities of lesser size, no definition of urbanism can hope to be completely satisfying as long as numbers are regarded as the sole criterion. Moreover, it is not difficult to demonstrate that communities of less than the arbitrarily set number of inhabitants lying within the range of influence of metropolitan centers have greater claim to recognition as urban communities than do larger ones leading a more isolated existence in a predominantly rural area. Finally, it should be recognized that census definitions are unduly influenced by the fact that the city, statistically speaking, is always an administrative concept in that the corporate limits play a decisive role in delineating the urban area. Nowhere is this more clearly apparent than in the concentrations of population on the peripheries of great metropolitan centers which cross arbitrary administrative boundaries of city, county, state, and nation.

As long as we identify urbanism with the physical entity of the city, viewing it merely as rigidly delimited in space, and proceed as if urban attributes abruptly ceased to be manifested beyond an arbitrary boundary line, we are not likely to arrive at any adequate conception of urbanism as a mode of life. The technological developments in transportation and communication which virtually mark a new epoch in human history have accentuated the role of cities as dominant elements in our civilization and have enormously extended the urban mode of living beyond the confines of the city itself. The dominance of the city, especially of the great city, may be regarded as a consequence of the concentration in cities of industrial and commercial, financial and administrative facilities and activities, transportation and communication lines, and cultural and recreational equipment such as the press, radio stations, theaters, libraries, museums, concert halls, operas, hospitals, higher educational institutions, research and publishing centers, professional oganizations, and religious and welfare institutions. Were it not for the attraction and suggestions that the city exerts through these instrumentalities upon the rural population, the differences between the rural and the urban modes of life would be even greater than they are. Urbanization no longer denotes merely the process by which persons are attracted to a place called the city and incorporated into its system of life. It refers also to that cumulative accentuation of the characteristics distinctive of the mode of life which is associated with the growth of cities, and finally to the changes in the direction of modes of life recognized as urban which are apparent among people, wherever they may be who have come under the spell of the influences which the city exerts by virtue of the power of its institutions and personalities operating through the means of communication and transportation.

The shortcomings which attach to number of inhabitants as a criterion of urbanism apply for the most part to density of population as well. Whether we accept the density of 10,000 persons per square mile as Mark Jefferson[4] proposed, or 1,000, which Willcox[5] preferred to regard as the criterion of urban settlements, it is clear that unless density is correlated with significant social characteristics it can furnish only an arbitrary basis for differentiating urban from rural communities. Since our census enumerates the night rather than the day population of an area, the locale of the most intensive urban life—the city center—generally has low population density, and the industrial and commercial areas of the city, which contain the most characteristic economic activities underlying urban society, would scarcely anywhere be truly urban if density were literally interpreted as a mark of urbanism. Nevertheless, the fact that the urban community is distinguished by a large aggregation and relatively dense concentration of population can scarcely be left out of account in a definition of the city. But these criteria must be seen as relative to the general cultural context in which cities arise and exist and are sociologically relevant only in so far as they operate as conditioning factors in social life.

The same criticisms apply to such criteria as the occupation of the inhabitants, the existence of certain physical facilities, institutions, and forms of political organization. The question is not whether cities in our civilization or in others do exhibit these distinctive traits, but how potent they are in molding the character of social life into its specifically urban form. Nor in formulating

[4]"The Anthropogeography of Some Great Cities," *Bull. American Geographical Society,* XLI (1909), 537–66.

[5]Walter F. Willcox, "A Definition of 'City' in Terms of Density," in E. W. Burgess, *The Urban Community* (Chicago, 1926), p. 119.

a fertile definition can we afford to overlook the great variations between cities. By means of a typology of cities based upon size, location, age, and function, such as we have undertaken to establish in our recent report to the National Resources Committee,[6] we have found it feasible to array and classify urban communities ranging from struggling small towns to thriving world-metropolitan centers; from isolated trading-centers in the midst of agricultural regions to thriving world-ports and commercial and industrial conurbations. Such differences as these appear crucial because the social characteristics and influences of these different "cities" vary widely.

A serviceable definition of urbanism should not only denote the essential characteristics which all cities—at least those in our culture—have in common, but should lend itself to the discovery of their variations. An industrial city will differ significantly in social respects from a commercial, mining, fishing, resort, university, and capital city. A one-industry city will present different sets of social characteristics from a multi-industry city, as will an industrially balanced from an imbalanced city, a suburb from a satellite, a residential suburb from an industrial suburb, a city within a metropolitan region from one lying outside, an old city from a new one, a southern city from a New England, a middle-western from a Pacific Coast city, a growing from a stable and from a dying city.

A sociological definition must obviously be inclusive enough to comprise whatever essential characteristics these different types of cities have in common as social entities, but it obviously cannot be so detailed as to take account of all the variations implicit in the manifold classes sketched above. Presumably some of the characteristics of cities are more significant in conditioning the nature of urban life than others, and we may expect the outstanding features of the urban-social scene to vary in accordance with size, density, and differences in the functional type of cities. Moreover we may infer that rural life will bear the imprint of urbanism in the measure that through contact and communication it comes under the influence of cities. It may contribute to the clarity of the statements that follow to repeat that, while the locus of urbanism as a mode of life is, of course, to be found characteristically in places which fulfil the requirements we shall set up as a definition of the city, urbanism is not confined to such localities but is manifest in varying degrees wherever the influences of the city reach.

While urbanism, or that complex of traits which makes up the characteristic mode of life in cities, and urbanization, which denotes the development and extensions of these factors, are thus not exclusively found in settlements which are cities in the physical and demographic sense, they do, nevertheless, find their most pronounced expression in such areas, especially in metropolitan cities. In formulating a definition of the city it is necessary to exercise caution in order to avoid identifying urbanism as a way of life with any specific locally or historically conditioned cultural influences which, while they may signifi-

[6] *Op. cit.,* p. 8.

cantly affect the specific character of the community, are not the essential determinants of its character as a city.

It is particularly important to call attention to the danger of confusing urbanism with industrialism and modern capitalism. The rise of cities in the modern world is undoubtedly not independent of the emergence of modern power-driven machine technology, mass production, and capitalistic enterprise. But different as the cities of earlier epochs may have been by virtue of their development in a preindustrial and precapitalistic order from the great cities of today, they were, nevertheless, cities.

For sociological purposes a city may be defined as a relatively large, dense, and permanent settlement of socially heterogeneous individuals. On the basis of the postulates which this minimal definition suggests, a theory of urbanism may be formulated in the light of existing knowledge concerning social groups.

III. A THEORY OF URBANISM

In the rich literature on the city we look in vain for a theory of urbanism presenting in a systematic fashion the available knowledge concerning the city as a social entity. We do indeed have excellent formulations of theories on such special problems as the growth of the city viewed as a historical trend and as a recurrent process,[7] and we have a wealth of literature presenting insights of sociological relevance and empirical studies offering detailed information on a variety of particular aspects of urban life. But despite the multiplication of research and textbooks on the city, we do not as yet have a comprehensive body of compendent hypotheses which may be derived from a set of postulates implicitly contained in a sociological definition of the city, and from our general sociological knowledge which may be substantiated through empirical research. The closest approximations to a systematic theory of urbanism that we have are to be found in a penetrating essay, "Die Stadt," by Max Weber,[8] and a memorable paper by Robert E. Park on "The City: Suggestions for the Investigation of Human Behavior in the Urban Environment."[9] But even these excellent contributions are far from constituting an ordered and coherent framework of theory upon which research might profitably proceed.

In the pages that follow we shall seek to set forth a limited number of identifying characteristics of the city. Given these characteristics we shall then indicate what consequences or further characteristics follow from them in the light of general sociological theory and empirical research. We hope in this manner to arrive at the essential propositions comprising a theory of urbanism. Some of these propositions can be supported by a considerable body of already

[7] See Robert E. Park, Ernest W. Burgess, et al., The City (Chicago, 1925), esp. chaps. ii and iii; Werner Sombart, "Städtische Siedlung, Stadt," Handwörterbuch der Soziologie, ed. Alfred Vierkandt (Stuttgart, 1931); see also bibliography.

[8] Wirtschaft und Gesellschaft (Tübingen, 1925), Part II, chap. viii, pp. 514–601.

[9] Park, Burgess, et al., op. cit., chap. i.

available research materials; others may be accepted as hypotheses for which a certain amount of presumptive evidence exists, but for which more ample and exact verification would be required. At least such a procedure will, it is hoped, show what in the way of systematic knowledge of the city we now have and what are the crucial and fruitful hypotheses for future research.

The central problem of the sociologist of the city is to discover the forms of social action and organization that typically emerge in relatively permanent, compact settlements of large numbers of heterogeneous individuals. We must also infer that urbanism will assume its most characteristic and extreme form in the measure in which the conditions with which it is congruent are present. Thus the larger, the more densely populated, and the more heterogeneous a community, the more accentuated the characteristics associated with urbanism will be. It should be recognized, however, that in the social world institutions and practices may be accepted and continued for reasons other than those that originally brought them into existence, and that accordingly the urban mode of life may be prepetuated under conditions quite foreign to those necessary for its origin.

Some justification may be in order for the choice of the principal terms comprising our definition of the city. The attempt has been made to make it as inclusive and at the same time as denotative as possible without loading it with unnecessary assumptions. To say that large numbers are necessary to constitute a city means, of course, large numbers in relation to a restricted area or high density of settlement. There are, nevertheless, good reasons for treating large numbers and density as separate factors, since each may be connected with significantly different social consequences. Similarly the need for adding heterogeneity to numbers of population as a necessary and distinct criterion of urbanism might be questioned, since we should expect the range of differences to increase with numbers. In defense, it may be said that the city shows a kind and degree of heterogeneity of population which cannot be wholly accounted for by the law of large numbers or adequately required by means of a normal distribution curve. Since the population of the city does not totally reproduce itself, it must recruit its migrants from other cities, the countryside, and—in this country until recently—from other countries. The city has thus historically been the melting-pot of races, peoples, and cultures, and a most favorable breeding-ground of new biological and cultural hybrids. It has not only tolerated but rewarded individual differences. It has brought together people from the ends of the earth *because* they are different and thus useful to one another, rather than because they are homogeneous and like-minded.[10]

There are a number of sociological propositions concerning the relation-

[10]The justification for including the term "permanent" in the definition may appear necessary. Our failure to give an extensive justification for this qualifying mark of the urban rests on the obvious fact that unless human settlements take a fairly permanent root in a locality the characteristics of urban life cannot arise, and conversely the living together of large numbers of heterogeneous individuals under dense conditions is not possible without the development of a more or less technological structure.

ship between *(a)* numbers of population, *(b)* density of settlement, *(c)* heterogeneity of inhabitants and group life, which can be formulated on the basis of the observation and research.

SIZE OF THE POPULATION AGGREGATE

Ever since Aristotle's *Politics*,[11] it has been recognized that increasing the number of inhabitants in a settlement beyond a certain limit will affect the relationships between them and the character of the city. Large numbers involve, as has been pointed out, a greater range of individual variation. Furthermore, the greater the number of individuals participating in a process of interaction, the greater is the *potential* differentiation between them. The personal traits, the occupations, the cultural life, and the ideas of the members of an urban community may, therefore, be expected to range between more widely separated poles than those of rural inhabitants.

That such variations should give rise to the spatial segregation of individuals according to color, ethnic heritage, economic and social status, tastes and preferences, may readily be inferred. The bonds of kinship, of neighborliness, and the sentiments arising out of living together for generations under a common folk tradition are likely to be absent or, at best, relatively weak in an aggregate the members of which have such diverse origins and backgrounds. Under such circumstances competition and formal control mechanisms furnish the substitutes for the bonds of solidarity that are relied upon to hold a folk society together.

Increase in the number of inhabitants of a community beyond a few hundred is bound to limit the possibility of each member of the community knowing all the others personally. Max Weber, in recognizing the social signifi-

[11]See esp. vii. 4. 4–14. Translated by B. Jowett, from which the following may be quoted:
"To the size of states there is a limit, as there is to other things, plants, animals, implements; for none of these retain their natural power when they are too large or too small, but they either wholly lose their nature, or are spoiled. . . . [A] state when composed of too few is not as a state ought to be, self-sufficing; when of too many, though self-sufficing in all mere necessaries, it is a nation and not a state, being almost incapable of constitutional government. For who can be the general of such a vast multitude or who the herald, unless he have the voice of a Stentor?
"A state then only begins to exist when it has attained a population sufficient for a good life in the political community: it may indeed somewhat exceed this number. But, as I was saying, there must be a limit. What should be the limit will be easily ascertained by experience. For both governors and governed have duties to perform; the special functions of a governor are to command and to judge. But if the citizens of a state are to judge and to distribute offices according to merit, then they must know each other's characters; where they do not possess this knowledge, both the election to offices and the decision of lawsuits will go wrong. When the population is very large they are manifestly settled at haphazard, which clearly ought not to be. Besides, in an overpopulous state foreigners and metics will readily acquire the rights of citizens, for who will find them out? Clearly, then, the best limit of the population of a state is the largest number which suffices for the purposes of life, and can be taken in at a single view. Enough concerning the size of a city."

cance of this fact, pointed out that from a sociological point of view large numbers of inhabitants and density of settlement mean that the personal mutual acquaintanceship between the inhabitants which ordinarily inheres in a neighborhood is lacking.[12] The increase in numbers thus involves a changed character of the social relationships. As Simmel points out:

> [If] the unceasing external contact of numbers of persons in the city should be met by the same number of inner reactions as in the small town, in which one knows almost every person he meets and to each of whom he has a positive relationship, one would be completely atomized internally and would fall into an unthinkable mental condition.[13]

The multiplication of persons in a state of interaction under conditions which make their contact as full personalities impossible produces that segmentalization of human relationships which has sometimes been seized upon by students of the mental life of the cities as an explanation for the "schizoid" character of urban personality. This is not to say that the urban inhabitants have fewer acquaintances than rural inhabitants, for the reverse may actually be true; it means rather that in relation to the number of people whom they see and with whom they rub elbows in the course of daily life, they know a smaller proportion, and of these they have less intensive knowledge.

Characteristically, urbanites meet one another in highly segmental roles. They are, to be sure, dependent upon more people for the satisfactions of their life-needs than are rural people and thus are associated with a greater number of organized groups, but they are less dependent upon particular persons, and their dependence upon others is confined to a highly fractionalized aspect of the other's round of activity. This is essentially what is meant by saying that the city is characterized by secondary rather than primary contacts. The contacts of the city may indeed be face to face, but they are nevertheless impersonal, superficial, transitory, and segmental. The reserve, the indifference, and the blasé outlook which urbanites manifest in their relationships may thus be regarded as devices for immunizing themselves against the personal claims and expectations of others.

The superficiality, the anonymity, and the transitory character of urban-social relations make intelligible, also, the sophistication and the rationality generally ascribed to city-dwellers. Our acquaintances tend to stand in a relationship of utility to us in the sense that the role which each one plays in our life is overwhelmingly regarded as a means for the achievement of our own ends. Whereas, therefore, the individual gains, on the one hand, a certain degree of emancipation or freedom from the personal and emotional controls of intimate groups, he loses, on the other hand, the spontaneous self-expres-

---

[12]*Op. cit.,* p. 514.

[13]Georg Simmel, "Die Grossstädte und das Geistesleben," *Die Grossstadt,* ed. Theodor Petermann (Dresden, 1903), pp. 187–206.

sion, the morale, and the sense of participation that comes with living in an integrated society. This constitutes essentially the state of *anomie* or the social void to which Durkheim alludes in attempting to account for the various forms of social disorganization in technological society.

The segmental character and utilitarian accent of interpersonal relations in the city find their institutional expression in the proliferation of specialized tasks which we see in their most developed form in the professions. The operations of the pecuniary nexus leads to predatory relationships, which tend to obstruct the efficient functioning of the social order unless checked by professional codes and occupational etiquette. The premium put upon utility and efficiency suggests the adaptability of the corporate device for the organization of enterprises in which individuals can engage only in groups. The advantage that the corporation has over the individual entrepreneur and the partnership in the urban-industrial world derives not only from the possibility it affords of centralizing the resources of thousands of individuals or from the legal privilege of limited liability and perpetual succession, but from the fact that the corporation has no soul.

The specialization of individuals, particularly in their occupations, can proceed only, as Adam Smith pointed out, upon the basis of an enlarged market, which in turn accentuates the division of labor. This enlarged market is only in part supplied by the city's hinterland; in large measure it is found among the large numbers that the city itself contains. The dominance of the city over the surrounding hinterland becomes explicable in terms of the division of labor which urban life occasions and promotes. The extreme degree of interdependence and the unstable equilibrium of urban life are closely associated with the division of labor and the specialization of occupations. This interdependence and instability is increased by the tendency of each city to specialize in those functions in which it has the greatest advantage.

In a community composed of a larger number of individuals than can know one another intimately and can be assembled in one spot, it becomes necessary to communicate through indirect mediums and to articulate individual interests by a process of delegation. Typically in the city, interests are made effective through representation. The individual counts for little, but the voice of the representative is heard with a deference roughly proportional to the numbers for whom he speaks.

While this characterization of urbanism, in so far as it derives from large numbers, does not by any means exhaust the sociological inferences that might be drawn from our knowledge of the relationship of the size of a group to the characteristic behavior of the members, for the sake of brevity the assertions made may serve to exemplify the sort of propositions that might be developed.

Density

As in the case of numbers, so in the case of concentration in limited space, certain consequences of relevance in sociological analysis of the city emerge. Of these only a few can be indicated.

As Darwin pointed out for flora and fauna and as Durkheim[14] noted in the case of human societies, an increase in numbers when area is held constant (i.e., an increase in density) tends to produce differentiation and specialization, since only in this way can the area support increased numbers. Density thus reinforces the effect of numbers in diversifying men and their activities and in increasing the complexity of the social structure.

On the subjective side, as Simmel has suggested, the close physical contact of numerous individuals necessarily produces a shift in the mediums through which we orient ourselves to the urban milieu, especially to our fellow-men. Typically, our physical contacts are close but our social contacts are distant. The urban world puts a premium on visual recognition. We see the uniform which denotes the role of the functionaries and are oblivious to the personal eccentricities that are hidden behind the uniform. We tend to acquire and develop a sensitivity to a world of artefacts and become progressively farther removed from the world of nature.

We are exposed to glaring contrasts between splendor and squalor, between riches and poverty, intelligence and ignorance, order and chaos. The competition for space is great, so that each area generally tends to be put to the use which yields the greatest economic return. Place of work tends to become dissociated from place of residence, for the proximity of industrial and commercial establishments makes an area both economically and socially undesirable for residential purposes.

Density, land values, rentals, accessibility, healthfulness, prestige, aesthetic consideration, absence of nuisances such as noise, smoke, and dirt determine the desirability of various areas of the city as places of settlement for different sections of the population. Place and nature of work, income, racial and ethnic characteristics, social status, custom, habit, taste, preference, and prejudice are among the significant factors in accordance with which the urban population is selected and distributed into more or less distinct settlements. Diverse population elements inhabiting a compact settlement thus tend to become segregated from one another in the degree in which their requirements and modes of life are incompatible with one another and in the measure in which they are antagonistic to one another. Similarly, persons of homogeneous status and needs unwittingly drift into, consciously select, or are forced by circumstances into, the same area. The different parts of the city thus acquire specialized functions. The city consequently tends to resemble a mosaic of social worlds in which the transition from one to the other is abrupt. The juxtaposition of divergent personalities and modes of life tends to produce a relativistic perspective and a sense of toleration of differences which may be regarded as prerequisites for rationality and which lead toward the secularization of life.[15]

---

[14]E. Durkheim, *De la division du travail social* (Paris, 1932), p. 248.

[15]The extent to which the segregation of the population into distinct ecological and cultural areas and the resulting social attitude of tolerance, rationality, and secular mentality are functions of density as distinguished from heterogeneity is difficult to determine. Most likely we are dealing here with phenomena which are consequences of the simultaneous operation of both factors.

The close living together and working together of individuals who have no sentimental and emotional ties foster a spirit of competition, aggrandizement, and mutual exploitation. To counteract irresponsibility and potential disorder, formal controls tend to be resorted to. Without rigid adherence to predictable routines a large compact society would scarcely be able to maintain itself. The clock and the traffic signal are symbolic of the basis of our social order in the urban world. Frequent close physical contact, coupled with great social distance, accentuates the reserve of unattached individuals toward one another and, unless compensated for by other opportunities for response, gives rise to loneliness. The necessary frequent movement of great numbers of individuals in a congested habitat gives occasion to friction and irritation. Nervous tensions which derive from such personal frustrations are accentuated by the rapid tempo and the complicated technology under which life in dense areas must be lived.

Heterogeneity

The social interaction among such a variety of personality types in the urban milieu tends to break down the rigidity of caste lines and to complicate the class structure, and thus induces a more ramified and differentiated framework of social stratification than is found in more integrated societies. The heightened mobility of the individual, which brings him within the range of stimulation by a great number of diverse individuals and subjects him to fluctuating status in the differentiated social groups that compose the social structure of the city, tends toward the acceptance of instability and insecurity in the world at large as a norm. This fact helps to account, too, for the sophistication and cosmopolitanism of the urbanite. No single group has the undivided allegiance of the individual. The groups with which he is affiliated do not lend themselves readily to a simple hierarchical arrangement. By virtue of his different interests arising out of different aspects of social life, the individual acquires membership in widely divergent groups, each of which functions only with reference to a single segment of his personality. Nor do these groups easily permit of a concentric arrangement so that the narrower ones fall within the circumference of the more inclusive ones, as is more likely to be the case in the rural community or in primitive societies. Rather the groups with which the person typically is affiliated are tangential to each other or intersect in highly variable fashion.

Partly as a result of the physical footlooseness of the population and partly as a result of their social mobility, the turnover in group membership generally is rapid. Place of residence, place and character of employment, income and interests fluctuate, and the task of holding organizations together and maintaining and promoting intimate and lasting acquaintanceship between the members is difficult. This applies strikingly to the local areas within the city into which persons become segregated more by virtue of differences in race, language, income, and social status, than through choice or positive attraction to people like themselves. Overwhelmingly the city-dweller is not a home-owner and since a transitory habitat does not generate binding traditions and sentiments, only rarely is he truly a neighbor. There is little opportunity for the individual to obtain a conception of the city as a whole or to survey his place in the total scheme. Consequently he finds it difficult to determine what is to his own "best interests" and to decide between the issues and leaders presented to him by the agencies of mass suggestion. Individuals who are thus detached from the organized bodies which integrate society comprise the fluid masses that make collective behavior in the urban community so unpredictable and hence so problematical.

Although the city, through the recruitment of variant types to perform its diverse tasks and the accentuation of their uniqueness through competition and the premium upon eccentricity, novelty, efficient performance, and inventiveness, produces a highly differentiated population, it also exercises a leveling influence. Wherever large numbers of differently constituted individuals congregate, the process of depersonalization also enters. This leveling tendency inheres in part in the economic basis of the city. The development of large cities, at least in the modern age, was largely dependent upon the concentrative force of steam. The rise of the factory made possible mass production for an impersonal market. The fullest exploitation of the possibilities of the division of labor and mass production, however, is possible only with standardization of processes and products. A money economy goes hand in hand with such a system of production. Progressively as cities have developed upon a background of this system of production, the pecuniary nexus which implies the purchasability of services and things has displaced personal relations as the basis of association. Individuality under these circumstances must be replaced by categories. When large numbers have to make common use of facilities and institutions, an arrangement must be made to adjust the facilities and institutions to the needs of the average person rather than to those of particular individuals. The service of the public utilities, of the recreational, educational, and cultural institutions must be adjusted to mass requirements. Similarly, the cultural institutions, such as the schools, the movies, the radio, and the newspapers, by virtue of their mass clientele, must necessarily operate as leveling influences. The political process as it appears in urban life could not be understood without taking account of the mass appeals made through modern propaganda techniques. If the individual would participate at all in the social, political, and economic life of the city, he must subordinate some of his individuality to the demands of the larger community and in that measure immerse himself in mass movements.

IV. THE RELATION BETWEEN A THEORY OF URBANISM AND SOCIOLOGICAL RESEARCH

By means of a body of theory such as that illustratively sketched above, the complicated and many-sided phenomena of urbanism may be analyzed in terms of a limited number of basic categories. The sociological approach to the city thus acquires an essential unity and coherence enabling the empirical investigator not merely to focus more distinctly upon the problems and processes that properly fall in his province but also to treat his subject matter in a more integrated and systematic fashion. A few typical findings of empirical research in the field of urbanism, with special reference to the United States, may be indicated to substantiate the theoretical propositions set forth in the preceding pages, and some of the crucial problems for further study may be outlined.

On the basis of the three variables, number, density of settlement, and degree of heterogeneity, of the urban population, it appears possible to explain the characteristics of urban life and to account for the differences between cities of various sizes and types.

Urbanism as a characteristic mode of life may be approached empirically from three interrelated perspectives: (I) as a physical structure comprising a population base, a technology, and an ecological order; (2) as a system of social organization involving a characteristic social structure, a series of social institutions, and a typical pattern of social relationships; and (3) as a set of attitudes and ideas, and a constellation of personalities engaging in typical forms of collective behavior and subject to characteristic mechanisms of social control.

Urbanism in Ecological Perspective

Since in the case of physical structure and ecological processes we are able to operate with fairly objective indices, it becomes possible to arrive at quite precise and generally quantitative results. The dominance of the city over its hinterland becomes explicable through the functional characteristics of the city which derive in large measure from the effect of numbers and density. Many of the technical facilities and the skills and organizations to which urban life gives rise can grow and prosper only in cities where the demand is sufficiently great. The nature and scope of the services rendered by these organizations and institutions and the advantage which they enjoy over the less developed facilities of smaller towns enhances the dominance of the city and the dependence of ever wider regions upon the central metropolis.

The urban-population composition shows the operation of selective and differentiating factors. Cities contain a larger proportion of persons in the prime of life than rural areas which contain more old and very young people. In this, as in so many other respects, the larger the city the more this specific characteristic of urbanism is apparent. With the exception of the largest cities, which have attracted the bulk of the foreign-born males, and a few other special types of cities, women predominate numerically over men. The heterogeneity of the urban population is further indicated along racial and ethnic lines. The foreign born and their children constitute nearly two-thirds of all the inhabitants of cities of one million and over. Their proportion in the urban population declines as the size of the city decreases, until in the rural areas they comprise only about one-sixth of the total population. The larger cities similarly have attracted more Negroes and other racial groups than have the smaller communities. Considering that age, sex, race, and ethnic origin are associated with other factors such as occupation and interest, it becomes clear that one major characteristic of the urban-dweller is his dissimilarity from his fellows. Never before have such large masses of people of diverse traits as we find in our cities been thrown together into such close physical contact as in the great cities of America. Cities generally, and American cities in particular, comprise a motley of peoples and cultures, of highly differentiated modes of life between which there often is only the faintest communication, the greatest indifference and the broadest tolerance, occasionally bitter strife, but always the sharpest contrast.

The failure of the urban population to reproduce itself appears to be a biological consequence of a combination of factors in the complex of urban life, and the decline in the birth-rate generally may be regarded as one of the most significant signs of the urbanization of the Western world. While the proportion of deaths in cities is slightly greater than in the country, the outstanding difference between the failure of present-day cities to maintain their population and that of cities of the past is that in former times it was due to the exceedingly high death-rates in cities, whereas today, since cities have become more livable from a health standpoint, it is due to low birth-rates. These biological characteristics of the urban population are significant sociologically, not merely because they reflect the urban mode of existence but also because they condition the growth and future dominance of cities and their basic social organization. Since cities are the consumers rather than the producers of men, the value of human life and the social estimation of the personality will not be unaffected by the balance between births and deaths. The pattern of land use, of land values, rentals, and ownership, the nature and functioning of the physical structures, of housing, of transportation and communication facilities, of public utilities—these and many other phases of the physical mechanism of the city are not isolated phenomena unrelated to the city as a social entity, but are affected by and affect the urban mode of life.

Urbanism as a Form of Social Organization

The distinctive features of the urban mode of life have often been described sociologically as consisting of the substitution of secondary for primary contacts, the weakening of bonds of kinship, and the declining social significance of the family, the disappearance of the neighborhood, and the undermining of the traditional basis of social solidarity. All these phenomena can be substantially verified through objective indices. Thus, for instance, the low and declining urban-reproduction rates suggest that the city is not conducive to the traditional type of family life, including the rearing of children and the maintenance of the home as the locus of a whole round of vital activities. The transfer of industrial, educational, and recreational activities to specialized institutions outside the home has deprived the family of some of its most characteristic historical functions. In cities mothers are more likely to be employed, lodgers are more frequently part of the household, marriage tends to be postponed, and the proportion of single and unattached people is greater. Families are smaller and more frequently without children than in the country. The family as a unit of social life is emancipated from the larger kinship group characteristic of the country, and the individual members pursue their own diverging interests in their vocational, educational, religious, recreational, and political life.

Such functions as the maintenance of health, the methods of alleviating the hardships associated with personal and social insecurity, the provisions for education, recreation, and cultural advancement have given rise to highly specialized institutions on a community-wide, statewide, or even national basis. The same factors which have brought about greater personal insecurity also underlie the wider contrasts between individuals to be found in the urban world. While the city has broken down the rigid caste lines of preindustrial society, it has sharpened and differentiated income and status groups. Generally, a larger proportion of the adult-urban population is gainfully employed than is the case with the adult-rural population. The white-collar class, comprising those employed in trade, in clerical, and in professional work, are proportionately more numerous in large cities and in metropolitan centers and in smaller towns than in the country.

On the whole, the city discourages an economic life in which the individual in time of crisis has a basis of subsistence to fall back upon, and it discourages self-employment. While incomes of city people are on the average higher than those of country people, the cost of living seems to be higher in the larger cities. Home ownership involves greater burdens and is rarer. Rents are higher and absorb a larger proportion of the income. Although the urban-dweller has the benefit of many communal services, he spends a large proportion of his income for such items as recreation and advancement and a smaller proportion for food. What the communal services do not furnish the urbanite must purchase, and there is virtually no human need which has remained unexploited by commercialism. Catering to thrills and furnishing means of escape from drudgery, monotony, and routine thus become one of the major functions of urban recreation, which at its best furnishes means for creative self-expression and spontaneous group association, but which more typically in the urban world results in passive spectatorism on the one hand, or sensational record-smashing feats on the other.

Being reduced to a stage of virtual impotence as an individual, the urbanite is bound to exert himself by joining with others of similar interest into organized groups to obtain his ends. This results in the enormous multiplication of voluntary organizations directed toward as great a variety of objectives as there are human needs and interests. While on the one hand the traditional ties of human association are weakened, urban existence involves a much greater degree of interdependence between man and man and a more complicated, fragile, and volatile form of mutual interrelations over many phases of which the individual as such can exert scarcely any control. Frequently there is only the most tenuous relationship between the economic position or other basic factors that determine the individual's existence in the urban world and the voluntary groups with which he is affiliated. While in a primitive and in a rural society it is generally possible to predict on the basis of a few known factors who will belong to what and who will associate with whom in almost every relationship of life, in the city we can only project the general pattern of group formation and affiliation, and this pattern will display many incongruities and contradictions.

Urban Personality and Collective Behavior

It is largely through the activities of the voluntary groups, be their objectives economic, political, educational, religious, recreational, or cultural, that the urbanite expresses and develops his personality, acquires status, and is able to carry on the round of activities that constitute his life-career. It may easily be inferred, however, that the organizational framework which these highly differentiated functions call into being does not of itself insure the consistency and integrity of the personalities whose interests it enlists. Personal disorganization, mental breakdown, suicide, delinquency, crime, corruption, and disorder might be expected under these circumstances to be more prevalent in the urban than in the rural community. This has been confirmed in so far as comparable indices are available; but the mechanisms underlying these phenomena require further analysis.

Since for most group purposes it is impossible in the city to appeal individually to the large number of discrete and differentiated individuals, and since it is only through the organizations to which men belong that their interests and resources can be enlisted for a collective cause, it may be inferred that social control in the city should typically proceed through formally organized groups. It follows, too, that the masses of men in the city are subject to manipulation by symbols and stereotypes managed by individuals working from afar or operating invisbly behind the scenes through their control of the instruments of communication. Self-government either in the economic, the political, or the cultural realm is under these circumstances reduced to a mere figure of speech or, at best, is subject to the unstable equilibrium of pressure groups. In view of the ineffectiveness of actual kinship ties we create fictional kinship groups. In the face of the disappearance of the territorial unit as a basis of social solidarity we create interest units. Meanwhile the city as a community resolves itself into a series of tenuous segmental relationships superimposed upon a territorial base with a definite center but without a definite periphery and upon a division of labor which far transcends the immediate locality and is world-wide in scope. The larger the number of persons in a state of interaction with one another the lower is the level of communication and the greater is the tendency for communication to proceed on an elementary level, i.e., on the basis of those things which are assumed to be common or to be of interest to all.

It is obviously, therefore, to the emerging trends in the communication system and to the production and distribution technology that has come into existence with modern civilization that we must look for the symptoms which will indicate the probable future development of urbanism as a mode of social life. The direction of the ongoing changes in urbanism will for good or ill transform not only the city but the world. Some of the more basic of these factors and processes and the possibilities of their direction and control invite further detailed study.

It is only in so far as the sociologist has a clear conception of the city as a social entity and a workable theory of urbanism that he can hope to develop a unified body of reliable knowledge, which what passes as "urban sociology" is certainly not at the present time. By taking his point of departure from a theory of urbanism such as that sketched in the foregoing pages to be elaborated, tested, and revised in the light of further analysis and empirical research, it is to be hoped that the criteria of relevance and validity of factual data can be determined. The miscellaneous assortment of disconnected information which has hitherto found its way into sociological treatises on the city may thus be sifted and incorporated into a coherent body of knowledge. Incidentally, only by means of some such theory will the sociologist escape the futile practice of voicing in the name of sociological science a variety of often unsupportable judgments concerning such problems as poverty, housing, city-planning, sanitation, municipal administration, policing, marketing, transportation, and other technical issues. While the sociologist cannot solve any of these practical problems—at least not by himself—he may, if he discovers his proper function, have an important contribution to make to their comprehension and solution. The prospects for doing this are brightest through a general, theoretical, rather than through an *ad hoc* approach.

The Evolution of the American City and the Emergence of Anomie: A Culture Case Study of Buffalo, New York: 1810–1910*

Elwin H. Powell

Sociologists have often postulated a relationship between urbanism and anomie.[1] The city is pictured as a 'motely of social worlds which touch but do not interpenetrate' (Park), as a 'society of strangers' (Meyer). More a population aggregate than a community the city is functionally integrated through the cash nexus, but there is 'no communication and no consensus . . . [and] human relations are symbiotic rather than social' (Park). Men are isolated from one another and alienated from the larger society; anomie is reflected in social pathologies as well as in the decay of public life (de Grazia). Lewis Mumford describes the modern megalopolis in four words: 'external regularity; internal disruption'.[2]

Seeking an explanation for the character of urban life sociologists first turned to demography and ecology. For R. E. Park human society consisted

---

*Revision of a paper read before the Western New York Sociological Society, Fall, 1959. For criticism I am indebted to Dr. Sidney Willhelm of San Francisco State College.

[1] The concept of anomie is used here as a virtual equivalent of alienation; for amplification see Elwin H. Powell, 'Occupation, Status and Suicide: Toward a Redefinition of Anomie', *American Sociological Review,* 23 (April 1958), 131–9.

[2] The spread of anomie is a dominant motif in the literature of urban sociology, see Louis Wirth, 'Urbanism as a Way of Life', *Reader in Urban Sociology,* eds. Paul Hatt and Albert J. Riess (Glencoe, Ill.: Free Press, 1951), 32–49; Georg Simmel, 'The Metropolis and Mental Life', ibid., 563–74; R. E. Park, *Human Communities,* ed. E. C. Hughes (Glencoe, Ill.: Free Press, 1952), 240–62, *et passim;* Julie Meyer, 'The City and the Stranger', *American Journal of Sociology,* LVI (March 1951), 476–83. In the 1920's and 1930's the University of Chicago Press published a series of empirical monographs liking social and personal disorganization to urbanism, see Nels Anderson, *The Hobo* (1923); Clifford Shaw, *Delinquency and Urban Areas* (1934); Harvey Zorbaugh, *The Gold Coast and the Slum* (1932); R. E. L. Faris and H. W. Dunham, *Mental Disorders in Urban Areas* (1939). For a recent statement of the same hypothesis, see Marshall Clinard, *The Sociology of Deviant Behavior* (New York: Rinehart, 1956). For an overview of anomie in modern society, Sebastian de Grazia, *The Political Community: A Study of Anomie* (Chicago: University of Chicago Press, 1948). On the historical development from the metropolis to the megalopolis, Lewis Mumford, *Culture of Cities* (New York: Harcourt, Brace, 1938).

SOURCE: Elwin H. Powell, "The Evalution of the American City and the Emergence of Anomie: A Culture Case Study of Buffalo, New York: 1810–1910," *British Journal of Sociology,* 13 (June 1962), 156–159. Reprinted by permission.

of an ecological base and a cultural superstructure, and the former determined the latter.[3] Following Simmel and Durkheim, Louis Wirth reasoned that 'as the number of people interacting [dynamic density] increase, social relations become superficial and segmentalized, producing the "schizoid character of the urban personality" '. The anonymity and transience of urban life engenders a sophisticated and calculating self-centredness. 'No single group has the undivided allegiance of the individual . . . and there is little opportunity for the individual to obtain a conception of the city as a whole or to survey his place in the total scheme of things.'[4] Or, as Park put it, 'man gains his freedom but loses his direction'.[5] The demographic-ecological thesis can be represented schematically as follows:

$$\text{Dynamic Density} \longrightarrow \begin{bmatrix} \text{Heterogeneity} \\ \text{Division of Labour} \longrightarrow \text{Anonymity} \longrightarrow \text{Anomie} \\ \text{Mobility} \end{bmatrix}$$

Kingsley Davis follows a similar argument: population density gives rise to heterogeneity, anonymity, and finally 'an atomization of the constituent individuals'.[6] Following the dissolution of communal solidarity there is a competitive struggle for existence, and competition is the foundation of the laws of urban ecology.

Yet the demographic-ecological framework has never proved completely satisfactory as an explanation of the urban way of life. First, it may be culturally limited; not all cities correspond to the American pattern.[7] Secondly, there are serious logical contradictions in the conceptual scheme itself.[8] And finally, as Walter Firey has shown, the 'laws' of ecology are not 'natural' but cultural phenomena. Firey demonstrated that the ecological configuration was partially the product of social institutions. Similarly in a chapter on 'localized anomie' Firey maintains that the deterioration of communal and kinship solidarity, so characteristic of the American city, is a function of the economic system rather than urbanism as such. Furthermore the economic order is ultimately the creation of cultural values.[9]

The present paper is an attempt to delineate some of the historical and institutional sources of the anomie of urban life.

[3]For a critique of Park's position, William L. Kolb, 'The Structure and Function of Cities', *Economic Development and Cultural Change,* III (1954), 30–50.

[4]Wirth, 'Urbanism as a Way of Life', op. cit., 32–49; especially 40–3.

[5]Park, *Human Communities,* 91–5.

[6]Kingsley Davis, *Human Society* (New York: Macmillan, 1949), 329–36. Cf. Robert C. Angell, *The Integration of American Society* (New York: McGraw-Hill, 1941), p. 201, on the relationship between urban anonymity and the weakening of the moral community.

[7]Cf. Fustel de Coulanges, *The Ancient City* (New York: Doubleday Anchor, 1956), for notable exceptions.

[8]Ruth Alihan, *Social Ecology* (New York: Columbia University Press, 1938).

[9]Walter Firey, *Land Use in Central Boston* (Cambridge: Harvard University Press, 1947), 290–2; 323–40, *et passim.*

METHOD: HISTORICAL

Sociologists have not availed themselves of the relative abundance of historical material on the American city.[10] Reference is occasionally made to Adna Weber and Arthur Schlesinger, senr., but the raw data from the archives are rarely used. Several people have written on the pre-industrial city, and the late Howard Becker was working on a typology of the Greek city.[11] Yet the twenty-five page bibliography of the 1957 edition of the Hatt and Reiss *Reader in Urban Sociology* contains hardly a reference to the nineteenth-century American city.[12] This is especially unfortunate because the transition from a rural to an urban society began immediately after the Civil War and reached fruition in the decisive period between 1890 and 1910 when the 'core culture' which has more or less prevailed since then came into being. To fully understand the urban present it is necessary to know at least the broad contours of the past.

DATA: BUFFALO, NEW YORK: 1810–1910

Demographically Buffalo's development typifies the American city. Almost a small town until the 1850's, it was a full-grown metropolis by the turn of the century, afterwards spreading out into a megalopolis. Between 1810 and 1850 the population doubled each decade, growing from a village of 1,508 to a city of 42,261 at mid-century. Table I gives data on growth since 1850. The first settlers were New Englanders moving west. In 1830 some 10 percent of the population was foreign-born, mainly German and Irish stock. By 1860 the population was nearly half German—30,000. Polish immigration began in the 1880's and 1890's; Italians came in large numbers around the turn of the century. By the time of the First World War the foreign-born (one-third of the city) population was 26 per cent Polish, 17 per cent German, 13 per cent Italian, with the remainder of Irish, English and Eastern European descent.[13] While Buffalo was once called a Polish city there is today little to distinguish it from other heavy-industry centres of the north-east.

(1) *Buffalo as Community: 1810–1860.* Although Buffalo was primarily a commercial centre there was still a strong sense of social solidarity in the

[10]For a review of the literature, Blake McKelvey, 'American Urban History Today', *American Historical Review,* LVII (July 1952), 919–29.

[11]Howard Becker, 'Culture Case Study and Greek History', *American Sociological Review,* 23 (Oct. 1958), 489–504; Gideon Sjoberg, *The Pre-industrial City* (Glencoe, Ill.: Free Press, 1960); Horace Miner, *The Primitive City of Timbuctoo* (Princeton: Princeton University Press, 1953).

[12]The historical sense seems better developed in European urban sociology, see David Glass, *The Town and a Changing Civilization* (London: Jane Lane, 1935); Ruth Glass, 'Urban Sociology in Great Britain: A Trend Report', *Current Sociology,* IV (1955), 5–76.

[13]Niles Carpenter, 'Nationality, Color and Economic Opportunity in the City of Buffalo', *University of Buffalo Studies,* V (1926–7), 96–194.

1830's and 1840's.[14] One writer speaks of the community as 'a band of brothers and sisters'—doubtless an exaggeration. Nevertheless, both necessity and common values created a kind of mutual dependence which is seldom found in the modern city. Eight months of the year, from April to December, were devoted to business but the other four months of ice-bound winter were 'quite generally given up to social enjoyment. . . . One never expected to be without several friends on any evening where there was not an important social affair taking place. . . . It was not uncommon . . . to write three hundred or four hundred invitations to a party.'[15] The society is described as 'full of ceremony and courtly usage, at the same time quaintly provincial. . . .' The public lecture— on subjects ranging from animal magnetism to 'The Progress of Literature in the 13th and 14th Centuries'—was a popular entertainment, and many activities revolved around the church. Of course there were outsiders, e.g. an anomic waterfront element, who did not participate fully in the cultural life of the community, but the open frontier siphoned off many of the misfits and 'riff-raff'. The resident population thought of themselves as simple, democratic folk possessed of that sense of equality which de Tocqueville made the key to American character.[16]

The extremes of wealth and poverty were less pronounced than in subsequent decades. Few people lived off the unearned increment of capital; the owners of property were usually the managers of their holdings. Most establishments employed no more than twenty or so workers; manufacturing (ship building, iron working) was still a handicraft.[17] Like the merchant the artisan served a small personally-known clientele, and there is no record of serious and sustained labour trouble (though there were occasional riots). The workers, as Professor Horton comments, 'were not aiming at working class solidarity but tried rather through individual exertions to rise above their class and enter business or the professions'.[18] Classes were not segregated ecologically; of the four residential wards of the city the assessed value of real estate was approximately the same in each—$2,500,000.[19] A businessman's 'word was as good

[14]The early Buffalo (c. 1810–30) was a stage coach town, its social life revolving around the tavern, Robert W. Bingham, *Cradle of the Queen City* (Buffalo: Buffalo Historical Society, 1931). Cf. Carl Bridenbaugh, *Cities in the Wilderness* (New York: Ronald Press, 1938), p. 107.

[15]Martha Fitch Poole, 'The Social Life of Buffalo in the 1830's and 49's', *Publications of the Buffalo Historical Society*, XVII (1913), 67–90. Hereafter abbreviated *PBHS*. For a similar picture, *The Journal of Mary Peacock* (Buffalo: Privately Printed, 1938). This document was written in 1838.

[16]See Frank M. Hollister, 'Some Early Buffalo Characters', *PBHS,* XVII (1913), 67–90; Julia Snow, 'Early Recollections of Buffalo', ibid., 129–64.

[17]Cf. Carl Bridenbaugh, *The Colonial Craftsman* (New York: New York University Press, 1950), 65–124, for a similar situation in an earlier period.

[18]John T. Horton, *History of Northwestern New York* (New York: Lewis Historical Publishing Co., 1947), 80–3. This remarkable book is an untapped mine of sociological data and has a significance far beyond the sphere of local history.

[19]*Proceedings of the Board of Supervisors of Erie County* (Buffalo: C. E. Young, 1852), p. 10.

as his bond' and merchants freely borrowed money from one another when low on cash.[20] As late as 1840 the city council had no fixed time to meet; members simply gathered in a local tavern or hotel when there was business to be discussed. Buffalo had only one policeman until the mid-'forties and did not have a uniformed police force until 1866. Seemingly informal (primary group) control was sufficient to maintain order and carry on the business of the community (although it is also possible that more disorder could be tolerated in this early period, when the social structure still had a certain looseness about it). But by the late 'forties as Mrs. Poole reflects, 'changes were foreshadowed. . . . The introduction of the railway brought strangers of every condition and kind to our doors. That exclusiveness which the locality, surroundings, climate and conditions of the times forced upon us was now at an end, never to return.'[21] Both the sources and the profundity of the 'change' eluded most of the observers of the time. There was an imperceptible hardening of class lines, a gradual closing of the avenues of social ascent, a solidification of the power of the ruling élite.

(2) *Buffalo as Class Society: 1860–1910.*   While the nature of the city did not change overnight, by the late 1860's the outlines of a new society were clearly visible.[22] At the top of the social pyramid were men of great wealth; at the bottom was an industrial proletariat, a detached and indigent population. Arrests for both major and minor crimes increased sharply in the 1860's, as indicated in Table I. By the 1870's around 5 per cent of the population was receiving poor relief from the city. Of the 7,696 people on relief in 1879, 17 per cent were native-born Americans, 36 per cent were Irish, 30 per cent German and the remainder of miscellaneous European stocks.[23] Vagrants were sent to the 'poor farm' for 30 days; petty thieves received as much as 60 days in the workhouse for such crimes as stealing a coat or a pair of boots.[24] This was the age of the vagabond when tramps roamed the country as 'pitiful caricatures of the pioneer'.[25]

Some sense of the time can be gained from a review of the chronic labour trouble of the period. Railroading was the primary industry of Buffalo, and when in 1877 wages were reduced from $1.50 to $1.38 a day (12 hours) a major strike was precipitated. The local press insisted that the 'strikers' rebellion'

[20]W. H. Glover and Frank W. Copley, 'Spaulding as Mayor of Buffalo', *Niagara Frontier,* 7 (Spring, 1960), 3–10, for a picture of the 1850's.

[21]Poole, op. cit., 493.

[22]For an overview of the period, Charles Hunt Page, *Class and American Sociology: From Ward to Ross* (New York: Dial Press, 1940), 3–25.

[23]Data from *The Mayor's Annual Message to the City Council: 1879.*

[24]*Buffalo Express,* January 17; August 1, 1877.

[25]Arthur Schlesinger, *The Rise of the City, 1878–98* (New York: Macmillan, 1933), p. 119. The author also notes a 50 per cent rise in the number of prison inmates from 1880–90 and a growth in the murder rate from 24.7 (1880) to 68.5 (1890) to 107.2 (1898) per million of the population while the murder rate was declining in European countries such as Germany and England . . . Fundamental blame was attached to unhealthy urban growth. Essentially Buffalo follows the national pattern.

must be put down, and for that purpose the state militia was finally called to the scene. After the return to normalcy the press seemed puzzled that neither the railroad nor the employees 'consider that they owe any sort of allegiance to each other'. Of course the workers 'had a right to decline to work at the reduced pay, but there their rights ceased'. However just their complaint 'there can be no toleration of the strikers' course. For the right of a person to employ labourers to work at any price they may agree upon without interference is one without which society cannot exist.'[26] Although the press assumed the 1877 strike would 'make the corporations more solicitous to avoid giving occasion for strikes in the future', the same scene on a larger scale was re-enacted in 1892. After the local police proved unable to subdue 700 striking railroad switchmen, 8,000 troops were dispatched to Buffalo. The switchmen finally capitulated, saying they could not fight the U.S. Army and a half-dozen corporations too, but for several days martial law reigned; the saloons were closed (often at bayonet point) and the streets of the city were deserted.[27] The railway workers were the first to unionize and later the crafts followed suit, saying simply: 'We organize because we must.' Concentrated capital created conditions where it was no longer possible to bargain on an individual basis.

The decade of the 1890's was the high noon of Buffalo capitalism. The city boasted 60 millionaires, twice the number in all the United States in 1850. Congruent with the prevailing myth men were said to have acquired their fortunes through hard work, thrift and individual genius—the virtues of the Protestant Ethic. One writer contends that none of the Buffalo millionaires inherited great wealth, and the assertion contains a kind of literal truth: there was no great wealth to inherit in 1850. But inherited position had a decisive effect on individual destiny. The ten richest families had been well established in the city since 1840. Between 1860 and 1890 when the fortunes were made the population of the city trebled—from 81,000 to 244,000—and the businessman or landowner already established in the community was bound to prosper. Without question the rich got richer, and there is some evidence that the poor became poorer; during the period the per capita personal wealth appears to have declined (see Table I). A more intangible change also occurred; men came to look differently on wealth and poverty. Increasingly business and labour inhabited different social worlds. Writing in a Buffalo union publication Samuel Gompers stated the case clearly, 'Modern society is based on one simple fact, the practical separation of the capitalist class from the great mass of workers. It is not so much a difference in industrial rank as social status . . . a distinction scarcely noticeable in the United States before the previous generation.'[28]

In the 1890's the separation acquired even a physical or ecological dimen-

[26] *Buffalo Express,* July 21; 26; 27, 1877.
[27] *Buffalo Courier,* August 16, 1892.
[28] *History of the United Trades and Labor Council of Erie County* (Buffalo: 1897), p. 505.
Cf. Richard Hofsteader, *The Age of Reform* (New York: Alfred A. Knopf, 1955), 62–70.

TABLE I. POPULATION, PROPERTY AND CRIME IN Buffalo, 1850–1908

		Property*				Crime†	
	Popula-	Real		Personal		Arrests per 1000	
Year	tion	Millions of Dollars	Per capita Dollars	Millions of Dollars	Per capita Dollars	Male	Female
1850	42,261	15.3	352	2.03	48.2	—	—
1855	74,214	27.3	368	6.66	99.5	55.0	13.3
1860	81,129	28.1	298	5.89	72.5	49.1	17.3
1865	94,210	25.8	274	7.73	82.2	113.5	48.2
1870	117,714	30.8	262	6.54	56.0	100.0	30.4
1875	134,557	34.9	260	6.10	45.6	—	—
1880	155,134	81.7	525	7.52	48.4	99.0	18.3
1885	205,400	99.9	483	8.46	41.2	75.5	13.5
1890	255,664	151.3	591	11.0	43.2	121.0	17.3
1895	304,025	220.2	720	14.3	47.2	131.0	13.3
1900	352,387	223.0	635	9.4	26.7	—	—
1905	376,587	241.9	645	7.4	19.7	104.0	13.3
1908	400,641	269.4	636	7.3	18.4	160.0	13.9

*Data on Property Valuations from Truman C. White (ed.), *Erie County* (Boston: Boston History Company, Publishers, 1898), 441; and the *Proceedings of the Board of Supervisors of Erie County* for the years 1900, 1904, 1908. Data can only be regarded as a rough estimate.

†Rates are based on data from *Proceedings of the Board of Supervisors of Erie County,* 1875–6, for the years 1855–75; and from the *Annual Reports of the Buffalo Police Department* for the years 1876 through 1908. Again the data must be taken as only approximations.

sion. Upper-class families of enormous wealth, Anglo-Saxon origin and Protestant religion built three- and four-storey palaces along Delaware Avenue.

> 'This fashionable section was only a small part of the city [writes Mable Dodge Luhan], but it seemed to us the only real Buffalo. . . . On Delaware Avenue you knew everyone you met on the street, but people never talked to each other except of outward things. There was hardly any real intimacy between friends and people had no confidence in each other . . . they neither showed their feelings nor talked about them. . . . In those days only the outermost rim of life was given any conscious attention.'[29]

The life of the upper class was sombre and humourless, bearing almost no resemblance to the musical comedy conception of a 'gay nineties', and a mood of alienation permeated the reflective writing of the time.[30]

A small and literate patrician element looked with longing to the past, a spirit embodied in Buffalo's most accomplished poet, David Gray. Indepen-

[29]Mable Dodge Luhan, *Intimate Memories: Background* (New York: Harcourt Brace, 1933), 3.
[30]*Buffalo Poets* (Buffalo: Privately Printed, 1893).

dently wealthy and a Buffalo newspaper editor for forty years Gray could speak with equal force to the intellectual and the business community. With a pessimism faintly suggestive of Henry Adams, Gray's last years were spent in bewildered revolt against progress, industrialism and the city.[31] But the 'new rich' greeted the future with brassy optimism. Progress meant money, and money was the sacred value around which all else revolved. As Mrs. Luhan says of her grandfather: 'He had a sense not only of the importance but the holiness of money.'[32]

Money was the cornerstone of the polity as well as the economy. Thrift was the highest civic virtue, and at the dedication of the new city and county hall in the 1870's the noblest words the orator could find are these, 'The people . . . have secured a building at less cost than has been expended for any similar structure in this country.'[33] The theme is reiterated on every ceremonial occasion, even down to the present. Thus from the 1870's on the annual message of the mayor to the city council begins with a *ritual of frugality*. In 1875 Mayor Dayton told the council, 'For the first time in years the questions of government—municipal, state and national—are now considered as ones of finance and political economy. Men everywhere are . . . governing their actions by business principles.'[34] Even Grover Cleveland, whose rapid rise to national fame began as a reform mayor of Buffalo, climaxed his first address to the council in this vein: 'We are . . . trustees and agents of our fellow citizens, holding their funds in sacred trust.'[35] The philosophy of politics as business reaches something of a high point in 1895 when Mayor Jewett told the council, 'Enterprizes are attracted by a wise, conservative and business-like government. . . . To me the city of Buffalo appears to be, not a political hive, but a vast business corporation.'[36] Except for the abortive effort at reform between 1898 and 1910 when plans for municipal socialism (city ownership of utilities) were seriously promoted by even the local business class, there has scarcely been a departure from the credo of laissez-faire capitalism.[37]

Around the turn of the century the economic base of the city was changing. Ownership and control of key industries were passing to outside interests.[38]

[31] *David Gray: Letters, Poems and Selected Prose* (ed.) J. N. Larned (Buffalo: Courier Company, 1888); James Fraser Gluck, 'David Gray: Some Reflections on his Work and Life (A Memorial)', *PBHS* (1889).

[32] Luhan, op. cit., 153.

[33] *Memorial of the City and County Hall Opening Ceremonies* (Buffalo: Courier Company, 1876), 137.

[34] *Annual Message of the Mayor of the City of Buffalo, 1875.*

[35] Ibid., 1882.

[36] Ibid., 1895.

[37] *Proceedings of the Common Council,* 1908 (Buffalo: Enquirer Press, 1909), 3–5; 23–4, indicates there were strong pressures for municipal ownership of gas, light and street car companies as well as unsuccessful efforts to break the grip of the railroads which had paralysed harbour development for over forty years.

[38] By the 1930's two-thirds of the work force was employed by outside controlled industry and only one-half of the downtown retail business was locally owned. Lewis Froman, *The Ownership and Control of Buffalo Business* (Buffalo: Whitney Graham, 1942), p. 44.

The formation of the Lackawanna Steel Company in 1901 was the prototype of subsequent industrial development. The company was founded with a capital investment of $30,000,000, 17 per cent of which was local. Ten years later local ownership had dwindled to 7 per cent. Only two of the twenty-man board of directors were Buffalonians, but the company was handed a *carte blanche* by the city. No building restrictions were imposed and there was no protest against health and safety conditions even though there were as many as 4,000 injuries a year and one fatality a day in a work force of 6,000. By 1906 the steel works covered 1,500 acres and had an authorized capital stock of $60,000,000 (doubled since 1901) and in that year alone sold over $28,000,000 in products. Yet the employees, mainly Polish and Slavic immigrants, worked twelve hours a day, seven days a week, at wages ranging from ten to twenty cents an hour.[39]

Worse than wage slavery was the threat of unemployment. From the 1870's on unemployment rates were abnormally high and the census of 1900—a prosperous time—records the figures shown in Table II.

TABLE II. UNEMPLOYMENT FOR MALES OVER 10 YEARS OF AGE IN 1900

Occupation	Number in Labour Force	Unemployed				
		1–3 months	4–6 months	7–12 months	Total	Per cent
Professional	5,081	161	136	74	371	7.3
Domestic and Personal Service	23,681	2,712	4,198	1,356	8,266	35.3
Trade Transport	34,330	1,354	1,705	666	3,725	10.9
Manufacturing and Mechanical	42,354	4,383	3,969	1,685	10,037	23.4
Total	106,340	8,675	10,108	3,817	22,600	19.8

Data from Department of Commerce and Labour, Bureau of the Census, *Occupations at the Twentieth Census.* Special Reports (Washington: U.S. Government Printing Office, 1904), p. 432.

With heavy industry came the slums, where in Hobbesian style the life of man was 'bitter, brutish and brief'. The Buffalo of 1910 was a replica of Upton Sinclair's *Jungle.* Fifty to sixty people crowded into ten-room houses in the steel districts, and sometimes boarders could not rent rooms but only spaces on beds for a night or day turn. Ninety-four per cent of the Poles in Buffalo had an income of less than $635, the estimated living wage for the time, and the Hungarian settlement held 'the astonishing record of 10,000 human beings without a single bathtub'.[40] One observer notes that

[39] *Buffalo Times,* January 3, June 3, 1906; *Buffalo Express,* March 26, 1906; March 2, 1909.
[40] *Buffalo Express,* March 15, 1910; *Buffalo News,* February 2, 1908.

at night gangs roam the streets and come toward each other . . . roaring at the top of their voices. When they meet they start fighting simply for the sake of fighting which has become a sport for these people. They use clubs, knives and revolvers. . . . Police are called but refuse to come to the area. . . . Children have no place to play except with the pigs and goats who wallow about in the slime and swamps.[41]

This latter observation is verified by photographs published in the local press.

While the lot of the craftsman had improved, the unskilled factory worker, isolated from the larger community and unprotected by union power, was hardly more than a piece of machinery. The personnel policy of Lackawanna Steel was both a cause and a symbol of this new way of life.

Of the five or six thousand employees [writes the *Buffalo Times*], everyone is so recorded that not a man can loaf or beat his time a minute without the heads of different departments being cognizant of the fact and his wage cut accordingly. When a man is hired, a card record is taken . . . and he is given a number. . . . After assuming this number the laborer loses his name and thereafter is known only by the figures on his coat.[42]

While material conditions have improved since 1910, with the further regimentation of the work force still others have 'lost their name' and become a cipher in a ledger.

INTERPRETATION: ANOMIE AS A PRODUCT OF CAPITALISM

Outwardly placid, the nineteenth century closed on a note of foreboding. Metaphorically speaking the century ended at the Pan American Exposition in Buffalo where a Polish 'anarchist' assassinated President William McKinley.[43] The act seemed to materialize the secret fears which the wealthy had harboured for 20 years. Earlier Buffalo Congressman James O. Putnam had warned: 'We are rapidly becoming a nation of great cities. In them gather the dangerous elements of society. In them anarchy hatches its plots of murder and lights its revolutionary fires. . . .'[44] The prophesy was more a projection of guilt than a rational assessment of the radical movement; nevertheless, the Buffalo of 1900 was anything but confident. 'The Gilded Age,' as Professor Horton remarks, 'was an age of innocence only for sheltered dowagers and debutantes; it was an age of apprehension.'[45]

[41] *Buffalo Express,* April 7, 1907.

[42] *Buffalo Times,* September 11, 1904. The item appears under the caption: 'Wonderful Work at the Plant of Lackawanna Steel.'

[43] Robert J. Donovan, *The Assassins* (New York: Harpers, 1955), 82–107, points out that Leon Czologosz, McKinley's assassin, was not a member of any anarchist organization but a schizoid personality with the delusion he was an anarchist. The best account of the event and times is Emma Goldman's *Living My Life* (New York: A. Knopf, 1931).

[44] Quoted in Horton, *History of Northwestern New York,* p. 256.

[45] Ibid., 293.

In the 1840's the young men of Buffalo were advised that success came only through a wise self-reliance and was 'incompatible with all presumption upon Destiny and excluded all dependence on Adventious Circumstance'.[46] By the turn of the century the advice seemed all but irrelevant; the lives of most people were shaped by circumstances quite beyond their own control. For the working-class unemployment came like a natural disaster, unrelated to the actions of men. Even the merchant class, supposedly the incarnation of individual initiative, owed its affluence as much to the mysterious dynamics of population growth and industrial expansion as to its own efforts. Success was largely the consequence of being at the right place at the right time with the right connections. In addition, there was the fortuitous gyration of the business cycle, which, defined as beyond rational control, actually became so. More than ever chance seemed to rule the affairs of men.[47] With the separation of the social classes it became increasingly difficult for either class to gain a rational comprehension of the actions of the other. With the emergence of the trans-local corporation remote authorities could make decisions affecting the lives of thousands who had no alternative but acquiescence. A people who a century earlier had conquered nature was now unable to master its own creation—the social environment.[48] Both individually and collectively, men seemed impotent in the face of the urban problem, and there was a general retreat into the sphere of private life.

In the progressive period in Buffalo (1900–10) there was an heroic effort at municipal reform, which in the end accomplished little. Once the labour movement was co-opted into the corporate structure, the energy for social transformation was dissipated. In the 1890's labour was explicitly socialistic, calling for collective ownership of all means of production and distribution as well as higher pay and an eight-hour day. In Buffalo by 1910 the wages of craftsmen had been raised substantially, but the proposals for collective ownership were abandoned. Henceforth, the A.F. of L. asked for its members nothing more than 'the right to sell their labour to the best advantage of themselves'; far from revolutionary, 'the principle upon which organized labour is founded . . . is the best bulwark of society against the threat of socialism'.[49] The demand for radical reform subsided as the principle of self interest, the spirit of capitalism, prevailed.

Since its foundation the American city has been dominated by the eco-

[46]Rev. Laurens P. Hicock, D.D., *A Wise Self Reliance Secures Success: An Address before the Young Men's Association of the City of Buffalo* (Buffalo: Jewett, Thomas, 1848).

[47]George A. Dunlap, *The City in the American Novel* (Philadelphia: University of Pennsylvania, 1934), 11–41. See especially the analysis of the 'economic chance world' in novels of William Dean Howells.

[48]Lewis Mumford, *City Development: Studies in Disintegration and Renewal* (New York: Harcourt Brace, 1945), p. 14. 'The steel town . . . was an environment much more harsh, antagonistic and brutal than anything the pioneers had encountered.'

[49]*United Trades and Labor Council of Erie County: Official Program and Journal* (Buffalo: William Grazer, 1913), p. 3.

nomic institution—first the market, then the corporation. Neither local political nor religious institutions were able to regulate economic activity; indeed, both merely reinforced the existing system. The key to the city is the economic institution:

First, the business ideology was clearly embodied in municipal organization. From the 1870's onward the objective of local government was the creation of a climate favourable to business enterprise, which means minimal taxation and control. If the purpose of the city was to stimulate investment what better incentive than a compliant administration. Given this definition of the situation it was inevitable that the 'spirit of graft and lawlessness', as Lincoln Steffens called it, should assert itself.[50] Under laissez-faire capitalism the city could play at best *only a regulative not a productive* role in economic life. As early as 1873 the socialists had proposed public works programmes to solve the unemployment problem, but the most Buffalo offered the indigent was the county poor farm. Private charities were left to cope with all the problems created by starvation wages, immigration and unemployment.

Secondly, the industrial corporation as the main employer of men determined their style of life in countless ways. First it created an 'employee mentality', a submissiveness quite at odds with the ideal of self-reliance. Occupying a role of passive subordination eight or twelve hours a day did not condition men to take an active part in a democratic community. There was an active and anarchic rebellion, an aggression bred of frustration and expressed in crime, but no interest in social reconstruction. The insecurity of wage-labour and unemployment also contributed materially to the high crime rates of the urban slums. The slum was the product of industrial capitalism; it was created *in* not *by* the city. As we have seen, it was corporate policy (of the railroads in the nineteenth century and the steel mills in the twentieth) which precipitated the bitterest labour trouble in Buffalo. Given the premise of profit-making it was inevitable that wages should be cut to the subsistence level. For the middle class, status in the corporation was beginning to replace status in the territorial community as the primary bond upon which one's fate depended. Since its ownership was translocal, the corporation had only a nominal and pecuniary interest in the city of Buffalo. In the nineteenth century the local capitalist élite, while amassing wealth, still took pride in the city, and established organizations of enduring benefit to the community: a remarkable park system, a museum of natural history, art galleries, libraries and the historical society. But as the power and autonomy of the local élite declined, the city lost much of its colour and high culture.[51]

[50]Lincoln Steffens, *Shame of the Cities* (New York: Sagamore Press, 1957), p. 40. 'In all cities in 1900 the better classes—the business men—are the sources of corruption, but they are so rarely pursued and caught that we do not fully realize whence the trouble comes. Thus most cities blame the politicians and the ignorant and vicious poor.'

[51]For a savage account of Buffalo in the 1930's see Wyndham Lewis, *American I Presume* (New York: Howell Soskin, 1940), '. . . a dark and massive patch upon the landscape, with a gilded thread running down the middle . . . around which oceans of aliens surge and stagnate . . .' (p. 107).

Finally, the ecology of the city is a product of economic institutions rather than sub-social, biotic competition. A 'cultural institution'—the railroads—blocked the development of a 'natural' harbour for seventy-five years. The spatial order of the American city is rational only in serving the ends of profit for the property holders. In the context of the needs of the community land use may be quite irrational. For instance, the city of Buffalo has been desperately deficient in park space for forty years; yet more and more public land is being sold to private interests.[52] This is not an expression of the natural law of ecology but the cultural law of profit.

CONCLUSION

Urban sociology links the nature of the city to its demographic-ecological composition. The size and heterogeneity of the modern city creates an anonymous milieu which 'individuates the person and secularizes society' (Park). The city dissolves the primary group; the result is isolation and finally disorientation or anomie. Yet in the evolution of Buffalo from a cohesive community to an atomized society it is not the process of urbanization but the development of the economic institution which is the decisive factor. The social character of the American city—the anomie of the urban way of life—is a product of the spirit of capitalism.

[52]The most recent instance was in 1954 when a 1,000-acre farm designated for park use was sold to Republic Steel. Alice Grailcourt, *The Buffalo Common Council at Work* (unpublished M.A., University of Buffalo, 1956).

Urbanism and Suburbanism as Ways of Life: A Re-evaluation of Definitions
Herbert J. Gans

The contemporary sociological conception of cities and of urban life is based largely on the work of the Chicago School, and its summary statement in Louis Wirth's essay, "Urbanism as a Way of Life." (40)* In that paper, Wirth developed a "minimum sociological definition of the city" as "a relatively large, dense and permanent settlement of socially heterogeneous individuals." (40, p. 50). From these prerequisites, he then deduced the major outlines of

*I am indebted to Richard Dewey, John Dyckman, David Riesman, Melvin Webber, and Harold Wilensky for helpful comments on earlier drafts of this essay.

SOURCE: Arnold Rose, ed., *Human Behavior and Social Process* (Boston: Houghton Mifflin Company, 1962), pp. 625–648. Reprinted by permission.

the urban way of life. As he saw it, number, density, and heterogeneity created a social structure in which primary-group relationships were inevitably replaced by secondary contacts that were impersonal, segmental, superficial, transitory, and often predatory in nature. As a result, the city dweller became anonymous, isolated, secular, relativistic, rational, and sophisticated. In order to function in the urban society, he was forced to combine with others to organize corporations, voluntary associations, representative forms of government, and the impersonal mass media of communications (40, pp. 54–60). These replaced the primary groups and the integrated way of life found in rural and other pre-industrial settlements.

Wirth's paper has become a classic in urban sociology, and most texts have followed his definition and description faithfully (5). In recent years, however, a considerable number of studies and essays have questioned his formulations (1, 5, 13, 15, 17, 19, 20, 23, 24, 27, 28, 30, 35, 38, 41).[1] In addition, a number of changes have taken place in cities since the article was published in 1938, notably the exodus of white residents to low- and medium-priced houses in the suburbs, and the decentralization of industry. The evidence from these studies and the changes in American cities suggest that Wirth's statement must be revised.

There is yet another, and more important reason for such a revision. Despite its title and intent, Wirth's paper deals with urban-industrial society, rather than with the city. This is evident from his approach. Like other urban sociologists, Wirth based his analysis on a comparison of settlement types, but unlike his colleagues, who pursued urban-rural comparisons, Wirth contrasted the city to the folk society. Thus, he compared settlement types of pre-industrial and industrial society. This allowed him to include in his theory of urbanism the entire range of modern institutions which are not found in the folk society, even though many such groups (e.g., voluntary associations) are by no means exclusively urban. Moreover, Wirth's conception of the city dweller as depersonalized, atomized, and susceptible to mass movements suggests that his paper is based on, and contributes to, the theory of the mass society.

Many of Wirth's conclusions may be relevant to the understanding of ways of life in modern society. However, since the theory argues that all of society is now urban, *his analysis does not distinguish ways of life in the city from those in other settlements within modern society.* In Wirth's time, the comparison of urban and pre-urban settlement types was still fruitful, but today, the primary task for urban (or community) sociology seems to me to be the analysis of the similarities and differences between contemporary settlement types.

This paper is an attempt at such an analysis; it limits itself to distinguishing ways of life in the modern city and the modern suburb. A re-analysis of Wirth's conclusions from this perspective suggests that his characterization of the

---

[1] I shall not attempt to summarize these studies, for this task has already been performed by Dewey (5), Reiss (23), Wilensky (38), and others.

urban way of life applies only—and not too accurately—to the residents of the inner city. The remaining city dwellers, as well as most suburbanites, pursue a different way of life, which I shall call "quasi-primary." This proposition raises some doubt about the mutual exclusiveness of the concepts of city and suburb and leads to a yet broader question: whether settlement concepts and other ecological concepts are useful for explaining ways of life.

THE INNER CITY

Wirth argued that number, density, and heterogeneity had two social consequences which explain the major features of urban life. On the one hand, the crowding of diverse types of people into a small area led to the segregation of homogeneous types of people into separate neighborhoods (40, p. 56). On the other hand, the lack of physical distance between city dwellers resulted in social contact between them, which broke down existing social and cultural patterns and encouraged assimilation as well as acculturation—the melting pot effect (40, p. 52). Wirth implied that the melting pot effect was far more powerful than the tendency toward segregation and concluded that, sooner or later, the pressures engendered by the dominant social, economic, and political institutions of the city would destroy the remaining pockets of primary-group relationships (40, pp. 60–62). Eventually, the social system of the city would resemble Tönnies' *Gesellschaft*—a way of life which Wirth considered undesirable.

Because Wirth had come to see the city as the prototype of mass society, and because he examined the city from the distant vantage point of the folk society—from the wrong end of the telescope, so to speak—his view of urban life is not surprising. In addition, Wirth found support for his theory in the empirical work of his Chicago colleagues. As Greer and Kube (19, p. 112) and Wilensky (38, p. 121) have pointed out, the Chicago sociologists conducted their most intensive studies in the inner city.[2] At that time, these were slums recently invaded by new waves of European immigrants and rooming house and skid row districts, as well as the habitat of Bohemians and well-to-do Gold Coast apartment dwellers. Wirth himself studied the Maxwell Street Ghetto, an inner-city Jewish neighborhood then being dispersed by the acculturation and mobility of its inhabitants (39). Some of the characteristics of urbanism which Wirth stressed in his essay abounded in these areas.

Wirth's diagnosis of the city as *Gesellschaft* must be questioned on three counts. First, the conclusions derived from a study of the inner city cannot be

[2]By the *inner city*, I mean the transient residential areas, the Gold Coasts and the slums that generally surround the central business district, although in some communities they may continue for miles beyond that district. The *outer city* includes the stable residential areas that house the working- and middle-class tenant and owner. The *suburbs* I conceive as the latest and most modern ring of the outer city, distinguished from it only by yet lower densities, and by the often irrelevant fact of the ring's location outside the city limits.

generalized to the entire urban area. Second, there is as yet not enough evidence to prove—nor, admittedly, to deny—that number, density, and heterogeneity result in the social consequences which Wirth proposed. Finally, even if the causal relationship could be verified, it can be shown that a significant proportion of the city's inhabitants were, and are, isolated from these consequences by social structures and cultural patterns which they either brought to the city, or developed by living in it. Wirth conceived the urban population as consisting of heterogeneous individuals, torn from past social systems, unable to develop new ones, and therefore prey to social anarchy in the city. While it is true that a not insignificant proportion of the inner city population was, and still is, made up of unattached individuals (26), Wirth's formulation ignores the fact that this population consists mainly of relatively homogeneous groups, with social and cultural moorings that shield it fairly effectively from the suggested consequences of number, density, and heterogeneity. This applies even more to the residents of the outer city, who constitute a majority of the total city population.

The social and cultural moorings of the inner city population are best described by a brief analysis of the five types of inner city residents. These are:

1. the "cosmopolites";
2. the unmarried or childless;
3. the "ethnic villagers";
4. the "deprived"; and
5. the "trapped" and downward mobile.

The "cosmopolites" include students, artists, writers, musicians, and entertainers, as well as other intellectuals and professionals. They live in the city in order to be near the special "cultural" facilities that can only be located near the center of the city. Many cosmopolites are unmarried or childless. Others rear children in the city, especially if they have the income to afford the aid of servants and governesses. The less affluent ones may move to the suburbs to raise their children, continuing to live as cosmopolites under considerable handicaps, especially in the lower-middle-class suburbs. Many of the very rich and powerful are also cosmopolites, although they are likely to have at least two residences, one of which is suburban or exurban.

The unmarried or childless must be divided into two subtypes, depending on the permanence or transience of their status. The temporarily unmarried or childless live in the inner city for only a limited time. Young adults may team up to rent an apartment away from their parents and close to job or entertainment opportunities. When they marry, they may move first to an apartment in a transient neighborhood, but if they can afford to do so, they leave for the outer city or the suburbs with the arrival of the first or second child. The permanently unmarried may stay in the inner city for the remainder of their lives, their housing depending on their income.

The "ethnic villagers" are ethnic groups which are found in such inner city neighborhoods as New York's Lower East Side, living in some ways as they did when they were peasants in European or Puerto Rican villages (15). Although they reside in the city, they isolate themselves from significant contact with most city facilities, aside from workplaces. Their way of life differs sharply from Wirth's urbanism in its emphasis on kinship and the primary group, the lack of anonymity and secondary-group contacts, the weakness of formal organizations, and the suspicion of anything and anyone outside their neighborhood.

The first two types live in the inner city by choice; the third is there partly because of necessity, partly because of tradition. The final two types are in the inner city because they have no other choice. One is the "deprived" population: the very poor; the emotionally disturbed or otherwise handicapped; broken families; and, most important, the non-white population. These urban dwellers must take the dilapidated housing and blighted neighborhoods to which the housing market relegates them, although among them are some for whom the slum is a hiding place, or a temporary stop-over to save money for a house in the outer city or the suburbs (27).

The "trapped" are the people who stay behind when a neighborhood is invaded by non-residential land uses or lower-status inmigrants, because they cannot afford to move, or are otherwise bound to their present location (27).[3] The "downward mobiles" are a related type; they may have started life in a higher class position, but have been forced down in the socio-economic hierarchy and in the quality of their accommodations. Many of them are old people, living out their existence on small pensions.

These five types all live in dense and heterogeneous surroundings, yet they have such diverse ways of life that it is hard to see how density and heterogeneity could exert a common influence. Moreover, all but the last two types are isolated or detached from their neighborhood and thus from the social consequences which Wirth described.

When people who live together have social ties based on criteria other than mere common occupancy, they can set up social barriers regardless of the physical closeness or the heterogeneity of their neighbors. The ethnic villagers are the best illustration. While a number of ethnic groups are usually found living together in the same neighborhood, they are able to *isolate* themselves from each other through a variety of social devices. Wirth himself recognized this when he wrote that "two groups can occupy a given area without losing their separate identity because each side is permitted to live its own inner life and each somehow fears or idealizes the other." (39, p. 283). Although it is true that the children in these areas were often oblivious to the social barriers set up by their parents, at least until adolescence, it is doubtful whether their acculturation can be traced to the melting pot effect as much as to the pervasive

---

[3]The trapped are not very visible, but I suspect that they are a significant element in what Raymond Vernon has described as the "gray areas" of the city (32).

influence of the American culture that flowed into these areas from the outside.[4]

The cosmopolites, the unmarried, and the childless are *detached* from neighborhood life. The cosmopolites possess a distinct subculture which causes them to be disinterested in all but the most superficial contacts with their neighbors, somewhat like the ethnic villagers. The unmarried and childless are detached from neighborhood because of their life-cycle stage, which frees them from the routine family responsibilities that entail some relationship to the local area. In their choice of residence, the two types are therefore not concerned about their neighbors, or the availability and quality of local community facilities. Even the well-to-do can choose expensive apartments in or near poor neighborhoods, because if they have children, these are sent to special schools and summer camps which effectively isolate them from neighbors. In addition, both types, but especially the childless and unmarried, are transient. Therefore, they tend to live in areas marked by high population turnover, where their own mobility and that of their neighbors creates a universal detachment from the neighborhood.[5]

The deprived and the trapped do seem to be affected by some of the consequences of number, density, and heterogeneity. The deprived population suffers considerably from overcrowding, but this is a consequence of low income, racial discrimination, and other handicaps, and cannot be considered an inevitable result of the ecological make-up of the city.[6] Because the deprived have no residential choice, they are also forced to live amid neighbors not of their own choosing, with ways of life different and even contradictory to their own. If familial defenses against the neighborhood climate are weak, as is the case among broken families and downward mobile people, parents may lose their children to the culture of "the street." The trapped are the unhappy people who remain behind when their more advantaged neighbors move on; they must endure the heterogeneity which results from neighborhood change.

Wirth's description of the urban way of life fits best the transient areas of the inner city. Such areas are typically heterogeneous in population, partly because they are inhabited by transient types who do not require homogeneous neighbors or by deprived people who have no choice, or may themselves be quite mobile. Under conditions of transience and heterogeneity, people interact

---

[4]If the melting pot has resulted from propinquity and high density, one would have expected second-generation Italians, Irish, Jews, Greeks, Slavs, etc. to have developed a single "pan-ethnic culture," consisting of a synthesis of the cultural patterns of the propinquitous national groups.

[5]The corporation transients (36, 38), who provide a new source of residential instability to the suburb, differ from city transients. Since they are raising families, they want to integrate themselves into neighborhood life, and are usually able to do so, mainly because they tend to move into similar types of communities wherever they go.

[6]The negative social consequences of overcrowding are a result of high room and floor density, not of the land coverage of population density which Wirth discussed. Park Avenue residents live under conditions of high land density, but do not seem to suffer visibly from overcrowding.

only in terms of the segmental roles necessary for obtaining local services. Their social relationships thus display anonymity, impersonality, and superficiality.[7]

The social features of Wirth's concept of urbanism seem therefore to be a result of residential instability, rather than of number, density, or heterogeneity. In fact, heterogeneity is itself an effect of residential instability, resulting when the influx of transients causes landlords and realtors to stop acting as gatekeepers—that is, wardens of neighborhood homogeneity.[8] Residential instability is found in all types of settlements, and, presumably, its social consequences are everywhere similar. These consequences cannot therefore be identified with the ways of life of the city.

THE OUTER CITY AND THE SUBURBS

The second effect which Wirth ascribed to number, density, and heterogeneity was the segregation of homogeneous people into distinct neighborhoods,[9] on the basis of "place and nature of work, income, racial and ethnic characteristics, social status, custom, habit, taste, preference and prejudice." (40, p. 56). This description fits the residential districts of the *outer city*.[10] Although these districts contain the majority of the city's inhabitants, Wirth went into little detail about them. He made it clear, however, that the sociopsychological aspects of urbanism were prevalent there as well (40, p. 56).

Because existing neighborhood studies deal primarily with the exotic sections of the inner city, very little is known about the more typical residential neighborhoods of the outer city. However, it is evident that the way of life in these areas bears little resemblance to Wirth's urbanism. Both the studies which question Wirth's formulation and my own observations suggest that the common element in the ways of life of these neighborhoods is best described as *quasi-primary*. I use this term to characterize relationships between neighbors. Whatever the intensity or frequency of these relationships, the interaction

---

[7]Whether or not these social phenomena have the psychological consequences Wirth suggested depends on the people who live in the area. Those who are detached from the neighborhood by choice are probably immune, but those who depend on the neighborhood for their social relationships—the unattached individuals, for example—may suffer greatly from loneliness.

[8]Needless to say, residential instability must ultimately be traced back to the fact that, as Wirth pointed out, the city and its economy attract transient—and, depending on the sources of outmigration, heterogeneous—people. However, this is a characteristic of urban-industrial society, not of the city specifically.

[9]By neighborhoods or residential districts I mean areas demarcated from others by distinctive physical boundaries or by social characteristics, some of which may be perceived only by the residents. However, these areas are not necessarily socially self-sufficient or culturally distinctive.

[10]For the definition of *outer city,* see Footnote 2.

is more intimate than a secondary contact, but more guarded than a primary one.[11]

There are actually few secondary relationships, because of the isolation of residential neighborhoods from economic institutions and workplaces. Even shopkeepers, store managers, and other local functionaries who live in the area are treated as acquaintances or friends, unless they are of a vastly different social status or are forced by their corporate employers to treat their customers as economic units (30). Voluntary associations attract only a minority of the population. Moreover, much of the organizational activity is of a sociable nature, and it is often diffiicult to accomplish the association's "business" because of the members' preference for sociability. Thus it would appear that interactions in organizations, or between neighbors generally, do not fit the secondary-relationship model of urban life. As anyone who has lived in these neighborhoods knows, there is little anonymity, impersonality or privacy.[12] In fact, American cities have sometimes been described as collections of small towns.[13] There is some truth to this description, especially if the city is compared to the actual small town, rather than to the romantic construct of anti-urban critics (33).

Postwar suburbia represents the most contemporary version of the quasi-primary way of life. Owing to increases in real income and the encouragement of home ownership provided by the FHA, families in the lower-middle class and upper working class can now live in modern single-family homes in low-density subdivisions, an opportunity previously available only to the upper and upper-middle classes (34).

The popular literature describes the new suburbs as communities in which conformity, homogeneity, and other-direction are unusually rampant (4, 32). The implication is that the move from city to suburb initiates a new way of life which causes considerable behavior and personality change in previous urbanites. A preliminary analysis of data which I am now collecting in Levittown, New Jersey, suggests, however, that the move from the city to this predominantly lower-middle-class suburb does not result in any major behavioral changes for most people. Moreover, the changes which do occur reflect the move from the social isolation of a transient city or suburban apartment building to the quasi-primary life of a neighborhood of single-family homes.

[11]Because neighborly relations are not quite primary, and not quite secondary, they can also become *pseudo-primary;* that is, secondary ones disguised with false affect to make them appear primary. Critics have often described suburban life in this fashion, although the actual prevalence of pseudo-primary relationships has not been studied systematically in cities or suburbs.

[12]These neighborhoods cannot, however, be considered as urban folk societies. People go out of the area for many of their friendships, and their allegiance to the neighborhood is neither intense nor all-encompassing. Janowitz has aptly described the relationship between resident and neighborhood as one of "limited liability." (20, Chapter 7)

[13]Were I not arguing that ecological concepts cannot double as sociological ones, this way of life might best be described as small-townish.

Also, many of the people whose life has changed reported that the changes were intended. They existed as aspirations before the move, or as reasons for it. In other words, the suburb itself creates few changes in ways of life. Similar conclusions have been reported by Berger in his excellent study of a working class population newly moved to a suburban subdivision (4).

A COMPARISON OF CITY AND SUBURB

If urban and suburban areas are similar in that the way of life in both is quasi-primary, and if urban residents who move out to the suburbs do not undergo any significant changes in behavior, it would be fair to argue that the differences in ways of life between the two types of settlements have been overestimated. Yet the fact remains that a variety of physical and demographic differences exist between the city and the suburb. However, upon closer examination, many of these differences turn out to be either spurious or of little significance for the way of life of the inhabitants (34).[14]

The differences between the residential areas of cities and suburbs which have been cited most frequently are:

1.   Suburbs are more likely to be dormitories.
2.   They are further away from the work and play facilities of the central business districts.
3.   They are newer and more modern than city residential areas and are designed for the automobile rather than for pedestrian and mass-transit forms of movement.
4.   They are built up with single-family rather than multi-family structures and are therefore less dense.
5.   Their populations are more homogeneous.
6.   Their populations differ demographically: they are younger; more of them are married; they have higher incomes; and they hold proportionately more white collar jobs (8, p. 131).

Most urban neighborhoods are as much dormitories as the suburbs. Only in a few older inner city areas are factories and offices still located in the middle of residential blocks, and even here many of the employees do not live in the neighborhood.

The fact that the suburbs are farther from the central business district is often true only in terms of distance, not travel time. Moreover, most people make relatively little use of downtown facilities, other than workplaces (12, 21). The downtown stores seem to hold their greatest attraction for the upper-middle class (21, pp. 91–92); the same is probably true of typically urban

---

[14]They may, of course, be significant for the welfare of the total metropolitan area.

entertainment facilities. Teen-agers and young adults may take their dates to first-run movie theatres, but the museums, concert halls, and lecture rooms attract mainly upper-middle-class ticket-buyers, many of them suburban.[15]

The suburban reliance on the train and the automobile has given rise to an imaginative folklore about the consequences of commuting on alcohol consumption, sex life, and parental duties. Many of these conclusions are, however, drawn from selected high-income suburbs and exurbs, and reflect job tensions in such hectic occupations as advertising and show business more than the effects of residence (29). It is true that the upper-middle-class housewife must become a chauffeur in order to expose her children to the proper educational facilities, but such differences as walking to the corner drug store and driving to its suburban equivalent seem to me of little emotional, social, or cultural import.[16] In addition, the continuing shrinkage in the number of mass-transit users suggests that even in the city many younger people are now living a wholly auto-based way of life.

The fact that suburbs are smaller is primarily a function of political boundaries drawn long before the communities were suburban. This affects the kinds of political issues which develop and provides somewhat greater opportunity for citizen participation. Even so, in the suburbs as in the city, the minority who participate are the professional politicians, the economically concerned businessmen, lawyers and salesmen, and the ideologically motivated middle- and upper-middle-class people with better than average education.

The social consequences of differences in density and house type also seem overrated. Single-family houses on quiet streets facilitate the supervision of children; this is one reason why middle-class women who want to keep an eye on their children move to the suburbs. House type also has some effects on relationships between neighbors, insofar as there are more opportunities for visual contact between adjacent homeowners than between people on different floors of an apartment house. However, if occupants' characteristics are also held constant, the differences in actual social contact are less marked. Homogeneity of residents turns out to be more important as a determinant of sociability than proximity. If the population is heterogeneous, there is little social contact between neighbors, either on apartment-house floors or in single-family-house blocks; if people are homogeneous, there is likely to be considerable social contact in both house types. One need only contrast the apartment house located in a transient, heterogeneous neighborhood and exactly the same structure in a neighborhood occupied by a single ethnic group. The former is a lonely, anonymous building; the latter, a bustling micro-society. I have observed similar patterns in suburban areas: on blocks where people are homo-

---

[15]A 1958 study of New York theater goers showed a median income of close to $10,000 and 35 per cent were reported as living in the suburbs (10).

[16]I am thinking here of adults; teen-agers do suffer from the lack of informal meeting places within walking or bicycling distance.

geneous, they socialize; where they are heterogeneous, they do little more than exchange polite greetings (16).

Suburbs are usually described as being more homogeneous in house type than the city, but if they are compared to the outer city, the differences are small. Most inhabitants of the outer city, other than well-to-do homeowners, live on blocks of uniform structures as well—for example, the endless streets of rowhouses in Philadelphia and Baltimore or of two-story duplexes and six-flat apartment houses in Chicago. They differ from the new suburbs only in that they were erected through more primitive methods of mass production. Suburbs are of course more predominantly areas of owner-occupied single homes, though in the outer districts of most American cities homeownership is also extremely high.

Demographically, suburbs as a whole are clearly more homogeneous than cities as a whole, though probably not more so than outer cities. However, people do not live in cities or suburbs as a whole, but in specific neighborhoods. An analysis of ways of life would require a determination of the degree of population homogeneity within the boundaries of areas defined as neighborhoods by residents' social contacts. Such an analysis would no doubt indicate that many neighborhoods in the city as well as the suburbs are homogeneous. Neighborhood homogeneity is actually a result of factors having little or nothing to do with the house type, density, or location of the area relative to the city limits. Brand new neighborhoods are more homogeneous than older ones, because they have not yet experienced resident turnover, which frequently results in population heterogeneity. Neighborhoods of low- and medium-priced housing are usually less homogeneous than those with expensive dwellings because they attract families who have reached the peak of occupational and residential mobility, as well as young families who are just starting their climb and will eventually move to neighborhoods of higher status. The latter, being accessible only to high-income people, are therefore more homogeneous with respect to other resident characteristics as well. Moreover, such areas have the economic and political power to slow down or prevent invasion. Finally, neighborhoods located in the path of ethnic or religious group movement are likely to be extremely homogeneous.

The demographic differences between cities and suburbs cannot be questioned, especially since the suburbs have attracted a large number of middle-class child-rearing families. The differences are, however, much reduced if suburbs are compared only to the outer city. In addition, a detailed comparison of suburban and outer city residential areas would show that neighborhoods with the same kinds of people can be found in the city as well as the suburbs. Once again, the age of the area and the cost of housing are more important determinants of demographic characteristics than the location of the area with respect to the city limits.

CHARACTERISTICS, SOCIAL ORGANIZATION, AND ECOLOGY

The preceding sections of the paper may be summarized in three propositions:

1. As concerns ways of life, the inner city must be distinguished from the outer city and the suburbs; and the latter two exhibit a way of life bearing little resemblance to Wirth's urbanism.
2. Even in the inner city, ways of life resemble Wirth's description only to a limited extent. Moreover, economic condition, cultural characteristics, life-cycle stage, and residential instability explain ways of life more satisfactorily than number, density, or heterogeneity.
3. Physical and other differences between city and suburb are often spurious or without much meaning for ways of life.

These propositions suggest that the concepts urban and suburban are neither mutually exclusive, nor especially relevant for understanding ways of life. They—and number, density, and heterogeneity as well—are ecological concepts which describe human adaptation to the environment. However, they are not sufficient to explain social phenomena, because these phenomena cannot be understood solely as the consequences of ecological processes. Therefore, other explanations must be considered.

Ecological explanations of social life are most applicable if the subjects under study lack the ability to *make choices,* be they plants, animals, or human beings. Thus, if there is a housing shortage, people will live almost anywhere, and under extreme conditions of no choice, as in a disaster, married and single, old and young, middle and working class, stable and transient will be found side by side in whatever accommodations are available. At that time, their ways of life represent an almost direct adaptation to the environment. If the supply of housing and of neighborhoods is such that alternatives are available, however, people will make choices, and if the housing market is responsive, they can even make and satisfy explicit *demands.*

Choices and demands do not develop independently or at random; they are functions of the roles people play in the social system. These can best be understood in terms of the *characteristics* of the people involved; that is, characteristics can be used as indices to choices and demands made in the roles that constitute ways of life. Although many characteristics affect the choices and demands people make with respect to housing and neighborhoods, the most important ones seem to be *class*—in all its economic, social and cultural ramifications—and *life-cycle stage.*[17] If people have an opportunity to choose, these two characteristics will go far in explaining the kinds of housing and

[17]These must be defined in dynamic terms. Thus, class includes also the process of social mobility, stage in the life-cycle, and the processes of socialization and aging.

neighborhoods they will occupy and the ways of life they will try to establish within them.

Many of the previous assertions about ways of life in cities and suburbs can be analyzed in terms of class and life-cycle characteristics. Thus, in the inner city, the unmarried and childless live as they do, detached from neighborhood, because of their life-cycle stage; the cosmopolites, because of a combination of life-cycle stage and a distinctive but class-based subculture. The way of life of the deprived and trapped can be explained by low socio-economic level and related handicaps. The quasi-primary way of life is associated with the family stage of the life-cycle, and the norms of child-rearing and parental role found in the upper working class, the lower-middle class, and the non-cosmopolite portions of the upper-middle and upper classes.

The attributes of the so-called suburban way of life can also be understood largely in terms of these characteristics. The new suburbia is nothing more than a highly visible showcase for the ways of life of young, upper-working-class and lower-middle-class people. Ktsanes and Reissman have aptly described it as "new homes for old values." (22). Much of the descriptive and critical writing about suburbia assumes that as long as the new suburbanites lived in the city, they behaved like upper-middle-class cosmopolites and that suburban living has mysteriously transformed them (7; 14, pp. 154–162; 25; 36). The critics fail to see that the behavior and personality patterns ascribed to suburbia are in reality those of class and age (6). These patterns could have been found among the new suburbanites when they still lived in the city and could now be observed among their peers who still reside there—if the latter were as visible to critics and researchers as are the suburbanites.

Needless to say, the concept of "characteristics" cannot explain all aspects of ways of life, either among urban or suburban residents. Some aspects must be explained by concepts of social organization that are independent of characteristics. For example, some features of the quasi-primary way of life are independent of class and age, because they evolve from the roles and situations created by joint and adjacent occupancy of land and dwellings. Likewise, residential instability is a universal process which has a number of invariate consequences. In each case, however, the way in which people react varies with their characteristics. So it is with ecological processes. Thus, there are undoubtedly differences between ways of life in urban and suburban settlements which remain after behavior patterns based on residents' characteristics have been analyzed, and which must therefore be attributed to features of the settlement (11).

Characteristics do not explain the causes of behavior; rather, they are clues to socially created and culturally defined roles, choices, and demands. A causal analysis must trace them back to the larger social, economic, and political systems which determine the situations in which roles are played and the cultural content of choices and demands, as well as the opportunities for their achievement.[18] These systems determine income distributions, educational and occupational opportunities, and in turn, fertility patterns, child-rearing methods, as well as the entire range of consumer behavior. Thus, a complete analysis of the way of life of the deprived residents of the inner city cannot stop by indicating the influence of low income, lack of education, or family instability. These must be related to such conditions as the urban economy's "need" for low-wage workers, and the housing market practices which restrict residential choice. The urban economy is in turn shaped by national economic and social systems, as well as by local and regional ecological processes. Some phenomena can be explained exclusively by reference to these ecological processes. However, it must also be recognized that as man gains greater control over the natural environment, he has been able to free himself from many of the determining and limiting effects of that environment. Thus, changes in local transportation technology, the ability of industries to be footloose, and the relative affluence of American society have given ever larger numbers of people increasing amounts of residential choice. The greater the amount of choice available, the more important does the concept of characteristics become in understanding behavior.

Consequently, the study of ways of life in communities must begin with an analysis of characteristics. If characteristics are dealt with first and held constant, we may be able to discover which behavior patterns can be attributed to features of the settlement and its natural environment.[19] Only then will it be possible to discover to what extent city and suburb are independent—rather than dependent or intervening—variables in the explanation of ways of life.

This kind of analysis might help to reconcile the ecological point of view with the behavioral and cultural one, and possibly put an end to the conflict between conceptual positions which insist on one explanation or the other (9). Both explanations have some relevance, and future research and theory must clarify the role of each in the analysis of ways of life in various types of settlement (6, p. xxii). Another important rationale for this approach is its usefulness for applied sociology—for example, city planning. The planner can recommend changes in the spatial and physical arrangements of the city. Frequently, he seeks to achieve social goals or to change social conditions through physical solutions. He has been attracted to ecological explanations because these relate behavior to phenomena which he can affect. For example, most planners tend to agree with Wirth's formulations, because they stress

[18]This formulation may answer some of Duncan and Schnore's objections to socio-psychological and cultural explanations of community ways of life (9).

[19]The ecologically oriented researchers who developed the Shevsky-Bell social area analysis scale have worked on the assumption that "social differences between the populations of urban neighborhoods can conveniently be summarized into differences of economic level, family characteristics and ethnicity." (3, p. 26). However, they have equated "urbanization" with a concept of life-cycle stage by using family characteristics to define the index of urbanization (3, 18, 19). In fact, Bell has identified suburbanism with familism (2).

number and density, over which the planner has some control. If the undesirable social conditions of the inner city could be traced to these two factors, the planner could propose large-scale clearance projects which would reduce the size of the urban population, and lower residential densities. Experience with public housing projects has, however, made it apparent that low densities, new buildings, or modern site plans do not eliminate anti-social or self-destructive behavior. The analysis of characteristics will call attention to the fact that this behavior is lodged in the deprivations of low socio-economic status and racial discrimination, and that it can be changed only through the removal of these deprivations. Conversely, if such an analysis suggests residues of behavior that can be attributed to ecological processes or physical aspects of housing and neighborhoods, the planner can recommend physical changes that can really affect behavior.

A RE-EVALUATION OF DEFINITIONS

The argument presented here has implications for the sociological definition of the city. Such a definition relates ways of life to environmental features of the city qua settlement type. But if ways of life do not coincide with settlement types, and if these ways are functions of class and life-cycle stage rather than of the ecological attributes of the settlement, a sociological definition of the city cannot be formulated.[20] Concepts such as city and suburb allow us to distinguish settlement types from each other physically and demographically, but the ecological processes and conditions which they synthesize have no direct or invariate consequences for ways of life. The sociologist cannot, therefore, speak of an urban or suburban way of life.

CONCLUSION

Many of the descriptive statements made here are as time-bound as Wirth's.[21] Twenty years ago, Wirth concluded that some form of urbanism would eventually predominate in all settlement types. He was, however, writing during a time of immigrant acculturation and at the end of a serious depression, an era of minimal choice. Today, it is apparent that high-density, heterogeneous surroundings are for most people a temporary place of resi-

[20]Because of the distinctiveness of the ways of life found in the inner city, some writers propose definitions that refer only to these ways, ignoring those found in the outer city. For example, popular writers sometimes identify "urban" with "urbanity," i.e., "cosmopolitanism." However, such a definition ignores the other ways of life found in the inner city. Moreover, I have tried to show that these ways have few common elements, and that the ecological features of the inner city have little or no influence in shaping them.

[21]Even more than Wirth's they are based on data and impressions gathered in the large Eastern and Midwestern cities of the United States.

dence; other than for the Park Avenue or Greenwich Village cosmopolites, they are a result of necessity rather than choice. As soon as they can afford to do so, most Americans head for the single-family house and the quasi-primary way of life of the low-density neighborhood, in the outer city or the suburbs.[22]

Changes in the national economy and in government housing policy can affect many of the variables that make up housing supply and demand. For example, urban sprawl may eventually outdistance the ability of present and proposed transportation systems to move workers into the city; further industrial decentralization can forestall it and alter the entire relationship between work and residence. The expansion of present urban renewal activities can perhaps lure a significant number of cosmopolites back from the suburbs, while a drastic change in renewal policy might begin to ameliorate the housing conditions of the deprived population. A serious depression could once again make America a nation of doubled-up tenants.

These events will affect housing supply and residential choice; they will frustrate but not suppress demands for the quasi-primary way of life. However, changes in the national economy, society, and culture can affect people's characteristics—family size, educational level, and various other concomitants of life-cycle stage and class. These in turn will stimulate changes in demands and choices. The rising number of college graduates, for example, is likely to increase the cosmopolite ranks. This might in turn create a new set of city dwellers, although it will probably do no more than encourage the development of cosmopolite facilities in some suburban areas.

The current revival of interest in urban sociology and in community studies, as well as the sociologist's increasing curiosity about city planning, suggest that data may soon be available to formulate a more adequate theory of the relationship between settlements and the ways of life within them. The speculations presented in this paper are intended to raise questions; they can only be answered by more systematic data collection and theorizing.

REFERENCES

1. Axelrod, Morris, "Urban Structure and Social Participation," *American Sociological Review*, Vol. 21 (February 1956), 13–18.

2. Bell, Wendell, "Social Choice, Life Styles and Suburban Residence," in William M. Dobriner (ed.), *The Suburban Community* (New York: G. P. Putnam's Sons, 1958), 225–247.

3. Bell, Wendell, and Maryanne T. Force, "Urban Neighborhood Types and Par-

[22]Personal discussions with European planners and sociologists suggest that many European apartment dwellers have similar preferences, although economic conditions, high building costs, and the scarcity of land make it impossible for them to achieve their desires.

ticipation in Formal Associations," *American Sociological Review,* Vol. 21 (February 1956), 25–34.

4. Berger, Bennett, *Working Class Suburb: A Study of Auto Workers in Suburbia* (Berkeley, Calif.: University of California Press, 1960).

5. Dewey, Richard, "The Rural-Urban Continuum: Real but Relatively Unimportant," *American Journal of Sociology,* Vol. 66 (July 1960), 60–66.

6. Dobriner, William M., "Introduction: Theory and Research in the Sociology of the Suburbs," in William M. Dobriner (ed.), *The Suburban Community* (New York: G. P. Putnam's Sons, 1958), pp. xiii-xxviii.

7. Duhl, Leonard J., "Mental Health and Community Planning," in *Planning 1955* (Chicago: American Society of Planning Officials, 1956), pp. 31–39.

8. Duncan, Otis Dudley, and Albert J. Reiss, Jr., *Social Characteristics of Rural and Urban Communities, 1950* (New York: John Wiley & Sons, 1956).

9. Duncan, Otis Dudley, and Leo F. Schnore, "Cultural, Behavioral and Ecological Perspectives in the Study of Social Organization," *American Journal of Sociology,* Vol. 65 (September 1959), 132–155.

10. Enders, John, *Profile of the Theater Market* (New York: Playbill, undated and unpaged).

11. Fava, Sylvia Fleis, "Contrasts in Neighboring: New York City and a Suburban Community," in William M. Dobriner (ed.), *The Suburban Community* (New York: G. P. Putnam's Sons, 1958), pp. 122–131.

12. Foley, Donald L. "The Use of Local Facilities in a Metropolis," in Paul Hatt and Albert J. Reiss, Jr. (eds.), *Cities and Society* (Glencoe, Ill.: The Free Press, 1957), pp. 237–247.

13. Form, William H., *et al.* "The Compatibility of Alternative Approaches to the Delimitation of Urban Sub-areas," *American Sociological Review,* Vol. 19 (August 1954), 434–440.

14. Fromm, Erich, *The Sane Society* (New York: Rinehart & Co., Inc., 1955).

15. Gans, Herbert J., *The Urban Villagers: A Study of the Second Generation Italians in the West End of Boston* [Boston: Center for Community Studies, December 1959 (mimeographed)].

16. Gans, Herbert J., "Planning and Social Life: An Evaluation of Friendship and Neighbor Relations in Suburban Communities," *Journal of the American Institute of Planners,* Vol. 27 (May 1961), 134–140.

17. Greer, Scott, "Urbanism Reconsidered: A Comparative Study of Local Areas in a Metropolis," *American Sociological Review,* Vol. 21 (February 1956), 19–25.

18. Greer, Scott, "The Social Structure and Political Process of Suburbia," *American Sociological Review,* Vol. 25 (August 1960), 514–526.

19. Greer, Scott, and Ella Kube, "Urbanism and Social Structure: A Los Angeles Study," in Marvin B. Sussman (ed.), *Community Structure and Analysis* (New York: Thomas Y. Crowell Company, 1959), pp. 93–112.

20. Janowitz, Morris, *The Community Press in an Urban Setting* (Glencoe, Ill.: The Free Press, 1952).

21. Jonassen, Christen T., *The Shopping Center Versus Downtown* (Columbus, Ohio: Bureau of Business Research, Ohio State University, 1955).

22. Ktsanes, Thomas, and Leonard Reissman, "Suburbia: New Homes for Old Values," *Social Problems,* Vol. 7 (Winter 1959–60), 187–194.

23. Reiss, Albert J., Jr., "An Analysis of Urban Phenomena," in Robert M. Fisher (ed.), *The Metropolis in Modern Life* (Garden City, N.Y.: Doubleday & Company, Inc., 1955), pp. 41–49.

24. Reiss, Albert J., Jr., "Rural-Urban and Status Differences in Interpersonal Contacts," *American Journal of Sociology,* Vol. 65 (September 1959), 182–195.

25. Riesman, David, "The Suburban Sadness," in William M. Dobriner (ed.), *The Suburban Community* (New York: G. P. Putnam's Sons, 1958), pp. 375–408.

26. Rose, Arnold M., "Living Arrangements of Unattached Persons," *American Sociological Review,* Vol. 12 (August 1947), 429–435.

27. Seeley, John R., "The Slum: Its Nature, Use and Users," *Journal of the American Institute of Planners,* Vol. 25 (February 1959), 7–14.

28. Smith, Joel, William Form, and Gregory Stone, "Local Intimacy in a Middle-Sized City," *American Journal of Sociology,* Vol. 60 (November 1954), 276–284.

29. Spectorsky, A. C., *The Exurbanites* (Philadelphia: J. B. Lippincott Co., 1955).

30. Stone, Gregory P., "City Shoppers and Urban Identification: Observations on the Social Psychology of City Life," *American Journal of Sociology,* Vol. 60 (July 1954), 36–45.

31. Strauss, Anselm, "The Changing Imagery of American City and Suburb," *Sociological Quarterly,* Vol. 1 (January 1960), 15–24.

32. Vernon, Raymond, *The Changing Economic Function of the Central City* (New York: Committee on Economic Development, Supplementary Paper No. 1, January 1959).

33. Vidich, Arthur J., and Joseph Bensman, *Small Town in Mass Society: Class, Power and Religion in a Rural Community* (Princeton, N.J.: Princeton University Press, 1958).

34. Wattell, Harold, "Levittown: A Suburban Community," in William M. Dobriner (ed.), *The Suburban Community* (New York: G. P. Putnam's Sons, 1958), pp. 287–313.

35. Whyte, William F., Jr., *Street Corner Society* (Chicago: The University of Chicago Press, 1955).

36. Whyte, William F., Jr., *The Organization Man* (New York: Simon & Schuster, 1956).

37. Wilensky, Harold L., "Life Cycle, Work, Situation and Participation in Formal Associations," in Robert W. Kleemeier, *et al.* (eds.), *Aging and Leisure: Research Perspectives on the Meaningful Use of Time* (New York: Oxford University Press, 1961), Chapter 8.

38. Wilensky, Harold L., and Charles Lebeaux, *Industrial Society and Social Welfare* (New York: Russell Sage Foundation, 1958).

39. Wirth, Louis, *The Ghetto* (Chicago: The University of Chicago Press, 1928).

40. Wirth, Louis "Urbanism as a Way of Life," *American Journal of Sociology,* Vol. 44 (July 1938), 1–24. Reprinted in Paul Hatt and Albert J. Reiss, Jr. (eds.), *Cities and Society* (Glencoe, Ill.: The Free Press, 1957), pp. 46–64. [All page references are to this reprinting of the article.]

41. Young, Michael, and Peter Willmott, *Family and Kinship in East London* (London: Routledge & Kegan Paul, Ltd., 1957).

The Local Community as an Ecology of Games*
Norton E. Long

The local community whether viewed as a polity, an economy, or a society presents itself as an order in which expectations are met and functions performed. In some cases, as in a new, company-planned mining town, the order is the willed product of centralized control, but for the most part the order is the product of a history rather than the imposed effect of any central nervous system of the community. For historic reasons we readily conceive the massive task of feeding New York to be achieved through the unplanned, historically developed cooperation of thousands of actors largely unconscious of their collaboration to this individually unsought end. The efficiency of this system is attested to by the extraordinary difficulties of the War Production Board and Service of Supply in accomplishing similar logistical objectives through an explicit system of orders and directives. Insofar as conscious rationality plays a role, it is a function of the parts rather than the whole. Particular structures working for their own ends within the whole may provide their members with goals, strategies, and roles that support rational action. The results of the interaction of the rational strivings after particular ends are in part collectively functional if unplanned. All this is the well-worn doctrine of Adam Smith, though one need accept no more of the doctrine of beneficence than that an unplanned economy can function.

While such a view is accepted for the economy, it is generally rejected for the polity. Without a sovereign, Leviathan is generally supposed to disintegrate and fall apart. Even if Locke's more hopeful view of the naturalness of the social order is taken, the polity seems more of a contrived artifact than the economy. Furthermore, there is both the hangover of Austinian sovereignty and the Greek view of ethical primacy to make political institutions seem different in kind and ultimately inclusive in purpose and for this reason to give them an over-all social directive end. To see political institutions as the same kind of thing as other institutions in society rather than as different, superior, and inclusive (both in the sense of being sovereign and ethically more significant) is a form of relativistic pluralism that is difficult to entertain. At the local

---

*This paper is largely based on a year of field study in the Boston Metroplitan area made possible by grants from the Stern Family Foundation and the Social Science Research Council. The opinions and conclusion expressed are those of the author alone.

SOURCE: Norton E. Long, "The Local Community as an Ecology of Games," *American Journal of Sociology,* 64 (November 1958), 251–261. Copyright 1958 by the University of Chicago. Reprinted by permission of the author and publisher, the University of Chicago Press.

level, however, it is easier to look at the municipal government, its departments, and the agencies of state and national government as so many institutions, resembling banks, newspapers, trade unions, chambers of commerce, churches, etc., occupying a territorial field and interacting with one another. This interaction can be conceptualized as a system without reducing the interacting institutions and individuals to membership in any single comprehensive group. It is psychologically tempting to envision the local territorial system as a group with a governing "they." This is certainly an existential possibility and one to be investigated. However, frequently, it seems likely, systems are confused with groups, and our primitive need to explain thunder with a theology or a demonology results in the hypostatizing of an angelic or demonic hierarchy. The executive committee of the bourgeoisie and the power elite make the world more comfortable for modern social scientists as the Olympians did for the ancients. At least the latter-day hypothesis, being terrestrial, is in principle researchable, though in practice its metaphysical statement may render it equally immune to mundane inquiry.

Observation of certain local communities makes it appear that inclusive over-all organization for many general purposes is weak or non-existent. Much of what occurs seems to just happen with accidental trends becoming cumulative over time and producing results intended by nobody. A great deal of the communities' activities consist of undirected co-operation of particular social structures, each seeking particular goals and, in doing so, meshing with others. While much of this might be explained in Adam Smith's terms, much of it could not be explained with a rational, atomistic model of calculating individuals. For certain purposes the individual is a useful way of looking at people; for many others the role-playing member of a particular group is more helpful. Here we deal with the essence of predictability in social affairs. If we know the game being played is baseball and that X is a third baseman, by knowing his position and the game being played we can tell more about X's activities on the field than we could if we examined X as a psychologist or a psychiatrist. If such were not the case, X would belong in the mental ward rather than in a ball park. The behavior of X is not some disembodied rationality but, rather, behavior within an organized group activity that has goals, norms, strategies, and roles that give the very field and ground for rationality. Baseball structures the situation.

It is the contention of this paper that the structured group activities that coexist in a particular territorial system can be looked at as games. These games provide the players with a set of goals that give them a sense of success or failure. They provide them determinate roles and calculable strategies and tactics. In addition, they provide the players with an elite and general public that is in varying degrees able to tell the score. There is a good deal of evidence to be found in common parlance that many participants in contemporary group structures regard their occupations as at least analogous to games. And, at least in the American culture, and not only since Eisenhower, the conception of being on a "team" has been fairly widespread.

Unfortunately, the effectiveness of the term "game" for the purposes of this paper is vitiated by, first, the general sense that games are trivial occupations and, second, by the pre-emption of the term for the application of a calculus of probability to choice or decision in a determinate game situation. Far from regarding games as trivial, the writer's position would be that man is both a game-playing and a game-creating animal, that his capacity to create and play games and take them deadly seriously is of the essence, and that it is through games or activities analogous to game-playing that he achieves a satisfactory sense of significance and a meaningful role.

While the calculability of the game situation is important, of equal or greater importance is the capacity of the game to provide a sense of purpose and a role. The organizations of society and polity produce satisfactions with both their products and their processes. The two are not unrelated, but, while the production of the product may in the larger sense enable players and onlookers to keep score, the satisfaction in the process is the satisfaction of playing the game and the sense in which any activity can be grasped as a game.

Looked at this way, in the territorial system there is a political game, a banking game, a contracting game, a newspaper game, a civic organization game, an ecclesiastical game, and many others. Within each game there is a well-established set of goals whose achievement indicates success or failure for the participants, a set of socialized roles making participant behavior highly predictable, a set of strategies and tactics handed down through experience and occasionally subject to improvement and change, an elite public whose appro-bation is appreciated, and, finally, a general public which has some apprecia-tion for the standing of the players. Within the game the players can be rational in the varying degrees that the structure permits. At the very least, they know how to behave, and they know the score.

Individuals may play in a number of games, but, for the most part, their major preoccupation is with one, and their sense of major achievement is through success in one. Transfer from one game to another is, of course, possible, and the simultaneous playing of roles in two or more games is an important manner of linking separate games.

Sharing a common territorial field and collaborating for different and particular ends in the achievement of over-all social functions, the players in one game make use of the players in another and are, in turn, made use of by them. Thus the banker makes use of the newspaperman, the politician, the contractor, the ecclesiastic, the labor leader, the civic leader—all to further his success in the banking game—but, reciprocally, he is used to further the others' success in the newspaper, political, contracting, ecclesiastical, labor, and civic games. Each is a piece in the chess game of the other, sometimes a willing piece, but, to the extent that the games are different, with a different end in view.

Thus a particular highway grid may be the result of a bureaucratic depart-ment of public works game in which are combined, though separate, a profes-sional highway engineer game with its purposes and critical elite onlookers; a departmental bureaucracy; a set of contending politicians seeking to use the highways for political capital, patronage, and the like; a banking game concerned with bonds, taxes, and the effect of the highways on real estate; newspapermen interested in headlines, scoops, and the effect of highways on the papers' circulation; contractors eager to make money by building roads; ecclesiastics concerned with the effect of highways on their parishes and on the fortunes of the contractors who support their churchly ambitions; labor leaders interested in union contracts and their status as community influentials with a right to be consulted; and civic leaders who must justify the contributions of their bureaus of municipal research or chambers of commerce to the social activity. Each game is in play in the complicated pulling and hauling of siting and constructing the highway grid. A wide variety of purposes is subserved by the activity, and no single overall directive authority controls it. However, the interrelation of the groups in constructing a highway has been developed over time, and there are general expectations as to the interaction. There are also generalized expectations as to how politicians, contractors, newspapermen, bankers, and the like will utilize the highway situation in playing their particular games. In fact, the knowledge that a banker will play like a banker and a newspaperman like a newspaperman is an important part of what makes the situation calculable and permits the players to estimate its possibilities for their own action in their particular game.

While it might seem that the engineers of the department of public works were the appropriate protagonists for the highway grid, as a general activity it presents opportunities and threats to a wide range of other players who see in the situation consequences and possibilities undreamed of by the engineers. Some general public expectation of the limits of the conduct of the players and of a desirable outcome does provide bounds to the scramble. This public expectation is, of course, made active through the interested solicitation of newspapers, politicians, civic leaders, and others who see in it material for accomplishing their particular purposes and whose structured roles in fact require the mobilization of broad publics. In a sense the group struggle that Arthur Bentley described in his *Process of Government* is a drama that local publics have been taught to view with a not uncritical taste. The instruction of this taste has been the vocation and business of some of the contending parties. The existence of some kind of over-all public puts general restraints on gamesmanship beyond the norms of the particular games. However, for the players these are to all intents as much a part of the "facts of life" of the game as the sun and the wind.

It is perhaps the existence of some kind of a general public, however rudimentary, that most clearly differentiates the local territorial system from a natural ecology. The five-acre woodlot in which the owls and the field mice, the oaks and the acorns, and other flora and fauna have evolved a balanced system has no public opinion, however rudimentary. The co-operation is an unconscious affair. For much of what goes on in the local territorial system co-operation is equally unconscious and perhaps, but for the occasional social scientist, unnoticed. This unconscious co-operation, however, like that of the

five-acre woodlot, produces results. The ecology of games in the local territorial system accomplishes unplanned but largely functional results. The
games and their players mesh in their particular pursuits to bring about
over-all results; the territorial system is fed and ordered. Its inhabitants are
rational within limited areas and, pursuing the ends of these areas, accomplish
socially functional ends.

While the historical development of largely unconscious co-operation between the special games in the territorial system gets certain routine, over-all
functions performed, the problem of novelty and breakdown must be dealt
with. Here it would seem that, as in the natural ecology, random adjustment
and piecemeal innovation are the normal methods of response. The need or
cramp in the system presents itself to the players of the games as an opportunity for them to exploit or a menace to be overcome. Thus a transportation
crisis in, say, the threatened abandonment of commuter trains by a railroad
will bring forth the players of a wide range of games who will see in the
situation opportunity for gain or loss in the outcome. While over-all considerations will appear in the discussion, the frame of reference and the interpretation of the event will be largely determined by the game the interested parties
are principally involved in. Thus a telephone executive who is president of the
local chamber of commerce will be playing a civic association, general business
game with concern for the principal dues-payers of the chamber but with a
constant awareness of how his handling of this crisis will advance him in his
particular league. The politicians, who might be expected to be protagonists
of the general interest, may indeed be so, but the sphere of their activity and
the glasses through which they see the problem will be determined in great part
by the way they see the issue affecting their political game. The generality of
this game is to a great extent that of the politician's calculus of votes and
interests important to his and his side's success. To be sure, some of what
Walter Lippmann has called "the public philosophy" affects both politicians
and other game-players. This indicates the existence of roles and norms of a
larger, vaguer game with a relevant audience that has some sense of cricket.
This potentially mobilizable audience is not utterly without importance, but
it provides no sure or adequate basis for support in the particular game that
the politician or anyone else is playing. Instead of a set of norms to structure
enduring role-playing, this audience provides a cross-pressure for momentary
aberrancy from gamesmanship or constitutes just another hazard to be calculated in one's play.

In many cases the territorial system is impressive in the degree of intensity
of its particular games, its banks, its newspapers, its downtown stores, its
manufacturing companies, its contractors, its churches, its politicians, and its
other differentiated, structured, goal-oriented activities. Games go on within
the territory, occasionally extending beyond it, though centered in it. But,
while the particular games show clarity of goals and intensity, few, if any, treat
the territory as their proper object. The protagonists of things in particular are
well organized and know what they are about; the protagonists of things in

general are few, vague, and weak. Immense staff work will go into the development of a Lincoln Square project, but the twenty-two counties of metropolitan New York have few spokesmen for their over-all common interest and not enough staff work to give these spokesmen more substance than that required for a "do-gooding" newspaper editorial. The Port of New York Authority exhibits a disciplined self-interest and a vigorous drive along the lines of its developed historic role. However, the attitude of the Port Authority toward the general problems of the metropolitan area is scarcely different than that of any private corporation. It confines its corporate good citizenship to the contribution of funds for surveys and studies and avoids acceptance of broader responsibility. In fact, spokesmen for the Port vigorously reject the need for any superior level of structured representation of metropolitan interests. The common interest, if such there be, is to be realized through institutional interactions rather than through the self-conscious rationality of a determinate group charged with its formulation and attainment. Apart from the newspaper editorial, the occasional politician, and a few civic leaders the general business of the metropolitan area is scarcely anybody's business, and, except for a few, those who concern themselves with the general problems are pursuing hobbies and causes rather than their own business.

The lack of over-all institutions in the territorial system and the weakness of those that exist insure that co-ordination is largely ecological rather than a matter of conscious rational contriving. In the metropolitan area in most cases there are no over-all economic or social institutions. People are playing particular games, and their playgrounds are less or more than the metropolitan area. But even in a city where the municipal corporation provides an apparent overall government, the appearance is deceptive. The politicians who hold the offices do not regard themselves as governors of the municipal territory but largely as mediators or players in a particular game that makes use of the other inhabitants. Their roles, as they conceive them, do not approach those of the directors of a TVA developing a territory. The ideology of local government is a highly limited affair in which the office-holders respond to demands and mediate conflicts. They play politics, and politics is vastly different from government if the latter is conceived as the rational, responsible ordering of the community. In part, this is due to the general belief that little government is necessary or that government is a congery of services only different from others because it is paid for by taxes and provided for by civil servants. In part, the separation of economics from politics eviscerates the formal theory of government of most of the substance of social action. Intervention in the really important economic order is by way of piecemeal exception and in deviation from the supposed norm of the separation of politics and economics. This ideal of separation has blocked the development of a theory of significant government action and reduced the politician to the role of registerer of pressure rather than responsible governor of a local political economy. The politics of the community becomes a different affair from its government, and its government is so structured as to provide the effective actors in it neither a sense of general responsibility nor the roles calling for such behavior.

The community vaguely senses that there ought to be a government. This is evidenced in the nomination by newspapers and others of particular individuals as members of a top leadership, a "they" who are periodically called upon to solve community problems and meet community crises. Significantly, the "they" usually are made up of people holding private, not public, office. The pluralism of the society has separated political, ecclesiastical, economic, and social hierarchies from one another so that the ancient union of lords spiritual and temporal is disrupted. In consequence, there is a marked distinction between the status of the "they" of the newspapers and the power elite of a C. Wright Mills or a Floyd Hunter. The politicians have the formal governmental office that might give them responsible governing roles. However, their lack of status makes it both absurd and presumptuous that they should take themselves so seriously. Who are they to act as lords of creation? Public expectation neither empowers nor demands that they should assume any such confident pose as top community leaders. The latter position is reserved for a rather varying group (in some communities well defined and clear-cut, in others vague and amorphous) of holders for the most part of positions of private power, economic, social, and ecclesiastical. This group, regarded as the top leadership of the community, and analogous to the top management of a corporation, provides both a sense that there are gods in the heavens whose will, if they exercise it, will take care of the community's problems and a set of demons whose misrule accounts for the evil in the world. The "they" fill an office left vacant by the dethronement of absolutism and aristocracy. Unlike the politicians in that "they" are only partially visible and of untested powers, the top leadership provides a convenient rationale for explaining what goes on or does not go on in the community. It is comforting to think that the executive committee of the bourgeoisie is exploiting the community or that the beneficent social and economic leaders are wearying themselves and their digestions with civic luncheons in order to bring parking to a congested city.

Usually the question is raised as to whether *de facto* there is a set of informal power-holders running things. A related question is whether community folklore holds that there is, that there should be, and what these informal power-holders should do. Certainly, most newspapermen and other professional "inside dopesters" hold that there is a "they." In fact, these people operate largely as court chroniclers of the doings of the "they." The "they," because they are "they," are newsworthy and fit into a ready-made theory of social causation that is vulgarized widely. However, the same newspaperman who could knowingly open his "bird book" and give you a run-down on the local "Who's Who" would probably with equal and blasphemous candor tell you that "they" were not doing a thing about the city and that "they" were greatly to be blamed for sitting around talking instead of getting things done. Thus, as with most primitive tribes, the idols are both worshiped and beaten, at least verbally. Public and reporters alike are relieved to believe both that there is a "they" to make civic life explicable and also to be held responsible for what occurs. This belief in part creates the role of top leadership and demands that it somehow be filled. It seems likely that there is a social-psychological table of organization of a community that must be filled in order to remove anxieties. Gordon Childe has remarked that man seems to need as much to adjust to an unseen, socially created spiritual environment as to the matter-of-fact world of the senses.

The community needs to believe that there are spiritual fathers, bad or good, who can deal with the dark: in the Middle Ages the peasants combated a plague of locusts by a high Mass and a procession of the clergy who damned the grasshoppers with bell, book, and candle. The Hopi Indians do a rain dance to overcome a drought. The harassed citizens of the American city mobilize their influentials at a civic luncheon to perform the equivalent and exorcise slums, smog, or unemployment. We smile at the medievals and the Hopi, but our own practices may be equally magical. It is interesting to ask under what circumstances one resorts to DDT and irrigation and why. To some extent it is clear that the ancient and modern practice of civic magic ritual is functional —functional in the same sense as the medicinal placebo. Much of human illness is benign; if the sufferer will bide his time, it will pass. Much of civic ills also cure themselves if only people can be kept from tearing each other apart in the stress of their anxieties. The locusts and the drought will pass. They almost always have.

While ritual activities are tranquilizing anxieties, the process of experimentation and adaptation in the social ecology goes on. The piecemeal responses of the players and the games to the challenges presented by crises provide the social counterpart to the process of evolution and natural selection. However, unlike the random mutation of the animal kingdom, much of the behavior of the players responding within the perspectives of their games is self-conscious and rational, given their ends in view. It is from the over-all perspective of the unintended contribution of their actions to the forming of a new or the restoration of the old ecological balance of the social system that their actions appear almost as random and lacking in purposive plan as the adaptive behavior of the natural ecology.

Within the general area of unplanned, unconscious social process technological areas emerge that are so structured as to promote rational, goal-oriented behavior and meaningful experience rather than mere happenstance. In these areas group activity may result in cumulative knowledge and self-corrective behavior. Thus problem-solving in the field of public health and sanitation may be at a stage far removed from the older dependence on piecemeal adjustment and random functional innovation. In this sense there are areas in which society, as Julian Huxley suggests in his *The Meaning of Evolution,* has gone beyond evolution. However, these are as yet isolated areas in a world still swayed by magic and, for the most part, carried forward by the logic of unplanned, undirected historical process.

It is not surprising that the members of the "top leadership" of the territorial system should seem to be largely confined to ritual and ceremonial roles. "Top leadership" is usually conceived in terms of status position rather than specifiable roles in social action. The role of a top leader is ill defined and to a large degree unstructured. It is in most cases a secondary role derived from a primary role as corporation executive, wealthy man, powerful ecclesiastic, holder of high social position, and the like. The top-leadership role is derivative from the other and is in most cases a result rather than a cause of status. The primary job is bank president, or president of Standard Oil; as such, one is naturally picked, nominated, and recognized as a member of the top leadership. One seldom forgets that one's primary role, obligation, and source of rational conduct is in terms of one's business. In fact, while one is on the whole pleased at the recognition that membership in the top leadership implies—much as one's wife would be pleased to be included among the ten best-dressed women—he is somewhat concerned about just what the role requires in the expenditure of time and funds. Furthermore, one has a suspicion that he may not know how to dance and could make a fool of himself before known elite and unknown, more general publics. All things considered, however, it is probably a good thing for the business, the contacts are important, and the recognition will be helpful back home, in both senses. In any event, if one's committee service or whatever concrete activity "top leadership" implies proves wearing or unsatisfactory, or if it interferes with business, one can always withdraw.

A fair gauge of the significance of top-leadership roles is the time put into them by the players and the institutionalized support represented by staff. Again and again the interviewer is told that the president of such-and-such an organization is doing a terrific job and literally knocking himself out for such-and-such a program. On investigation a "terrific job" turns out to be a few telephone calls and, possibly, three luncheons a month. The standard of "terrific job" obviously varies widely from what would be required in the business role.

In the matter of staffing, while the corporation, the church, and the government are often equipped in depth, the top-leadership job of port promotion may have little more than a secretary and an agile newspaperman equipped to ghost-write speeches for the boss. While there are cases where people in top-leadership positions make use of staff from their own businesses and from the legal mill with which they do business, this seems largely confined to those top-leadership undertakings that have a direct connection with their business. In general, top-leadership roles seem to involve minor investments of time, staff, and money by territorial elites. The absence of staff and the emphasis on publicity limit the capacity of top leadership for sustained rational action.

Where top leaderships have become well staffed, the process seems as much or more the result of external pressures than of its own volition. Of all the functions of top leaderships that of welfare is best staffed. Much of this is the result of the pressure of the professional social worker to organize a concentration of economic and social power sufficient to permit him to do a job. It is true, of course, that the price of organizing top leadership and making it manageable by the social workers facilitated a reverse control of themselves

—a control of whose galling nature Hunter gives evidence. An amusing side-light on the organization of the "executive committee of the bourgeoisie" is the case of the Cleveland Fifty Club. This club, supposedly, is made up of the fifty most important men in Cleveland. Most middling and even upper executives long for the prestige recognition that membership confers. Reputedly, the Fifty Club was organized by Brooks Emery, while he was director of the Cleveland Council on World Affairs, to facilitate the taxation of business to support that organization. The lead time required to get the august members of the Fifty Club together and their incohesiveness have severely limited its possibilities as a power elite. Members who have tried to turn it to such a purpose report fairly consistent failure.

The example of the Cleveland Fifty Club, while somewhat extreme, points to the need on the part of certain activities in the territorial system for a top leadership under whose auspices they can function. A wide variety of civic undertakings need to organize top prestige support both to finance and to legitimate their activities. The staff man of a bureau of municipal research or the Red Feather Agency cannot proceed on his own; he must have the legitimatizing sponsorship of top influentials. His task may be self-assigned, his perception of the problem and its solution may be his own, but he cannot gain acceptance without mobilizing the influentials. For the success of his game he must assist in creating the game of top leadership. The staff man in the civic field is the typical protagonist of things in general—a kind of entrepreneur of ideas. He fulfils the same role in his area as the stock promoter of the twenties or the Zeckendorfs of urban redevelopment. Lacking both status and a confining organizational basis, he has a socially valuable mobility between the specialized games and hierarchies in the territorial system. His success in the negotiation of a port authority not only provides a plus for his taxpayers federation or his world trade council but may provide a secure and lucrative job for himself.

Civic staff men, ranging from chamber of commerce personnel to college professors and newspapermen, are in varying degrees interchangeable and provide an important network of communication. The staff men in the civic agencies play similar roles to the Cohens and Corcorans in Washington. In each case a set of telephone numbers provides special information and an effective lower-echelon interaction. Consensus among interested professionals at the lower level can result in action programs from below that are bucked up to the prestige level of legitimitization. As the Cohens and Corcorans played perhaps the most general and inclusive game in the Washington bureaucracy, so their counterparts in the local territorial system are engaged in the most general action game in their area. Just as the Cohens and Corcorans had to mobilize an effective concentration of top brass to move a program into the action stage, so their counterparts have to mobilize concentrations of power sufficient for their purposes on the local scene.

In this connection it is interesting to note that foundation grants are being used to hire displaced New Deal bureaucrats and college professors in an attempt to organize the influentials of metropolitan areas into self-conscious governing groups. Professional chamber of commerce executives, immobilized by their orthodox ideology, are aghast to see their members study under the planners and heretics from the dogmas of free-enterprise fundamentalism. The attempt to transform the metropolitan appearance of disorder into a tidy territory is a built-in predisposition for the self-constituted staff of the embryonic top metropolitan management. The major disorder that has to be overcome before all others is the lack of order and organization among the "power elite." As in the case of the social workers, there is thrust from below to organize a "power elite" as a necessary instrument to accomplish the purposes of civic staff men. This is in many ways nothing but a part of the general groping after a territorial government capable of dealing with a range of problems that the existing feudal disintegration of power cannot. The nomination of a top leadership by newspapers and public and the attempt to create such a leadership in fact by civic technicians are due to a recognition that there is a need for a leadership with the status, capacity, and role to attend to the general problems of the territory and give substance to a public philosophy. This involves major changes in the script of the top-leadership game and the self-image of its participants. In fact, the insecurity and the situational limitations of their positions in corporations or other institutions that provide the primary roles for top leaders make it difficult to give more substance to what has been a secondary role. Many members of present top leaderships are genuinely reluctant, fearful, and even morally shocked at their positions' becoming that of a recognized territorial government. While there is a general supposition that power is almost instinctively craved, there seems considerable evidence that at least in many of our territorial cultures responsibility is not. Machiavellian *virtu* is an even scarcer commodity among the merchant princes of the present than among their Renaissance predecessors. In addition, the educational systems of school and business do not provide top leaders with the inspiration or the know-how to do more than raise funds and man committees. Politics is frequently regarded with the same disgust as military service by the ancient educated Chinese.

It is possible to translate a check pretty directly into effective power in a chamber of commerce or a welfare agency. However, to translate economic power into more general social or political power, there must be an organized purchasable structure. Where such structures exist, they may be controlled or, as in the case of *condottieri,* gangsters, and politicians, their hire may be uncertain, and the hired force retains its independence. Where businessmen are unwilling or unable to organize their own political machines, they must pay those who do. Sometimes the paymaster rules; at other times he bargains with equals or superiors.

A major protagonist of things in general in the territorial system is the newspaper. Along with the welfare worker, museum director, civic technician, etc., the newspaper has an interest in terms of its broad reading public in agitating general issues and projects. As the chronicler of the great, both in its general news columns and in its special features devoted to society and business, it provides an organizing medium for elites in the territory and provides them with most of their information about things in general and not a little of inside tidbits about how individual elite members are doing. In a sense, the newspaper is the prime mover in setting the territorial agenda. It has a great part in determining what most people will be talking about, what most people will think the facts are, and what most people will regard as the way problems are to be dealt with. While the conventions of how a newspaper is to be run, and the compelling force of some events limit the complete freedom of a paper to select what events and what people its public will attend to, it has great leeway. However, the newspaper is a business and a specialized game even when its reporters are idealists and its publisher rejoices in the title "Mr. Cleveland." The paper does not accept the responsibility of a governing role in its territory. It is a power but only a partially responsible one. The span of attention of its audience and the conventions of what constitute a story give it a crusading role at most for particular projects. Nonetheless, to a large extent it sets the civic agenda.

The story is told of the mayor of a large eastern metropolis who, having visited the three capital cities of his constituents—Rome, Dublin, and Tel Aviv —had proceeded home via Paris and Le Havre. Since his staff had neglected to meet the boat before the press, he was badgered by reporters to say what he had learned on his trip. The unfortunate mayor could not say that he had been on a junket for a good time. Luckily, he remembered that in Paris they had been having an antinoise campaign. Off the hook at last, he told the press that he thought this campaign was a good thing. This gave the newsmen something to write about. The mayor hoped this was the end of it. But a major paper felt in need of a crusade to sponsor and began to harass the mayor about the start of the local antinoise campaign. Other newspapers took up the cry, and the mayor told his staff they were for it—there had to be an antinoise campaign. In short order, businessmen's committees, psychiatrists, and college professors were mobilized to press forward on a broad front the suppression of needless noise. In vindication of administrative rationality it appeared that an antinoise campaign was on a staff list of possibilities for the mayor's agenda but had been discarded by him as politically unfeasible.

The civic technicians and the newspapers have somewhat the same relationship as congressional committee staff and the press. Many members of congressional committee staffs complain bitterly that their professional consciences are seared by the insistent pressure to seek publicity. But they contend that their committee sponsors are only impressed with research that is newsworthy. Congressional committee members point out that committees that do not get publicity are likely to go out of business or funds. The civic agency head all too frequently communicates most effectively with his board through his success in getting newspaper publicity. Many a civic ghost-writer has found his top leader converted to the cause by reading the ghosted speech he delivered at the civic luncheon reported with photographs and editorials in the press. This is even the case where the story appears in the top leader's own paper. The need of the reporters for news and of the civic technicians for publicity brings the participants of these two games together. As in the case of the congressional committee, there is a tendency to equate accomplishment with publicity. For top influentials on civic boards the news clips are an important way of keeping score. This symbiotic relation of newsmen and civic staff helps explain the heavy emphasis on ritual luncheons, committees, and news releases. The nature of the newspapers' concern with a story about people and the working of marvels and miracles puts a heavy pressure for the kind of story that the press likes to carry. It is not surprising that civic staff men should begin to equate accomplishment with their score measured in newspaper victories or that they should succumb to the temptation to impress their sponsors with publicity, salting it to their taste by flattering newspaper tributes to the sponsors themselves. Despite the built-in incapacity of newspapers to exercise a serious governing responsibility in their territories, they are for the most part the only institutions with a long-term general territorial interest. In default of a territorial political party or other institution that accepts responsibility for the formulation of a general civic agenda the newspaper is the one game that by virtue of its public and its conventions partly fills the vacuum.

A final game that does in a significant way integrate all the games in the territorial system is the social game. Success in each of the games can in varying degrees be cashed in for social acceptance. The custodians of the symbols of top social standing provide goals that in a sense give all the individual games some common denominator of achievement. While the holders of top social prestige do not necessarily hold either top political or economic power, they do provide meaningful goals for the rest. One of the most serious criticisms of a Yankee aristocracy made by a Catholic bishop was that, in losing faith in their own social values, they were undermining the faith in the whole system of final clubs. It would be a cruel joke if, just as the hardworking upwardly mobile had worked their way to entrance, the progeny of the founders lost interest. The decay of the Union League Club in *By Love Possessed* is a tragedy for more than its members. A common game shared even by the excluded spectators gave a purpose that was functional in its time and must be replaced—hopefully, by a better one. A major motivation for seeking membership in and playing the top-leadership game is the value of the status it confers as a counter in the social game.

Neither the civic leadership game nor the social game makes the territorial ecology over into a structured government. They do, however, provide important ways of linking the individual games and make possible cooperative action on projects. Finally, the social game, in Ruth Benedict's sense, in a general way patterns the culture of the territorial ecology and gives all the players a set of vaguely shared aspirations and common goals.

B SOCIAL PATTERNS AND PROCESS

Urban Neighborhood Types and Participation in Formal Associations*

Wendell Bell and Maryanne T. Force

This paper reports part of a study of social participation conducted in San Francisco in the spring of 1953. The investigation rested upon two main notions:

First, that the major social roles which an individual occupies regulate the amount and nature of his participation in society. For example, if one knew a person's economic, family, and ethnic status, his age and sex, his aspirations or expectations regarding the roles he might achieve, and his status history with respect to these types of statuses, one should be able to predict closely that person's participation in the various activities of society.

Second, that the social type of neighborhood in which an urbanite lives is an efficient indicator of his social participation and may be a significant factor

*The writers wish to express their appreciation to the Carnegie Corporation of New York and the Stanford University Committee for Research in the Social Sciences who furnished funds for the execution of the study of which this report is part. Harry V. Kincaid and Marion D. Boat made important contributions to this study, and we gratefully acknowledge their aid.

SOURCE: Wendell Bell and Maryanne T. Force, "Urban Neighborhood Types and Participation in Formal Association," *American Sociological Review,* 21 (February 1956), 25–34. Reprinted by permission.

in its own right in shaping his social participation. It has been contended, for example, that social differences between the populations of urban neighborhoods can be conveniently summarized into differences of economic level, family characteristics, and ethnicity.[1] It is our hypothesis that neighborhood populations having different configurations with respect to these three variables will have different patterns of social participation.

This paper will be limited to an examination of the relationship between amount of formal association participation and certain of the above mentioned individual status and neighborhood differences. Other papers are in preparation dealing with additional aspects of individual social participation.

Following Komarovsky, all formally organized groups are included in our definition of formal associations ". . . except economic concerns (stores, corporations), governmental agencies, and schools."[2] Thus, all non-profit formal organizations are included unless they are part of the governmental body. "Their functions are characterized by explicit regularity and standardization —such as being identified by a name, or having officers, or having a written constitution, or having regular meetings."[3] This follows generally accepted definitions of "voluntary associations," "formal organizations," or "formal groups."

DESCRIPTION OF THE SAMPLE

Selection of the Neighborhoods.   Using the census tract scores given in *Social Area Analysis*[4] four census tracts were selected in San Francisco in which to conduct the study of social participation. The identifying place names, census tract designations, and index scores for the four tracts selected are given in Table 1. It was decided to hold ethnicity constant as far as possible, so all four of the tracts selected contain relatively few nonwhites and few members of foreign-born groups, as indicated by their relatively low scores on the index of ethnic status. Census tracts N-8 (located in the Mission district) and M-6 (located in the Outer Mission district) have low scores on the index of economic status relative to the scores of the other census tracts in the San Francisco Bay Region. The Mission population, however, is a rooming-house district with a relatively low score on the index of family status, having a low fertility ratio, many women in the labor force, and few single-family detached

[1]Eshref Shevky and Wendell Bell, *Social Area Analysis,* Stanford: Stanford University Press, 1955.

[2]Mirra Komarovsky, "A Comparative Study of Voluntary Organizations of Two Suburban Communities," *Sociological Problems and Methods,* Volume 27, Publications of the American Sociological Society, 1933, p. 84.

[3]Morris Axelrod, "A Study of Formal and Informal Group Participation in a Large Urban Community," unpublished Ph.D. dissertation (microfilmed), University of Michigan, 1953, pp. 14–15.

[4]Shevky and Bell, *op. cit.,* pp. 61–66.

dwellings. The population of Outer Mission has a relatively high score on the index of family status and is characterized by high fertility ratios, few women in the labor force, and many single-family detached dwellings. Census tract B-6 is in the Pacific Heights district and is a high-rent apartment house area, having a relatively high economic level, but a low score on family status. Census tract O-7 contains the district known as St. Francis Wood and, like Pacific Heights, contains a population having high economic status, but like Outer Mission is a single family home area characterized by a high score on family status.

TABLE 1. IDENTIFYING PLACE NAMES, CENSUS TRACT DESIGNATIONS, AND INDEX SCORES FOR THE FOUR STUDY TRACTS*

Index	Mission (N-8)	Pacific Heights (B-6)	Outer Mission (M-6)	St. Francis Wood (O-7)
Economic status†	46	96	43	92
Family status‡	28	9	67	70
Ethnic status§	14	7	20	6

*Index scores can vary approximately from 0 to 100.
†Composed of measures of occupation and education.
‡Composed of measures of fertility, women not in the labor force, and single family detached dwelling units.
§Per cent of persons in the census tract who are nonwhite or foreign born white from Southern and Eastern Europe, Asia, and French Canada.

Selection of the Respondents. A probability area sample was selected for each of the study census tracts. First, a complete list of dwelling units in each of the tracts was compiled by means of standard block listing procedures. Second, a sampling interval (k) was established for each tract, and a sample of dwellings drawn by taking a random number from 1 to k and selecting every kth dwelling unit thereafter. Third, within each sample dwelling one male over the age of 21 was selected as the respondent, thus eliminating from the study social participation differences resulting from the differential requirements of the roles of the two sexes. Dwellings containing no males over age 21 were removed from the sample, and in those which contained two or more males over age 21 one male was selected randomly from a respondent selection table provided on each interview schedule. In order to assure randomness in the sample no substitutions were allowed.

Response Rates. St. Francis Wood (high family and high economic status) had the highest per cent of completed interviews with 90.8 per cent of the number of qualified respondents in the sample fully completing their interviews. Pacific Heights (low family and high economic status) had a response rate of 84.9 per cent, Mission (low family and low economic status) had 83.9 per cent, and Outer Mission (high family and low economic status) had 83.3 per cent. Refusal rates were higher in the two low economic status neighborhoods than in the two high economic status neighborhoods, but refusals accounted for most of the loss in completed interviews in all four neighborhoods. People seemed to be more suspicious of the interviewers in Outer Mission than in the other tracts, although a recent robbery in Mission influenced several respondents not to open the doors to their rooms until they had made certain of the identity of the interviewer. The resistance occurred in spite of several articles in the metropolitan papers describing the study, television programs featuring a discussion of the study, advance letters to the respondents, official credentials carried by each interviewer, and the co-operation of the Police Department in identifying *bona fide* interviewers to the householders.

AMOUNT OF PARTICIPATION BY NEIGHBORHOOD

Number of Formal Group Memberships.   One measure of formal group participation used in many previous studies and employed in this study is the sheer number of memberships in formal associations. Table 2 contains the per cent of persons in each neighborhood who belong to a certain number of formal organizations.[5] From Table 2 it can be seen that in each of the different neighborhoods more than 76 per cent of the men belong to at least one formal group. This finding is comparable to the findings of other studies of formal group membership in urban areas. Goldhamer[6] in his study of Chicago residents found that 70 per cent of the men belonged to one or more formal groups, and Axelrod[7] found that 80 per cent of the men in his Detroit sample belonged to at least one formal group.

However, these figures indicate considerably higher membership in one or more formal associations than is given in some other studies of formal participation among urban dwellers, especially among those men who are blue-collar workers. Komarovsky,[8] for example, reports that 60 per cent of the working class men belong to no formal associations. Dotson[9] presents similar findings for a later period in New Haven. It is not clear whether the inconsistency of our findings with those of Komarovsky and Dotson is due to regional differ-

[5]General church membership is not included, but memberships in church-connected groups are included throughout this paper.

[6]Herbert Goldhamer, "Some Factors Affecting Participation in Voluntary Associations," unpublished Ph.D. dissertation (microfilmed), University of Chicago, 1942.

[7]Axelrod, *op. cit.*

[8]Mirra Komarovsky, "The Voluntary Associations of Urban Dwellers," *American Sociological Review,* 11 (December, 1946), pp. 686–98.

[9]Floyd Dotson, "Patterns of Voluntary Association Among Urban Working-Class Families," *American Sociological Review,* 16 (October, 1951), pp. 687–93.

ences, Komarovsky's low response rate (29 per cent of the questionnaires were returned), Dotson's small sample of men (N = 50), or variations in degree of unionization. (If memberships in labor unions were not counted in our two low economic level neighborhoods, then our findings would correspond to theirs.)

Although the data shown in Table 2 support the contention that the formal association is widespread throughout diverse social groupings in an urban environment, only about a third or less of the men in every neighborhood, except St. Francis Wood, belong to three or more formal associations.

TABLE 2. PER CENT OF MEN HAVING MEMBERSHIP IN A CERTAIN NUMBER OF FORMAL ASSOCIATIONS

Number of Groups	Low Family Low Econ. (Mission) Per Cent	Low Family High Econ. (Pacific Heights) Per Cent	High Family Low Econ. (Outer Mission) Per Cent	High Family High Econ. (St. Francis Wood) Per Cent
Seven or more	1.7	11.0	0	19.0
Six	0	2.6	0	4.2
Five	1.2	3.2	1.2	11.9
Four	2.3	7.3	2.9	13.7
Three	11.6	11.5	8.8	17.3
Two	22.1	23.0	22.4	13.7
One	37.8	19.9	44.7	13.1
None	23.3	21.5	19.4	7.1
Not ascertained	0	0	0.6	0
Total	100.0	100.0	100.0	100.0
Number of cases	(172)	(191)	(170)	(168)

Comparing the tracts with respect to the number of formal group memberships, we find that the high economic status tracts contain relatively more men who belong to a greater number of formal associations than do the low economic status tracts. The largest percentage (66.1 per cent) of men belonging to three or more associations is in St. Francis Wood, and the next largest percentage (35.6 per cent) is in Pacific Heights. The two low economic level neighborhoods at each level of family status have significantly (p < .01) lower percentages of men who report that they belong to three or more associations wtih 16.8 per cent so reporting in Mission and 12.9 per cent so reporting in Outer Mission.

Differences between neighborhoods having different family status, holding economic status constant, are not consistent, although at the high economic level St. Francis Wood, having high family status, has a much larger percentage of men who belong to three or more associations than does Pacific Heights, the low family status neighborhood. Pacific Heights also contains a larger percentage of men who belong to no associations than does St. Francis Wood.

Attendance at Formal Group Meetings. The mere number of member-ships does not give adequate information regarding the amount of participa-tion in formal associations, since membership in some cases may be only nominal. Table 3 contains the frequency of attendance at all formal association meetings for these men who report belonging to at least one such organiza-tion.[10]

TABLE 3. PER CENT OF FORMAL ASSOCIATION MEMBERS WHO ATTEND A SPECIFIED NUMBER OF MEETINGS

Frequency of Attendance	Low Family Low Econ. (Mission) Per Cent	Low Family High Econ. (Pacific Heights) Per Cent	High Family Low Econ. (Outer Mission) Per Cent	High Family High Econ. (St. Francis Wood) Per Cent
More than once a week	8.3	30.9	6.6	26.9
About once a week	8.3	15.4	10.9	14.1
A few times a month	28.8	17.4	16.1	23.1
About once a month	17.4	6.7	16.1	6.4
A few times a year	19.0	12.1	25.5	19.9
About once a year	6.1	3.4	6.6	3.8
Never	12.1	14.1	17.5	5.8
Not ascertained	0	0	0.7	0
Total	100.0	100.0	100.0	100.0
Number of members	(132)	(149)	(137)	(156)

In St. Francis Wood only 5.8 per cent, in Mission 12.1 per cent, in Pacific Heights 14.1 per cent, and in Outer Mission 17.5 per cent of the members of formal groups do not attend meetings. Thus, the vast majority of the members in each of the neighborhoods, in excess of 82 per cent, attend at least one meeting a year.

This finding is fairly consistent with those of Axelrod[11] who found that 22

[10]General church attendance is not included here or elsewhere in this paper, but attendance at meetings of church-connected groups is included.

[11]Axelrod, *op. cit.*

per cent of the men who belong to formal groups in Detroit attended no formal group meetings during a three month period, although Dotson[12] found that of the number of memberships held by men in his sample in New Haven as many as one-third were inactive.

When the members in the four neighborhoods are compared with respect to the frequency of formal association attendance, marked differences between neighborhoods appear. Again, the greatest amount of formal participation occurs among the persons who live in the high economic status neighborhoods. Men living in St. Francis Wood and Pacific Heights who belong to formal associations attend more frequently than those living in Mission and Outer Mission. In Pacific Heights 30.9 per cent of the members attend meetings more than once a week compared to only 8.3 per cent in Mission (p < .01); in St. Francis Wood 26.7 per cent of the members attend meetings more than once a week compared to only 6.6 per cent in Outer Mission (p < .01).

Considering those men who belong to formal associations but who attend only about once a year or less, it may be noted that Pacific Heights, the high economic, low family status neighborhood, has almost as large a percentage of men who are relatively isolated from social contacts in formal groups as the two low economic status neighborhoods. Since Pacific Heights, Mission, and Outer Mission are the neighborhoods with the largest percentages of men who do not belong to formal groups, it is evident that sizeable segments of the population in these three neighborhoods are socially isolated from this form of participation. This is consistent with the general conclusion of Komarovsky who says with respect to formal group participation that a large segment of the population, particularly the lower social and economic level ". . . is cut off from channels of power, information, growth and a sense of participation in purposive social action."[13] We would add to this generalization that even on the higher economic levels a significant segment of those men living in neighborhoods of low family status are similarly isolated.

Office Holding in Formal Associations.   Generally, holding positions of leadership in a formal association denotes more active participation in the group than not holding positions of leadership. Thus, a third measure of formal association participation used in this study, and one which indicates the relative power position of the individual within the association, is whether or not the individual holds office in the formal associations to which he belongs. Table 4 contains a summary presentation of this material. Consistent with our other findings, the high economic status neighborhoods contain a larger percentage of members who hold office in a formal association than do the low economic status neighborhoods at each level of family status. Pacific Heights (24.5 per cent) contains a larger percentage than Mission (13.0 per cent) (p < .05), and St. Francis Wood (34.8 per cent) contains a larger percentage than Outer Mission (11.6 per cent) (p < .01).

[12]Dotson, *op. cit.*
[13]Komarovsky, 1946, *op. cit.,* p. 698.

TABLE 4. PER CENT OF FORMAL ASSOCIATION MEMBERS WHO HOLD OFFICES

Holds Office	Low Family Low Econ. (Mission) Per Cent	Low Family High Econ. (Pacific Heights) Per Cent	High Family Low Econ. (Outer Mission) Per Cent	High Family High Econ. (St. Francis Wood) Per Cent
Yes	13.0	24.5	11.6	34.8
No	86.3	74.8	87.7	65.2
Not ascertained	0.7	0.7	0.7	0
Total	100.0	100.)	100.0	100.0
Number of cases	(131)	(151)	(138)	(155)

Although no difference appears between the two low economic status neighborhoods, the relative number of office holders is somewhat higher in St. Francis Wood (high economic and high family status) than it is in Pacific Heights (high economic and low family status). Our findings consistently show that the higher economic status neighborhoods contain relatively more men who belong to formal associations, more members who frequently attend meetings, and more members who hold office in formal associations when compared with neighborhoods of a lower economic level.

The differences by family status are not so large nor so consistent, although at the high economic status level, the lower family status neighborhood contains a higher percentage of men who are socially isolated with respect to formal association participation by all three measures of participation used here than the higher family status neighborhood contains.

INDIVIDUAL AND NEIGHBORHOOD CHARACTERISTICS

Education, Occupation, and Income.   Thus far in the analysis the discussion has been limited to the formal association participation of men as that behavior is related to the social type of neighborhood in which the men live. In effect, we have been assigning to each man his neighborhood scores for economic and family status, and relating his formal association behavior to these scores. However, the neighborhoods are not completely homogeneous with respect to economic and family status; that is, each man by some measure of his own individual economic or family status does not necessarily have a score which equals the average for his neighborhood. A neighborhood's score has been referred to as a unit variable, and an individual's own score as a personal variable.[14] In this section we wish to explore further the relationship between economic position and formal association by tabulating these two types of variables simultaneously.

Since the most significant and consistent findings concern economic and not family status, the study neighborhoods have been grouped so that the two low economic status neighborhoods, Mission and Outer Mission, are together, and the two high economic status neighborhoods, Pacific Heights and St. Francis Wood, are together. Education, occupation, and annual family income were taken as measures of personal economic status. As is shown in Table 5, the high economic status neighborhoods contain relatively more men with higher education, with white collar occupations, and with higher incomes; and the low economic status neighborhoods contain relatively more men with lower education, blue collar occupations, and lower incomes. However, there is a small percentage of men living in the high economic status neighborhoods who have either relatively low education, blue collar jobs, or relatively low incomes, that is, who would be classified as low economic status on the basis of personal variables even though they are living in high economic status neighborhoods. Similarly, there are in the low economic status neighborhoods small percentages of men who would be classified as high economic status on the basis of their personal ratings on education, occupation, and income. The question arises whether differences in amount of formal association participation between high and low economic status neighborhoods still exist when controls are introduced for personal economic status.

Table 6 shows the per cent of men who attend formal association meetings frequently by the average economic status of the neighborhood and by the respondent's own education, occupation, and family income. Comparing the percentages *within each neighborhood,* the general tendency is for relatively more frequent attenders to have higher education, white collar occupations, and higher incomes. This, of course, is consistent with the findings of many studies which have related such measures to formal association participation.

Of particular interest here, however, is the comparison of amount of formal association participation between neighborhoods, holding personal education, occupation, and income constant. For example, a larger percentage of the men who have been to college are frequent attenders in the high economic status neighborhoods than in the low economic status neighborhoods. This is also true of the men in the less educated categories. At each of the educational levels the men living in the higher economic status neighborhoods are more likely to be frequent attenders than are the men living in the lower economic status neighborhoods. ($\Sigma\chi^2 = 15.78$, $p < .01$)

Although not statistically significant, a similar tendency can be seen when personal occupation and income are held constant. Men with high occupations

---

[14]Paul F. Lazarsfeld and Allen H. Barton, "Qualitative Measurement in the Social Sciences: Classification, Typologies, and Indices," in Daniel Lerner and Harold D. Lasswell (editors), *The Policy Sciences,* Stanford: Stanford University Press, 1951, pp. 187–92.

TABLE 5. PER CENT OF MEN HAVING SELECTED SOCIO-ECONOMIC CHARACTERISTICS BY NEIGHBORHOOD

Socio-Economic Characteristics	Neighborhood Characteristics	
	Low Economic Status (Mission and Outer Mission) Per Cent	High Economic Status (Pacific Heights and St. Francis Wood) Per Cent
Education		
Some college or more	9.6	50.4
Completed high school only	24.6	25.6
Some high school	23.7	13.1
Grade school or less	42.1	10.9
Not ascertained	0.0	0.0
Total	100.0	100.0
Number of cases	(342)	(359)
Occupation		
Profs., mgrs., props., and offs.	12.9	67.4
Sales, clerical, and kind. workers	8.5	21.2
Craftsmen, foremen, and operatives	57.0	8.6
Service workers and laborers	21.6	2.5
Not ascertained	0.0	0.3
Total	100.0	100.0
Number of cases	(342)	(359)
Income		
$10,000 and over	2.0	41.5
6,000–9,999	18.4	28.7
3,000–5,999	65.0	20.9
0–2,999	14.0	5.3
Not ascertained	0.6	3.6
Total	100.0	100.0
Number of cases	(342)	(359)

TABLE 6. PER CENT OF MEN WHO ATTEND FORMAL ASSOCIATION MEETINGS FREQUENTLY BY NEIGHBORHOOD AND INDIVIDUAL SOCIO-ECONOMIC CHARACTERISTICS*

	Neighborhood Characteristics	
Individual Socio-Economic Characteristics	Low Economic Status (Mission and Outer Mission) Per Cent	High Economic Status (Pacific Heights and St. Francis Wood) Per Cent
Education		
Some college or more	27.3	46.4
	(33)	(181)
Completed high school only	14.5	28.3
	(83)	(92)
Some high school	17.3	30.4
	(81)	(46)
Grade school or less	7.6	23.1
	(144)	(39)
Occupation		
Profs., mgrs., props., and offs.	32.6	42.7
	(43)	(241)
Sales, clerical, and kind. workers	20.7	26.3
	(29)	(76)
Craftsmen, foremen, and operatives	9.3	22.6
	(194)	(31)
Service workers and laborers	10.8	33.3
	(74)	(9)
Income		
$10,000 and over	0.0	53.4
	(4)	(148)
6,000–9,999	16.9	29.1
	(65)	(103)
3,000–5,999	13.1	20.0
	(222)	(75)
0–2,999	12.5	15.8
	(48)	(19)

*Men were classified frequent attenders if they attended meetings 37 or more times per year. The total number of cases on which the percentage is based is given in parentheses in each case.

are more likely to be frequent attenders if they live in the high economic status neighborhoods. The same is true for the other occupational groups. For example, men who are service workers and laborers are more likely to be frequent attenders if they live in the high economic status neighborhoods. A similar tendency occurs between the two neighborhoods when comparing men who have similar incomes. Those who live in the high economic status neighborhoods are somewhat more likely than those who live in the low economic status neighborhoods to be frequent attenders at formal association meetings. Thus, differences in formal association participation still exist when comparing the low with the high economic status neighborhoods, even when certain measures of personal economic status are controlled.

There seem to be at least two explanations for these findings. First, the neighborhood characteristics may be an index to the self image of the individual, and second, the type of neighborhood in which a person lives may itself be a factor in the kinds of pressures which are brought upon the individual to participate in formal associations.

In the first instance the lower economic status persons who live in high economic status neighborhoods and the higher economic status persons who live in low economic status neighborhoods may be the "deviants" who are found in many stratification studies; that is, they may be those whose objective class position does not seem congruent with their own placement of themselves. The economic characteristics of the neighborhoods in which they live, however, may give important objective clues regarding their group identification and, thereby, give indications of certain kinds of behavioral and attitudinal correlates.

The second case would involve the effect of the neighborhood in determining the role expectations of the individual after the individual became a part of the neighborhood. For example, persons living in high economic status neighborhoods may come under much greater pressures to participate in certain types of associations than do persons living in low economic status neighborhoods. Neighborhood improvement associations, civic groups, welfare and charitable organizations, etc., are more likely to have members from high economic status neighborhoods than from low economic status neighborhoods.

Family Characteristics.   Within each of the four neighborhoods the number of formal association memberships, as well as the frequency of attendance at formal association meetings, was tabulated against marital status, age of children, employment status of wife, and type of dwelling (single family detached vs. two or more family dwelling). Although other writers report relationships between formal association participation and these variables, we find no consistent trends when making comparisons within each of the neighborhoods.

Age Differences.   Many writers have investigated the relationship between age and formal association participation. Axelrod,[15] for example, in his Detroit

[15]Axelrod, *op. cit.*

study finds that formal association membership starts out relatively low in early adulthood, reaches a peak in the forties, and then declines to a new low by the sixties. He also finds this same pattern for the very active participants. Goldhamer found that when participation is measured by frequency of attendance, the young men tend to exceed the older men and that participation tends to decline in the oldest age group (fifty and over).[16] From his study of persons aged 65 and over living in a California community of retired people, McKain noted that formal association participation declined with advanced years; about 50 per cent of those over age 65 reported that they gave less time to associations than they did when they were 50 years of age, only 1 per cent said that their social activities had increased.[17] These findings have been interpreted by some as indicating a structural relationship between the adult life cycle and formal association participation: ties with formal associations preventing many formal associations in the twenties; consolidation of occupational position, a home and a family leading the individual to join associations in the thirties; formal associations becoming an end in themselves in the forties and occupying more time; children grown to adulthood, retirement, and loss of physical stamina and vigor resulting in less and less formal association participation at the older age groups.[18]

Annual formal association attendance by age is given in Table 7 for each of the four study neighborhoods in San Francisco. These data require a revision of the above view, and constitute some evidence of the degree of difference in life styles of segments of the population at different levels of economic status. In each of the high economic status neighborhoods *the per cent of men who are active participants increases with increasing age.* No such relationship, however, occurs between age and formal association participation among the men who live in the low economic status neighborhoods. On the contrary, in these neighborhoods the smallest percentage of men who attend meetings "seldom or never" is in the middle age group and the largest percentage, who are thus "socially isolated," is in the older age group. Thus, the relationship between age and formal association participation in the low economic status neighborhoods approximates that found by most other writers, but we find an entirely different pattern in the high economic status neighborhoods.

There is some corroboration of our findings in Webber's study.[19] In Orlando, Florida he found that the older age group, which he defined as 70 or older, had a slightly greater nonmembership and slightly lower incidence of membership in two or more associations. However, he found the opposite relationship in a generally higher economic status community, West Palm Beach, where those under age 70 reported considerably higher nonmember-

[16]Goldhamer, *op. cit.*

[17]Walter C. McKain, Jr. "The Social Participation of Old People in a California Retirement Community," unpublished Ph.D. dissertation, Harvard University, 1947.

[18]Axelrod, *op. cit.*

[19]Irving L. Webber, "The Organized Social Life of the Retired in Two Florida Communities," *American Journal of Sociology,* 59 (January, 1954), pp. 340–46.

TABLE 7. ANNUAL FORMAL ASSOCIATION ATTENDANCE BY NEIGHBORHOOD AND AGE*

	Age		
Neighborhood	21–39 Per Cent	40–59 Per Cent	60 and Over Per Cent
Low family, low econ. (Mission)			
Attendances per year:			
37 or more	18.9	7.3	16.2
5–36	33.9	54.9	10.8
0–4	47.2	37.8	73.0
Total	100.0	100.0	100.0
	(53)	(82)	(37)
Low family, high econ. (Pacific Heights)			
Attendances per year:			
37 or more	28.3	35.6	43.9
5–36	32.6	19.6	17.5
0–4	39.1	44.8	38.6
Total	100.0	100.0	100.0
	(46)	(87)	(57)
High family, low econ. (Outer Mission)			
Attendances per year:			
37 or more	10.4	16.7	16.7
5–36	29.9	37.5	16.7
0–4	59.7	45.8	66.6
Total	100.0	100.0	100.0
	(67)	(72)	(30)
High family, high econ. (St. Francis Wood)			
Attendances per year:			
37 or more	21.4	38.0	53.1
5–36	53.6	33.3	25.0
0–4	25.0	28.7	21.9
Total	100.0	100.0	100.0
	(28)	(108)	(32)

*The numbers on which the percentages are based are given in parentheses.

ship, and somewhat lower proportions in one or more associations. He also found that persons over age 70 in the latter community were more likely to attend five to nine meetings per month.[20]

In addition (see Table 7) the reported relationships between participation and neighborhood still hold within the three different age groups. The largest percentages of men who are frequent attenders live in Pacific Heights and St. Francis Wood, and Pacific Heights has a relatively larger number of men who attend seldom or never than does St. Francis Wood.

SUMMARY

This paper has attempted to relate amount of formal association participation to some of the social types of neighborhoods in which men live and to certain social roles which men occupy. A brief review of the findings follows:

1. Although the four urban neighborhoods studied were widely divergent with respect to economic level and extent of family life, over three-fourths of the men hold membership in at least one formal group, and a relatively small percentage of these are inactive.
2. Men living in the high economic status neighborhoods belong to the greater number of associations, attend more frequently, and hold office more than men living in low economic status neighborhoods.
3. Comparing the two high economic status neighborhoods, the low family status neighborhood contains relatively more men who belong to no formal associations, who never attend meetings if they do belong, and who do not hold office than does the high family status neighborhood. No such relationship appears when comparing the two low economic status neighborhoods.
4. Within each of the neighborhoods persons of higher economic status, as indicated by their own individual educational level, income, and occupation, generally have a greater amount of associational participation than do individuals of lower economic status. However, holding individual economic status constant, persons living in the high economic status neighborhoods still have more associational participation than those living in the low economic status neighborhoods. Thus the economic characteristics of the neighborhood population as a unit may be an important indicator of the economic reference group for those living in the neighborhood, and may define a set of general societal expectations with respect to associational behavior for the residents.
5. It was reported that individual family status characteristics within each of the neighborhoods, such as marital status, age of children, employment

[20]Foskett has recently reported similar findings for two Oregon communities. See John M. Foskett, "Social Structure and Social Participation," *American Sociological Review,* 20 (August, 1955), pp. 431–38.

status of wife, etc., showed no consistent relationship to formal association participation.

6. Finally, the relationship between age roles and associational participation depends upon economic level. In the high economic status neighborhoods the percentage of frequent attenders increases with increasing age, but in the low economic status neighborhoods no such trend exists. In fact, in the latter type of neighborhoods the relationship between age and participation tended to follow the pattern most often reported in other studies with the older aged persons being the most isolated and the middle aged persons the least isolated.

Geographic Mobility and Extended Family Cohesion*
Eugene Litwak

This is the second of two companion papers, both of which seek to demonstrate that *modified* extended family relations are consistent with democratic industrial society.[1] These papers, then, attempt to modify Parson's hypothesis that the isolated nuclear family is the only type which is functional for such a society.[2] Because Parsons so clearly relates his hypothesis to a more general theory of class and business organization there is considerable value in keeping his point of view in the forefront of discussion, for its modification under such circumstances provides rich intellectual dividends.

Parsons assumes only one kind of extended family relational pattern, the "classical" type exemplified in the Polish and Irish peasant families.[3] There is some evidence, however, for the existence of a modified[4] extended family that

*The author wishes to express his thanks to Glenn H. Beyer, Director of the Cornell Housing Research Center for permitting use of the data in this study, and to Paul F. Lazarsfeld, Arthur R. Cohen, and Bernard Barber for their helpful comments, although they are not necessarily in agreement with the author's point of view.

[1]The first paper is Eugene Litwak, "Occupational Mobility and Extended Family Cohesion," *American Sociological Review,* 25 (February, 1960), pp. 9–21.

[2]Talcott Parsons, "The Social Structure of the Family," in Ruth N. Ashen, editor, *The Family: Its Function and Destiny,* New York: Harper, 1949, pp. 191–192.

[3]These families were marked by geographical propinquity, occupational integration, strict authority of extended family over nuclear family, and stress on extended rather than nuclear family relations.

[4]The modified extended family differs from past extended families in that it does not require geographical propinquity, occupational nepotism, or integration, and there are no strict authority relations, but equalitarian ones. Family relations differ from those of the isolated nuclear family in that significant aid is provided to nuclear families, although this aid has to do with standard of living (housing, illness, leisure pursuits) rather than occupational appointments or promotions.

SOURCE: Eugene Litwak, "Geographic Mobility and Extended Family Cohesion," *American Sociological Review,* 25 (June 1960), 385–394. Reprinted by permission.

is theoretically more relevant and empirically more predictive than either of the two alternatives posed by Parsons' hypothesis—the isolated nuclear family and the classical extended family.[5] The present inquiry supplements the earlier paper by demonstrating that modified extended family relations can be maintained despite differential geographical mobility. The first part of this paper examines the assumptions underlying Parsons' point of view as well as the modification suggested herein. In the second part empirical evidence is presented to show that extended family identification can be maintained despite geographical mobility.

GEOGRAPHICAL MOBILITY AND EXTENDED FAMILY ANOMY

There are at least three arguments which support the view that extended family relations are not consistent with geographical mobility: (1) individuals who are strongly attached to their extended families will be reluctant to move even if better jobs are available elsewhere; (2) it is unlikely that identification with extended family will be retained where only one nuclear family moves while the rest of the extended family remains behind; and (3) it is financially more difficult to move a large family and locate jobs for many individuals simultaneously.

The first and third of these propositions suggest that individuals with extended family ties are unlikely to move. The second proposition suggests that if they do move individuals are unlikely to retain their extended family identification with those who remain behind. These arguments can be buttressed by the more general analysis of Homans, who points out that contact is one of the four major prerequisites for primary group cohesion.[6] Since these are familiar arguments they need not be elaborated.

GEOGRAPHICAL MOBILITY AND EXTENDED FAMILY COHESION

In this analysis, major attention is given to propositions which are contrary to those stated above, namely, the following: (1) individuals who are part of a modified extended family grouping are in a better position to move because the latter legitimizes such moves, and as a consequence provides economic, social, and psychological support; (2) extended family relations can be maintained over great geographical distances because modern advances in communication techniques have minimized the socially disruptive effects of geographic distance; and (3) financial difficulties of moving extended families

---

[5]The counter hypothesis advanced in this paper is a modification of Parsons' position in that it accepts his analysis that the classical extended family is disfunctional for contemporary society, but it rejects his view that the isolated nuclear family is the only theoretically meaningful alternative.

[6]George C. Homans, *The Human Group,* New York: Harcourt, Brace, 1950, p. 36.

in a bureaucratic industrialized society are minimized because family coalescence takes place when the family is at its peak earning capacity and when it is least likely to disrupt the industrial organization.

1. *Modified Extended Families Aid Geographical Mobility.* Implicit in the argument that extended family relations lead to a reluctance to move is the view that extended families cannot legitimize geographical mobility. If it can be demonstrated that in current society the contrary is the case, then it can also be shown that such families have far greater facilities than the isolated nuclear family for encouraging spatial movement.

Past instances of legitimation of such movement by the extended family help to clarify the point. In situations of economic or political catastrophe (the Irish potato famine or the Russian pogroms), the extended family encouraged mobility. Given this type of situation, the extended family had at least two advantages over the isolated nuclear family. First, its greater numbers permitted easier accumulation of capital to finance the trip of any given nuclear family. This led to a push and pull kind of migration, with the migrant sending money to help those who had remained behind. Secondly, because of its close ties and size the extended family had superior lines of communication. Thus the migrant became a communication outpost for those who remained behind, providing information on jobs, housing, local social customs, and language. Those who had migrated earlier also could aid the newcomer at the most difficult point of migration.[7]

In a mature industrial society there is great institutional pressure on the extended family to legitimate differential geographical mobility among its nuclear family members. This pressure derives from the fact that the extended family can never fully control the economic destiny of its nuclear sub-parts. Although the extended family provides important aid, the major source of economic support for the nuclear family must come from its own occupational success, which is based much more on merit than nepotism. As a consequence, if the extended family wants to see its member nuclear families become successful, it must accept one of the chief prerequisites to occupational success— geographical mobility.[8]

In other words, it is postulated that a semi-independent relation links the nuclear family to the extended family. Because the extended family cannot offer a complete guarantee of occupational success it legitimates the moves of nuclear family members. On the other hand, receiving as it does significant aid

[7]Of the large literature on this point, see e.g., Walter Firey, *Land Use in Central Boston,* Cambridge: Harvard University Press, 1947, pp. 184–186.

[8]C. Wright Mills, C. Senior, and R. K. Goldsen in the *Puerto Rican Journey,* New York: Harper, 1950, p. 51, provide some indirect evidence on legitimation when they point out that the Puerto Rican migrant rarely moves out of a sense of economic necessity but because of a desire for economic betterment. They also show that these migrants rely on extended family communications before migrating (pp. 53–55). These facts illustrate that for the lowest income strata of migrants there has been a legitimation of geographical mobility for maximizing goals. This would seem to be doubly true of the middle-class migrant since he is economically better off to start with.

in achieving many of its goals, the nuclear family retains its extended family connections despite geographical distance.

2. *Extended Family Identification Is Retained Despite Breaks in Face-To-Face Contact.* There are two reasons why extended families can provide important supplements to nuclear family goal achievement despite geographical distance and therefore two reasons why extended family identification can be maintained despite breaks in face-to-face contact.[9] As noted above, the rapid development of techniques of communication has made it relatively easy for family members to keep contact despite great distances. Nor does distance, in a money economy, prevent or seriously hinder such aids to family members as help in times of illness, emergency loans or gifts, home purchase, and the like—all at long range.

3. *Geographical Coalescence Takes Place at Peaks of Earning Power.* Although the extended family encourages mobility when it is occupationally rewarding, it does not do so when such moves no longer bring rewards. Given the character of large-scale organizations, there are regular occasions when geographical mobility is not linked to occupational rewards, for example, when the individual is at the peak of his career. The career in the large organization is one in which the individual moves up until he reaches a position from which he can no longer advance; here he remains until he retires. Careers of bureaucrats are rarely downward. Two aspects of this situation are particularly important in the present context: (1) once a person has advanced as far as he can occupationally his working efficiency is no longer tied to geographic moves; and (2) it is at this point that the nuclear family is in the best economic position to support moves of extended family. At this period of his life, the careerist can seek a position near his extended family if he can find a job which matches his present one. Or he can encourage retired parents to settle near him. In short, it is suggested that when the extended family does coalesce it does not lead to undue financial strain (trying to locate jobs for many people simultaneously), nor is it likely to mean an irrational distribution of labor since it involves either retired people or job exchanges between people on the same occupational level.

FINDINGS

In order to test alternative propositions about the relationship between family structure and geographical mobility, data from a survey of 920 white

---

[9]In addition to these assumptions, two more general ones should be made. First, it is assumed (in counter-distinction to W. F. Ogburn, for example, in "The Changing Functions of the Family," *Selected Studies in Marriage and the Family,* New York: Henry Holt, 1953, pp. 74–75) that extended families have not lost their functions. See Litwak, *op. cit.* Secondly, it is assumed that extensive family activity does not lead to occupational nepotism *(ibid.);* but Parsons' hypothesis states that extended family structures will collapse, or nepotism will destroy the industrial order.

married women living in the Buffalo, New York, urban area were analyzed. The sample is biased in the direction of white, younger, middle-class, native-born individuals and as such is not representative of the total population.[10] However, the bias is a useful one since this is the very group which should most likely illustrate Parsons' hypothesis.[11] If it can be shown that his hypothesis does not hold for this group, then it is unlikely to hold for any division of the society.

1. *Mobility Reduces Extended Family Face-To-Face Contact.* The common basis for the opposing views—that geographical mobility is or is not antithetical to extended family relations—should be made explicit so that it is not mistaken for the main issue. Both positions are in agreement that geographical mobility generally reduces extended family face-to-face contact. Of the respondents in this study, 52 per cent with relatives living in the city received one or more family visits a week. In contrast, only four per cent of those with no such nearby relatives received visits this frequently.

2. *Breaks in Face-To-Face Contact Do Not Reduce Extended Family Identification.* Central to the argument advanced in this paper is the view that geographical distance between relatives does not necessarily lead to a loss of extended family identification. In order to measure family orientation, all individuals were asked to respond to the following statements: (1) "Generally I like the whole family to spend evenings together." (2) "I want a house where family members can spend time together." (3) "I want a location which would make it easy for relatives to get together." (4) "I want a house with enough room for our parents to feel free to move in." These items formed a Guttman scale pattern.[12] Individuals who answered items 3 or 4 positively[13] were considered to be oriented toward the extended family. Those who answered items 1

[10]The field study was conducted in the Buffalo area between June and October, 1952. For details of the study and the sampling, see Glenn H. Beyer, Thomas W. Mackesey, and James E. Montgomery, *Houses Are for People: A Study of Home Buyer Motivations,* Ithaca: Cornell University Housing Research Center, 1955. Some special features of the sample should be noted here. The sample cannot be considered to be a random one. Being a study designed to investigate housing, five or six different sampling procedures based on neighborhood and housing design were used. The varied nature of the sample complicates the problem of the appropriate statistical test. Therefore the argument must rest heavily on its theoretical plausibility and its consistency with other relevant studies. However, if the assumptions of a random area sample are made, and the sign and Wilcoxon signed-ranks tests are used, then all major findings are significant at the .05 level and beyond. The signs for these tests were always taken from the most complex table in which the given variables appeared.

[11]Parsons, *op. cit.,* pp. 180–181.

[12]Although these items were dichotomized to form a Guttman scale pattern, it is not argued that they meet all of the requirements for such a scale. See Eugene Litwak, *Primary Group Instruments of Social Control in Industrial Society: The Extended Family and the Neighborhood,* unpublished Ph.D. thesis, Columbia University, 1958, pp. 43–47.

[13]The fact that only four per cent of the population answered item 4 positively means that item 3 defines extended family orientation for most of the population. In this connection, no assumption is made that this operational definition exhausts the meaning of extended family orientation; it is only assumed that it will correlate highly with any other measures of extended family orientation.

or 2, but not 3 or 4, positively were considered to be nuclear family oriented. Those who answered none[14] of the questions positively were classified as non-family oriented.

In order to measure the effects of distance between relatives on family identification, all respondents were divided into two categories, those who had relatives living in town and those who did not. The data presented in Table 1 indicate that geographical distance does not mean a loss of identity. Those who are geographically distant from their relatives are as likely as those who live nearby to retain their extended family identification (22 and 20 per cent, respectively).

Table 1 very likely underestimates the relationship between mobility and extended family identification, since there may have been many individuals who either moved to the community because their relatives lived there or encouraged relatives to come later. In such cases family identification would

TABLE 1. GEOGRAPHICAL DISTANCE DOES NOT LEAD TO A LOSS OF EXTENDED FAMILY IDENTIFICATION

	Percentage Extended Family Oriented	Percentage Nuclear Family Oriented	Percentage Non-Family Oriented	Total
Relatives living in town	20	52	28	100 (643)*
Relatives living out of town	22	58	20	100 (272)

*In this and the following tables the figures in parentheses indicate the population base for a given percentage. For tests of significance in these tables, see Footnote 10.

have been maintained initially despite geographical distance. To deal with this question, all respondents again were divided, this time between those who spent their first 20 years in the city under study and those who were raised elsewhere. If the latter are considered to be migrants, it can be seen from Table 2 that the migrants (23 per cent) are more likely than the non-migrants (18 per cent) to be identified with their extended families.

3. *Close Identification with Extended Family Does Not Prevent Nuclear Families from Moving Away.* Are people who are close to their extended families likely to leave them in order to advance themselves occupationally? To measure the likelihood of persons moving from the community for occupational reasons, the respondents were asked the following question: "Is there a good chance that your husband might take a job out of town?" Those who

[14]Because some people may have interpreted "family" to mean only extended family, it is possible that in this non-family oriented group there are some people who are nuclear family oriented. This plus the fact that the items were dichotomized to maximize their scaling properties suggests that little reliance should be placed on the absolute percentage of people exhibiting each value position but only on their differential distribution in various groups.

TABLE 2. MIGRANTS ARE NOT LESS EXTENDED FAMILY IDENTIFIED THAN NON-MIGRANTS

	Percentage Extended Family Oriented	Percentage Nuclear Family Oriented	Percentage Non-Family Oriented	Total
Spent major part of first 20 years in city	18	51	31	100 (504)
Spent major part of first 20 years out of the city	23	56	21	100 (416)

answered "yes" were classified as potential migrants. To test the likelihood of leaving their relatives, only respondents with relatives in town were examined. It can be seen from Table 3 that those individuals more closely identified with the extended family also were more likely to leave the city and presumably their nearby relatives (23 and 14 per cent, respectively).

TABLE 3. STRONG IDENTIFICATION WITH RELATIVES DOES NOT PREVENT PEOPLE FROM TAKING JOBS ELSEWHERE

	Among Those with Relatives in the City the Percentage Saying Good Chance Husband Will Take Job Out of Town
Extended family orientation	23 (128)
Nuclear family orientation	18 (336)
Non-family orientation	14 (184)

The same point can be made for the general population if the figures from Tables 1 and 2 are calculated to show how likely family oriented persons are to be migrants. Table 4 presents results which are consistent with Table 3. People are likely to move, then, even when they are strongly identified with their families, and once having moved away from them, they are likely to retain their family identity.

TABLE 4. PEOPLE IDENTIFIED WITH EXTENDED FAMILY ARE AS LIKELY OR MORE LIKELY TO BE MIGRANTS THAN OTHERS

	Percentage Raised Out of Town	Percentage Having No Relatives in the City
Extended family oriented	51 (187)	32 (187)
Nuclear family oriented	47 (493)	31 (493)
Non-family oriented	37 (240)	23 (240)

4. *Bureaucratic Career and Extended Family Mobility.* The analysis is thus far consistent with the view that in modern bureaucratic society extended family relations can retain their viability despite differential rates of geographic mobility. To be fully consistent, however, it should be shown that extended family movement is related to career development in the way anticipated by the foregoing discussion. For it was pointed out that it is only when the individual is on the upswing of his career that mobility will be encouraged, while it will be discouraged when he reaches the peak.

In order to measure career stages individuals were asked: "Within the next ten years, do you expect the head of the household will be making: a. a great deal more than now; b. somewhat more than now; c. same as now; d. other, e.g., retired, don't know, etc." Those who said that they expected to earn "a great deal more" income were assumed to be on the upswing of their careers, those who named "somewhat more" were assumed to be fast approaching the peak, while all others were assumed to have reached the peak or plateau of their careers.[15] Table 5 confirms the view that bureaucratic development is congenial to family movement when people are upwardly mobile: 39 per cent of those on the upswing were migrants, while only 16 per cent of those who had reached their career plateaus were migrants.

TABLE 5. THOSE ON THE UPSWING OF THEIR CAREER ARE LIKELY TO BE MIGRANTS

	Within the Next Ten Years	*Percentage Without Relatives Living in the City*
Upswing of career	Expect to make a great deal more than now	39 (183)
Medium point	Expect to make somewhat more than now	29 (603)
Peak of career or plateau	Expect to make the same or somewhat less than now	16 (134)

Two additional bits of evidence supplement this point. First, if the hypothesis advanced in this paper is correct, the individuals who are both extended family oriented and rising in their careers should be most mobile because they have the advantage of aid from their extended families. Comparatively speaking, extended family identity should not lead to mobility when individuals have reached the career plateau. Table 6 suggests that this is the case. When individuals are moving ahead occupationally, those who are psychologically close to their families are much more mobile than those who dissociate them-

[15] Since 95 per cent of the sample subjects were 45 or younger, and since the study was conducted during a period of great prosperity, virtually no one said he expected to earn less than now.

TABLE 6. EXTENDED FAMILY IDENTIFICATION IS LIKELY TO ENCOURAGE GEOGRAPHICAL MOBILITY WHEN INDIVIDUALS ARE ON THE UPSWING OF THEIR CAREERS

Within the Next Ten Years	Percentage Having No Relatives in the City		
	Extended Family Oriented	Nuclear Family Oriented	Non-Family Oriented
Upswing of career: Expect to make a great deal more than now	47 (49)*	40 (107)	22 (27)
Medium point of career: Expect to make somewhat more than now	30 (112)	31 (322)	27 (169)
Peak or plateau of career: Expect to make the same or less than now	12 (26)	22 (63)	11 (45)

*This cell reads as follows: 47 per cent of the 49 people who are extended family oriented and who expect to make a great deal more in the future have no relatives in the city.

selves from their families (47 and 22 per cent, respectively, are mobile). In contrast, among people at the career peak, the extended family oriented are no more mobile than the non-family oriented (12 and 11 per cent, respectively).

The second bit of evidence which supports the view that extended family aid encourages mobility on the upswing of the career and discourages it otherwise involves the direction of the move. Individuals who have reached the career plateau *might possibly* still move if such moves meant bringing them closer to their extended family. To investigate this possibility, respondents were asked: "Compared to your last house is your present house closer, the same, or farther away from your family?" Table 7 shows that where individuals are climbing the ladder they are as likely, if not more likely, to move away from their relatives when they are identified with their extended families as when they are not (53 per cent as compared to 37 and 48 per cent). However, where individuals have reached the occupational plateau, those who are identified with their extended families are less likely to move away from them (38 per cent as compared to 62 and 53 per cent).

In short, the evidence presented here indicates that the career strongly influences the extent and the direction of geographical mobility in a manner consistent with the view that extended family relations are viable in contemporary bureaucratic society.

5. *Bureaucratic and Non-Bureaucratic Careers.* This index of career, however, does not necessarily imply a *bureaucratic* career. Earlier discussions often assume that careers take place in a bureaucratic context. Therefore, the findings of this study should be further differentiated in terms of bureaucratic and non-bureaucratic occupations. In order to isolate the non-bureaucratic career, working-class persons whose fathers were also from a working-class occupational group were segregated from the rest of the population. Non-manual middle-class and upper-class individuals are more likely to follow bureaucratic careers, involving standard promotional steps associated with geographical mobility.[16]

[16]On the basis of the U. S. Census's occupational categories, the husband and the husband's father were classified into: (1) professional, technical, and kindred, and managers, officials, and proprietors; (2) clerical and kindred workers, and sales workers; or (3) all others except farmers or farm help. Husbands' and husbands' fathers' occupations were cross classified to provide four occupational categories: (1) upper-class husbands whose parents were upper-class; (2) husbands whose parents were from a higher occupational group; (3) husbands whose parents were from a lower occupational group; (4) working-class husbands whose parents were working-class. Two groups were eliminated: all individuals of farm background; and middle-class individuals of middle-class parentage (excluded because of the small number of cases). The stationary upper-class group is considered to approximate most closely the bureaucratic occupations, while the stationary manual groups are assumed to be the polar opposite. Here "upper-class" does not refer to an old-line "aristocracy" but to a professional-managerial occupational grouping. By definition, all people in administrative positions in large-scale organizations and professionals are included in the upper-class or upwardly mobile occupational groups. There remains the question of whether or not they constitute a sufficiently large number within the overall classification to give a distinct direction. Gold and Slater in a study based upon a random sample of the Detroit area point out that in the one category roughly similar in age and occupation to the "upper-class" in this investigation, 74 per cent of the individuals were members of a bureaucratic organization. Martin Gold and Carol Slater, "Office, Factory, Store—and Family: A Study of Integration Setting," *American Sociological Review,* 23 (February, 1958), pp. 66, 69.

TABLE 7. EXTENDED FAMILY IDENTIFICATION IS LIKELY TO ENCOURAGE MOVES* AWAY FROM THE EXTENDED FAMILY WHEN PEOPLE ARE ON THE UPSWING OF THEIR CAREERS

	Percentage Whose Last Move Carried Them Farther from Their Families		
	Extended Family Oriented	Nuclear Family Oriented	Non-Family Oriented
Expect to make a great deal more in 10 years	53 (49)**	37 (67)	48 (27)
Expect to make somewhat more	52 (112)	56 (322)	59 (169)
Expect to make the same or less	38 (26)	62 (63)	53 (45)

*Those with relatives in the city were classified together with those without relatives, since the same statistical pattern occurred in each case.
**This figure reads 53 per cent of 49 people who were extended family oriented and who expected to earn a great deal more in the next ten years moved farther away from their families.

In contrast, these features do not necessarily mark occupational advancement among manual workers. In this group occupational success may mean the achievement of plant seniority or the opening of a small business.[17] In such cases success is negatively related to future geographic mobility. As a consequence, a manual worker who envisions an upswing in his career may encourage family members to settle nearby because future success is closely linked to present location. Thus, it is expected that occupational advance has far different meanings for members of the working class and for the middle- and upper-class persons.

In Table 8 it can be seen that the only instances of upswings in careers leading to geographic mobility occur among members of the upper class (43 per cent of those who are on the upswing have no relatives in the community compared to 23 per cent of those who have achieved a plateau). For members of the stationary working class, occupational advancement is least likely, comparatively speaking, to result in geographical mobility (10 per cent of those on the upswing and 12 per cent of those on the plateau have relatives in the city).

Table 8 more than any other should indicate the limitations of the present hypothesis. The latter cannot claim to explain any major features of current American society but only the behavior of members of that group which is often thought to be prototypical of future American society—those belonging to bureaucratic occupations. It is assumed here that future societies will in fact become increasingly bureaucratized. Since Parsons' analysis is largely concerned with this same group,[18] it is maintained that this study provides evidence contrary to his hypothesis.

6. *The Extended Family and Emotional, Social, and Economic Aid.* Extended families have a unique function in providing aid to those who are moving. This is based partly on the fact that family membership is defined in terms of blood ties and therefore is least pervious to changes in social contact, and partly on the fact that the individual receives his earliest and crucial socialization with people who eventually become extended family members. The individual might find voluntary associations of lesser help than family aid, because new personal contacts must be established when one moves, and old contacts tend to have no continuing meaning when geographical contact is broken. Aid from neighbors has somewhat the same character. This point emerges clearly when newcomers to a neighborhood are compared with long-term residents in terms of the average amount of social participation in various areas of life. Table 9 shows that family contacts are as likely, if not more likely, to occur among newcomers than among long-term residents. In contrast, neighborhood and club affiliations are likely to increase the longer individuals

[17]See, e.g., Seymour Martin Lipset and Reinhard Bendix, "Social Mobility and Occupational Career Patterns," in Bendix and Lipset, editors, *Class, Status and Power,* Glencoe, Ill.: Free Press, 1953, pp. 457–459.
[18]Parsons, *op. cit.,* pp. 180–181.

TABLE 8. ONLY AMONG UPPER- AND MIDDLE-CLASS BUREAUCRATIC OCCUPATIONS DO CAREER LINES PLAY A ROLE

	Percentage Having No Relatives in the City			
Within the Next Ten Years	Stationary Upper-Class*	Upwardly Mobile	Downwardly Mobile	Stationary Manual Workers
Upswing of career Expect to make a great deal more than now	43 (76)**	39 (72)	40 (25)	10 (10)
Medium point of career Expect to make somewhat more than now	42 (146)	39 (183)	26 (99)	11 (176)
Peak or plateau of career Expect to make the same or less than now	23 (26)	13 (32)	28 (18)	12 (58)

*For a definition of occupational classification, see footnote 16.
**This cell should read as follows: 43 per cent of the 76 people who were stationary upper-class and who had high expectations of future economic improvement had no relatives in the city.

live in the neighborhood.[19] This suggests the unique function of the extended family during the moving crisis.

TABLE 9. THE EXTENDED FAMILY MEETS THE NEEDS OF RECENT MOVERS[a]

	Percentage Receiving Frequent Family Visits[b]	Percentage Belonging to More Than One Club[c]	Percentage Knowing Five or More Neighbors[d]	Total Population
Respondents Having No Relatives in the City				
Newcomers	22	25	38	110
Long-term residents	16	51	63	166
Difference	08	−26	−25	
Respondents Having Relatives in the City				
Newcomers	54	44	41	163
Long-term residents	49	43	60	485
Difference	05	01	−19	

[a]The respondents were divided between the newcomers or those people who had lived in their houses nine months or less and the long-term residents or all others.

[b]When no relatives in the city a frequent visit is defined as one or more family visits a month —either invited or non-invited. When relatives live in the city a frequent visit is defined as one or more family visits a week.

[c]This is the closest approximation to the average number of clubs to which the population belonged.

[d]This is the closest approximation to the average number of neighbors the respondents knew well enough to call on.

SECONDARY EVIDENCE

The evidence presented above consistently documents the position that extended family relations are not antithetical to geographical mobility in bureaucratic industrialized society. In fact, at times such relationships actually encourage mobility. The limits of the sample, however, place severe restrictions on the general application of these data. It is of some importance, therefore, to seek in other researches supportive evidence for extended family viability.

[19]The striking differences between respondents with relatives living in the city and those without nearby relatives, shown in Table 9, are discussed in an unpublished paper, Eugene Litwak, "Voluntary Associations and Primary Group Development in Industrial Society."

First, as a necessary but not sufficient condition, it should be shown that extended family relations are fairly extensive in American society today. In recent years, four studies that provide data on extended family visiting have been carried out, respectively, in Los Angeles, Detroit, San Francisco, and Buffalo. Three of these indicate that close to 50 per cent of the residents made one or more such visits a week. And three of the four investigations, on the basis of comparisons of family, neighbors, friends, and voluntary associations, conclude that the family relationships were either the most frequent or the most vital. These findings, as limited as they are, strongly suggest that extended family relations are extensive.[20]

What is of even greater interest is that these studies indicate that middle-class white persons share this viability with others and that these relations are highly important ones. Thus Sussman, in a study of middle-class white Protestant families, shows that 80 per cent of the family relationships studied involved giving aid, and in 70 per cent of the cases respondents felt that the recipients would suffer loss of status if the aid were not continued. Moreover, this aid had much more to do with standard of living than with locating jobs or helping people to advance in them through nepotism.[21] This investigation was supplemented by a study by Bell and Boat which indicates that 76 per cent of the low income and 84 per cent of the high income subjects could count on extended family aid in cases of illness lasting a month or longer; they also report that 90 per cent of the respondents indicated that at least one member of the extended family was a close friend.[22] Studies on working class families,[23] Puerto Rican families,[24] Negro families,[25] and Italian families[26] indicate that extended family relations in these cases are viable and warm.

Although these relations are of a far different character from the middle-class family contacts discussed in this paper,[27] the studies of working-class and ethnic groups do provide insight into the extension and warmth of extended family relations in all strata of contemporary society. They do not by themselves refute Parsons' formulation because he assumes that extended family

[20]Morris Axelrod, "Urban Structure and Social Participation," *American Sociological Review,* 21 (February, 1956), pp. 13–18; Wendell Bell and Marion D. Boat, "Urban Neighborhoods and Informal Social Relations," *American Journal of Sociology,* 62 (January, 1957), pp. 391–398; Scott Greer, "Urbanism Reconsidered," *American Sociological Review,* 21 (February, 1956), p. 22; Litwak, *Primary Group Instruments . . . , op. cit.,* p. 82.

[21]Marvin B. Sussman, "The Help Pattern in Middle Class Family," *American Sociological Review,* 18 (February, 1953), pp. 22–28 *passim.*

[22]Bell and Boat, *op. cit.,* p. 396.

[23]Michael Young and Peter Willmott, *Family and Kinship in East London,* London: Routledge and Kegan Paul, 1957, pp. 159–166.

[24]Mills, Senior, and Goldsen, *op. cit.,* pp. 115, 117.

[25]E. Franklin Frazier, "The Impact of Urban Civilization Upon Negro Family Life," P. K. Hatt and A. S. Reiss, Jr., editors, *Cities and Societies: The Revised Reader in Urban Sociology,* Glencoe, Ill.: Free Press, 1957, pp. 495–496.

[26]Firey, *op. cit.,* pp. 184–186.

[27]Cf. Litwak, "Occupational Mobility and Extended Family Cohesion," *op. cit.*

relations are declining, not that they have disappeared. However, they buttress the alternative hypothesis advanced here since they do suggest a basic prerequisite of that hypothesis, namely, that extended family relations are viable in contemporary urban society.

CONCLUSIONS

It is argued, then, that these relations can retain their social significance under industrial bureaucratic pressures for geographical mobility. Evidence has been presented that is inconsistent with Parsons' hypothesis. Two theoretical points support this contrary view: first, that the extended family relationship which does not demand geographical propinquity (not examined by Parsons) is a significant form of social behavior; second, that theoretically the most efficient organization combines the ability of large-scale bureaucracy to handle uniform situations with the primary group's ability to deal with idiosyncratic situations. These two theoretical points suggest that there is both a need and a capacity for extended families to exist in modern society.

The data presented here (and in the earlier companion paper) demonstrate that persons separated from their families retained their extended family orientation; those with close family identification were as likely, if not more likely, to leave their family for occupational reasons; those on the upswing of their careers were apt to move away from their families and to receive family support; those on the career plateau were not likely to move or to move toward their family; that considerations of this kind hold only for bureaucratic occupations; and that the modified extended family seems to be uniquely suited to provide succor during periods of movement. These findings suggest interesting questions for future research. With respect to the family system, there is a need to isolate the mechanisms by which the nuclear family retains its semi-independence while receiving aid from the extended family.[28] It is also important to specify in greater detail the limits of the modified extended family organization in terms of time (does it extend over two or three generations?) and social distance (is it limited, for example, to parents and married children or siblings?). Concerning the occupational system, it is important to identify the type of bureaucratic structure which permits the family to be linked with occupations without affecting productivity.[29] For the analysis of class structure, the question arises as to how likely it is that extended family relations become significant factors blurring class identification without reducing occupational mobility.

[28]Cf. Eugene Litwak, "The Use of Extended Family Groups in the Achievement of Social Goals: Some Policy Implications," *Social Problems,* forthcoming.

[29]Cf. Litwak, "Occupational Mobility and Extended Family Cohesion," *op. cit.;* and *Primary Group Instruments . . . , op. cit.,* pp. 6–30.

Some Sources of Residential Satisfaction in an Urban Slum

Marc Fried and Peggy Gleicher

The gradual deterioration of older urban dwellings and the belief that such areas provide a locus for considerable social pathology have stimulated concern with altering the physical habitat of the slum. Yet the technical difficulties, the practical inadequacies, and the moral problems of such planned revisions of the human environment are also forcing themselves upon our attention most strikingly.[1] While a full evaluation of the advantages and disadvantages of urban renewal must await studies which derive from various disciplines, there is little likelihood that the vast sums currently available will be withheld until there is a more systematic basis for rational decisions. Thus it is of the utmost importance that we discuss all aspects of the issue as thoroughly as possible and make available even the more fragmentary findings which begin to clarify the many unsolved problems.

Since the most common foci of urban renewal are areas which have been designated as slums, it is particularly important to obtain a clearer picture of so-called slum areas and their populations. Slum areas undoubtedly show much variation, both variation from one slum to another and heterogeneity within urban slum areas. However, certain consistencies from one slum area to another have begun to show up in the growing body of literature. It is quite notable that the available systematic studies of slum areas indicate a very broad working-class composition in slums, ranging from highly skilled workers to the nonworking and sporadically working members of the "working" class. Moreover, even in our worst residential slums it is likely that only a minority of the inhabitants (although sometimes a fairly large and visible minority) are afflicted with one or another form of social pathology. Certainly the idea that social pathology in any form is decreased by slum clearance finds little support in the available data. The belief that poverty, delinquency, prostitution, and alcoholism magically inhere in the buildings of slums and will die with the demolition of the slum has a curious persistence but can hardly provide adequate justification for the vast enterprise of renewal planning.

[1]Herbert Gans. "The Human Implications of Current Redevelopment and Relocation Planning." *Journal of the American Institute of Planners,* Vol. 25, No. 1 (February 1959), pp. 15–25.

SOURCE: Marc Fried and Peggy Gleicher, "Some Sources of Residential Satisfaction in an Urban Slum," *Journal of the American Institute of Planners,* 27 (November 1961), 305–315. Reprinted by permission of the *Journal of the American Institute of Planners.*

In a larger social sense, beyond the political and economic issues involved, planning for urban renewal has important human objectives. Through such planning we wish to make available to a larger proportion of the population some of the advantages of modern urban facilities, ranging from better plumbing and decreased fire hazards to improved utilization of local space and better neighborhood resources. These values are all on the side of the greater good for the greatest number. Yet it is all too apparent that we know little enough about the meaning and consequences of differences in physical environment either generally or for specific groups. Urban renewal may lead, directly and indirectly, to improved housing for slum residents. But we cannot evaluate the larger effects of relocation or its appropriateness without a more basic understanding than we now have of the meaning of the slum's physical and social environment. This report is an initial essay toward understanding the issue. We shall consider some of the factors that give meaning to the residential environment of the slum dweller. Although the meaning of the environment to the resident of a slum touches only one part of the larger problem, it is critical that we understand this if we are to achieve a more effectively planned and designed urban environment.[2]

II. THE SIGNIFICANCE OF THE SLUM ENVIRONMENT

People do not like to be dispossessed from their dwellings, and every renewal project that involves relocation can anticipate considerable resistance, despite the best efforts to insure community support.[3] It is never quite clear whether most people object mainly to being forced to do something they have not voluntarily elected to do; or whether they simply object to relocation, voluntary or involuntary. There is, of course, considerable evidence for the commitment of slum residents to their habitat. Why this should be so is less clear and quite incomprehensible in the face of all middle-class residential values. In order to evaluate the issue more closely we shall consider the problem of the meaning and functional significance of residence in a slum area. Although we are primarily concerned with a few broadly applicable generalizations, a complete analysis will take better account of the diversities in the composition of slum populations.

[2]This is one of a series of reports on the meaning and significance of various aspects of working-class life. This group of studies will provide a basis for a subsequent analysis of the impact of relocation through a comparison of the pre-relocation and the post-relocation situation. The population of the original area was predominantly white, of mixed ethnic composition (mainly Italian, Polish, and Jewish). The many ethnic differences do not vitiate the larger generalizations of this study.

[3]This does not seem limited to contemporary relocation situations. Firey reports a similar phenomenon in Boston during the nineteenth century. Walter Firey, *Land Use in Central Boston* (Cambridge: Harvard University Press, 1947).

The fact that more than half the respondents in our sample[4] have a long-standing experience of familiarity with the area in which they lived before relocation suggests a very basic residential stability. Fifty-five per cent of the sample first moved to or were born in the West End approximately 20 years ago or more. Almost one fourth of the entire sample was born in the West End. Not only is there marked residential stability within the larger area of the West End, but the total rate of movement from one dwelling unit to another has been exceedingly low. Table 1 gives the distribution of movement from one dwelling unit to another within the ten years prior to the interview. It is readily evident that the largest proportion of the sample has made very few moves indeed. In fact, a disproportionate share of the frequent moves is made by a small group of relatively high-status people, largely professional and semiprofessional people who were living in the West End only temporarily. Regardless of which criterion we use, these data indicate that we cannot readily accept those impressions of a slum which suggest a highly transient population. An extremely large proportion shows unusual residential stability, and this is quite evenly distributed among the several levels of working-class occupational groups.

TABLE 1. NUMBERS OF MOVES IN PREVIOUS TEN YEARS

Moves	Number	Per cent
Totals	473	100
None	162	34
One	146	31
Two	73	15
Three or more	86	19
No answer	6	1

The Slum Environment as Home

What are the sources of this residential stability? Undoubtedly they are many and variable, and we could not hope to extricate the precise contribution of each factor. Rents were certainly low. If we add individually expended heating costs to the rental figures reported we find that 25 per cent were paying $34 a month or less, and 85 per cent paying $54 a month or less. But though

[4]These data are based on a probability sample of residents from the West End of Boston interviewed during 1958–1959. The sampling criteria included only households in which there was a female household member between the ages of 20 and 65. The present analysis is based on the pre-relocation data from the female respondents. Less systematic pre-relocation data on the husbands are also available, as well as systematic post-relocation data for both wives and husbands and women without husbands.

this undoubtedly played a role as a background factor, it can hardly account for the larger findings. Low rental costs are rarely mentioned in discussing aspects of the West End or of the apartment that were sources of satisfaction. And references to the low West End rents are infrequent in discussing the sources of difficulty which people expected in the course of moving. In giving reasons for having moved to the last apartment they occupied before relocation, only 12 per cent gave any type of economic reason (including decreased transportation costs as well as low rents). Thus, regardless of the practical importance that low rents must have had for a relatively low income population, they were not among the most salient aspects of the perceived issues in living in the West End.

On the other hand, there is considerable evidence to indicate that living in the West End had particular meaning for a vast majority of West End residents. Table 2 shows the distribution in response to the question, "How do you feel about living in the West End?", clearly indicating how the West End was a focus for very positive sentiments.

That the majority of West Enders do not remain in or come back to the West End simply because it is practical (inexpensive, close to facilities) is further documented by the responses of the question, "Which neighborhood, this one or any other place, do you think of as your real home, that is where you feel you really belong?" It is quite striking that fully 71 per cent of the people named the West End as their real home, only slightly less than the proportion who specify liking the West End or liking it very much. Although there is a strong relationship between liking the West End and viewing it as home, 14 per cent of those who view the West End as home have moderately or markedly negative feelings about the area. On the other hand, 50 per cent of those who do not regard the West End as home have moderately or markedly positive feelings about the area. Thus, liking the West End is not contingent on experiencing the area as that place in which one most belongs. However, the responses to this item give us an even more basic and global sense of the meaning the West End had for a very large proportion of its inhabitants.

TABLE 2. FEELINGS ABOUT THE WEST END

Feelings	Number	Per cent	
Totals	473	100	
Like very well	174	37	75
Like	183	38	
Mixed like-dislike	47	10	14
Indifferent	18	4	
Dislike	25	5	10
Dislike very much	23	5	
No answer	3	1	

These responses merely summarize a group of sentiments that pervade the interviews, and they form the essential context for understanding more discrete meanings and functions of the area. There are clearly differences in the details, but the common core lies in a widespread feeling of belonging someplace, of being "at home" in a region that extends out from but well beyond the dwelling unit. Nor is this only because of familiarity, since a very large proportion of the more recent residents (64 per cent of those who moved into the West End during 1950 or after) also showed clearly positive feelings about the area. And 39 per cent of those who moved in during 1950 or after regard the West End as their real home.[5]

Types of Residential "Belonging"

Finer distinctions in the quality and substance of positive feelings about the West End reveal a number of variations. In categorizing the qualitative aspects of responses to two questions which were analyzed together ("How do you feel about living in the West End?" and "What will you miss most about the West End?"), we distinguished three broad differences of emphasis among the positive replies. The three large categories are: (1) *integral belonging:* sense of *exclusive* commitment, taking West End for granted as home, thorough familiarity and security; (2) *global commitment:* sense of profound gratification (rather than familiarity), pleasure in West End and enjoyment; and (3) *discrete satisfaction:* specific satisfying or pleasurable opportunities or atmosphere involving no special commitment to *this* place.

Only a small proportion (13 per cent) express their positive feelings in terms of logically irreplaceable ties to people and places. They do so in often stark and fundamental ways: this is my home; it's all I know; everyone I know is here; I won't leave. A larger group (38 per cent) are less embedded and take the West End less for granted but, nonetheless, express an all-encompassing involvement with the area which few areas are likely to provide them again. Their replies point up a less global but poignant sense of loss: it's one big happy family; I'll be sad; we were happy here; it's so friendly; it's handy to everything and everyone is congenial and friendly. The largest group (40 per cent) are yet further removed from a total commitment but, in spite of the focused and discrete nature of their satisfaction with the interpersonal atmosphere or the convenience of the area, remain largely positive in feeling.

Differences in Foci of Positive Feelings

Thus, there is considerable variability in the depth and type of feeling implied by liking the West End; and the West End as home had different

---

[5]It is possible, of course, that we have obtained an exaggerated report of positive feelings about the area because of the threat of relocation. Not only does the consistency of the replies and their internal relationships lead us to believe that this has not caused a major shift in response, but, bearing in mind the relative lack of verbal facility of many of the respondents and their frequent tendencies to give brief replies, we suspect that the interview data often lead to underestimating the strength of sentiment.

connotations for different people. For a large group, the West End as home seems to have implied a comfortable and satisfying base for moving out into the world and back. Among this group, in fact, the largest proportion were more concerned with accessibility to other places than with the locality itself. But for more than half the people, their West End homes formed a far more central feature of their total life space.

There is a difference within this larger group between a small number for whom the West End seems to have been the place *to* which they belonged and a larger number for whom it seems rather to have been the place *in* which they belonged. But for the larger group as a whole the West End occupied a unique status, beyond any of the specific attributes one could list and point to concretely. This sense of uniqueness, of home, was not simply a function of social relationships, for the place in itself was the object of strong positive feelings. Most people (42 per cent) specify both people and places or offer a global, encompassing reason for their positive feelings. But almost an equally small proportion (13 per cent and 10 per cent, respectively) select out people or places as the primary objects of positive experience.

With respect to the discrete foci for positive feelings, similar conclusions can be drawn from another question: "Which places do you mostly expect to miss when you leave the West End?" In spite of the place-orientation of the question, 16 per cent specify some aspect of interpersonal loss as the most prominent issue. But 40 per cent expect to miss one of the places which is completely identified with the area or, minimally, carries a specific local identity. The sense of the West End as a local region, as an area with a spatial identity going beyond (although it may include) the social relationships involved, is a common perception. In response to the question: "Do you think of your home in the West End as part of a local neighborhood?"[6] 81 per cent replied affirmatively. It is this sense of localism as a basic feature of lower-class life and the functional significance of local interpersonal relationships and of local places which have been stressed by a number of studies of the working class[7] and are documented by many aspects of our data.

In summary, then, we observe that a number of factors contribute to the special importance that the West End seemed to bear for the large majority of its inhabitants.

1. Residence in the West End was highly stable, with relatively little movement from one dwelling unit to another and with minimal transience into

---

[6] This question is from the interview designed by Leo Srole and his associates for the Yorkville study in New York.

[7] The importance of localism in working-class areas has been most cogently described by Richard Hoggart. *The Uses of Literacy* (London: Chatto and Windus, 1857), and by Michael Young and Peter Willmott, *Family and Kinship in East London* (Glencoe: The Free Press, 1957). In our own data, the perception of the area as a local neighborhood is largely independent of the individual's own commitment to the area.

and out of the area. Although residential stability is a fact of importance in itself, it does not wholly account for commitment to the area.

2. For the great majority of the people, the local area was a focus for strongly positive sentiments and was perceived, probably in its multiple meanings, as home. The critical significance of belonging in or to an area has been one of the most consistent findings in working-class communities both in the United States and in England.

3. The importance of localism in the West End, as well as in other working-class areas, can hardly be emphasized enough. This sense of a local spatial identity includes both local social relationships and local places. Although oriented around a common conception of the area as "home," there are a number of specific factors dominating the concrete meaning of the area for different people.

We now turn to a closer consideration of two of these sets of factors: first, the interpersonal networks within which people functioned, and, in the subsequent section, the general spatial organization of behavior.

III. SOCIAL RELATIONSHIPS IN PHYSICAL SPACE

Social relationships and interpersonal ties are not as frequently isolated for special attention in discussing the meaning of the West End as we might have expected. Despite this relative lack of exclusive salience, there is abundant evidence that patterns of social interaction were of great importance in the West End. Certainly for a great number of people, local space, whatever its independent significance, served as a locus for social relationships in much the same way as in other working-class slum areas.[8] In this respect, the urban slum community also has much in common with the communities so frequently observed in folk cultures. Quite consistently, we find a strong association between positive feelings about the West End and either extensive social relationships or positive feelings about other people in the West End.[9] The availability of such interpersonal ties seems to have considerable influence on feelings about the area, but the absence of these ties does not preclude a strongly positive feeling about the West End. That is, despite the prominence of this pattern, there seem to be alternative sources of satisfaction with the area for a minority of the people.

[8]Many of the studies of working-class areas make this point quite clear. Cf. Hoggart. *op. cit.;* Young and Willmott, *op. cit.;* Herbert Gans, *The Urban Villagers* (Glencoe: The Free Press, forthcoming); J. M. Mogey, *Family and Neighbourhood* (London: Oxford University Press, 1956); Madeline Kerr, *People of Ship Street* (London: Routledge and Kegan Paul, 1958).

[9]These associations between feelings about the West End and interpersonal variables include interpersonal relationships outside the West End as well. Thus there is the possibility that an interrelated personality variable may be involved. We shall pursue this in subsequent studies.

The Place of Kinship Ties

Following some of the earlier studies of membership in formal organizations, which indicated that such organizational ties were infrequent in the working class, increasing attention has been given to the importance of kinship ties in lower-class groups.[10] Despite the paucity of comparative studies, most of the investigations of working-class life have stressed the great importance of the extended-kinship group. But the extended-kinship group, consisting of relationships beyond the immediate family, does not seem to be a primary source of the closest interpersonal ties. Rather, the core of the most active kinship ties seems to be composed of nuclear relatives (parents, siblings, and children) of both spouses.[11] Our data show that the more extensive these available kinship ties are within the local area, the greater the proportion who show strong positive feeling toward the West End. These data are given in Table 3 and show a quite overwhelming and consistent trend in this direction. Other relationships point to the same observation: the more frequent the contact with siblings or the more frequent the contact with parents or the greater the desire to move near relatives, the greater the proportion who like the West End very well.

TABLE 3. EXTENSIVENESS OF KIN IN WEST END BY FEELINGS ABOUT WEST END

Extensiveness of kin in West End	Number of respondents	Totals	Feelings about West End (per cent)		
			Strongly positive	Positive	Mixed negative
None	193	100	29	46	25
Few	150	100	37	38	25
Some	67	100	45	31	24
Many	52	100	58	27	15

The Importance of the Neighbor Relationship

Important as concrete kinship ties were, however, it is easy to overestimate their significance and the relevance of kinship contacts for positive feelings about the residential area. Studies of the lower class have often neglected the importance of other interpersonal patterns in their concentration on kinship.

[10] The importance of kinship ties for working-class people was particularly brought to the fore by Floyd Dotson, "Patterns of Voluntary Association Among Urban Working Class Families," *American Sociological Review*, 1951, Vol. 25. pp. 687–693.

[11] This point is made by Young and Willmott, *op. cit.* In this regard as in many others, the similarity of the East End of London and the West End of Boston is quite remarkable.

Not only are other social relationships of considerable significance, but they also seem to influence feelings about the area. The similar effects of both sets of relationships is evident in Table 4, which presents the association between feelings about the West End and the personal importance of relatives versus friends.[12] A greater proportion (50 per cent) have a strong preference for relatives, but a large group (31 per cent) indicates a strong preferential orientation to friends. More relevant to our immediate purpose, there is little difference among the three preference groups in the proportions who have strong positive feelings about the West End.

TABLE 4. PREFERENCE FOR RELATIVES OR FRIENDS BY FEELINGS ABOUT WEST END

Preference for relatives or friends	Number of responents	Feelings about West End (per cent)			
		Totals	Strongly positive	Postive	Mixed negative
Relatives preferred	232	100	39	39	22
Mixed preferences	81	100	35	32	33
Friends preferred	148	100	36	42	22

In view of the consistency in the relations between a wide variety of interpersonal variables and feelings about the West End, it seems likely that there are alternative paths to close interpersonal ties of which kinship is only one specific form.[13] In fact, the single most powerful relation between feelings about the West End and an interpersonal variable is provided by feelings about West End neighbors (Table 5). Although the neighbor relationship may subsume kinship ties (i.e., when the neighbors are kin), the association between feelings about neighbors and feelings about the West End is stronger than the association between feelings about the West End and any of the kinship variables. Beyond this fact, the frequent references to neighbors and the stress on *local* friendships lead us to suggest that the neighbor relationship was one of the most important ties in the West End. And, whether based on prior kinship

[12]The "Preference for Relatives or Friends" item is based on four separate questions presenting a specific situation and asking if the respondent would prefer to be associated with a relative or friend in each situation.

[13]We do not mean to imply that this exhausts the special importance of kinship in the larger social structure. There is also evidence to suggest that some of the basic patterns of the kinship relationship have influenced the form of interpersonal ties more generally in the urban working class. This issue is discussed in Marc Fried and Erich Lindemann, "Sociocultural Factors in Mental Health and Illness," *American Journal of Orthopsychiatry,* 1961, Vol. 31, pp. 87–101, and will be considered further in subsequent reports.

affiliation or not, it formed one of the critical links between the individual (or family) and the larger area and community.

TABLE 5. CLOSENESS TO NEIGHBORS BY FEELINGS ABOUT WEST END

Closeness to neighbors	Number of respondents	Feelings about West End (per cent)			
		Totals	Strongly positive	Positive	Mixed negative
Very positive	78	100	63	28	9
Positive	265	100	37	42	21
Negative	117	100	20	39	41

Localism in Close Interpersonal Ties

Since the quality of feeling about the West End is associated with so wide a diversity of interpersonal relationships, it is not surprising that the majority of people maintained their closest ties with West Enders. The distribution of relationships which were based in the West End or outside the West End are given in Table 6. The striking proportion whose closest ties are all or mostly from the West End is clearly evident. As we would expect on the basis of the previous results, the more exclusively a person's closest relationships are based in the West End, the greater the likelihood that he will have strong positive feelings about the West End.

TABLE 6. WEST END DWELLING OF FIVE CLOSEST PERSONS

Five closest persons	Number	Per cent
Totals	473	100
All West End	201	42 ⎱ 60
Mostly West End	85	18 ⎰
Equally West End and outside	13	3
Mostly outside West End	70	15 ⎱ 25
All outside West End	46	10 ⎰
Unspecified	58	12

A few significant factors stand out clearly from this analysis.

1. Although the kinship relationship was of considerable importance in the West End, as in other working-class communities, there were a number of alternative sources of locally based interpersonal ties. Among these, we suggest that the neighbor relationship is of particular importance, both in its own right and in its effect on more general feelings about the area.
2. There is considerable generality to the observation that the greater one's interpersonal commitments in the area, in the form of close contact or strongly positive feelings, the greater the likelihood of highly positive feelings about the area as a whole. This observation holds for all the forms of interpersonal relationship studied.

What is perhaps most striking about the social patterns of the West End is the extent to which all the various forms of interpersonal ties were localized within the residential area. Local physical space seems to have provided a framework within which some of the most important social relationships were embedded. As in many a folk community[14] there was considerable overlap in the kinds of ties which obtained: kin were often neighbors; there were many interrelated friendship networks; mutual help in household activities was both possible and frequent; many of these relationships had a long and continuous history; and the various ties often became further intertwined through many activities within a common community.

The street itself, favorite recreation areas, local bars, and the settlement houses in the area all served as points of contact for overlapping social networks. Thus the most unique features of this working-class area (although common to many other working-class areas) were: (a) the interweaving and overlap of many different types of interpersonal contacts and role relationships, and (b) the organization and concrete manifestation of these relationships within a common, relatively bounded spatial region. It is these characteristics which seem to have given a special character and meaning both to the quality of interpersonal relationships and to the area within which these relationships were experienced.

We have repeatedly stressed the observation that, granting the importance of local social relationships, the meaning of "localism" in the West End included places as well as people. It is difficult to document the independent significance of either of these factors, but the importance of the physical space of the West End and the special use of the area are evident in many ways. Previously we indicated the importance of physical areas and places as sources of satisfaction in the West End. We now wish to consider more systematically the way in which the physical space of the area is subjectively organized by a large proportion of the population. In understanding the importance of such subjective spatial organization in addition to the significance of local social

---

[14]Ward Goodenough gives an excellent description of a similar pattern on Truk. Cf. Ward Goodenough, *Property, Kin, and Community on Truk* (New Haven: Yale University Publications in Anthropology, No. 46, 1951).

relationships, we can more adequately appreciate the enormous and multiply derived meaning that a residential area may have for people.

IV. SUBJECTIVE SPATIAL ORGANIZATION

There is only a fragmentary literature on the psychological, social, or cultural implications of spatial behavior and spatial imagery. The orientation of the behavioral sciences to the history, structure, and dynamics of social relationships has tended to obscure the potential significance of the nonhuman environment generally and, more specifically, that aspect of the nonhuman environment which we may designate as significant space. Although there have been a number of important contributions to this problem, we are far from any systematic understanding of the phenomena.[15] We do not propose to discuss the problems or concepts, but only to start with a few very primitive considerations and to observe the working-class relationship to space in several respects. We are primarily concerned with the way in which space is organized or structured in defining the usable environment and in providing restrictions to or freedom for mobility in space.[16] In this way we may hope to see more broadly the constellation of forces which serve to invest the residential environment of the working class with such intense personal meaning.

Spatial Usage Patterns in the Middle Class

There are undoubtedly many differences among people in the way space is organized, according to personality type, physiological disposition, environmental actualities, social roles, and cultural experience. We wish to focus only on some of those differences which, at the extremes, distinguish the working class quite sharply from higher-status groups. Although we do not have comparative data, we suggest that in the urban middle class (most notably among relatively high-status professional and business groups) space is characteristically used in a highly *selective* way. The boundary between the dwelling unit

[15]There are a number of rich and provocative discussions of selected aspects of space-oriented behavior. Cf. Paul Schilder, *The Image and Appearance of the Human Body* (London: Kegan Paul, Trench, Trubner, and Co., 1935); and *Mind: Perception and Thought in Their Constructive Aspects* (New York: Columbia University Press, 1942); Erik Homburger Erikson, "Configurations in Play—Clinical Notes," *Psychoanalytic Quarterly,* 1937, Vol. 6, pp. 139–214; H. A. Witkin, *Personality Through Perception* (New York: Harper, 1954); Edward T. Hall, "The Language of Space," *Landscape,* Fall 1960. The studies of the animal ecologists and the experimental studies of spatial orientation have considerable bearing on these issues. A recent contribution to the literature of urban planning, Kevin Lynch's *The Image of the City* (Cambridge: The Technology Press, 1960) bears directly on the larger problems of spatial orientation and spatial behavior in the urban environment, and its analytic framework has proved useful in the present formulations.

[16]We shall not touch on a related problem of considerable interest, the basic modes of conceiving or experiencing space in general. We assume a close relation between general conceptions of space and ways of using spatial aspects of specific parts of the environment, but an analysis of this problem is beyond the scope of the present discussion.

and the immediate environs is quite sharp and minimally permeable. It is, of course, possible to go into and out of the dwelling unit through channels which are specifically designated for this purpose. But walls are clear-cut barriers between the inside of the dwelling unit and the outer world. And even windows are seldom used for any interchange between the inner world of the dwelling unit and the outside environment (except for sunlight and air). Most of us take this so much for granted that we never question it, let alone take account of it for analytic purposes. It is the value of the "privacy of the home." The dwelling unit may extend into a zone of lawn or garden which we tend and for which we pay taxes. But, apart from this, the space outside the dwelling unit is barely "ours."

As soon as we are in the apartment hallway or on the street, we are on a wholly *public* way, a path to or from someplace rather than on a bounded space defined by a subjective sense of belonging.[17] Beyond this is a highly individualized world, with many common properties but great variability in usage and subjective meaning. Distances are very readily transgressed; friends are dispersed in many directions; preferred places are frequently quite idiosyncratic. Thus there are few physical areas which have regular (certainly not daily) widespread common usage and meaning. And contiguity between the dwelling unit and other significant spaces is relatively unimportant. It is primarily the channels and pathways between individualized significant spaces which are important, familiar, and common to many people. This orientation to the use of space is the very antithesis of that localism so widely found in the working class.

The Territorial Sense in the Working Class

Localism captures only a gross orientation toward the social use of an area of physical space and does not sufficiently emphasize its detailed organization. Certainly, most middle-class observers are overwhelmed at the degree to which the residents of any working-class district and, most particularly, the residents of slums are "at home" in the street. But it is not only the frequency of using the street and treating the street outside the house as a place, and not simply as a path, which points up the high degree of permeability of the boundary between the dwelling unit and the immediate environing area. It is also the use

[17]The comment of one reader to an early draft of this paper is worth quoting, since it leads into a fascinating series of related problems. With respect to this passage, Chester Hartman notes: "We tend to think of this other space as anonymous and public (in the sense of belonging to everyone, i.e., no one) when it does not specifically belong to us. The lower-class person is not nearly so alienated from what he does not own." To what extent is there a relationship between a traditional expectation (even if occasionally belied by reality) that only *other* people own real property, that one is essentially part of a "property-less class" and a willingness to treat any property as common? And does this provide a framework for the close relationship between knowing and belonging in the working class in contrast to the middle-class relationship between owning and belonging? Does the middle-class acceptance of legal property rights provide a context in which one can *only* belong if one owns. From a larger psychological view, these questions are relevant not merely to physical space and physical objects but to social relationships as well.

of all channels between dwelling unit and environment as a bridge between inside and outside: open windows, closed windows, hallways, even walls and floors serve this purpose. Frequently, even the sense of adjacent human beings carried by noises and smells provides a sense of comfort. As Edward Ryan points out:[18]

> Social life has an almost uninterrupted flow between apartment and street: children are sent into the street to play, women lean out the windows to watch and take part in street activity, women go "out on the street" to talk with friends, men and boys meet on the corners at night, and families sit on the steps and talk with their neighbors at night when the weather is warm.

It is not surprising, therefore, that there is considerable agreement between the way people feel about their apartments and the way they feel about the West End in general (Table 7). Without attempting to assign priority to feelings about the apartment or to feelings about the West End, it seems likely that physical barriers which are experienced as easily permeable allow for a ready generalization of positive or negative feelings in either direction.

TABLE 7. FEELINGS ABOUT THE APARTMENT BY FEELINGS ABOUT WEST END

Feelings about apartment	Number of respondents	Feelings about West End (per cent)			
		Totals	Like very well	Like	Mixed-dislike
Like	367	100	43	40	17
Mixed-indifferent	41	100	20	42	39
Dislike	60	100	12	30	58

We would like to call this way of structuring the physical space around the actual residential unit a *territorial* space, in contrast to the selective space of the middle class. It is territorial in the sense that physical space is largely defined in terms of relatively bounded regions to which one has freedom or restriction of access, and it does not emphasize the path function of physical space in allowing or encouraging movements to or from other places.[19] There is also evidence, some of which has been presented in an earlier section, that

[18]This comment is a fragment from a report on ethnographic observations made in the area.

[19]These formulations, as previously indicated, refer to modal patterns and do not apply to the total population. Twenty-six per cent do select out the "accessibility" of the area, namely, a path function. The class difference, however, is quite striking, since 67 per cent of the highest-status group give this response, but only 19 per cent of the lowest-status group and between 28 per cent and 31 per cent of the middle- (but still low-status) groups select out various types of "accessibility."

it is territorial in a more profound sense: that individuals feel different spatial regions belong to or do not belong to them and, correspondingly, feel that they belong to (or in) specific spatial regions or do not belong.[20]

Spatial Boundaries in the Local Area

In all the previous discussion, the West End has been treated as a whole. People in the area did, in fact, frequently speak of the area as a whole, as if it were an entity. However, it is clear that the area was differently bounded for different people. Considering only the gross distinction between circumscribing the neighborhood as very small, localized space in contrast to an expansive conception of the neighborhood to include most of the area, we find that the sample is about equally split (Table 8). It is apparent, therefore, that the territorial zone may include a very small or a very large part of the entire West End, and for quite a large proportion it is the former. For these people, at least, the boundary between dwelling unit and street may be highly permeable: but this freedom of subjective access does not seem to extend very far beyond the area immediately adjacent to the dwelling unit. It is also surprising how little this subjective sense of neighborhood size is affected by the extensiveness of West End kin or of West End friends. This fact tends to support the view that there is some degree of independence between social relationships and spatial orientations in the area.[21]

TABLE 8. AREA OF WEST END "NEIGHBORHOOD"

Neighborhood	Number	Per cent
Totals	473	100
Much of West End: all of area, West End specified, most of area, large area specified	191	40
Part of West End: one or two streets or less, a small area, a store	207	44
People, not area: the people around	17	4
Not codeable	58	12

[20]Without attempting, in this report, a "depth" psychological analysis of typical patterns of working-class behaviors, we should note the focal importance of being accepted or rejected, of belonging or being an "outsider." Preliminary evidence from the post-relocation interviews reveals this in the frequent references to being unable to obtain an apartment because "they didn't want us" or that the landlord "treated us like dirt." It also emerges in the frequently very acute sensitivity to gross social-class differences, and a sharp sense of not belonging or not fitting in with people of higher status. Clarification of this and related problems seems essential for understanding the psychological and social consequences of social-class distinctions and has considerable implications for urban residential planning generally and urban renewal specifically.

[21]The social-class patterning is also of interest. Using the occupation of the head of household as the class criterion, there is almost no difference among the three working-class status levels in the area included as a neighborhood (the percentages who say "much or all of the area" for these three groups are, respectively, 51 per cent, 46 per cent, and 48 per cent). But only 38 per cent of the high-status group include much or all of the West End in their subjective neighborhood.

Thus, we may say that for almost half the people, there is a subjective barrier surrounding the immediately local area. For this large group, the barrier seems to define the zone of greatest personal significance or comfort from the larger area of the West End. However, it is clearly not an impermeable barrier. Not only does a large proportion of the sample fail to designate this boundary, but even for those who do perceive this distinction, there is frequently a sense of familiarity with the area beyond.[22] Thus, when we use a less severe criterion of boundedness than the local "neighborhood" and ask people how much of the West End they know well, we find that a very large proportion indeed indicate their familiarity with a large part or most of the area (Table 9).[23] Although almost half the people consider "home ground" to include only a relatively small local region, the vast majority is easily familiar with a greater part of the West End. The local boundaries within the West End were, thus, boundaries of a semi-permeable nature although differently experienced by different people.

TABLE 9. AREA OF WEST END KNOWN WELL

Area	Number	Per cent	
Totals	473	100	
Just own block	27	6	20
A few blocks	65	14	
Large part	66	14	64
Most of it	237	50	
Uncodeable	78	16	

The Inner-Outer Boundary

These distinctions in the permeability of the boundaries between dwelling unit and street and across various spaces within the larger local region are brought even more sharply into focus when we consider the boundary surrounding the West End as a whole. The large majority may have been easily familiar with most or all of the West End. But it is impressive how frequently such familiarity seems to stop at the boundaries of the West End. In comparison with the previous data, Table 10 demonstrates the very sharp delineation of the inner space of the West End from the outer space surrounding the West

[22]Of those who include only part of the West End in their designation of their neighborhood, 68 per cent indicate they know a large part or most of the West End well. Naturally, an even higher percentage (87 per cent) of those who include much or all of the West End in their neighborhood are similarly familiar with a large part or all of the area.

[23]We used the term "neighborhood" for want of a better term to designate the immediate local area of greatest significance. On the basis of his ethnographic work, however, Edward Ryan points out that this term is rarely used spontaneously by West Enders.

End. The former is generally well explored and essentially familiar, even though it may not be considered the area of commitment. The latter is either relatively unknown by many people or, if known, it is categorized in a completely different way. A relatively large proportion are familiar with the immediately adjacent areas which are directly or almost directly contiguous with the West End (and are often viewed as extensions of the West End), but only slightly more than a quarter (26 per cent) report familiarity with any other parts of the Boston area. Thus there seems to be a widely experienced subjective boundary surrounding the larger local area and some of its immediate extensions which is virtually impermeable. It is difficult to believe that people literally do not move out of this zone for various activities. Yet, if they do, it apparently does not serve to diminish the psychological (and undoubtedly social) importance of the boundary.[24]

TABLE 10. FAMILIAR AREAS OF BOSTON

Area	Number	Per cent
Totals	473	101
West End only: no other area, none	141	30
Adjacent area: North End, esplanade	216	46
Contiguous areas: East Boston, Cambridge	98	21
Nearby areas: Revere, Malden, Brookline	12	3
Metropolitan Boston, beyond "nearby" areas	1	0
Outside Boston area	3	1
No answer	2	0

These data provide considerable evidence to support, if they do not thoroughly validate, the view that the working class commonly organizes physical space in terms of a series of boundaries. Although we do not mean to imply any sense of a series of concentric boundaries or to suggest that distance alone is the critical dimension, there seems to be a general tendency for the permeability of these boundaries to decrease with increasing distance from the dwelling unit. Significant space is thus subjectively defined as a series of contiguous regions with the dwelling unit and its immediately surrounding local area as the central region. We have referred to this way of organizing physical space as *territorial* to distinguish it from the more highly *selective* and individualized use of space which seems to characterize the middle class. And we suggest that it is the territorial conception and manner of using physical

[24]Unfortunately, we do not have data on the actual frequency of use of the various areas outside the West End. Thus we cannot deal with the problem of the sense of familiarity in relation to actual usage patterns. However, in subsequent reports, we hope to pursue problems related to the bases for defining or experiencing physical-spatial boundaries and the various dimensions which affect the sense of commitment to and belonging in physical areas.

space which provides one of the bases for the kind of localism which is so widely found in working-class areas.

In conjunction with the emphasis upon local social relationships, this conception and use of local physical space give particular force to the feeling of commitment to, and the sense of belonging in, the residential area. It is clearly not just the dwelling unit that is significant but a larger local region that partakes of these powerful feelings of involvement and identity. It is not surprising, therefore, that "home" is not merely an apartment or a house but a local area in which some of the most meaningful aspects of life are experienced.

V.   CONCLUSIONS

The aims of urban renewal and the sources of pressure for renewal are manifold: among the objectives we may include more rational and efficient use of land, the elimination of dilapidated buildings, increase in the municipal tax base, and the improvement of living conditions for slum dwellers. Although the social benefit to the slum dweller has received maximum public attention, it is always unclear how the life situation (or even the housing situation) of the working-class resident of a slum is supposed to be improved by slum clearance or even slum improvement. Public housing has not proved to be an adequate answer to this problem for many reasons. Yet public housing is the only feature of renewal programs that has even attempted to deal seriously with this issue.

In recent years, a number of reports have suggested that concern about slum conditions has been used to maneuver public opinion in order to justify use of eminent domain powers and demolition, largely for the benefit of middle- and upper-status groups. Although we cannot evaluate this political and economic issue, we do hope to understand the ways in which dislocation from a slum and relocation to new residential areas has, in fact, benefited or damaged the working-class residents involved. It is all too apparent, however, that the currently available data are inadequate for clarifying some of the most critical issues concerning the effects of residential relocation upon the subject populations.

We know very little about slums and the personal and social consequences of living in a slum. We know even less about the effects of forced dislocation from residential areas on people in general and on working-class people specifically. But rational urban planning which, under these circumstances, becomes urban *social* planning, requires considerable knowledge and understanding of people and places affected by the plans. It is incumbent upon us to know both what is wrong with the slum and with slum life and what is right about slums and living in slums.[25] It is essentially this question, formulated as the meaning

[25]There is, of course, the evident danger of considering a social pattern on the basis of "right" and "wrong" which, inevitably, merely reproduce our own transitory values. A careful and thorough analysis, however, provides its own correctives to our all-too-human biases.

and consequences of living in a slum, that has motivated our inquiry into the sources of residential satisfaction in an urban slum. In turn, this study provides one of the bases for understanding the ways in which dislocation and relocation affect the patterns of personal and social adaptation of former residents of a slum.

In studying the reasons for satisfaction that the majority of slum residents experience, two major components have emerged. On the one hand, the residential area is the region in which a vast and interlocking set of social networks is localized. And, on the other, the physical area has considerable meaning as an extension of home, in which various parts are delineated and structured on the basis of a sense of belonging. These two components provide the context in which the residential area may so easily be invested with considerable, multiply determined meaning. Certainly, there are variations both in the importance of various factors for different people and in the total sense which people have of the local area. But the greatest proportion of this working-class group (like other working-class slum residents who have been described) shows a fairly common experience and usage of the residential area. This common experience and usage is dominated by a conception of the local area beyond the dwelling unit as an integral part of home. This view of an area as home and the significance of local people and local places are so profoundly at variance with typical middle-class orientations that it is difficult to appreciate the intensity of meaning, the basic sense of identity involved in living in the particular area. Yet it seems to form the core of the extensive social integration that characterizes this (and other) working-class slum populations.

These observations lead us to question the extent to which, through urban renewal, we relieve a situation of stress or create further damage. If the local spatial area and an orientation toward localism provide the core of social organization and integration for a large proportion of the working class, and if, as current behavioral theories would suggest, social organization and integration are primary factors in providing a base for effective social functioning, what are the consequences of dislocating people from their local areas? Or, assuming that the potentialities of people for adaptation to crisis are great, what deeper damage occurs in the process? And, if there are deleterious effects, are these widespread or do they selectively affect certain predictable parts of the population? We emphasize the negative possibilities because these are closest to the expectations of the population involved and because, so frequently in the past, vague positive effects on slum populations have been arbitrarily assumed. But it is clear that, in lieu of or along with negative consequences, there may be considerable social benefit.

The potential social benefits also require careful, systematic evaluation, since they may manifest themselves in various and sometimes subtle ways. Through a variety of direct and intervening factors, the forced residential shift may lead to changes in orientations toward work, leading to increased satisfaction in the occupational sphere; or, changes may occur in the marital and total familial relationship to compensate for decreased kinship and friendship contacts and, in turn, lead to an alternative (and culturally more syntonic) form of interpersonal satisfaction; or, there may be either widespread or selective decreases in problems such as delinquency, mental illness, and physical malfunctioning.

A realistic understanding of the effects, beneficial and/or deleterious, of dislocation and relocation from an urban slum clearly requires further study and analysis. Our consideration of some of the factors involved in working-class residential satisfaction in the slum provides one basis for evaluating the significance of the changes that take place with a transition to a new geographic and social environment. Only the careful comparison of pre-relocation and post-relocation data can begin to answer these more fundamental questions and, in this way, provide a sound basis for planning urban social change.

The City as a Mosaic of Social Worlds—the Neighbourhood and Behaviour
Duncan W. G. Timms

*   *   *

THE NEIGHBOURHOOD AND BEHAVIOUR

Apart from ethnographic studies[5] of the way of life in certain specified areas of the city, three major sources of material are available for an analysis of the relationship between residence and behaviour: studies of the association between propinquity and friendship, studies concerned with explicating the socio-cultural factors involved in deviant behavior, and studies concerned with the relationship between area of residence and educational experience. We shall look at some examples of each in turn.

Propinquity and Friendship

The most comprehensive analysis of the relationship between residential location and patterns of informal social relations is the study by Festinger, Schachter and Back, set in a housing estate developed for married veteran

[5]E. g. the work of the Institute for Community studies.

SOURCE: Duncan W. G. Timms, from *The Urban Mosaic* (London: Cambridge University Press, 1971), pp. 9–15, 16–26, 34–35. Reprinted by permission.

students attending the Massachusetts Institute of Technology.[6] The study is concerned with the patterns of friendship and communication at the intra-neighbourhood level. The population of the estate was highly homogeneous in terms of age, family characteristics, and socio-economic background and its inhabitants had few or no previous contacts in the community. In such a situation Festinger *et al.* hypothesize that 'friendships are likely to develop on the basis of the brief and passive contacts made going to and from home or walking about the neighbourhood'.[7] These passive contacts, in turn, are likely to be mediated through proximity and through those locational effects which require people to use the same paths in their movement about the estate. The influence of proximity is measured through physical distance; that of locational effects through 'functional distance', an index of 'the number of passive contacts that position and design encourage'.[8] In both cases the data obtained are in striking agreement with the hypothesis. Comparing actual friendship choices with possible choices, there is a marked inverse relationship between friendship nomination and distance. Within each of the courts into which the estate is divided the highest ratio of actual to possible friendships is reported for immediate neighbours, those respectively two and three distance units away have successively smaller ratios, while no choices at all are made to those who live four units away. There is a similar effect in the case of choices given outside the nominator's court. 'The greater the physical separation between any two points in these communities, the fewer the friendships.'[9] The effects of functional distance are revealed in the tendency for the residents of end houses to receive significantly fewer friendship nominations than those living in any other position. On the basis of their findings, the authors posit that 'The closer together a number of people live, and the greater the extent to which functional proximity factors cause contacts among these people, the greater the probability of friendships forming and the greater the probability of group formation.'[10] The groups formed on the basis of the two proximity factors not only provide the framework for informal communication within the estate, but also serve as the providers of consensual opinions and attitudes. Thus each court is reported as developing its own group standards and to possess its own machinery for sanctioning conformity. Individuals who deviate from the group norm tend to be isolated within their court. The ecological structure of the estate provides the framework for its socio-cultural structure.[11]

[6]L. Festinger, S. Schachter and K. Back, *Social Pressures in Informal Groups* (London, 1950).
[7]*Ibid.* p. 34.
[8]*Ibid.* p. 35.
[9]*Ibid.* p. 44.
[10]*Ibid.* p. 161.
[11]Similar findings are reported by Caplow and Forman for a student housing project at the University of Minnesota. Caplow and Forman show that while length of residence is associated with number of acquaintances it has little association with number of friends. Friendship choices are overwhelmingly local. See T. Caplow and R. Forman, 'Neighbourhood interaction in a homogeneous community', *Am. Sociol. Rev.* 15 (1950), 357–67.

Festinger *et al.* point out that the locale of their study is unusual in the homogeneity of its population and suggest that ecological factors may be much less important in determining friendship and group formation in less 'artificial' communities. An analysis of a new middle-class housing estate on the fringes of an Australian city, however, provides striking corroboration for their assertion of the relationship between proximity and friendship.[12]

The locale of the study is the first part of what is planned to become one of the largest private enterprise housing developments in Australia. The initial development of Waratah[13] took place in the early 1960s on a site some 7½ miles from the centre of one of the State capitals in an area 'across the river' from some of the best-known high status residential districts in the city. The estate is designed to be a 'model suburb', with shopping facilities, golf courses, an Olympic-sized swimming pool, a sports oval and parks, primary and secondary schools. At the time of the study, however, much of this lay in the future and the immediate concern is with the sixty-six households resident on the site some two years after the estate was opened. Median length of residence is ten months.

Community participation and the goal of 'togetherness' are themes stressed by both the developers of Waratah and by its residents. The amount of friendship interaction on the estate, as ascertained by a sociometric technique, is generally high. The fourteen women who leave Waratah for work tend to be socially isolated within the estate, but the great majority of the remainder are active participants in the local interaction system. Two-thirds of the women are members of one large network. The effects of distance on friendship interaction are marked, even though no houses are separated by more than half-a-mile.

Table 1 shows the relationship between the ratio of actual to possible friendship choices made by the women on the estate and straight-line distance. Women living within a radius of 100 yards of the respondent are more than ten times as likely to be chosen as friends as are those living more than 400 yards away. More than two-thirds of all the friendship nominations directed to estate residents involve women living in the same street as their chooser; nearly half of all reciprocal friendships involve immediate neighbours.

The emphasis given to social participation in Waratah poses a problem for those in a less-advantageous location. To a large extent the esteem accorded to a Waratah woman is a function of her participation. Those who are socially isolated tend to exhibit alienation.[14] The spatial patterning of the population, as reflected in the map of demographic potential,[15] reveals a close relationship

[12]D. W. G. Timms, 'Anomia and social participation amongst suburban women' (University of Auckland, 1969), mimeo paper.

[13]The name is fictitious.

[14]The measure of alienation is Srole's 'Anomia Scale'. See L. Srole, 'Social integration and certain corollaries', *Am. Sociol. Rev.* 21 (1956), 709–16.

[15]Demographic potential may be interpreted as a measure of aggregate accessibility. See J. Q. Stewart, 'Demographic gravitation', *Sociometry,* 11 (1948), 31–58.

with the patterning of alienation. Those women who are physically isolated tend also to be socially isolated—and they respond to their frustration by rejecting their rejectors. The influence of microgeography is as pronounced in Waratah as it is in the estate studied by Festinger *et al.*, notwithstanding the differences in population characteristics. In both estates the physical arrangement is reflected not only in the patterning of the informal contacts between residents but also in the patterning of residents' attitudes.

TABLE I. THE RELATIONSHIP BETWEEN FRIENDSHIP CHOICES AND PHYSICAL DISTANCE IN WARATAH

Distance in yards	Actual choices given	Number of possible choices	Choices given Possible choices
100	156	703	0.22
200	105	1120	0.09
300	67	1046	0.06
400	17	556	0.03
500+	6	586	0.01

Although proximity makes interaction easier and contact more likely, the relationship between the physical structure of the community and the pattern of its friendships should not be exaggerated. As Kuper states: 'The siting factors, with their planned and unplanned consequences, only provide a potential base for neighbour relations. There is no simple mechanical determination by the physical environment.'[16] Contact may lead to hostility rather than friendship and there are many instances of physically adjacent households who have little to do with each other. Different groups differ in their dependence on local friendship opportunities: the effects of proximity are probably more pronounced for women, especially those with young children, for the aged and for the infirm than they are for men, for the middle-aged, and for the fit. Proximity is most likely to lead to friendship when the persons concerned are similar in other ways. According to Gans, propinquity brings contact, but the development of contact into positive affect depends on social homogeneity.[17] Because the population of the city is residentially differentiated into more or less homogeneous areas, however, proximity is able to exert a considerable influence on the patterning of urban social relationships, especially for those individuals and groups who for one reason or another spend much of their time within their local vicinity.

The relationship between residential differentiation, propinquity, and social interaction is further explored in a series of studies concerned with the premarital residence patterns of marriage partners. The concern here is with

[16]L. Kuper (ed.), *Living in Towns* (London, 1953), p. 27.
[17]H. J. Gans, 'Planning and social life', *Journ. Am. Inst. Planners,* 27 (1961), 136–7.

inter-neighbourhood rather than intra-neighbourhood patterns. In a review by Katz and Hill,[18] it is shown that the original finding by Bossard,[19] that the frequency of marriage decreases as the distance between the two parties increases, is generally supported. Katz and Hill explain the relationship in terms of a theory which combines elements of normative, segregational, and interactional perspectives. Traditional normative views of mate selection stress the role of cultural factors in delimiting a field of eligible marriage partners. Generally the emphasis in urban-industrial society is on the advantages of marrying within the group. Since groups having different cultures are residentially segregated by neighbourhood, the emphasis on endogamous marriage will be reflected in the propinquity of eventual marriage partners. Persons who deviate from the group expectations on the choice of marriage partners may be expected to show relatively greater distances to their eventual mates than will those who conform to the local norm. Katz and Hill further elaborate the theory by pointing out that the time-cost expenses of interaction vary according to distance and to the number of intervening opportunities. Drawing on Stouffer's model of intervening opportunities and interaction[20] they suggest that *(a)* marriage is subject to normative evaluations and expectations; *(b)* that within a field of normatively defined eligibles the probability of marriage varies directly with the probability of interaction; and *(c)* that the probability of interaction varies as the ratio of eligible interaction partners at a given distance to the intervening opportunities: thus the probability of marriage reflects the combined effects of the normative divisions of society, the patterns of residential differentiation, and the time-cost implications of proximity *v.* distance. In an analysis of Oslo material, Ramsøy[21] is able to show that each factor has an independent influence. Beshers[22] has suggested that recognition of the relationship between the probability of marriage and propinquity may be an important element in a family's residential location. Where there are fears that normative constraints against the choice of the 'wrong' marriage partner are breaking down, it may be necessary for the parents of eligible children to relocate in a neighbourhood which contains only the 'right' sort of potential mates. Who daughter marries reflects who daughter meets—and who daughter meets reflects where she lives. Since marriage is so closely entwined with the social stratification system and forms one of the most important dimensions for the evaluation of a family's social rank there is a strong motivation to ensure that it is guided along the 'right' lines. Residential differentiation both allows and facilitates such guidance.

[18]A. M. Katz and R. Hill, 'Residential propinquity and marital selection', *Marr. and Fam. Living,* 20 (1958), 27–34.
[19]J. H. S. Bossard, 'Residential propinquity as a factor in marriage selection', *Am. J. Soc.* 38 (1933), 219–24.
[20]S. A. Stouffer, 'Intervening opportunities', *Am. Sociol. Rev.* 5 (1940), 845–67.
[21]N. R. Ramsøy, 'Assortative mating and the structure of cities', *Am. Sociol. Rev.* 31 (1966) 773–86.
[22]L. M. Beshers, *Urban Social Structure* (New York, 1962), pp. 104–7.

The Neighbourhood and Deviant Behavior

The connexion between deviant behavior and residential location is a major element in most sociological discussions of deviancy. A large volume both of research and of theory has been directed towards the explication of the connexion, but a fully integrated and verified series of propositions relating deviancy to neighbourhood is still awaited. Rather than attempt a general synthesis all that will be attempted here is to present a selection of some of the more important work which bears on the connexion of neighbourhood to deviancy.

It has long been recognized in the scientific literature that both the total amount and the types of deviant behaviour exhibited by residents of various districts differ considerably. In the nineteenth century, Mayhew provided a detailed description of the variation in crime and other forms of proscribed behaviour which characterized the various districts of London.[23] He pointed out that the major 'rookeries' of crime in the metropolis have had a long history, such areas as St Giles and Spitalfields having been the 'nests of London's beggars, prostitutes, and thieves' for several centuries. On the basis of his interviews and observations in the field, Mayhew was impressed by the socio-cultural roots of criminality. Anticipating the Lombrosian viewpoint, in which criminality was related *inter alia* with physiologic and genetic characteristics, Mayhew states in 1862:

> But crime, we repeat, is an effect with which the shape of the head and the form of the features appear to have no connexion whatever . . . Again we say that the great mass of crime in this country is committed by those who have been bred and born to the business, and who make a regular trade of it.[24]

Mayhew's conclusions have been generally corroborated by later investigators.

A milestone in the development of modern criminology was reached with the publication, in 1929, of the first of a series of reports on criminality and delinquency authored by Shaw and McKay.[25] Working essentially within the Chicago ecological tradition, Shaw and McKay produced a mass of data showing the variation in 'delinquency rates' in the different natural areas first of Chicago, and then of several other American cities. Aware of the dangers of ecological determinism they also pay considerable attention to the role of individual factors as intervening variables in the relationship between group characteristics and individual behaviour. The methodological concern they

---

[23] H. Mayhew, *London Labour and the London Poor* (London, 1864), esp. vol. 4.

[24] H. Mayhew, *The Criminal Prisons of London* (London, 1862), p. 383.

[25] C. R. Shaw, F. M. Zorbaugh, H. D. McKay and L. Cottrell, *Delinquency Areas* (Chicago, 1929); C. R. Shaw and H. D. McKay, *Social Factors in Juvenile Delinquency* (Washington, 1931); C. R. Shaw, *The Jackroller* (Chicago, 1930); C. R. Shaw, H. D. McKay, and J. F. McDonald, *Brothers in Crime* (Chicago, 1938); C. R. Shaw, H. D. McKay, *Juvenile Delinquency and Urban Areas* (Chicago, 1942). For extended discussions of the work of Shaw and McKay, see Burgess and Bogue, *Contributions to Urban Sociology*, pp. 591–615 and T. Morris, *The Criminal Area* (London, 1957), pp. 65–91.

display with regard to 'situational analysis' and the combination of ecological data with individual case studies, a precursor of the modern emphasis on 'contextual' effects,[26] enables Shaw and McKay to avoid many of the pitfalls of ecological determinism which some writers have seen as being characteristic of all ecological research.[27] By calculating delinquency rates, the number of offenders per thousand population at risk, Shaw and McKay are able to show not only that there are gross differences in the aggregate rates for different parts of the city, but also that there are slighter but still significant differences in the distribution of the different age groups of offenders. Thus the truants and the juvenile delinquents are concentrated in the slum districts and near large industrial areas, while the adult offenders are primarily concentrated in the rooming-house areas on the fringe of the central business district. Common to all the high rate areas, however, are the facts of physical deterioration and obsolescence, taken to be symptoms of some underlying malaise which is thought to be related to the uncontrolled nature of the city's growth. Shaw and McKay show that areas which were characterized by high rates of delinquency in the late 1920s had also been so characterized in 1900, notwithstanding considerable changes in the national, ethnic, and occupational composition of their populations. They suggest that the explanation of this stability lies in the development of 'delinquent norms' in the delinquent areas and in the normative confusion which results from rapid population movements. Great stress is laid on the importance of neighbourhood play-groups and of the family in the development of the child's attitudes and behaviour tendencies. It is pointed out that in areas characterized by a confusion of values and norms many of the standards upheld by the child's peers might be antithetical to those of his parents. Case studies of individual delinquents are used to illustrate the argument.

*   *   *

The volumes authored by Shaw and McKay contain the seeds of most of the subsequent approaches to the sociology of delinquency. Their emphasis on the role of delinquent traditions finds echoes in Cohen's theory of the delinquent contraculture, Miller's concern with the focal concerns of lower-class culture, and the Sherifs' emphasis on the role of the local neighbourhood as a reference group.[29] Their concern with the intervening effects of social integration is reflected in the Sutherland-Cressey theory of differential associa-

[26]E.g. M. W. Riley, *Sociological Research* (New York, 1963), vol. 1, pp. 644–738.

[27]Cf. C. T. Jonassen, 'A revaluation and critique of some of the methods of Shaw and Mckay', *Am. Sociol. Rev.* 14 (1949), 608–15. See also R. S. Sterne, 'Components and stereotypes in ecological analyses of social problems', *Urb. Aff. Quart.* 3 (1967), 1, 3–21.

[29]A. K. Cohen, *Delinquent Boys* (New York, 1955); W. B. Miller, 'Lower class culture as a generating milieu of gang delinquency', *J. Soc. Issues,* 14 (1958), 5–19; Sherif and Sherif, *Reference Groups.* A wide selection of sociological theories relating to criminality and juvenile deliquency is contained in M. E. Wolfgang, L. Savitz and N. Johnston (eds), *The Sociology of Crime and Delinquency* (New York, 1962).

tion[30] and in the demonstration by Maccoby *et al.* that high delinquency areas
are characterized by significantly higher degrees of social disintegration than
otherwise similar low delinquency areas.[31] In each case there is a clear assumption that *where* an adolescent lives will have a major effect on the chances of
his becoming delinquent.

To Cohen the delinquent sub-culture is a collective innovation developed
by low status youths in face of the problem of having to deal with the insecurity
and feelings of inferiority which are engendered in them as a result of their
unfortunate experiences at the hands of an essentially middle-class society. The
conflict between neighbourhood values and those of the wider community are
brought into especially sharp focus in the school system. Since their family and
peer-group backgrounds ill-prepare them for successful participation in the
competitive educational system designed by and for the middle classes, the
lower-class youths tend to find themselves at the bottom of the school's status
hierarchy. The feelings of status inferiority, combined with a general ambivalence to middle-class values, are brought together in the development of a set
of group norms based on an inversion of what are perceived as being the central
middle-class values. A central role in the process is played by the realization
by the low-class youths that they are not alone in their situation and the
consequent associational nature of their solution to their problems. There is
a clear analogy with the Marxist theory of developing class interest and conflict. The new set of norms provide a new set of status dimensions based on
an inversion of middle-class values. Within the local peer-group context the
disenchanted low status youth may hope to achieve high rank by demonstrating his alienation from conventional, middle-class norms. The adolescent peer-
group provides both the incentive and the opportunity for the disadvantaged
youth to develop his own bases of value.

Cohen's emphasis on the reaction-formation nature of the delinquent contraculture has been sharply criticized by other writers. Miller, in particular,
presents a theory of the relationship between lower-class culture and gang
delinquency which is in sharp disagreement with the Cohen model. To Miller

> the cultural system which exerts the most direct influence on (gang) behaviour is
> that of the lower class community itself—a long-established, distinctively patterned
> tradition with an integrity of its own—rather than a so-called delinquent subculture
> which has arisen through conflict with middle class culture.[32]

The bases of the lower-class culture are seen as lying in the common adaptations made by the unsuccessful immigrants and down-trodden Negroes who

[30]D. R. Cressey, 'Epidemiology and individual conduct', *Pac. Sociol. Rev.* 3 (1960), 47–54.
Reprinted in Wolfgang *et al., Sociology of Crime*, pp. 81–90.

[31]E. E. Maccoby, J. P. Johnson and R. M. Church, 'Community integration and the social
control of juvenile delinquency', *J. Soc. Issues* 14 (1958).

[32]Miller, 'Lower class culture'. Quote from Wolfgang *et al., Sociology of Crime*, p. 267.

inhabit the central city slums. Rather than an ideological reaction-formation, Miller sees the content of the lower-class culture as an effective adaptation to the local reality. Central to the culture are a series of focal concerns—trouble, toughness, smartness, excitement, autonomy, and fate. The world of the lower-class adolescent is effectively structured in terms of these concerns. Brought up in a home environment characterized by 'serial monogamy', in which effective male models are absent, the adolescent is thrown upon the company of his peers to search for a satisfactory identity and status in terms of the street group's codes. Like Thrasher before him,[33] Miller emphasizes that much of the lower-class street gang's behaviour is non-delinquent. Because of the nature of the lower-class focal concerns and the relatively easy rewards associated with some illegal activities in the lower-class community, however, the adolescent lower-class gang also provides a likely setting for the occurrence of delinquent behaviour.

A problem common to all sub-cultural theories of delinquent behaviour is that of explaining why not all inhabitants of the relevant neighbourhoods appear to become delinquent. To some extent the problem may be illusory: thus Kobrin and Mays show that there may be a very considerable difference between the 'official' delinquency rates and rates computed on more direct evidence of actual behaviour.[34] Kobrin suggests that even the more inclusive official records indicate the proportion of delinquents to be approximately two-thirds of the age eligibles in high rate areas. The proportion is presumably considerably higher if all those who are not apprehended are added. On the other hand it remains apparent that a certain proportion of juveniles in delinquent areas appear to be able to escape the coercive effects of their environment. Part of the answer probably lies in the detailed organization of the community. The work of Shaw and McKay is replete with suggestions about the effects of differences in the internal structuring of social relationships in the neighbourhood. In an analysis of two working-class neighbourhoods in Boston the main correlate of criminality is found to be the extent of integration into the ongoing interaction system of the local community.[35] In the high rate neighbourhood the inhabitants neither know nor want to know as many of their neighbours as do those in the low rate area. There is no apparent difference between the areas in beliefs about the 'wrongness' or the 'seriousness' of delinquent activities, but in the high rate neighbourhood there is a strong feeling against disciplining other people's children and 'interfering in the affairs of other people's kids'. Within the high rate neighbourhood itself the delinquent families are yet further isolated and there is little interaction between 'law-abiders' and offenders. There are few differences between the neighbour-

---

[33]Thrasher, *The Gang.*

[34]S. Kobrin, 'The conflict of values in delinquency areas', *Am. Sociol. Rev.* 16 (1951), 653–61; rep. in Wolfgang *et al., Sociology of Crime,* pp. 295–66; J. B. Mays, *On the Threshold of Delinquency* (Liverpool, 1958).

[35]Maccoby *et al.,* 'Community integration'.

hoods in most of their characteristics, but the high rate neighbourhood is considerably less homogeneous in its ethnic and religious composition. A similar emphasis on the significance of local interaction networks follows from Sutherland's hypothesis about differential association. According to this view 'criminal behaviour is learned in interaction with persons in a pattern of communication'. When persons become criminals 'they do so because of an excess of definitions favourable to violation of law over definitions unfavourable to violation of law'.[36] The associations which a person has are seen as being determined in the general context of social organization. The role of locality factors is thus likely to be high. In support of the hypothesis of differential association Wootton states that, on the basis of her experience as a Juvenile Court Magistrate, she has

> been very impressed by the part which casual acquaintances appear to play in determining who does and who does not step over the line in districts in which court appearances are not at all unusual. The arrival of a particular family in a particular street may have devastating consequences for the children of neighbours with hitherto blameless records.[37]

In one of the most well-known studies produced by the Chicago ecological school, Thrasher suggests that one of the factors which facilitates the evolution of the spontaneous play-group of childhood into a delinquent gang is the availability of outlets for stolen goods in certain inner city areas.[38] The presence of junk dealers and the 'no-questions-asked' attitude of many adult buyers helps to make larceny easy and profitable. Extensions of this concern with the local integration of adults and juveniles in explaining the development of different forms of delinquent behaviour have been made by Kobrin and, more generally, by Cloward and Ohlin.[39] Kobrin is particularly concerned with 'differences in the degree to which integration between the conventional and criminal value systems is achieved'. In neighbourhoods where there is a high degree of integration, adult deviancy 'tends to be systematic and organized'. Not only may the more successful violators become the administrators of organized crime but they may also maintain membership in conventional institutions such as the local church, political parties, and unions. Delinquent activity in such areas is essentially 'an apprenticeship in crime'. The contrasting type of delinquent area is one in which there is little organized adult activity in crime although many adults in these areas may commit individual violations. Frequently such areas have recently suffered from population turnover so that the carriers of conventional codes are momentarily disorganized.

---

[36] E. G. Sutherland and D. R. Cressey, *Principles of Criminology* (Philadelphia, 1960), pp. 74–81.

[37] B. Wootton, *Social Science and Social Pathology* (London, 1959), p. 68.

[38] Thrasher, *The Gang.*

[39] Kobrin, 'Conflict of values'; R. A. Cloward and L. E. Ohlin, *Delinquency and Opportunity* (New York, 1961).

In such circumstances juveniles are exposed to norms favouring both violation and non-violation and, at the same time, are insulated from the effective control of either sort of adult model. In these disorganized areas 'the delinquencies of juveniles tend to acquire a wild, untrammelled character . . . The escape from controls originating in any social structure, other than that provided by unstable groupings of the delinquents themselves, is complete'.[40]

The Cloward and Ohlin approach to the explanation of the different forms which may be taken by gang delinquency in the city represent a consolidation of the anomie orientation of such writers as Durkheim and Merton[41] with the socio-cultural orientation of Shaw and McKay and Sutherland. The theory which Cloward and Ohlin present is probably the most ambitious since Shaw and McKay. Expressed more formally than Kobrin's hypothesis, the 'theory of delinquency and differential opportunities' nonetheless leads to similar conclusions. Cloward and Ohlin suggest that in order to become a criminal the individual must have access to illegitimate means. As in the case of any other achieved status 'the individual must have access to appropriate environments for the acquisition of the values and skills associated with the performance of a particular role, and he must be supported in the performance of the role once he has learned it'.[42]

In the same way as legitimate opportunities, illegitimate opportunities are differentially available. Given a predisposition to deviate, resulting from a socially structured inability to reach valued ends by legitimate means, 'the nature of the delinquent response that may result will vary according to the availability of various illegitimate means'.[43] According to the availability of illegitimate means in the local community two main types of delinquent response are postulated: the criminal gang and the conflict gang. A third type, the retreatist gang, is believed to be the result of a double failure: a lack of success in both the legitimate and illegitimate structures. The criminal gang is characteristic of the integrated delinquent area in which illegitimate means are readily available in both the learning and supportive roles. Close bonds exist between adult violators and juveniles and there is a readily available infrastructure of such supportive statuses as fences, shady lawyers, junk men, and the like. In such a neighbourhood the child not only has the opportunity to perform in an illegitimate way but is likely to be shown that such performances may be highly rewarding. The delinquent subculture which arises in such circumstances 'is a more or less direct response to the local milieu'. A stable neighbourhood organized around illegitimate values results in stable criminality. The conflict sub-culture, on the other hand, is believed to be characteristic of disorganized low status neighbourhoods. In areas characterized by

[40]Kobrin, in Wolfgang et al., Sociology of Crime, p. 264.
[41]See M. B. Clinard (ed.), Anomie and Social Structure (New York, 1964).
[42]Cloward and Ohlin, in Wolfgang et al., Sociology of Crime, p. 256.
[43] Ibid. p. 258.

high rates of vertical and geographic mobility, massive housing projects in which 'site tenants' are not awarded priority in occupancy, so that traditional residents are dispersed and 'strangers' reassembled; and changing land use, as in the case of residential areas that are encroached upon by the expansion of adjacent commercial and industrial areas . . . transiency and instability become the over-riding features of social life.[44]

Under these conditions Cloward and Ohlin suggest that there will be many influences on the young making for violent behaviour. In the disorganized areas the adolescent is cut off from both legitimate and illegitimate opportunity structures. His chances of success in the conventional world are slight, yet there are few effective illegitimate models from which he can learn and few supportive agencies available should he attempt to use illegitimate means. The resulting discontent is subject to little social control and the adolescents must rely upon their own resources for achieving prestige: 'Under these conditions, tendencies towards aberrant behaviour become intensified and magnified.' Violence is seized upon as an avenue for the attainment of prestige not only because it expresses pent-up frustration, but also because it is an activity in which the inhabitants of disorganized areas are not at a relative disadvantage. 'The principal prerequisites for success are "guts" and the capacity to endure pain. One doesn't need "connections", "pull", or elaborate technical skills in order to achieve "rep".'[45]

As a result, in the disorganized neighbourhoods of the city, the play-groups of children become the conflict gangs of adolescence, with each gang jealously guarding its 'turf'. The third class of delinquent adaptation identified by Cloward and Ohlin is the retreatist sub-culture organized around the consumption of drugs. In essence they suggest that 'retreatist behaviour emerges among some lower-class adolescents because they have failed to find a place for themselves in criminal or conflict subcultures'.[46] Faced with the same anomic situation as others in their neighbourhood as far as legitimate opportunity structures are concerned, their attempts to use illegitimate means are unsuccessful. If they are able to adjust their aspirations downwards Cloward and Ohlin suggest they may be able to make the stable 'corner boy' adaptation outlined by Whyte;[47] 'but for those who continue to exhibit high aspirations under conditions of double failure, retreatism is the expected result'.[48] Although the empirical basis of the Cloward and Ohlin thesis is scant it remains probably the most systematic attempt yet published to relate neighbourhood socio-cultural characteristics to juvenile delinquency.

Attention so far has been concentrated almost wholly on studies relating

[44] *Ibid.* p. 282.
[45] *Ibid.* p. 283.
[46] *Ibid.* p. 287.
[47] W. F. Whyte, *Street Corner Society* (Chicago, 1955).
[48] Cloward and Ohlin, in Wolfgang *et al., Sociology of Crime,* p. 287.

the neighbourhood to the delinquent activity of adolescents. Work relating other forms of deviant behaviour to the neighbourhood is also relevant to our purpose. In fact, however, with the exception of a few ecological studies concerned with the more severe psychiatric disorders and with suicide, there is little material available relating community characteristics to deviant behaviour other than that committed by juveniles. Adult criminals generally appear as rather shadowy figures on the fringes of the investigator's concern with delinquent youth or else are seen as merely grown-up versions of the latter. Little material is available on the community background of alcoholism or of much adult drug addiction. The oft-remarked association between 'suburban neurosis' and the consumption of barbiturates by women has little research evidence to bear it up. Analysis of the local participation of such 'deviants' and the content of local sub-cultures should be a rewarding exercise.

The classic ecological study of the residential distribution of psychotic patients is Faris and Dunham's *Mental Disorders in Urban Areas,* a study of Chicago and of Providence, Rhode Island.[49] Replication of their work in a series of other American cities,[50] and in Bristol, Luton and Derby,[51] has generally led to a corroboration of their pioneer findings. Faris and Dunham's study is based on data relating to nearly 29,000 patients admitted to four state mental hospitals during the period 1922 to 1934. The area framework for the ecological analysis consists of the sub-communities defined in the Chicago 'Community Fact Books'. Both the rates for all psychoses and those for different diagnoses show systematic variations between the various areas of the city. The general pattern is very similar to that of the delinquency rates established by Shaw and McKay: high rates are clustered around the central business district while there are progressively lower rates towards the periphery of the city. The distribution of schizophrenia, general paresis, drug addiction, and alcoholic psychoses parallels that for the total series, with the highest rates occurring in neighbourhoods characterized by low socio-economic status and rapid population turnover. With the exception of the few high rate areas most neighbourhoods have a low frequency of these psychoses. Both male and

[49]R. E. L. Faris and H. W. Dunham, *Mental Disorders in Urban Areas* (Chicago, 1939).

[50]E. W. Mowrer, *Disorganization, Personal and Social* (New York, 1942), chaps 15–16; H. W. Dunham, 'Current status of ecological research in mental disorder', *Soc. Forces,* 25 (1947), 321–6; S. A. Queen, 'Ecological study of mental disorders', *Am. Sociol. Rev.* 5 (1940), 201–9; C. W. Schroeder, 'Mental disorders in cities', *Am. J. Sociol.* 48 (1942), 40–7. For a general criticism of the ecological approach in the investigation of psychiatric disorders see M. L. Kohn and J. A. Clausen, 'The ecological approach in social psychiatry', *Am. J. Sociol.* 60 (1954), 140–51.

[51]E. H. Hare, 'Mental illness and social conditions in Bristol', *J. Ment. Sci.* 102 (1956), 349; E. H. Hare, 'Family setting and the urban distribution of schizophrenia', *J. Ment. Sci.* 102 (1956), 753; D. W. G. Timms, 'The Distribution of Social Defectives in Two British Cities: A Study in Human Ecology', unpub. Ph.D. dissertation, University of Cambridge, 1963; D. W. G. Timms, 'The spatial distribution of social deviants in Luton, England', *Aust. N.Z. J. Sociol.* I (1965), 38–52.

female and native-born and foreign-born populations show the same general distribution pattern. The rates of schizophrenia for Whites are highest in areas where Negroes are in the majority, while those for Negroes are highest in areas where Whites are in the majority. In contrast with the findings on schizophrenia, patients diagnosed as having a manic-depressive psychosis show a virtually random residential distribution. Although the highest incidence rates occur in the inner city there is no general gradient towards the outskirts and inter-area variation is slight. The correlation between the incidence rates of schizophrenia and manic-depressive psychoses is little different from zero.

The distribution of hospitalized mental patients in the English towns of Luton and Derby closely follows the Chicago pattern.[52] In Luton the neighbourhoods within a half-mile radius of the city centre have a total first admission rate which is more than twice that of neighbourhoods located more than two miles from the centre. In Derby there is a threefold difference between neighbourhoods in the two zones. In both towns both the total rates and the rates for schizophrenia are highest in those neighbourhoods which combine low status with high residential mobility. The correlation between schizophrenia and the manic-depressive psychoses is insignificant in Luton but significant and positive in Derby. No convincing explanation of the difference in the two towns is forthcoming and the Derby pattern stands as a deviation from that reported in the majority of other analyses.

Although there is an impressive consistency in the findings on the distribution of the major psychoses in Western cities there is little evidence of consistency in the attempts which have been made to explain the findings. Faris and Dunham's preferred explanation is couched in terms of social isolation, but alternative explanations have been proposed which stress differential community attitudes and reactions to abnormal behaviour, the drift of schizophrenics (and other deviants) to disorganized communities, and differences in family socialization patterns.[53] The social isolation hypothesis has also been proposed as an explanation of suicide which has been shown to have a distribution pattern which is very similar to that of schizophrenia.[54]

In essence the social isolation hypothesis suggests 'that extended isolation of the person produces the abnormal traits of behaviour and mentality'.[55] A vicious circle of seclusion and rejection ends in the person's withdrawal from reality. 'Any factor which interferes with social contacts with other persons produces isolation. The role of an outcast has tremendous effects on the development of the personality.'[56] According to Sainsbury:

[52]Timms, 'Distribution of Social Defectives'.

[53]See S. K. Weinberg, 'Urban areas and hospitalized psychotics', in S. K. Weinberg (ed.), *The Sociology of Mental Disorders* (Chicago, 1967), pp. 22–6.

[54]P. Sainsbury, *Suicide in London* (London, 1955); J. P. Gibbs (ed.), *Suicide* (New York, 1968), esp. Introduction and chap. 2.

[55]Faris and Dunham, *Mental Disorders in Urban Areas,* p. 173.

[56]*Ibid.* p. 177.

That the differential distribution of suicide rates within the city corresponds with the areas of social disorganization, mobility and isolation, seems well founded. These statistics raise the question whether social disorganization causes suicide. The evidence suggests that it does. The interpretation offered is that high mobility and social isolation preclude a stable social framework by which the individual may orientate himself, so that he pursues an anonymous and aimless existence devoid of meaning, which induces an ennui culminating in suicide.'[57]

Similarly Gibbs postulates that

> *disruption of social relations* is *the* etiological factor in suicide, whether variation in the rate or the individual case. The general thesis is stated formally as two propositions: (1) the greater the incidence of disrupted social relations in a population, the higher the suicide rate of that population; and (2) all suicide victims have experienced a set of disrupted social relations that is not found in the history of nonvictims.[58]

The evidence in favour of the general thesis concerning the noxious effects of social isolation is strong, but there is little material available for specifying the precise effects of different types and different lengths of isolation. If both schizophrenia and suicide (as well as drug addiction and alcoholic psychosis) are seen as resulting from a disruption of social relationships, what determines which reaction takes place? Are disruptions equally significant whenever they occur? In their 1939 statement, Faris and Dunham suggest 'Normal mentality and behaviour develops over a long period of successful interaction between the person and . . . organized agencies of society. Defects in mentality and behaviour may result from serious gaps in any part of the process.'[59] In earlier statements, Faris concentrated on a postulated incongruity between intra-familial and extra-familial orientations towards the child and suggested that these could be subsumed under a model of the 'typical process' of schizophrenia which has its roots in childhood difficulties of relating to others. Parental over-solicitude produces a 'spoiled child' type of personality which is subject to persecution, discrimination or rejection by its neighbourhood peers. In the face of continued lack of success at making friends in the neighbourhood the child eventually gives up, 'from this time their interest in sociability declines and they slowly develop the seclusive personality that is characteristic of the schizophrenic'.[60] As a result of a lack of experience with interacting with others the person is deficient in his understanding of relational behaviour and may therefore be expected to react towards others in unconventional and culturally

---

[57]Sainsbury, *Suicide in London.*
[58]Gibbs, *Suicide,* p. 173. Italics in original.
[59]Faris and and Dunham, *Mental Disorders in Urban Areas,* p. 153.
[60]R. E. L. Faris, 'Cultural isolation and the schizophrenic personality', *Am. J. Sociol.* 40 (1937), 456–7.

inappropriate ways. In this model Faris appears to anticipate one of the major aspects of the aetiological scheme outlined by the authors of the Stirling County study.[61] In what is the most comprehensive analysis of the relationship between community characteristics and psychiatric morbidity yet published, Leighton *et al.* advance the theory that the major environmental factor in the aetiology of mental disorder is social disintegration, as indicated by such measures as poverty, cultural mixing, decline in religious behaviour, broken homes, and poor communication. The disintegrated community is one which lacks a patterned and stable network of interaction and reciprocity; it resembles a 'collectivity' rather than a society. The theory is stated strongly:

> Our casual orientation may be illustrated by the following hypothetical situations. If you were to introduce a random sample of symptomatically unimpaired people into the Disintegrated Areas in numbers small enough so they produced no significant change in the socio-cultural system, we think most of these individuals would become impaired. Conversely, if you were to take people out of the Disintegrated Areas and make a place for them in a well integrated community, we believe many would show marked reduction or disappearance of impairment.[62]

Rather than a direct causal link between the experience of living in a disintegrated community and the development of disorders, Leighton *et al.* suggest a more complicated two-step process. Life in communities characterized by a variety of indices suggesting social disintegration has certain noxious effects on the 'essential psychical condition', probably as a result of interference with the individual's needs for recognition and affiliation. Faced with this disturbance, the personality system may still avoid breakdown if it can substitute more gratifying objects for those causing the original maladjustment. Here again, the inhabitant of the disintegrated area is handicapped. 'The culture of the Disintegrated Areas is extremely poor in the number and complexity of objects available for this kind of adjustment.' Moreover, even if such objects are available, the breakdown of social relationships in the disintegrated neighbourhood means that the disturbed local inhabitant has little likelihood of finding them. Few guides exist

> and those that do exist seem far more likely to foster than to prevent the emergence of self-defeating sequences and the ultimate emergence of symptoms. Concretely, there is not much to prevent and often much to encourage a person with a disturbed essential psychical condition seeking relief by withdrawing to daydreams, building

[61]As of late 1969 three volumes had been published in the *Stirling County Study of Psychiatric Disorder and Sociocultural Environment:* vol. I, *My Name is Legion,* by A. H. Leighton (New York, 1959); vol. 2, *People of Cove and Woodlot,* by C. C. Hughes, M. A. Tremblay, R. N. Rapoport and A. H. Leighton (New York, 1960); and vol. 3, *The Character of Danger,* by P. C. Leighton, J. S. Harding, D. S. Macklin, A. M. Macmillan, and A. H. Leighton (New York, 1963).

[62]Leighton *et al., Character of Danger,* p. 369.

satisfactions on paranoid systems of thought, forgetting the past and blotting out the future, sinking into chronic states of apathy, depression, and anxiety, or masking the disturbed feelings by means of alcohol, sex, fighting, stealing, and other forms of excitement.[63]

The disintegrated areas described in the Stirling County study are small rural slums.

> All are outside of towns either just or quite far. They are strings of houses stretching along the highway or along a gravel road from a cross-road. All are situated on submarginal, unproductive land, overcut, untilled . . . The houses are mostly poorly built, of rough lumber, often with a tarpaper finish. Many are quite dilapidated. The interior is much like the outside—poorly furnished and poorly kept.

The inhabitants are the remnants of former industries, stranded when the latter foundered. Their ethnic and religious background is diverse. Occupationally they are unemployed or seasonal workers.

> There is very little social cohesion, organisation, or leadership in any of these neighbourhoods. The prevailing attitudes toward each other are hostility and suspicion, toward the rest of the world, a rather hopeless envy; toward themselves the feeling that they are a worthless lot . . . They are not acceptable socially in any circles except their own, so little visiting is done outside.[64]

Similar communities exist in the peripheral zones of many New World cities. In Australia, shanty towns containing mixed aboriginal and immigrant populations occur on the outskirts of many Queensland and New South Wales cities. Their characteristics—physical, social, and reputational—appear to be identical with those described in rural Nova Scotia.

Peripheral slums occupy one of the two major zones in transition which characterize the ecological structure of the city—zones which are in the process of major changes in function.[65] The other zone in transition, that surrounding the central business district, contains what is probably the core of the city's deviant areas. The characteristics of the rural slum have much in common with those of the unstable slums and rooming-house districts which typically occur around the borders of the city centre. The combination of low socio-economic status and high rates of population mobility appears to provide a fertile environment for deviant behaviour wherever it occurs.

*   *   *

[63] *Ibid.* p. 389.

[64] *Ibid.* pp. 405–6

[65] The concept of the 'zone in transition' is developed in E. W. Burgess 'The growth of the city', in R. E. Park, E. W. Burgess and R. D. McKenzie (eds.), *The City* (Chicago, 1925), pp. 47–62. Reprinted in Theodorson, *Studies in Human Ecology*, pp. 37–44.

The Neighbourhood, the Child, and Education

*   *   *

The child's conception of social reality is built up in the process of his interaction with his family, his peers, the other adults in his community, and those agencies of the wider society, particularly the school, with which he comes into contact. By comparing his experiences and his attitudes with those of his play-mates he can obtain consensual validation for his behaviour. By imitating the available adult models he can incorporate their roles into his future repertoire. By conforming with the normative expectations of those who have power over him he can gain acceptance into the group. In each case the earliest experiences may be expected to set the tone for much of what follows. The significance of neighbourhood for personality development is that most of these early experiences may be expected to take place within the bounds of the local area. Both the informal groupings of the playgroup and the family and the formal groupings of the school are based on a territorial delimitation of the community. The residential differentiation of the urban population ensures that this delimitation is unlikely to throw up random aggregates. Rather, there will be certain consistent patterns. In their turn these patterns will affect the personality development of the individual. Where the child is met with congruent reactions from family, neighbours, peers, and external agents he is likely to grow up with an integrated and secure sense of his own identity and of his own worth. Where the reactions conflict, the resulting personality may also be full of ambiguities and self-doubts. The residential differentiation of the community, aided and abetted by the geographical variation in educational facilities, has significance far beyond the immediate situation of the individual.

Overview of the Neighbourhood and Human Behaviour

The consequences for human behaviour of residence in one neighbourhood rather than another are mediated by the network of social relationships which connect the individual with his family, with peer-groups, with voluntary associations, and with a plethora of other groups. The neighbourhood is important because so many of these relationships depend on face-to-face contact and this form of interaction is particularly sensitive to spatial distance. A large variety of social processes takes place more forcefully when they occur within a face-to-face context. Although developments in communications technology have vastly increased the range over which meaningful interaction can take place it remains true that no other form of contact can approach the face-to-face meeting when evaluatively-charged material is to be transmitted. Face-to-face contact brings into play a host of ancillary communication systems— primarily gestural in form—which provide a richness of content which is lost in less intimate forms of interaction. These ancillary systems appear to be particularly influential in the transmission of attitudinal and evaluative information. The importance of non-verbal cues for the interpretation of meaning suggests that face-to-face contact is not only the most influential form of interaction, but also that it is an essential aspect of the human socialization process. Not only is the occurrence of face-to-face contact dependent on spatial proximity, but the groups in which it occurs most frequently, notably the family and the peer group, are themselves the objects of residential segregation. A child born in one neighbourhood rather than another is likely to belong to a particular type of family and to be exposed to a particular set of extra-familial stimuli. It is because people are segregated over the neighbourhood of the city in a systematic rather than a random fashion, and that the probability of contact varies according to propinquity, that the neighbourhood has significance for human behaviour. This significance is most pronounced for those who are essentially restricted to the neighbourhood—the young, the old, and those who care for them—but the effects of neighbourhood experiences on the developing personality may be apparent throughout life. The effects of residential differentiation are far-reaching.

Urban Differentiation, Characteristics of Boards of Directors, and Organizational Effectiveness[1]
Mayer N. Zald

Organizations are affected by the social, demographic, and ecological characteristics of the communities in which they are located. As larger urban centers differentiate into subcommunities and neighborhoods of different sizes and functions (as shown in land usages), organizations with similar products and goals are likely to find wide variations in support. At the very least, "demand" for organizational products varies according to the "wants" of the population in the area it serves.

Not only does urban differentiation lead to variation in the demand for services but it also leads to variation in a community's ability to provide a

[1]This paper is one of several based on a study of the Young Men's Christian Association of Metropolitan Chicago. The larger study was supported by a grant from the National Institutes of Health (GM-10777). Support for this phase of the study was received from the President's Joint Committee on the Prevention of Juvenile Delinquency and Youth Crime (HEW-66216). I am indebted to Phillips Cutright, Ray Elling, and Ollie Lee for their critical reactions to earlier versions of the paper. Charles Kamen, Mary Queeley, Patricia Denton, and Sue Ann Sanders assisted in the collection and analysis of data.

SOURCE: Mayer Zald, "Urban Differentiation, Characteristics of Boards of Directors, and Organizational Effectiveness," *American Journal of Sociology,* 73 (November 1967), 261–272. Copyright 1967 by the University of Chicago. Reprinted by permission of the author and the publisher, the University of Chicago Press.

support base for the organization. In this study we are concerned with the ability of different subcommunities to provide a pool of potential board members for a non-profit service organization, the Young Men's Christian Association of Metropolitan Chicago. Board members are expected, among other things, to make financial contributions, to provide leadership for the organization, and to add legitimation to its activities. *To the extent that urban differentiation restricts organizational access to a pool of potential board members with organizationally enhancing characteristics, we would expect lower organizational effectiveness.* For example, organizations in slum areas may find it difficult to locate board members with "desirable" attributes among the residents of the area because the *supply* of potential board members is restricted. Only if such organizations can link themselves to individuals and groups with no immediate connection to the area can they find the requisite board leadership. The Jacksonian emphasis on democratic participation in our society suggests that such a situation is bad since dependence on "outside" leadership leads to a devitalization of local institutions: "social absenteeism" leads either to an absence of leadership or to a leadership without real commitment and involvement. (A secondary concern of this paper will be to examine the correlates of board members' spatial connection to the areas in which agencies are located.) Regardless of this emphasis on participation, however, the necessity of recruiting board members, wherever they can be found, and of competing with other organizations in so doing suggests that organizations may vary in their *attractiveness* to potential board members. To understand fully the ability of organizations to recruit "good" board members, demographic factors influencing supply *and* organizational factors influencing attractiveness must be taken into account.

The foregoing statements represent sociological truisms, for the notions of both markets and, in more general terms, support bases represent part of the stock-in-trade of most sociological analysts of organization. But while quantitative studies of the relation of retail businesses to their support bases have been done,[2] there are few, if any, quantitative studies of other aspects of organizational support bases as they are linked to urban differentiation.[3]

This paper presents evidence on the relation of the ecological and demographic characteristics of the areas served by branches of the Young Men's

[2]Brian J. L. Berry, *Commercial Structure and Commercial Blight,* Research Paper No. 85 (Chicago: University of Chicago Geography Department, 1963).

[3]Studies of urban ecology in the Park-Burgess tradition did examine these linkages in a qualitative fashion. For a recent comparative and quantitative study, one aspect of which focuses on this problem, see Peter Rossi, *Why Families Move: A Study in the Social Psychology of Urban Residential Mobility* (Glencoe, Ill.: Free Press, 1955), pp. 55–62. See also L. V. Blankenship and R. H. Elling, "Organizational Support and Community Power Structure: The Hospital," *Journal of Health and Human Behavior,* III, No. 4 (1962), 257–68; and R. H. Elling and S. Halebsky, "Organizational Differentiation and Support: A Conceptual Framework," *Administrative Science Quarterly,* VI (1961), 185–210.

Christian Association to some characteristics of their boards of directors. However, it is important to do more than just demonstrate differences among boards since such differences are important only if they have organizational consequences. We will, therefore, also be concerned with several outcome or effectiveness criteria. After first describing the research site, we will relate measures of the demographic and ecological base to board-member characteristics. Then we shall demonstrate the correlation of board-member characteristics to organizational effectiveness.

RESEARCH SITE

The Young Men's Christian Association of Metropolitan Chicago is the world's largest urban association of YMCA's. In 1961, when this study was begun, it had thirty-seven departments (branches), over two thousand employees (including close to three hundred professionals), an annual budget of over fifteen million dollars, and roughly one thousand board members of local departments.

Historically, the association has had a strong emphasis on the importance of laymen to the operation and control of the organization; the YMCA was an association of lay members who, in the tradition of Protestant Congregationalism, governed their own organization. Thus, even while bureaucratization and professionalization have occurred, an emphasis has been maintained on the importance and involvement of the boards of directors.[4]

The thirty-seven departments of the Chicago YMCA were located in the inner city, outer ring, and suburban areas; they did not, however, encompass the whole metropolitan area. Gary, Oak Park, and Evanston, for instance, had YMCA's which were not part of the metropolitan association, while the North Shore suburbs (Lake Forest, Winnetka, Glencoe, etc.) had never organized YMCA's. Most departments were identified with a community area, and all except three had delimited service areas. These three exceptions served the total community (i.e., the "Loop" area) and were excluded from further analysis. Obviously, the different areas are likely to develop different kinds of YMCA's, and historically there has been a tendency for larger departments to locate near commercial and industrial centers while smaller departments locate primarily in residential areas.

[4]For the history of the YMCA in the United States, see C. Howard Hopkins, *The History of the YMCA in North America* (New York: Association Press, 1951). For a history of the Chicago association, see Emmett Dedmon, *Great Enterprises* (Chicago: Rand McNally & Co., 1957). Owen Pence's *The YMCA and Social Need* (New York: Association Press, 1939) is a good sociological analysis of the transformation of the organization. For a shorter study of the transformation of the YMCA, see Mayer N. Zald and Patricia Denton, "From Evangelism to General Service: On the Transformation of the YMCA," *Administrative Science Quarterly*, VIII (1962), 214–34.

Three points regarding the departments studied should be noted. First, the boards of directors of each department were selected by the individual departments and were—except in unusual cases—self-perpetuating. Thus no central allocating or recruiting mechanism existed that would substantially influence the ability of local departments to compete for board members. Second, because the departments varied in size and program, there was some variation in the attractiveness of individual departments to potential board members.[5] Finally, the departments existed in all areas of the city, thus providing a wide variance in demographic base.

The analysis strategy is as follows. The next section presents correlation coefficients relating selected demographic characteristics to characteristics of board members. Then, the relation of board characteristics to several outcome measures—indexes of board and departmental effectiveness—is considered. Finally, the discussion is complicated by presentation of alternative explanations of results—on the one hand, considering the value of the correlations of demographic and outcome variables with those of board characteristics and outcome; and, on the other, the alternative value of departmental expense (which indexes both attractiveness and internal organizational features) as an explanatory variable.

DEMOGRAPHIC CORRELATES OF BOARD–MEMBER CHARACTERISTICS

The land use patterns of the city affect the supply of potential board members by bringing into the areas served by the departments people with

[5]Underlying this paper, though not tested in it, is an embryonic theory of the supply, demand, and recruitment of board members of voluntary associations. To state the theory briefly: the "supply" of potential board members varies in quality and number depending upon the occupational, educational, income, and elite composition of the available population. It is also affected by such attitudinal dimensions as the "associational-regarding" sentiments in the population. The "demand" for board members depends upon the number of associations attempting to gain or increase public legitimation and support and the need of these organizations for leadership for internal management. The competition among organizations leads to a distribution of the supply according to the differential attractiveness of organizations.

In general, larger organizations are more attractive than small ones because they permit a wider scope of action, a perception of greater community value, and a larger stage for self-aggrandizement. In general, organizations that deal with central or important societal values (e.g., hospitals and universities) are more attractive than those that deal with more peripheral values (e.g., community centers providing recreation for slum children).

As Ray Elling and Ollie Lee have noted in a personal communication, the above theory omits the processes and mechanisms of recruitment and involvement. Specifically, organizations that have "quality" or "power" boards find it easier to recruit others of similar standing both because of the associational and interpersonal networks in which the board members move and because others are attracted to boards that already have people of prestige on them. Once on a board, a person's awareness, interest, and involvement may develop.

different social attributes which may be considered more or less desirable. The purpose of this section is to correlate demographic variables (presumptively indexing potential supply) with the actual socioeconomic characteristics and work-residence patterns of board members of different departments.

Demographic Characteristics. Four measures of the departmental area are employed: total population residing in the service area, median family income of the resident families, per cent white of the resident population, and total number employed in the area (regardless of whether the population lives in the area). The first three variables were obtained from census tabulations.[6] Where census tracts lay in two or more departments, the figures were apportioned according to the proportion of the tract's land area lying in each service area.

The fourth variable could not be obtained from census reports, but data were available on the number employed in each postal zone.[7] Where postal zones overlapped two or more departments, a land use map, a postal zone map, and maps of departmental areas were used to apportion the number of employed.[8]

All four of these variables are conceived as supply variables, with larger scores representing a larger pool of potential board members. The first three variables index the pool of potential board members living in the area, while the last variable indexes, presumptively, the pool of business leaders associated with a larger working force.

Aggregate Measures of Board Characteristics. Measures on board composition come from one source, a board rating questionnaire filled in by the executive secretary of each department.[9] These measures fall into two groups:

[6] *Bureau of the Census Report PHC-1, for the Chicago Standard Metropolitan Statistical Area, 1960* (Washington: U.S. Government Printing Office) and the *Local Community Fact Book Chicago Metropolitan Area, 1960* (Chicago: Chicago Community Inventory, University of Chicago, 1960). The data are summarized by departmental areas in Mayer N. Zald and Charles S. Kamen, *Selected Characteristics of the Residents of the Service Areas of the Local Departments of the Metropolitan Chicago Young Men's Christian Association* (Chicago: YMCA of Chicago, 1964).

[7] *Employed Workers Covered by the Illinois Unemployment Compensation Act, 1955–1961, with Breakdowns for Chicago Postal Zones and Major Suburban Communities* (Chicago: Illinois State Employment Service, June 15, 1962 [mimeographed]), and *Suburban Factbook* (Chicago: Northeastern Illinois Metropolitan Area Planning Commission, 1960–61).

[8] The procedures used are presented in more detail in Charles S. Kamen. *The Boards of Directors of the Chicago YMCA: Correlaries of Board Member Participation* (Chicago: YMCA of Metropolitan Chicago, October, 1963), Appendix II.

[9] It is appropriate to note that these data, although crucial to this paper, were not collected as part of the larger study design. Fortuitously, I had learned that one of the metropolitan office staff was planning to gather information from the executives of each department about the training of board members. He expanded his program-oriented survey to include questions relevant to our study. The questionnaire was so structured that the secretary entered information from his records and perceptions on *each* board member. These were then summarized for each department by our research staff.

measures of socio-economic status, and measures of the spatial location of work and residence. The measures of socioeconomic status are drawn from the executives' description of board members' occupations. These we summarized into six categories: "business leaders," "middle management," "profession-als," "religious leaders, ministers," "labor leaders," and "other." The percent-ages in the last three categories were very small and will not concern us further.[10] The first three comprise the status measures used.

The executive secretary also indicated whether each board member lived and worked within the departmental area. This information was used to de-velop four measures: per cent live in-work in, per cent live in-work out, per cent live out-work in, and per cent live out-work out. These measures can be considered a rough measure of "social absenteeism" or, conversely, of leader-ship resources within an area.

Results. We have used product-moment correlations of the *t-* scored aggregate measures to examine the relations of demographic characteristics to board characteristics (and to facilitate later analysis as well).

Table 1 presents demographic correlates of the residence patterns of board members. These data examine the search for departmental leadership in differ-entiated community areas. The subject of interest is the extent to which a community area provides a pool of leaders within its boundaries; or, if you prefer the Jacksonian understanding, to what extent are organizations led by people with local orientations and maximum commitment to local institu-tions.[11]

Two key conclusions emerge from an examination of the pattern of correla-tions. First, the larger the number of people employed in an area the less likely are board members to live in the area (work in-live in, $r = -.33$; work out-live in, $r = -.44$). Departments situated in industrial and commercial subcom-munities do not recruit from among local residents. Furthermore, boards in areas having large concentrations of employment also tend to recruit board

[10]At one point, a sheer average of Duncan socio-economic ratings of occupations was contemplated, but the special nature of our population invalidated such a measure. In particular, Duncan scores result in highest scores being given all professionals. Yet, both the YMCA secretar-ies and I believed that many of the business leaders who would have scored only moderately on the Duncan index had much higher prestige, wealth, and social standing than many of the professionals. To give but one example, a multimillionarie who was a nationally known realtor and builder of apartment complexes would have received a score of 76 if classified as self-employed, real estate, or 51 if classified as self-employed builder, while any lawyer would have received a score of 93. Many of the businessmen came from the upper strata of occupations that have wide intraposition variance, but Duncan scores reflect only the general standing of the occupation.

[11]This issue has plagued much of the discussion of local government and suburbanization. Does "social absenteeism" increase as local leadership sources move to the suburbs? Data not presented indicate that people who live and work outside of the areas whose boards they serve *do not* contribute less to those organizations. It may be that social absenteeism separates organizations from potential board members rather than lowering their commitment once they have joined. See Kamen, *op. cit.* (n. 8 above).

members who *work outside* of that area (work out-live out, $r = .36$). These boards are not dependent on local leadership pools alone.

TABLE 1.   CORRELATIONS BETWEEN DEMOGRAPHIC CHARACTERISTICS OF DEPART-MENTAL AREAS AND RESIDENCE PATTERNS OF BOARD MEMBERS   (N=34)

Demographic Characteristics of Area	*Work-Residence Patterns*			
	Work in-Live in	Work out-Live in	Work in-Live out	Work out-Live out
Total number of people employed in area*	−.33	−.44	.16	.36
Total number of people living in area*	−.11	−.22	.18	.02
Median income of residents in area*	.56	.24	−.21	−.42
Percentage of white residents in area*	.19	.15	.05	−.22

*Excludes three departments, two of whose service areas are city wide and the third of which is restricted to a hospital complex. These departments had a predominantly work in-live out pattern. Inclusion would have raised the correlation of number employed with work in-live out.

Second, the median income of the population residing within a community area is the best single predictor of the residence pattern of board members. Departments serving areas of high-average income are much more likely to recruit board members residing in the area than are departments in low-income areas. The same pattern holds for departments serving high-percentage white areas. (Median income and percentage white are correlated .74 over departmental areas.)

The main conclusion to be drawn from the above data is that increasing residential *poverty* in an area correlates positively with increasing departmental recruitment of non-residents, either of people who only work in the area or, if necessary, of those who both live and work outside of the area the department serves. (As is shown below, however, in terms of its contribution to organizational and board effectiveness, the ability to recruit from the area the department serves may be a mixed blessing.) In general, then, the potential supply, measured in this gross way, is related to the recruitment of locally based board members.

In terms of its contribution to organizational effectiveness, the socioeconomic composition of a board's members is more important than their work-residence pattern. How, then, do the supply variables relate to our measures of socioeconomic characteristics?[12] In Table 2 the largest correlations are those between *number employed* and *number residing* in an area and percentage business leaders. As size of work force and of resident population increases, the aggregate status of board members increases. Median income is of little value in predicting the aggregate status of board members.

TABLE 2. CORRELATION COEFFICIENTS OF DEMOGRAPHIC CHARACTERISTICS OF DEPARTMENTAL AREAS AND OF WORK-RESIDENCE PATTERNS WITH SOCIOECONOMIC CHARACTERISTICS OF BOARD MEMBERS (N=34)

Demographic Characteristics	SES Measures (%)		
	Business Leaders	Middle Management	Professional
1. Total number of people employed in area	.54	−.21	−.17
2. Total number of people residing in area	.33	−.27	−.17
3. Median income of residents in area	−.05	.02	−.06
4. Percentage white residents in area	−.04	.27	−.23
5. Work in-live in	−.39	.09	.24
6. Work out-live in	−.28	.12	.10
7. Work in-live out	.33	−.03	0
8. Work out-live out	.19	−.10	−.06

[12]A word is in order regarding the measurement of socioeconomic status. The three measures of occupational status are not fully independent of each other. As noted above, the executive secretary was asked to place each board member in one of the following six categories. (1) professional leader—doctor, lawyer, etc.; (2) business leader—officer of firm or corporation; (3) middle management in business or industry; (4) religious leader; (5) labor leader; or (6) other. Thus, while there are five degrees of freedom, a high percentage in one category limits the variation in the other categories. Furthermore, in actuality, most board members were placed in one of the three categories which we are reporting. In no department did the percentage falling outside of these categories rise above 42 per cent. The "other" category was typically the largest of the discarded three; it was extremely heterogeneous, including retired people from diverse occupations as well as housewives and others. The intercorrelations among the three measures of SES reported in Table 2 are:

Per Cent	1	2	3
1. Business leaders		−57	−.23
2. Middle management			−.47
3. Professional			

The fact that the intercorrelations of the first three variables do not account for more than 40 per cent of variance suggests that their lack of independence does not prohibit substantive interpretations of correlations with other variables.

How can we explain these findings? The bottom half of Table 2 helps to unravel these relationships. The correlations indicate that departments with larger proportions of members living within the area are more likely to have boards with lower aggregate status (compare percentage business leaders, rows 5 and 6 with rows 7 and 8). On the other hand, departments that attract board members living outside the area are more likely to have boards with higher aggregate status. Often these members are people who reside in areas lacking YMCA's (e.g., the North Shore communities). Paradoxically, then, given the social ecology of Chicago, the location of departments within areas favorable to local recruitment of leadership limits the over-all status of the board that is actually attracted. (Presumably, these departments would recruit higher-status board members were mechanisms for attracting them available.)

The foregoing analysis demonstrates that the work-residence patterns of board members are related to urban differentiation in land uses and that urban differentiation is also related to the socioeconomic status of the board members that are attracted. From the point of view of organizational analysis, however, urban differentiation and its correlates are only important as they affect organizational functioning. What, then, is the effect of these factors on organizational effectiveness?

BOARD CHARACTERISTICS AND EFFECTIVENESS

The measurement and conceptualization of both board and organizational effectiveness present a complex problem. The examination of organizational effectiveness involves many different facets—efficiency ratios, morale, actual attainment of goals, indirect measurement of goal attainment, community and membership commitment, and so on. Examination of the effectiveness of boards presents a similar welter of possibilities—the extent of public and personal financial support that is given or raised by the board, the knowledge-ability and intelligence that are evidenced in decisions made by the boards, the success of boards in linking the organization to other organizations and sources of support, the relation of the board to the power structure of the community, and so on. Here we restrict ourselves to four easily quantified types of measures: financial contributions of board members, program participation, board attendance, and global ratings of organizational and departmental effectiveness.

Financial Contribution. The executive secretary of each department extracted from organizational records each board-member's contributions for 1961 and 1962. Our measure, a direct measure of board effectiveness in contributing money, is the percentage of board members contributing an average of more than fifty dollars a year. While there might be even better measures of financial contribution (e.g., the ability of board members to influence Community Fund allocations, or the amount that board members raise from people not on the board), this measure has the dual advantages of precision and easy availability.

Program Participation. The percentage of board members involved in direct program leadership measures the extent to which board members lead specific programs (e.g., youth groups, athletic coaching, and the like). From the viewpoint of YMCA ideology, which stresses that the YMCA is an *association* of members, not a hierarchical organization, program participation is a direct measure of effectiveness. (In other organizations, of course, board participation might represent potential interference with and complication of staff duties.)

Meeting Attendance. One expectation of individual board members is that they know their department and help to shape policy by attendance at both board and committee meetings. Most departments convene the full board nine or ten times a year, and the committees meet as required. Our measure is the percentage of a department's board members attending more than the grand median of number of meetings attended by the board members of all departments. (Because the executive secretary keeps attendance records, each member's attendance is known.) It should be noted that no claim is made that decisions of the full board are actually determinative. As in other organizations, key decisions are often pre-arranged among staff and key committees. Certainly, however, we would expect attendance at meetings to relate to knowledge and awareness, all other factors being equal.

Ratings of Board and Departmental Effectiveness. These ratings are essentially "reputational" measures of departmental and board effectiveness. Two knowledgeable staff members of the metropolitan office rated each board and each department on the following three phrases: "over-all efficiency," "quality of programming" and "board strength." "Board strength" is a reputational measure of board effectiveness,[13] while the former two probe departmental effectiveness. These measurements are reliable and distinct, and use of a forced-comparison ranking procedure provided a normal distribution of departments on each of the variables.[14]

[13]The phrase "board strength" was purposefully employed. No other phrase captured as well the tenor of staff discussions in evaluating boards. Usually a strong board was also considered a good one. Some boards were considered passive and weak, others independent-minded and strong. It might have been possible to separate the dimensions of independence/non-independence vis-à-vis the metropolitan office from the dimension of strength. Our observations suggest that only a few boards were considered both strong and independent.

[14]For details, see Appendix I, by Mary Queeley, in Kamen, *op. cit.* (n. 8 above). Since the metropolitan office staff tend to push for liberal program innovations, the use of their ratings might be thought to lead to an ideological bias in the ratings. The raters used, however, were both conservative and liberal; different raters were used for different dimensions. Finally, examination of the actual rankings revealed that several departments considered to be "innovative" were ranked down on some variables while several considered conservative were ranked upward on others. Inter-rater reliabilities are $r = .86$ for efficiency, $r = .73$ for board strength, and $r = .74$ for quality of program. Quality of program correlates .65 with efficiency and .67 with board strength. Efficiency correlates .63 with board strength.

Results. Table 3 presents correlations of board-member characteristics with the measures of effectiveness. The lower panels correlate selected demographic characteristics, residence patterns, and departmental expense with the measures of effectiveness. These latter coefficients allow us to examine the extent to which factors other than the characteristics of board members are helpful in determining effectiveness.

Column 1, top panel, clearly demonstrates that the percentage of board members rated as business leaders is directly related to level of contribution.[15] The percentage of middle management and professional is either uncorrelated or slightly inversely correlated with contribution levels. In the first instance, then, the expectation that attracting upper management to board membership would have a positive effect on contributions seems to be borne out. The low correlations found (none above .3) in reading down column 2 suggest that there is a slight tendency for boards with more well-to-do members to have lower attendance rates while boards with higher percentages of professionals may have slightly higher attendance rates. In a sense, then, the organization can trade attendance for contributions and vice versa. But the correlations are so low that a firm generalization is not warranted. Column 3 shows that departments with higher-status board members have low, direct-participation rates ($r = - .58$). Again, participation is inversely related to status.

Substantial correlations are found between metropolitan staff ratings of the departments and characteristics of the boards. First, it is clear that the metropolitan office staff considers strongest those boards with the highest percentage of business leaders. The correlation of .67 (with business leadership) is among the largest found in this study. It is also clear that having well-to-do boards correlates positively with quality of department programs and with over-all efficiency. Although the picture is more complex than this statement indicates, it appears that having strong boards leads to greater effectiveness, both of program and of efficiency. The data seem to imply that boards do make a difference (and in the direction that most agency executives would predict). To sum up the first panel, then, it appears that the members of more well-to-do boards contribute more money than those on less well-to-do boards; the well-to-do boards also contribute to a more effective department. On the other hand, departments with more middle management and professional leadership tend to have higher meeting attendance and higher program participation.

The second panel of Table 3 presents relationships between the two demographic measures which were most importantly associated with the characteristics of board members—number of employees in area and median income of residents—and the measures of board and organizational effectiveness. The low correlation of median income of residents with the measures of effectiveness indicates that this aspect of the areas has but little association with the

[15]This is not surprising. The percentage business leaders correlates .89 with a measure based on the executive secretaries' perception of each board member's annual income.

TABLE 3. CORRELATIONS OF BOARD CHARACTERISTICS, SELECTED DEMOGRAPHIC CHARACTERISTICS, RESIDENCE PATTERNS, AND DEPARTMENTAL EXPENSE WITH MEASURES OF EFFECTIVENESS (N=34)

	% Above $50 Contribution	% Above Median Meeting Attendance	% Direct Program Participation	Board Strength	Over-all Efficiency	Quality of Program
Board characteristics (%):						
Business leaders	.43	−.23	−.58	.67	.48	.42
Middle management	−.17	.19	.20	−.57	−.33	−.35
Professional leaders	−.09	.21	.26	−.13	−.32	−.07
Demographic characteristics of area:						
Number employed	.01	−.05	−.34	.35	.46	.21
Median income of residents	−.17	−.25	−.08	.04	.09	.19
Residence patterns:						
Work in-live in	−.35	−.05	−.42	.02	−.16	.11
Work in-live out	.29	.14	−.30	−.12	−.02	−.15
Departmental expense	.18	−.01	−.32	.71	.50	.48

outcome variables. None of the correlations accounts for as much as 10 per cent of the variance.

The other demographic variable, number employed in area, has little correlation with three of our six measures. It does have substantial (for this study) correlation, however, with two of the ratings made by the metropolitan staff and with program participation. Looking ahead to the fourth panel, we find a similar pattern of correlation between departmental expense and ratings of boards by metropolitan staff. And we have already noted the relatively substantial correlations of these outcome measures with the status of board members. Thus, both empirically and analytically the question of the determinants of these ratings remains ambiguous. These relations will be discussed in the final section.

Before leaving these zero-order relationships, however, we should mention the correlations in the third panel of Table 3. The correlation of percentage work in-live out patterns with contributions is due to its correlation with the percentage of business leaders on the board (see panel 2, Table 2). The percentage work in-live in has only slight correlation with all measures of effectiveness except direct program participation. The work in-live in pattern operates in an opposite way from the work in-live out pattern. Board members who both live in and work in are more likely to take a part in the program but less likely to contribute financially.

The over-all pattern emerging from Table 3 is that departments with high-status boards are associated with higher contribution levels and with generally better efficiency, program quality, and board strength. On the other hand they tend to have lower participation in direct program activities. Boards recruiting "locals" obtain slightly higher rates of program participation but little else. The data presented, then, certainly tend to confirm the basic proposition: Board composition is related to both board and organization effectiveness.

DEPARTMENTAL EXPENSE, BOARD CHARACTERISTICS, AND MEASURES OF EFFECTIVENESS

Earlier we noted that the YMCA of Chicago had often located its larger branches in areas with large business and manufacturing concentration. In fact, departmental expense correlates .45 with total employment in the area. Furthermore, we postulated that board members were more attracted to large organizations than small. We then argued that the larger YMCA's were in a better position to compete for those board members considered most desirable. In our data the attractiveness of a larger organization is evidenced by a zero order correlation of .50 between departmental expense and percentage business leadership. The weight of all these factors suggests that the system functions so that those organizations which tend to be the most attractive to board members with the most desirable characteristics (from the organization's viewpoint) are also those located in areas with the largest pool of potential board members—a situation conducive to the "rich getting richer."

The question emerges as to whether the rich do actually get richer. Does the recruitment of "superior boards" actually lead to more effective operation, or is the association of board characteristics with several measures of effectiveness merely spurious, the correlation being simply a function of the fact that more effective organizations, as here measured, are also larger ones?

This question gains added meaning when the staffing pattern of the YMCA is considered. As a general rule the career of executive secretaries takes the following pattern: executive secretaries are recruited from among the "better" of the lower professionals (business managers, program secretaries, boys' work secretaries, and the like). A new executive secretary is usually placed first in one of the smaller departments. As he proves his ability to administer and build a department, he is promoted to a larger department. As a result, the executive secretaries of the larger departments are generally those with the most experience and, supposedly, competence. One skill expected of secretaries is competence at recruiting good board members. Thus it may be that many of the findings from correlating departmental effectiveness with board characteristics may simply be a function of the department's size and the quality of its secretary. Moreover, larger departments may also be more effective because they benefit from greater division of labor.

Unfortunately, we do not have a rating of executive effectiveness so staff quality cannot be separated from department size. We can, however, begin to separate department size (seen as a composite of staff quality *and* the advantages of a division of labor) from the effects of having boards with higher percentages of business leaders.

First, examination of column 1, Table 3, indicates that larger size of department does not correlate highly with the average donations of board members ($r = .18$). Thus, while departments with higher average expense do tend to have higher average contributions, the relationship is loose, and contributions are not automatic. Although we lack quantitative data on this question, our observations suggest that a department's ability to obtain large contributions from its board members depends on either a general understanding that board membership entails large donations (one smaller department had a standing rule that members must be able to donate one hundred dollars a year) or a demonstrated need. The larger departments are sometimes money-making operations and, unless the secretary and board created special projects, they find it difficult to justify a heavy emphasis on contributions. Thus, while having wealthier members *permits* a department to obtain larger contributions, this factor is operative only when a need can be justified.

A more convincing way to examine the contribution of board characteristics and departmental size to organizational effectiveness is to compare partial correlations. Table 4 presents partial and multiple correlations of departmental expense and percentage business leaders to four measures of effectiveness (the three global ratings and percentage of members contributing more than fifty dollars annually). It is clear that board strength is related to both the percentage of business leaders on the board and the size of the organization. Larger departments are able to attract and utilize board members in such a way that the metropolitan staff sees them as being "strong." The multiple correlation of .80 suggests that the major components of strength are caught in the two independent variables. Both departmental expense and business leadership make independent, though smaller, contributions to quality of program ratings and to over-all efficiency. Adequate measurement of *staff* effectiveness might show these relations to be spurious, yet at this point we cannot rule out the contribution of boards to effectiveness. Finally, the partial correlations make it clear that when the status of board members is partialled out, departmental size is *uncorrelated* with amount of contribution.

TABLE 4.   PARTIAL AND MULTIPLE CORRELATION OF FOUR MEASURES OF EFFECTIVENESS WITH DEPARTMENTAL EXPENSE AND PERCENTAGE BUSINESS LEADERSHIP
Variables:
  1 = Board strength
  2 = Quality of program
  3 = Over-all efficiency
  4 = % above $50 contribution
  5 = % business leadership
  6 = Departmental expense
Partial Correlations:
  15.6 = .52
  16.5 = .48
  25.6 = .28
  26.5 = .25
  35.6 = .31
  36.5 = .35
  45.6 = .40
  46.5 = .04
Multiple Correlations:
  1.56 = .80
  2.56 = .48
  3.56 = .57
  4.56 = .43

SUMMARY AND CONCLUSIONS

This paper has attempted to bring together several areas of sociological analysis. In particular, we have shown that the processes of urban differentiation have consequences for the ability of a service organization to attract social support; the status of boards of directors is related to the income structure of residents in an area and the number of people employed in the area. Furthermore, we have shown that, within the limits of our data, the characteristics of a board are related to the effectiveness of an organization; higher-status boards, contributing greater financial aid, are likely to be associated with departments that are rated as more effective in program quality, level of efficiency, and board strength. On the other hand, these boards may show lower meetings attendance rates and less participation in programs. Furthermore, an analysis using partial correlation showed that these relationships are not merely a spurious correlate of departmental size (although they may be spuriously related to executive and staff competence, which was not measured). Departmental size is interrelated with demographic characteristics of areas, with ability to attract high status boards, and with measures of effectiveness.

More important, however, than the specific associations shown is the general line of analysis implied. On the one hand, the process of metropolitan differentiation has consequences which are rarely considered in ecology texts. Here we have attempted to link urban ecology with organizational theory; the two are joined both through the concept of a support base and through the factors determining organizational location. Furthermore, we have quantitatively shown some effects of support base on organizational effectiveness. Too often both of these concepts are left unmeasured and vacuous.

This study has certain limits which should be noted. First, the role of staff has not been adequately examined. More important for the major analytic theme, however, we have studied the YMCA in vacuo, yet it must compete for board members with other organizations in its areas. There is not only a supply of potential board members, there is also a demand function at work.

And not only must the YMCA compete for board members but the effectiveness of its boards is related to the linkages they establish with other organizations and centers of power. Our general postulate would be that the higher the status of the board the more likely the organization is to command resources and legitimacy from the society. A more subtle analysis, however, would show that high status alone is insufficient; depending on the functions to be served, a balance in board recruitment may be necessary. The professional who assumed that only status was of importance in recruiting boards would be mistaken. Indeed, for certain specific issues, decisions, or linkages, general social status might even hinder the appropriate action.

In spite of the limitations of this study, however, its central thrust should be noted: The study of boards of directors cannot be limited to Veblenesque caricature in which board members conspicuously consume community prestige; instead, it must be seen as an integral part of organizational theory.

C URBAN POLITICAL PROCESS

The "Liberation" of Gary, Indiana
Edward Greer

In silhouette, the skyline of Gary, Indiana, could serve as the perfect emblem of America's industrial might—or its industrial pollution. In the half-century since they were built, the great mills of the United States Steel Corporation —once the largest steel complex on earth—have produced more than a quarter-trillion tons of steel. They have also produced one of the highest air pollution rates on earth. Day and night the tall stacks belch out a ruddy smoke that newcomers to the city find almost intolerable.

Apart from its appalling physical presence, the most striking thing about Gary is the very narrow compass in which the people of the city lead their lives. Three-quarters of the total work force is directly employed by the United States Steel Corporation. About 75 percent of all male employment is in durable goods manufacture and in the wholesale-retail trades, and a majority of this labor force is blue-collar. This means that the cultural tone of the city is solidly working-class.

But not poor. Most Gary workers own their own homes, and the city's median income is 10 percent above the national average. The lives of these

SOURCE: Edward Greer, "The Liberation of Gary, Indiana," *Trans-action,* 8 (January 1971), 30–39, 63. Copyright © January 1971 by Trans-action, Inc., New Brunswick, New Jersey. Reprinted by permission.

people, however, are parochial, circumscribed, on a tight focus. With the exception of the ethnic clubs, the union and the Catholic church, the outstanding social edifices in Gary are its bars, gambling joints and whorehouses.

COMPANY TOWN

The city of Gary was the largest of all company towns in America. The United States Steel Corporation began construction in 1905, after assembling the necessary parcel of land on the Lake Michigan shore front. Within two years, over $40 million had been invested in the project; by now the figure must be well into the billions.

Gary was built practically from scratch. Swamps had to be dredged and dunes leveled; a belt-line railroad to Chicago had to be constructed, as well as a port for ore ships and of course a vast complex of manufacturing facilities including coke ovens, blast furnaces and an independent electrical power plant. The city was laid out by corporation architects and engineers and largely developed by the corporation-owned Gary Land Company, which did not sell off most of its holdings until the thirties. Even though the original city plan included locations for a variety of civic, cultural and commercial uses (though woefully little for park land), an eminent critic, John W. Reps, points out that it "failed sadly in its attempt to produce a community pattern noticeably different or better than elsewhere."

The corporation planned more than the physical nature of the city. It also had agents advertise in Europe and the South to bring in workers from as many different backgrounds as possible to build the mills and work in them. Today over 50 ethnic groups are represented in the population.

This imported labor was cheap, and it was hoped that cultural differences and language barriers would curtail the growth of a socialist labor movement. The tough, pioneer character of the city and the fact that many of the immigrant workers' families had not yet joined them in this country combined to create a lawless and vice-ridden atmosphere which the corporation did little to curtail. In much more than its genesis and name, then, Gary is indelibly stamped in the mold of its corporate creators.

LABOR AND THE LEFT

During the course of the First World War, government and vigilante repression broke the back of the Socialist party in small-town America, though it was not very strong to begin with. Simultaneously, however, the Left grew rapidly as a political force among the foreign-born in large urban centers. As the war continued, labor peace was kept by a combination of prosperity (full employment and overtime), pressures for production in the "national interest," and Wilsonian and corporate promises of an extension of democracy in the workplace after the war was over. The promises of a change in priorities proved empty, and in 1919 the long-suppressed grievances of the steelworkers broke forth. Especially among the unskilled immigrant workers, demands for an industrial union, a reduction of the workday from 12 to eight hours and better pay and working conditions sparked a spontaneous movement for an industry–wide strike.

For a time it appeared that the workers would win the Great Steel Strike of 1919, but despite the capable leadership of William Z. Foster the strike was broken. The native white skilled labor aristocracy refused to support it, and the corporation imported blacks from the South to scab in the mills. This defeat helped set back the prospect of militant industrial trade unionism for almost a generation. And meanwhile, racism, a consumer-oriented culture (especially the automobile and relaxed sexual mores) and reforms from above (by the mid-twenties the eight-hour day had been voluntarily granted in the mills) combined to prevent the Left from recovering as a significant social force.

It was in the period between World War I and the depression that a substantial black population came to Gary. Before the war only a handful of black families lived there, and few of them worked in the mills. During World War I, when immigration from abroad was choked off, blacks were encouraged to move to Gary to make up for the labor shortage caused by expanding production. After the war this policy was continued, most spectacularly during the strike, but rather consistently throughout the twenties. In 1920 blacks made up 9.6 percent of the population; in 1930 they were 17.8 percent—and they were proportionately represented in the steel industry work force.

When the CIO was organized during the depression, an interracial alliance was absolutely essential to the task. In Gary a disproportionate number of the union organizers were black; the Communist party's slogan of "black and white unite and fight" proved useful as an organizing tactic. Nevertheless, it was only during World War II (and not as the result of the radicals' efforts) that black workers made a substantial structural advance in the economy. Demography, wartime full employment and labor shortages proved more important to the lot of black workers than their own efforts and those of their allies.

As after the First World War, so after the second, there came a repression to counter the growth of the Left. The Communist component of the trade union movement was wiped out, and in the general atmosphere of the early cold war black people, too, found themselves on the defensive. At the local level in Gary, the remaining trade union leaders made their peace with the corporation (as well as the local racketeers and Democratic party politicians), while various campaigns in the forties to racially integrate the schools and parks failed utterly.

Finally, in the early fifties, the inherently limited nature of the trade union when organized as a purely defensive institution of the working class—and one moreover that fully accepts capitalist property and legal norms—stood fully

revealed. The Steelworkers Union gave up its right to strike over local grievances, which the Left had made a key part of its organizing policy, in return
for binding arbitration, which better suited the needs and tempers of the
emerging labor bureaucrats.

CORPORATE RACISM

The corporation thus regained effective full control over the work process.
As a result, the corporation could increase the amount of profit realized per
worker. It could also intensify the special oppression of the black workers;
foremen could now assign them discriminatorily to the worst tasks without
real union opposition. This corporate racism had the additional benefit of
weakening the workers' solidarity. For its part, the union abolished shop
stewards, replacing them with one full-time elected "griever." This of course
further attenuated rank-and-file control over the union bureaucracy, aided in
depoliticizing the workers and gave further rein to the union's inclination to
mediate worker/employer differences at the point of production, rather than
sharpen the lines of struggle in the political economy as a whole.

The corporate and union elites justified this process by substantial wage
increases, together with other benefits such as improved pension and welfare
plans. For these gains a price was paid. Higher product prices, inflation and
a rising tax burden on the workers all ensued from the union's passive acceptance of corporate priorities.

There were extremely important racial consequences as well. For as the
union leadership was drawn further and further into complicity with corporate
goals, a large segment of the industrial working class found itself in the
apparently contradictory position of opposing the needs of the poorest workers
for increased social welfare services. A large part of the material basis for white
working-class racism originates here. Gary steelworkers, struggling to meet
their home mortgage payments, are loath to permit increased assessments for
additional municipal services which they view as mostly benefitting black
people.

UNITED STATES STEEL

Needless to say, the corporation helped to develop, promote and protect
the Gary working class's new ways of viewing itself and its world.

In the mill, the corporation systematically gave the black workers the
dirtiest jobs (in the coke plants, for example) and bypassed them for promotion
—especially for the key skilled jobs and as foremen. Nor has that policy
changed. Although about a third of the employees in the Gary Works are
black, and many of them have high seniority, and although virtually all the
foremen are promoted directly from the ranks without needing any special

qualifications, there are almost no black (or Spanish-speaking) foremen. According to figures submitted by the United States Steel Corporation to the Gary Human Relations Commission, as of 31 March 1968, out of a total of 1,011 first-line supervisors (foremen) only 22 were black.

The corporation not only practices racism directly, it also encourages it indirectly by supporting other discriminatory institutions in Gary. Except for some free professionals and small business, the entire business community is a de facto fief of the corporation. The Gary Chamber of Commerce has never to my knowledge differed from the corporation on any matter of substance, though it was often in its economic self-interest to do so. This has been true even with regard to raising the corporation's property assessment, which would directly benefit local business financially. And in its hiring and sales practices, as well as in its social roles, this group is a leading force for both institutional racism and racist attitudes in the community. For instance, it is well known that the local banks are very reluctant to advance mortgage money in black areas of town, thus assuring their physical decline. White workers then draw the reasonable conclusion that the movement of blacks into their neighborhoods will be at the expense of the value of their homes and react accordingly. The local media, completely dependent financially on the local business community, can fairly be described as overtly racist. The story of the voting fraud conspiracy to prevent the election of the present mayor, Richard Hatcher, a black man, didn't get into the local paper until days after it made the front page of the *New York Times*.

The newspaper publisher is very close to the national Catholic hierarchy and the local bishop, who in turn is closely linked to the local banks. The church is rhetorically moderately liberal at the diocesan level, but among the ethnic parishes the clergy are often overtly racist.

POLITICAL CONSIDERATIONS

While the United States Steel Corporation has an annual budget of $5 billion, the city of Gary operates on some $10 million annually. (This figure applies only to municipal government functions; it excludes expenditures by the schools, welfare authorities, the Sanitary Board and the Redevelopment Commission.)

And the power of the city government, as is usually the case in this country, is highly fragmented. Its legal and financial authority is inadequate to carry out the public functions for which it bears responsibility. The power of the mayor is particularly limited. State civil service laws insulate school, welfare, fire and police personnel from the control of City Hall. Administrative agencies control key functions such as urban renewal, the low income housing authority, sanitation, the park system and the board of health. Appointive boards, with long and staggered terms of tenure, hire the administrators of these agencies; and although in the long run a skillful mayor can obtain substantial control over their operations, in the short run (especially if there are sharp policy differences) his power may well be marginal.

Two other structural factors set the context in which local government in Gary—and in America generally—is forced to operate. First, key municipal functions increasingly depend upon federal aid; such is the case with the poverty program, urban renewal, low income housing and, to a substantial degree, welfare, education and even police and sanitation. Thus, the priorities of the federal government increasingly shape the alternatives and options open to local officials, and their real independence is attenuated.

Second, the tax resources of local governments—resting for the most part on comparatively static real estate levies—are less and less able to meet the sharply rising costs of municipal services and operations. These costs reflect the increased social costs of production and welfare, costs that corporations are able to pass on to the general public.

This problem is particularly acute in Gary because of the ability of the corporation to remain grossly underassessed. As a result, there are implacable pressures to resist expansion of municipal services, even if the need for them is critical. In particular, since funds go to maintain existing services, it is virtually impossible for a local government to initiate any substantive innovations unless prior funding is assured. In this context, a sustained response to the urban crisis is prevented not only by a fragmentation of power but also by a lack of economic resources on a scale necessary to obtain significant results.

For the city of Gary, until the election of Mayor Hatcher, it was academic to talk about such considerations as the limits of local government as an instrument of social change and improvement of the general welfare. Before him, municipal government had been more or less content simply to mediate between the rackets on the one hand and the ethnic groups and business community on the other.

The Democratic party, structured through the Lake County machine, was the mechanism for accomplishing a division of spoils and for maintaining at least a formal legitimacy for a government that provided a minimum return to its citizenry. Left alone by the corporation, which subscribed to an inspired policy of live and let live where municipal politics were concerned, this political coalition governed Gary as it saw fit.

In return for the benevolent neutrality of the corporation toward its junior partner, the governing coalition refrained from attempting to raise the corporation's tax assessments or to otherwise insinuate itself into the absolute sovereignty of the corporation over the Gary Works. Air pollution activities were subjected only to token inspection and control, and in the entire history of the city the Building Department never sent an inspector into the mill. (These and other assertions about illegal or shady activities are based on reports from reliable informants and were usually verified by a second source. I served under Mayor Hatcher as director of the Office of Program Coordination until February 1969.)

In this setting—particularly in the absence of a large middle class interested in "good government" reform—politics was little more than a racket, with the city government as the chief spoils. An informal custom grew up that representatives of different ethnic minorities would each hold the mayor's office for one term. The mayor then, in association with the county officials, would supervise the organized crime (mostly gambling, liquor and prostitution) within the community. In effect, the police force and the prosecutor's office were used to erect and centralize a protection racket with the mayor as its director and organized crime as its client. Very large sums of money were involved, as indicated by the fact that one recent mayor was described by Internal Revenue officials as having an estimated annual income while in office of $1.5 million.

Besides the racket of protecting criminal activity, other sources of funds contributed to the large illicit incomes of city officials. There were almost 1,000 patronage jobs to distribute to supporters or sell to friends. There were proceeds from a myriad of business transactions and contracts carried out under municipal authority. Every aspect of municipal activity was drawn into the cash nexus.

For instance, by local ordinance one had to pass an examination and pay a $150 fee for a contractor's license to do repair or construction work within city limits. The licensing statute was enacted to maintain reasonable standards of performance and thus protect the public. In reality, as late as 1967, passing the exam required few skills, except the ability to come up with $1,200 for the relevant officials, or $1,500 if the applicant was unfortunate enough to have black skin.

Gary municipal affairs also had a racist quality. The black population continued to rise until in the early sixties it composed an absolute majority. Yet the benefits of the system just outlined were restricted to the less scrupulous of the leaders of other ethnic groups, which constituted altogether only 40 percent of the population. The spoils came from all; they were distributed only among whites.

And this was true not only for illegal spoils and patronage but also for legitimate municipal services. As one example, after Hatcher became mayor, one of the major complaints of the white citizenry concerned the sharp decline in the frequency of garbage collection. This resulted, not from a drop in efficiency of the General Services division, as was often charged, but from the fact that the garbage routes were finally equalized between white and black areas.

In short, the city government was itself just another aspect of the institutionalized structure of racism in Gary. To assure the acquiescence of Gary's blacks to the system, traditional mechanisms of repression were used: bought black politicians and ward leaders, token jobs, the threat of violence against rebels and the spreading of a sense of impotence and despair. For instance, it was a Gary tradition for the Democratic machine to contribute $1,500 each week to a black ministers' alliance for them to distribute to needy parishioners

—with the tacit understanding that when elections came around they would help deliver the vote.

HATCHER'S CAMPAIGN

The successful insurgency of Richard Gordon Hatcher destroyed the core of this entire relationship.

Hatcher developed what can best be described as a black united front, inasmuch as it embraced all sectors of the black community by social class, occupation, ideology and temperament. The basis of this united front was a commonly held view that black people as a racial group were discriminated against by the politically dominant forces. Creating it required that Hatcher bridge existing divisions in the black community, which he did by refusing to be drawn into a disavowal of any sector of the black movement either to his left or right—except for those local black politicals who were lackeys of the Democratic machine. Despite immense public pressure, for example, Hatcher refused to condemn Stokeley Carmichael, even though scurrilous rightwing literature was widely circulated calling him a tool of Carmichael and Fidel Castro. Actually, the rumor that hurt Hatcher the most was the false assertion that he was secretly engaged to a white campaign worker—and it was so damaging in the black community that special pains had to be taken to overcome it.

Muhammad Ali was brought to the city to campaign for Hatcher, but Hubert Humphrey was not invited because of the bitter opposition of white antiwar elements within his campaign committee. It is worth noting that a substantial portion of Hatcher's financial and technical assistance came from a very small group of white liberals and radicals, who, while they played a role disproportionate to their numbers, suffered significant hostility from their white neighbors for involving themselves openly with Hatcher. Their support, however, made it possible for the campaign to appeal, at least rhetorically, to all the citizens on an interracial basis.

Of course, this support in the white community did not translate into votes. When the count was complete in the general election, only 13 percent of Gary's overwhelmingly Democratic white voters failed to bolt to the Republicans; and if one omits the Jewish professional and business section of town, that percentage falls to 6 percent (in blue-collar Glen Park)—a figure more explicable by polling booth error than goodwill.

Even in the Democratic primary against the incumbent mayor, Hatcher barely won, although he had the support of a large majority of the Spanish-speaking vote and overwhelming support (over 90 percent) of the black vote. His victory was possible, moreover, only because the white vote was split almost down the middle due to the entry of an insurgent and popular "backlash" candidate.

Hatcher's primary victory was particularly impressive given the obstacles he had to face. First, his entire primary campaign was run on less than $50,000, while the machine spent an estimated $500,000 in cash on buying black votes alone. Second, the media was openly hostile to Hatcher. And third, efforts were made to physically intimidate the candidate and his supporters. Death threats were common, and many beatings occurred. Without a doubt, the unprecedented action of the Hatcher organization in forming its own self-defense squads was essential in preventing mass intimidation. It was even necessary on primary day for armed groups to force open polls in black areas that would otherwise have remained inoperative.

These extraordinary methods demonstrated both how tenuous are the democratic rights of black people and what amazing organization and determination are necessary to enforce them when real shifts of power appear to be at stake. When the primary results came in, thousands of black citizens in Gary literally danced in the streets with joy; and everyone believed that the old Gary was gone forever.

HATCHER'S TEMPTATIONS

Immediately after the primary victory, the local alignment of forces was to some degree overshadowed by the rapid interposition of national ones. Until Hatcher won the primary, he was left to sink or swim by himself; after he established his own independent base of power, a new and more complex political process began: his reintegration into the national political system.

The county Democratic machine offered Hatcher a bargain: its support and $100,000 for the general election campaign in return for naming the chief of police, corporation counsel and controller. Naturally, Hatcher refused to accept a deal that would have made him a puppet of the corrupt elements he was determined to oust from power. Thereupon the county machine (and the subdistrict director of the Steelworkers Union) declared itself for, and campaigned for, the Republican.

But the question was not left there. To allow the Democratic party to desert a candidate solely because he was black would make a shambles of its appeal to black America. And dominant liberal forces within the Democratic party clearly had other positive interests in seeing Hatcher elected. Most dramatically, the Kennedy wing of the Democratic party moved rapidly to adopt Hatcher, offering him sorely needed political support, financial backing and technical assistance, without any strings attached. By doing this, it both solidified its already strong support from the black community and made it more reasonable for blacks to continue to place their faith in the Democratic party and in the political system as a whole.

As a necessary response to this development (although it might have happened anyway), the Johnson-Humphrey wing of the Democratic party also offered support. And this meant that the governor of Indiana and the Indiana State Democratic party endorsed Hatcher as well—despite the opposition of the powerful Lake County machine. Thus Hatcher achieved legitimacy within the political system—a legitimacy that he would need when it came to blocking a serious voting fraud plot to prevent his winning the election.

Despite clear evidence of what was happening, the Justice Department nevertheless refused to intervene against this plot until Hatcher's campaign committee sent telegrams to key federal officials warning them that failure to do so would result in a massive race riot for which the federal officials would be held publicly responsible. Only by this unorthodox maneuver, whose credibility rested on Hatcher's known independent appeal and constituency, was the federal executive branch persuaded to enforce the law. Its intervention, striking 5,000 phony names from the voters rolls, guaranteed a Hatcher victory instead of a Hatcher defeat.

The refusal of the Justice Department to move except under what amounted to blackmail indicated that the Johnson-Humphrey wing of the party was not enthusiastic about Hatcher, whose iconoclastic and often radical behavior did not assure that he would behave appropriately after he was in power. But its decision finally to act, together with the readiness of the Kennedy forces to fully back Hatcher, suggests that there was a national strategy into which the Hatcher insurgency could perhaps be fitted.

My own view of that national strategy is that the federal government and the Democratic party were attempting to accommodate themselves to rising black insurgency, and especially electoral insurgency, so as to contain it within the two-party system. This strategy necessitated sacrificing, at least to a degree, vested parochial interests such as entrenched and corrupt machines.

Furthermore, black insurgency from below is potentially a force to rationalize obsolete local governments. The long-term crisis of the cities, itself reflecting a contradiction between public gain and private interest, has called forth the best reform efforts of the corporate liberal elite. Centered in the federal government, with its penumbra of foundations, law firms and universities, the political forces associated with this rationalizing process were most clearly predominant in the Kennedy wing of the Democratic party.

The economic forces whose interests are served by this process are first the banks, insurance companies and other sections of large capital heavily invested in urban property and, more generally, the interests of corporate capital as a whole—whose continued long-range profit and security rest on a stable, integrated and loyal population.

Thus the support given to Hatcher was rational to the system as a whole and not at all peculiar, even though it potentially implied economic and political loss for the corporation, United States Steel, whose operations on the spot might become more difficult. The interests of the governing class as a whole and of particular parts of it often diverge; this gap made it possible for Hatcher to achieve some power within the system. How these national factors would shape the amount and forms of power Hatcher actually obtained became quite evident within his first year of office.

MOSAIC OF BLACK POWER

When I arrived in the city five months after the inauguration, my first task was to aid in the process of bringing a semblance of order out of what can fairly be described as administrative chaos.

When the new administration took over City Hall in January 1968 it found itself without the keys to offices, with many vital records missing (for example, the file on the United States Steel Corporation in the controller's office) and with a large part of the city government's movable equipment stolen. The police force, for example, had so scavenged the patrol cars for tires and batteries that about 90 percent of them were inoperable. This sort of thing is hardly what one thinks of as a normal process of American government. It seems more appropriate to a bitter ex-colonial power. It is, in fact, exactly what happened as the French left Sekou Toure's Guinea.

There were no funds available. This was because the city council had sharply cut the municipal budget the previous summer in anticipation of a Hatcher victory. It intended, if he lost, to legislate a supplemental appropriation. But when he won without bringing in a council majority with him, its action assured that he would be especially badly crippled in his efforts to run the city government with a modicum of efficiency. Moreover, whenever something went wrong, the media could and did blame the mayor for his lack of concern or ability.

Not only did Richard Hatcher find his position sabotaged by the previous administration even before he arrived, but holdovers, until they were removed from their positions, continued to circumvent his authority by design or accident. And this comparatively unfavorable situation extended to every possible sphere of municipal activities.

Another problem was that the new administrators had to take over the management of a large, unwieldly and obsolete municipal system without the slightest prior executive experience. That there were no black people in Gary with such experience in spite of the high degree of education and intelligence in the black community is explicable only in terms of institutionalized racism —blacks in Gary were never permitted such experiences and occupational roles. Hatcher staffed his key positions with black men who had been school-teachers, the professional role most closely analogous to running a government bureaucracy. Although several of these men were, in my view, of outstanding ability, they still had to learn everything by trial and error, an arduous and painful way to maintain a complex institution.

Furthermore, this learning process was not made any easier by the unusually heavy demands placed on the time of the mayor and his top aides by the national news media, maneuvering factions of the Democratic party, a multiplicity of civil rights organizations, universities and voluntary associations and others who viewed the mayor as a celebrity to be importuned, exploited or displayed. This outpouring of national interest in a small, parochial city came on top of, and was almost equal to, the already heavy work load of the mayor.

Nor were there even clerical personnel to answer the mail and phone calls, let alone rationally respond to the deluge. The municipal budget provided the mayor with a single secretary; it took most of the first summer to make the necessary arrangements to pay for another two secretaries for the mayor's own needs. One result was that as late as June 1968 there was still a two-month backlog of personal mail, which was finally answered by much overtime work.

In addition to these problems there were others, not as common to American politics, such as the threat of violence, which had to be faced as an aspect of daily life. The problem of security was debilitating, especially after the King and Kennedy assassinations. In view of the mayor's aggressive drive against local organized crime, the race hatred whipped up during and after the campaign by the right wing and the history of violence in the steel town, this concern with security was not excessive, and maintaining it was a problem. Since the police were closely linked with the local Right, it was necessary to provide the mayor with private bodyguards. The presence of this armed and foreboding staff impaired efficiency without improving safety, especially since the mayor shrugged off the danger and refused to cooperate with these security efforts.

In addition, the tremendous amounts of aid we were offered by foundations, universities and federal officials proved to be a mixed blessing. The time needed to oversee existing processes was preempted by the complex negotiations surrounding the development and implementation of a panoply of new federal programs. There had never been a Concentrated Employment Program in Gary, nor a Model Cities Program, nor had the poverty program been locally controlled. Some of these programs weren't only new to Gary, they hadn't been implemented anywhere else either. The municipal bureaucracy, which under previous administrations had deliberately spared itself the embarrassment of federal audits, didn't have the slightest idea as to how to utilize or run these complex federal programs. Moreover, none of the experts who brought this largesse to Gary had a clear understanding of how it was to be integrated into the existing municipal system and social structure. These new federal programs sprang up overnight—new bureaucracies, ossified at birth— and their actual purposes and effects bore little relation to the legislative purposes of the congressional statutes that authorized them.

Needless to say, ordinary municipal employees experienced this outside assistance as a source of confusion and additional demoralization, and their efficiency declined further. Even the new leadership was often overwhelmed by, and defensive before, the sophisticated eastern federal bureaucrats and private consultants who clearly wanted only to help out America's first black mayor. The gifts, in other words, carried a fearful price.

BUREAUCRATIC ENEMIES

Except for the uniformed officials and the schools, which were largely outside the mayor's control, the standing city bureaucracy was a key dilemma for Mayor Hatcher.

The mayor had run on a reform program. His official campaign platform placed "good government" first, ahead of even tax reform and civil rights. Hatcher was deeply committed to eliminating graft and corruption, improving the efficiency of municipal government—especially the delivery of services to those sectors of the citizenry that had been most deprived—and he did not view his regime as merely the substitution of black faces for white ones in positions of power.

But he also had a particular historic injustice to rectify: the gross under-representation of blacks in the city government, and their complete exclusion from policy-making positions. Moreover, implicit in his campaign was a promise to reward his followers, who were mostly black. (At least most participants in the campaign assumed such a promise; Hatcher himself never spoke about the matter.)

Consequently, there was tremendous pressure from below to kick out everyone not covered by civil service protection and substitute all black personnel in their places. But to do so would have deepened the hostility of the white population and probably weakened Hatcher's potential leverage in the national Democratic party. He resisted this pressure, asserting that he believed in an interracial administration. However, in addition to this belief (which, as far as I could determine, was genuine), there were other circumstances that dictated his course of action in this matter.

To begin with, it was always a premise of the administration that vital municipal services (police and fire protection, garbage collection, education, public health measures) had to be continued—both because the people of Gary absolutely needed them and because the failure to maintain them would represent a setback for black struggles throughout the country.

It also appeared that with a wholesale and abrupt transition to a totally new work force it would be impossible to continue these services, particularly because of a lack of the necessary skills and experiences among the black population—especially at the level of administration and skilled technical personnel. In this respect Hatcher faced the classic problem faced by all social revolutions and nationalist movements of recent times: after the seizure of power, how is it possible to run a complex society when those who traditionally ran it are now enemies?

The strategy Hatcher employed to meet this problem was the following. The bulk of the old personnel was retained. At the top level of the administration (personal staff, corporation counsel, chief of police, controller) new, trustworthy individuals were brought in. Then, gradually, new department heads were chosen, and new rank-and-file people included. If they had the skill already, they came at the beginning; if they didn't, they were brought in at a rate slow enough to provide for on-the-job training from the holdovers, without disrupting the ongoing functions of the particular department.

The main weakness of this gradualist strategy was that it permitted the old bureaucracy to survive—its institutional base was not destroyed.

The result was that the new political priorities of the administration could not be implemented with any degree of effectiveness in a new municipal political practice. City government remained remarkably like what it had been in the past, at least from the perspective of the average citizen in the community. While the political leadership was tied up with the kinds of problems I noted earlier, the bureaucracy proceeded on its own course, which was basically one of passive resistance. There were two aspects to this: bureaucratic inertia, a sullen rejection of any changes in established routine that might cause conflicts and difficulties for the employees; and active opposition based on politics and racism, to new methods and goals advocated by the mayor.

To cite just one example, the mayor decided to give a very high priority to enforcement of the housing codes, which had never been seriously implemented by preceding administrations. After much hard work, the Building Department was revamped to engage in aggressive inspection work. Cases stopped being "lost," and the number of inspections was increased by 4,000 percent while their quality was improved and standardized. Then it was discovered that cases prepared for legal enforcement were being tabled by the Legal Department on grounds of technical defects.

I personally ascertained that the alleged legal defects were simply untrue. I then assumed that the reason for the legal staff's behavior was that they were overburdened with work. Conferences were held to explain to them the mayor's priorities so they could rearrange their work schedule. Instead, a series of bitter personal fights resulted, culminating in my removal from that area of work since the staff attorneys threatened to resign if there were continued interference with their professional responsibility. In the course of these disputes, both black and white attorneys expressed the opinion that they did not consider themselves a legal aid bureau for Gary's poor, and furthermore the root of the city's housing problem was the indolent and malicious behavior of the tenants. In their view, it was therefore unjust to vigorously enforce the existing statutes against the landlords. Thus, despite the administration's pledge, black ghetto residents did not find their lives ameliorated in this respect.

Gradually, then, the promise of vast change after the new mayor took office came to be seen as illusory. Indeed, what actually occurred was much like an African neocolonial entity: new faces, new rhetoric and people whose lives were scarcely affected except in their feelings towards their government.

This outcome was not due to a failure of good faith on the part of the Hatcher administration. Nor does it prove the fallacious maximalist proposition that no amelioration of the people's conditions of life is possible prior to a revolution. Instead, it was due to the decline of the local mass base of the Hatcher administration and the array of national political forces confronting it.

Most black people in Gary were neither prepared nor able to take upon themselves the functions performed for them by specialized bureaucracies. They relied upon the government for education, welfare, public health, police and fire protection, enforcement of the building codes and other standards, maintenance of the public roads and the like. Unable to develop alternative popularly based community institutions to carry on these functions by democratic self-government, the new administration was forced to rely upon the city bureaucracy—forced to pursue the option that could only result in minor changes.

ABORTED LIBERATION

The most significant consequence of the Hatcher administration's failure to transcend the structural terrain on which it functioned was political, the erosion of popular support after the successful mobilization of energies involved in the campaign. The decline of mass participation in the political process contributed in turn to the tendency of the new regime to solve its dilemmas by bureaucratic means or by relying on outside support from the federal government.

The decline in mass support ought not to be confused with a loss of votes in an election. Indeed, Hatcher is now probably as secure politically as the average big city mayor. The point is that the mass of the black population is not actively involved in helping to run the city. Thus, their political experiences are not enlarged, their understanding of the larger society and how it functions has not improved, and they are not being trained to better organize for their own interests. In short, the liberating process of the struggle for office was aborted after the initial goal was achieved—and before it could even begin to confront the profound problems faced by the mass of urban black Americans.

For example, after the inauguration, old supporters found themselves on the outside looking in. For the most part, since there was no organized effort to continue to involve them (and indeed to do so could not but conflict with the dominant strategy of the administration), they had to be content to remain passive onlookers. Moreover, the average citizen put a lot of faith in the mayor and wanted to give him an opportunity to do his job without intruding on the process.

Even among the most politicized rank-and-file elements there was a fear of interfering. Painfully conscious of their lack of training and experience, they were afraid of "blowing it." Instead they maintained a benevolent watchfulness, an attitude reinforced by the sense that Hatcher was unique, that his performance was some kind of test of black people as a race. (Whites were not the only people encouraged by the media to think in these terms.) There were of course some old supporters who were frankly disillusioned: they did not receive the patronage or other assistance they had expected: they were treated rudely by a bureaucratic holdover or were merely unable to reach the ear of a leader who was once accessible as a friend.

The ebbing away of popular participation could be seen most markedly in the Spanish-speaking community, which could not reassure itself with the symbolic satisfaction of having a member of its group in the national spotlight. With even less education and prior opportunity than the blacks, they found that the qualifications barrier to municipal government left them with even less patronage than they felt to be their due reward. This feeling of betrayal was actively supported by the former machine politicians and criminal elements, who consciously evoked ethnic prejudices to isolate the mayor and weaken his popular support.

What happened in the first year of the new administration, then, was a contradiction between efficiency and ethnic solidarity. At each point the mayor felt he had to rely upon the expert bureaucracy, even at the cost of increasing his distance from his mass base. And this conflict manifested itself in a series of inexorable political events (the appointment of outside advisors, for example), each of which further contributed to eroding the popular base of the still new leadership.

As Antonio Gramsci pointed out, beneath this contradiction lies a deeper one: a historic class deprivation—inflicted on the oppressed by the very structure of the existing society—which barred the underclass from access to the skills necessary for it to run the society directly in its own interests and according to its own standard of civilization. Unless an oppressed social group is able to constitute itself as what Gramsci characterizes as a counterhegemonic social bloc, its conquest of state power cannot be much more than a change in leaders. Given the overall relation of forces in the country at large, such an undertaking was beyond the power of the black community in Gary in 1968. Therefore, dominant national political forces were able quickly to reconstitute their overall control.

NATIONAL POWER

What happened to Richard Hatcher in Gary in his first year as mayor raises important questions—questions that might be of only theoretical interest if he were indeed in a unique position. He is not. Carl Stokes, a black, is mayor of Cleveland. Charles Evers, a black, is mayor of Fayette, Mississippi. Thomas Bradley, a black, very nearly became mayor of Los Angeles. Kenneth Gibson, a black, is now mayor of Newark. The list will grow, and with it the question of how we are to understand the mass participation of blacks in electoral politics in this country and the future of their movement.

I believe that until new concepts are worked out, the best way of understanding this process is by analogy with certain national liberation movements in colonial or neocolonial countries. Of course, the participants—in Gary as in Newark—are Americans, and they aren't calling for a UN plebiscite. But they were clearly conscious of themselves as using elections as a tool, as a step toward a much larger (though admittedly ill-defined) ultimate goal—a goal whose key elements of economic change, political power, dignity, defense of a "new" culture and so forth are very close to those of colonial peoples. It is because Hatcher embraced these larger objectives (without, of course, using precisely the rhetoric) that his campaign can be thought of as part of a nationalist process that has a trajectory quite similar to that of anticolonial liberation movements.

In its weakened local posture, the Hatcher administration was unable to resist successfully a large degree of cooptation by the national political authorities. Despite a brave vote at the Democratic National Convention for Reverend Channing Philips, Hatcher was essentially forced to cooperate with the national government and Democratic party—even to the extent of calling on the sheriff of Cook County to send deputies to reinforce the local police when a "mini-riot" occurred in the black ghetto.

Without either a nationally coordinated movement or an autonomous base of local insurgency—one capable of carrying out on a mass scale government functions outside the official structure—Hatcher's insurgency was contained within the existing national political system. Or, to express it somewhat differently, the attempt by black forces to use the electoral process to further their national liberation was aborted by a countervailing process of neocolonialism carried out by the federal government. Bluntly speaking, the piecemeal achievement of power through parliamentary means is a fraud—at least as far as black Americans are concerned.

The process by which the national power maintained itself, and even forced the new administration to aid it in doing so, was relatively simple. As the gap between the popular constituency and the new government widened, like many another administration, Hatcher's found itself increasingly forced to rely upon its "accomplishments" to maintain its popularity and to fulfill its deeply held obligation to aid the community.

Lacking adequate autonomous financial resources—the mill remained in private hands, and it still proved impossible to assess it for tax purposes at its true value—accomplishments were necessarily dependent upon obtaining outside funds. In this case, the funds had to come from the federal government, preferably in the form of quick performance projects to maintain popular support and to enable everyone to appear to be doing something to improve matters.

These new programs injected a flow of cash into the community, and they created many new jobs. In his first year in office, the mayor obtained in cash or pledges more federal funds than his entire local budget. Hopes began to be engendered that these programs were the key to solving local problems, while the time spent on preparing them completed the isolation of the leadership from the people.

Then, too, the stress of this forced and artificial growth created endless opportunities for nepotism and even thievery. Men who had never earned a decent living before found themselves as high-paid executives under no requirement to produce any tangible results. Indeed, federal authorities seemed glad to dispense the funds without exercising adequate controls over their expenditures. A situation arose in which those who boasted of how they were hustling the system became prisoners of its largesse.

Even the most honest and courageous leader, such as Mayor Hatcher, could not help but be trapped by the aid offered him by the federal authorities. After all, how can any elected local executive turn down millions of dollars to dispense with as he sees fit to help precisely those people he was elected to aid: The acceptance of the help guaranteed the continuation of bonds of dependence. For without any real autonomous power base, and with new vested interests and expectations created by the flow of funds into the community, and with no available alternate path of development, the relation of power between the local leader and the national state was necessarily and decisively weighted toward the latter.

In Gary, Indiana, within one year after the most prodigious feat in the history of its black population—the conquest of local political power—their insurgency has been almost totally contained. It is indeed difficult to see how the existing administration can extricate itself from its comparative impasse in the absence of fresh national developments, or of a new, more politically coherent popular upsurge from below.

There is, however, no doubt that the struggle waged by the black people of Gary, Indiana, is a landmark on their road to freedom; for the experiences of life and struggle have become another part of their heritage—and thus a promise for us all.

Citizen Participation in Social Policy: The End of the Cycle?*

Jon Van Til
Sally Bould Van Til

The participation of citizens is a basic aspect of liberal democracy. The process of democratic governance is often valued more highly than its end product, as Mill (1875:39) argued: "The most important point of excellence which any

*A revised version of a paper read at the meetings of the American Sociological Association September 4, 1969.

SOURCE: Jon Van Til and Sally Bould Van Til, "Citizen Participation in Social Policy: The End of the Cycle?" *Social Problems,* 17 (Winter 1970), pp. 313–323. Reprinted by permission of the publisher, The Society for the Study of Social Problems.

form of government can possess is to promote the virtue and intelligence of the people themselves." To Mill, and the Anglo-American tradition that followed him, political participation was to be a great force for citizen education as well as system legitimation.

The concept of "citizen participation" is a uniquely American variant of the general concept of participation. It has become a key element in the post-war development of programs to contend with the crisis in the American city and society—particularly in the programs of urban renewal, community action, and model cities. However, the poverty program, with its bold attempt to foster citizen participation, has inspired as thorough a denunciation of the concept of citizen participation as was brought forth by the urban renewal program. Social scientists and government officials seem to have arrived at similar conclusions from these two experiences: citizen participation in social policy defeats the instrumental goals of policy reform and implementation.

A TYPOLOGY OF MEANINGS OF CITIZEN PARTICIPATION

This paper distinguishes between six forms of citizen participation in recent social policy and notes certain patterns by which two modes appear to predominate. In urban renewal programs, for example, the concept was originally interpreted to mean the involvement of civic leaders in an advisory capacity to the local planning agency. Over time, however, the concept began to include the activities of ordinary citizens in quite different roles. We contend that the variety of meanings of citizen participation in urban renewal may be comprehended by a typology that distinguishes between two aspects of participation: the range of citizenry involved, and the focus of their participation.[1]

Citizen participation in renewal involved either civic leaders only, or civic leaders as well as citizens affected by the renewal. Thus, the range of participation involved elites only, or non-elites as well as elites. Similarly, the focus of issues to which the participants directed their attention varied between questions of both ends and means, and questions of means only. In the first case, the focus of participation was on both the politics and administration of renewal; in the latter, the focus was only on administration. Table I presents four types of meanings of citizen participation that emerge from the combination of the two dimensions.

[1]Neither of these dimensions is particularly precise, but both are venerable ones in the literature of political sociology. The elite—non-elite distinction has been used outstandingly by William Kornhauser (1959); the politics-administration distinction is considered useful by Herbert Simon (1957).

CITIZEN PARTICIPATION IN URBAN RENEWAL

The "elite coalition," the involvement of elite only in questions of policy implementation, was the original form of citizen participation in urban renewal. It met the requirements of the "workable program," which demanded only the existence of a community-wide committee, which, it is suggested, should contain at least one representative of each civic group interested in the program (U.S. Housing and Home Finance Agency, 1961: 4). This type of participation stresses the values of cooperation, education, and consensus; it rather clearly implies that what is crucial is the harmonious realization of the renewal plans as drawn up by the experts.[2]

Evidence from early renewal experiences in Newark, Boston, New York, and San Francisco, indicates the presence of this form (cf. McQuade, 1966; Kaplan, 1963). In Newark, for example, Kaplan notes (1963:12) that the renewal officials often say that "their clearance decisions are made on the basis of 'technical' rather than 'political' criteria, and that the projects are planned in a 'nonpolitical' environment." The elites who rubber-stamp the plans generally do not challenge that assumption, which typically reflects the coincidence of their preferences with the plans that are drawn.

TABLE 1. A TYPOLOGY OF MEANINGS OF CITIZEN PARTICIPATION IN URBAN RENEWAL

Participation Is By	Participation Focuses On	
	Administrative Concerns Only	Political and Administrative Concerns
Elites only	Elite coalition	Politics of renewal
Elites and non-elites	Citizen advice	Pluralist participation

The effect of the "elite coalition" is clearly reflected in the goal-displacement that has been evident in the urban renewal program. The legislation embodied two potentially conflicting goals for renewal; the redevelopment of the center city and the provision of low-cost housing. In that the former purpose has been given higher priority than the latter, the elite coalition has had its way. Urban renewal has to date destroyed far more low-income housing than it has built (cf. Greer, 1965:3; Anderson, 1964:67).

The elite coalition often yielded to the "politics of renewal;" where compe-

[2]For instance, the Journal of Housing stated on its cover in July, 1956: "The only possible conclusion is that, in the long run, the cause of urban renewal will be advanced by having the public aware of what is going on and how it affects them. Citizen participation can save both time and money."

tition for the scarce values of land use is concerned, the conflicting interests of political elites are often manifested. Citizen participation in the politics of renewal means little more than the struggle for control of renewal planners among competing political elites. The politics of renewal shows more than the inescapability of political conflict in renewal; it also reveals how far from the interests of those citizens whose lives are touched by renewal plans are concepts of citizen participation that make room for elites only. The best studies of renewal politics (Rossi and Dentler, 1961:287; Meyerson and Banfield, 1964; Kaplan, 1963) demonstrate that the big decisions in renewal are made at supra-neighborhood levels and that non-elite participation in renewal conflict is often passive in nature.

Gradually, renewal programs elicited the participation of citizens directly affected by the plans. Such "pluralist participation" saw non-elites organizing to gain access to decisions formerly made by elites (cf. Kornhauser, 1959); it also took the form in most cases, of opposing the renewal of their neighborhoods. As citizens learned of renewal experiences in other areas of their city, they became more likely to organize to meet programs proposed for their community. The first encounter between citizens and the elite coalition tended to produce an easy win for the latter—as in Lake Meadows in Chicago, the West End in Boston, and Kips Bay and Stuyvesant Town in New York (cf. Wilson, 1966:409–410; Bellush and Hausknecht, 1967:191). As the opposition became more organized, however, delays were won in implementation, and sometimes a veto was achieved.

One observer of the mobilization of residents, William Brussat (n.d.:8), noted that "People in the mass do not produce positive, systematic programs. They are constitutionally incapable . . . of making complex decisions. But the negative decision is a simple decision, and the negative power of the grass roots is incontestable. The grass roots has the power of the veto." Kaplan (1963:164) and Wilson (1966:409) have noted the rise of such veto groups, and have pessimistically evaluated their impact on the planning process.[3]

The negative consequences of the involvement of non-elites as veto groups in the renewal process, coupled with the attractiveness of the idea of the participation of non-elites, have led to the development of the fourth type of citizen participation, where non-elites serve as "citizen advisors." Such involvement may range from the merest leg-work of collecting an audience for a meeting, to a rather full participation in the planning of the project itself.

---

[3]These sentiments are still heard in high circles. One high governmental official criticized Mayor Lindsay's renewal program in New York: "Community groups have gotten two very distinct ideas. One is that there's money in this, that if you raise enough hell there's money in it. Second, the city has made very clear that until it is satisfied that a particular community group is representative and makes known what it wants, the city isn't going to do anything. I think it's wild" (The New York Times, November 9, 1969).

Citizen participation is currently manifested in urban renewal programs through the Neighborhood Development Programs. At this writing, it is too early to judge the success of this form of "pluralist participation."

Experiences in Dyersburg, Tennessee, and Washington, D.C., have been described in demonstration reports as providing extensive administrative experiences for ordinary citizens (cf. Nixon and Boyd, 1957; District of Columbia, 1964).

The demonstration report on a conservation project in the Adams-Morgan section of Washington concluded (District of Columbia, 1964: vii): "Encouraging citizen involvement in planning and improvement programs through the organization of a citizens' planning committee turned out to be the strongest single stimulus to citizen participation in Adams-Morgan." The involvement of citizens in planning is a risky business, for their competence in this area is generally suspect. Nonetheless, the Washington report recommends (1964:8) that the advice of the citizens' committee be carried out, informed by "careful technical guidance" from professional planners. While the participation of non-elites as citizen advisors provides for optimism with regard to the extension of participation in democratic society, its application was limited to those neighborhoods in which old housing was to be rehabilitated and not cleared. Its incidence was so atypical in the renewal experience that it did not affect the scholarly consensus about participation of non-elites in renewal. Thus Kaplan (1963:164) argued that renewal was inescapably involved in the process of elite politics, but urged that it be kept as far out of the realm of mass politics as possible. And Rossi and Dentler (1961:285) denied the non-elite citizen the right to amend the plans lest "the overall features of renewal are . . . undermined by small concessions that, when aggregated, amount to serious departures from the grander conception."

It is difficult to reconcile this outpouring of pessimistic conclusions toward citizen participation of non-elites in the renewal programs with the new optimism that surrounded the involvement of poor people in the war on poverty. Did not the planners know the potential explosiveness inherent in asking for the participation of the lower class in a middle class world?

It appears clear that they did not. The poverty program framers were affiliated with a different political climate. Drawing on the experience of the Ford Foundation grey area studies, and the work of the President's Committee on Juvenile Delinquency, as well as the growing emphasis on "participatory democracy," an active role for the poor was conceived (cf. Marris and Rein, 1967).

CITIZEN PARTICIPATION IN THE WAR ON POVERTY

Most broadly, the poverty program began on the sole optimistic note of the urban renewal program, seeking to develop a role for non-elites, in this case the poor, as citizen advisors. A program designed to rehabilitate people, rather than buildings, necessarily required the active involvement of the poor. Maximum feasible participation, it followed, was necessary to enable the poor to escape from the "culture of poverty" in the bootstrapping manner of previous

Americans. Nevertheless, the precise role of the poor in relation to this clause was never clarified either by the framers of the legislation, or by the Congress as the bill sped through (cf. Rubin, 1967:5–6)."[4]

The primary intention of the community action programs was generally interpreted as involving the poor in a largely administrative role (Donovan, 1967:43)[5]; but the period of non-controversial implementation was short-lived, if it in fact existed at all in the large cities. Citizen participation in the war on poverty became embroiled in ideological issues much more quickly than it did in the urban renewal case. The vagueness of the legislative intent lent fuel to that debate (cf. Raab, 1966:47), and two new conceptions of non-elite participation emerged. One position contended that the poor should have an influential, if not controlling voice, in administering their program; another claimed that the poor should be allowed to deal with political as well as administrative questions. This was almost revolutionary; never before had the poor been given credit for much expertise regarding the area of their own experience.

TABLE 2.   A TYPOLOGY OF MEANINGS OF CITIZEN PARTICIPATION IN SOCIAL POLICY

	Participation Focuses on	
Participation Is By	Administrative Concerns Only	Political and Administrative Concerns
Elites Only	Elite coalition	Politics of reform
Elites and non-elites	Citizen advice	Pluralist participation
Non-elites only	Client participation	Grassroots participation

To accommodate this new conception of citizen participation, we must add a third level to our model, one that deals with the participation of non-elites only. Its administrative focus we shall call "client participation," and its political focus "grassroots participation."

The overall intent of the poverty program being largely administrative implies that the innovative potential of such participation was originally seen in the form of "client participation," the structure of which was defined by

[4]The task force apparently had in mind only two rather diffuse meanings for the concept. One was a concern that not all the newly-created jobs go to the middle-class professionals and that the poor themselves were to be employed by their program. Secondly, as the legislation appeared before the passage of the 1964 Civil Rights Act, this clause was to be a protection against the exclusion of Negroes in the prgorams in the south (Moynihan, 1966:6).

[5]Donovan quotes Attorney General Robert F. Kennedy in his testimony before a House committee: "This bill calls for maximum feasible participation of residents. This means the involvement of the poor in planning and implementing programs: giving them a real voice in their institutions."

Frank Riessman (1965a, 1966; Riessman and Rein, 1965). Here, the emphasis was placed upon organizing and directing the demands of the poor toward the institutions which serve them so as to make those institutions more responsive to their poor clients. The clients become a "third force;" the model maintains the need for the direct involvement of the poor in helping themselves, while also seeking to meet the O.E.O. directive of a "quiet revolution."

O.E.O. was clearly sympathetic to this interpretation of citizen participation in its definition of the problem of the poor, being "that they are not in a position to influence the policies, procedures, and objectives of the organizations responsible for their welfare" (O.E.O. Workbook quoted in Donovan, 1967:43).

Nevertheless, such participation was not agreeable to the middle-class professionals who ran the service agencies, nor to city hall, nor to the radical organizers with even more ambitious plans for the poor. Even as the program was being formulated, the conflict in the Mobilization for Youth program over the involvement of the poor in running their schools indicated the political potential of client participation (cf. Riessman, 1965b).

It is not surprising, then, that the poverty program became embroiled in political questions, at both elite and non-elite levels. With few exceptions, such as Mayor Daley of Chicago and Mayor Shelley of San Francisco, traditional political elites did not initiate poverty programs. Nevertheless, they quickly became involved when their authority was challenged by grassroots participation or, as was more likely, by aspiring leaders of ethnic groups heretofore excluded from power in the pluralist polity. The nature of the concerns of local elites was clarified at the Mayors' Conference in 1965. While their proposed resolution blamed the participation of the poor for "fostering class struggle" (cf. Newsweek, 1965:24), the real threat came not from the poor themselves, but from leaders who utilized the "participation of the poor" in their bid for power through ethnic politics (cf. Raab, 1966:54–56). As Mayor Shelley of San Francisco astutely noted, the poverty program "has the potential for setting up a great political organization. Not mine" (quoted in Kramer, 1969:60).

Thus, the leadership of the Black community, which had emerged in the civil rights struggle, was quick to demand a central role for the poor whose interests they were prepared to represent. Often it was the leaders of CORE, or other civil rights militants who pressed for this "representation" (Kramer, 1969:168; Raab, 1966:54). Other ethnic groups, a large proportion of whom were also found in the ranks of the poor, were also quick to demand greater representation. Often the need to "organize the poor" was recognized only after these new leaders came into power (Kramer, 1969:107).

Grassroots participation, the participation of non-elites alone in political and administrative questions, was thus more frequently discussed than found in reality. Such participation required a period of organizing the poor. Often this organization, as indicated above, was directed toward ends of boosting the mobility of individuals aspiring to be elites rather than the creation of powerful indigenous organizations among the poor themselves. The "Alinsky model," as found in the Syracuse University Community Action Training Center (cf. Knoll and Witcover, 1966), was rare indeed. In some cases the organizing of the poor led to the development of groups that became chapters of the Welfare Rights Organization (cf. Kramer, 1969:102). But these limited attempts met with ultimate defeat. The funds for the Syracuse University project were discontinued; W.R.O. has persisted only outside the boundaries of the war on poverty. And even before the Green amendment, the Kentucky political elite had successfully moved to exclude Appalachian volunteers and Vista volunteers, the primary sources of grassroots organizing in their community action programs *(The New York Times,* Aug. 19, 1967, and Sept. 29, 1967).

In the area of practical application, then, the revolutionary new concept of non-elite participation failed to materialize. Even the less politicized of the two modes, the third force strategy of client participation, did not succeed in gaining a significant foothold. The program which Riessman describes as most closely conforming to it, the non-university Syracuse Crusade for Opportunity, has been involved in a crisis of leadership, with political attacks from both right and left *(The Wall Street Journal,* August 25, 1967:1). To remain effective yet non-political is very difficult indeed. The third force may be either "cooled out" by the service agency or co-opted for the interests of city hall (cf. Riessman and Rein, 1965:13; Shostak, 1965).

Faced with these forces, it is not surprising that poverty programs retreated to the second rung of our typology, to modes involving more traditional participation of both elites and non-elites. On that level, however, the bid for power by blacks and other groups of poor usually resulted in stalemate, as in the renewal experience. The Green amendment, placing the final power in the hands of traditional political elites, as well as the new challenges to old leadership within the ethnic groups, have both contributed to this situation; the poor, seeing little in the program to help them, lose interest. Generally, enough pressure remains in the program to provide some services. Thus, the program, now old and weary, becomes depoliticized.

By this cycle, many programs end up at the point which the majority of programs never left. The role of the poor, or their representatives, is to advise service agencies. The middle-class professional plays the key role, both in planning and implementation. The involvement of the poor, once the subject of strong O.E.O. directives, is limited to individuals who are either hired by the program or "representatives" chosen by it. The proposal emerges as a non-controversial consensus of service agencies to improve institutional output, integrate delivery, and promote civic well-being (cf. Kramer and Denton, 1967:79–80; Jencks, 1966:21–22; Levitan, 1969:115–116).

The inability to withstand the pressures of majority interest and minority dissensus thus forced a retreat of the poverty program from the more radical interpretations of citizen participation to which it gave birth. The Green amendment of 1967 is in one sense only a legitimation of O.E.O.'s increasing reluctance to sponsor programs which were controversial. The amendment was proposed to resolve a basic contradiction between traditional American beliefs and the proposed participation of the poor in policy-making. Those who pay, say; or as Mrs. Green (quoted in *The New York Times,* Nov. 8, 1967) put it in defending her amendment for local control: "those who are helping to pay shall have a voice through elected officials."

Thus, the tie between political and economic power is maintained, and the programs are saved from domination by the poor. Again the power to propose is guarded by elites; non-elites may merely accept or reject what is offered them. Perhaps the primary legacy of the program is found in the new political elites that have risen from the ranks of minorities formerly unrepresented in the pluralism of city politics.[6] One New York observer notes also the rise of a new class of bureaucrats, the "povertycrats" *(The New York Times,* Nov. 9, 1969).

PARTICIPATION IN THE MODEL CITIES PROGRAM

Even before the Green amendment resolved the participation dilemma in favor of elites, Congress had already defined a new approach to citizen participation in the third post-war attack on the urban crisis. While the model cities program, too, calls for widespread citizen participation, it is clear that this time the framers, learning from past experience, had developed a clearer conception of its meaning. Participation on the part of the poor was to focus on developing their "patience" and "understanding." The tactic of "involvement" is seen as "essential to quelling frustration." While they may have available to them channels to express "desires and identify with the projects being planned . . . the actual planning and decision-making rest with the demonstration city agencies" *(The Wall Street Journal,* Oct. 31, 1966). Thus, this new program was clear in its evaluation of maximum feasible participation of non-elites: it was impractical, inefficient, and politically dangerous. Concerning the advisory and planning body, the suggestion (U.S. Dept. of Housing and Urban Development, 1967:7) is that "the ultimate manifestation of public commitment is the appointment of a Board whose members represent and speak for the power structure of the community."

The model cities program, then, attempted to formalize the retreat from the less traditional modes of client and grassroots participation which the poverty program had introduced. In part, this was achieved because the poor were weary. Nevertheless, this "professionalization of reform" (the phrase is Moynihan's, 1969: ch.2) has not occurred without some protest. In Philadelphia one secretary resigned, charging that the council's professional staff stifles

---

[6]Ironically, President Nixon now proposes that O.E.O. focus primarily on innovation—an area it has already seemingly exhausted.

true citizen participation in the program and "too many interested and hopeful participants have fallen away" *(The Philadelphia Inquirer,* March 29, 1968).

In spite of the new limited form of participation, the poor and their allies have again attempted to make their voices heard. Too often this repeats the cycle toward stalemate, for while the city proposes and the community opposes, Congress cuts the overall model cities budget, assuring the perpetuation of the status quo. The major result of this new attempt at participation by non-elites may very well be the modest goal originally proposed in the legislation of providing "maximum opportunities for employing residents of the area in all phases of the program" (Demonstration Cities and Metropolitan Development Act of 1966, Title I, Section 103, a, 2). If this process is successful in opening well-paying construction jobs to blacks, it will be no mean accomplishment for non-elite citizen participation. This meaning, however, hardly embodies the high ideals normally attributed to the concept.

CONCLUSION

Our examination of the changing meanings of citizen participation leads us to conclude that in both the urban renewal and community action experiences, there are strong tendencies leading toward the stalemate of citizen groups and political elites, on both matters of administrative and political concern. Rather than the emergence of a creative "pluralist participation," in which elites and non-elites seek an accommodation of their interests, we find an inability of social policy to provide solutions by the mutual adjustment of the interests involved.[7] Elites tend to resist yielding the power to propose solutions to problems to non-elites. And, as the war on poverty indicates, non-elites eventually tire of this stalemate, and citizen participation comes to mean little more than the presence of a few "citizen advisors," attached to a service agency that serves as a buffer between the poor and an affluent society. When aroused again by a new social plan, as the model cities program, we already find signs of a similar progression through the cycle of participation once more toward stalemate.

Among academic analysts of social policy, civic leaders, and new left critics, the conclusion is now abroad that citizen participation has failed. Civic leaders attribute the failure to the intractable nature of the poor; the new left attributes it to the intractable nature of the "power structure;" many academics seem to have concluded that a combination of the two explanations is sufficient.

James Q. Wilson (1966b:29), for example, concludes that "effective local planning requires *less,* not more citizen participation." Citizen participation

---

[7]Gusfield (1962:25) has noted that such stalemates often occur in pluralist systems and may lead to periodic crises within them.

raises "unrealistic expectations" for non-elite citizens who have, according to Bellush and Hausknecht (1967b:279ff), neither "morale-cohesion," "capacity for effective membership," "leadership," "knowledge," or "awareness," all seen as "prerequisites for participation." According to Banfield and Wilson (1964), they lack the necessary "community-regarding and public-regarding political ethos." Such conclusions incline these academic critics favorably toward the "professionalization of reform."

We suggest that these interpretations, while not inappropriate to the analysis of the social experiments we have treated in this paper, ought not be used to imply the failure of all forms of citizen participation. We contend that non-elites can behave in "public-regarding" ways if provided the proper situation by social policy. As the Cahns (1968:217) note:

> People respond to the terms of the question put. . . . Until recently, there has been no attempt to create forums in which the poor have been asked to make decisions as composite human beings, as human beings who have something valid to say about the allocation of resources from the point of view of the entire community. Instead, they have been forced into the role of responding as selfish, dependent individuals. By confining the poor to speaking in that role, professionals purport to prove an incapacity to function responsibly in any other role.

Similarly, Liebow (1967:64–65) notes that the poor characteristically do not defer gratifications because they have little to gain in the long run, not because they cannot behave in orientation to the future.

The cycle of citizen participation, we believe, must be moved off its direction toward stalemate by the development of a fully democratic urban pluralism. We do not think it necessary to conclude, as have some social scientists, that democracy does not work among the poor because it is inefficient and raises conflicts. Rather, we believe that the experience with citizen participation in recent social policy demonstrates the critical importance of the development of new institutional forms that will represent the interests of the poor and will build those interests into the larger political and social structure such that these purposes can be achieved. It is growing too late to paper over class conflicts and subcultural differences with the explanation that participation will not work. The crisis of our times is too immediate, and its potential for social chaos is great.

Social policy regarding the poor seems inevitably involved in political questions in which both the poor and the non-poor are critically interested. The critical challenge to American social policy in the decades ahead lies in developing means whereby the interests of the poor may be accommodated without arousing the countervailing power of the non-poor against them so that change is stalemated. The alternatives to such institutional innovation would appear to be repression or rebellion.

REFERENCES

Anderson, Martin, *The Federal Bulldozer*, (Cambridge M.I.T. Press, 1964).

Bellush, Jewell, and Murray Hausknecht, "Urban renewal and the reformer," in Bellush and Hausknecht (eds.), *Urban Renewal: People, Politics, and Planning*, (Garden City: Anchor Books, 1967), pp. 189–197.

——— "Planning, participation, and urban renewal," in Bellush and Hausknecht (eds.), *Urban Renewal: People, Politics, and Planning*, (Garden City: Anchor Books, 1967), pp. 278–286.

Brussat, William K., *Citizens Organization for Neighborhood Conservation*, (Chicago: National Association of Housing and Renewal Officials).

Chan, Edgar S., and Jean Camper, "Citizen participation," in Hans B. Speigel (ed.), *Citizen Participation in Urban Development*, (Washington, D.C.: NTL Institute for Applied Behavioral Science, 1968), pp. 211–224.

District of Columbia Office of Urban Renewal, *Adams-Morgan: Democratic Action to Serve a Neighborhood* (Washington, D.C., 1964).

Donovan, John C., *The Politics of Poverty*, (New York: Pegasus, 1967).

Greer, Scott, *Urban Renewal and American Cities*, (Indianapolis: Bobbs-Merrill, 1965).

Gusfield, Joseph R., "Mass society and extremist politics," *American Sociological Review* 27 (February 1962), 19–30.

Jencks, Christopher, "Accommodating Whites: A new look at Mississippi," *The New Republic* 139 (April 16, 1966), 19–22.

Kaplan, Harold, *Urban Renewal Politics: Slum Clearance in Newark*, (New York: Columbia University Press, 1963).

Knoll, Erwin, and Jules Witcover, "Organizing the poor," Pp. 247–253 in Herman P. Miller (ed.), *Poverty American Style*, (Belmont, California: Wadsworth Publishing Co., 1966), pp. 247–253.

Kornhauser, William, *The Politics of Mass Society*, (New York: The Free Press, 1959).

Kramer, Ralph M., *The Participation of the Poor*, (Englewood Cliffs: Prentice-Hall, 1969).

Kramer, Ralph, and C. Denton, "Organization of a community action program: A Comparative case study," *Social Work* 12 (October 1967), 68–80.

Levitan, Sar A., *The Great Society's Poor Law: A New Approach to Poverty*, (Baltimore: Johns Hopkins Press, 1969).

Marris, Peter, and Martin Rein: *Dilemmas of Social Reform*, (New York: Atherton, 1967).

McQuade, Walter, "Urban renewal in Boston," in James Q. Wilson (ed.), *Urban Renewal: The Record and the Controversy*, (Cambridge: M.I.T. Press, 1966), pp. 259–277.

Meyerson, Martin, and Edward C. Banfield, *Politics, Planning and the Public Interest* (New York: The Free Press, 1964).

Mill, John Stuart, *Considerations on Representative Government*, (New York: Henry Holt and Company, 1875).

Moynihan, Daniel P., "What is community action?" *The Public Interest* 2 (Fall 1966): 3–8.

———*Maximum Feasible Participation: Community Action in the War on Poverty.* (New York: The Free Press, 1969).

Newsweek, "Shriver and the war on poverty." *Newsweek* 66 (September 13, 1965): 22–29.

Nixon, William Bishop, and Joseph M. Boyd, Jr., *Citizen Participation in Urban Renewal.* (Nashville: Tennessee State Planning Commission, 1957).

Raab, Earl, "What war and which poverty?" *The Public Interest* 1 (Spring 1966): 45–56.

Riessman, Frank, "Anti-poverty programs and the role of the poor." Pp. 403–412 in Margaret Gordon (ed.), *Poverty in America.* (San Francisco: Chandler, 1965).

———"Mobilizing the poor," *Commonweal* 82 (May 21, 1965): 285–289.

———"The new anti-poverty ideology." *Poverty and Human Resources Abstracts I* (July-August 1966): 5–16.

Riessman, Frank, and Martin Rein, "The third force: an anti-poverty ideology," *American Child* 47 (November 1965): 10–14.

Rossi, Peter H., and Robert A. Dentler, *The Politics of Urban Renewal* (New York: The Free Press of Glencoe, 1961).

Rubin, Lillian, "Maximum feasible participation, the origins, implications and present status," *Poverty and Human Resources Abstracts* 2 (November-December 1967), 5–18.

Shostak, Arthur, "Containment, co-optation or codetermination." *American Child* 47 (November 1965), 15–19.

Simon, Herbert A., *Administrative Behavior* (2nd ed.), (New York: Macmillan, 1957).

U.S. Housing and Home Finance Agency, *Urban Renewal,* (Washington, D.C., 1961).

U.S. Department of Housing and Urban Development, *Strengthening Community Services in Low Income Areas: A Field Guide* 7 (Washington, D.C., 1967).

Wilson, James Q., "Citizen participation in urban renewal," in Wilson (ed.), *Urban Renewal: The Record and the Controversy,* (Cambridge: M.I.T. Press, 1966), pp. 407–421.

———"The war on cities," *The Public Interest* 3 (Spring 1966), 27–44.

Wilson, James Q., and Edward Banfield, "Public-regardingness as a value premise in voting behavior," *American Political Science Review* 58 (December 1964), 876–887.

The Vertical Axis of Community Organization and the Structure of Power

John Walton

*   *   *

In the relatively brief period since its inception, the study of community power structure has attracted a wide range of enthusiasts. Researchers of diverse backgrounds have found their particular interests coalesce around the assumption that local leadership processes are of central importance to the explanation of community action. The research implications of this approach have been explored in a variety of areas including urban renewal, social welfare, health and hospital services, community conflict and ethnic relations.[2] Though often divided on issues of how the leadership process is organized and the extent to which power is effectively exercised, investigators are in agreement concerning the viability of research problems suggested by the approach.

In addition to these fertile substantive applications, much has been done to develop the research methods of power-structure studies.[3] The conflict which prevailed a few years ago between proponents of rival methods seems to have subsided with the recognition that different methods tap different dimensions of the total power scene. Investigators now appear to agree on the

[2]See, for example, Amos Hawley, "Community Power and Urban Renewal Success," *American Journal of Sociology,* 68 (Jan., 1963), pp. 422–431; Warner Bloomberg and Morris Sunshine, *Suburban Power Structures and Public Education: A Study of Values, Influence and Tax Effort* (Syracuse: University Press, 1963); Ralph B. Kimbrough, *Political Power and Education Decision Making* (Chicago: Rand McNally and Co., 1964); Irving A. Fowler, "Local Industrial Structure, Economic Power and Community Welfare," *Social Problems,* 6 (Summer, 1958), pp. 41–51; Ivan Belknap and John Steinle, *The Community and Its Hospitals* (Syracuse: Syracuse University Press, 1963); Floyd Hunter, Ruth Conner Schaffer and Cecil G. Sheps, *Community Organization: Action and Inaction* (Chapel Hill: University of North Carolina Press, 1956); James S. Coleman, *Community Conflict* (New York: The Free Press, 1957); William A. Gamson, "Rancorous Conflict in Community Politics," *American Sociological Review,* 31 (Feb., 1966), pp. 71–81; James McKee, "Community Power and Strategies in Race Relations," *Social Problems,* 6 (Winter, 1958–1959), pp. 41–51.

[3]L. Vaughn Blankenship, "Community Power and Decision Making: A Comparative Evaluation of Measurement Techniques," *Social Forces,* 43 (Dec., 1964), pp. 207–216; William V. D'Antonio and Eugene Erickson, "The Reputational Technique as a Measure of Community Power: An Evaluation Based on Comparative and Longitudinal Studies," *American Sociological Review,* 27 (June, 1962), pp. 362–376; Linton C. Freeman, *et al.,* "Locating Leaders in Local Communities: A Comparison of Some Alternative Approaches," *American Sociological Review,* 28 (Oct., 1963), pp. 791–798.

SOURCE: John Walton, from "The Vertical Axis of Community Organization and the Structure of Power," *Social Science Quarterly,* 48 (december 1967), 353–368.

need for methodologically balanced, comparative and longitudinal studies. This trend is manifest in several notable works that have appeared recently.[4]

In spite of these convergences, however, there has been almost no progress in one vital respect; the development of theoretical explanation of the reported findings. Elaborate documentation of the atheoretical character of the field hardly seems necessary. One has only to peruse a portion of the literature to discover that the principal issues are almost entirely concerned with method and conflicting interpretations of how broadly power is distributed. Only rarely do we find some of the initial steps in theorizing represented by conceptual considerations and the development of propositional inventories.[5]

The purpose of this paper is to develop a theoretical explanation of how power is distributed in local communities, and to consider briefly how various power arrangements may account for different forms of community action. The analysis incorporates earlier theoretical discussions of the community and a systematic review of the power-structure literature. Anticipating the conclusions for a moment, it will be argued that as communities become increasingly interdependent with extracommunity institutions, changes in the local normative order ensue producing more competitive power arrangements.

Starting with a review of previous research, the argument moves on to consider the adequacy of certain theoretical approaches and, finally, to develop the propositions concerning power structure and community action.

FINDINGS OF PREVIOUS RESEARCH

In an earlier paper the findings of thirty-three power-structure studies dealing with fifty-five communities were analyzed in order to determine the relationship between a number of substantive and methodological variables and the dependent variable, type of power structure.[6] Subsequently that analysis was replicated using a somewhat larger number of studies.[7] The selection of studies was intended to be exhaustive of the published literature in social science devoted specifically to the study of community power structure. By dealing with the published literature the examination excluded some unpublished studies, especially dissertations. Confining the analysis to the social

---

[4]Robert Presthus, *Men at the Top: A Study in Community Power* (New York: Oxford University Press, 1964); Robert E. Agger, Daniel Goldrich and Bert E. Swanson, *The Rulers and the Ruled: Political Power and Impotence in American Communities* (New York: John Wiley and Sons, 1964); William V. D'Antonio and William H. Form, *Influentials in Two Border Cities: A Study in Community Decision-Making* (Notre Dame: University of Notre Dame Press, 1965).

[5]For some efforts in this direction see Agger, *et al., The Rulers;* Presthus, *Men at the Top;* M. Herbert Danzger, "Community Power Structure: Problems and Continuities," *American Sociological Review,* 24 (Oct., 1964), pp. 707–717.

[6]John Walton, "Substance and Artifact: The Current Status of Research on Community Power Structure," *American Journal of Sociology,* 71 (Jan., 1966), pp. 430–438.

[7]John Walton, "A Systematic Survey of Community Power Research" in Michael T. Aiken and Paul E. Mott, *The Structure of Community Power: Readings* (in press).

science literature excluded journalistic reports. Finally, the criterion that the research be specifically concerned with community power excluded a number of community studies dealing with stratification, local government and related aspects of social and political life. These criteria were employed in a screening of the literature, and the resulting list of studies was checked against several lengthy bibliographies to insure its inclusiveness. Thus the studies are regarded as a universe, defined by the above criteria, rather than a sample.

Each study was reviewed and, when sufficient information was available, coded in terms of a number of self-explanatory independent variables *(e.g., region, population size, industrialization, economic diversity, etc.).* Similarly, the type of power structure identified in each report was coded in terms of four categories: 1) Pyramidal—a monolithic, monopolistic, or single cohesive leadership group; 2) Factional—at least two durable factions that compete for advantage; 3) Coalitional—leadership varies with issues and is made up of fluid coalitions of interested persons and groups; 4) Amorphous—the absence of any persistent pattern of leadership or power exercised on the local level. Table 1 indicates those few associations which were found to be significant or meaningful.[8]

In contrast to these positive findings, a large number of variables, including region, population size, population composition, industrialization, economic diversity and type of local government, were *not* found to be related to type of power structure.

Taking these results as a summary of the present status of research, it appears that no firm generalizations are suggested. The findings fail to conform to any neat pattern such as an association between competitive power structures and greater complexity of local social and economic organization. The inadequacies of such an explanation are underscored by the negative findings. The evidence may, however, be suggestive of some less obvious explanation. In order to explore that possibility we shall look at some implicitly theoretical positions in the area of community power and a major theoretical work on American communities, asking, in both cases, how they square with the above findings and how they might inform the present analysis.

TABLE 1.[9] COMMUNITY CHARACTERISTICS AND COMMUNITY POWER STRUCTURE[10]

	Pyramidal	Factional, Coalitional and Amorphous	Total
Absentee Ownership[11]			
Present	2	18	20
Absent	12	9	21

[8]A complete summary of the findings, positive and negative, is to be found in Walton, *op. cit.*

[9]The cell entries in the table represent communities, rather than studies, since a single study often dealt with two or more towns.

[10]The variable power structure was originally coded in terms of four categories. The categories are collapsed here to avoid small N's and to provide a contrast between more and less concentrated power arrangements.

Total	14	27	41
	$Q=-.85$ $.01>p>.001$		
Economic Resources[12]			
Adequate	9	17	26
Inadequate	6	5	11
Total	15	22	37
	$Q=-.39$ $.30>p>.20$		
Type of City[13]			
Independent	14	22	36
Satellite	2	10	12
Total	16	32	48
	$Q=-.52$ $.20>p>.10$		
Party Competition			
Competitive	0	10	10
Noncompetitive	10	12	22
Total	10	22	32
	$Q=-1.0$ $.02>p>.01$		
Change in Power Structure			
Dispersion	2	17	19
Concentration	0	0	0
No Change	3	4	7
Oscillation	2	1	3
Decline Locally	1	2	3
Total	8	24	32

[11]The N's in each of these subtables vary because the studies coded do not provide uniform data on each variable.

[12] Operational definitions of the following three variables are indicated by the type of information coded under each category. Adequate economic resources—includes towns with reportedly prosperous business communities and low rates of poverty and unemployment; inadequate economically—underdeveloped with high rates of poverty and unemployment. Independent city—includes central cities of metropolitan areas and independent manufacturing, commercial or agricultural centers; satellite city—suburb or town dominated by a nearby city. Party competition—the existence of two or more local parties (or affiliates in formally nonpartisan cities) which regularly contend for public office; noncompetitive—a one-party town.

[13]When the zero-order level findings on economic resources and type of city are examined controlling for research method, a factor associated with type of power structure identified, the differences here do not persist. The findings are reported here because they are suggestive and because the low quality of the data may be obscuring significant associations. That is, the lower the quality of the data, the more difficult it is to demonstrate statistically significant relationships and the more likely it is that such relationships may be obscured. In the present context I have gone beyond a strict interpretation of the earlier findings in an attempt to draw some meaningful generalizations.

THEORETICAL APPROACHES

In one of the first attempts to bring some order out of the confusion of results, David Rogers developed a series of propositions concerning community political systems.[14] His dependent variable, type of political system, was made up of the categories monolithic and pluralistic. In stating the relationship between these and a number of characteristics of community social structure, Rogers hypothesized that the following would be associated with a pluralistic system: a high degree of industrialization, a large population, a socially heterogeneous population, a policy differentiated from the kinship and economic systems, a local government of extensive scope, two or more political parties and the unionization, or other political and economic organization, of working-class groups. The underlying theme in this series of propositions, what has been referred to as the implicit theory, centers on the effects of industrialization, and attendant processes of urbanization and bureaucratization, the outcome of these being structural differentiation which contributes to a pluralistic power situation. The approach is, of course, central to contemporary social science whether stated in terms of *gemeinschaft* and *gesellschaft* or any other of a variety of polar types.

Amos Hawley has presented a somewhat more specific approach.[15] Here power is defined as a system property whose distribution can be measured by the ability to mobilize resources and personnel. In any total system, such as a community, this ability lies in the various component sub-systems and is exercised through their managerial functions. Hence, operationally, the greater the number of managerial personnel, the greater the concentration of power. If we grant that success in a collective action requires the mobilization of resources and personnel, and that this ability is greatest where power is most highly concentrated, then it follows that the greater the concentration of power in a community the greater the *probability* of success in any collective action. In a recent paper, inspired in part by the Hawley piece, Edgar Butler and Hallowell Pope have suggested another measure of power concentration, the number of profile or key industries and the concentration of managerial functions within these.[16]

It should be noted that the Hawley and Butler and Pope papers are concerned chiefly with community action; for each the premise is that more concentrated power situations are conducive to concerted action. Unlike Rogers they are not trying to explain patterns of power distribution but,

[14]David Rogers, "Community Political Systems: A Framework and Hypotheses for Comparative Studies," in Bert E. Swanson (ed.), *Current Trends in Comparative Community Studies* (Kansas City, Mo.: Community Studies, Inc., 1962).

[15]Hawley, *op. cit.*

[16]Edgar W. Butler and Hallowell Pope, "Community Power Structures, Industrialization and Public Welfare Programs," paper read at the 61st annual meeting of the American Sociological Association, Miami Beach, Florida, August, 1966.

rather, employ these to explain community action. Nevertheless, they are pertinent here because they imply a theoretical position involving the saliency of managerial functions in the determination of community power structures.

How do these explanatory schemes square with the findings culled from the existing literature? Considering first the hypotheses formulated by Rogers, the evidence runs counter to his notions of the effects of industrialization, population size and population heterogeneity. On the positive side, his proposition about political parties, though not entirely equivalent to party competition, is supported. Unfortunately, no data are available on the remaining three propositions. What evidence we have, however, indicates that Roger's propositions do not fare very well within the present context, though they may have greater predictive power in a cross cultural or historical perspective. For our purposes the implication is that the theoretical approach implicit in these propositions is in need of revision. Perhaps it will be necessary to abandon the simplified notion of a unilinear relationship between the growing complexity of industrial society and more pluralistic local power arrangements, in favor of a more limited, yet more discriminating explanation.[17]

The evidence presented previously is not directly relevant to the Hawley and Butler and Pope approaches since these attempt to explain community action. If, however, we assume with these authors that concentrated power structures are associated with community action, and then examine the antecedent link in their chain of reasoning, we find that those community characteristics allegedly conducive to power concentration (*i.e.* ones engendering a large number of managerial functions)—industrialization, economic diversity, proportion of absentee ownership, and economic resources—are either unrelated or associated with the less concentrated power structures in our data. This fact can hardly be taken as a refutation of the positions presented. What it does indicate is that the number of managerial functions appears to be a poor indicator of type of power structure (though it may indicate the number of potentially powerful people in community action).

In short, the analysis thus far demonstrates the need for theoretical statements which are both more explicit and account better for the available data.

As we shall see, Roland Warren's analysis of *The Community in America*[18] provides a pertinent general framework for dealing theoretically with the specific questions of power structure. Warren's central thesis is that American communities are undergoing a drastic transformation of their entire structure

[17]This conclusion applies to similar propositional inventories based on the "evolutionary" or "continuum" notion. See, for example, Delbert C. Miller and William H. Form, *Industry, Labor and Community* (New York: Harper Bros., 1960).

[18]Roland L. Warren, *The Community in America* (Chicago: Rand McNally, 1963), and "Toward a Reformulation of Community Theory," *Human Organization,* 15 (Summer, 1962), pp. 8–11.

and function; "[this] 'great change' in community living includes the increasing orientation of local community units toward extra-community systems of which they are a part, with a decline in community cohesion and autonomy."[19] Although Warren analyzes these changes along seven fundamental dimensions of community life, a summary statement indicates their relevance for present purposes:

> In the first place, they signalize the increasing and strengthening of the external ties which bind the local community to the larger society. In the process, various parts of the community—its educational system, its recreation, its economic units, its governmental functions, its religious units, its health and welfare agencies, and its voluntary associations—have become increasingly oriented toward district, state, regional, or national offices and less and less oriented toward each other.
>
> In the second place, as local community units have become more closely tied in with state and national systems, much of the decision-making prerogative concerning the structure and function of these units has been transferred to the headquarters or district offices of the systems themselves, thus leaving a narrower and narrower scope of functions over which local units, responsible to the local community, exercise autonomous power.[20]

On the basis of these observations concerning the "great change" and with the simultaneous recognition that communities (*i.e.* "combinations of social units and systems which perform the major functions having locality reference") do persist as meaningful units, Warren finds useful a distinction between the *horizontal* and *vertical axes* of community organization. The vertical axis refers to connections between community organizations and extracommunity centers, and the horizontal axis refers to connections between community organizations. The "great change" involves an increase in the former type of connections often at the cost of the latter.

In what follows several propositions will be developed which relate Warren's approach specifically to the question of how power is distributed on the local level. We will find that his concept of a vertical axis of community organization has particular importance for this analysis.

AN EXPLANATION OF DIFFERENTIAL PATTERNS OF COMMUNITY POWER STRUCTURE

Power is defined here as *the capacity to mobilize resources for the accomplishment of intended effects with recourse to some type of sanction(s) to encour-*

[19]Warren, *The Community in America,* p. 53.
[20]*Ibid.,* p. 5.

age compliance.[21] This definition includes the elements of both potential and actualized power in that capacity for mobilizing resources refers to potential while the application of sanctions refers to actualized power. *Capacity* also implies a distinction from *right* such that *authority* is not confused with the definition. Following Lasswell and Kaplan, the threat of sanctions, positive or negative, distinguishes *influence* from power—*i.e.* influence refers only to the capacity to mobilize resources.

Power structure is defined as *the characteristic pattern within a social organization whereby resources are mobilized and sanctions employed in ways that affect the organization as a whole.*

For the sake of simplicity we will deal here with competitive and monopolistic power structures.[22] Monopolistic power structures characterize social organizations in which the capacity for mobilizing resources and recourse to sanctions are the exclusive property of a group with similar interests. In competitive situations the capacity for mobilizing resources and recourse to sanctions are possessed by two or more groups with different interests.

The basic assumption of the theoretical statement to be developed here is that a monopoly of power produces a situation in which consensus is the most important factor underlying the use of power. This consensus may, but need not imply agreement on values and objectives. What it does imply is agreement concerning the capabilities of those holding power to realize their own intentions over a wide range of community relevant issues. In such a monopolistic situation expectations concerning the norms prescribed by the existing power arrangement tend to be widely recognized. That is, the limits of allowable (nonsanctionable) deviance and opposition are narrow and clear. As a result of these congruent expectations, potential rather than manifest power is more commonly the mechanism by which compliance is encouraged; overt conflict and coercion are relatively infrequent occurrences because compliance can be realized without them. Merriam captured the sense of this assumption when

[21]This definition derives from a number of discussions of the concept of power. Some of the most relevant writings include Bertrand Russell, *Power: A New Social Analysis* (New York: Barnes and Noble, 1962); Max Weber, *The Theory of Social and Economic Organization* (trans. by A. M. Henderson and Talcott Parsons; New York: Oxford University Press, 1947); Talcott Parsons, "On the concept of Political Power," *Proceedings of the American Philosophical Society,* 107 (June, 1963), pp. 232–262; Harold Lasswell and Abraham Kaplan, *Power and Society: A Framework for Political Inquiry* (New Haven: Yale University Press, 1950).

[22]This is not meant to imply that such a dichotomy is the most useful framework, though it tends to pre-occupy the literature, *e.g.,* Presthus, *Men at the Top;* D'Antonio and Form, *Influentials.* Etzioni has offered four types of control structures based on the means of control available to various positions within an organization; see *A Comparative Analysis of Complex Organizations* (New York: Free Press, 1961). Agger, *et al., The Rulers,* characterizes power structures with two variables, "distribution of power" and "convergence of leadership ideology" and a resulting fourfold table. Construing the second variable as an indicator of leadership cohesiveness, the formulation provides an important distinction between truly competitive systems and cases where power is shared among a number of groups but similarity of interests unites them in a monopolistic power arrangement. Many controversies in the field stem from a failure to make this distinction.

he wrote "Power is not strongest when it uses violence, but weakest."[23]

By contrast, in competitive situations the exercise of power moves from a reliance on consensus to more overt applications of sanctions. This becomes necessary to the extent that competing groups become capable of restricting the scope of each other's sanctions. Claims to power must be supported by effective action. Greater normative diversity, with attendant diversity in expectations, characterizes this situation. Such circumstances result in a greater incidence of conflict stemming from the fact that those who would exercise power are required to make evident their claim through the use of sanctions.

It should be added that each of these circumstances contains elements of the other. Monopolistic power arrangements do, at times, generate divergent norms and expectations just as they occasionally have recourse to overt applications of coercion. More importantly, the role of consensual expectations and potential power are critical to all forms of social organization and can be observed in many of the transactions carried on in competitive power settings. In this connection conflict is probably most characteristic of those transitional periods in which power is becoming more or less diffused since it is at this point that the normative order is most uncertain and expectations least clear.[24] In the event that this transition is one from monopolistic to competitive it may culminate in a new set of rules defining community power arrangements which, while more conducive to conflict than the monopolistic situation, produces less conflict than the transitional phase.

Because at first glance this assumption may appear to be a truism, its nontrivial character will be demonstrated. Presthus' study of two New York communities which differed on a pluralist-elitist continuum is valuable here. Discussing the more elitist of the two, Presthus reasons:

> In Riverview sharper class and economic differences and resulting disparities in expectations, values and consensus seem to have placed a premium on more centralized, imperative leadership. As organizational theory and studies of group behavior suggest, social support, shared values, and common expectations make possible the minimization of overt power and authority. When community consensus is limited, leaders tend to function in a more unilateral manner.[25]

Here the minimization of overt power and authority is equated with a more pluralistic (competitive) power situation. The present argument agrees with

[23]In a more elaborate statement Merriam writes, "In most communities the use of force is relatively uncommon in proportion to the number of regulations, and the success of the organization is not measured by the amount of violence in specific cases but by the extent to which violence is avoided and other substitutes discovered." Charles E. Merriam, *Political Power,* Collier Books Edition (New York: Macmillan, 1964), p. 36.

[24]Although the present concern is with community conflict, this argument closely parallels Durkheim's thesis on suicide and changes in the normative order.

[25]Presthus, *Men at the Top,* p. 427.

the prior notion that common expectations result in a minimization of overt power (and conflict), but this is taken to be characteristic of a monopolistic situation. Thus, when community consensus is limited the leadership process tends to be more competitive.[26]

Obviously the relationship identified in my assumption may operate in either direction—*i.e.* changes in the competitiveness of the power situation can produce changes in norms and expectations and, similarly, changes in norms and expectations can lead to changes in power arrangements. In this approach we are concerned with developing an explanation of the change in power structures, that is, in the latter direction of the causal complex.

In this section we have reasoned that normative expectations bear a particular relationship to power structure and that conflict can be taken as an indicator of that relationship.[27] In what follows an attempt will be made to elaborate the connection between normative expectations and types of power structure in terms of the data drawn from existing community studies.

Returning to the data in Table 1, we can now raise the question of how the ideas presented would account for the findings. It will be recalled that the data indicate a relationship between competitive power structures and the presence of absentee-owned corporations, competitive party politics, adequate economic resources and satellite status. Further, in those communities where change was studied, the trend was in the direction of a greater dispersion of power. Do these findings suggest some underlying explanation?

Upon closer examination the evidence does point to an explanation. Each of the variables associated with competitive power structures reflects the interdependence of the community and extracommunity centers of power or increased emphasis on the vertical axis. For example, a high proportion of absentee-owned industry suggests that many community relevant decisions are controlled by the personnel and interests of national corporate bodies whose influence may stem from either a deliberate intervention in local affairs or from the more characteristic aloofness to local responsibility.[28] Similarly competitive political parties may often reflect the involvement of county, state and national

[26]A more precise treatment of this relationship would specify types of conflict and how these are associated with various power arrangements. For example, monopolistic power structures may suppress dissent and conflict, they may manage it within innocuous limits or they may engender revolutionary conflict. Competitive power structures, on the other hand, may encourage conflict which results in a stalemate or ineffective argument and nonrevolutionary change.

[27]James S. Coleman, *Community Conflict* (New York: Free Press, 1957) accords with this point by arguing that whenever the pattern of control is so complete that certain elements can see no way of moving into a position of power, there may be sporadic conflict but no organized opposition (nor, presumably, regular conflict).

[28]For studies documenting this, see, Robert O. Schulze, "The Bifurcation of Power in a Satellite City" in Morris Janowitz (ed.), *Community Political Systems* (Glencoe: The Free Press, 1961), pp. 19–80; Roland J. Pellegrin and Charles H. Coates, "Absentee-owned Corporations and Community Power Structure," *American Journal of Sociology*, 61 (March, 1956), pp. 413–419.

party organizations in a struggle for control of local constituencies.[29] While it could be reasonably argued that inadequate economic resources result in substantial intervention and control by state and federal agencies which extend aid to local bodies, the position taken here is that communities with more adequate economic resources maintain a greater number of interdependent ties to extracommunity institutions such as suppliers, markets, investors and other economic units. Finally, in the case of type of city, the connection is apparent. Suburban municipalities and smaller towns which form satellites of larger urban centers are interdependent in a variety of economic and political activities including municipal services, jobs, consumer behavior, *etc.* If, at points, the relationship between each of these variables and community interdependence is not unambiguous, the position taken here is enhanced by the pattern they suggest when taken together.

Drawing together all that has been said up to this point, the proposition which seems best to account for the findings can be stated as follows: to the extent that the local community becomes increasingly interdependent with respect to extracommunity institutions.(or develops along its vertical axis) the structure of local leadership becomes more competitive.[30]

Theoretically this proposition derives from the more general statement concerning norms and power arrangements. That is, the mechanism by which interdependence, or increasing relevance of the vertical axis of community organization, affects the distribution of community power is the disruption of the local normative order associated with the existing power structure. Development along the vertical axis involves the introduction of new interests and new institutional relationships implying new definitions of the community, and these have the effect of disrupting consensual normative expectations.

In addition to a differentiation of allegiance, these changes include the introduction of new *resources* and *sanctions* into the community. Local organizations with vertical ties to extracommunity institutions frequently share in the capital and human resources of the larger entity making it possible for them to sustain a broader scope of activities than would otherwise be the case. For example, absentee-owned corporations may receive funds and skilled person-

[29]On this point there is little evidence pro or con, and I present it only as a plausible hypothesis.

[30]It should be noted that the inferences about change are drawn primarily from cross-sectional data and thus run the risk of incorrectly inferring trends. Given the nature of available data, there is no alternative other than recommending future longitudinal studies following the lead of Agger, *et al., The Rulers,* and D'Antonio and Form, *Influentials.* Other studies which attempt to replicate earlier work include Delbert C. Miller, "Decision-Making Cliques in Community Power Structures: A Comparative Study of an American and an English City," *American Journal of Sociology,* 64 (Nov., 1958), pp. 299–310; David A. Booth and Charles R. Adrian, "Power Structure and Community Change: A Replication Study of Community A," *Midwest Journal of Political Science,* 6 (Aug., 1962), pp. 277–296; Donald A. Clelland and William H. Form, "Economic Dominants and Community Power: A Comparative Analysis," *American Journal of Sociology,* 69 (March, 1964), pp. 511–521; M. Kent Jennings, *Community Influentials: The Elites of Atlanta* (New York: Free Press, 1964).

nel for a desired expansion of local operations making them more important as local tax contributors, employers and suppliers. Such resources carry with them potential sanctions. In the above example some of these would include the threat to locate elsewhere,[31] threat of cutbacks or other actions having an adverse effect on the local economy, support or nonsupport in local elections. What has been said here of absentee-owned corporations could also be said, though perhaps in less dramatic ways, of other vertical community organizations. The point to be emphasized is that these organizations introduce new sources of power into the local picture and, being interdependent, they also have stakes in the local decision-making process which occasionally must be defended. The greater the number of community organizations with vertical ties, the more frequent and the more inclusive are contests surrounding the decision-making process.

In summary, the theoretical statement advanced here states that the introduction of organizations with vertical ties produces a greater interdependence between community and extracommunity centers of power. This interdependence brings changes in the local normative order, as well as new resources and sanctions, creating circumstances conducive to the emergence of competing power centers. Accordingly, variables which reflect the interdependence of the community and the "carrying society"—absentee ownership, party competition, adequate economic resources and satellite status—are associated with competitive power structures; whereas those variables which reflect only intracommunity change—economic diversity, population increase, *etc.*—are not so associated.[32]

Parenthetically, it is instructive to note certain parallels between this argument and Banfield's theoretical treatment of the exercise of power. Defining power as "the ability to establish control over another" (*i.e.* "the ability to cause another to give or withhold action"),[33] Banfield states that any actor has a limited stock of power which he spends or invests in ways that he believes will maintain and enhance his ability to control. When "investment opportunities" change so does the structure of influence. For example, he offers the

[31]For a discussion of this ploy and other sanctions available to economic institutions, see Arnold Rose, *The Power Structure: Political Processes in American Society* (New York: Oxford University Press, 1967), Chapter 3.

[32]The point to be emphasized here is that greater complexity and specialization are not necessarily conducive to the changes under consideration, but only insofar as these developments produce greater interdependence. At some point, of course, complexity and specialization do necessitate greater interdependence, but it would seem that this is not always the case at every level of community development. We would expect that some of these variables are confounded in such a way that increasing size, for example, will be related to competitive power structures at that point in a community's development when size and interdependence vary together. According to this argument, such as an association would be spurious. This may be the case, though the available data are too crude and provide too few observations to allow an unequivocal solution.

[33]Edward C. Banfield, *Political Influence: A New Theory of Urban Politics* (New York: Free Press Paperback Edition, 1965), p. 348.

following proposition; "As the number of autonomous actors increases, control tends to become less structured. Structures of control—*i.e.* relationships which are stable from proposal to proposal—are expensive to maintain. The value of a structure—and thus the amount that will be invested in it—tends to decline as the outcome of the process becomes less and less subject to control."[34] In the present context the number of "autonomous actors" increases as a result of changes in normative expectations and the effectiveness of sanctions. Similarly, the result here is a less concentrated structure of power.

Returning to our own explanatory scheme, one loose end can be tied up. The findings on change in Table 1 indicated that community power structures are tending to become more competitive. This trend is a predictable consequence of the spread of "metropolitan dominance"[35] and its implications for greater community interdependence. That is, if Bogue and others are correct —and there seems to be ample evidence that they are—the spread of metropolitan dominance would lead one to predict a corresponding trend toward competitive power arrangements. Such is, in fact, what the findings indicate.

Discussing the effects of increasing interdependence, Greer summarizes the consequences for the "locality group" in terms of a loss of autonomy, exposure to conflicting norms and the fragmentation of local normative order. In connection with the latter he identifies many of the events and explanations embodied in the theoretical statement developed here.

> Fragmentation of the local normative order is a predictable consequence; some of the members of the local group must conform to patterns from afar, since they are dependent upon the large, extended organization for their livelihood. Others take advantage of the local group's loss of coercive power to exploit added degrees of freedom; they experiment with new means to old ends, they exercise freedom of choice. Others, still, are dependent upon the local order for social position and rewards; their life is controlled by its norms, but with the attrition of dependence (and therefore the basis for order), they find it impossible to communicate or to enforce compliance. (The cutting edge of the sanctions depended, after all, upon the interdependence of the local group.) When individuals become committed to groups centering outside the locality, the new dependence brings a measure of independence from their neighbors.[36]

This fragmentation of the local normative order, accomplished through changes in expectations concerning power leads, according to this theoretical statement, to changes in the structure of community power; specifically it leads to more competitive power arrangements.

[34] *Ibid.*, p. 318.
[35] Don J. Bogue, *The Structure of the Metropolitan Community* (Ann Arbor: Horace H. Rackham School of Graduate Studies, University of Michigan, 1949).
[36] Scott Greer, *The Emerging City: Myth and Reality* (New York: The Free Press, 1962), pp. 50–51.

METROPOLITAN POLITICS AND COMMUNITY ACTION

Since the purpose of this paper was to develop an explanation of how power is distributed in local communities, *and* how power arrangements may account for community action, some comments on the latter question are called for. This may be particularly useful for two reasons; first, the foregoing analysis bears directly on the subject of community action and, second, the discussion serves to integrate another perspective on power and decision-making into this explanation.

In his well known essay describing the local community as an "ecology of games,"[37] Norton Long argues that the concept of "power structure" suffers from misplaced concreteness, that when we look more closely at cities we find no such structured decision-making institution.

What is characteristic of metropolitan areas is the lack of overall decision-making institutions. This does not mean that there are not institutions with power in metropolitan areas. It does mean that there are no institutions with sufficient power and overall responsibility to make decisions settling metropolitan issues and solving metropolitan problems . . .[38]

Rather, Long conceives of metropolitan issues as having careers in which interested and powerful parties—governments, groups and institutions—interact and "develop a system of largely unintended cooperation through which things get done . . ."[39] In this process actors deal with metropolitan problems from a limited point of view: *i.e.* one confined to their particular interest and institutional base.

There are at least two reasons why Long's empirically persuasive approach has stymied students of community power. One would appear to be the fact that much of this research has been conducted in places other than metropolitan areas where decisions settling local issues are possible. Second, the well known controversy over pluralism and elitism in the literature—because it is a debate over who makes local decisions, a small, cohesive group or a large, diverse one—may have obscured the possibility that no one makes such decisions.

In the present explanation metropolitan areas are prototypes of interdependent, vertically organized communities. Here we would expect a highly fragmented and competitive power arrangement in which the scope of any group or institution would be limited to prime interest areas. That is, the competitive process would militate against generalized influence and require

[37]Norton E. Long, "The Local Community as an Ecology of Games," *American Journal of Sociology,* 44 (Nov., 1958), pp. 251–266.
[38]Norton E. Long, *The Polity* (Chicago: Rand McNally, 1962), p. 157.
[39]*Ibid.*

that actors work to maintain their position within the system. Long and Banfield concur with this prediction in the stress they put on metropolitan politics as going systems in which institutions and groups seek to maintain and enhance their power in particular areas, public policy representing the results of their cooperation.[40]

Under these circumstances we would expect to find a fragmented and competitive pattern of community action. Community action in American cities seems increasingly to fit this pattern. The most apparent illustrations are found in the activities of civil rights, anti-poverty and peace groups which often possess resources conferred by extracommunity institutions and which are beginning to seriously involve themselves in the local political process. Here, of course, they encounter opposition from other local and vertically organized groups. As a result coordinated community action becomes more problematic and public policy represents less a reflection of consensus than a byproduct of the competitive process in which power is differentially exercised. Discussing the resurgence of radical politics in Chicago, Cleveland, Pittsburgh, Gary and several other cities, one author concludes "In the midwest, this tendency is general, and holds promise of becoming the outstanding fact of urban political life in America by the end of the decade."[41] In another vein, several studies which have touched on the consequences of increasing involvement of the federal government in local affairs find, contrary to political folklore, an enhancement of competitive, democratic processes.[42]

Notable among deviant cases is the Vidich and Bensman study[43] where involvement of state and county governments resulted in an abdication of responsibility on the part of local leaders. While it is significant that these changes diluted the power of Springdale's elite, it is also recognized that the consequences of extracommunity involvement were not those we would predict. In this regard the theory presented here may be in need of modification. Recalling that Springdale is a town of 2,500 people and that its extracommunity ties center chiefly around state subsidies, it is reasonable to infer that both the nature of the community and of the vertical ties are contingent elements in the theory presented here. Perhaps it is the case, for example, that changes along the vertical axis lead to greater competitiveness only in those communities which possess a certain minimum of institutional viability and that without this the same changes spell the demise of local leadership.

[40]Also relevant to this characterization is Wallace S. Sayre and Herbert Kaufman, *Governing New York City: Politics in the Metropolis* (New York: Russell Sage Foundation, 1960).

[41]Stephen A. Booth. "The New Politics Goes Local," *The Nation,* Vol. 204, No. 22 (May 29, 1967).

[42]Presthus, *Men at the Top;* William V. D'Antonio, "Community Leadership in an Economic Crisis: Testing Ground for Ideological Cleavage," *American Journal of Sociology,* 71 (May, 1966), pp. 688–700.

[43]*Small Town in Mass Society* (Princeton: Princeton University Press, 1958).

CONCLUSIONS

The explanation offered here represents an attempt to push the study of community power beyond a disproportionate emphasis on technique and toward a concern for testing propositions derived from explicit theoretical statements. There seems little doubt that this alternative is best suited for resolving the controversies over how power is distributed in local communities, and for generalizing research in this area to the larger problems of social organization and change.

The theory developed in this paper states that the introduction into the local community of the institutions and influence of nation-urban culture produces a "fragmentation of local normative order" or a disruption of consensual expectations concerning the norms prescribed by existing power arrangements. As expectations are altered and interests are differentiated, new resources are exploited for the creation of competing power groups.

The theory, as we have said, focuses on one direction of influence in what is undoubtedly a complex process. In so doing, however, it has the virtue of generating a number of testable propositions. Future comparative studies could evaluate, on the basis of first-hand data, the fundamental proposition regarding community interdependence and the advent of competitive power arrangements. A sampling of related propositions includes:

1. Changes, other than interdependence, which challenge the local normative order lead to more competitive power arrangements.
2. Intracommunity change which does not challenge the normative order does not lead to greater competitiveness.
3. Vertical ties which do not alter the normative order do not lead to the exploitation of new resources and more competitive power arrangements.
4. Normative diversity within a community leads to a greater frequency of application of overt sanctions (Presthus).
5. The greater the number of vertical ties in a community, the smaller the scope of local power groups.
6. The greater the number of vertical ties (and competitiveness) the more difficult (less frequent) is coordinated community action.

In addition to suggesting propositions the theory implies a new direction for research in that it locates the source of local change in the relationship between the community and extracommunity institutions. It is expected that researchers will find this theory informative as they become increasingly aware of what it implies for the choice of an appropriate unit of analysis in future community power studies. If the theory is correct the appropriate unit of analysis is not the community per se but, rather, the relationship between the community and the institutions of national-urban culture.

A Note on Walton's Analysis of Power Structure and Vertical Ties

Roland L. Warren

John Walton's analysis of community power structures is important not only in that it goes beyond a mere equating of competitive power structures with size of population, but also because it suggests a theoretical explanation for competitiveness in power structures which is both plausible and frought with substantive implications. Although the analysis is plausible and significant, the variables on which it is based can be challenged on the basis of their validity as indicators of interdependence; and, of course, additional, more deliberately designed research would be needed to establish firmly the relationship between community interdependence and competitive power structures which is derived from the present analysis.

But that is for the future. Let us examine the analysis itself, in relation to the data on which it is based, and then go on to consider some of the implications of the relationship, if it is corroborated by subsequent research.

Walton concludes that four variables show a statistically significant relationship to competitive power structures. These are absentee ownership, adequate economic resources, satellite status and political party competition. These otherwise purely empirical relationships are given theoretical meaning by the observation that they are all indicators of a community's dependence on the surrounding society. Such dependence, linking community units to extracommunity systems, introduces new resources and sanctions into the community and brings about a fragmentation of the local normative order and, through this, a number of competing power centers.

Consequently, those communities with the greatest dependence on vertical ties, as indicated by these four variables, will show the greatest pluralism, or diversity, or competitiveness of power structures. In oversimplified terms, the greater and more numerous the vertical ties, the more pluralistic the power structure; the fewer and weaker the vertical ties, the more monolithic the power structure.

Because of the great significance of this thesis, it is doubly important to note that the reasoning on which it is based, though entirely plausible, is still extremely tenuous. A key point in the analysis is the extent to which the four indicators actually constitute valid and powerful operational measures of

SOURCE: Roland L. Warren, "A Note on Walton's Analysis of Power Structure and Vertical Ties," *Social Science Quarterly*, 48 (December 1967), 369–372. Reprinted by permission.

strength of vertical ties. Taken individually, both absentee-owned industry and competitive political parties would seem to be plausible indicators of community interdependence, for the reasons which Walton suggests. On the other hand, he is understandably temperate in assertions about the variable of adequate economic resources. I doubt strongly that this variable would have occurred to him in advance as something especially to test for, had it not been one which showed an empirical relationship to competitive power structures in the direction indicated. It certainly would not have occurred to me. Probably on this one, we should simply reflect on the note written in the margin of a preacher's sermon: "Weak point. Pound the pulpit!" and then go on to the next point.

The fourth variable, or attribute, is that of being a satellite community. Here again, the reasoning is plausible, but would require more refined consideration of whether the dimensions of interdependence which satellite status indicates are relevant to the dimensions of interdependence which could be the basis for a plausible theoretical association between interdependence and competitive power structures. Those aspects of interdependence which could be theoretically derived from satellite status would have to be specified, operationalized, and then tested for degree of association with competitive power structure, before one could draw a valid conclusion on this question.

Yet, taken all in all, the distributions would indicate the plausibility of the theoretical explanation, and would strongly support the desirablity of pursuing this new, rich vein.

One other aspect of the analysis suggests the need for greater clarification in the theoretical explanation of the data. This has to do with the use of the community's "normative order" as an important variable, a variable which is sometimes treated as an independent variable, at other times as an intermediate variable. The question is whether this variable is not superfluous. It does not seem to be necessary to the theoretical explanation, and rather seems to have the status only of a theoretical construct, not too clearly defined, which accounts for nothing and simply clutters the analysis. Further, it lends itself to reification and what, it would seem to me at least, is a deliberate reversal of the direction of the imputed relationship.

Thus, we get the statement: "In the present context the number of 'autonomous actors' increases as a result of changes in normative expectations and the effectiveness of sanctions." But there is nothing in either the data or in the theoretical reasoning to lend support to normative expectations as an independent variable. Put quite simply, ties to extracommunity systems give local community units access to resources and sanctions which may be relatively independent of other local community units, and often subjects them to constraints which are determined by extracommunity systems. Both of these aspects quite plausibly operate to fragmentalize the community power structure. In doing so, they may also fragmentalize the community's "normative expectations," all depending on what this term means. But it is the existence of independent sources of resources and sanctions, and of independent constraints, which fragmentalizes the community power structure—not the fragmentalizing of the community's normative structure as such.

Hence, in my judgment, the concept of fragmentation of normative structure should either be abandoned or clarified. Incidentally, the work of Levine and his associates lends both data and analysis which support this thesis. Their analysis of the health field indicates among other things that those health agencies which are least dependent upon other local community agencies for their necessary resources are least likely to collaborate with them.[1]

But let us examine briefly some of the substantive implications of the thesis which Walton presents, for in acknowledging the above difficulties I do not mean to minimize either the brilliance of the analysis, the plausibity of the theoretical aspects, or the importance of the assertion.

Some time ago, I presented a seminar of graduate students with three values, or desiderata, which appear frequently in the literature of those who participate in community development as a social movement. These three values are: 1) Community autonomy (the community is master of its own fate), 2) Community viability (the community is capable of confronting its problems and making decisions and taking appropriate action) and 3) Citizen participation (there is broad participation in community organizations and in decision-making on community matters).

The assignment was to take, abstractly, a city of some 100,000 people in the continental United States, with a surrounding fringe population of perhaps another 100,000. What would a community of this size look like, in its social structure and behavior, which maximized these three values which are so often championed by "community-development" advocates? The students worked in three subgroups, each sketching out the implications for such a community of the maximization of *one* of these three values. In a subsequent plenary session, as each group reported and a general discussion ensued, two things became strikingly apparent.

The first was that each value could be maximized only at a price (in terms of the jeopardization of other values) which most communities would probably find excessive.

The second was that these three values could not be maximized simultaneously, for beyond a certain threshold they impeded each other. This was especially the case with viability and autonomy. One can be approximated only at increasing costs to the other.

Walton's thesis is of great substantive importance in this respect. For it implies that you must take your choice between autonomy and a democratic fragmentation of power structures. Those communities which are most auton-

[1]Sol Levine and Paul E. White, "Exchange as a Conceptual Framework for the Study of Interorganizational Relationships," *Administrative Science Quarterly,* 5 (March, 1961), pp. 583–601; and Sol Levine, Paul E. White, and Benjamin D. Paul, "Community Interorganizational Problems in Providing Medical Care and Social Service," *American Journal of Public Health,* 53 (August, 1963) pp. 1183–1195.

omous are the most monolithic in their power structures. Those communities
which are the least autonomous are the most pluralistic in their power structures. Thus, two different expectations or value aspirations for the "good"
community in the eyes of many community-development advocates are found
to be incompatible. One must therefore choose. Which do you want: Community autonomy at the sacrifice of broad distribution of power? or a democratically broad distribution of community power at the sacrifice of autonomy?

In this connection, a friend and colleague of mine was recently engaged in
developing a series of seminars in a fairly large metropolis, in which his explicit
goal was to bring together top leadership from different segments of community interests and organizations so that they could jointly confront community
problems at a more inclusive level. I asked him whether, inadvertently, he was
not trying to convert a pluralistic power structure into a monolithic one, and
how he could be sure that the community would benefit by the concerted
decision-making and action he hoped to further, rather than be harmed by it.
The works of political scientists such as Banfield and economists such as
Lindblom make a strong case for a plurality of decision-making centers at the
community level. Likewise, sociologists have indicated an implicit value preference for pluralistic power structures, without being so analytically specific
as to the fact that they are making this judgment and the reasons why they
make it.[2]

My friend responded by stating that his effort would not be justifiable if
it were not accompanied by an equal stress on community-wide values, as
opposed to the selfish values of this or that particular power group. Yet works
such as *Political Influence* and the *Intelligence of Democracy* make a strong
case that the community's inclusive interests are furthered by a fragmented
power structure rather than by a monolithic one (although Banfield, especially,
acknowledges that there may be a plausible justification for centralized decision-making, and even enumerates situations in which the juxtaposition of
opposing power centers may produce an inferior aggregate utility as compared
to a unified decision-making context).[3]

It is somewhat ironic that many of us tend to criticize the advocates of
decentralization, of "market choice" as opposed to centralized planning, as
somehow being nineteenth-century characters who do not adequately appreciate the obvious desirablity of centralized planning, while at the same time we
continue to make an implicit and largely unexamined value judgment against
the very monolithic power structures which are empirical examples of centralized planning.

In the immediately preceding remarks, it is quite apparent that many of

[2]Edward C. Banfield, *Political Influence* (New York: The Free Press of Glencoe, 1961), pp.
324 ff.; and Charles E. Lindblom, *The Intelligence of Democracy: Decision Making Through
Mutual Adjustment* (New York and London: The Free Press-Collier-Macmillan, Ltd., 1965),
passim.
[3]Banfield, *Political Influence,* pp. 355 ff.

the terms are being used in ambiguous senses, and that their full implications have not been precisely delineated. All the more reason why we should welcome the kind of coldly analytical study which Walton has produced, especially since his findings are so imbued with implications for social theory and social policy.

Part IV

URBAN SOCIETY:
EXPERIENCES AT
THE MARGIN

THE METROPOLIS IS A VAST MELTING POT OF DIVERSE PEOPLES. MIRRORING the society of which they are a part, cities concentrate and magnify the differences that exist within that society. Ethnic, religious, linguistic, and racial diversity is extensive. The newcomer and the long-settled resident, the urban sophisticate and the Appalachian migrant, share a similar geographic home but scarcely a common urban experience. Sharp disparities in wealth, status, and power are common. Thus, the urban population cannot be described as a totality, only as a set of diverse populations. The poor, particularly the minority-group poor, are a large and important segment of the urban population,[1] and this section describes some of the significant properties of their life and circumstances.

An analysis of the experiences of life for the urban poor would be incomplete without exploring the nature of the American response to the poor, particularly the less self-sufficient among them. To be poor in American society is to be severely stigmatized and to suffer a sense of being outside the mainstream of society (24). A condition of poverty is viewed as a moral defect. This attitude of derogation toward the poor by the broader society is compounded by a society stressing mobility, competitiveness, and achievement, a society enmeshed in materialist values and one that accords no legitimate or acceptable place in the social or moral order for those at the bottom. Not surprisingly, there is a tendency of "blaming the victim" (82) or his cultural properties for individual or group disabilities. The perception of the poor as "disreputable" or "undeserving" is reinforced by the continuance of racial animosity and the fact that minority groups are a significant portion of the urban poor (16), especially for those under sixty-five.[2] False analogies with previous immigrant experience and the absence of a genuine interrelationship between the urban poor and society contribute to the perpetuation of negative attitudes. In addition, governmental efforts to alleviate poverty and the public sense of possible policy options have been seriously compromised by other attitudes. There is the heritage, now somewhat weakened, of laissez-faire ideology and of antipathy to governmental control over private entrepreneurship in business, and financial, land, and construction activities. There is also the influence of the inequitable distribution of effective political and institutional power.

[1] There is no precise referent for the present discussion. The population with which we are concerned is essentially made up of the black, Mexican-American, and Puerto Rican inhabitants of the city who are poor and living predominantly in segregated areas within the city. No sharp boundary lines distinguish the poor from the nonpoor. We have in mind, however, an upper income figure of roughly between $5,000 and $6,000 a year for a family of four, thus encompassing somewhat more than half of the nonwhite urban population. However, even the more well-to-do ghetto resident shares many similar experiences with his poorer brethren.

[2] Many researchers have attempted to explain which population categories could be considered as poor, and what some of their demographic and geographic properties are. Several such efforts include 16, 30, 68, 75, 76, 97.

Economic disabilities are, of course, a major property of the population with which we are concerned.[3] A significant portion of the nonwhite urban population lives in conditions of poverty, about half the families securing too little to achieve even moderate standards of family needs. Many receive quite low wages. Unemployment and under-employment, especially compared to that of whites, is considerable and results in a significant ghetto population with insufficient job opportunities (3, 12, 41, 105). This is a condition aggravated by the changing character of employment itself. Not only is there a long-term decline of low-skilled jobs, or put differently, an increased demand for greater levels of educational achievement and the possession of special skills, but the principal location of industrial jobs is shifting to areas outside of the central city (3, 73, 81). The growth of employment opportunities in the metropolitan centers is in the white-collar and service fields; changing employment opportunities are thus partly discordant with the employment needs of the low-income, low-education, and low-skilled populations of our central cities. In contrast to the periods of heavy immigration to the United States when industrial expansion provided some diversity of employment and economic opportunities, even for those of moderate education and skills, such possibilities are today increasingly closed to the lower stratum of the population.

These circumstances are compounded by still other economic disabilities. Goods available in ghetto areas tend to be higher priced and of poorer quality. Opportunities for bargain shopping are lacking and exploitive credit practices and hidden finance charges are not unusual. The low-income population suffers exploitation through repossession of goods and wage garnishment and bears the brunt of a host of rather unsavory enterprises that seek to penalize the poor (3, 8, 94). Insurance and home mortgages are often unavailable or exceedingly costly.[4] These add to the economic plight of the poor. Related, is the severe absence of legal resources and their unfamiliarity with legal forms and rights (28, 93, 95, 98, 106).

As the selections reprinted here, as well as a host of other items make clear, to

[3]For a broad review of the economic conditions exhibited and experienced by the urban ghetto, see Bell (3). The end of her volume also contains a useful bibliography offering references for many of the points expressed here. The literature on poverty populations is extremely extensive and diverse. Some well-known volumes of collected essays dealing with many aspects of poverty and poverty populations include 20, 26, 45, 81. There are many general studies of individual urban minority populations. Some of the more well-known items include 7, 10, 36, 39, 55, 78, 89, 90. A number of summary reviews as well as items focusing on somewhat more particular properties of the poor include 4, 15, 31, 46, 62, 63, 69, 80. Reference will be variously made throughout the following discussion to additional sources relevant to various particular concerns. In this regard, however, many of the items that are later cited in relation to the culture-of-poverty concept are also especially pertinent to any interest in a delineation of the properties, life patterns and experiences of the urban poor.

[4]An important need of the poor is the ability to obtain credit and insurance at reasonable rates and moderately and honestly financed home purchases. See McPherson (60).

be poor and to live in the urban slums, particularly for a minority group, is not only to lack money but to experience wide-ranging physical inadequacies, personal disabilities, and other diverse strains.[5] More than a third of the low-income population lives in substandard housing, and adequate housing in the suburbs is beyond the reach of a significant portion of the American population (3, 86, 101, 102, 108). Convenient and economical transportation is frequently absent. Garbage collection is inadequate. The presence of rats and other vermin, the danger of lead-based paints, and high rates of drug addiction, violence, and crime compound the negative, frustrating, and soul-searing properties of the urban ghetto. Some of these are noted in the Report of the National Advisory Commission on Civil Disorders (99, 100). Their discussion of "Conditions of Life in the Racial Ghetto" provides additional elaboration by also describing the high incidence of disease, the significant proportion affected by chronic illness, and the lower availability and utilization of medical services (34, 35, 42).

The economic and physical properties of the ghetto only partially explain the nature of life at the margin. The existence of prejudice and the practice of discrimination, though reduced in scope from their earlier form, have importantly influenced the nature of the urban experience and minority-group disabilities. Prejudice and discrimination have created an antipathy which has adversely affected urban life and experience for minority populations, deepened the sense of marginality and powerlessness, made more difficult individual efforts at change as well as ameliorative national policy, and exacerbated relationships between the ghetto and external institutions.

An understanding of the circumstances of the ghetto population also requires recognition of the existence of severe personal, familial, and community disabilities.[6] There is a pervasive condition of insecurity, deprivation, and strain. More serious personal characteristics may also appear, such as a sense of hopelessness, ineffectiveness, and apathy. Some will experience difficulty establishing genuine relationships, especially of an enduring nature.[7] There is a disproportionate amount of family instability—family strife, unhappy and broken marriages, desertion, female-headed households, illegitimacy, and insufficient supervision of children. In such circumstances the ability of parents to provide offspring with adequate nurturance and role models for effective functioning is seriously undermined. Inadequate school performance, termination of education, delinquency, and drug addiction flaw the lives and qualify the prospects of many ghetto youths.

The educational experience of the ghetto child perhaps deserves special com-

[5] Relevant accounts are provided by many of the items listed in footnote 3.

[6] The items by Blum and Rossi (4) and Rossi and Blum (80) provide a comprehensive review of the literature on characteristics of the poor. Many of the citations in footnote 3 include discussions of the community properties of ghetto areas.

[7] There is also the contention that impoverished ghetto populations will develop negative images of self, a diminished sense of personal worth, and an insufficient clarity of self-identity. Clear support for such a view, however, is not provided by current research findings (4).

ment. In this regard there is by now an extensive, depressing,and widely recognized commentary on the quality of education in the ghetto (33, 43, 54). Essentially, the circumstances depicted are those of a steady decline in comparative performance with the child's continued schooling, with severe inadequacies in even rudimentary skills. The schools are frequently older, less well financed, and staffed by less skilled teachers, than those in the suburbs and more affluent areas. Too frequently the students confront an uncongenial and, at times, even hostile environment, one lacking flexibility and responsiveness to the distinctive needs and characteristics of the lower-income child and minority-group culture. Frequently this is also a segregated education (14). Diverse programs for change have been suggested and some instituted, but the situation has not greatly improved (22, 27, 38, 61, 88).

The bases or roots of these diverse phenomena and disabilities are various and each may to some extent, of course, be productive of the other. More fundamentally, the personal and familial properties develop as a consequence of conditions of poverty, minimal resources, the experience of erratic employment and menial jobs, marginality, the defeats and derogation suffered in transactions with societal institutions, invidious ghetto membership in American society, and the failure to attain the "universal" values and performance standards of the broader society. The latter conditions suggest that the circumstances of poverty assume especially serious personal and familial consequences in light of the particular characteristics of the values and institutions of the society—such as the stress on competitive success and mobility, mass consumer practices, cultural uniformity, and invidious class and communal group status and values.[8] The appearance of such consequences, however, seems to be minimized where poor minority populations possess distinctive cultural properties that maximize a sense of individual dignity, commitment, group support, efficaciousness, and independence. On the whole, though, these are lacking in contemporary ghetto populations.[9]

[8]The reader familiar with Oscar Lewis' work will, of course, recognize the preceding as similar to the perspective that he develops, though the present writer in other respects takes exception to Lewis' culture-of-poverty concept.

[9]What is involved here is that the response to circumstances of poverty and the relationship to the external, dominant society is mediated by individual involvement in an independent culture of an extensive and sustaining quality. Thus, while situational and environmental circumstances such as impoverishment, denial, estrangement, hostility, or the like are of major importance, they prove especially consequential where the individual lacks other sources of nurturance, group involvement, sense of personal worth, standards of personal commitment, purpose, and performance that are at times provided by some of the old, respected, and fully elaborated cultures that some religious and ethnic populations possess. At times these cultures may also provide a set of values which stress continued application and denial as a means of success, or a turning inward toward group commitment and involvement as a satisfactory criterion of individual performance and worth. These too mitigate some of the negative personal, familial and community effects of poverty conditions.

The urban ghetto exhibits severe disabilities at the community level, as well as at the level of the individual and family. Effective community institutions (within the sphere of legitimate or legal activities) are frequently lacking, as is a strong sense of community for many residents. In effect, this is an accentuation of a condition which, at least to some extent, prevails throughout contemporary urban society. The obstacles to community and effective organizational functioning and citizen involvement, however, are heightened in the ghetto. These include the sense of hopelessness, cynicism, powerlessness, and the social estrangement generated by the circumstances of the poor. Further, where families are large, jobs scarce, income limited, baby sitters costly, and personal concerns limited by financial, familial, health, and housing problems, the ability and interest to relate to the community, as well as to share in community organizations and enterprise is seriously undermined. The weakness of community-based institutions is variously exhibited. The church is often ineffective and irrelevant to many of the needs and concerns of the community. Civic organizations are usually weak, and local-based political organization and activity is slight. The poor are not involved in politics, are uninformed, and generally lack interest in the political scene. Existing political groups provide only slight representation to the poor and minority groups. The weakness of community that the lack of involvement and debilitated community institutions partly reflect creates a rather anomalous situation. It makes any effort at community control and the decentralization of institutional and political structures a precarious undertaking. Yet, at the same time, a possible consequence of such institutional and political innovation could be the revitalization of community. We return more fully to this question in the concluding section of the volume.

The circumstances of poverty populations have at times been characterized as constituting a distinctive culture, or rather, a subculture within the broader society. In effect, some students have postulated a culture of poverty (9, 23, 49, 50, 51, 52, 53), and a diverse literature has sought to delineate distinctive social and cultural properties of the poor or of elements within such populations. Usually this takes the direction of stressing the presumed presence of such characteristics, values, and personal properties as a consensual marriage, matriarchal and unstable families, low motivation and achievement levels, little ability to defer gratification, impulsiveness, fatalism, dependency, feelings of inferiority, a sense of marginality, weak ego structure, provincialism, and lack of participation in community or broader societal institutions (9, 13, 23, 52, 53, 67, 71). The way of life and values of the poor are viewed as continuing over time, being transmitted intergenerationally and seriously minimizing the possibility of change through alteration of the situational or environmental conditions that the poor experience. Thus, the major contentions are that some portion of the poor exhibit a distinctive subculture, that this is transmitted between generations, that its properties pose a very substantial impediment to changing the impoverished condition of this population, and that consequently situational or environmental change (for instance, guaranteed family income, increased employment opportunities, and creation of nonalienating institutions) would be insufficient for the achievement of an alteration in the characteristics or disabilities of those within the culture of poverty.

While the issues surrounding the culture-of-poverty concept are still strongly debated, the weight of scholarly opinion and available research findings suggest that the principal contentions involved in this concept are not clearly supported. The culture-of-poverty enthusiasts have been effectively criticized for deriving culture principally from overt behavior and not attending to the values or aspirations that people hold. Hyman Rodman has, in this connection, suggested the existence of a "value stretch" (79). The poor are perceived as holding conventional societal norms, but due to their daily life circumstances they may diverge from these in their behavior, and even develop alternate values to rationalize or adjust to their existential conditions (21, 25, 44, 55, 78).[10] Thus, the poor are viewed as sharing both the broader societal norms and, in addition, developing a distinct set of norms to accord with the circumstances that they confront. Gans aptly quotes Hylan Lewis' remark that "it is important not to confuse basic life chance and actual behavior with basic cultural values and preferences" (21, p. 209).

A middle-class bias has also, in some respects, been exhibited in the culture-of-poverty argument and in supporting research. There has been a failure to take into account the circumstances of the poor as these influence the individual's response to, and negotiation of, those situations and phenomena (e.g., use of money, attitudes toward education, and life goals) utilized by social scientists to evaluate such qualities as achievement motivation (37, 84), ambition or aspiration level (40, 64), and patterns of deferred gratification (64).[11] In many of these efforts inadequate attention has been paid to the *relative* distance between present circumstances and personal goals and to the question of what would be realistic ambitions, goals, motivations, or gratifications in light of existing conditions. What has been emphasized is the absolute level of the goal. Yet, an apparently "high" goal may for a middle-class individual differ little from prevailing family and individual circumstances, and a presumably more modest goal for a poor person may, in light of existing conditions, actually signify a considerably greater relative level of ambition.

Most students would agree that some value differences do exist between the poor and other elements of society. However, these are generally perceived as differences of degree, not qualitative differences. In addition, the diversity present among the poor, as among other elements in American society, further minimize the ability to

[10]A contrary perspective in regard to some of the relevant empirical findings is provided by Henriques (32).

[11]For additional discussions, including some of a more comprehensive nature see such items as 6, 11, 18, 85, 92, 104.

establish a distinct and qualitatively different poverty segment. Further, such differences as are established appear to be essentially a response to economic, social, political, and other situational circumstances. The processes of individual change reflected in both historical and contemporary patterns of mobility suggest that, on the whole, changing situations produce alterations in personal behavior and values. This may be retarded where conditions have been such as to produce a strongly apathetic, fatalistic, and despairing populace. Yet even in such circumstances it does not appear that one is dealing with an intergenerational phenomenon in terms of cultural transmission. Nor are the members of such a population unable to change when effective communication can be established that succeeds in conveying the possibility of change and the personal, familial, and community rewards following from change.

It is difficult to support the contention that a distinct set of traits are transmitted from generation to generation, in terms other than as a response to the continuance of social and economic conditions interrelated with poverty itself. Neither the strength of these presumed distinctive traits, the socialization practices of those in poverty, nor the patterns of social interaction among the poor are such as to provide any considerable confidence in the ability of a culture of poverty to be passed from one generation to the next. While there may be an internalization and conversion of some situational responses into culture patterns, this seems of a quite restricted nature and of limited viability over any period of time where situational circumstances are changing. Of course, culture patterns do continue over time and may be strongly resistant to change. However, this involves both strong individual identity with, and commitment to, these patterns and a number of supportive and socializing institutions. These conditions are found within those religious, ethnic, and communal populations which have succeeded in transmitting their distinct "designs for living" over many generations, often in strongly hostile environments. However, these conditions for intergenerational cultural survival do not exist among the poor. While much of the research on these questions is quite incomplete (107), the careful research of Louis Kriesberg (44) provides strong support for the contention that, at least among the poor, husbandless, urban mothers that he studied, poverty-associated conditions did "not appear to be transmitted in any major way" (44, p. 297). He found little distinctive family, income, and welfare dependency, or social patterns in the previous generation of his "mothers in poverty." In a different direction, an imaginative analysis by Otis D. Duncan (17) has documented the fact that racial properties are more significant in determining the continuance of income disparities than the social and economic properties of one's family of origin.

The preceding comments suggest that an alteration of the situational factors within which poverty families are implicated would provide the opportunity for a large majority to achieve situations of economic, social, and family viability. Unfortunately, social policy has not been formulated in such terms. It has tended to define the life of the poor as reflecting the disabilities and inadequacies of the individual or his family.

In a different vein, Herbert Gans has responded to the controversy surrounding the concept of a culture of poverty by suggesting that, "if the culture of poverty is defined as those cultural patterns that keep people poor, it would be necessary to also include in the term the persisting cultural patterns among the affluent that, deliberately or not, keep their fellow citizens poor" (21, p. 216). This, of course, opens up a whole new perspective on poverty and social policy, one requiring more far-reaching and radical change than has been attempted in the past. The absence of a program elaborated in such terms signifies, however, a continuation of a poverty population.

A frequent omission in analyses concerning the culture of poverty and in a great deal of the literature on urban ghetto populations is a discussion of the strengths or positive qualities of the individuals and families of the ghetto. In spite of adverse circumstances, including low income, many do function effectively. A large proportion of the population is employed, and most families are stable. Children are raised in a nurturant setting, succeed in establishing stable lives, and some find the means to improve their own circumstances above that of their parents. For many the ghetto experience, even recognizing its pain, limited opportunities, and severe hardships, still does not prevent attaining many of the personal and family satisfactions that we ordinarily identify with as typical for the average citizen, though these may be somewhat more qualified. Even some presumed disabilities may actually be used to serve constructive ends. Thus, female-headed households may serve to diminish potential strife and raise family cohesion over what might prevail were a male head present. And the harsh circumstances confronted by the young may at times steel them for later difficulties and produce a realistic assessment of life and opportunities that makes possible a more effective adjustment to the constraints and blocked opportunities of their environment. The stress throughout the present introduction on the strains and disabilities suffered by the ghetto population is not to deny the preceding but to suggest something of the dimensions and range of differences that exist between the poor of the ghetto and the broader population.

The relationship of the individual and his community to the external agencies and personnel that impinge upon the ghetto has received little attention in the preceding discussion. These are, however, an important aspect of any overall description of the circumstances of urban neighborhoods and ghetto populations. We have in mind here the presence on the local community level of such governmental agencies as those in the area of housing, health, and urban renewal, as well as school, police, and welfare institutions. The selections by Lyford (56) and by Boesel and his colleagues (5) provide vivid and illuminating treatment in these regards. Lyford's discussion is an especially powerful and disturbing account of the arrogance and alien power of these institutions and their personnel. He sharply depicts the futility of seeking to communicate with powerful and removed city bureaucracies, or of attempting to secure an accurate accounting of policy and intentions from them. He points to the discrepancies between actual deeds or inaction, as the case may be, and presumed policy. Their response to criticism and questions is irrelevant. Their commitments to local areas are ignored or altered at will. They are unresponsive to any but organized pressure, and they use a multitude of regulations to avoid responsibility and action. Not only is it a situation where the institutions of local government both ignore and mistreat the powerless citizens of the local community, but these same institutions generally function so as to advance the interests of elements in the private business sector, whether landlords, banks, or other groups, who misuse, and profit from, the local community. The type of circumstances treated by Lyford contributes significantly to the creation of a sense of hostility, cynicism, frustration, defeat, and powerlessness.

"White Institutions and Black Rage," the essay by David Boesel and his associates, provides a useful extension of Lyford's discussion. It offers a brief review of the attitudes of the members of several institutions that function within the ghetto but whose origin and character are established outside the community. The authors interviewed employers, merchants, teachers, social workers, police and political party workers. While some of these, especially the merchants and police, were suspicious and had a distorted perception of the circumstances of the black population, perhaps an even more important finding was the belief that the problems of the ghetto population or its difficulty with social institutions (e.g., the schools) developed from the inadequacies or disabilities of the residents of the ghetto. In other words, neither institutional failures nor strains within the local population were perceived by the members of these external agencies as arising from the functioning or practices of the institutions themselves. Rather, they were viewed as accounted for by the characteristics of the ghetto or its population. One has here a reflection of the common practice of "blaming the victim" (82). Certainly there resides, in these circumstances as well as in those recounted in Lyford's biting piece, a major impetus behind the growing demand for institutional decentralization and local control.

The social, economic, and political plight of the urban poor has been a long-standing condition. While greater public concern is now being expressed, the programs developed in the last decade or so, as well as earlier efforts, have been woefully inadequate.[12] While the brevity of our discussion does not permit their consideration, we can close by at least pointing to the nature of their insufficiencies. Such observations will be a helpful prelude to the more extended treatment of urban dilemmas in our concluding section.

A basic failing of social policy has been its adherence to a belief in the individual, rather than institutional, origins of poverty. Thus social policy has avoided the fundamental fact that the condition of the urban poor is principally one that requires an alteration of their economic circumstances and related institutional structures. The welfare program, for instance, has clearly provided little other than a minimal exis-

---

[12]For evaluations of past and current policy efforts in the poverty and welfare field, as well as for new program suggestions, see 48, 70, 74, 77, 91, 96.

tence, and not even that for everyone in need (77, 91). Nor has it even functioned so as to encourage or make possible a condition of self-reliance and family improvement. Only an adequate income maintenance program could begin to achieve such an end. Yet, little has been done either to provide for some type of guaranteed annual income or even to assure more jobs and better remuneration on many existing low-paying ones. Without such an effort many of the programs that have been developed have only a peripheral usefulness in respect to the core problems of those who live on the margins of American society. Even in their own terms, however, many of these programs, e.g., in housing, education, job training, model cities, and nursery care, have been meager and insufficient, frequently in conception and funding, often in administration and execution. Broadly conceived and more fundamental efforts would require significant constraints upon vested private interests and well-organized power structures, such as banks, realtors, the construction industry, trade unions, the educational hierarchy, and local political leadership. Not surprisingly, therefore, the formulation of policy has been timid and involved little alteration of existing circumstances.

The immediate circumstances and prospect, then, of the urban poor is not very salutary. One hopes that perhaps in the long run more imaginative and responsive public policy, greater use of public power for public ends, and increased availability of resources will combine with a growing consciousness, organization, and vitality among the minority poor of the urban ghettos to provide the circumstances for alleviating the disproportionate poverty, social and physical decay, personal disabilities, and estrangement that have been sketched in the present account.

REFERENCES

1. Allen, Vernon L., *Psychological Factors in Poverty* (Chicago:Markham Publishing Co., 1970).

2. _____, "The Psychology of Poverty: Problems and Prospects," in Vernon L. Allen, ed., *Psychological Factors in Poverty* (Chicago: Markham Publishing Co., 1970), pp. 367–383.

3. Bell, Carolyn Shaw, *The Economics of the Ghetto* (New York: Pegasus, 1970), paper.

4. Blum, Zahava D., and Rossi, Peter H., "Social Class Research and Images of the Poor: A Bibliographic Review," in Daniel P. Moynihan, ed., *On Understanding Poverty* (New York: Basic Books, 1969), pp. 343–397.

5. Boesel, David, et al., "White Institutions and Black Rage," *Trans-action,* 6 (March 1969), 24–31.

6. Bruckham, Idel R., "The Relationship between Achievement Motivation and Sex, Age, Social Class, School Stream and Intelligence," *British Journal of Social and Clinical Psychology,* 5 (September 1966), 211–220.

7. Brown, Claude, *Manchild in the Promised Land* (New York: Macmillan, 1965).

8. Caplovitz, David, *The Poor Pay More: Consumer Practices of Low Income Families* (New York: Fress Press, 1963).

9. Chilman, Catherine S., *Growing Up Poor,* Publication No. 13, Welfare Administration, U.S. Department of Health, Education, and Welfare (Washington: U.S. Government Printing Office, 1966).

10. Clark, Kenneth B., *Dark Ghetto Dilemmas of Social Power* (New York: Harper and Row, 1965).

11. Crockett, Harry J., Jr., "Psychological Origins of Mobility," in Neil J. Smelser and Seymour M. Lipset, eds., *Social Structure and Mobility in Economic Development* (Chicago: Aldine, 1966), pp. 280–309.

12. Cummings, Laurie D., "The Employed Poor: Their Characteristics and Occupations," *Monthly Labor Review,* 88 (July 1965), 828–884.

13. Davis, Allison, "Child Rearing in the Class Structure of American Society," in *The Family in a Democratic Society,* Anniversary Papers of the Community Service Society of New York (New York: Columbia University Press, 1949), pp. 56–69.

14. Dentler, Robert A., et al., *The Urban R's: Race Relations as the Problem in Urban Education* (New York: Praeger, 1967).

15. Deutsch, Martin, *The Disadvantaged Child* (New York: Basic Books, 1967).

16. Downs, Anthony, *Who Are the Urban Poor?* CFD Supplementary Paper, No. 26 (New York: Committee for Economic Development, 1968).

17. Duncan, Otis D., "Inheritance of Poverty or Inheritance of Race?" in Daniel P. Moynihan, ed., *On Understanding Poverty* (New York: Basic Books, 1969), pp. 85–110.

18. Featherman, David L., "Achievement Orientations and Socioeconomic Career Attainments," *American Sociological Review,* 37 (April 1972), 131–143.

19. Ferguson, Robert H. "Unemployment, Its Scope, Measurement and Effect on Poverty," Bulletin 53–2 (Ithaca: School of Industrial Relations, Cornell University, 1965).

20. Ferman, Louis A., et al., eds., *Poverty in America: A Book of Readings* (Ann Arbor: The University of Michigan Press, 1968).

21. Gans, Herbert J., "Culture and Class in the Study of Poverty: An Approach to Anti-Poverty Research," in Daniel P. Moynihan, ed., *On Understanding Poverty* (New York: Basic Books, 1969), pp. 201–228.

22. Gittel, Marilyn, ed., *Educating an Urban Population* (New York: Sage Publications, 1967).

23. Gladwin, Thomas, *Poverty U.S.A.* (Boston: Little, Brown, 1967).

24. Goffman, Erving, *Stigma: Notes on the Management of Spoiled Identity* (Englewood Cliffs, N.J.: Prentice-Hall, 1963).

25. Goode, William, "Illegitimacy in the Caribbean Social Structure," *American Sociological Review,* 25 (February 1960), 21–30.

26. Gordon, Margaret S., ed., *Poverty in America* (San Francisco: Chandler, 1965).

27. Gross, Ronald and Beatrice, eds., *Radical School Reform* (New York: Simon and Schuster, 1969).

28. Grosser, Charles F., and Edward V. Sparer, "Legal Services for the Poor: Social Work and Social Justice," *Social Work,* 11 (January 1966), 81–87.

29. Guttentag, Marcia, "Group Cohesiveness, Ethnic Organization, and Poverty," *Journal of Social Issues,* 26 (Spring 1970), 105–132.

30. Haber, Alan, "Poverty Budgets: How Much Is Enough?" *Poverty and Human Resources Abstracts,* 1 (May-June 1966), 5–14.

31. Harrington, Michael, *The Other America* (New York, Macmillan, 1962).

32. Henriques, Fernando, *Family and Colour in Jamaica* (London: Eyre and Spottiswoode, 1953).

33. Herndon, James, *The Way Its Spozed to Be* (New York: Simon and Schuster, 1968).

34. Hunt, Eleanor P., "Infant Mortality and Poverty Areas," *Welfare in Review,* 5 (August-September 1967), 1–12.

35. Hurley, Rodger L., *Poverty and Mental Retardation* (New York: Random House, 1969).

36. Jacobs, Paul, *Prelude to Riot, A View of Urban American From the Bottom* (New York: Random House, 1966).

37. Kahl, Joseph A., "Some Measurements of Achievement Orientation," *American Journal of Sociology,* 70 (May 1965), 669–681.

38. Keach, Everett T., et al., eds., *Education and Social Crisis: Perspectives on Teaching Disadvantaged Youth* (New York: John Wiley, 1967).

39. Keil, Charles, *Urban Blues* (Chicago: University of Chicago Press, 1966).

40. Keller, Suzanne, and Zavalloni, Marisa, "Ambition and Social Class: A Respecification," *Social Forces,* 43 (October 1964), 58–70.

41. Keyserling, Leon H., *The Role of Wages in a Great Society, Stressing Minimum-Wage Gains to Help the Working Poor* (Washington: Conference on Economic Progress, 1966).

42. Kosa, John, et al., *Poverty and Health, A Sociological Analysis* (Cambridge: Harvard University Press, 1969).

43. Kozol, Jonathan, *Death at an Early Age* (Boston: Houghton Mifflin, 1967).

44. Kriesberg, Louis, *Mothers in Poverty: A Study of Fatherless Families* (Chicago: Aldine, 1970).

45. Larner, Jeremy, and Howe, Irving, eds., *Poverty: Views From the Left* (Clifton, N.Y.: William Morrow, 1968).

46. Leacock, Eleanor Burke, ed., *The Culture of Poverty, A Critique* (New York: Simon and Schuster, 1971).

47. Lebeaux, Charles, "Life on A.D.C.: Budgets of Despair," in Louis A. Ferman, et al., eds., *Poverty in America, A Book of Readings* (Ann Arbor: The University of Michigan Press, 1968), 519–529.

48. Levitan, Sar A., et al., eds., *Towards Freedom from Want* (Madison, Wis.: Industrial Relations Research Association, 1968).

49. Levy, Gerald F., *Ghetto School, Class Warfare in an Elementary School* (New York: Pegasus, 1970), paper.

50. Lewis, Oscar, *Five Families: Mexican Case Studies in the Culture of Poverty* (New York: Basic Books, 1959).

51. _____, *The Children of Sanchez* (New York: Random House, 1961).

52. _____, *Pedro Martinez* (New York: Random House, 1964).

53. _____, "The Culture of Poverty," *Scientific American,* 215 (October 1966), 19–25.

54. _____, *La Vida: A Puerto Rican Family in the Culture of Poverty—San Juan and New York* (New York: Random House, 1966).

55. Liebow, Elliot, *Tally's Corner: A Study of Negro Streetcorner Men* (Boston: Little, Brown, 1967).

56. Lyford, Joseph, "The Airtight Cage," in *The Airtight Cage* (New York: Harper & Row, 1966), pp. 301–317, 329–333.

57. _____, *The Airtight Cage* (New York: Harper and Row, 1966).

58. Matza, David, "The Disreputable Poor," in Reinhard Bendix and Seymour M. Lipset, eds., *Class, Status, and Power* (New York: The Free Press, 1966), pp. 289–302.

59. _____, "Poverty and Disrepute," in Robert K. Merton and Robert A. Nisbet, eds., *Contemporary Social Problems,* 3rd ed. (New York: Harcourt, Brace, Jovanovich, Inc., 1971), pp. 601–656.

60. McPherson, James Alan, " 'In My Father's House There Are Many Mansions, and I'm Going to Get Me Some of Them Too!' The Story of the Contract Buyers League," *The Atlantic,* 229 (April 1972), 51–82.

61. Miller, Harry L., ed., *Education for the Disadvantaged: Current Issues and Research* (New York: The Free Press, 1967).

62. Miller, Henry, "Characteristics of AFDC Families," *Social Service Review,* 39 (December 1965), 339–409.

63. Miller, S. M., "The American Lower Classes : A Typological Approach," *Social Research,* 31 (Spring 1964), 1–22.

64. Miller, S. M., et al., "Poverty and Self-indulgence: A Critique of the Non-deferred Gratification Pattern," in Louis Ferman, et al., eds., *Poverty in America* (Ann Arbor: University of Michigan Press, 1968), pp. 416–432.

65. Miller, S. M., and Riessman, Frank, "The Working Class Sub-culture: A New View," *Social Problems,* 9 (Summer 1961), 86–97.

66. Miller, S. M., and Roby, Pamela A., *The Future of Inequality* (New York: Basic Books, 1970).

67. Miller, Walter B., "Lower Class Culture as a Generating Milieu of Gang Delinquency," *Journal of Social Issues,* 14 (Summer 1958), 5–19.

68. Mooney, Joseph D., "Urban Poverty and Labor Force Participation," *American Economic Review,* 57 (March 1967), 104–119.

69. Moore, William, Jr., *The Vertical Ghetto, Everyday Life in an Urban Project* (New York: Random House, 1969).

70. Morgan, James N., et al., *Income and Welfare in the United States* (New York: McGraw-Hill, 1962).

71. Moynihan, Daniel P., "The Negro Family: The Case for National Action," in Lee Rainwater and William L. Yancey, eds., *The Moynihan Report and the Politics of Controversy* (Cambridge, Mass.: M.I.T. Press, 1967).

72. Moynihan, Daniel P., ed., *On Understanding Poverty: Perspectives from the Social Sciences* (New York: Basic Books, 1968).

73. National Committee Against Discrimination in Housing, *The Impact of Housing Patterns* (New York, 1968).

74. National Conference on Social Welfare, *Social Welfare Forum, 1966* (New York: Columbia University Press, 1966).

75. Orshansky, Mollie, "Recounting the Poor—A Five-Year Review," *Social Security Bulletin,* 29 (April 1966), 20–37.

76. ———, "The Shape of Poverty in 1966," *Social Security Bulletin,* 31 (March 1968), 3–32.

77. Piven, Frances Fox, and Cloward, Richard A., *Regulating the Poor: The Functions of Public Welfare* (New York: Pantheon, 1971).

78. Rainwater, Lee, *Behind Ghetto Walls, Black Families in a Federal Slum* (Chicago: Aldine, 1970).

79. Rodman, Hyman, "The Lower Class Value Stretch," *Social Forces,* 42 (December 1963), 205–215.

80. Rossi, Peter H., and Blum, Zahava D., "Class, Status, and Poverty," in Daniel P. Moynihan, ed., *On Understanding Poverty* (New York: Basic Books, 1969), 36–63.

81. Russell, Joe L., "Changing Patterns in Employment of Nonwhite Workers," *Monthly Labor Review,* 89 (May 1966), 503–599.

82. Ryan, William, *Blaming the Victim* (New York: Pantheon, 1971).

83. Ryscavage, Paul M., and Willacy, Hazel M., "Employment of the Nation's Urban Poor," *Monthly Labor Review,* 91 (August 1968), 15–21.

84. Scanzoni, John, "Socialization, Achievement, and Achievement Values," *American Sociological Review,* 32 (June 1967), 449–456.

85. Schneider, Louis, and Lysgaard, Sverre, "Deferred Gratification Pattern," *American Sociological Review,* 18 (April 1953), 142–149.

86. Schorr, Alvin L., *Slums and Social Insecurity: An Appraisal of the Effectiveness of Housing Policies in Helping to Eliminate Poverty in the United States,* Research Report No. 1, Division of Research Statistics. Social Security Administration, U.S. Department of Health, Education, and Welfare (Washington: U.S. Government Printing Office, 1963).

87. _____, *Explorations in Social Policy* (New York: Basic Books, 1968).

88. Schreiber, Daniel, ed., *Profile of the School Dropout: A Reader on America's Major Educational Problem* (New York: Random House, 1967).

89. Senior, Clarence, *The Puerto Ricans: Strangers—Then Neighbors* (Chicago: Quadrangle Books, 1965).

90. Sexton, Patricia Cayo, *Spanish Harlem, An Anatomy of Poverty* (New York: Harper, 1965).

91. Steiner, Gilbert, *The State of Welfare,* The Brookings Institution (Washington: The Brookings Institution, 1971).

92. Straus, Murray A., "Deferred Gratification, Social Class, and the Achievement Syndrome," *American Sociological Review,* 27 (June 1962), 326–335.

93. Stumpf, Harry P., "Law and Poverty: A Political Perspective," *Wisconsin Law Review,* (No. 3 1968), 694–733.

94. Sturdivant, Frederick D., "Better Deal for Ghetto Shoppers," *Harvard Business Review* (March-April 1968), 130–136.

95. Ten Broek, Jacob, ed., *The Law of the Poor* (San Francisco: Chandler, 1966).

96. Thurow, Lester C., *Poverty and Discrimination* (Washington: The Brookings Institution, 1969).

97. U. S. Department of Commerce, Bureau of the Census. "Poverty Areas in 100 Largest Metropolitan Areas," Supplementary Report PC(SI)-54, 1960 Census (Washington: U.S. Government Printing Office, 1967).

98. ———, Department of Health, Education, and Welfare. Welfare Administration, *The Extension of Legal Services to the Poor* (Washington: U. S. Government Printing Office, 1965).

99. ———, National Advisory Commission on Civil Disorders, *Report of the National Advisory Commission on Civil Disorders,* "Unemployment, Family Structure, and Social Disorganization" (Washington: U. S. Government Printing Office, 1968), pp. 123–130.

100. ———, ———, *Report of the National Advisory Commission on Civil Disorders,* "Conditions of Life in the Racial Ghetto," (Washington: U.S. Government Printing Office, 1968), pp. 133–141.

101. ———, National Commission on Urban Problems, *Building the American City* (Washington: U.S. Government Printing Office, 1969).

102. ———, The President's Committee on Urban Housing, *A Decent Home,* The Report of the President's Committee on Urban Housing (Washington: U.S. Government Printing Office, 1969).

103. Valentine, Charles A., *Culture and Poverty, Critique and Counter-Proposals* (Chicago: University of Chicago Press, 1968).

104. Veroff, Joseph, et al., "The Use of Thematic Apperception to Assess Motivation in a Nationwide Interview Study," *Psychological Monographs,* 74, no. 12 (1960).

105. Wachtel, Dawn, D., *The Working Poor* (Springfield, Va.: U.S. Clearinghouse for Federal Scientific and Technical Information, U.S. Department of Commerce, 1968).

106. Wald, Patricia M., *Law and Poverty: 1965,* Report to the National Conference on Law and Poverty (Washington: U.S. Government Printing Office, 1965).

107. Weissberg, Norman C., "Intergenerational Welfare Dependency: A Critical Review," *Social Problems,* 18 (Fall 1970), 257–274.

108. Wilner, Daniel M., et al., *The Housing Environment and Family Life, A Longitudinal Study of the Effects of Housing on Morbidity and Mental Health* (Baltimore: John Hopkins, 1962).

109. Winter, J. Alan, ed., *The Poor: A Culture of Poverty or a Poverty of Culture?* (Grand Rapids, Mich.: Eerdmans, 1969).

Population Characteristics and Properties of Ghetto Life

National Advisory Commission on
Civil Disorders

UNEMPLOYMENT, FAMILY STRUCTURE AND SOCIAL DISORGANIZA-TION

Recent Economic Trends

The Negro population in our country is as diverse in income, occupation, family composition, and other variables as the white community. Nevertheless, for purposes of analysis, three major Negro economic groups can be identified.

The first and smallest group consists of middle and upper income individuals and households whose educational, occupational, and cultural characteristics are similar to those of middle and upper income white groups.

The second and largest group contains Negroes whose incomes are above the "poverty level" but who have not attained the educational, occupational, or income status typical of middle-class Americans.

The third group has very low educational, occupational, and income attainments and lives below the "poverty level."

A recent compilation of data on American Negroes by the Departments of Labor and Commerce shows that although incomes of both Negroes and whites have been rising rapidly,

> Negro incomes still remain far below those of whites. Negro median family income was only 58 percent of the white median in 1966.
>
> Negro family income is not keeping pace with white family income growth. In constant 1965 dollars, median nonwhite income in 1947 was $2,174 lower than median white income. By 1966, the gap had grown to $3,036.
>
> The Negro upper income group is expanding rapidly and achieving sizeable income gains. In 1966, 28 percent of all Negro families received incomes of $7,000 or more, compared with 55 percent of white families. This was 1.6 times the proportion of Negroes receiving comparable incomes in 1960, and four times greater than the proportion receiving such incomes in 1947. Moreover, the proportion of Negroes employed in high-skill, high-status, and well-paying jobs rose faster than comparable proportions among whites from 1960 to 1966.

SOURCE: From "Unemployment, Family Structure, and Social Disorganization," *Report of the National Advisory Commission on Civil Disorders* (Washington, D.C.: U. S. Government Printing Office, 1968), pp. 123–130, 133–140.

As Negro incomes have risen, the size of the lowest income group has grown smaller, and the middle and upper groups have grown larger—both relatively and absolutely.

Group	Percentage of Negro families		Percentage of white families	
	1947	1960	1966	1966
$7,000 and over	7	17	28	55
$3,000 to $6,999	29	40	41	33
Under $3,000	65	44	32	13

About two-thirds of the lowest income group—or 20 percent of all Negro families—are making no significant economic gains despite continued general prosperity. Half of these hard-core disadvantaged—more than 2 million persons—live in central-city neighborhoods. Recent special censuses in Los Angeles and Cleveland indicate that the incomes of persons living in the worst slum areas have not risen at all during this period, unemployment rates have declined only slightly, the proportion of families with female heads has increased, and housing conditions have worsened even though rents have risen.

Thus, between 2.0 and 2.5 million poor Negroes are living in disadvantaged neighborhoods of central cities in the United States. These persons comprise only slightly more than 1 percent of the Nation's total population, but they make up about 16 to 20 percent of the total Negro population of all central cities, and a much higher proportion in certain cities.

Unemployment and Underemployment

The Critical Significance of Employment. The capacity to obtain and hold a "good job" is the traditional test of participation in American society. Steady employment with adequate compensation provides both purchasing power and social status. It develops the capabilities, confidence, and self-esteem an individual needs to be a responsible citizen, and provides a basis for a stable family life. As Daniel P. Moynihan has written:

The principal measure of progress toward equality will be that of employment. It is the primary source of individual or group identity. In America what you do is what you are: to do nothing is to be nothing; to do little is to be little. The equations are implacable and blunt, and ruthlessly public.

For the Negro American it is already, and will continue to be, the master problem. It is the measure of white bona fides. It is the measure of Negro competence, and also of the competence of American society. Most importantly, the linkage between problems of employment and the range of social pathology that afflicts the Negro community is unmistakable. Employment not only controls the present for the Negro American but, in a most profound way, it is creating the future as well.

For residents of disadvantaged Negro neighborhoods, obtaining good jobs is vastly more difficult than for most workers in society. For decades, social, economic, and psychological disadvantages surrounding the urban Negro poor have impaired their work capacities and opportunities. The result is a cycle of failure—the employment disabilities of one generation breed those of the next.

Negro Unemployment. Unemployment rates among Negroes have declined from a post-Korean War high of 12.6 percent in 1958 to 8.2 percent in 1967. Among married Negro men, the unemployment rate for 1967 was down to 3.2 percent.[1]

Notwithstanding this decline, unemployment rates for Negroes are still double those for whites in every category, including married men, as they have been throughout the postwar period. Moreover, since 1954, even during the current unprecedented period of sustained economic growth, unemployment among Negroes has been continuously above the 6 percent "recession" level widely regarded as a sign of serious economic weakness when prevalent for the entire work force.

While the Negro unemployment rate remains high in relation to the white rate, the number of additional jobs needed to lower this to the level of white unemployment is surprisingly small. In 1967, approximately 3 million persons were unemployed during an average week, of whom about 638,000, or 21 percent, were nonwhites. When corrected for undercounting, total nonwhite unemployment was approximately 712,000 or 8 percent of the nonwhite labor force. To reduce the unemployment rate to 3.4 percent, the rate prevalent among whites, jobs must be found for 57.5 percent of these unemployed persons. This amounts to nearly 409,000 jobs, or about 27 percent of the net number of new jobs added to the economy in the year 1967 alone and only slightly more than one-half of 1 percent of all jobs in the United States in 1967.

The Low-Status and Low-Paying Nature of Many Negro Jobs. Even more important perhaps than unemployment is the related problem of the undesirable nature of many jobs open to Negroes. Negro workers are concentrated in the lowest skilled and lowest paying occupations. These jobs often involve substandard wages, great instability and uncertainty of tenure, extremely low status in the eyes of both employer and employee, little or no chance for meaningful advancement, and unpleasant or exhausting duties. Negro men in particular are more than three times as likely as whites to be in unskilled or service jobs which pay far less than most:

[1] Adjusted for Census Bureau undercounting.

Type of occupation	Percentage of male workers in each type of occupation, 1966		Median earnings of all male civilians in each occupation, 1965
	White	Nonwhite	
Professional, technical, and managerial	27	9	$7,603[1]
Clerical and sales	14	9	5,532[1]
Craftsmen and foremen	20	12	6,270
Operatives	20	27	5,046
Service workers	6	16	3,436
Nonfarm laborers	6	20	2,410
Farmers and farm workers	7	8	1,669[1]

[1]Average of two categories from normal Census Bureau categories as combined in data presented in The Social and Economic Conditions of Negroes in the United States (BLS No. 332).

This concentration in the least desirable jobs can be viewed another way by calculating the changes which would occur if Negro men were employed in various occupations in the same proportions as the male labor force as a whole (not solely the white labor force).

Type of occupation	Number of male nonwhite workers, 1966			
	As actually distributed[1]	If distributed the same as all male workers	Difference	
			Number	Percent
Professional, technical, and managerial	415,000	1,173,000	+758,000	+183
Clerical and sales	415,000	628,000	+213,000	+51
Craftsmen and foremen	553,000	894,000	+341,000	+62
Operatives	1,244,000	964,000	−280,000	−23
Service workers	737,000	326,000	−411,000	−56
Nonfarm laborers	922,000	340,000	−582,000	−63
Farmers and farm workers.	369,000	330,000	−39,000	−11

[1]Estimates based upon percentages set forth in BLS No. 332, p. 41.

Thus, upgrading the employment of Negro men to make their occupational distribution identical with that of the labor force as a whole would have an immense impact upon the nature of their occupations. About 1.3 million nonwhite men—or 28 percent of those employed in 1966—would move up the employment ladder into one of the higher status and higher paying categories. The effect of such a shift upon the incomes of Negro men would be very great.

Using the 1966 job distribution, the shift indicated above would produce about
$4.8 billion more earned income for nonwhite men alone if they received the
1965 median income in each occupation. This would be a rise of approximately
30 percent in the earnings actually received by all nonwhite men in 1965 (not
counting any sources of income other than wages and salaries).

Of course, the kind of "instant upgrading" visualized in these calculations
does not represent a practical alternative for national policy. The economy
cannot drastically reduce the total number of low-status jobs it now contains,
or shift large numbers of people upward in occupation in any short period.
Therefore, major upgrading in the employment status of Negro men must
come through a faster relative expansion of higher level jobs than lower level
jobs (which has been occurring for several decades), an improvement in the
skills of nonwhite workers so they can obtain a high proportion of those added
better jobs, and a drastic reduction of discriminatory hiring and promotion
practices in all enterprises, both private and public.

Nevertheless, this hypothetical example clearly shows that the concentration of male Negro employment at the lowest end of the occupational scale is
greatly depressing the incomes of U.S. Negroes in general. In fact, this is the
single most important source of poverty among Negroes. It is even more
important than unemployment, as can be shown by a second hypothetical
calculation. In 1966, there were about 724,000 unemployed nonwhites in the
United States on the average, including adults and teenagers, and allowing for
the Census Bureau undercount of Negroes. If every one of these persons had
been employed and had received the median amount earned by nonwhite males
in 1966 ($3,864), this would have added a total of $2.8 billion to nonwhite
income as a whole. If only enough of these persons had been employed at that
wage to reduce nonwhite unemployment from 7.3 percent to 3.3 percent—the
rate among whites in 1966—then the income gain for nonwhites would have
totaled about $1.5 billion. But if nonwhite unemployment remained at 7.3
percent, and nonwhite men were upgraded so that they had the same occupational distribution and incomes as all men in the labor force considered together, this would have produced about $4.8 billion in additional income, as
noted above (using 1965 earnings for calculation). Thus the potential income
gains from upgrading the male nonwhite labor force are much larger than
those from reducing nonwhite unemployment.

This conclusion underlines the difficulty of improving the economic status
of Negro men. It is far easier to create new jobs than either to create new jobs
with relatively high status and earning power, or to upgrade existing employed
or partly employed workers into such better quality employment. Yet only
such upgrading will eliminate the fundamental basis of poverty and deprivation among Negro families.

Access to good-quality jobs clearly affects the willingness of Negro men
actively to seek work. In riot cities surveyed by the Commission with the
largest percentage Negroes in skilled and semiskilled jobs, Negro men participated in the labor force to the same extent as, or greater than, white men.

Conversely, where most Negro men were heavily concentrated in menial jobs, they participated less in the labor force than white men.

Even given similar employment, Negro workers with the same education as white workers are paid less. This disparity doubtless results to some extent from inferior training in segregated schools, and also from the fact that large numbers of Negroes are only now entering certain occupations for the first time. However, the differentials are so large and so universal at all educational levels that they clearly reflect the patterns of discrimination which characterize hiring and promotion practices in many segments of the economy. For example, in 1966, among persons who had completed high school, the median income of Negroes was only 73 percent that of whites. Even among persons with an eighth-grade education, Negro median income was only 80 percent of white median income.

At the same time, a higher proportion of Negro women than white women participates in the labor force at nearly all ages except 16 to 19. For instance, in 1966, 55 percent of nonwhite women from 25 to 34 years of age were employed, compared to only 38 percent of white women in the same age group. The fact that almost half of all adult Negro women work reflects the fact that so many Negro males have unsteady and low-paying jobs. Yet even though Negro women are often better able to find work than Negro men, the unemployment rate among adult nonwhite women (20 years old and over) in 1967 was 7.1 percent, compared to the 4.3 percent rate among adult nonwhite men.

Unemployment rates are, of course, much higher among teenagers, both Negro and white, than among adults; in fact about one-third of all unemployed Negroes in 1967 were between 16 and 19 years old. During the first 9 months of 1967, the unemployment rate among nonwhite teenagers was 26.5 percent; for whites, it was 10.6 percent. About 219,300 nonwhite teenagers were unemployed.[2] About 58,300 were still in school but were actively looking for jobs.

Subemployment in Disadvantaged Negro Neighborhoods. In disadvantaged areas, employment conditions for Negroes are in a chronic state of crisis. Surveys in low income neighborhoods of nine large cities made by the Department of Labor late in 1966 revealed that the rate of unemployment there was 9.3 percent, compared to 7.3 percent for Negroes generally and 3.3 percent for whites. Moreover, a high proportion of the persons living in these areas were "underemployed," that is, they were either part-time workers looking for fulltime employment, or full-time workers earning less than $3000 per year, or had dropped out of the labor force. The Department of Labor estimated that this underemployment is 2½ times greater than the number of unemployed in these areas. Therefore, the "subemployment rate," including both the unemployed and the underemployed, was about 32.7 percent in the nine areas surveyed, or 8.8 times greater than the overall unemployment rate for all U.S. workers. Since underemployment also exists outside disadvantaged neighborhoods, comparing the full subemployment rate in these areas with the unem-

[2]After adjusting for Census Bureau undercounting.

ployment rate for the Nation as a whole is not entirely valid. However, it provides some measure of the enormous disparity between employment conditions in most of the Nation and those prevalent in disadvantaged Negro areas in our large cities.

The critical problem is to determine the actual number of those unemployed and underemployed in central-city Negro ghettos. This is summarized in the following table:

Group	Nonwhite subemployment in disadvantaged areas of all central cities, 1967		
	Unemploy-ment	Under-employment	Total sub-employment
Adult men	102,000	230,000	332,000
Adult women	118,000	266,000	384,000
Teenagers	98,000	220,000	318,000
Total	318,000	716,000	1,034,000

Therefore, in order to bring subemployment in these areas down to a level equal to unemployment alone among whites, enough steady, reasonably paying jobs (and the training and motivation to perform them) must be provided to eliminate all underemployment and reduce unemployment by 65 percent. For all three age groups combined, this deficit amounted to 923,000 jobs in 1967.

The Magnitude of Poverty in Disadvantaged Neighborhoods

The chronic unemployment problems in the central city, aggravated by the constant arrival of new unemployed migrants, is the fundamental cause of the persistent poverty in disadvantaged Negro areas.

"Poverty" in the affluent society is more than absolute deprivation. Many of the poor in the United States would be well off in other societies. Relative deprivation—inequality—is a more useful concept of poverty with respect to the Negro in America because it encompasses social and political exclusions as well as economic inequality. Because of the lack of data of this type, we have had to focus our analysis on a measure of poverty which is both economic and absolute—the Social Security Administration's "poverty level"[3] concept. It is clear, however, that broader measures of poverty would substantiate the conclusions that follow.

In 1966, there were 29.7 million persons in the United States—15.3 percent of the Nation's population—with incomes below the "poverty level," as defined by the Social Security Administration. Of these, 20.3 million were white (68.3 percent), and 9.3 million nonwhite (31.7 percent). Thus, about 11.9

[3]$3335 per year for an urban family of four.

percent of the Nation's whites and 40.6 percent of its nonwhites were poor under the the Social Security definition.

The location of the Nation's poor is best shown from 1964 data as indicated by the following table:

Group	Percentage of those in poverty in each group living in—			
	Metropolitan areas		Other areas	Total
	In central cities	Outside central cities		
Whites	23.8	21.8	54.4	100
Nonwhites	41.7	10.8	47.5	100
Total	29.4	18.4	52.2	100

SOURCE: Social Security Administration.

The following facts concerning poverty are relevant to an understanding of the problems faced by people living in disadvantaged neighborhoods.[4]

- In central cities 30.7 percent of nonwhite families of two or more persons lived in poverty compared to only 8.8 percent of whites.
- Of the 10.1 million poor persons in central cities in 1964, about 4.4 million of these (43.6 percent) were nonwhites, and 5.7 million (56.4 percent) were whites. The poor whites were much older on the average than the poor nonwhites. The proportion of poor persons 65 years old or older was 23.2 percent among whites, but only 6.8 percent among nonwhites.
- Poverty was more than twice as prevalent among nonwhite families with female heads than among those with male heads, 57 percent compared to 21 percent. In central cities, 26 percent of all nonwhite families of two or more persons had female heads, as compared to 12 percent of white families.
- Among nonwhite families headed by a female, and having children under 6, the incidence of poverty was 81 percent. Moreover, there were 243,000 such families living in poverty in central cities—or over 9 percent of all nonwhite families in those cities.
- Among all children living in poverty within central cities, nonwhites outnumbered whites by over 400,000. The number of poor nonwhite children equalled or surpassed the number of white poor children in every age group.

Two stark facts emerge:

- 54 percent of all poor children in central cities in 1964 were nonwhites.
- Of the 4.4 million nonwhites living in poverty within central cities in 1964, 52 percent were children under 16 and 61 percent were under 21.

[4]Source: Social Security Administration; based on 1964 data.

Number of Children Living in Poverty (Millions)

Age group	White	Nonwhite	Percent of total nonwhite
Under 6	0.9	1.0	53
6 to 15	1.0	1.3	57
16 to 21	0.4	0.4	50
Total	2.3	2.7	54

Since 1964, the number of nonwhite families living in poverty within central cities has remained about the same; hence, these poverty conditions are probably still prevalent in central cities in terms of absolute numbers of persons, although the proportion of persons in poverty may have dropped slightly.[5]

The Social Impact of Employment Problems in Disadvantaged Negro Areas

Unemployment and the Family. The high rates of unemployment and underemployment in racial ghettos are evidence, in part, that many men living in these areas are seeking, but cannot obtain, jobs which will support a family. Perhaps equally important, most jobs they can get are at the low end of the occupational scale, and often lack the necessary status to sustain a worker's self-respect, or the respect of his family and friends. These same men are also constantly confronted with the message of discrimination: "You are inferior because of a trait you did not cause and cannot change." This message reinforces feelings of inadequacy arising from repeated failure to obtain and keep decent jobs.

Wives of these men are forced to work and usually produce more money. If the men stay at home without working, their inadequacies constantly confront them and tensions arise between them and their wives and children. Under these pressures, it is not surprising that many of these men flee their responsibilities as husbands and fathers, leaving home, and drifting from city to city, or adopting the style of "street corner men."

Statistical evidence tends to document this. A close correlation exists between the number of nonwhite married women separated from their husbands each year and the unemployment rate among the nonwhite males 20 years old and over. Similarly, from 1948 to 1962, the number of new Aid to Families

[5]For the Nation as a whole, the proportion of nonwhite families living in poverty, dropped from 39 percent to 35 percent from 1964 to 1966 (defining "family" somewhat differently from the definition used in the data above). The number of such families declined from 1.9 million to 1.7 million. However, the number and proportion of all nonwhites living in central cities rose in the same period. As a result, the number of nonwhite families living in so-called "poverty areas" of large cities actually rose from 1,561,000 in 1960 to 1,588,000 in 1966.

with Dependent Children cases rose and fell with the nonwhite male unemployment rate. Since 1963, however, the number of new cases—most of them Negro children—has steadily increased even though the unemployment rate among nonwhite males has declined. The impact of marital status on employment among Negroes is shown by the fact that in 1967 the proportion of married men either divorced or separated from their wives was more than twice among unemployed nonwhite men as among employed nonwhite men. Moreover, among those participating in the labor force, there was a higher proportion of married men with wives present than with wives absent.

UNEMPLOYMENT RATE AND PARTICIPATION IN TOTAL LABOR FORCE, 25 TO 54-YEAR-OLD NONWHITE MEN, BY MARITAL STATUS, MARCH, 1967

	Unemployment rate, nonwhite	Labor force participation (percent), nonwhite
Married, wife present	3.7	96.7
Other (separated, divorced, widowed)	8.7	77.6

Fatherless Families.   The abandonment of the home by many Negro males affects a great many children growing up in the racial ghetto. As previously indicated, most American Negro families are headed by men, just like most other American families. Yet the proportion of families with female heads is much greater among Negroes than among whites at all income levels, and has been rising in recent years.

PROPORTION OF FAMILIES OF VARIOUS TYPES (IN PERCENT)

Date	Husband-Wife		Female head	
	White	Nonwhite	Female	Nonwhite
1950	88.0	77.7	8.5	17.6
1960	88.7	73.6	8.7	22.4
1966	88.8	72.7	8.9	23.7

This disparity between white and nonwhite families is far greater among the lowest income families—those most likely to reside in disadvantaged big-city neighborhoods—than among higher income families. Among families with incomes under $3,000 in 1966, the proportion with female heads was 42 percent for Negroes but only 23 percent for whites. In contrast, among families with incomes of $7,000 or more, 8 percent of Negro families had female heads compared to 4 percent of whites.

The problems of "fatherlessness" are aggravated by the tendency of the poor to have large families. The average poor, urban, nonwhite family contains 4.8 persons, as compared with 3.7 for the average poor, urban, white family. This is one of the primary factors in the poverty status of nonwhite households in large cities.

The proportion of fatherless families appears to be increasing in the poorest Negro neighborhoods. In the Hough section of Cleveland, the proportion of families with female heads rose from 23 to 32 percent from 1960 to 1965. In the Watts section of Los Angeles it rose from 36 to 39 percent during the same period.

The handicap imposed on children growing up without fathers, in an atmosphere of poverty and deprivation, is increased because many mothers must work to provide support. The following table illustrates the disparity between the proportion of nonwhite women in the child-rearing ages who are in the labor force and the comparable proportion of white women:

Age group	Percentage of women in the labor force	
	Nonwhite	White
20 to 24	55	51
25 to 34	55	38
35 to 44	61	45

With the father absent and the mother working, many ghetto children spend the bulk of their time on the streets—the streets of a crime-ridden, violence-prone, and poverty-stricken world. The image of success in this world is not that of the "solid citizen," the responsible husband and father, but rather that of the "hustler" who promotes his own interests by exploiting others. The dope sellers and the numbers runners are the "successful" men because their earnings far outstrip those men who try to climb the economic ladder in honest ways.

Young people in the ghetto are acutely conscious of a system which appears to offer rewards to those who illegally exploit others, and failure to those who struggle under traditional responsibilities. Under these circumstances, many adopt exploitation and the "hustle" as a way of life, disclaiming both work and marriage in favor of casual and temporary liaisons. This pattern reinforces itself from one generation to the next, creating a "culture of poverty" and an ingrained cynicism about society and its institutions.

The "Jungle." The culture of poverty that results from unemployment and family disorganization generates a system of ruthless, exploitative relationships within the ghetto. Prostitution, dope addiction, casual sexual affairs, and crime create an environmental jungle characterized by personal insecurity and tension. The effects of this development are stark:

• The rate of illegitimate births among nonwhite women has risen sharply in the past two decades. In 1940, 16.8 percent of all nonwhite births were illegitimate. By 1950 this proportion was 18 percent; by 1960, 21.6 percent; by 1966, 26.3 percent. In the ghettos of many large cities, illegitimacy rates exceed 50 percent.

• The rate of illegitimacy among nonwhite women is closely related to low income and high unemployment. In Washington, D.C., for example, an analysis of 1960 census tracts shows that in tracts with unemployment rates of 12 percent or more among nonwhite men, illegitimacy was over 40 percent. But in tracts with unemployment rates of 2.9 percent and below among nonwhite men, reported illegitimacy was under 20 percent. A similar contrast existed between tracts in which median nonwhite income was under $4,000 (where illegitimacy was 38 percent) and those in which it was $8,000 and over (where illegitimacy was 12 percent).

• Narcotics addiction is also heavily concentrated in low-income Negro neighborhoods, particularly in New York City. Of the 59,720 addicts known to the U.S. Bureau of Narcotics at the end of 1966, just over 50 percent were Negroes. Over 52 percent of all known addicts lived within New York State, mostly in Harlem and other Negro neighborhoods. These figures undoubtedly greatly understate the actual number of persons using narcotics regularly—especially those under 21.

• Not surprisingly, at every age from 6 through 19, the proportion of children from homes with both parents present who actually attend school is higher than the proportion of children from homes with only one parent or neither present.

• Rates of juvenile delinquency, venereal disease, dependency upon AFDC support, and use of public assistance in general are much higher in disadvantaged Negro areas than in other parts of large cities. Data taken from New York City contrasting predominantly Negro neighborhoods with the city as a whole clearly illustrate this fact.

SOCIAL DISTRESS—MAJOR PREDOMINATELY NEGRO NEIGHBORHOODS IN NEW YORK CITY AND THE CITY AS A WHOLE

	Juvenile delinquency [1]	Venereal disease [2]	ADC [3]	Public assistance [4]
Brownsville	125.3	609.9	459.0	265.8
East New York	98.6	207.5	148.6	71.8
Bedford-Stuyvesant	115.2	771.3	337.1	197.2
Harlem	110.8	1,603.5	265.7	138.1
South Bronx	84.4	308.3	278.5	165.5
New York City	52.2	269.1	120.7	60.8

[1]Number of offenses per 1,000 persons 7–20 years (1965).
[2]Number of cases per 100,000 persons under 21 years (1964).
[3]Number of children in aid to dependent children cases per 1,000 under 18 years, using 1960 population as base (1965).
[4]Welfare assistance recipients per 1,000 persons, using 1960 population as base (1965).

In conclusion: in 1965, 1.2 million nonwhite children under 16 lived in central city families headed by a woman under 65. The great majority of these children were growing up in poverty under conditions that make them better candidates for crime and civil disorder than for jobs providing an entry into American society.

* * *

CONDITIONS OF LIFE IN THE RACIAL GHETTO

The conditions of life in the racial ghetto are strikingly different from those to which most Americans are accustomed—especially white, middle-class Americans. We believe it important to describe these conditions and their effect on the lives of people who cannot escape from the ghetto.[1]

Crime and Insecurity

Nothing is more fundamental to the quality of life in any area than the sense of personal security of its residents, and nothing affects this more than crime.

In general, crime rates in large cities are much higher than in other areas of our country. Within such cities, crime rates are higher in disadvantaged Negro areas than anywhere else.

The most widely used measure of crime is the number of "index crimes" (homicide, forcible rape, aggravated assault, robbery, burglary, grand larceny, and auto theft) in relation to population. In 1966, 1,754 such crimes were reported to police for every 100,000 Americans. In cities over 250,000, the rate was 3,153, and in cities over 1 million, it was 3,630—or more than double the national average. In suburban areas alone, including suburban cities, the rate was only 1,300, or just over one-third the rate in the largest cities.

Within larger cities, personal and property insecurity has consistently been highest in the older neighborhoods encircling the downtown business district. In most cities, crime rates for many decades have been higher in these inner areas than anywhere, except in downtown areas themselves, where they are inflated by the small number of residents.

High crime rates have persisted in these inner areas even though the ethnic character of their residents continually changed. Poor immigrants used these areas as "entry ports," then usually moved on to more desirable neighborhoods as soon as they acquired enough resources. Many "entry port" areas have now become racial ghettos.

The difference between crime rates in these disadvantaged neighborhoods and in other parts of the city is usually startling, as a comparison of crime rates

[1]We have not attempted here to describe conditions relating to the fundamental problems of housing, education, and welfare, which are treated in detail in later chapters.

in five police districts in Chicago for 1965 illustrates. These five include one high-income, all-white district at the periphery of the city, two very low-income, virtually all-Negro districts near the city core with numerous public housing projects, and two predominantly white districts, one with mainly lower middle-income families, the other containing a mixture of very high-income and relatively low-income households. The table shows crime rates against persons and against property in these five districts, plus the number of patrolmen assigned to them per 100,000 residents, as follows:

INCIDENCE OF INDEX CRIMES AND PATROLMEN ASSIGNMENTS PER 100,000 RESIDENTS IN 5 CHICAGO POLICE DISTRICTS, 1965

Number	High-income white district	Low middle-income white district	Mixed high- and low-income white district	Very low income Negro district No. 1	Very low income Negro district No. 2
Index crimes against persons	80	440	338	1,615	2,820
Index crimes against property	1,038	1,750	2,080	2,508	2,630
Patrolmen assigned	93	133	115	243	291

These data indicate that:

• Variations in the crime rate against persons within the city are extremely large. One very low income Negro district had 35 times as many serious crimes against persons per 100,000 residents as did the high-income white district.

• Variations in the crime rate against property are much smaller. The highest rate was only 2.5 times larger than the lowest.

• The lower the income in an area, the higher the crime rate there. Yet low-income Negro areas have significantly higher crime rates than low-income white areas. This reflects the high degree of social disorganization in Negro areas described in the previous chapter, as well as the fact that poor Negroes as a group have lower incomes than poor whites as a group.

• The presence of more police patrolmen per 100,000 residents does not necessarily offset high crime in certain parts of the city. Although the Chicago Police Department had assigned over three times as many patrolmen per 100,000 residents to the highest crime areas shown as to the lowest, crime rates in the highest crime area for offenses against both persons and property combined were 4.9 times as high as in the lowest crime area.

Because most middle-class Americans live in neighborhoods similar to the more crime-free district described above, they have little comprehension of the sense of insecurity that characterizes the ghetto resident. Moreover, official statistics normally greatly understate actual crime rates because the vast majority of crimes are not reported to the police. For example, studies conducted for the President's Crime Commission in Washington, D.C., Boston, and Chicago, showed that three to six times as many crimes were actually committed against persons and homes as were reported to the police.

Two facts are crucial to an understanding of the effects of high crime rates in racial ghettos; most of these crimes are committed by a small minority of the residents, and the principal victims are the residents themselves. Throughout the United States, the great majority of crimes committed by Negroes involve other Negroes as victims. A special tabulation made by the Chicago Police Department for the President's Crime Commission indicated that over 85 percent of the crimes committed against persons by Negroes between September, 1965, and March, 1966, involved Negro victims.

As a result, the majority of law-abiding citizens who live in disadavantaged Negro areas face much higher probabilities of being victimized than residents of most higher income areas, including almost all suburbs. For nonwhites, the probability of suffering from any index crime except larceny is 78 percent higher than for whites. The probability of being raped is 3.7 times higher among nonwhite women, and the probability of being robbed is 3.5 times higher for nonwhites in general.

The problems associated with high crime rates generate widespread hostility toward the police in these neighborhoods for reasons described elsewhere in this Report. Thus, crime not only creates an atmosphere of insecurity and fear throughout Negro neighborhoods but also causes continuing attrition of the relationship between Negro residents and police. This bears a direct relationship to civil disorder.

There are reasons to expect the crime situation in these areas to become worse in the future. First, crime rates throughout the United States have been rising rapidly in recent years. The rate of index crimes against persons rose 37 percent from 1960 to 1966, and the rate of index crimes against property rose 50 percent. In the first 9 months of 1967, the number of index crimes was up 16 percent over the same period in 1966, whereas the U.S. population rose about 1 percent. In cities of 250,000 to 1 million, index crime rose by over 20 percent, whereas it increased 4 percent in cities of over 1 million.[2]

[2]The problem of interpreting and evaluating "rising" crime rates is complicated by the changing age distribution of the population, improvements in reporting methods, and the increasing willingness of victims to report crimes. Despite these complications, there is general agreement on the serious increase in the incidence of crime in the United States.

Second, the number of police available to combat crime is rising much more slowly than the amount of crime. In 1966, there were about 20 percent more police employees in the United States than in 1960, and per capita expenditures for police rose from $15.29 in 1960 to $20.99 in 1966, a gain of 37 percent. But over the 6-year period, the number of reported index crimes had jumped 62 percent. In spite of significant improvements in police efficiency, it is clear that police will be unable to cope with their expanding workload unless there is a dramatic increase in the resources allocated by society to this task.

Third, in the next decade, the number of young Negroes aged 14 to 24 will increase rapidly, particularly in central cities. This group is responsible for a disproportionately high share of crimes in all parts of the Nation. In 1966, persons under 25 years of age comprised the following proportions of those arrested for various major crimes: murder, 37 percent; forcible rape, 64 percent; robbery, 71 percent; burglary, 81 percent; larceny, about 77 percent; and auto theft, 89 percent. For all index crimes together, the arrest rate for Negroes is about four times higher than that for whites. Yet the number of young Negroes aged 14 to 24 in central cities will rise about 63 percent from 1966 to 1975, as compared to only 32 percent for the total Negro population of central cities.[3]

Health and Sanitation Conditions

The residents of the racial ghetto are significantly less healthy than most other Americans. They suffer from higher mortality rates, higher incidence of major diseases, and lower availability and utilization of medical services. They also experience higher admission rates to mental hospitals.

These conditions result from a number of factors.

These factors are aggravated for Negroes when compared to whites for the simple reason that the proportion of persons in the United States who are poor is 3.5 times as high among Negroes (41 percent in 1966) as among whites (12 percent in 1966).

Poverty. From the standpoint of health, poverty means deficient diets, lack of medical care, inadequate shelter and clothing and often lack of awareness of potential health needs. As a result, almost 30 percent of all persons with family incomes less than $2,000 per year suffer from chronic health conditions that adversely affect their employment—as compared with less than 8 percent of the families with incomes of $7,000 or more.

Poor families have the greatest need for financial assistance in meeting medical expenses. Only about 34 percent of families with incomes of less than

[3]Assuming those cities will experience the same proportion of total United States Negro population growth that they did from 1960 to 1966. The calculations are derived from population projections in Bureau of the Census, *Population Estimates,* Current Population Reports, Series P-25, No. 381. Dec. 18, 1967, p. 63.

$2,000 per year use health insurance benefits, as compared to nearly 90 percent of those with incomes of $7,000 or more.[4]

Maternal Mortality. Mortality rates for nonwhite mothers are four times as high as those for white mothers. There has been a sharp decline in such rates since 1940, when 774 nonwhite and 320 white mothers died for each 100,000 live births. In 1965, only 84 nonwhite and 21 white mothers died per 100,000 live births—but the gap between nonwhites and whites actually increased.

Infant Mortality. Mortality rates among nonwhite babies are 58 percent higher than among whites for those under 1 month old and almost three times as high among those from 1 month to 1 year old. This is true in spite of a large drop in infant mortality rates in both groups since 1940.

NUMBER OF INFANTS WHO DIED PER 1,000 LIVE BIRTHS

Year	Less than 1 month old		1 month to 1 year old	
	White	Nonwhite	White	Nonwhite
1940	27.2	39.7	16.0	34.1
1950	19.4	27.5	7.4	17.0
1960	17.2	26.9	5.7	16.4
1965	16.1	25.4	5.4	14.9

Life Expectancy. To some extent because of infant mortality rates, life expectancy at birth was 6.9 years longer for whites (71.0 years) than for nonwhites (64.1 years) in 1965. Even in the prime working ages, life expectancy is significantly lower among nonwhites than among whites. In 1965, white persons 25 years old could expect to live an average of 48.6 more years, whereas nonwhites 25 years old could expect to live another 43.3 years, or 11 percent less. Similar but smaller discrepancies existed at all ages from 25 through 55; some actually increased slightly between 1960 and 1965.

Lower Utilization of Health Services. A fact that also contributes to poorer health conditions in the ghetto is that Negro families with incomes similar to those of whites spend less on medical services and visit medical specialists less often.

[4]Public programs of various kinds have been providing significant financial assistance for medical care in recent years. In 1964, over $1.1 billion was paid out by various governments for such aid. About 52 percent of medical vendor payments came from Federal Government agencies, 33 percent from states, and 12 percent from local governments. The biggest contributions were made by the Old Age Assistance Program and the Medical Assistance for the Aged Program. The enactment of Medicare in 1965 has significantly added to this flow of public assistance for medical aid. However, it is too early to evaluate the results upon health conditions among the poor.

PERCENT OF FAMILY EXPENDITURES SPENT FOR MEDICAL CARE, 1960–61

Income group	White	Nonwhite	Ratio, white to nonwhite
Under $3,000	9	5	1.8:1
$3,000 to $7,499	7	5	1.4:1
$7,500 and over	6	4	1.5:1

Since the lowest income group contains a much larger proportion of non-white families than white families, the overall discrepancy in medical care spending between these two groups is very significant, as shown by the following table:

HEALTH EXPENSES PER PERSON PER YEAR FOR THE PERIOD FROM JULY TO DECEMBER

Income by racial group	Expenses					
	Total medical	Hospital	Doctor	Dental	Medicine	Other
Under $2,000 per family per year:						
White	$130	$33	$41	$11	$32	$13
Nonwhite	63	15	23	5	16	5
$10,000 and more per family per year:						
White	179	34	61	37	31	16
Nonwhite	133	34	50	19	23	8

These data indicate that nonwhite families in the lower income group spent less than half as much per person on medical services as white families with similar incomes. This discrepancy sharply declines but is still significant in the higher income group, where total nonwhite medical expenditures per person equal, on the average, 74.3 percent of white expenditures.

Negroes spend less on medical care for several reasons. Negro households generally are larger, requiring greater nonmedical expenses for each household and leaving less money for meeting medical expenses. Thus, lower expenditures per person would result even if expenditures per household were the same. Negroes also often pay more for other basic necessities such as food and consumer durables, as discussed in the next part of this chapter. In addition, fewer doctors, dentists, and medical facilities are conveniently available to Negroes than to most whites—a result both of geographic concentration of doctors in higher income areas in large cities and of discrimination against Negroes by doctors and hospitals. A survey in Cleveland indicated that there were 0.45 physicians per 1,000 people in poor neighborhoods, compared to 1.13 per 1,000 in nonpoverty areas. The result nationally is fewer visits to physicians and dentists.

PERCENT OF POPULATION MAKING ONE OR MORE VISITS TO INDICATED TYPE OF MEDICAL SPECIALIST FROM JULY 1963 TO JUNE 1964

Type of medical specialist	Family incomes of $2,000–$3,999		Family incomes of $7,000–$9,999	
	White	Nonwhite	White	Nonwhite
Physician	64	56	70	64
Dentist	31	20	52	33

Although widespread use of health insurance has led many hospitals to adopt nondiscriminatory policies, some private hospitals still refuse to admit Negro patients or to accept doctors with Negro patients. And many individual doctors still discriminate against Negro patients. As a result, Negroes are more likely to be treated in hospital clinics than whites and they are less likely to receive personalized service. This conclusion is confirmed by the following data:

PERCENT OF ALL VISITS TO PHYSICIANS FROM JULY 1963 TO JUNE 1964, MADE IN INDICATED WAYS

Type of visit to physician	Family Incomes of $2,000–$3,000		Family Incomes of $7,000–$9,999	
	White	Nonwhite	White	Nonwhite
In physician's office	68	56	73	66
Hospital clinic	17	35	7	16
Other (mainly telephone)	15	9	20	18
Total	100	100	100	100

Environmental Factors. Environmental conditions in disadvantaged Negro neighborhoods create further reasons for poor health conditions there. The level of sanitation is strikingly below that which is prevalent in most higher income areas. One simple reason is that residents often lack proper storage facilities for food—adequate refrigerators, freezers, even garbage cans, which are sometimes stolen as fast as landlords can replace them.

In areas where garbage collection and other sanitation services are grossly inadequate—commonly in the poorer parts of our large cities—rats proliferate.

It is estimated that in 1965, there were over 14,000 cases of ratbite in the United States, mostly in such neighborhoods.

The importance of these conditions was outlined for the Commission as follows:[5]

> Sanitation Commissioners of New York City and Chicago both feel this [sanitation] to be an important community problem and report themselves as being under substantial pressure to improve conditions. *It must be concluded that slum sanitation is a serious problem in the minds of the urban poor and well merits, at least on that ground, the attention of the Commission.* A related problem, according to one Sanitation Commissioner, is the fact that residents of areas bordering on slums feel that sanitation and neighborhood cleanliness is a crucial issue, relating to the stability of their blocks and constituting an important psychological index of "how far gone" their area is.
>
> * * * There is no known study comparing sanitation services between slum and non-slum areas. The experts agree, however, that there are more services in the slums on a quantitative basis, although perhaps not on a per capita basis. In New York, for example, garbage pickups are supposedly scheduled for about six times a week in slums, compared to three times a week in other areas of the city; the comparable figures in Chicago are two to three times a week versus once a week.
>
> The point, therefore, is not the relative quantitative level of services but the peculiarly intense needs of ghetto areas for sanitation services. This high demand is the product of numerous factors including: (1) higher population density; (2) lack of well managed buildings and adequate garbage services provided by landlords, number of receptacles, carrying to curbside, number of electric garbage disposals; (3) high relocation rates of tenants and businesses, producing heavy volume of bulk refuse left on streets and in buildings; (4) different uses of the streets—as outdoor living rooms in summer, recreation areas—producing high visibility and sensitivity to garbage problems; (5) large numbers of abandoned cars; (6) severe rodent and pest problems; (7) traffic congestion blocking garbage collection; and (8) obstructed street cleaning and snow removal on crowded, car-choked streets. Each of these elements adds to the problem and suggests a different possible line of attack.

Exploitation of Disadvantaged Consumers by Retail Merchants

Much of the violence in recent civil disorders has been directed at stores and other commercial establishments in disadvantaged Negro areas. In some cases, rioters focused on stores operated by white merchants who, they apparently believed, had been charging exorbitant prices or selling inferior goods. Not all the violence against these stores can be attributed to "revenge" for such practices. Yet it is clear that many residents of disadvantaged Negro neighborhoods believe they suffer constant abuses by local merchants.

Significant grievances concerning unfair commercial practices affecting

[5]Memorandum to the Commission dated Nov. 16, 1967, from Robert Patricelli, minority counsel, Subcommittee on Employment Manpower and Poverty, U.S. Senate.

Negro consumers were found in 11 of the 20 cities studied by the Commission. The fact that most of the merchants who operate stores in Negro areas are white undoubtedly contributes to the conclusion among Negroes that they are exploited by white society.

It is difficult to assess the precise degree and extent of exploitation. No systematic and reliable survey comparing consumer pricing and credit practices in all-Negro and other neighborhoods has ever been conducted on a nationwide basis. Differences in prices and credit practices between white middle-income areas and Negro low-income areas to some extent reflect differences in the real costs of serving these two markets (such as differential losses from pilferage in supermarkets), but the exact extent of these cost differences has never been estimated accurately. Finally, an examination of exploitative consumer practices must consider the particular structure and functions of the low-income consumer durables market.

Installment Buying.   This complex situation can best be understood by first considering certain basic facts:

- Various cultural factors generate constant pressure on low-income families to buy many relatively expensive durable goods and display them in their homes. This pressure comes in part from continuous exposure to commerical advertising, especially on television. In January, 1967, over 88 percent of all Negro households had TV sets. A 1961 study of 464 low-income families in New York City showed that 95 percent of these relatively poor families had TV sets.
- Many poor families have extremely low incomes, bad previous credit records, unstable sources of income or other attributes which make it virtually impossible for them to buy merchandise from established large national or local retail firms. These families lack enough savings to pay cash, and they cannot meet the standard credit requirements of established general merchants because they are too likely to fall behind in their payments.
- Poor families in urban areas are far less mobile than others. A 1967 Chicago study of low-income Negro households indicated their low automobile ownership compelled them to patronize neighborhood merchants. These merchants typically provided smaller selection, poorer services and higher prices than big national outlets. The 1961 New York study also indicated that families who shopped outside their own neighborhoods were far less likely to pay exorbitant prices.
- Most low-income families are uneducated concerning the nature of credit purchase contracts, the legal rights and obligations of both buyers and sellers, sources of advice for consumers who are having difficulties with merchants and the operation of the courts concerned with these matters. In contrast, merchants engaged in selling goods to them are very well informed.
- In most states, the laws governing relations between consumers and merchants in effect offer protection only to informed, sophisticated parties with understanding of each other's rights and obligations. Consequently, these laws are little suited to protect the rights of most low-income consumers.

In this situation, exploitative practices flourish. Ghetto residents who want to buy relatively expensive goods cannot do so from standard retail outlets and are thus restricted to local stores. Forced to use credit, they have little understanding of the pitfalls of credit buying. But because they have unstable incomes and frequently fail to make payments, the cost to the merchants of serving them is significantly above that of serving middle-income consumers. Consequently, a special kind of merchant appears to sell them goods on terms designed to cover the high cost of doing business in ghetto neighborhoods.

Whether they actually gain higher profits, these merchants charge higher prices than those in other parts of the city to cover the greater credit risks and other higher operating costs inherent in neighborhood outlets. A recent study conducted by the Federal Trade Commission in Washington, D.C., illustrates this conclusion dramatically. The FTC identified a number of stores specializing in selling furniture and appliances to low-income households. About 92 percent of the sales of these stores were credit sales involving installment purchases, as compared to 27 percent of the sales in general retail outlets handling the same merchandise.

The median income annually of a sample of 486 customers of these stores was about $4,200, but one-third had annual incomes below $3,600, about 6 percent were receiving welfare payments, and another 76 percent were employed in the lowest paying occupations (service workers, operatives, laborers and domestics), as compared to 36 percent of the total labor force in Washington in those occupations.

Definitely catering to a low-income group, these stores charged significantly higher prices than general merchandise outlets in the Washington area. According to testimony by Paul Rand Dixon, Chairman of the FTC, an item selling wholesale at $100 would retail on the average for $165 in a general merchandise store and for $250 in a low-income specialty store. Thus, the customers of these outlets were paying an average price premium of about 52 percent.

While higher prices are not necessarily exploitative in themselves, many merchants in ghetto neighborhoods take advantage of their superior knowledge of credit buying by engaging in various exploitative tactics—high-pressure salesmanship, "bait advertising," misrepresentation of prices, substitution of used goods for promised new ones, failure to notify consumers of legal actions against them, refusal to repair or replace substandard goods, exorbitant prices or credit charges, and use of shoddy merchandise. Such tactics affect a great many low-income consumers. In the New York study, 60 percent of all households had suffered from consumer problems (some of which were purely their own fault). About 23 percent had experienced serious exploitation. Another 20 percent, many of whom were also exploited, had experienced repossession, garnishment, or threat of garnishment.

Garnishment. Garnishment practices in many states allow creditors to deprive individuals of their wages through court action, without hearing or trial. In about 20 states, the wages of an employee can be diverted to a creditor merely upon the latter's deposition, with no advance hearing where the employee can defend himself. He often receives no prior notice of such action and is usually unaware of the law's operation and too poor to hire legal defense. Moreover, consumers may find themselves still owing money on a sales contract even after the creditor has repossessed the goods. The New York study cited earlier in this chapter indicated that 20 percent of a sample of low-income families had been subjected to legal action regarding consumer purchases. And the Federal Trade Commission study in Washington, D.C., showed that, on the average, retailers specializing in credit sales of furniture and appliances to low-income consumers resorted to court action once for every $2,200 of sales. Since their average sale was for $207, this amounted to using the courts to collect from one of every 11 customers. In contrast, department stores in the same area used court action against approximately one of every 14,500 customers.[6]

Variations in Food Prices. Residents of low-income Negro neighborhoods frequently claim that they pay higher prices for food in local markets than wealthier white suburbanites and receive inferior quality meat and produce. Statistically reliable information comparing prices and quality in these two kinds of areas is generally unavailable. The U.S. Bureau of Labor Statistics, studying food prices in six cities in 1966, compared prices of a standard list of 18 items in low-income areas and higher income areas in each city. In a total of 180 stores, including independent and chain stores, and for items of the same type sold in the same types of stores, there were no significant differences in prices between low-income and high-income areas. However, stores in low-income areas were more likely to be small independents (which had somewhat higher prices), to sell low-quality produce and meat at any given price, and to be patronized by people who typically bought smaller sized packages which are more expensive per unit of measure. In other words, many low-income consumers in fact pay higher prices, although the situation varies greatly from place to place.

Although these findings must be considered inconclusive, there are significant reasons to believe that poor households generally pay higher prices for the food they buy and receive lower quality food. Low-income consumers buy more food at local groceries because they are less mobile. Prices in these small stores are significantly higher than in major supermarkets because they cannot achieve economies of scale and because real operating costs are higher in low-income Negro areas than in outlying suburbs. For instance, inventory "shrinkage" from pilfering and other causes is normally under 2 percent of sales but can run twice as much in high-crime areas. Managers seek to make up for these added costs by charging higher prices for food or by substituting lower grades.

These practices do not necessarily involve exploitation, but they are often perceived as exploitative and unfair by those who are aware of the price and quality differences involved but unaware of operating costs. In addition, it is probably that genuinely exploitative pricing practices exist in some areas. In

---

[6]Assuming their sales also averaged $207 per customer.

either case, differential food prices constitute another factor convincing urban Negroes in low-income neighborhoods that whites discriminate against them.

The Airtight Cage

Joseph P. Lyford

BUREAUCRACY

Father Browne, who often speaks in cartoons, says that New York City government is like the Empire State Building without elevators. Somewhere up on top is the administrative apparatus, the public is in the basement, and in between is a vast air space occupied by the civil service. The consequence of this three-tiered arrangement is that the unaffiliated citizen lives in nearly total bewilderment about his government and, on their side, the administrative officials work in general ignorance of what their own bureaucracies are doing to the citizen. Presumably it was a suspicion of this latter fact that impelled Mayor Wagner to rent himself a private mailbox (Box 100) to which he asked citizens to write and tell him the truth about his subordinates.

Although there was no reason to suppose that Box 100 was anything but another public-relations effort, some people took it seriously for a time. Peter Slevin, a member of the Irish junta of Stryckers Bay Neighborhood Council, used to send off communications to Box 100 regularly. "I wrote to Wagner, I wrote to the commissioner, I wrote to everybody," he says. "I have my own typewriting machine at home, and I send letters in complaining about the block, and also the whole neighborhood—how it is run ragged and all the different illegal things that are going on. I complain about the police department and the narcotics division.

"The only answer they will ever give you if you write to that Box 100 is a little made-up-in-advance letter of the mayor's. The last time I wrote him, I complained about the Housing and Redevelopment Board and I put a note on the bottom of my card saying I didn't want the made-up letter, I wanted an answer from the mayor himself. Now, what do you think I got? I got the made-up letter. It told me that the mayor had turned my letter over to the Housing and Redevelopment Board, the same outfit I was complaining about."

A different style of frustration lies in wait for the citizen who thinks he can accomplish something by interrogating public officials at public meetings—by

SOURCE: Joseph P. Lyford, from *The Airtight Cage: A Study of New York's West Side* (New York: Harper & Row, 1966), pp. 301–317, 329–333. Copyright © 1966 by Joseph P. Lyford. Reprinted by permission of Harper & Row, Publishers, Inc.

"putting them on the spot," as the saying goes. Ordinarily these inquisitions are an unmitigated fizzle. An individual who tangles with the head of a bureaucracy will find himself fighting way out of his class. Any commissioner worth his salt can dispose of any critic by telling him that "the situation you describe is certainly not typical," implying that a minor subordinate has goofed, or he will tell the citizen that he is "not in possession of all the facts." This latter rejoinder will almost always dispose of the case, because it is true; if the citizen had all the facts he would know a great deal more than the commissioner.

The cold gray truth about the futility of individual protest has been demonstrated over and over on the West Side. One of the many examples was the meeting called by the FDR-Woodrow Wilson Democratic Club to air objections to the way in which the urban renewal plan was being implemented. The platform groaned under the weight of several city commissioners and state and federal housing officials, and for a few moments at the outset it seemed as if, having flushed them out in the open, an aroused public would make short work of the bureaucrats. But every time a housewife, local politician, businessman, tenant, or organizational representative rose to shout his grievances, the appropriate official would suffocate him with an involved technical explanation of the city's program as it was supposed to work on paper. The more outraged the plaintiff the easier it was to strangle him with his own innocence. One of these was Elemer Vadasz, the owner of André's Pastry Shop, who said in apoplexy that the city was forcing him to vacate but had done nothing about its promises to relocate him properly. The Commissioner of Relocation patiently described the relocation program for commercial tenants and enumerated several forms that had to be filled out by businessmen to qualify. Then the commissioner elicited the fact that Vadasz had not filled out one of the forms, and with the exposure of this crime against the state the pastry shop owner was done for—at least for that night.*

Another speaker, Aramis Gomez, who at the time was still the neighborhood's official angry Puerto Rican (he was later to be appointed to a government job), attacked the Department of Real Estate for alleged failures to maintain properly buildings it had taken over in the urban renewal area. The Commissioner of Real Estate recalled irritably that he had once told Gomez that if he had any complaints he should report them to the commissioner, but that Gomez had never done so and, therefore, Gomez had no business bringing up his charges in a public meeting. This seemed to satisfy the audience, a good part of which was hostile to Gomez on general principles, and the scuffle ended without any further inquiry into whether Gomez's charges were, in fact, true.

---

*Later Vadasz became so vocal that the Department of Relocation made a special project of him. News photographers were invited to take a picture of Vadasz as he received a check for $3,000 from the Commissioner of Relocation. Other displaced commercial tenants continued to have just as much difficulty as ever in relocating their businesses, and many of them found that private developers, approved by the city, were charging exorbitant rents for space in the urban renewal area.

The same commissioner handled Mrs. Marianne Jacobs, whose husband owns a local drugstore, with equal dispatch. Mrs. Jacobs stated she had talked to several tenants in city-owned buildings and had discovered they had not received rent reductions promised them by the city. The commissioner said this could not be so and explained the department's policy. Standing up for several minutes while a commissioner explains department policy will take the steam out of anybody and eventually Mrs. Jacobs sat down, never to regain the floor again. And so the meeting went, with the professionals taking the amateurs in stride, shriveling enormous personal crises to the status of petty complaints, responding to requests for information by offering the official philosophy. The common thread that stitched all the official responses together was their irrelevance to the questions. Such confrontations give the bystander the feeling of traveling through one of those amusement park concessions where iron bars turn out to be rubber and there are mirrors that make a man seem seven feet tall or seven inches short.

Of course there were roads besides Box 100 or public meetings open to the citizen seeking redress from his government. For instance, one could complain into a microphone attached to the mayor's "gripemobile," a contraption which rolled from borough to borough and gave citizens the illusion they were getting through to His Honor himself. Its value seemed to be largely therapeutic. The citizen might also try to call somebody up on the telephone or even barge into the bureaucratic establishment and demand an audience with the man in charge. These forays were easily sidetracked. People as well as letters always seemed to be addressing themselves to the wrong department, and on those rare occasions when the city answered a letter the signatures at the bottom were so illegible that it was impossible to tell with whom one was communicating. The corporation counsel's office had a standard signature that resembled a tightly coiled spring and could not have been deciphered by an archaeologist. A telephone call to a city agency was tantamount to wandering through a pitch-black cave, full of voices telling the citizen he had the wrong extension.

I used to keep a record of such phone calls. The following entry is rather typical: "Called WOrth 4–5656, asked for the Department of Real Estate, was given extension. Explained I wanted to find out about mortgages on my house, which had been taken over by the city. Switched to another extension. When I repeated reason for my call man said I should call Extension 462. He clicked for the switchboard, could not get it, then said, 'I guess it must be their coffee break,' and advised me to hang up and call WOrth 4–5656 again and ask for Extension 462. Did so, got 462, explained what I wanted, was transferred to Extension 415. Explained to information officer at 415 who said I had wrong extension and that Housing and Redevelopment Board had nothing to do with mortgages. He suggested I call the City Urban Renewal Maintenance Corporation. I said I had already called that office, which had referred me to the Department of Real Estate, which had referred me to the Housing and Redevelopment Board. The information officer replied, 'I can't help you; we shouldn't even be discussing this.' Repeated to information officer that I had been shuttled to him through several other extensions. 'Why did they misinform you?' he said. 'Tell me who referred you to me and I'll call him and tell him to stop.' I said I didn't know the names of the persons at Extensions 415 or 462. 'How do you expect help if you don't know people's names?' the information officer said. 'Could you tell me what department I should call to get the information I need?' I asked. 'Aren't you the information officer?' The information officer replied, 'Particularly no, in general yes.' He suggested I call a Mr. Pignato in the Department of Real Estate. 'You are wasting my time,' he said, and hung up."

I called WOrth 4–5656 again and asked for Mr. Pignato. Mr. Pignato's secretary answered and said it was the wrong place, that I should call the City Urban Renewal Maintenance Corporation. I said I had already talked to the City Urban Renewal Maintenance Corporation. Another man got on the line and said I should call the corporation counsel. Even better, he said, I should hire a lawyer. I called the corporation counsel's office. The man who answered told me to hire an attorney.

If anyone feels that this example exaggerates the norm, he is free to pick up a telephone and experiment for himself.

Although there is an infinite variety of bureaucrats and bureaucracies, in New York City they have certain common characteristics, one of which is an almost pathological fear of the inquisitive citizen. A request to a minor official for the type of information which is usually available in the mayor's annual report brings the response that the caller must first get "clearance" from the commissioner himself. I once called the office of the Commissioner of Welfare to ask about the salary scales of welfare investigators, and was told that information was "not to be given out." A Columbia Journalism School student produced a near panic at the West Side office of the Department of Relocation when she appeared with a notebook: a social worker who agreed to take her with him on his rounds was considered a fool by his colleagues for exposing himself to publicity. The "thou shalt not talk" rule is so firmly established that a school superintendent could once tell me before several associates, without a shade of embarrassment, that in interviewing school principals I should remember that "principals are not allowed to state opinions, they are only allowed to state the facts." Apprehensiveness about the public is widespread in every city department.

Another trait of most commissioners is their emphasis on "positive accomplishments." While such emphasis, as Dr. Norman Vincent Peale has often said, may be necessary for one's self-esteem and reputation as a go-getter, it results in the propagation of totally bloodless and unrealistic pictures of the social and economic disasters which have overtaken the people. Even when a commissioner will talk frankly, the comments about his departmental program have an academic quality about them and they grossly understate the crises. Former Commissioner of Hospitals Ray Trussell was one of the most intelligent and candid, but after listening to him one is simply not prepared for the shock of inspecting actual conditions in a city hospital. Representative John

Lindsay's election campaign description of conditions in Harlem Hospital, based on what the hospital staff itself had to say, captured far more of the desperateness of the situation.

The reason commissioners talk as they do is mainly because they neglect their first responsibility to themselves, which is to do their own reporting. Inevitably the commissioner comes to see the picture through the eyes of subordinates who long ago became professional expediters. He succumbs to the built-in rationalizations of the administrator. He becomes the victim of his own public relations department, and after he has given the same speech over and over he believes it.

It might be instructive to select one city commissioner and get some idea of how he operated, and then look at the experience of one of the families who became entangled in his department. Perhaps the most interesting example of a bureaucrat was Milton Mollen, chairman of Housing and Redevelopment during most of the Wagner administration. His agency was one which had a persistent and determining influence on the life of the people in the area. Chairman Mollen himself was the most plausible and politically successful of the city's commissioners and at the same time one of the most resistant to public criticism. No other commissioner had as large a public relations apparatus, nor did any other receive such recognition and rewards. The mayor eventually promoted Mollen to the post of city Housing Coordinator, and later, in a political switch, Mollen sought and received the nomination for comptroller on the Republican-Liberal ticket of John Lindsay in the mayoralty campaign of 1965.

In contrast to Boston's Edward Logue and Pittsburgh's Bernard Loshbough, two of the country's most effective redevelopment experts, Mollen brought little special experience to the city's Housing and Redevelopment Board. He had previously been with the corporation counsel's office, was admittedly a political appointment, and his function as chairman of the Housing and Redevelopment Board was to act as the mayor's political agent. This in turn explains why the personnel policies of the Housing and Redevelopment Board were so different from those of Loshbough and Logue. Whereas the latter insisted on keeping their agencies free of political appointments, technical experts in New York found themselves very much subordinated to the political wing of the agency.

A basic part of Mollen's announced policy as commissioner was what he called an "open-door policy" at housing and redevelopment headquarters. In his many speeches to West Side organizations, he would declare that "we ask you, the people of the community, if you have any problems, do not hesitate to bring them to us." But the ordinary citizen who took Chairman Mollen up on his invitation invariably found that the chairman and his chief subordinates were prepared to repel all boarders. If a citizen managed to see anyone in the department, it was one of the many members of HRB's huge public relations staff. Most likely he would be referred to a "community relations" specialist, a kind and patient listener named Elizabeth Kempton, who had no authority to deal with anyone's problems and who was able to give only routine information—the type the citizen usually already had himself. In other words, without a personal introduction to the chairman from a local Democratic leader, the citizen might as well spend his time hollering up a stovepipe.

Those who did manage to breach the walls of the chairman's office ordinarily found a third party present at all discussions—a self-assured, youngish man in a gray flannel suit who was the chairman's chief public relations adviser. This gentleman, Robert Seaver, seemed to operate on the assumption that a citizen who came to him for help thereby placed himself in a position of inferiority and therefore could be treated with as much rudeness as the occasion seemed to demand. Information on department policy was proffered as if it were classified material, with Seaver even going so far as to tell me once that he was "not to be quoted" on anything he had to say—a rather remarkable statement for a public relations man. Seaver displayed another common characteristic of city officials, a mild paranoia about the press. In my first meeting with him he complained about the activities of one Woody Klein, a *World-Telegram and Sun* reporter (later appointed press officer to Mayor Lindsay), who would call up the office for information without giving his name, keep track of the number of times he was shunted around to different extensions, and then write a story about the run-around for his paper. Such behavior, Seaver felt, was dirty pool.

The chairman himself was an affable, preoccupied man, slow to passion except when his department was criticized. His private interviews were exact replicas of his public speeches. One got the theoretical picture of urban renewal presented as an actual fact, in attractively worded generalities, accompanied by interpolations from the omnipresent Seaver. One always had the impression, in listening to Chairman Mollen, that the real Chairman Mollen had already left the office for another appointment. Unlike other commissioners, the chairman never admitted that there were serious shortcomings in his department's operation. At a meeting of the Park West Village tenants' association, for instance, he rejected criticism of his Area Services North office, declaring that the tenants of the urban renewal area were grateful for its work —a statement that could not have been made by anyone with the slightest firsthand knowledge of the tenants' real feelings. However, the discrepancies between official policy and operational fact were no problem for Chairman Mollen, since he was addressing himself mainly to the sophisticated middle-class types who came to meetings—the people who had "weight" in the community. Such hearers, with little or no personal involvement in the urban renewal program, were quite willing to accept Mr. Mollen's advertisements at their face value.

One of those who learned not to take Chairman Mollen at face value was a man we shall here call José Rodriguez. Rodriguez is one of those uninfluential citizens whose fate helps illustrate the nature of man's relationship to his government in the twentieth century. The Rodriguez family's personal education about the democratic system began in earnest when José, his wife Christine, and their two young children moved into a rooming house in the West Nineties and acquired a notoriously callous landlord. The Rodriguezes liked their new location because it was just across the street from a new elementary school, and only a couple of blocks from a junior high school. Local authorities also had reason to be pleased with the advent of the Rodriguezes. Although both parents were employed, they took an interest in local affairs. On several occasions Rodriguez helped out with special events at public schools and hospitals, and both children quickly made an excellent impression on their teachers.

Rodriguez's income and that of his wife, who worked in a laundry, enabled them to pay on time each month their $110 rent for the new place, which consisted of two and a half rooms on the basement floor. It became apparent soon after they moved in that they were not getting anywhere near their money's worth. The apartment, no better and no worse than hundreds of decomposed compounds which flourish under the city's so-called rent control program, was badly in need of painting and plastering. Holes in the floor were covered by carpet or cardboard, and a large opening under the kitchen sink produced frequent visits from rats in the basement. Rodriguez also found that the toilet bowl was coming loose and water ran over the bathroom floor. The apartment was also overrun with cockroaches. Rodriguez asked for exterminator service, to which he was entitled. The landlord refused it. Nor did the landlord pay for a stove and kitchen sink which Rodriguez had bought for the kitchen, although the original equipment had been so decayed as to be unusable.

When Rodriguez found that he would not get his landlord to clean the filthy hallways or get rid of the vermin, he phoned the Department of Health until a department official told him curtly to buy himself a can of insecticide and stop bothering the department. Next he complained to the office of Area Services North, a local agency of the Housing and Redevelopment Board, which was charged with seeing that private landlords in the urban renewal area maintained their buildings properly and kept them free of code violations. Rodriguez's experience with Area Services North was typical; nothing happened.

So he wrote to Chairman Mollen himself. When the chairman also refused to do anything about the complaint, Rodriguez decided to write to the then candidate for the U.S. Senate, Robert Kennedy. The letter described the family's living conditions and declared that city agencies entrusted with the enforcement of health and building codes had failed to cooperate with the tenants.

"How much can a human being take?" Rodriguez concluded. "Please, Mr. Kennedy, help us."

A week or so later, he received an answer.

"I was shocked to hear of your plight," wrote Kennedy, "and I am certainly going to do everything I can to help you and your fellow tenants." What Kennedy meant by "help" was that he had referred Rodriguez's letter to

Chairman Mollen, "who has assured me that he will have your situation thoroughly investigated."

Five weeks later, Rodriguez received a letter from Mollen describing the results of the "thorough investigation" the chairman had promised Mr. Kennedy.

"A check, both at our office and with the Department of Buildings, revealed that certain violations existed on said premises." Mollen also wrote that the attorney for the landlord had stated that several violations had been removed and that other violations existed because of Rodriguez's continued refusal to allow repairmen to enter his apartment.

Chairman Mollen then proceeded to give the back of his hand to the family Rodriguez. "In your complaint to Senator-elect Kennedy you stated that various city agencies involved in code enforcement had neglected to cooperate with the tenants. I am certain that if you cooperate the city will do all it can to see that conditions are improved."

At no time during Mollen's "investigation" did any representative of the Housing and Redevelopment Board or of any code-enforcement agency take the trouble to talk to Rodriguez or to look at his apartment to see if, in fact, any violations had been removed. Nor was Rodriguez ever given an opportunity to respond to the charges—which were untrue—that he had refused entry to any workman hired by the landlord. By his own admission Chairman Mollen's sole source of information was the landlord's attorney. Apparently no city official had the time to make an on-the-spot investigation. However, shortly before he wrote to Rodriguez, Chairman Mollen attended a tree-planting ceremony a few blocks from the apartment, at which occasion his photograph was taken for the Spanish newspaper *El Diario*.

Such rebuffs as Mollen's letter dealt the Rodriguez family a double blow. Not only did it mean they could expect little help from the authorities, but it also was the signal to the landlord that he could harass them with impunity. This landlord was not accustomed to having his tenants complain, and he decided to get rid of the troublemakers as quickly as possible. Until their arrival he had operated the building and another even more decrepit one on the same street in defiance of all manner of fire, occupancy, building, and health regulations without any protest from his tenants. Most of them were Puerto Ricans desperate for a place to live, who were jammed into these buildings in violation of occupancy regulations; any complaints about their treatment would have meant their immediate eviction. A measure of the landlord's control over the tenants was the fact that he even distributed their mail. There were no regulation mailboxes in the Rodriguezes' house: the postman dropped the mail into the slot of a padlocked box to which the landlord had the only key. Rodriguez protested to the U.S. Post Office, but the postal authorities did nothing about it.

For nearly a year the landlord carried out a campaign of harassment to drive the Rodriguez family out of the house. He served several eviction notices, and on more than six different occasions he appeared at the door of their apartment with summonses charging Rodriguez with assault, theft, disorderly behavior, nonpayment of rent, or threats of violence. On most of these occasions, he was accompanied by a policeman who had been told by the landlord that Rodriguez was dangerous. To answer each summons or notice of eviction, Rodriguez had to take the better part of a day to find a lawyer, prepare a defense, call witnesses, and travel downtown to criminal court or the agency where a hearing was to be held. The summonses forced him to absent himself from his union hiring hall, thereby losing a chance at any employment opportunity which might turn up that day.

The truth of the landlord's charges can be judged by the fact that in some cases he did not even appear to press his complaint, and in all cases the charges against Rodriguez were dismissed. But, although he lost each time, the landlord succeeded in irritating and worrying the family, keeping it in a constant state of insecurity, using up Rodriguez's time, causing him expense, and interfering with his employment.

In the opinion of this observer, Rodriguez won his rounds in court in spite of the judicial procedure because he could speak English (although with a heavy accent), because he kept his temper both in and out of court, in spite of considerable provocation in both places, and because he kept a complete file of documents bearing on his case. Finally, he had some friends who were occasionally able to get him a lawyer without charge. Had he lacked any of these assets, it is difficult to say whether he would be a free man today. The proceedings in court had very little resemblance to the administration of justice as it is discussed in bar association meetings. Rodriguez was merely one of a long line of people—largely Negroes and Puerto Ricans—who were handled on an assembly-line basis by an overworked, harried judge who sometimes did not appear to understand the charges. There would be a "Now what's this all about?," then, after a few moments of confused argument, the magistrate would berate both plaintiff and defendant, tell them to stop picking on each other, and threaten them both with jail if they ever appeared before him again. Or he might just postpone things by granting the landlord an adjournment, thereby prolonging Rodriguez's discomfort a little longer.

On one occasion when Rodriguez took the offensive and filed charges against the landlord for failing to render services and correct violations, the head of a city agency appeared as a witness for the landlord himself, appealing to the judge to postpone a decision on the case until her agency had had time to make an inspection of the Rodriguez apartment—a plea which came months after Rodriguez had vainly appealed to her agency and to her boss, Chairman Mollen, for just such an inspection. When the inspection was finally held, the two inspectors became angry at Rodriguez for having invited one of his friends to be present as a witness, and Rodriguez was never allowed to see the report of the inspection.

The conclusion to the harassment of Rodriguez could have been predicted. For one thing, Rodriguez began to run out of lawyers. Friendly attorneys were willing to help on a one-shot basis, but when the next summons was served they were always too busy. Rodriguez appealed to local civil rights groups, to Puerto Rican organizations, to the FDR-Woodrow Wilson Democratic Club, and got promises of help, but the help never materialized.

One night Rodriguez was arrested and arraigned in the 24th Precinct police station, charged by the landlord with assault. This case was also thrown out of court, but it was Rodriguez's last victory. During a summer rainstorm a few weeks later, a marshal knocked at the Rodriguez door with a court order evicting the family for nonpayment of rent. The order had been signed without Rodriguez's ever having had a hearing on the charges, which were false. So the Rodriguez family and all its belongings were moved out onto the sidewalk, and all a handful of friendly neighbors could do was to cover the furniture with plastic to keep it dry. Then the Rodriguezes were transported to a fifth-floor walkup apartment in a frightful city-owned building a block or so away.

The unaffiliated poor are not the only ones whose nonviolent protests fail consistently. The experiences of many West Side homeowners who are pushed against the cutting edge of the urban renewal apparatus also illustrate the futility of resistance, even by those who—unlike the poor—know some of their rights and are in a position to put up a defense. The fundamental weakness of the homeowners' position is that they are an infinitesimal and unorganized minority and, therefore, are not taken seriously by public officials. Another handicap of the homeowner is that, despite official proclamations to the contrary, private homeownership is not compatible with the theory behind the city's real-estate policies. The earth of Manhattan is seen by the Commissioner of Real Estate as a source of tax revenue to be cultivated as intensively as possible. That is to say, the ideal use of land is that which provides the greatest dollar return per square foot. One might say that the city's preferred crop is the "money bush." It is obvious that a four-story, eighteen-foot-wide house is not a money bush, but a pestiferous weed to be plowed under to make way for apartment houses, parking lots, office buildings, and other money bushes.

A third handicap for the homeowner trying to defend himself is that local politicians, if they concern themselves at all about the area's tenants, logically concentrate their efforts on protecting large numbers of people in far worse shape than the private homeowner, who is supposed—sometimes incorrectly —to be able to take care of himself financially no matter what the city decides to do to him. In a sense, it is his very insignificance that makes the homeowner historically important. His fate is another example of how the bureaucracy disposes of the type of citizen it deems irrelevant.

My own campaign to prevent the city from taking over my home at 33 West Ninety-second Street is an interesting case history of what happens to the individual who attempts to do battle with his government. The house . . . was a twenty-foot brownstone that had been rehabilitated and converted into apartments at a cost of approximately $35,000 in addition to the purchase price. The rehabilitation had been carried out by a private builder in 1959 and 1960, with a permit from the Department of Buildings. On completion of the renovation, the private builder had received a certificate of occupancy from the department. I assumed that, in line with the announced policy of the Housing and Redevelopment Board of conserving "sound structures," my house would not be eventually condemned by the urban renewal authorities. I did not realize at the time that the preliminary urban renewal plan had marked it for condemnation under the mistaken assumption that the house was a one-family dwelling in a state of disrepair—something I discovered in my first conversation with a city appraiser. Since the house was located next to a modern apartment building and was on the edge, not in the middle, of an urban renewal site to the east, it was not an obstruction to new construction on that site. In addition to the foregoing reasons for preserving the house, it provided modern housing at middle-income rents and it was one of the few good brownstones in the area that were open to Negro tenants.

On my first attempt to talk to the Housing and Redevelopment Board, and after I had informed it of its mistake in classifying the house as a single-family dwelling, I found it was not going to change its decision to condemn. What the Housing and Redevelopment Board had presented to the community as a "preliminary plan" was as far as my case was concerned "a final and unalterable" plan. I was never able to get an appointment with any Housing and Redevelopment Board official who had the power to change the decision. Each time I sought an interview, I was referred to a community relations person who would tell me that she was "sorry" and that "nothing could be done" about my case. She did arrange one meeting for me with several officials, but even as I talked I realized that this was not a discussion but simply a *pro forma* occasion at which I was to be administered the last rites. My listeners wore the solemn, polite expressions of politicians at the wake of a constituent they knew but slightly.

Nevertheless, I persisted in trying to find out the board's reasons for condemning my home. With the board's arguments before me, I would have some basis for deciding on whether to give up or prepare a rebuttal. But I was never able to learn why the board had decided on condemnation; I was told over and over simply that "the plan cannot be changed." When I asked to see an architect's plan for the construction which included my site, I was told I could not see any such plan. I did not even find out if there was a plan. Finally I was told sympathetically that I would be happier if I stopped fighting.

Since patients do not ordinarily agree to an amputation without some sort of an explanation from the doctor, I tried to get the information I wanted from other sources. Eventually I managed to learn, by talking to tenants and owners of nearby condemned properties, that my house site was part of a package. My land would be part of a T-shaped plot on which a private developer would erect a luxury apartment house with an entrance on Central Park West, with apartments renting at around four hundred dollars a month. I also learned that the land on which my house stood would be part of the garden area for the apartment house. In other words the city of New York was using its condemnation powers to displace me and my family and tear down a valuable brownstone to plant bushes.

I discussed my situation with Mrs. Robert Landy, a resident of 325 Central Park West. Her building and my house were part of the same parcel. Mrs. Landy and her fellow tenants were as indignant as I about the plan for our part of the block, since their building was attractive, roomy, and excellently maintained. A typical apartment of five rooms—which I inspected—rented for $140 a month and could not have been duplicated for twice that rent in any new construction.

Mrs. Landy said she had had the same difficulties I had had in getting information from the Housing and Redevelopment Board. All that the tenants of 325 Central Park West could find out was that their building was supposed to be "structurally unsound," and that it was supposed to have "wooden beam supports." The tenants had argued in vain that the house was in perfectly satisfactory condition and that it did not have the alleged "wooden beam supports." However, the board told the tenants that the plan could not be changed and that they would not discuss it further. Later, HRB public relations man Seaver repeated to me what I had heard from Mrs. Landy, that 325 was "structurally unsound," that it had "wooden beam supports," and that it must go.

Although we were presumably in the same boat—part of the same "unalterable plan"—my fate and that of the people in 325 Central Park West were quite different. The tenants of 325 organized, hired a lawyer to fight their case, and generated political pressure on their own behalf. They invited Chairman Mollen and other HRB officials to a progressive dinner party in the house at 325. Subsequently it happened that one day without fanfare the Housing and Redevelopment Board removed 325 Central Park West from the condemned list, acknowledging in so doing the fact that 325 was structurally sound and did not have, as was originally supposed, "wooden beam supports." Today the tenants of 325 are turning the building into a cooperative.

Once the plan for 325 had been changed it seemed to me more logical than ever that my house could be saved since the "unalterable plan" would have to be redrawn entirely. I was wrong again. The HRB continued to refuse to discuss the case of my house, and at this point I gave up. But any expectation that my unconditional surrender would end my troubles with the city was unfounded. Now began a new series of difficulties, this time with the Department of Real Estate, the Department of Relocation, the City Urban Renewal Maintenance Co. (CURMCO), and the office of the corporation counsel. I shall only attempt to report on a few of these difficulties.

To begin with, the city of New York does not do business with a property owner it is about to dispossess. It ignores him. From the time the first city appraiser looked at my house until the day three years later when the city took title to it, I did not receive one signed communication from any city agency informing me that the government wished to take my home, what its procedure would be, or when it proposed to take action. During this period, the city made no attempt to negotiate the sale of the house, to tell me what it proposed to pay for it, or what steps I would be expected to take in handling my part of the transaction. I tried many times to discover what the city proposed to do with me—information to which I felt I had a special right since I was not giving my property up of my own free will. In all this time I received just one piece of "correspondence"; an almost illegible mimeographed sheet, with no explanatory letter or any identification of the sender, telling me that legal steps had been taken to condemn my property.

On February 1, 1963, a man rang my doorbell, identified himself as a city employee, and proceeded to nail up a yellow sign on the wall which stated that the premises now belonged to the city of New York and all tenants thenceforth should pay their rent to the City Urban Renewal Corporation office at 203 West Ninety-third Street. In this manner I was notified that I had ceased to own my own home and that I was now a tenant of the city (rent unspecified). Not until three months later did a city representative telephone me with an offer for my house of several thousand dollars less than the purchase price. When I refused the offer I discovered that the city was haggling; a few days later it increased its offer several thousand dollars to approximately what I had paid for my home. Even then the offer represented a substantial loss to me because I had put additional money into the house since purchasing it and I was losing a source of income as well. The city's second and final offer was accompanied by the common persuader used on recalcitrants, an ultimatum that if I did not accept the offer and chose to fight the case in court, it would take me two years to get my money.

While such a threat usually worked in situations where the recalcitrant had to have money immediately to move elsewhere, I was in a position where I could go to court, and the court's final award to me was $6,000 more than the city's first offer. After paying the lawyer's fees I cleared just about what I had paid for my house. I did not receive the final bulk payment for my property for twenty-two months after the city had seized it, during which time the city paid me 4 percent interest on the money it owed me while I was borrowing money at 6 percent in order to purchase another place to live.

My experience with the house also gave me a chance to learn something about the Department of Relocation. One of the city's alleged reasons for putting me out of my house three or four years before it planned to tear it down was that it wanted to use the apartments to relocate some of the people being evicted from condemned buildings in other parts of the urban renewal area. However, most of the apartments in my house remained vacant after the city took it over, despite the shortage of good housing in the area. After a few months, the city abandoned any pretense of maintaining the premises, with the result that the boiler of a new furnace blew up, and the two or three people still living in the building were without heat or hot water. Meanwhile city employees systematically pillaged the house. A maintenance man appropriated the furnace's expensive electronic control system, the front doors were smashed in by raiders, broken glass was strewn about the house, and policemen in uniform entered vacant apartments and made off with the refrigerators.

Today the house is still standing, an empty piece of wreckage which once housed six families. I never walk on Ninety-second Street now because I don't want to see it again.

*   *   *

The government of the city has taken on many of the basic characteristics of the large, private aggregations of money and power, and has thereby become more and more the enemy of community. If the two circles of power, public and private, once functioned as countervailing forces against each other, they are now in important respects each other's agents. The corporation on one hand has become to a greater and greater degree a producer for government, and as part of the arrangement it professes a new sense of responsibility for the public welfare. On the other hand, the government agency has adopted the organization and technical innovations of the private sector and tailors its welfare programs and regulatory activities to conform to the accumulating pressures of a vast array of private interests. The resulting situation is exactly the opposite of the socialization which state power is supposed to be bringing about. Far from cutting away the base of the private sector, the governmental bureaucracy has become a means through which private power—from banks to labor unions—has strengthened its grip on the development of the city, and has subordinated the general welfare to the private interest.

One can pick at random any one of thousands of case histories of the West Side poor to find an individual illustration of what happens to the unaffiliated citizen at the hands of government agencies infiltrated with the private interest and paralyzed by the weight of their own anatomy. And examples of the private invasion of the public sphere can be found in every phase of municipal government:* Bernard Weissbourd's remark that the self-defeating nature of public housing policies is determined by the private developers who are its enemies can be paraphrased to fit almost any other area of municipal governmental policy; land use, taxation, city planning, urban renewal, assessments, health and welfare programs, housing, the courts and law enforcement. The very size of government, once seen as a threat to the private sector, has made it more susceptible to private pressure. In Lincoln Steffens' day the pressure was erratic and personal, today the science of applying pressure and yielding to it has been automated along with everything else, to the point where the private interest controls not merely individual people but the whole climate in which the governmental apparatus functions.

The division of executive government power into impersonal and nearly autonomous agencies and "authorities" has put them as far out of the range of public protest as a private monopoly like the New York Telephone Company. The New York Port Authority is one example of enormous governmental power which has accumulated out of nowhere and operates primarily

---

*The situation in the city parallels that in the federal government, where agencies such as the Federal Communications Commission, Food and Drug Administration, and others are dominated by the industries they were created to regulate.

as a promoter of private business interests. The experience of confronting a public agency and a private monopoly like Consolidated Edison is practically identical—in both cases one is dealing with organizations preoccupied with internal security and populated in the lower reaches by a professional class fearful of innovation and responsibility and unresponsive to any outside stimulus except organized pressure. When such government agencies are allowed to dominate the life of the poor to the minutest detail, they isolate them from participation in community life.

When even a middle-class citizen with financial and political resources has difficulty in defending himself against arbitrary government action, the position of the poor becomes hopeless. The commitments an agency makes to one of its impoverished wards are not written down, and they can be changed, lied about, or abrogated at will. The low-income Negro or Puerto Rican learns that the administrative agency is indefatigable in calling him to account for the smallest infractions, but when he seeks protection from that agency he finds that his rights are ephemeral and that his case disintegrates in a mass of technicalities. He learns that a code-enforcement agency takes little initiative on his behalf and has no will to protect him. Rather, on rare occasions when he insists on his rights vigorously, at some time or another agency officials may conspire against him, because they consider the complainant a troublemaker, or because they have been corrupted by the person who has violated the rights of the complainant.

Like the public agency, the law and the judicial process also seem to work most effectively when it is the poor who are being prosecuted. The fact is no secret. Some state bar associations openly acknowledge this to be the case, and when he was attorney general, Robert Kennedy paid a great deal of attention to the problem. Patricia Wald's report to the 1965 National Conference on Law and Poverty catalogues dozens of ways in which the judicial system is rigged against the indigent, and although she draws her illustrations from many cities, she could have found all the examples she needed in the life of the West Side poor. Given this situation, it is no surprise that the minority groups' hatred and fear of legal authority has occasionally fanned an isolated act of rebellion into a sustained outbreak of mass violence.

Perhaps because they are temporary political appointees and therefore in a more exposed and precarious position, the top administrative officials in the New York City government have been more sensitive to criticism than the eternal civil service employees beneath them. But when a commissioner admits his agency operates inefficiently or unjustly "at times," he almost always concludes by a remark that there are a few rotten apples in every barrel. The condition of the barrel is never questioned. One also hears from commissioners that the city is too big and the budget too small: the manner in which a department has used its resources is never discussed. Underlying all the apologies is the assumption, which the public shares, that the city is doomed. In the face of such an attitude, of course, it becomes impossible to reduce waste, reorganize departments, or create an atmosphere that would encourage innovation. The defeatism partly explains why, even when a costly budget increase is approved, the money is channeled into expansion of the administrative apparatus rather than into improvement of direct public services.

One impressive characteristic of the civil service and political appointees in the lower levels of the bureaucracy is their peculiar attitude toward the citizen they are supposed to serve—especially if he is poor and raises a fuss. Regardless of the employee's racial or ethnic background, he very often reacts in a negative way to any situation which jiggles his procedure-centered world. Life in a municipal office building creates its own rigid habit patterns and psychological attitudes, and outsiders had better beware of them. The civil service worker in some ways resembles a member of one of the more ingrown trade unions. If he has a social attitude he lays it away when he goes on the job.

The huge mass of administrative regulations is a boon to certain agency officials, protecting the mind that avoids responsibility and shies away from the special case. It provides dozens of legal pretexts for inaction. Worst of all, the almost unlimited power which administrative rules confer on the official often results in a subconscious attitude that he personally owns the services his department is supposed to provide the public. To understand fully the results of this proprietary attitude, one must have undergone some of the insulting interrogations to which applicants for public housing are often subjected. The applicant is frequently treated as a suppliant who, if he happens to rub the official the wrong way, can be groundlessly accused of everything from immorality to cheating on his income-tax returns. Since such comments are always informal and made without witnesses present, the applicant has no recourse—he might as well be arguing with a policeman.

A bureaucratic system riddled with such attitudes will respond only if it is badly frightened. But systems don't frighten easily. Even though individual employees may be constitutionally apprehensive, the system in which they work has dispersed responsibility so widely that it is almost impossible to call anybody to account: therefore inefficiency is pursued without interruption almost as a matter of policy.

Some elements of new life have managed to take root in fissures of the bureaucratic rock. For instance, in two of the city's most absurdly organized and top-heavy agencies—the Department of Welfare and the Board of Education—case workers and teachers with a social direction to their thinking have bucked the system and forced policy and organizational changes. The pressure of the teachers, made possible by their new union (the United Federation of Teachers, AFL-CIO) has given them a small voice in influencing the educational program, while the case workers' strike against the Department of Welfare has emphasized the unworkability of traditional approaches to welfare problems. It is unlikely, however, that such low-level pressures can ever force the administrative organization to be more responsive to the poor. For one thing, the pressures are too isolated. Also, as reformers achieve substantial successes, they lose their revolutionary impulses and tend to become accretions to the system. This tendency is already noticeable among the teachers, whose union is becoming more preoccupied with teachers' prerogatives and less and less interested in general improvements in the educational system which might interfere with these prerogatives. The union's drive to prevent school principals from observing teachers in class once the teacher's probationary period is over is an indication of this trend.

White Institutions & Black Rage
David Boesel, Richard Berk,

W. Eugene Groves, Bettye Eidson &

Peter H. Rossi

Five summers of black rebellion have made it clear that the United States is facing a crisis of proportions not seen since the Great Depression. And one of the root causes of this crisis, it has also become clear, is the performance of white institutions, especially those institutions in the ghetto. Some of these institutions—police and retail stores, for example—have done much to antagonize Negroes; others, such as welfare departments and black political organizations, have tried to help and have failed.

Why have these white institutions helped engender black rage? One way to find out might be to study the attitudes of the men working for them—to discover what their personnel think about the racial crisis itself, about their own responsibilities, about the work they are doing. Therefore, at the request of the National Advisory Commission on Civil Disorders (the riot commission), we at Johns Hopkins University visited 15 Northern cities and questioned men and women working for six different institutional groups: major employers, retail merchants, teachers, welfare workers, political workers (all Negro), and policemen. All of the people we questioned, except the employers, work right in the ghetto, and are rank-and-file employees—the cop on the beat, the social caseworker, and so on.

EMPLOYERS' SOCIAL RESPONSIBILITY

The "employers" we questioned were the managers or personnel officers of the ten institutions in each city that employed the most people, as well as

SOURCE: David Boesel, Richard Berk, W. Eugene Groves, Bettye Eidson, and Peter Rossi, "White Institutions & Black Rage," *Trans-action*, 6 (March 1969), pp. 24–31. Copyright © March 1969 by Trans-action, Inc., New Brunswick, New Jersey. Reprinted by permission.

an additional 20 managers or personnel officers of the next 100 institutions. As such, they represented the most economically progressive institutions in America. And in their employment policies we could see how some of America's dominant corporate institutions impinge on the everyday lives of urban Negroes.

Businessmen are in business to make a profit. Seldom do they run their enterprises for social objectives. But since it is fashionable these days, most of the managers and personnel officers we interviewed (86 percent, in fact) accepted the proposition that they "have a social responsibility to make strong efforts to provide employment for Negroes and other minority groups." This assertion, however, is contradicted by unemployment in the Negro community today, as well as by the hiring policies of the firms themselves.

Businessmen, as a whole, do not exhibit openly racist attitudes. Their position might best be described as one of "optimistic denial"—the gentlemanly white racism evident in a tacit, but often unwitting, acceptance of institutional practices that subordinate or exclude Negroes. One aspect of this optimistic denial is a nonrecognition of the seriousness of the problems that face black people. Only 21 percent of our sample thought that unemployment was a very serious problem in the nations' cities, yet 26 percent considered air pollution very serious and 31 percent considered traffic very serious. The employers' perspective is based upon their limited experience with blacks, and that experience does not give them a realistic picture of the plight of Negroes in this country. Employers don't even think that racial discrimination has much to do with the Negroes' plight; a majority (57 percent) felt that Negroes are treated at least as well as other people of the same income, and an additional 6 percent felt that Negroes are treated *better* than any other part of the population.

This optimistic denial on the part of employers ("things really aren't that bad for Negroes") is often combined with a negative image of Negroes as employees. Half of those employers interviewed (51 percent) said that Negroes are likely to have higher rates of absenteeism than whites, so that hiring many of them would probably upset production schedules. Almost a third thought that, because Negro crime rates are generally higher than white crime rates, hiring many Negroes could lead to increased theft and vandalism in their companies. About a fifth (22 percent) thought that hiring Negroes might bring "agitators and troublemakers" into their companies, and another one-fifth feared that production costs might rise because Negroes supposedly do not take orders well.

The employer's views may reflect not only traditional white prejudices, but also some occasional experience he himself has had with Negroes. Such experiences, however, may stem as much from the employer's own practices and misconceptions as from imputed cultural habits of Negroes. As Elliott Liebow observed in his study of Negro street-corner men *(Talley's Corner),* blacks have learned to cope with life by treating menial, low-status, degrading jobs in the same way that the jobs treat them—with benign nonconcern.

Most of the employers believe that Negroes lack the preparation for anything but menial jobs. A full 83 percent said that few Negroes are qualified for professional jobs, and 69 percent thought that few are qualified for skilled positions. When it comes to unskilled jobs, of course, only 23 percent of the employers held this view. The employers seem to share a widespread assumption—one frequently used as a cover for racism—that for historical and environmental reasons Negroes have been disabled to such an extent as to make them uncompetitive in a highly competitive society. And while it is certainly true that black people have suffered from a lack of educational and other opportunities, this line of thinking—especially among whites—has a tendency to blame the past and the ghetto environment for what is perceived as Negro incompetence, thus diverting attention from *present* institutional practices. So, many employers have developed a rhetoric of concern about upgrading the so-called "hard-core unemployed" in lieu of changing their employment policies.

To a considerable extent our respondents' assessment of Negro job qualifications reflects company policy, for the criteria used in hiring skilled and professional workers tend to exclude Negroes. The criteria are (1) previous experience and (2) recommendations. It is evident that because Negroes are unlikely to have *had* previous experience in positions from which they have long been excluded, and because they are unlikely to have had much contact with people in the best position to recommend them, the criteria for "qualification" make it probable that employers will consider most Negroes unqualified.

NEGROES GET THE WORST JOBS

In short, the employers' aversion to taking risks (at least with people), reinforced by the pressure of labor unions and more general discriminatory patterns in society, means that Negroes usually get the worst jobs.

Thus, although Negroes make up 20 percent of the unskilled workers in these large corporations, they fill only a median of one percent of the professional positions and only 2 percent of the skilled positions. Moreover, the few Negroes in the higher positions are unevenly distributed among the corporations. Thirty-two percent of the companies don't report Negroes in professional positions, and 24 percent do not report any in skilled positions. If these companies are set aside, in the remaining companies the median percentage of Negroes in the two positions rises to 3 percent and 6 percent respectively. Further, in these remaining companies an even larger percentage (8 percent in both cases) of *current* positions are being filled by Negroes—which indicates, among other things, that a breakthrough has been accomplished in some companies, while in others Negro employment in the upper levels remains minimal or nonexistent.

Even among those companies that hire blacks for skilled jobs, a Negro applicant's chances of getting the job are only one-fourth as good as those of his white counterpart. For professional positions, the chances are more nearly equal: Negro applicants are about three-fourths as likely to get these jobs as are white applicants. It seems that Negroes have come closest to breaking in at the top (though across all firms only about 4 percent of the applicants for professional positions are Negro). The real stumbling-block to equal employment opportunities seems to be at the skilled level, and here it may be that union policies—and especially those of the craft unions—augment the employers' resistance to hiring Negroes for and promoting Negroes to skilled positions.

What do urban Negroes themselves think of employers' hiring practices? A survey of the same 15 cities by Angus Campbell and Howard Schuman, for the riot commission, indicates that one-third (34 percent) of the Negro men interviewed reported having been refused jobs because of racial discrimination, and 72 percent believed that some or many other black applicants are turned down for the same reason. Almost as many (68 percent) think that some or many black people miss out on promotions because of prejudice. And even when companies do hire Negroes (presumably in professional positions), this is interpreted as tokenism: 77 percent of the black respondents thought that Negroes are hired by big companies for show purposes.

The companies we studied, which have little contact with the ghetto, are very different from the other institutions in our survey, whose contact with the ghetto is direct and immediate. The corporations are also up-to-date, well-financed, and innovative, while the white institutions inside the ghetto are outdated, underfinanced, and overloaded. In historical terms, the institutions in the ghetto represent another era of thought and organization.

GHETTO MERCHANTS

The slum merchants illustrate the tendency of ghetto institutions to hark back to earlier forms. While large corporations cooperate with one another and with the government to exert substantial control over their market, the ghetto merchant still functions in the realm of traditional laissez-faire. He is likely to be a small operator, economically marginal and with almost no ability to control his market. His main advantage over the more efficient, modern retailer is his restricted competition, for the ghetto provides a captive market. The difficulty that many blacks have in getting transportation out of the ghetto, combined with a lack of experience in comparative shopping, seems to give the local merchant a competitive aid he sorely needs to survive against the lower prices and better goods sold in other areas of the city.

The merchants in our study also illustrate the free-enterprise character of ghetto merchandising. They run very small operations—grocery stores, restaurants, clothing and liquor stores, and so on, averaging a little over three employees per business. Almost half of them (45 percent) find it difficult to "keep up with their competition" (competition mainly *within* the ghetto). Since there are almost no requirements for becoming a merchant, this group is the most heterogeneous of all those studied. They have the widest age range (from 17 through 80), the highest percentage of immigrants (15 percent), and the lowest educational levels (only 16 percent finished college).

Again in contrast to the large corporations, the ghetto merchant must live with the harsh day-to-day realities of violence and poverty. His attitudes toward Negroes, different in degree from those of the employers, are at least partly a function of his objective evaluations of his customers.

Running a business in a ghetto means facing special kinds of "overhead." Theft is an especially worrisome problem for the merchants; respondents mentioned it more frequently than any other problem. There is, of course, some basis in fact for their concern. According to the riot commission, inventory losses—ordinarily under 2 percent of sales—may be twice as great in high-crime areas (most of which are in ghettos). And for these small businesses such losses may cut substantially into a slender margin of profit.

Thus it is not surprising that, of all the occupational groups interviewed in this study, the retail merchants were among the most likely to consider Negroes violent and criminal. For example, 61 percent said that Negroes are more likely to steal than whites, and 50 percent believed that Negroes are more likely to pass bad checks. No wonder, then, that black customers may encounter unusual surveillance and suspicion when they shop.

Less understandable is the ghetto merchant's apparent ignorance of the plight of ghetto blacks. Thus, 75 percent believe that blacks get medical treatment that is equal to or better than what whites get. A majority think that Negroes are not discriminated against with regard to treatment by the police, recreation facilities and so forth. Logically enough, 51 percent of the merchants feel that Negroes are making too many demands. This percentage is the second-highest measured (the police were the least sympathetic). So the merchants (like all other groups in the survey except the black politicians) are inclined to emphasize perceived defects in the black community as a major problem in their dealings with Negroes.

The shaky economic position of the merchants, their suspicion of their Negro customers, and the high "overhead" of doing business in the ghetto (because of theft, vandalism, bad credit risks) lead many merchants to sell inferior merchandise at higher prices—and to resort to other stratagems for getting money out of their customers. To elicit responses from the merchants on such delicate matters, we drew up a series of very indirect questions. The responses we obtained, though they no doubt understate the extent to which ghetto merchants provide a poor dollar value per unit of goods, are nevertheless revealing. For example, we asked the merchants to recommend various ways of "keeping up with business competition." Some 44 percent said that you should offer extra services; over a third (36 percent) said you should raise prices to cover unusually high overhead; and the same number (36 percent) said that you should buy "bargain" goods at lower prices, then sell them at regular prices. (To a small merchant, "bargain goods" ordinarily means "seconds," or slightly spoiled merchandise, because he doesn't do enough volume to gain real discounts from a wholesaler.) A smaller but still significant segment (12 percent) said that one should "bargain the selling price with each customer and take whatever breaks you can get."

The Campbell-Schuman study indicates that 56 percent of the Negroes interviewed felt that they had been overcharged in neighborhood stores (24 percent said often); 42 percent felt that they had been sold spoiled or inferior goods (13 percent said often). Given the number of ghetto stores a customer may visit every week, these data are entirely compatible with ours. Since one-third of the merchants indicated that they were not averse to buying "bargain" goods for sale in their stores, it is understandable that 42 percent of the Negroes in these areas should say that at one time or another they have been sold inferior merchandise.

It is also understandable that during the recent civil disorders many Negroes, unable to affect merchants by routine methods, struck directly at the stores, looting and burning them.

TEACHERS IN THE GHETTO

Just as ghetto merchants are in a backwater of the economy, ghetto schools are in a backwater of the educational system, experimental efforts in some cities notwithstanding.

Negroes, of course, are most likely to be served by outmoded and inadequate schools, a fact that the Coleman Report has documented in considerable detail. In metropolitan regions of the Northeast, for example, 40 percent of the Negro pupils at the secondary level attended schools in buildings over 40 years old, but only 15 percent of the whites did; the average number of pupils per room was 35 for Negroes but 28 for whites.

The teachers covered in our survey (half of whom were Negro) taught in ghetto schools at all levels. Surprisingly, 88 percent said that they were satisfied with their jobs. Their rate of leaving, however, was not consistent with this. Half of the teachers had been in their present schools for no more than four years. Breaking the figures down year by year, we find that the largest percentage (17 percent) had been there only one year. In addition, the teachers' rate of leaving increased dramatically after they had taught for five years.

While the teachers thought that education was a major problem for the cities and especially for the ghettos, they did not think that ghetto schools were a source of the difficulty. A solid majority, comparing their own schools with others in the city, thought that theirs were average, above average, or superior in seven out of eight categories. The high quality of the teaching staff, so rated by 84 percent of the respondents, was rivaled only by the high quality of the textbooks (again 84 percent). The one doubtful area, according to the teachers, was the physical plant, which seemed to them to be just barely competitive;

in this respect, 44 percent considered their own schools below average or inferior.

The teachers have less confidence in their students than in themselves or their schools. On the one hand, they strongly reject the view that in ghetto schools education is sacrificed to the sheer need for order: 85 percent said it was not true that pupils in their schools were uneducable, and that teachers could do little more than maintain discipline. On the other hand, the teachers as a group could not agree that their students were as educable as they might be. There was little consensus on whether their pupils were "about average" in interest and ability: 28 percent thought that their pupils were; 41 percent thought it was partially true that they were; and 31 percent thought it was not true. But the teachers had less difficulty agreeing that their students were *not* "above average in ability and . . . generally co-operative with teachers." Agreeing on this were 59 percent of the teachers, with another 33 percent in the middle.

The real problem with education in the ghetto, as the teachers see it, is the ghetto itself. The teachers have their own version of the "Negro disability" thesis: the "cultural deprivation" theory holds that the reason for bad education in the ghetto is the student's environment rather than the schools. (See "How Teachers Learn to Help Children Fail," by Estelle Fuchs, September, 1968.) Asked to name the major problems facing their schools, the teachers most frequently mentioned community apathy; the second most-mentioned problem, a derivation of the first, was an alleged lack of preparation and motivation in the students. Fifty-nine percent of the teachers agreed to some extent that "many communities provide such a terrible environment for the pupils that education doesn't do much good in the end."

Such views are no doubt detrimental to education in the ghetto, for they imply a decided fatalism as far as teaching is concerned. If the students are deficient—improperly motivated, distracted, and so on—and if the cause of this deficiency lies in the ghetto rather than in the schools themselves, then there is little reason for a teacher to exert herself to set high standards for her students.

There is considerable question, however, whether the students in ghetto schools are as distracted as the teachers think. Events in the last few years indicate that the schools, especially the high schools and the junior high schools, are one of the strongest focuses of the current black rebellion. The student strike at Detroit's Northern High School in 1966, for example, was cohesive and well-organized. A boycott by some 2,300 students, directed against a repressive school administration, lasted over two weeks and resulted in the dismissal of the principal and the formation of a committee, including students, to investigate school conditions. The ferment in the ghetto schools across the country is also leading to the formation of permanent and independent black students' groups, such as the Modern Strivers in Washington, D.C.'s Eastern High, intent on promoting black solidarity and bringing about changes in the educational system. In light of such developments, there is reason to think that the teachers in the survey have overestimated the corrosive effects of the ghetto environment on students—and underestimated the schools' responsibility for the state of education in the ghetto.

SOCIAL WORKERS AND THE WELFARE ESTABLISHMENT

Public welfare is another area in which old ideas have been perpetuated beyond their time. The roots of the present welfare-department structure lie in the New Deal legislation of the 1930s. The public assistance provisions of the Social Security Act were designed to give aid to the helpless and the noncompetitive: the aged, the blind, the "permanently and totally" disabled, and dependent children. The assumption was that the recipient, because of personal disabilities or inadequacies, could not make his way in life without outside help.

The New Deal also provided work (e.g., the W.P.A.) for the able-bodied who were assumed to be unemployed only temporarily. But as the Depression gave way to the war years and to the return of prosperity, the massive work programs for the able-bodied poor were discontinued, leaving only those programs that were premised on the notion of personal disability. To a considerable extent today's Negro poor have had to rely on the latter. Chief among these programs, of course, is Aid for Dependent Children, which has become a mainstay of welfare. And because of racial discrimination, especially in education and employment, a large part of the Negro population also experiences poverty as a permanent state.

While most of the social workers in our survey showed considerable sympathy with the Negro cause, they too felt that the root of the problem lay in weaknesses in the Negro community; and they saw their primary task as making up the supposed deficiency. A hefty majority of the respondents (78 percent) thought that a large part of their responsibility was to "teach the poor how to live"—rather than to provide the means for them to live as they like. Assuming disability, welfare has fostered dependency.

The social workers, however, are unique among the groups surveyed in that they are quite critical of their own institution. The average welfare worker is not entirely at one with the establishment for which she works. She is likely to be a college graduate who regards her job as transitional. And her lack of expertise has its advantages as well as its disadvantages, for it means that she can take a more straightforward view of the situations she is confronted with. She is not committed to bureaucracy as a way of life.

The disparity between the welfare establishment and the average welfare worker is evident in the latter's complaints about her job. The complaints she voices the most deal *not* with her clients, but with the welfare department itself and the problems of working within its present structure—the difficulty of getting things done, the red tape, the lack of adequate funds, and so on. Of the five most-mentioned difficulties of welfare work, three dealt with such intra-agency problems; the other two dealt with the living conditions of the poor.

There is a good deal of evidence to support the social worker's complaints. She complains, for example, that welfare agencies are understaffed. The survey indicates that an average caseload is 177 people, each client being visited about once a month for about 50 minutes. Even the most conscientious of caseworkers must be overwhelmed by such client-to-worker ratios.

As in the case of the schools, welfare has engendered a countervailing force among the very people it is supposed to serve. Welfare clients have become increasingly hostile to the traditional structure and philosophy of welfare departments and have formed themselves into an outspoken movement. The welfare-rights movement at this stage has aims: to obtain a more nearly adequate living base for the clients, and to overload the system with demands, thus either forcing significant changes or clearing the way for new and more appropriate institutions.

BLACK POLITICAL PARTY WORKERS

Usually when segments of major social institutions become incapable of functioning adequately, the people whom the institutions are supposed to serve have recourse to politics. In the ghetto, however, the political machinery is no better off than the other institutions. Around the turn of the century Negroes began to carve out small niches for themselves in the politics of such cities as Chicago and New York. Had Negro political organizations developed along the same lines as those of white ethnic groups, they might today provide valuable leverage for the ghetto population. But this has not happened. For one thing, the decline of the big-city machine, and its replacement in many cities by "nonpolitical" reform governments supported by a growing middle class, began to close off a route traditionally open to minority groups. Second, black politicians have never been regarded as fullfledged political brokers by racist whites, and consequently the possibility of a Negro's becoming a powerful politician in a predominantly white city has been foreclosed (the recent election of Carl Stokes as Mayor of Cleveland and Richard D. Hatcher, Mayor of Gary, Indiana, would be exceptions). Whites have tended to put aside their differences when confronting Negro political efforts; to regard Negro demands, no matter how routine, as racial issues; and hence to severely limit the concessions made to black people.

Today the sphere of Negro politics is cramped and closely circumscribed. As Kenneth B. Clark has observed, most of the Negroes who have reached high public office have done so *not* within the context of Negro politics, but through competition in the larger society. In most cities Negro political organizations are outmoded and inadequate. Even if, as seems probable, more and more Negro mayors are elected, they will have to work within the antiquated structure of urban government, with sharply limited resources. Unless things change, the first Negro mayor of Newark, for example, will preside over a bankrupt city.

Our survey of Negro political workers in the 15 cities documents the inadequacy of Negro politics—and the inadequacy of the larger system of urban politics. The political workers, understandably, strongly sympathize with the aspirations of other black people. As ghetto politicians, they deal with the demands and frustrations of other blacks day after day. Of all the groups surveyed, they were the most closely in touch with life in the ghetto. Most of them work in the middle and lower levels of municipal politics; they talk with about 75 voters each week. These political workers are, of course, acutely aware of the precipitous rise in the demands made by the black community. Most (93 percent) agreed that in the last few years people in their districts have become more determined to get what they want. The strongest impetus of this new determination comes from the younger blacks: 92 percent of the political workers agreed that "young people have become more militant." Only a slight majority, however (56 percent), said the same of middle-aged people.

Against the pressure of rising Negro demands, urban political organizations formed in other times and on other assumptions, attentive to other interests, and constrained by severely limited resources, find themselves unable to respond satisfactorily. A majority of the political workers, in evaluating a variety of services available to people in their districts, thought that all except two—telephone service and the fire department—were either poor or fair. Worst of the lot, according to the political workers, were recreation, police protection, and building inspection.

In view of these respondents, the black community has no illusions about the ability of routine politics to meet its needs. While only 38 percent of the political workers thought that the people in their districts regarded their councilmen as friends fighting for them, 51 percent said that the people considered their councilmen "part of the city government which must be asked continually and repeatedly in order to get things done." (Since the political workers were probably talking about their fellow party members, their responses may have been more favorable than frank. A relatively high percentage of "don't know" responses supports this point.)

Almost all the Negro politicians said that they received various requests from the voters for help. Asked whether they could respond to these requests "almost always, usually, or just sometimes," the largest percentage (36 percent) chose "sometimes"—which, in context, is a way of saying "seldom." Another 31 percent said they "usually" could respond to such requests, and 19 percent said "almost always." Logically enough, 60 percent of the political workers agreed that in the last few years "people have become more fed up with the system, and are becoming unwilling to work with politicians." In effect, this is an admission that they as political workers, and the system of urban politics to which they devote themselves, are failing.

When economic and social institutions fail to provide the life-chances that a substantial part of a population wants, and when political institutions fail to provide a remedy, the aspirations of the people begin to spill over into forms of activity that the dominant society regards either as unacceptable or illegitimate—crime, vandalism, noncooperation, and various forms of political protest.

Robert M. Fogelson and Robert D. Hill, in the *Supplemental Studies* for the riot commission, have reported that 50 percent to 90 percent of the Negro males in ten cities studied had arrest records. Clearly, when the majority of men in a given population are defined as criminals—at least by the police—something more than "deviant" behaviour is involved. In effect, ghetto residents—and especially the youth—and the police are in a state of subdued warfare. On the one hand, the cities are experiencing a massive and as yet inchoate social rising of the Negro population. On the other hand, the police —devoted to the racial status quo and inclined to overlook the niceties of mere law in their quest for law and order—have found a variety of means, both conventional and otherwise, for countering the aims of Negroes. In doing so, they are not only adhering to the norms of their institution, but also furthering their personal goals as well. The average policeman, recruited from a lower- or middle-class white background, frequently of "ethnic" origins, comes from a group whose social position is marginal and who feel most threatened by Negro advances.

The high arrest rate in the Negro community thus mirrors both the push of Negroes and the determined resistance of the police. As the conflict intensifies, the police are more and more losing authority in the eyes of black people; the young Negroes are especially defiant. Any type of contact between police and black people can quickly lead to a situation in which the policeman gives an order and the Negro either defies it or fails to show sufficient respect in obeying it. This in turn can lead to the Negro's arrest on a disorderly conduct charge or on a variety of other charges. (Disorderly conduct accounted for about 17 percent of the arrests in the Fogelson-Hill study.)

POLICE HARASSMENT TECHNIQUES

The police often resort to harassment as a means of keeping the Negro community off-balance. The riot commission noted that:

> Because youths commit a large and increasing proportion of crime, police are under growing pressure from their supervisors—and from the community—to deal with them forcefully. "Harassment of youths" may therefore be viewed by some police departments—and members even of the Negro community—as a proper crime prevention technique.

The Commission added that "many departments have adopted patrol practices which, in the words of one commentator, have 'replaced harassment by individual patrolmen with harassment by entire departments.' "

Among the most common of the cops' harassment techniques are breaking up street-corner groups and stop-and-frisk tactics. Our study found that 63 percent of the ghetto police reported that they "frequently" were called upon to disperse loitering groups. About a third say they "frequently" stop and frisk people. Obviously then, the law enforcer sometimes interferes with individuals and groups who consider their activities quite legitimate and necessary. Black people in the ghetto—in the absence of adequate parks, playgrounds, jobs, and recreation facilities, and unwilling to sit in sweltering and overcrowded houses with rats and bugs—are likely to make the streets their front yards. But this territory is often made uninhabitable by the police.

Nearly a third of the white policemen in our study thought that most of the residents of their precinct (largely Negro) were not industrious. Even more striking about the attitudes of the white police working in these neighborhoods is that many of them deny the fact of Negro inequality: 20 percent say the Negro is treated better than any other part of the population, and 14 percent say he is treated equally. As for their own treatment of Negroes, the Campbell-Schuman survey reported that 43 percent of the black men, who are on the streets more than the women, thought that police use insulting language in their neighborhoods. Only 17 percent of the white males held this belief. Of the Negro men, 20 percent reported that the police insulted them personally and 28 percent said they knew someone to whom this had happened; only 9 percent and 12 percent, respectively, of the whites reported the same. Similarly, many more blacks than whites thought that the police frisked and searched people without good reason (42 percent compared to 12 percent); and that the police roughed up people unnecessarily (37 percent as compared to 10 percent). Such reports of police misconduct were most frequent among the younger Negroes, who, after all, are on the receiving end most often.

The policeman's isolation in the ghetto is evident in a number of findings. We asked the police how many people—of various types—they knew well enough in the ghetto to greet when they saw them. Eighty-nine percent of the police said they knew six or more shopowners, managers, and clerks well enough to speak with, but only 38 percent said they knew this many teenage or youth leaders. At the same time, 39 percent said that most young adults, and 51 percent said that most adolescents, regard the police as enemies. And only 16 percent of the white policemen (37 percent of the blacks) either "often" or "sometimes" attended meetings in the neighborhood.

The police have wound up face to face with the social consequences of the problems in the ghetto created by the failure of other white institutions—though, as has been observed, they themselves have contributed to those problems in no small degree. The distant and gentlemanly white racism of employers, the discrimination of white parents who object to having their children go to school with Negroes, the disgruntlement of white taxpayers who deride the present welfare system as a sinkhole of public funds but are unwilling to see it replaced by anything more effective—the consequences of these and other forms of white racism have confronted the police with a massive control problem of the kind most evident in the riots.

In our survey, we found that the police were inclined to see the riots as the long range result of faults in the Negro community—disrespect for law, crime, broken families, etc.—rather than as responses to the stance of the white community. Indeed, nearly one-third of the white police saw the riots as the result of what they considered the basic violence and disrespect of Negroes in general, while only one-fourth attributed the riots to the failure of white institutions. More than three-fourths also regarded the riots as the immediate result of agitators and criminals—a suggestion contradicted by all the evidence accumulated by the riot commission. The police, then, share with the other groups—excepting the black politicians—a tendency to emphasize perceived defects in the black community as an explanation for the difficulties that they encounter in the ghetto.

The state of siege evident in many police departments is but an exaggerated version of a trend in the larger white society. It is the understandable, but unfortunate, response of people who are angry and confused about the wide-spread disruption of traditional racial patterns and who feel threatened by these changes. There is, of course, some basis for this feeling, because the Negro movement poses challenges of power and interest to many groups. To the extent that the movement is successful, the merchants, for example, will either have to reform their practices or go out of business—and for many it may be too late for reform. White suburbanites will have to cough up funds for the city, which provides most of them with employment. Police departments will have to be thoroughly restructured.

The broad social rising of Negroes is beginning to have a substantial effect upon all white institutions in the ghetto, as the situation of the merchants, the schools, and the welfare establishment illustrates. Ten years ago, these institutions (and the police, who have been affected differently) could operate pretty much unchecked by any countervailing power in the ghetto. Today, both their excesses and their inadequacies have run up against an increasingly militant black population, many of whom support violence as a means of redress. The evidence suggests that unless these institutions are transformed, the black community will make it increasingly difficult for them to function at all.

Part V

URBAN DILEMMAS
AND SOLUTIONS:
THE NATURE OF
"URBAN" PROBLEMS
AND STRATEGIES
FOR CHANGE

ONE OF THE MAJOR PERSPECTIVES PRESENTED IN THIS UNIT IS THAT "URBAN' problems originate in nonlocal national circumstances and institutions. As a corollary, we suggest that there is a national character or scope to those disabilities so frequently identified as "urban" problems. Neither in their derivation or location can they be referred to with accuracy as "urban" problems, though some do assume a starker and more visible character in the urban centers. Of greater import is the necessity of understanding that the circumstances of the cities, as well as other communities in American society, reflect—often in an unintended fashion—policies and decisions made elsewhere, both by the private and public sector. Such a comprehension is crucial, particularly when one's attention turns to efforts to change.

In considering the federal and, to some extent, state government, there are many examples of diverse policies, apparently quite removed from contemporary urban dilemmas, which have nonetheless significantly contributed to the appearance of such disabilities. Thus, it is not unreasonable to suggest that federal housing subsidies and the activities of federal and state savings and loan associations have subsidized low-density middle-income living in the suburbs. Hence, these post-World War II housing policies have not only financed the flight of the white population to the suburbs but they have also meant the absence of any adequate programs for multi-dwelling construction within the cities. Some public housing was of course built, but the program was quite inadequate in scope and in many respects poorly carried out. In fact, the policy of locating public housing projects in the inner city has contributed to keeping lower-income people in the city and has strengthened patterns of segregation.

Such patterns have been even more directly strengthened by Federal Housing Authority policy that sanctioned residential segregation for housing built under its programs. The lack of a site selection policy by the Department of Housing and Urban Development for federally assisted housing programs had similar consequences. Urban renewal has further compounded an inadequate housing situation by destroying three times as many homes as it has built. Moreover federal highway policies aided the movement of more privileged population elements out of the city and added to the congestion within the society. This cannot be dissociated from the failure to provide funds for other types of transportation, i.e., intra- and intercity mass transport. These policies also play a part in accounting for the decline of urban tax revenue. Nor can we ignore farm policy which has encouraged mechanization, failed to aid the poor farmer, and helped produce the exodus of many millions ill-equipped for life in the cities that lacked the resources to sustain them. (82)

Conversely, if government policy were altered and enforced with increased funding in the areas of housing, urban renewal, transportation, business subsidies and tax policies, with the employment of minority-group members in the construction industry and the facilitation of minority group business enterprise, this would significantly encourage a number of changes that would have a vital role in resolving what has been

573

referred to as the "urban crisis." These could very likely include an increase in employment, the growth of a minority-group middle-class business sector, altered nonsegregated suburban and urban patterns of residential location, continuance of central city business activities, innovation and construction of public transport systems, and growth of antipollution practices.

Of course, such changes assume the desire and the political will to allocate sufficient resources and to develop policies toward these ends, rather than the ones that permit a freer rein to corporate and business enterprise, profiteering by land speculators, high profits by the construction industry, middle-class ability to secure government-backed funding and tax concessions for single family suburban residence, and the exclusion of minority groups and the less affluent from wide sections of the metropolitan region. The organization, strength, and considerable political effectiveness of special interest groups buttressed by an American ideology that has hampered significant governmental action for a broader public good has seriously compromised such an effort. A major emphasis of this unit is the inability of the market mechanism and local government to resolve the "urban crisis." The need for vigorous federal action and strong constraints where needed is stressed.

The themes and issues developed in the present discussion and in the readings are not limited, of course, to the perspective and analysis just offered. A close relationship, however, is exhibited by some selections. This is especially true for the major focus of concern in this unit—urban dilemmas and solutions related to the ghetto and minority populations, especially those centering around poverty. Hence, the need is stressed for emphasizing action programs developed at a national level.

In other areas we also suggest the significant limitations in strategies of change that is based, for example, on concepts of neighborhood action, community participation, and control, albeit the still valid and useful qualities of such strategies are pointed out. Thus, the need is recognized for community-based protest, political organization, and control in order to stimulate responsive governmental policy or to meet problems of personal estrangement and ineffectiveness. In another direction, the reader will find that our discussion and selections dealing with ghetto disabilities and remedial policy considers the nature, role, and problematic qualities of planning. Special attention is given to distinguishing between physical and social planning and noting the insufficiency of the former. Consideration is also given to the political and administrative fragmentation of metropolitan areas and the further impediments this contributes to effective action by individual urban centers; proposals for reform are suggested and discussed. We also introduce, though with somewhat qualified enthusiasm, the increasingly popular proposal of new town construction, as a means of responding to increased urban growth and creating an attractive residential and community environment. The possible potential application of the new town concept as a means of achieving desegregation is the major positive quality stressed in the selection pertaining to this matter. Throughout much of our comments and in the individual selections runs a criticism of the inadequacies of present programs of amelioration.

*   *   *

In "The Metropolitan Problem" Luther Gulick (39) partially develops two major themes that are dominant elements in our present discussion. He stresses that the "market mechanism" and "local municipal action" are seriously ineffective for attaining adequate physical and social urban properties. Further, they have contributed to some of the urban disabilities. In effect, his discussion provides a brief but effective summary of some of the inadequacies of laissez-faire ideology and practice. Gulick points to the failure of the laissez-faire market mechanism to take into account future needs and patterns of growth, a necessity if coordination is to be achieved among different business sectors. It does not fit isolated individual business enterprise into any broader rationalized plan. Private investment is lacking where a profit cannot be achieved, which means the neglect and underdevelopment of various important but unprofitable individual and community needs. Nor are efforts by local public authorities, Gulick points out, likely to be able to remedy the inadequacies of the private sector. Reflecting the increasing scale of modern society, the scope of "urban" problems extends beyond the boundaries of the community. Furthermore, local communities lack adequate financial resources. With metropolitan fragmentation, they lack even the political resources for effective action.

Gulick's discussion points to the inadequacies of the traditional approach. It also calls attention, though it provides very little elaboration, to the origin of urban disabilities in the functioning of nonlocal national institutions—mass marketing, corporate structures, and ineffectiveness of the national laissez-faire economy. He also introduces our suggestion that the disabilities of the cities are general societal problems, though they may in some respects be especially concentrated within the cities.

While Gulick gives predominant though not exclusive attention to the inability of the untempered market mechanism to meet urban physical needs, we would go much further in suggesting that a host of social disabilities also follow from the laissez-faire, corporate-centered character of the American economy. Reservations in regard to Gulick's treatment also appear necessary in a couple of other regards. He gives little attention to the political basis of policy failure and to political obstacles to effective national action presented by the power of privileged interests.[1] Many of these benefit from policies productive of urban disabilities. Thus, his explanation of such disabilities as a product of spreading urban concentrations is too simple and is even belied by his brief recognition of the role of national institutional structures, though these are not made clear.

The problem of the ghetto and the question of its change is introduced by Warren's essay, "Politics and the Ghetto System" (78). It initially appeared as the opening commentary to a series of items principally concerned with political policy questions

[1]See, for example, Scott Greer (38) for an incisive treatment in the area of urban renewal and housing.

and the dissolution of ghetto problems. Warren focuses on the social system characteristics of the ghetto, the ghetto's relationship to the broader society and that of society to the ghetto, and the consequences these have for the possibilities of change. He makes a useful contribution in his perception of ghetto disabilities as set within a national context, with efforts at change requiring a far-reaching scope. Yet he does not lose sight of the vital stimulus to change that local-based organization and protest can play.

Warren conceptualizes the ghetto as a social system whose institutions are an extension of the broader society and reflect the character of the ghetto's relationship to that society. This social system is conceptualized in terms of five "locality-relevant" functions, production-distribution-consumption, socialization, social control, social participation, and mutual support. These, in effect, assume a character such that they assure the continued dependency and estrangement of the ghetto from the broader society. Our discussion and selections in the previous unit have introduced a number of related concerns. The ghetto thus "constitutes a system whose parts mutually reinforce one another" (78, p. 16). And he notes "the symbiotic reciprocation between ghetto conditions and the surrounding society" (78, p. 16) that reinforces the dependency and ineffectiveness of the ghetto and its population. Among other relevant points he gives brief attention to the domination of ghetto institutions by nonlocal people and external-based institutions. He provides a perceptive discussion of the issue of whether there is a conspiracy to keep blacks in subjection. He considers the absence of neighborhood autonomy and suggests that its importance is qualified in light of the city and even nationwide character of decision-making. From a political perspective these ghetto properties may be perceived as retarding change of ghetto circumstances. Warren suggests, however, that the greatest impetus for change will come from the ghetto itself. This touches on what may be the crucial importance of notions of community control and participation.

In "Social and Physical Planning for the Elimination of Urban Poverty" (32), Herbert Gans gives attention to two major concerns. One is the problem of urban poverty and its elimination. The relative efficacy of physical and social planning is discussed as a fundamental issue in efforts at planned change in this context. While Gans' discussion of urban poverty is within a somewhat restricted scope, it is useful for what it does cover and for a broader effort to which it alludes.

Gans discusses what he calls guided mobility planning. This is essentially an effort to overcome such lower-class cultural and personal styles and disabilities as may impede social and economic mobility. Thus, the focus is on more effective schooling, job training, the development of self-reliance, and the extension of social services. The liberal program of reform and, hence, the content of much of the war on poverty program in the 1960s, as of more traditional social work practice, were essentially of this character. There has been, however, considerable disappointment and growing reservations about the utility of such efforts (54). Our earlier discussion, including the treatment by Gans in "Culture and Class in the Study of Poverty" (29), to which we referred, suggested the limited appropriateness of a strategy that is basically defined in terms of the problem of lower-class life style.[2] It has its principal relevance for the most depressed sectors of the lower class. Such an appropriateness is not to be ignored, of course, but it means that much of the population that is poor and the general problem of poverty and the burden on city services and finances still continues. And the efficacy of such efforts, as we have noted, is somewhat doubtful, especially without any broader and more fundamental changes. In conjunction with these, however, some possibility for movement exists.[3]

Gans does, in fact, go beyond the limited confines of guided mobility planning. He suggests the need for a more far-reaching policy, one that "must be able to affect the economy, the political and social structures that shore up poverty and racial—as well as class—discrimination . . ." (32, p. 637). Regrettably, he does not distinguish between his initial statement of the nature of guided mobility planning and the character of the more far-reaching proposals for institutional change that he offers, tending to treat the latter as aspects of a more adequate guided mobility planning. It seems useful, however, to keep these separate, reserving such planning to refer merely to seeking alterations in the properties of lower-class members and not social structural change. He does, in fact, suggest a number of "changes . . . which require redistribution of power, income, privileges and the alteration of established social roles" (32, p. 637). These include the recommendation for an increase in industrial jobs, continued efforts to combat discrimination, and the management of at least some economic enterprise for social and economic ends, particularly so as to provide increased employment opportunities. He also suggests the alteration of judicial, political, and law enforcement institutions to help minimize lower-class estrangement, heighten integration with society, and increase institutional responsiveness to the poor. Given the importance of these suggestions and their absence from practical political or policy initiatives, it is unfortunate that he offers no elaboration.[4] The following comments attempt a brief but fuller discussion.[5]

[2]The reader may note that Gans seems to suggest a greater degree of lower-class cultural disability and distinctiveness than is expressed in our introductory comments for the preceding section, or in his own later essay, "Culture and Class in the Study of Poverty" (29).

[3]This possibility would be appreciably enhanced where policy is carried out in the context of the local community or neighborhood and through the involvement of the local population. While difficult of achievement, past experience in social change, conditions for personal commitment and personal change, and the character of community redevelopment or revitalization efforts point to its great importance.

[4]However, a somewhat more recent paper, "The City and the Poor" (28), does offer some additional discussion of a few of the suggested policies.

[5]Levitan (52) has outlined in some detail a fairly traditional, yet quite extensive series of programs to aid the poor. Brief but of a somewhat more fundamental nature is Wilbur Cohen's (16) suggestions for increased federal responsibility. For a critical valuation of various antipoverty and social welfare efforts, see Larner and Howe (51). Broad-ranging essays of some interest will be found in the collection by Waxman (79). A political analysis of President Johnson's War on Poverty is provided by Donovan's study (21).

We are in accord with Gans' suggestion that efforts to significantly diminish urban poverty have to involve a program of significant institutional change, both on the local and national level. The importance of action in the economic sphere, especially on the federal level, must be stressed. It is reasonable to suggest that economic factors significantly contribute to urban disabilities, both in terms of the impoverishment of a significant sector of the citizenry and a paucity of community resources. Individual poverty can be perceived as a basic disability of the metropolis, as well as a fundamental cause or contributor to other disabilities. Some attention has already been given to the former concern.

A number of observations can be made, however, about some of the broader consequences of individual poverty. The existence of poverty has greatly impeded residential and educational desegregation and integration. Class factors have at times been as consequential as that of race. Certainly a significant proportion of urban problems, particularly financial ones, stem from the existence of considerable poverty populations. Heavy welfare costs and other local governmental services reflect such populations and also contribute to other problems and costs. These include higher rates of crime and drug addiction, with the concomitant high social and financial burden. To some extent even business and middle-class suburban movement, with a consequent tax loss, reflect a social, physical, and financial decline of the cities, to which the existence of poverty populations contribute. Educational problems, delinquency, corruption, and political conflict in varying degrees reflect the presence of sizable poverty populations.

The circumstances of the disadvantaged, which go beyond merely low income, are due to a number of institutional factors. One, of course, is the unavailability of adequately remunerative employment. This reflects the nature of industrial change and growth, the nature and distribution of private investment and governmental programs, the character of changing occupational levels, and assumptions about needed skill levels. However, the plight of the poor, especially the minority group poor, also stems from discrimination. This has been especially true in the area of housing.[6] Of course, there are many urban problems, partly of an economic character, that are not meaningfully related to the existence of individual poverty. Some of these would include, for instance, the ability to finance the construction and operation of efficient and economic transportation, effective pollution control, the disposal of a growing amount of garbage and trash, the provision of adequate educational programs, and the availability of proper health facilities. However, were the burdens stemming from the costs of individual poverty eliminated, other costly needs could at least be better met.

A program addressed to the economic basis of city problems in individual poverty must be formulated both at the level of the citizen and the community. Gunnar

[6]For many years even the federal housing agencies encouraged residential segregation.

Myrdal, for instance, has vigorously urged a two-pronged economic policy directed toward improving the economic circumstances of the individual. In his "National Planning for Health Cities: Two Challenges to Affluence" (56), he recommends programs at the family as well as community and national level. The former would provide some form of guaranteed family income or income maintenance, as well as job training. The latter would focus on achieving an increased rate of economic growth—crucial for attaining increasing employment opportunities. "The greatest single factor that could improve the quality of urban life . . . would be an increase in the scarcity of labor . . . scarcity of labor promises in time to change the whole climate in which poor people live. Only a full-employment economy is a healthy society." Further, more rapid economic growth would increase tax yields and with higher incomes perhaps increase the willingness to shoulder higher tax rates.

An effective program for significantly diminishing poverty (or other urban disabilities) must be a national one. This partly follows from the basis of poverty and other urban problems in the functioning of national institutions. Thus, only federal policy, given the national reach of its policy and the power at its disposal, can reasonably be expected to have any hope of success in reducing unemployment and raising wages and incomes. This could be accomplished, for instance, by regulating the character of industrial expansion, plant location, and job creation, developing income maintenance programs, and developing programs likely to offer opportunities for employment, such as large-scale housing or environmental preservation programs. If such efforts are not sufficient to the task and government revenues are inadequate to supplement these deficiencies, then even more basic alteration of national priorities and use of public and private resources may be needed. At that point an even more fundamental role would have to be assumed by the federal government.[7] Action at the national level will also be more likely to enforce uniform standards, provide for greater intercommunity coordination, the enlargement of administrative units, and a more rationalized policy and functioning. In another direction, the ability to develop and execute an adequate program is considerably greater at the national level. The

---

[7]Thus, the argument can be made that (a) even full employment and an expanding economy may still leave conditions of poverty widespread, as well as adequate efforts at confronting other urban problems severely underfinanced. (b) And that government resources might be insufficient to provide directly either adequate income maintenance or aid for adequately resolving other problems, such as improved transportation, adequate public facilities and social services, pollution control and housing. If such a somber prospect is accepted (see 69), then a much more fundamental alteration of private resource allocation becomes essential. This could take the direction, for example, of abandoning a great deal of automobile and ancillary production (or wastage, depending on one's point of view), mass production and merchandizing of needless or redundant goods, and shifting the vast manpower, wealth, and material goods consumed in such frivolous and even societally suicidal areas into meeting more consequential human, community, and social needs. Clearly, the development and execution of a program at this level can only be envisioned under the principal aegis of the national government.

more conservative and provincial attitudes that prevail at the local level are more likely to block or seriously qualify any effective program. Vested interests are also more likely to be able to frustrate ameliorative policy at the local level. Conversely, the general public or broader publics within the society can marshal political resources at the national level (see 67).

It is not only in regard to the phenomenon of poverty, however, where a need exists for federal involvement. The national government has a crucial role to play in achieving such ends as adequate mass transportation, control over pollution, and the raising of environmental standards—all the way from industrial and car pollutants to constraining airplane noise, providing adequate and reasonably priced housing, and achieving economical and modern health facilities. The importance of federal action is partly accounted for by the factors noted just previously. However, the distinctive properties of the preceding areas of need reinforce the necessity for a high degree of involvement and responsibility on the federal level. Thus, one or more of the following is present in these areas: an intercity and interregional character, close interrelationship with other institutional areas, far-reaching ramifications and consequences of activities and decisions in any one sphere, complex and costly technological properties or processes, and nonlocal decision-making. Federal policy would appear to be the only level for effective public efforts to achieve integrated and rationalized policy on the development and location of facilities and services. It would encourage needed research and technological developments, the alteration and modernization of industrial processes, and the modification of market-based determinations in regard to the style and form, as well as conditions of development, availability, and production of some physical goods, such as housing, means of transportation, or land modes of functioning adjusted to social and other community needs.

The criticism of the traditional city planning approach is the second major concern of Gans' essay. He suggests that such an approach assumes that an alteration of the physical environment will effect social change. In part, his criticism is an argument against concentrating on neighborhood planning, zoning, and building construction until more basic problems and determinants of poverty and estrangement of a social, economic, and political nature are resolved. Thus, part of Gans' discomfort with reliance on physical planning rests on the sound principle that economic, social, and family disabilities have a social origin; and only an effort directly focused on causal properties can be soundly effective. From a closely related perspective he also criticizes physical planning where it focuses, as it usually does, on altering local neighborhood circumstances. He points out that "important aspects of life take place within the family, personal group, and on the job, and the neighborhood does not seem to affect these greatly" (32, p. 638). Actually, Gans rejects the dichotomy between physical and social planning, contending that it reflects the stress on methods rather than goals. Whether a planning activity is viewed as of a physical or social nature depends on the perspective used. If one is essentially concerned with the goals of any planning effort, then he suggests both types of factors or methods be utilized in an integrated fashion.[8]

It is not practical to pursue further the very brief introduction to the nature and uses of planning provided by Gans' selection. Reference can only be made to some of the principal concerns and problems in the area of planning. The question of what particular goals and purposes are established and by whom, whose goals are to be realized, and what are the order of priorities and the distribution of costs and gains is certainly an important one. Related is the issue of for whom does the planner work and to whom is he responsible. This is, of course, inseparable from the issue of being able to define what constitutes the public interest and the place of distinctive groups and interests within it. There is also the practical question, which at times assumes an ideological or value-laden character, of how diverse groups and interests can be involved in the development and execution of a plan in a representative fashion. One of the problems is how to evaluate the consequences of planning. While apparently obvious in some respects, it is in many instances a complex and not readily resolvable issue, principally because of possible unintended side effects or a certain indeterminance as to what might have transpired in the absence of such a plan. The often difficult estimate of the financial, social, cultural, political costs and gains, the groups advantaged and disadvantaged, and the alternative use of resources are other problems that compound the issue.[9]

Other types of problems are also present. Regardless of the type of planning involved or the nature of the resolution reached among diverse interests and community needs, the bases for serious differences remain. Both in the abstract as well as the particular case there is the question of how sufficient our factual basis of information and knowledge should be before proceeding to develop and execute a plan. Even if some agreement can be reached on the nature of the allocation of values, there is still considerable room for difference over the scope and comprehensiveness of any particular planning effort. Considerable attention could be given to the problem of effectuating plan objectives and yet minimizing the development of oppressive governmental bureaucracies and constraints. Involved, in part, is how to achieve broader

[8]Note could be taken of the fact, however, that we are increasingly beginning to recognize the need for some qualification of the contention that "so-called physical planning questions are receding in importance, and socio-economic and political ones are becoming more relevant" (32, p. 643)—given the growing concern with the quality of the environment. Of course, these also become socio-economic and political concerns at a very basic level.

[9]A fuller elaboration of the planning process would in some important respects require exploring the relationship and the similarities and differences in emphasis, techniques, procedures, and problems between city planning, national planning, and planning directed toward resolving urban problems. Our earlier discussion would suggest that an adequate attempt at the latter cannot be secured without attention to efforts at both the national as well as individual community level, especially the former. There exists today a lack of both theoretical and practical integration between these analytically distinct spheres.

societal and individual goals through the involvement of the local community and
individual citizenry. Certainly, there are also decisions, whether overt or not, that are
made and are often a source of contention in regard to the degree of governmental
involvement, the extent of centralization-decentralization procedures in the initial
planning and execution process, the degree of citizen and group participation, the
range and type of areas left for unrestrained developed and individual behavior, and
the degree of individual liberty and choice and its preservation against limitations by
private corporate structures or public pressures. The theoretical and practical issues
here are deserving of considerable treatment. The reader wishing to turn to discussions
of some of these or the preceding questions can consult a large and varied literature
(5, 19, 20, 22, 28, 30, 31, 55, 59, 60, 61, 65, 68, 74, 80, 84).

A broad discussion of planning, in terms of both the theory of planning and the
practical aspects of its application, would have to explore the constraints to effective
planning (including its execution), be they political, ideological, or administrative or
resource insufficiencies. Related and of particular interest is the relationship between
social values and institutional structures, on the one hand, and the type of planning
and goals developed and the ability of their execution on the other. As the reader may
well perceive, this has especial relevance for the United States, given its anti-statism
and laissez-faire ideology, antipathy to the idea of planning for social or public purposes, an extremely strong corporate structure and strategically placed upper class,
the fragmentation of public power, and the lack (somewhat diminished recently) of
well-developed publics reflective of the broader public interest. A fuller discussion
would have to develop the character of the kind of impediments that these ideological
and structural conditions pose for effective planning in the United States.

The Aronowitz (7) and Committee for Economic Development (17) selections
consider some suggested solutions to problems of effective government in urban
areas, including the relationship of the individual citizen to political and institutional
decision-making. Both the problems and proposed solutions are of consequence for
a number of other concerns. While these items focus on problems of government,
they do so from quite different perspectives. Aronowitz considers, in effect, a suggested form of citizen control that has appeared as a response to growing pressure
for local-based control (especially from minority groups) and for the diminution of
estrangement. The more comprehensive statement by the Committee for Economic
Development, under the direction of Alan Campbell, focuses principally on the problems of effective government for growing metropolitan areas, giving some attention
to the local level. While the Aronowitz piece appears guided by a concern for
increasing the ability of particular population groups to maximize their interest needs,
Campbell focuses on the city and the region's need for greater governmental effectiveness. The latter statement, focusing on the need for governmental effectiveness in an
administrative and politically fragmented region, stresses the possible usefulness of
alterations in the governmental system. The selection by Aronowitz, concerned with

the disabilities of a particular population in the spheres of political and economic power, does not interpret local-level changes in governmental structures as significantly altering such disabilities, since these depend fundamentally on the nationwide institutional apparatus. Aronowitz favors local control, but in most regards he sees its value as sharply limited. The CED statement accepts community control as desirable, but approaches it within the broader framework of the needs of urban regions for greater effectiveness. While both selections deal with frequently proposed changes, in important ways the type of problems they are concerned with are quite different, as is the level of analysis.

The increasing focus on community control reflects a number of relatively contemporary concerns and phenomena. In part, it is certainly a response to the ineffectiveness and unresponsiveness of existing political and governmental institutions at a time of heightened group consciousness, declining legitimacy of traditional authority, and increasing discomfort for many sectors of the population. In a related sense it also appears to reflect a need for affirmation of group dignity and individual "rights," particularly in a period of growing estrangement.

The stress on decentralization and community control is relevant. Thus, in an important sense it is an expression of an amorphous movement of increasing strength and importance that is directed toward enhancing the individual's control over his environment, not merely the local community, but whatever may be the locale or type of his institutional involvement. It may also be perceived, in one sense, as part of a general movement against what is sometimes too loosely labeled as mass society. More particularly it may be a response to the decline of publics in Mills' sense (54, pp. 302–304), the declining autonomy of various sectors of society, and the increasingly impersonal nature of government.

While to a small extent the stress on community control may be no more than a cathartic gesture, it seeks to secure more responsive policy from existing institutions and their personnel, particularly local-based ones. The present emphasis on community control would also appear partly to reflect the stimulus provided by the stress in the recent "war on poverty" on participation by the local community and its population in various community projects, planning, and action agencies. The reader will recall the selection by Van Til and Van Til in this respect. In practice the emphasis on community control as a movement is characterized by a variety of possible objectives and functions, ranging from the development of group consciousness and local leadership to the more publicly and frequently voiced demand for greater institutional responsiveness.

The reader should perhaps be cautioned against perceiving the concepts of community control and decentralization as having identical referents, since this is not always the case. Where community control involves citizen participation, particularly within a local or neighborhood framework, then there is likely to be a situation of institutional decentralization. The latter, however, need not involve the notion of citizen participation, as functions can be decentralized or dispersed without any greater citizen input or involvement.[10]

The essay by Aronowitz is principally addressed to only one issue in the area of community control and decentralization. However, it is an important one and provides a more explicit and extended focus on a theme struck both in Warren's discussion of neighborhood autonomy (78) and Gans' consideration of the appropriateness of focusing on the neighborhood (32). The inclusion of this selection also provides the opportunity to consider a number of the questions involved in these areas not covered by Aronowitz.

Aronowitz is essentially concerned with community control as a strategy for improving the circumstances of the ghetto, though he sees it as a too narrow and ineffective approach. Thus, he writes that the "political and economic thrust of the demand (for community control) . . . does not challenge the present means of allocating resources among various elements of the political economy. To a large degree, the emphasis on community control has turned black politics away from issues of national power and thus, in part, represents a step backwards" (7, p. 48). Most fundamentally, the prevailing impetus toward community control is interpreted as lacking an adequate conception of power, especially in its nationwide institutional character. Thus, he feels that it never comes to grips with the involvement of the ghetto and ghetto conditions in national economic structures. It does not, therefore, respond to the obstacles that really hinder improvement at the community level. And it is an approach inadequate for achieving even the somewhat limited objectives that Aronowitz enumerates as its aims.

Aronowitz also notes the fragmented character of the many community control efforts and the absence of broader alliances. He also notes that efforts for community control have lacked interracial and interclass cooperation. They have even heightened conflict, particularly where ghetto efforts for increased services means increased costs and taxes. While these conflicts are presumably not inherent in community control, under some circumstances they can readily surface. He does recognize, however, that some areas, notably that of health services, lend themselves to serving as links between classes and races.

While Aronowitz suggests several related positive features of community control, he offers little elaboration. The positive qualities to which he refers, the challenge to centralized bureaucracies and to indirect forms of government, have their greatest relevance to issues quite removed from that of the ghetto, urban poverty, and urban problems. They relate to changing the nature of the polity and the individual's place

[10]Increased citizen participation need not, of course, involve decentralization, though it would be facilitated by a dispersion of functions and authority. Where such participation takes place within smaller community or institutional units that were lacking earlier, then there has been a phenomenon of decentralization.

in it. Though the importance of this aspect of community control may be granted, as well as the major thrust of Aronowitz's criticism, other positive qualities should be noted. These may have an important bearing, directly and otherwise, on the disabilities suffered by local communities and ghetto populations.[11]

Many positive and significant consequences may be realized from community control. This is particularly true where control also involves the phenomenon of citizen participation.[12] The most readily voiced aim is that of attaining responsive policy and functioning, both by the private and public sector, by political actors, institutions, organizations, and professional associations. Involved here is the hope of more effective action on community problems, of the increased relevance of both policy and local-based institutions and actors to community needs. A major element is the attempt to have an impact on the functioning of the various human service institutions personnel, in areas such as education, health, social service, and welfare. An important purpose is securing the accountability to consumer and community of the institutions and personnel that exist in or deal with the local neighborhood. At the root is minimizing the manipulability of the local population by either public or private actors and institutions, regaining control by a citizenry over its own environment, and creating more effective and suitable policies and functioning. Part of the changes envisioned would mean a diminution in the rigidity, unimaginativeness, and stultifying nature of the large-scale bureaucratic enterprises that affect the community.

Of a different character is the possible effect on the community and individual that can, in some instances, be derived from community control, particularly where this involves increased citizen participation. The most effective community action and change develops in circumstances where there has been intimate and ongoing involvement by the community in all stages of community-based programs. A community must recognize its own problems, define its own goals, and establish the appropriate means, otherwise these exist in a condition of externality (17, 34, 71, 75, 77). For the individual community member a condition of community viability and individual involvement may be a means of overcoming apathy, hopelessness, and the demoralizing effects of impotence and frustration. It is a means of heightening a sense of individual dignity and raises the possibility of individual personal growth and the

[11]For a perceptive discussion of neighborhood autonomy the reader should see the brief treatment in Warren's selection. It elaborates some of the points noted in the following and also offers some discussion of other relevant considerations. The earlier selection by Van Til and Van Til, it will be recalled, provided a politically attuned conceptual analysis of the concept of citizen participation, introducing a number of basic considerations present in the broader issue of community control.

[12]For a wide-ranging, informed, and balanced analysis of the concept and practice of community control, see Altshuler (5). For some discussions ranging over a wide series of issues and processes, especially the question of the implication of the individual in processes of community development and change, see such items as 3, 8, 17, 34, 71, 72. See Spiegel (72) for a specific focus on citizen participation and for various bibliographic references in this regard.

development of skills and competence (17, pp. 301–308; 33, ch 9; 40). It is within the context of community control efforts that successful job training programs seem most practical, especially efforts to develop various human service workers or para-professionals.

Local community control and participation would seem to have considerable political import. It is helpful in developing leadership among disadvantaged and minority populations. It can be useful for developing political organization, creating a constituency and an organizational network; in effect, laying the foundation for reaching beyond the community to broader issues and populations and nationwide political efforts. Thus, while a major criticism of a focus on community control, a justifiable one, is its avoidance of the broader national basis of local community disabilities, in many instances the means for developing the ability to deal effectively with such exterior factors can in part involve beginning at the local community level. This need not be an exclusive strategy, but a vital part of a broader effort.

There are a number of constraints or obstacles to the achievement of the positive consequences that can come from community control. The extent to which these are present and how they are overcome will determine whether the potentials of community control will be realized. One important determinant is the extent to which community control takes place under circumstances where there is considerably increased citizen participation in those spheres where the local neighborhood now has increased responsibility. While the absence of such increased participation does not deny all positive consequences from community control, it does considerably diminish them. Other determinants of the outcome of community control are—the degree to which local elements can cooperate, the extent to which an effective coalition can be established between newly emerging elements and the older established organizations and power groups within and without the community, the extent to which political authorities and other organized interest groups (for example, the trade unions and professional associations) exhibit a hostile or cooperative stance, the degree of authority available to the local community in those spheres where it undertakes greater management, the amount of resources possessed by the local community (financial, political, and organizational), and the degree to which local efforts do not transgress prevailing political, economic, and ethical standards and do not endanger existing centers of power and the corporate, business, political, union, and professional actors involved therein.

Clearly, such possible constraints on the effectiveness of community control may not make one very sanguine. What is important is that these efforts at community control become part of a national program of revitalization, of a broad-ranging effort at action on political, social, and economic problems. The many issues, concentrations of power, and lack of acceptance that may undermine local government and citizen participation should be subjected to national debate and to national efforts at change. Obviously, this is a comprehensive undertaking involving much more organization, planning, and potential opposition than a program of community control handled at the local level and detached from any broader considerations or efforts. The latter is the easy response to pressures for change and more responsible government but would appear to be an approach doomed to confusion, disappointment, and, perhaps, even greater frustration and alienation. It should be noted that efforts at community control approached in a more comprehensive national framework would of necessity begin to meet the kind of objections that Aronowitz poses and the kind of needs which he sees as lacking in a concentration on community control alone.

As with most public questions and certainly in regard to issues of governance, the establishment of community control programs must resolve a diverse number of problems and issues. There is the need of arriving at some equitable determination of who constitutes the community and who represents it. For instance, what voice should be had by employed professionals, local businessmen, and others nonresident in the community? Do different minority elements secure some guaranteed representation, or does the majority rule? As in any society, but perhaps especially within the local community, the question of the definition and preservation of the rights and freedoms of minorities is especially important. Thus, the greater authority and freedom for community control also carries a danger of repression of those not in accord with community purposes. Another problem is the extent that it is appropriate for the society—or the local community—to constrain or define appropriate functioning of the personnel working in that community, such as medical, educational, social service workers, and businessmen. In some terms this may not pose too great an issue, general agreement on the preservation of individual civil liberties or the freedom to apply one's expertise, for example. The manner in which these definitions are applied, however, is open to considerable difference of opinion and grounds for considerable acrimony.

Of quite a different character is the problem of securing participation at the local community level from a generally apathetic and estranged population. As noted earlier, the general milieu and circumstances of the poor work against community organizational involvement. In a related direction, there is the potential devolution of power to the major community actors or organizational staff. There is also the need to minimize the not uncommon phenomenon of factionalism and infighting among local groups and attempts at self-aggrandizement. Community control may also produce an increased degree of narrowness and provincialism. Further, where increased participation is sought and attained, it may initially diminish the delivery and quality of local services, though the general atmosphere or context within which it is provided may be of a more "positive" character.

According to Aronowitz the attention to efforts at securing community control may shift energies and attention away from a focus on the major source of population disabilities and the locale of effective remedial policy. In effect, attention may be diverted from central decision-making points or institutions where the major allocation of resources and basic policy is established.

Another fundamental question, particularly from a broader societal perspective, is what type of activities can appropriately be decentralized for community control and participation. This involves a determination of the extent to which the broader society and populations within it are affected by the decisions made within the particular community, and if they are, the degree to which they can justifiably seek to shape that decision. Some institutional spheres are, of course, more clearly imbedded in a society-wide framework than others, transportation networks, for example. Yet, even in regard to the latter it could be argued with some justification that a society might reasonably impose on all its members certain standards of student achievement and areas of competence. And conversely, in regard to transportation networks, it can well be contended that a local area should be able to control some aspects of the local area operation and management of the transport in question and at least have some influence, even if not final determination, over the location and development of a transportation network.

These difficulties rest on the fact that society is a complex interrelated network of activities, with a high degree of integration; i.e., what happens or does not happen at one point carries considerable consequences for other points and populations within that society. At such points there arise difficult questions of what can appropriately be the scope of local authority. These difficulties, among others, are not suggested to deny the considerable merit of both decentralization and increased community control. The deficiencies of the present order of things are striking enough to suggest the usefulness of change. It is also possible to alleviate some of the problems in the sphere of community control. It should be possible to establish some viable division of tasks and authority between the local area and the broader society and some preservation of the autonomy and liberties of the individual while community needs are pursued.

There has been an increasing recognition of the need to adapt metropolitan and community governmental forms to the fact of rapid urban growth. Concomitant with such growth there has been a rise of public services, an overlap and duplication of facilities and services, a dispersion of population and facilities, a shrinking tax base, the growth of independent municipalities and special districts (9, 60), and generally increased economic and social interdependence under conditions of sharp political and administrative fragmentation. Thus, some form of metropolitan federation or government has been envisioned as a means of achieving more unified and coordinated policy, administration, and planning and extending the areas of tax jurisdiction to match governmental service boundaries. This would provide the basis for more effective action to meet the problems of the metropolis.[13] While most communities

[13]The literature on reforming the nature of government in metropolitan areas is extensive. Several representative items affording a wide coverage of issues and topics include 1, 2, 26, 35, 37, 42, 44, 48, 63, 66. For a useful and far-ranging summary review of the question of metropolitan governmental reform, see Bollens and Schmandt (10).

have rejected various forms of metropolitan federation or government, a few have accepted it in relatively recent years (36, 42, 43, 49, 70).

"Reshaping Government in Metropolitan Areas" (14, 15) interprets governmental reform as a significant basis for initiating efforts at beginning to resolve metropolitan problems in such areas as education, welfare, crime, housing, and transportation. It suggests that a new structure of metropolitan and community government will provide for a more adequate and equitable distribution of resources, permit increased efficiency in resource utilization, and allow for more rationally planned and coordinated administration and efforts at change. While stressing the need for more comprehensive and less fragmented political units with increased authority, the CED statement also recognizes the pressure for decentralization and the gain in community identity and vitality that the existence of such local units may make possible.[14]

The selection reprinted here is the introduction and summary of recommendations of a longer statement prepared by the Research and Policy Committee of the Committee for Economic Development. A forceful document, it builds on and responds to the considerable proposals, criticisms, and strong passions that have developed in recent years on the general issue of governance and control, more particularly, in regard to questions of metropolitical government or federation, decentralization, and community control. Recognizing the merits of both centralized and decentralized government, it has sought to combine the advantages of both, rather than submerge one within the other. It proposes utilizing the larger metropolitan unit as the arena for handling those functions that require area-wide planning and that benefit from economies of scale. Highly interdependent activities whose execution at the local level have significant consequences for the entire region require area-wide government. Other functions and activities, such as garbage collection, neighborhood-oriented programs, and some aspects of urban renewal and police activity could, it suggests, be left for community determination. However, the "emphasis is on the *sharing of power and responsibility* and not on the assignment of entire functions to either level" (14, p. 56). The constituent element of community-level government is seen as the "community district." In the suburbs this is usually the already political and administratively defined suburban municipality. Within the central city it refers to those subsections of the city that more or less constitute neighborhood communities. To diminish the bargaining over parochial interests, representation on area-wide governing councils would be by legislative district and not by community. The effort throughout the policy statement is on securing the advantages of regional government, yet maintaining the virtues of local decentralized units.

The proposal is a commendable effort, and many students of urban affairs would urge the importance of effecting the reforms proposed. A wide-ranging assessment of

---

[14]The reader may recall that the selection by Gulick briefly considered the insufficiencies of local governments.

such an approach, however, would require recognition of a number of factors. To an important degree the source of urban problems rests on the policies and inactions exhibited at the national level and reflects functioning of public and private institutions of a nationwide character. These are not readily influenced by local governmental reform. This also means that inadequacies in the structure of metropolitan government are not at the root of what are referred to as urban problems. However, this should not obscure the possibility of some alleviation of disabilities through action at the local level, including governmental reform. As the preceding reservation may suggest, though, even the "best" administrative arrangements do not assure that adequate policy will even be formulated, sufficient resources sought, or retrogressive interests overcome.[15] On the level of the plan itself, a not easily resolved difficulty resides in the effort to maintain conditions of both centralization and decentralization through an allocation and sharing of functions. The likelihood of an ongoing and sometimes acrimonious tension seems deeply rooted. Exception can also be taken to the nature of the allocation of functions between the metropolitan and community levels sketched in later portions of the statement. A number of serious difficulties also exist, not surprisingly, on the level of achieving the proposed governmental reforms and in their proper administration. Where metropolitan areas cross state boundaries, the very difficult problem arises of securing effective interstate government and state cooperation. Other political obstacles include minority group opposition to metropolitan federation or government because of its potential weakening of the growing black strength in the central city, the aversion of suburban communities to sharing responsibilities and authority with the central city, and the hesitancy of many communities to bind themselves to decisions of an area-wide agency.

The value of governmental reform for metropolitan areas might be increased and the possibility of its attainment furthered were it part of a more comprehensive national program of change and action addressed to urban disabilities. It would then be one of several coordinated means of altering the conditions that have produced what has been called the "urban crisis." Such an effort could also use the leverage of federal grants to secure the cooperation of communities in metropolitan governmental reform (64).

A popular solution to urban disabilities and the problem of rapid urban growth, particularly among some planners and social visionaries, has been the new town concept. Rather than directly confronting the problems frequently associated with the city, the thrust of the new town movement has been to build new communities, ones without the drawbacks of the present cities. This is to be achieved through an overall comprehensive plan embodying those physical and social qualities that the unplanned

[15]It has also been noted that the establishment of a central governmental authority for a metropolitan area does not guarantee effective administration. See Feldman and Jassy's earlier and hence tentative study of Dade County, Florida (26).

growth of our urban centers have lacked or seriously qualified. These are intended as self-sufficient communities where the diverse range of human needs and group life can be attained (11, 24, 33, 57, 73). The ideal of a socially and economically hetero-geneous community is often held out (14, p. 55).

This is a movement that had its earliest developed statement in Ebenezer Howard's *Garden Cities of Tomorrow* (47) and a decade later, in the early years of the twentieth century, was introduced to the United States in Patrick Geddes' *Cities in Evolution* (33). Lewis Mumford, Clarence Stein, and Catherine Bauer, among others, vigorously continued this early tradition.[16] Great Britain first sought to carry out Ebenezer Howard's ideas in the early twentieth century. Somewhat later a number of efforts were initiated in the United States (73). The best known were probably Radburn, New Jersey and the federal initiated greenbelt communities. Since the Second World War, the continental nations and Great Britain witnessed large-scale cen-trally initiated public efforts to create a large number of new towns to control the form of urban growth and to house an increasingly urban population. In the United States private developers have been very actvie (24). The most ambitious and best known of these latter efforts are Columbia (11) and Reston, in the Baltimore-Washington, D.C. metropolitan area (24).

Some of the philosophical impetus for the new town movement in the United States has come from a historical and cultural anti-urban bias, one that rejects the possibility of achieving the "good" life within the large urban center (57, 73). For the most part, however, the new towns have appeared and been proposed more pro-grammatically as an opportunity for starting from scratch in the effort to create a planned community and environment where the disadvantages of the urban com-munities can be avoided with a properly designed and planned community.

Several major advantages are imputed to these new towns, based in varying degrees on the assumptions of physical or environmental determinism and the virtues of a comprehensive centrally planned development. To an important extent the positive qualities presumably maximized with new towns are seen as the obverse of the negative properties of the central city. The new towns are perceived as a means of creating a socially and personally supportive and wholesome environment. Proper physical design, it is held, can reduce impersonality and increase the opportunities for

---

[16]Planned communities or new towns have in a general sense an ancient heritage, evidenced in the establishment of numerous communities in the Mediterranean basin through colonization efforts made to settle the surplus population of the societies of that area, two to three-and-a-half thousand years ago. Somewhat similar efforts characterized the growth of cities somewhat later on the European continent. More recent examples in America can be found in the early New England states and the experience of settlement consequent with the expansion of the western frontier, as well as in the early growth of a number of eastern and northwestern American cities. These are not examples, however, of a response to an aversion to the existing characteristics or qualities of the cities or urban life.

social contacts and shared everyday experiences. A physically and socially varied community, with a range of diverse activities or pursuits, is envisioned. The full range of man's economic, educational, social, cultural, and leisure needs are to be served, in an environment so ordered as to raise the quality of individual and group life. This includes a setting where nature is respected and the positive qualities of the urban and rural community are accessible in a distinctive blend. Also stressed is increased convenience and safety. Services and employment opportunities are to be present in the community, and physical and social congestion and traffic patterns are to be minimized. Also, it is suggested that planned rather than helter-skelter growth, carried out within an overall scheme and with at least minimally attractive standards, should heighten the aesthetic beauty, general attractiveness and human quality of the community. Properties of blight, decay, and pollution are to be sharply reduced (39, p. 376).

These are not the only qualities, however, that lie behind the new town urge. Current suggestions for the development of new towns are generally propounded within the context of an expected increase in the American urban population of several tens of million by the end of the century. The not unreasonable contention is that if past patterns were to prevail such growth would be encompassed within a gigantic and disastrous expansion of urban and suburban sprawl around and beyond many of our present cities and suburban centers. It would assume various forms— low-density contiguous growth, ribbon development along transportation axes, or a discontinuous patchwork or "leapfrog" sprawl (16, p. 219). Uncoordinated, lacking a planned and rationally timed conversion of land usage, guided by market considerations in an individual laissez-faire quest for profit, and carried out within the framework of the urge for individual home ownership and the transportation grid, the consequences of such growth may be various. There is the danger of irreparable destruction of the countryside, the creation of costly, wasteful, and inefficient utility services and transportation networks, the appearance of insufficient and not too accessible public and private services, the creation of a monotonous and unattractive physical and social environment with little exhilaration and too few of the qualities needed by diverse ages and population elements, and the development of communities lacking housing or open to the minority or less affluent sectors of the society. It has been contended, with some justification but considerable exaggeration that "the last vestiges of a community have disappeared" (23, p. 7).

Other properties of the litany of criticism of unplanned urban growth could be enumerated, but these should suffice. In contrast to the consequences of uncontrolled urban sprawl, an extensive nationwide program of new towns is seen as making possible more rational land usage with a possible conservation of land, retention of more open space, and the continued availability of land for varied nonresidential and nonbusiness usage. A more aesthetic and socially nurturant environment could be shaped. In addition such a program is visualized as likely to provide more convenient and efficient transportation, a more economic and effective placement and coordination of utilities (27), and greater availability and diversity of facilities and services. Growth would be channeled and shaped so as to serve man and his needs.

These are significant and worthy purposes toward which new towns aim and to some extent they are realizable. Yet, without wishing to disparage the preceding, some important exceptions and constraints should be noted. The new town expression partly reflects an animus toward the city that distorts the nature of the urban environment and how it is experienced. Secondly, the new town concept minimizes or ignores qualities of tradition, neighborhood distinctiveness, a certain ineffable vitality, and the openness and flexibility for adjustment, change, and new directions for growth evidenced by many of the larger metropolitan centers. These find little place in the prepackaged new towns. Little recognition is given to the obstacles to such qualities in the new towns or to the question of the adequacy of fit between the preplanned community and changing population and human needs.

The new town movement exaggerates the potentials of the new town, minimizes the difficulty of their attainment, and ignores the changes that aging, shifting population, pressures of growth, and surrounding environmental alteration may bring to such new communities. There is also the conundrum that a comprehensively planned community requires retention of significant decision-making authority within the hands of the planners, in the face of a growing community population with rising demands for significant involvement in community government and planning. The means of sharing or transferring control from planners to residents in a responsive fashion is not easily determined. Nor is it clear how the resident's contributions to the establishment of the nature and structure of the community is to be attained, when its form is essentially determined before the community population has materialized (4, 12). These comments leave aside the considerable technical problems of land acquisition, financing, economic viability, and consumer demand that are major obstacles to new town development.[17] While the problems present in urban sprawl are serious and of considerable magnitude, other options or programs than that of new towns are available. Unfortunately, the probability of such programs being adapted is still slight.

Weissbourd and Channick (82) vigorously stress a possible application of a new town program that is of a quite different character than the possible advantages cited previously. They urge a policy of encouraging new town construction as a means of providing homes for minority-group populations now trapped in the central city. This would, they suggest, advance the development of desegregated communities and facilities and afford an opportunity for residence closer to areas of growing employ-

[17]Federal legislation in 1966, further extended in 1968 and 1970, has provided some financial support for new towns. However, this is far from resolving the technical, economic, and political problems involved. See the discussion in Eichler and Kaplan (24).

ment. They desire the creation of a situation where the poor and minority-group populations will be free to settle where they wish. In this regard they propose a program of securing a proportion of blacks in the suburbs equal to that for the metropolitan area as a whole. This is to be achieved through a program involving the construction of 350,000 housing units a year within new towns, with the provision of rent supplements or other aid where necessary, to secure residence by poor blacks. The construction of new towns could be successfully encouraged, they suggest, by withdrawing present federal subsidies from suburban developments and high-income residences in the cities and providing it only for appropriately sited new towns. They would do the same for public support for roads and transport construction.

These projects would require minimal federal regulation or financing other than the rechanneling of present federal subsidies, so as to encourage concentrated efforts at new town construction with a portion of the homes available to blacks and low-income whites. With such a program, and the consequent movement of both blacks and whites out of the central city, they point out, vacancies would be created in urban residential neighborhoods. These could then be available for black occupancy and thus further speed the destruction of segregated ghetto areas.

Their proposal is a bold effort to meet one of the most vexatious and fundamental problems in American society, one that has proved extremely difficult to resolve with the traditional palliatives tried to date. Yet, their essay is open to a number of serious criticisms and qualifications. Without a more comprehensive program and supportive public authority and planning, significant questions exist as to the adequacy of available means for the successful establishment of new towns, nor can the existence of employment opportunities and a sound economic base be assumed for these towns or their populations. Further, in regard to these quite important details and mechanisms, a strategy of merely five years duration can scarcely be viewed as sufficient. The time to build a new town, not to speak of a national effort of the present scope is considerably longer. Their discussion may also be overly optimistic on the ease of achieving nonsegregated new town communities. To date this has been far from the case, with very few minority-group members being resident in such communities. While this undoubtedly will increase with rent supplements, there is no assurance that blacks or other minorities would readily move to communities where they will be a preponderant minority, nor that a reappearance of segregation patterns may not develop in new towns.[18]

It could be reasonably questioned whether federal efforts and funding should be channeled to only one type of settlement, housing, and community development program. Could the vast amount of resources that would of necessity be committed

[18]It does appear true, however, that starting with an integrated community, particularly if at a common economic class level, will appreciably raise the likelihood of the continuance of generally integrated circumstances.

to new towns be more usefully applied to other types of response to urban growth
and revitalization and the resolution of the problem of segregation and related social
ills? In a related direction, their suggested program appears to involve a partial abandonment and turning away from the central city. Some question could be raised as
to the desirability and cost of such a consequence. The observation may also be made
that both their proposal and the new town movement generally does not come to
terms with many of the problems present in the existing cities. It could carry the risk,
even, of ignoring them (4).

On balance, however, encouraging a program of new town construction, though
not at the cost of ignoring the central city and the disabilities present there, does have
much to commend it. It offers both a means of incorporating the possibilities that
Weissbourd and Channick have raised, as well as providing for a growth of communities and suburban areas with distinctly superior qualities to that ordinarily exhibited
with unplanned urban sprawl and suburban growth. It would also seem to lend itself
to some of the market and entrepreneurial dynamics presently exhibited by the
residential development industry.

REFERENCES

1. Advisory Commission on Intergovernmental Relations, *Alternative Approaches to Governmental Reorganization in Metropolitan Areas* (Washington, D.C.: Government Printing Office, 1962).

2. _____, *Performance of Urban Functions: Local and Areawide* (Washington, D.C.: Government Printing Office, 1963).

3. Aleshire, Robert A., "Planning and Citizen Participation: Costs Benefits and Approaches," *Urban Affairs Quarterly,* 5 (June 1970), 369–393.

4. Alonso, William, "What Are New Towns For?" *Urban Studies,* 7 (January 1970), 37–55.

5. Altshuler, Alan A., *Community Control: The Black Demand for Participation in Large American Cities* (New York: Pegasus, 1970, paper).

6. _____, "The Goals of Comprehensive Planning," *Journal of the American Institute of Planners,* 31 (August 1965), 186–195.

7. Aronowitz, Stanley, "The Dialectics of Community Control," *Social Policy,* 1 (May-June 1970), 47–51.

8. Biddle, William W., and Biddle, Loureide J., *The Community Development Process: the Rediscovery of Local Initiative* (New York: Holt, Rinehart and Winston, 1965).

9. Bollens, John C., *Special District Government in the United States* (Berkeley: University of California Press, 1957).

10. _____, and Schmandt, Henry J., *The Metropolis, Its People, Politics, and Economic Life* (New York: Harper, 1965), chaps. 14, 15, 16.

11. Breckenfeld, Gurney, *Columbia and the New Cities* (New York: Ives Washburn, 1971).

12. Brooks, Richard, "Social Planning in Columbia," *Journal of the American Institute of Planners,* 37 (November 1971), 373–379.

13. Burns, Wilfred, *New Towns for Old: The Technique of Urban Renewal* (London: Leonard Hill, 1963).

14. Clapp, James A., *New Towns and Urban Policy* (New York: Dunellen, 1971).

15. Clinard, Marshal B., *Slums and Community Development, Experiments in Self-Help* (New York: Free Press, 1966).

16. Cohen, Wilbur J., "Government Policy and the Poor: Past, Present, and Future," *The Journal of Social Issues,* 26 (Summer 1970), 1–9.

17. Committee for Economic Development, "Introduction and Summary of Recommendations," *Reshaping Government in Metropolitan Areas,* A Statement on National Policy by the Research and Policy Committee (New York: Committee for Economic Development, 1970), 9–22.

18. _____, *Reshaping Government in Metropolitan Areas,* A Statement on National Policy by the Research and Policy Committee (New York: Committee for Economic Development, 1970).

19. Davidoff, Paul, "Advocacy and Pluralism in Planning," *Journal of the American Institute of Planners,* 30 (November 1964), 331–338.

20. _____, and Reiner,Thomas, "A Choice Theory of Planning," *Journal of the American Institute of Planners,* 28 (May 1962), 103–115.

21. Donovan, John C., *The Politics of Poverty* (New York: Pegasus, 1967, paper).

22. Dyckman, John W., "Social Planning, Social Planners, and Planned Societies," *Journal of the American Institute of Planners,* 32 (March 1966), 66–76.

23. Eichler, Edward P., "Why New Communities?" in B. Rieden and W. Nash, eds., *Shaping an Urban Future* (Cambridge: MIT Press, 1966), pp. 95–114.

24. _____, and Kaplan, Marshall, *The Community Builders* (Berkeley: University of California Press, 1967).

25. Fainstein, Susan S., and Fainstein, Norman I., "City Planning and Political Values," *Urban Affairs Quarterly,* 6 (March 1971), 341–362.

26. Feldman, Mark B., and Jassy, Everett L., "The Urban County: A Study of New Approaches to Local Government in Metropolitan Areas," *Harvard Law Review,* 73 (January 1960), 526–582.

27. Fiser, Webb S., *Mastery of the Metropolis* (Englewood Cliffs, N.J.: Prentice Hall, 1962).

28. Gans, Herbert J., "The City and the Poor," in Paul Meadows and Ephraim H. Mizruchi, eds., *Urbanism, Urbanization, and Change: Comparative Perspectives* (Reading, Mass.: Addison-Wesley, 1969), pp. 542–543.

29. _____, "Culture and Class in the Study of Poverty: An Approach to Anti-Poverty Research," in Daniel P. Moynihan, ed., *On Understanding Poverty* (New York: Basic Books, 1969), pp. 201–228.

30. ———, "The Failure of Urban Renewal: A Critique and Some Proposals," *Commentary,* 39 (April 1965), 29–37.

31. ———, "Planning and Social Life," *Journal of the American Institute of Planners,* 27 (May 1961), 134–140.

32. ———, "Social and Physical Planning for the Elimination of Urban Poverty," in Bernard Rosenberg, et al., eds., *Mass Society in Crisis: Social Problems and Social Pathology* (New York: Macmillan, 1964), pp. 629–644.

33. Geddes, Patrick, *Cities in Evolution,* new and rev. ed. (New York: Oxford University Press, 1950).

34. Goodenough, Ward H., *Cooperation in Change: An Anthropological Approach to Community Development* (New York: Russell Sage Foundation, 1963).

35. Grant, Daniel R., "The Metropolitan Government Approach: Should, Can, and Will It Prevail?" *Urban Affairs Quarterly,* 3 (March 1968), 103–110.

36. ———, "Urban and Suburban Nashville: A Case Study in Metropolitanism," *The Journal of Politics,* 17 (February 1955), 82–99.

37. Greer, Scott, *Metropolitics, A Study of Political Culture* (New York: John Wiley, 1963).

38. ———, *Urban Renewal and American Cities* (Indianapolis: Bobbs-Merrill, 1965).

39. Gulick, Luther H., "The Metropolitan Problem," *The Metropolitan Problem and American Ideas* (New York: Knopf, 1962), pp. 9–27.

40. Haggstrom, Warren C., "The Power of the Poor," in Louis A. Ferman, et al., eds., *Poverty in America,* rev. ed. (Ann Arbor: The University of Michigan Press, 1968), pp. 457–476.

41. Hancock, Macklin I., "New Towns—Are They the Answer to Current 'Urban Sprawl'?" *Journal of Housing,* 22 (October 1965), 469–471.

42. Harvard, William C., and Corty, Floyd, *Rural-Urban Consolidation* (Baton Rouge: Louisiana State University Press, 1964).

43. Hawkins, Brett W., *Nashville Metro—The Politics of City-County Consolidation* (Nashville, Tenn.: University of Tennessee Press, 1966).

44. Hawley, Amos H., and Zimmer, Basil G., "Resistance to Unification in a Metropolitan Community," in Morris Janowitz, ed., *Community Political Systems* (New York: Macmillan, 1961), pp. 146–157.

45. Hertzen, Heikki von, and Spreiregen, Paul D., *Building a New Town, Finland's New Garden City, Tapiola* (Cambridge, Mass.: MIT Press, 1971).

46. Hoppenfeld, Morton, "A Sketch of the Planning-Building Process for Columbia, Maryland," *Journal of the American Institute of Planners,* 33 (November 1967), 398–409.

47. Howard, Ebenezer, *Garden Cities of Tomorrow,* 3rd ed. (Cambridge: MIT Press, 1965).

48. Jones, Victor, "The Organization of a Metropolitan Region," *University of Pennsylvania Law Review,* 105 (February 1957), 539–550.

49. Kaplan, Harold, *Urban Political Systems: A Functional Analysis of Metro Toronto* (New York: Columbia University Press, 1967).

50. Lansing, John B., et al., Planned Residential Environments (Ann Arbor, Mich: Survey Research Center, Institute for Social Research, University of Michigan, 1970).

51. Larner, Jeremy, and Howe, Irving, eds., *Poverty: Views from the Left* (New York: William Morrow, 1968, paper).

52. Levitan, Sar A., *Programs in Aid of the Poor for the 1970's,* Policy Studies in Employment and Welfare 1 (Baltimore: Johns Hopkins, 1969).

53. Meyerson, Martin, "Building the Middle-Range Bridge for Comprehensive Planning," *Journal of the American Institute of Planners,* 23 (Spring 1956), 58–64.

54. Miller, S. M., and Ruby, Pamela, "The War on Poverty Reconsidered," in Jeremy Larner, and Irving Howe, eds., *Poverty: Views from the Left* (New York: William Morrow, 1968).

55. Mills, C. Wright, *The Power Elite* (New York: Oxford University Press, 1957).

56. Myrdal, Gunnar, "National Planning for Health Cities: Two Challenges to Affluence," in Sam Bass Warner, Jr., ed., *Planning for a Nation of Cities* (Cambridge: MIT Press, 1966), pp. 3–22.

57. Osborn, Frederic J., and Whittick, Arnold, *The New Towns: The Answer to Megalopolis* (New York: McGraw-Hill, 1963).

58. Ostrom, Vincent, Tiebout, Charles M., and Warren, Robert, "The Organization of Government in Metropolitan Areas: A Theoretical Inquiry," *American Political Science Review,* 55 (December 1961), 831–842.

59. Perloff, Harvey S., "New Directions in Social Planning," *Journal of the American Institute of Planners,* 31 (November 1965), 297–303.

60. _____, "Social Planning in the Metropolis," in Leonard J. Duhl, ed., *The Urban Condition, People and Policy in the Metropolis* (New York: Basic Books, 1963), pp. 331–347.

61. Petersen, William, "On Some Meanings of 'Planning'," *Journal of the American Institute of Planners,* 32 (May 1966), 130–142.

62. Pock, Max A., *Independent Special Districts: A Solution to the Metropolitan Area Problem* (Ann Arbor: University of Michigan Law School Legislative Research Center, 1962).

63. Press, Charles, " 'Efficiency and Economy' Arguments for Metropolitan Reorganization," *Public Opinion Quarterly,* 28 (Winter 1964), 584–594.

64. Riesman, Frank, and Gartner, Alan, "Community Control and Radical Social Change," *Social Policy,* 1 (May-June 1970), 52–55.

65. Rosow, Irving, "The Social Effects of the Physical Environment," *Journal of the American Institute of Planners,* 27 (May 1961), 127–133.

66. Sandalow, Terrance, "Federal Grants and the Reform of State and Local Government," in John R. Crecine, ed., *Financing the Metropolis: Public Policy in Urban Economies,* vol. 4, Urban Affairs Annual Reviews (Beverly Hills, Calif.: Sage Publications, 1970), pp. 175–194.

67. Schattschneider, E. E., *The Semisovereign People, A Realist's View of Democracy in America* (New York: Holt, Rinehart and Winston, 1960).

68. Schorr, Alvin L., *Slums and Social Insecurity* (Washington, D.C.: U.S. Government Printing Office, 1963).

69. Schultze, Charles L., et al., Setting National Priorities: The 1973 Budget (Washington, D.C.: The Brookings Institution, 1972).

70. Sofen, Edward, *The Miami Metropolitan Experiment, A Metropolitan Action Study,* rev. ed. (Garden City, N.Y.: Doubleday, 1966, paper).

71. Spicer, Edward G., ed., *Human Problems in Technological Change: A Casebook* (New York: Russell Sage Foundation, 1952).

72. Spiegel, Hans B. C., ed., *Citizen Participation in Urban Development,* vol. 1, "Concepts and Issues" (Washington, D.C.: NTL Institute for Applied Behavioral Science, 1968, paper).

73. Stein, Clarence S., *Toward New Towns for America* (Liverpool: Eaton Press, 1951).

74. Stuart, Darwin G., "Rational Urban Planning: Problems and Prospects," *Urban Affairs Quarterly,* 5 (December 1969), 151–182.

75. Tumin, Melvin M., "Some Social Requirements for Effective Community Development," *Community Development Review,* 11 (December 1958).

76. United Nations, Department of Economic and Social Affairs, *Planning of Metropolitan Areas and New Towns* (New York: United Nations, 1969).

77. Warren, Roland L., *The Community in America,* 2nd ed. (Chicago: Rand McNally, 1972).

78. _____, "Politics and the Ghetto System," Roland L. Warren, ed., *Politics and the Ghetto* (New York: Atherton, 1969), pp. 11–30.

79. Waxman, Chaim I., *Poverty: Power and Politics* (New York: Grosset and Dunlap, 1968).

80. Webber, Melvin M., "The Prospects for Policies Planning," in Leonard J. Duhl, ed., *The Urban Condition: People and Policy in the Metropolis* (New York: Basic Books, 1963), pp. 391–430.

81. Weissbourd, Bernard, *Segregation, Subsidies, and Megalopolis,* Occasional Paper No. 2 on the City (Santa Barbara, Calif.: Center for the Study of Democratic Institutions, 1964).

82. _____, and Channick, Herbert, "An Urban Strategy," *The Center Magazine,* 1 (September 1968), 56–65.

83. White, Morton, and White, Lucia, *The Intellectual versus the City: From Thomas Jefferson to Frank Lloyd Wright* (Cambridge: Harvard University Press and MIT Press, 1962).

84. Wilner, Daniel M., et al., *The Housing Environment and Family Life* (Baltimore: Johns Hopkins Press, 1962).

The Metropolitan Problem
Luther H. Gulick

*   *   *

THE URBAN CONCENTRATION OF NATIONAL PROBLEMS

. . . The major unsolved problems of our society and government arise primarily from the new rapid urbanization of the country.

No one can ignore nonurban problems, especially conservation of soil, water, and other natural resources, and the upgrading of rural life and rural human resources. These problems have been recognized as "national problems" since at least 1862, when the Morrill Act was passed. As matters stand, electricity has now been extended to 96 per cent of our working farms; highways and schools are all but universal, and the rural areas, except in some parts of the "deep South," generally enjoy a public health and welfare service, in relation to their needs, on a par with the more populous sections of the country.

Rural income still suffers from waves of overproduction and from unequal competition with the managed-price sectors of our national economy. But this problem too has been accepted as a national responsibility since 1929, when the Federal Farm Board was set up.

But when you identify the things that are wrong in America today, and try to locate them on the map, you find that most of our current headaches arise out of spreading urban concentrations. Just run over the list:

slums; congestion; obsolete buildings and factories; juvenile and other crime; rackets; crowded schools; reduced standards of educational quality; deteriorating transportation with rising costs; increasing water and air pollution; traffic congestion and accidents; chronic unemployment; reduced individual and social responsibility; segregation and handicaps for minority groups; ugly and insulting "developments"; silly and extravagant mass "consumerism"; the needless destruction of natural values; and the deterioration of cultural standards and resources.

SOURCE: Luther H. Gulick, from *The Metropolitan Problem and American Ideas* (New York: Alfred A. Knopf, 1962), pp. 9–27. Reprinted by permission.

This concentration of problems occurs in the cities and their suburbs, first, because that is where the American people now live. In the last decade over two-thirds of our population growth took place around the big cities. This will be increasingly the case in the next decades, unless all signs fail.

Many of the discomforts and ugly aspects of rapid urbanization are, in fact, disequilibriums created by the pace of change. When human beings pour into cities, leaving behind their families, habits, disciplines, and associations, they inevitably create and are engulfed in social chaos. The great difficulty of the urban areas is that the new equilibriums develop only, if at all, out of so much human suffering. Those who do not fit into the new environment are powerless to fit themselves into the new pattern because of the massive complexity of city life.

A further reason for the concentration of these problems in and around the big cities is inherent in the nature of our new economy. This new economy is characterized by: (1) a tremendous new emphasis on consumption and capturing the fancy of the consumer; (2) large private management units; (3) domination of mass public taste through producers' and sales control over most mass communication media; (4) accelerated obsolescence both through rapid application of technological research and through the concentrated decision process; (5) the virtual collapse of "the market mechanism" as a regulator both of production and prices, and therefore of the allocation of scarce resources; and finally (6) universally available, individually owned mass transportation for people and goods. Though some of these characteristics are good in themselves, the combination is not. Together these forces are giving us a new pattern of urban concentration and scatteration, with a bringing together in the urban areas of most of the problems we have just listed as endemic to our present national life.

THE TRADITIONAL APPROACH

The traditional American approach designed to solve such problems comes straight out of Adam Smith. Each home owner, each shop owner, each factory owner, each tenant, each worker, each manager, each consumer, each farmer is expected to follow his own "best interest." He will live and work where he chooses, and sell, tear down, rebuild, or remodel his aging buildings to meet "the demand" and produce for himself the best possible money return. He will buy and sell "at market" and be governed accordingly. In the process, Adam Smith demonstrated, we will thus "automatically" get production to meet demand, competitive low prices, and a city, along with its suburbs, which is continually being brought up-to-date. Sections will change, of course, but we will always have a total social and economic system which is "the best possible" because, by definition, it is the sum total of individual decisions which are the best possible for each individual owner or tenant or worker or consumer, and, after all, the city is always the sum total of the people and their homes, the shops, public buildings and institutions, the factories, streets, and parks which make it. In other words, the economic laws of self-interest give us an "unseen hand" which will guide each and every individual to decisions which are, by definition, best for the entire community.

In cities, men have long recognized that some public controls were, nonetheless, essential to keep a reasonable street layout, to establish certain health and fire controls, and to support certain community services like water supply, sanitation, police protection, and control over markets, weights and measures, and housing safety. These governmental controls were adopted after the unhappy discovery that the "unseen hand" did not in fact give us the kind of a city we wanted to live in. In other words, private selfish decisions did not in fact add up to produce a city which satisfied the public interest.

These various community controls and community services have been found necessary from the day of Hammurabi (1960 B.C.) to the most recent American city zoning ordinance (A.D. 1960), not because of any political or economic theory, but because of hard experience and the desire to "do something" effective about a "crying need." The theories came after the fact, and now the theories begin to influence our actions and are frequently cited as justification for given policy lines. Theory was ever thus in social affairs.

No one would say that American political and economic theory and belief have departed from the initial solid commitment to private property, free enterprise, and the fundamental belief that the end product of selfish individual decisions, especially in the field of economics, will be the best possible world *provided* this dog-eat-dog system is qualified (a) by the establishment of public controls and services where free enterprise fails or individual selfish decisions fail to give us what we want; and (b) by a decent human sympathy for the weak.

We thus end up in the United States with (a) private capitalism, mitigated by increasing segments of public ownership; (b) free enterprise, restrained by increasing public controls to protect the public interest and sustain "the market mechanism"; and (c) extensive public and private charities. I shall come back to the discussion of some of the questions of theory and practice raised by these three categories later on.

The most visible departures from free-enterprise capitalism are found in the big urban centers. The big cities are heavily involved in public ownership and public regulation. Streets, water supplies, sewers, docks, air terminals, bridges, tunnels, schools and other public buildings, parks, recreation facilities, auditoriums, concert halls, and museums head the list.

Regulation of free enterprise is even more evident in the cities, with controls designed to protect health, safety, and morals in every conceivable way. The land-use controls are especially worth study. In many an American city the so-called "owner" of a piece of private land cannot build except for legally defined purposes, can use only a defined portion of his lot, and must then conform with legally defined standards as to his walls and windows, maximum height, foundations, roof, and the design and installation of his electric wiring, plumbing, heating, air conditioning, stairways, fire escapes, kitchens, and toilets. He may also be required to preserve shade trees, provide parking space on his land, and conform to community esthetic standards as well. These controls have all been developed in the public interest, though we can also show that, when properly administered, they add to the value of private land and to the security of the private investments involved.

When you look to see what American governments are now engaged in these many controls over business and property ownership, and what governmental units own the streets and public facilities, you find that the practical, operational responsibility for all this socialism has been placed on the local units of government: the cities, the counties, the towns, the villages, the school districts, and the other special districts of local government. While the federal government has its lands, dams, and navigable waters, and the states their lands, highways, and institutions, the major instrument of public ownership, of regulation of land use and improvements, and of public services and protection of personal safety in America is local municipal government.

This did not come about as a matter of social theory. It came about because the problems arose in the localities. The people most affected took what steps they could to establish the controls and the services they found to be needed. And, on the whole, this assignment of the work has worked well up to the present time. Each move was a pragmatic Yankee solution designed to meet a condition, not a theory.

THE BREAKDOWN

In the face of the radically changed requirements of metropolitan areas, this traditional approach has now broken down. The proof of this statement is everywhere. In every big city the slums are spreading faster than they are being cleared up. Circulation of people and goods is becoming less and less satisfactory and more and more costly. Even the delightful expansion of suburban life is beginning to run into difficulties as the suburbs "fill in"; and the service and control jobs are so big that the local governmental units involved are unequal to the tasks they face.

In spite of this accumulating evidence of failure on every hand, some people talk as though the old approach can save us. It is my contention that two of the chief props of the traditional approach have collapsed. They are the "market mechanism" and traditional "local municipal action."

POINTS OF FAILURE OF THE "MARKET MECHANISM"

At what points does the "unseen hand" fail to give us the kind of city we demand in the modern day and age? A comprehensive answer for this embarrassing question would be a large order, but we can list the easily recognizable factors to illustrate the point.

First comes the street layout. Private land owners and developers have never, anywhere in the world, laid out their lot lines and their building and development lines so that those of neighboring areas would add up to form a convenient, adequate, and integrated pattern for posterity or even for themselves. Left to themselves, land owners generally leave crooked, narrow, noncontinuous lanes which may look "picturesque" to tourists from abroad but which are totally unsatisfactory for any kind of sustained urban life, once industrialization has commenced.

Clearly the general street locations, widths, and specifications for an entire urbanized region must be rationalized under the hand of a single controlling governmental authority. No one will question this. However, this admission leads us a good deal farther than we have ever gone, now that the solidly built-up urban areas are so extended and the traffic has become so heavy and complex.

Another implication of this statement as to streets is that there must also be broad community control over land uses and densities of occupancy. This necessity arises from the fact that the circulation system, including the streets, and the related land uses are opposite sides of the same coin. Without the streets there is no urban land use; except for the land use, there is no need for streets. Each depends on and determines the other. Thus the seemingly simple agreement as to the need of unified public control over contiguous streets leads us far indeed in the modern urban setting.

Second, private enterprise will no longer give us any form of mass transportation (except elevators!) in an urban area without requiring substantial governmental action and participation. This arises in part because the public will not accept rates of fare adequate to attract the private investor—in an inflationary world—and will not give to private groups "monopolies" to use the public streets, or the public power of eminent domain.

As a result, government must be heavily involved in developing and regulating mass transportation, if not also in owning, operating, financing it, and conducting the developmental research required. Even taxicabs have to be limited as to number, regulated as to their service, and controlled as to their rates. The "unseen hand" will not attend to these matters.

Third are water supplies, sewers, and sewerage. The time has now passed when such community services can be supplied by private enterprise. Here and there, for a specific small operation, a developer can put in a few pipes, drains, and utility connections, and build private cesspools and septic tanks, but such arrangements are temporizing makeshifts in any large developing urbanized area and, in the long run, have to be tied into and controlled by a responsible governmental unit.

Electric power and telephones and occasionally gas are, however, still extended to the developing metropolitan areas in the United States by private utilities, under the general control of state public service commissions. In this we have been most fortunate. These private utilities have in fact a much better record of adjustment to increasing metropolitan demand than any other local urban services, in part because they are free to ignore existing small-government boundaries and because these services are the beneficiaries of extraordinary recent technological advances which have helped them to do a better job with very modest increases in costs and rates.

Fourth is the business of modernizing the older, obsolete, and no longer efficient neighborhoods and layout of the older urban community. The inability of private enterprise to act on this problem is not hard to explain. An obsolete neighborhood involves several or many blocks and scores or hundreds of individual properties. No one of these owners can reap a reward from individual efforts to improve his property unless all or most of his neighbors do so also *and at the same time.* One laggard can spoil the effort. Furthermore, even the street arrangement may need replanning and reconstruction, as where pedestrian malls, no-traffic sections, a revised ownership pattern, parking facilities, or large industrial or other plottages are called for. Urban renewal and modernization will, of course, be carried out primarily by private enterprise and with private investment, but only as part of a total scheme which establishes the new modern urban pattern, a thing which can be done only by governmental action. The "unseen hand" will not tear down existing obsolete buildings on a mass basis, but it will build individual new housing, new shops, new factories, new offices, *provided* a proper stage is first set by comprehensive public action.

Fifth is housing for the middle-income and low-income segments of the urban population. Private builders will build housing only for a profit. As a result, they will finance housing for the upper-middle and higher income brackets and for nobody else.

The major costs of housing, perhaps as much as 72 per cent, excluding the land, are for labor.[2] As a result, new housing is priced in large measure in relation to construction wages. Those who cannot afford existing rents, or capital charges for housing, are thus forever in a position where they cannot afford to meet the costs of new housing unless they have a wage rate on a par with or above the wage rates of the construction industry. While this relationship can be altered somewhat by free land, reductions in financing costs, increased economies in construction, and reduced taxes, the hard core of labor costs remains dominant. Thus, that part of the population with an annual earning rate below that of the construction industry, left to their own devices, will live overcrowded in various degrees of second-hand and substandard housing. The market mechanism cannot provide better housing than this.

This is in part due, of course, to changing standards of "decency." We now demand a kitchen and a flush toilet for each family, where once we were fighting only windowless rooms and the common backyard privy. It is also true that we now demand minimum provisions far in advance of "satisfactory" housing as seen in Asia. These observations are, however, beside the point for our people. We know more about health, and we know how the social costs

[2]Charles Abrams: *The Future of Housing* (New York: Harper & Brothers; 1946), chap. xiii.

rise when our people are submerged in crowded and hopeless indecency. And we know only too well that even our newest standards are still pitifully low.

Some social reformers have sought to meet this situation by reducing the cost of financing a home, by establishing a better "market," by making the construction of a home as efficient as assembling an automobile, by holding costs down, by encouraging the rise of wages of the tenants, by consumer education, and by more rigid local enforcement of housing standards. These efforts have accomplished a good deal. Incidentally, they also involve extensive governmental intervention in the economy.

Even the widespread increase of wage levels, which is frequently put forward as "the only real solution" of the bad housing problem, has its own built-in frustration—most of the labor cost of housing is paid at a rate higher than the general community wage average. General wage advances have not in fact been reflected in improved housing.[3] Apparently wage increases will solve the housing problem only when most people receive a wage above the average! Thus, when all is said and done in the most vigorous and dynamic cities, we still have more slums today than we had a generation ago.

The result is unacceptable in big urban areas. It produces expanding slums and all the social problems which gravitate to and are aggravated by substandard housing arrangements. If something is to be done about this situation, it can only be done by government. The "unseen hand" gives us no way out, and never can.

Sixth are health and welfare activities and all the standard community services. About these there is no argument now. Charitable people have undertaken part of the responsibility for very limited groups as a personal obligation, rather than for profit. But the main burden is now and will continue to be handled directly by government. No other arrangement is now possible. There is still an important job for private welfare activities, especially in experimental and demonstration work, but the major effort is now public.

Seventh are education and the many varied institutions which lift our life to new levels of achievement and enjoyment, such as schools, colleges, libraries, museums, adult education, parks, recreation, noncommercial leisure-time activities, and cultural and artistic enrichment. This is an area in which a few activities can always be organized for profit, such as some private trade schools and some recreations, like spectator sports and the commercial theaters. Fortunately there are still many avenues of service for generous and imaginative philanthropy, but any mass education or recreation or cultural enjoyment can be provided only through extensive public patronage and support of various kinds, running all the way from tax exemption to public construction of facilities and direct public tax support of certain activities. Modern society in the urban areas needs and demands a great deal that can never be developed without government backing and tax support. This will be increasingly the situation in the future.

[3]Abrams: *The Future of Housing,* p. 165.

These seven clearly identifiable points, at which *laissez faire* cannot produce the kind of urban structure and life we are willing to accept, amply justify the statement with which we started a few paragraphs ago: the market mechanism cannot save us.

CAN LOCAL GOVERNMENTS MEET THE SITUATION?

If the market mechanism cannot save us, can the local governments? Here again, the answer is "no." The proof is the accumulating evidence of failure everywhere, in spite of many heroic efforts.

The reason for these failures is most instructive. Why have the great cities been unable to use their traditional governmental powers to deal with slums, traffic congestion, mass transportation, urban obsolescence, and the problems of migration, education, and crime, of water supply and air and water pollution, of recreation and cultural and other needs?

There are three interrelated reasons for this local inability to act: *First,* every one of these problems spreads out over an area broader than the boundaries of the local governments in question. It is clear that our big urban complexes are now so closely tied together economically, socially, and structurally by daily human movements and activities that every problem is a "spill-over" from the next jurisdiction. Little can be done about one piece of such a problem. *Once an indivisible problem is divided, nothing effective can be done about it.*

This is especially true as to the entire circulation and mass-transportation system, the water supply, air and water pollution, and land-use control. Once these jobs are split up into fractions, they are undoable, like trying to leap across a river in two jumps or mop up a part of a spilled bottle of milk on the kitchen floor.

Spreading area-wide problems cannot be handled geographic piece by geographic piece. They must be tackled in their entirety, comprehensively, and are difficult enough even so.

Second is the problem of paying for the things that need doing. Almost everything we are talking about calls for increased governmental expenditures. Most big cities are already raising all the taxes they can legally. They are thus so "strapped" that there is little they can do about the new problems, especially such expensive projects as slum clearance, urban renewal, school expansion, recreation and cultural facilities, pollution controls, and mass transportation. Financing such activities is complicated further by the fact that many cities are losing taxable resources as the factories move or develop outside of town, and many of the city improvements are occasioned by, or are for the benefit of, the suburbs. Even among the suburbs, some are "have" and some "have-not" communities because of tax windfalls, a very serious matter when it comes to meeting school budgets, especially.

A few well-situated suburban enclaves can manage and finance their service and control needs, including a considerable part of the "spill-over" problems.

But even with all the tax revenues they need, they are powerless to meet their pollution-control, commuter, advanced-education, and broader cultural requirements within their own boundaries.

Because of the nature of the new spread-out urban development, the needs, the taxable resources, and the benefits do not match up geographically. This makes it impossible for local governments to proceed with any chance of success, except with an occasional service which can be made self-supporting. These self-supporting operations are generally paid for by the users regardless of geography, as anyone can see by watching the many state and county license plates of the cars and trucks that use any major bridge, tunnel, or throughway.

Most of the needed urban improvements we are talking about, though costly today, will pay for themselves many times over in years to come. To tap this newly created wealth and ability to pay, and to use these resources to meet the costs of action, are obviously both desirable and fair. The existing local tax and revenue system, with its small geographic divisions, is precisely the wrong approach, because the costs will often fall in one jurisdiction and the benefits in another.

Matching up the costs of a governmental activity with the benefited persons or property is important also as a matter of economic justice. It is also indispensable as a political matter, because the decision to go ahead will hardly be made by those who have to pay but who receive little commensurate benefit or addition to their taxpaying capacity.

We therefore need a new branch of economic science which will record and demonstrate what people and what property stand to gain by various types of governmental activity affecting the economy. Such a science will show, I am convinced, that, under modern conditions, each metropolitan complex is organically related to the state and the national economy, and the efficiency of each local unit is reflected in the broader picture. If so, the nation must be deeply concerned in the efficiency of the developing urban structure and in its physical and social institutions, including especially its developing man power (health and education), its circulation system (street patterns and mass transportation), its productive efficiency (urban renewal), and its utilization of national resources (water, pollution, etc.). Once a nation has grown together, knit into a modern integrated industrial, financial, transportational, and managerial structure, the efficiency level of the great urban complexes is an inseparable part of the total national structure.

If the real benefit from certain governmental programs in these four great sectors[4] is national as well as local, it is obviously unjust, and delaying, to place the burden for the work mainly on small local agencies. To think and act sensibly, we must match up the benefits, the costs, and the decisions to act.

Third, the final reason for the inability of local governments to solve problems arising from our current surge of metropolitan development is political. . . .

---

[4]I.e., man power, circulation, productive efficiency, and allocation of national resources.

Politics and the Ghetto System
Roland L. Warren

If the ghettos are not impervious to social intervention techniques, they are at least highly persistent, showing remarkable ability to absorb or ward off attempts at change.

The papers in this volume contain many statements indicating the essential inadequacy of the concerted efforts to date to "do something about" the ghettos, suggesting that much more massive programs must be implemented before basic change can be anticipated. They also point again and again to certain aspects of the ghettos and the situation surrounding them that offer formidable obstacles to the would-be reformer.

One can, of course, find "reasons" for the apparent impermeability of the ghettos and for the relative inadequacy of various efforts to make a marked impact on the configuration of ghetto life. Each point of intervention permits at most a minimal impact which is soon absorbed by the total situation.

Consider some of the apparently futile measures:

Low-cost housing projects, once considered a panacea, have in many instances become dangerous, slovenly, carelessly maintained, and poorly repaired.

In any case, subsidized low-cost housing units in the past three decades have totaled only 800,000, and even the inadequate funds appropriated for them have often not been fully utilized.

An urban renewal program which has as one of its goals "a decent home and a suitable living environment for every American family" has had the net impact of drastically reducing the amount of low-rent housing available to city dwellers.

New school programs designed to upgrade the quality of ghetto schools have been largely unsuccessful, and in any case must confront youngsters who, even as they enter the school, are retarded in their mental development. This retardation increases as they "progress" through the grades.

Job training programs show high dropout rates, and many of those persons who stay with the program are either unable to find work or find it only at menial low-wage occupations.

Welfare programs designed presumably to reduce dependency and to en-

SOURCE: Roland L. Warren, ed., from *Politics and the Ghettos* (New York: Atherton Press, 1969), pp. 11–30. Copyright © 1969 by Atherton Press. Reprinted by permission of Aldine.Atherton, Inc.

courage self-sufficient living have the effect of increasing dependency and discouraging self-sufficiency.

Efforts to develop personal, racial, and neighborhood pride in the ghettos and participation in community decision-making are cut back financially and are eventually placed under the control of local municipal authorities.

One could continue giving examples of programs that are either ineffectual or self-defeating, but there is no need to. Several aspects of the problem of the pertinacity of the ghettos are examined in the following papers. None of those papers takes direct occasion to examine the ghetto itself as a tenacious social system, a configuration of mutually supporting circumstances which assures self-perpetuation and whose exchange relationships with the surrounding society are such as, in aggregate, to preserve the system rather than to change it.

THE GHETTO AS A SOCIAL SYSTEM

It is unwise, as well as unnecessary, to impute to the ghetto as a social system a sort of independent, autonomous existence, deliberately perpetuating itself and fending off all attempts at change. Similarly, it would be tendentious and exaggerated to consider the ghetto simply as the product of a deliberate conspiracy on the part of "the power structure," "white racism," "the establishment," or other reified social phenomena mustered up as scapegoats in a reductionist explanation of a highly complex situation.

There is nevertheless much to support the desirability of looking at the ghetto as a system that perpetuates itself, deliberately or not, and whose relations to the surrounding environment are such as to support and reinforce this self-perpetuation.

To be sure, any social configuration which exists over a period of time can be thought of as a self-perpetuating system, and any such configuration can be shown to be related to larger, more inclusive systems in ways which support it and reinforce it. Yet, many social configurations are nevertheless transitory. Although they may persist for a short or a long time and are reinforced in this persistence through their relationships with their environment, eventually they tend to dissolve. But for the predictable future, the ghettos show little sign of dissolving.

In a sense, the question at issue is what set of circumstances or social policies or events could be expected to dissolve the ghettos rather than perpetuate them, and to dissolve them at a price which is acceptable within the broad scope of American democratic social values. One way of approaching this question is to look at the forces which perpetuate the ghetto configuration. Political processes and social policy, if they are to be relevant to an attack on the ghettos, must confront these forces and overcome them, or at least manipulate them in such fashion as to change the configuration.

A pattern is discernible in the social structure of the ghetto, through which the various parts fit together and reinforce one another. As a convenient outline for examining this pattern we can consider some of the basic social functions which are pertinent to people living in any locality. One such outline is that of five "locality-relevant" functions: Production-distribution-consumption, socialization, social control, social participation, and mutual support.

Production-Distribution-Consumption is a composite term used to designate the way people get their income and spend it. Ghetto industry is owned to an overwhelming extent by people who do not themselves live in the ghettos. Opportunities for the employment of ghetto dwellers are distributed throughout the city, and even in the suburbs (in the case of domestic help). But there is a high rate of unemployment and the employment available to ghetto dwellers is largely of the unskilled, menial, poorly paid type. Having relatively little experience with the possibilities for long-term saving, or for "rational" budgeting, many ghetto dwellers purchase on impulse and do not use optimally such money as they have. Many, though not all, ghetto stores overcharge the unwary purchaser and often strap him with usurious interest rates for installment purchases. An inordinate proportion of ghetto households are dependent on public assistance payments which bring with them types of agency surveillance which are enervating and degrading.

Socialization refers to the process by which people are trained to become members of society. While the family and the school are considered society's chief instruments for this process, others include churches and other formal institutions, as well as television shows, comic books, and the culture that is communicated by peer groups. The child learns from the people around him, including other children, how to "fit in" and "make a go of things." But what does the Negro ghetto-dwelling child learn? He learns, whether implicitly or explicitly, that he is not quite the equal of other Americans. He learns a way of life that is attuned to squalid and dilapidated living quarters, poor nutrition, an unpleasant experience at school, constant surveillance of his family by society's agents—welfare, probation, school, landlord, police—and he learns to keep his level of aspiration below that of most other Americans. If he wants to be a doctor or a lawyer or an engineer he is quietly and sympathetically counseled to become a medical technologist or a draftsman, or to settle for something less. He is shown daily through word and deed—in school, on the streets, in stores—that he is poor and different from the white majority, and this fact is often transmitted to him by blacks as well

Social Control is a process, vital to all societies, through which members are kept in line with group norms. It may be represented by the formal instruments of the police and courts or the informal constraints on conduct exercised by propaganda, gossip, or social approval and disapproval. It may be imposed from without or, as usually occurs in the process of socialization, may become internalized and speak with the voice of self-discipline or "conscience."

The ghetto dweller is in a special position with regard to the social control processes of the surrounding society. In the first place, the formal processes of social control may work with inordinate rigor on him if he violates one of society's norms. The youngster engaged in mischief in the ghetto is much more likely to be picked up by the police, much more likely to be brought to children's court, much more likely to be packed away to a training school. When he grows older, a similar situation prevails.

But not only the police and the courts are concerned with social control. Many of the institutions which are set up to serve the ghetto dweller turn out to be efforts to control him more than to serve him. Thus, the welfare department, designed to afford him a minimal income when needed, actually engages in exercising various types of control on his conduct. Even the presumably benevolent Police Athletic League or summer camp program may be more explicitly concerned with "preventing delinquency" than with affording the ghetto child a healthy opportunity for recreation. Somehow, the agencies that are supposed to help the ghetto dweller are difficult to enlist in his aid. The public health department can't do much about the rats; the better business bureau can't do much about the exorbitant tenement rents. The ghetto dweller may have to wait in line hours at the clinic; the housing code doesn't seem to ensure that the leaky plumbing is repaired, or that adequate heat is supplied in winter. And the police, presumably there to protect his person and his rights, are at times the most conspicuous violators of both.

Social Participation, thought of as membership in and activity in voluntary associations of various kinds, takes on a peculiar form in the ghetto. Various studies indicate a rather live informal network of kinship and friendship. But in terms of organizations that would represent their interests, ghetto residents are underorganized. Such organizations as exist are mostly not indigenous to the neighborhood but rather have been established by others on behalf of the residents. Indigenous organizations, on the other hand, tend, with certain exceptions, to be rather sporadic, often centering around the rise or eclipse of this or that individual leader who succeeds for a time in building an organization through his own personal leadership.

Mutual Support, earlier largely a function of the neighborhood and relatives and friends, has come in an urbanized society to be carried on increasingly under formally organized auspices such as social service agencies, hospitals, welfare departments, clinics, and visiting nurse services. We have already noted that such agencies tend in the ghetto to be oriented inordinately toward the function of social control. In addition, the services offered are often extremely poor, and many studies indicate that the ghetto dweller is the object of various forms of discrimination. For example, numerous studies show that both diagnosis and treatment for mental illness are systematically related to the social class of the recipient group. Likewise, the quality of health care has been shown in most studies to be inferior in the case of the ghetto dweller. And, like other agencies and organizations in the ghetto, the agencies of mutual support are typically run by people who do not live there, and who are different in race, in income, and in position in the larger society.

Even this cursory survey of the ghetto as a social system indicates two important points, quite aside from the inferiority of the quality of living conditions offered the ghetto resident. The first is that the ghetto constitutes a system whose parts mutually reinforce one another. As we look across these five locality-relevant functions, we see that they are performed in the ghetto in a manner that virtually assures dependency. Further, they do not train the individual to think of himself as a part of the larger society, but rather to look upon the institutions of the large society with fear, hostility, and rage.

The other is that the institutions of the ghetto are not those of the ghetto population, but are those of the surrounding society, warped in accordance with the fact that they are "serving" a disadvantaged group, a group for whom the larger values of basic human dignity, justice, and respect for the nobility of each person are somehow less binding.

Seen in this way, the relation of the ghetto to the surrounding society is characterized by reciprocal reinforcement. For on the one hand the public institutions of the ghetto are provided by the surrounding society, and geared to exert controls in the direction of conformity with the larger society, while at the same time providing the "mutual support" dictated by American values. But on the other hand they do so in a manner encouraging dependency, both psychological and economical; discouraging attempts to "break out" into the mainstream; and instilling fear and hatred of the school, the law, and social agencies; thus producing behavior that can be disclaimed with the self-righteous demeanor of people who have "given" much, only to find the recipients "undeserving." In the symbiotic reciprocation between ghetto conditions and the surrounding society, the ghettos constitute a physical locale where disadvantaged people, increasingly blacks, can be segregated from the view of more prosperous and advantaged people in an otherwise affluent society. These disadvantaged people may provide a source of cheap labor, during such times as cheap labor happens to be needed at the margins of economic production; and of course they constitute the occasion for a large and growing industry of social workers and other caretakers and research workers who earn a living above the poverty level by "serving" those below it.

Now of course, like other composites, this composite picture is somewhat imprecise. Not all these disadvantages apply to all black ghetto residents with equal weight. Some ghetto people are employed above the poverty level. Not every experience with the school or with a social service agency or with the welfare department is denigrating. There is an occasional black businessman. Occasionally, the complaint to the code enforcement authority or to the health department is heeded. Not all police are brutal. Not all stores are exploitative. Occasionally, there is an understanding judge. Yet, in the aggregate, the scales tip massively in the indicated direction for black ghetto residents.

This brief sketching out of the perduring systemic aspects of the ghetto configuration has not been given in order to "view with alarm." The point is, rather, to stress that this interrelated system has a great degree of coherence internally and has relationships with other systems in the larger society which make it difficult to change.

Most of the papers in this volume are explicitly concerned not with the internal coherence and pertinacity of the ghetto as a societal form, but rather with the way social policy relevant to the ghetto is developed in the broad confrontation of political forces in American society. One can hardly read these papers without being struck by the specific themes which cut across them, coming up repeatedly in different contexts, and being approached by the authors at times from essentially the same point of view, at times from directly opposite points of view. These themes are important not only because they belong to a diagnosis of the ghetto problem but because they in so many instances imply different types of political action, on which the authors disagree

COLONIALISM, CONSPIRACY, AND COLLECTIVE GUILT

The concept of *colonialism* as an analytical model for understanding social institutions in the ghetto is raised in the paper by Norton E. Long, who asserts with regard to ghetto residents: "Like other colonials, they must learn from their masters the ideology and techniques for their own liberation." Tom Hayden analyzes some of the criticisms that have been made against employing the concept of colonialism with respect to the ghettos, and in turn points out that the criticisms are peripheral and that the basic concept is valid. Robert H. Binstock goes on to point out an essential difference in the colonialism which is based on domination from abroad and that which characterizes American ghettos. In the American case, the "colonials" are not a small dominant minority whose resource base is thousands of miles away, but are a majority with potent resources which would make armed rebellion a carnage.

Whether or not they constitute colonialism, an essential characteristic of ghetto institutions is that they are dominated not by local people, but by others. The people who teach the schools, police the streets, operate the churches, run the social work agencies, provide health services, own the stores, run the industry, and fight the fires are not ghetto people; the organizations that employ them are not run by ghetto people; and the policies they follow are not set by ghetto people. Rather, whether one thinks of them as helpers or exploiters, they represent the functionaries in a process over which ghetto people have little control and with which they feel little sense of identification. In this sense, ghetto institutions are similar to those of an occupying power, and in this sense a diagnosis of the politics of welfare must address itself to the forms in which valid local representation may be attained, and how these forms can be achieved.

A second *theme,* which is only occasionally in the forefront of attention in these papers but lurks ubiquitously in the background, is perhaps best conveyed by the word *conspiracy.* The conspiracy theme relates to two orders of phenomena, one involving the dominant society surrounding the ghetto and the other involving ghetto residents themselves. It is perhaps best introduced by alluding to the consideration of the ghetto as a coherent social system. . . . One can approach the "conspiracy" issue by considering the proposition: *If it had been the conscious intent of white society to produce a subsystem within American society in which Negroes would be segregated and within which they would be controlled, exploited, and continually forced into a position of second-class citizenship, both in their own perception and in that of whites, such an intention could not have been fulfilled more effectively than by developing the present system of black ghettos.*

This proposition implies that the system works so well that it can hardly be by chance. It is, whether directly or indirectly, the solution of a white society of Judeo-Christian traditions to the problem of how to keep blacks in subjection while still maintaining an alleged loyalty to the ideal values. Hence, the police brutality, the failure to enforce housing codes, the shoddy treatment given welfare recipients, the physical neglect of street cleaning and ghetto public facilities, the failure to activate an adequate housing program, and so on, are not merely a series of coincidental "problems," failures to implement the American dream in a number of isolated cases. They are rather the result of a systematic policy, partly conscious, partly unconscious, of subjugation of black people by white people. This, it would seem, is the underlying rationale of the charges of white racism, and of the recent ascendancy of that term over the term that was much more common until fairly recently—racial discrimination.

The aggregate result, in other words, appears so purposeful and so coherent that the assumption of purposeful, deliberate collective intent seems the only logical one. The ghetto configuration works *as if* white society were definitely wanting it that way and consciously planning it that way. Hence, the "plot," or "conspiracy."

The issue seems unresolvable on this level of analysis, since different people may contemplate the same set of interconnected data and some will call them a conspiracy and others will not. The approach from social system theory is helpful for purposes of understanding what is involved. One of the principal concerns of general systems theory, for example, is the recognition that various systems function as though they had a purpose. Whether or not they can be called purposeful without imputing some kind of "conscious" purposefulness is a much debated issue, which even extends to cybernetic systems.[1] The "invisible hand" which Adam Smith saw guiding the market process illustrates another aspect of the phenomenon. Systems act in ways which, when observed, seem to imply purposive, aggregate, centralized direction, even where it can be readily demonstrated that such direction does not take place.

The point is somewhat more readily understood when Merton's distinction between manifest and latent functions is taken into account. Put most simply, Merton recognized that certain behaviors may have the explicit purpose of

[1] Cf. Walter Buckley, ed., *Modern Systems Research for the Behavioral Scientist: A Sourcebook* (Chicago: Aldine, 1968), especially Part V, Section A: "Cybernetics and Purpose."

accomplishing goal *A*, but quite apart from this may also operate in such a manner as to bring about the accomplishment of goal *B*, even when goal *B* was not consciously a part of the planning.[2]

To say this is not to establish that in the case of white racism there is no conspiracy, but rather merely to point out that the conspiracy issue cannot be demonstrated simply by pointing to the circumstance that any given system funcions "as if" there were conscious, deliberate purpose and controlled direction to the total system.

Interestingly, the issue is dramatized by the attitudes of various parties on the matter of "collective guilt" for white racism. For example, the National Advisory Commission on Civil Disorders concluded: "What white Americans have never fully understood—but what the Negro can never forget—is that white society is deeply implicated in the ghetto. White institutions created it, white institutions maintain it, and white society condones it."[3] Hubert H. Humphrey, who was Vice President at the time, stated in a prepared address: "The contention by the President's riot commission that white society condones negro slums comes dangerously close to a doctrine of group guilt."[4]

In relation to the "conspiracy" question, this concept of group guilt could lead to an interesting and lengthy digression. Let us permit ourselves only a brief one. Modern social philosophy does not quite countenance the justice of the Old Testament God in punishing the Egyptians for the misdeeds of their Pharaoh, for which they were not individually guilty. Likewise, there are many people who still remember with consternation the destruction of the entire community of Lidice, Czechoslovakia, by the Nazis in retribution for the slaying of a Gestapo leader there. Christianity, by and large, modified the doctrine of collective guilt or collective salvation, for that matter, and in effect placed both on a more individual basis, so that in this sense, at least, *Pilgrim's Progress* is the Christian counterpart of the book of Exodus. Despite the values which have been ascribed to this more individualized viewpoint, in which the matter of guilt or innocence came to be laid on the individual rather than the group and in which motivation, purity of heart, and questions of individual intent became uppermost, there appears today to be a growing body of thought which indicates that this individualization of moral responsibility involves a high price, particularly in complex societies where individuals are inextricably bound up in systemic networks whose aggregate effect may be largely unrelated to individual motivation and individual morality. The point has been well developed by Reinhold Niebuhr in his *Moral Man and Immoral Society*.[5] The relevance of the question for the ghettos is indicated by the

[2] Robert K. Merton, *Social Theory and Social Structure,* rev. ed. (New York: The Free Press of Glencoe, 1957), pp. 19ff.

[3] *Report of the National Advisory Commission on Civil Disorders* (New York: Bantam, 1968), p. 2.

[4] *The New York Times,* March 25, 1968.

[5] Reinhold Niebuhr, *Moral Man and Immoral Society: A Study in Ethics and Politics* (New York: Scribner's, 1932).

perplexity with which many white middle class "liberals" consider their own relationship to the ghetto problem and "white racism." They feel that in their own personal lives they have tried to free themselves from prejudice, have "given to worthy causes" on behalf of the Negro, have defended racial equality in country club locker rooms and civic associations to the point of infuriating their less enlightened friends, have gone out of their way to associate with Negroes on a basis of equality. They have voted for the political leader who seemed to be the most genuinely concerned about racial justice.

Yes, they live in a white suburb, while the black ghettos fester, but they have been trying for years to promote open housing in their own community. Yes, they earn their living from a company which has inordinately few Negro employees in the white collar brackets, and so on through the school, the church, social activities, and government; but they wish things were different.

Yet, earnest though they may be, they recognize that in all these cases they are participating in and benefiting from institutions that, despite their own wishes, are, in their totality, racist—at least in the sense that in their aggregate outcome they produce the various conditions described as racial injustice. Herein lies what appears to be valid in the issue of white racism and collective guilt.

Unfortunately, we do not have a social ethic which accommodates adequately the type of conceptual analysis and empirical finding which arises from a social system approach to the ghettos. We are left either with a stupendous aggregate evil, but no individual evildoers; or, taking the other horn of the dilemma, we are asked to feel individually guilty for circumstances over which we have no individual control. Meanwhile, the exploitative system persists and awaits an ethic which can adequately handle the individual's relationship to large, impersonal systems.

The other relevant aspect of the "conspiracy" question has been widely debated—the sense in which ghetto rioting and arson can be considered on the one hand to be merely a blind, visceral type of lashing out, a catharsis through rage—and the sense in which it can be considered as purposeful, goal oriented, a deliberate means of "telling Whitey how things are going to be." The National Advisory Commission on Civil Disorders was quite explicit about the widespread riots of 1967:

"On the basis of all the information collected the Commission concludes that the urban disorders of the summer of 1967 were not caused by, nor were they the consequence of, any organized plan or 'conspiracy.'"[6]

Yet, whether or not organized, many aspects of the rioting, particularly of the arson and looting, appeared to be purposive, as did the similar activity after the assassination of Dr. Martin Luther King, Jr. The distinction here is not whether the riots performed a (latent) function, but whether that function was significant in the motivation of the actors. The evidence to support the latter seems to be meager, at least for the vast majority of participants.

[6] *Report of the National Advisory Commission on Civil Disorders*, p. 202.

NEIGHBORHOOD AUTONOMY, BLACK POWER, AND THE REVOLUTIONARY FERMENT

A recurrent theme in the papers is that of *neighborhood autonomy*. It is perhaps best approached through the consideration of a point already raised: that the institutions of the ghetto, whether or not they are (manifestly) *for* ghetto residents, are not *by* them. Both Tom Hayden and Norton E. Long emphasize the great importance of neighborhood autonomy, and Daniel J. Elazar asserts that neighborhood autonomy, far from being opposed to a "creative federalism," is actually one of its preconditions. As Elazar points out, there has been a turnabout in which the "progressives," or "liberals," who for the past three decades have been advocating the centralization of decision-making into more and more inclusive units, especially the federal government, are now decrying the curse of bigness in bureaucracies, the essential oppression of the mass society, and are advocating participatory democracy on a decentralized basis, including neighborhood autonomy. More specifically, black leaders and white liberals are stressing the necessity of neighborhood autonomy in the ghettos, the necessity for ghetto people to control the institutions that influence their lives in their own neighborhoods.

The current zig-zagging course of the neighborhood autonomy issue is hardly unprecedented. The "neighborhood unit" as an important basis for association in addition to a mere aggregation of dwellings and facilities emerged several decades ago. The concept, expounded and promoted by Clarence Arthur Perry,[7] achieved wide popularity in subsequent decades among architects and city planners. But the idea of making much of the neighborhood as a *social* unit was attacked as largely anachronistic and irrelevant by planners such as Reginald Isaacs[8] and sociologists such as Richard Dewey.[9] During this same period, there was a great proliferation of neighborhood or community council organizations, neighborhood centers, Alinsky-type organizations, and other types of social arrangement designed to promote the values inherent in the neighborhood, which was perceived as a social unit under threat of engulfment by the institutions of mass society. Gradually, however, there grew the realization that the major institutions which control the lives of people in their neighborhoods are not controlled by those neighborhoods, either in the ghettos or elsewhere.

Now that the wheel has again turned, and the concern for neighborhood autonomy is being voiced loud and strong by or on behalf of ghetto residents, there remains the basic question as to how relevant the neighborhood is as a unit of social organization in a period when so many vital decisions and policies

---

[7]Clarence Arthur Perry, *The Neighborhood Unit,* Monograph I of Vol. 7, *Regional Survey of New York and Its Environs,* Committee on Regional Planning of New York, 1929.

[8]Reginald Isaacs, "Are Urban Neighborhoods Possible?" *Journal of Housing* (July 1948.)

[9]Richard Dewey, "The Neighborhood, Urban Ecology, and City Planners," *American Sociological Review,* 15:4 (August 1950).

affecting neighborhood living are made at the city-wide level or the state level, or, with increasing volume, at the national level. Putting this question in sharpened form: If Scarsdale cannot be autonomous, can Harlem? If Winchester cannot be autonomous, can Roxbury? If Grosse Point cannot be autonomous, can inner Detroit?

Yet, though underlining the issue, such questions do not help clarify it. Rather, the question is *what* types of power over *what* types of behavior or public or private facility are relevant for decentralization to the neighborhood level, and what types of transfers and transformations do these involve? A consideration of some fairly widespread demands of black power advocates indicates that there remain many highly relevant issues: control over decentralized functions of local government, such as police, sanitation, public welfare, health, and other facilities, by local ghetto residents; similar control over schools, devolvement of ownership of present ghetto business establishments to ghetto residents, and development of new, locally owned enterprises; encouragement of entrepreneurship by indigenous residents; reversal of the development toward city-wide "at large" election of council members, so as to move toward election by wards or districts—and, in general, substantial control by neighborhood residents over activities designed to serve ghetto people.

Certainly, these issues are relevant to the neighborhood level, and are somewhat different, though perhaps more pertinent, than those associated with earlier, well-meaning efforts toward "neighborhood improvement" endeavors. Yet, these issues exist only within the parameters of still larger issues: How much income is accessible to neighborhood residents through national and state public assistance or alternative income maintenance programs? How much money is available to neighborhood schools through federal and state funding? What kinds of loans for mortgages, business investment, and other purposes are available through the federal government? How much in federal or state funds comes into the municipal treasury and is thus available for the development and improvement of municipal services and facilities in the neighborhood? How much is available for low-cost housing? These are questions that are not immediately approachable through neighborhood organizations, and past attempts to coordinate neighborhood organizations across the country on behalf of social policies affecting *all* neighborhoods have usually been both miniscule and ineffective.

Closely related to the theme of neighborhood autonomy has been that of *black power*. There is obviously wide divergence between the views of Norton E. Long and those of Robert C. Wood. It would be gratuitous to seek here to add to the heated, many-sided literature on the subject of black power—except to note one related item, highly conspicuous by its omission from the papers included in this volume: the fact that the majority of the poor in the United States are white, and the implication of this for an evaluation of equating ghettos with blackness and neighborhood autonomy in the ghettos with black power.

Four aspects of this circumstance merit consideration here. First is the

importance of the fact that the war on poverty and the more recent Model
Cities program have come increasingly to be thought of, by blacks and whites
alike, as programs for blacks. This development, needless to say, has had both
positive and negative repercussions among various parts of the white population.

But second, the outcome has been that the poor white, whether in the city
ghetto or in disadvantaged rural areas, has been underrepresented both
numerically and—perhaps more important—symbolically in the decision-
making both by the poor and by the nonpoor as regards measures presumably
to benefit the poor.

Third, the comparative neglect of the white poor both numerically and
symbolically can but serve to strengthen a bitter and ironic aspect of the entire
race/poverty configuration: that often, the bitterest enemy of the poor black
is the poor white.

Fourth, the issue as stated by Norton E. Long, though clear, is somewhat
oversimplified. It is not a question of black cities for black people. It is rather
a question of the mixture of control of various groups, minorities and majorities, which remains whether the majority in a particular city, or city neighborhood, is black or white. Should a city whose voters are 51 percent black have
100 percent black control, and a city which is 51 percent white have 100
percent white control? Despite the prevalence of segregational practices aimed
at blacks, the ghettos—by any set of objective criteria of poverty of residents,
dilapidation of housing, or disadvantaged circumstances in other aspects of
social organization—are far from exclusively black. People with experience in
the competition among ethnic groups—blacks, Puerto Ricans, whites (including national-origin groups), Mexican-Americans—know that the ghetto problem cannot be approached realistically in terms of all-or-none Blackism. The
relations between a black majority and a white minority of heterogeneous
composition present an agenda concerning which many alternatives are possible—including the continuation of the oppression of minority groups, only this
time by blacks.

A final theme, which constituted part of the prescribed topic for Tom
Hayden's paper, is the *revolutionary ferment.* It was felt necessary or at least
desirable to single out the topic of the New Left and the "revolutionary
ferment" for special treatment as an emerging force in policy determination
processes with respect to the ghettos. Conceivably, one would have found
repeated allusion to it in most of the other papers, and indeed this might have
been the case if the authors had not known that it was to receive intensive
treatment in a separate paper.

Taken as a whole, the net impact of these papers would seem to indicate
the essential conservatism of the existing channels through which social policy
regarding the ghettos is formulated in the American political process. As Alan
D. Wade indicates, the process of decision-making around welfare politics at
the federal level as depicted in Charles I. Schottland's comprehensive analysis
is essentially conservative and elitist. On balance, one is justified in entertaining

doubts as to whether a great amount of impetus for change is to be expected from this source, or from the forces around the various State Houses of the nation, or from the complex metropolitan configurations of which the ghettos are an integral—and necessary—part.

Where, then, would be the new dynamic forces that could begin to alter the configuration of decision-making to such an extent that the most-needed changes will actually take place?

Perhaps the greatest dynamic is from the ghetto itself. For something is stirring there. One can think of this something in terms of four interrelated components. There is the growing process of organization of the poor to speak for their own interests, rather than being spoken for by the nonpoor. There are the riots, which dramatize the stirring of a mighty and potentially cataclysmic force capable of tearing the cities apart. There is black power, the increasing realization on the part of Negroes that they will not be given their share of the benefits of a highly productive society but will have to struggle for them as Negroes. And there is the growing surge toward decentralization, a surge which goes far beyond the question of whether this or that school system or this or that municipal service will be decentralized, and constitutes by now the proportions of a social movement.

Underlying all these, there is the revolutionary ferment—the noise from the streets, the daily-accumulating new ways of seeking to influence the decision-making process by other than conventionally sanctioned means. The ghettos are caught up in this revolutionary ferment, being, among other things, part of the symbols and part of the substance of a social order whose basic premises are undergoing critical scrutiny. This questioning of the fundamental principles of our society is occasioned because of both the gap between ideal values and social reality, and increasing skepticism as to whether the ideal values, themselves, are valid. But the ghettos are only part of the subject-matter of the rebellion. "Mass society" is also indicted. So is centralized power. So is American society's overelaboration of its material culture. Conventional methods for carrying on policy contest—the political debate, the ballot, the educational campaign, the political pressure group, the letter to the editor, the legal contest—are themselves under indictment as being patently inadequate to effect the changes that are indispensable if injustices such as those of the ghettos are to be eliminated.

As these words are being written, the hot summer of 1968 is coming upon us, the Poor People's March is taking place in Washington, and the President of the United States has acceded to Congressional demands for a 6 billion dollar budget cut. The implication is clear to thousands of Americans: the conventional channels of public policy formation in the United States are incapable of confronting the crisis unless they are constantly being pressed by the "noise from the streets." Even among the thousands who take recourse to norm-violating methods of social policy participation—the draft-card burners, the students who seize control of universities, the ghetto rioters, the peace vigilers, the armed black militants—there are many who prefer that the established system for policy-making not adapt itself to the pressure from the streets but instead be destroyed, to be replaced by an allegedly more equitable one.

Can the system right what an increasing number of people are coming to consider to be its tragic wrongs—both at home and abroad—before it disintegrates under the twin pressures of external rebellion and internal anomic immobilization? Or will it be destroyed? Or do we confront the prospect of still another century of exploitation and racial injustice?

These, it would appear, are the basic questions which underlie the politics of welfare today. In seeing this, the New Left raises the right questions, whether or not it supplies the right answers. (As a matter of fact, it supplies precious few answers, good or bad, which even attempt to present clear and viable alternatives to the status quo.)

As one black civil rights leader put it, "We must try to prevent riots like we had last summer but if they occur, we can't afford to waste them." He is not a militant. Quite the opposite. But he catches, in this statement, the sense that if the political system is to face up to its huge problems, it will need plenty of "push" from the outside. Here, the "outside" means all the unconventional methods of social policy participation that help make this an exciting and fateful era.

The forces at work are truly revolutionary. It would be foolish to take for granted that the changes they produce will occur peacefully.

Social and Physical Planning for the Elimination of Urban Poverty
Herbert J. Gans

City planning has traditionally sought community betterment through so-called *physical* methods, such as the creation of efficient land use and transportation schemes, the sorting out of diverse types of land use, and the renewal of technologically obsolescent areas and buildings to achieve functional, as well as esthetically desirable, arrangements of structures and spaces. This paper deals with a new planning concept which places greater emphasis on economic and social methods of improving community life. In some places it is called human renewal; in others, community development; in yet others, social planning. Although none of the names is quite appropriate, the programs to which they refer are of crucial importance to the future of the city, for they seek to do away with—or at least to decimate—urban poverty and the deprivation that accompanies it. If these programs succeed, they are likely to have a lasting impact on city planning and on the other professions concerned with planning for community welfare.

The fight against poverty is not new, of course, and, in fact, the elimination of urban deprivation was one of the goals of the founders of modern city planning. The planning movement itself developed partly in reaction to the conditions under which the European immigrants who came to American cities in the mid-19th century had to live. The reduction of their squalor was one of Frederick Law Olmstead's goals when he proposed the building of city parks so that the poor—as well as the rich—might have a substitute rural landscape in which to relax from urban life. It motivated the Boston civic leaders who first built playgrounds in the slums of that city, and the founders of the settlement house movement, notably Jane Addams, who argued strongly for city planning. It also sparked the efforts of those who built model tenements to improve the housing conditions of the poor. And Ebenezer Howard had this goal in mind when he proposed to depopulate the London slums through Garden Cities.

Most of these planning efforts were not aimed directly at the reduction of poverty and deprivation, but sought to use land planning, housing codes and occasionally zoning to eliminate slums and reduce densities in the tightly packed tenement neighborhoods. The apotheosis of this approach—slum clearance—followed upon the arrival of the newest wave of poor immigrants: the Southern Negroes, Puerto Ricans and Mexicans who came to the city during World War II and in the post-war era. After a decade of noting the effects of the federal slum clearance program, however, some observers became concerned because while this method was eliminating slums, it was not contributing significantly to the improvement of the slum dwellers' living conditions.

In many cases, the reduction in the already short supply of low cost housing brought about by slum clearance, together with faulty or nonexistent relocation planning sent slum dwellers into adjacent slums or forced them to overcrowd declining areas elsewhere. But even where slum clearance was accompanied by adequate relocation programs, the housing of poor people in decent low cost dwellings did not solve other—and equally pressing—problems, such as poverty, unemployment, illiteracy, alcoholism, and mental illness. Nor could rehousing alone do away with crime, delinquency, prostitution, and other deviant behavior. In short, it became clear that such physical changes as urban renewal, good housing, and modern project planning were simply not enough to improve the lives of the poverty-stricken.

As a result, planners and "housers" began to look for non-physical planning approaches.[1] In this process, they made contact with other professions

[1]Another impetus came from the fact that several cities scheduled urban renewal projects in their skid row areas, and programs to "rehabilitate" its residents were developed as part of the relocation plan.

that are concerned with the low-income population, for example, social workers. Working in tandem with them and others, they have developed new programs, bearing the various names indicated above. Most often they have been referred to as social planning, a term that had been coined by social workers to describe the coordination of individual social agency programs carried out by such central planning and budgeting agencies as the United Fund.[2]

Although the term has already received considerable attention in city planning circles, I prefer to use another term. Insofar as the programs seek to aid low income people to change their fortunes and their ways of living, they are attempts to guide them toward the social and economic mobility that more fortunate people have achieved on their own. For this reason, the programs might best be described as planning for *guided mobility*.

Such programs are now underway in many American cities. Some are designed as programs in juvenile delinquency prevention, which have come into being under the aegis of the President's Committee on Juvenile Delinquency and work mainly with young people.[3] Others are oriented toward low income people of all ages, and since planners have been most active in these, the rest of the article will deal primarily with such programs.[4] Although most of the programs are just getting started, some over-all similarities between them are apparent. Needless to say, any generalizations about them are preliminary, for the programs are likely to change as they progress from initial formulation to actual implementation.

The guided mobility plans and proposals which I have examined have four major programmatic emphases:

1. to develop new methods of education for children from low income and culturally deprived homes, so as to reduce functional illiteracy, school

[2]The term has also been applied to plans which attempt to outline social—that is, non-physical—goals for the entire society, a procedure that would be more aptly called *societal* planning.

[3]Of these, the leading program is New York's Mobilization for Youth. This is described in Mobilization for Youth, Inc., "A Proposal for the Prevention and Control of Delinquency by Expanding Opportunities" (New York, Dec. 1961, mimeographed).

[4]Examples of the many such plans are: Action for Boston Community Development, "A Proposal for a Community Development Program in Boston" (Boston, Mass., Dec. 1961, mimeographed); Action Housing, Inc., ". . . Urban Extension in the Pittsburgh Area" (Pittsburgh, Pa., Sept. 1961, mimeographed); City of Oakland, "Proposal for a Program of Community Development" (City of Oakland, Cal., June and Dec. 1961, mimeographed); Community Progress, Inc., "Opening Opportunities: New Haven's Comprehensive Program for Community Progress" (New Haven, Conn., April 1962, mimeographed); and Department of City Planning, "A Plan for the Woodlawn Community: Social Planning Factors" (Chicago, Ill., Jan. 1962, mimeographed). My comments about the plans below are based on a number of published and unpublished documents which I have examined, as well as on discussions about existing and proposed plans in which I have participated in several cities. My description of these plans is, in sociological terminology, an ideal type, and does not fit exactly any one of the plans now in existence.

dropouts and learning disabilities which prevent such children from competing in the modern job market in adulthood;

2. to reduce unemployment by new forms of job training among the young, by the retraining of adults and by the creation of new jobs in the community;

3. to encourage self-help on an individual and group basis through community organization methods that stimulate neighborhood participation; and

4. to extend the amount and quality of social services to the low income population. Among the latter are traditional casework services, new experiments for giving professional help to the hard-to-reach, multi-problem family and the provision of modern facilities and programs of public recreation, public health and community center activities.

The educational phase of guided mobility includes programs such as Higher Horizons, which attempt to draw bright children from the culturally restrictive context of low income environments, and to offer them the academic and cultural opportunities available to bright middle class children. There are also programs to help average and backward youngsters, using remedial reading and other devices to guide them during the early school years, so that they will develop the skills and motivations to stay in school until high school graduation. The occupational phase of the plans includes job programs which will employ young people in useful community projects, and in quasi-apprentice programs in private industry, as well as various vocational training and retraining programs for young and old alike. Meanwhile, added effort is scheduled to attract new industries, and thus to bring new jobs to the community.

The extension of social services, and the community organization phase of the programs use decentralization as a means of reaching the high proportion of low income people who usually abstain from community contact. The provision of social services to the hard-to-reach will be attempted by bringing programs to the neighborhood level, with neighborhood directors to supervise the process. In addition, the social agencies plan to coordinate their services, so that individual agencies working with the same individual or family know what the other is doing, and duplication and contradictions can be avoided. More neighborhood facilities will also be established, including community schools, public health clinics and recreation centers, sometimes grouped in a "services center," so that people will be encouraged to come there when they need help.

The decentralizing of community organization activities is intended to create a sense of neighborhood and an interest in neighborhood self-help. Community organizers will work in the neighborhood for this purpose, and will try to involve "natural leaders" living in the area, who can act as a bridge between the professionals, the city and the neighborhood population.

This is a very general description of the programs. In actuality, each community has a somewhat distinctive approach, or a different emphasis in the selection of programs, depending partly on the lineup of sponsoring agencies. But some city planners who have become interested in guided mobility programs are still preoccupied—and sometimes too much so—with traditional physical planning approaches, notably two: the realization of a neighborhood scheme—originally devised by Clarence Perry[5] and consisting of a small, clearly bounded residential area, built up at low density, with auto and pedestrian traffic carefully separated, considerable open space, and with a combination elementary school and neighborhood meeting place in its center; and the provision both in such neighborhoods and in the larger community of a standard array of public facilities for recreation, health, education, culture, and other community services.

The concern with neighborhood is of course traditional in city planning, and even the new challenge of finding non-physical ways of helping the low-income group has not diverted the planner from it. In some cities, guided mobility plans are thus almost appendages to physical planning programs, based on the traditional belief that the rebuilding of the city into a series of separate neighborhoods to encourage a small-townish middle class form of family life is a proper solution even for poverty. Elsewhere, the program may be an appendage of urban renewal activities, the main intent still being the upgrading of the physical neighborhoods. Thus, guided mobility is used partly to organize the neighborhood into undertaking—or helping the city with—this task. But in most cases, the neighborhood emphasis is based on a genuine concern that one of the causes of urban deprivation is to be found in the poor quality of neighborhood life.

The provision of public facilities is also a traditional planning emphasis, dating back to the days when the planner was an ally of the reformers who were fighting for the establishment of these facilities. Out of this has come the belief that public facilities are crucial agencies in people's lives, that up-to-date facilities and programs will encourage intensive use of them and that this in turn will help significantly in achieving the aims of guided mobility planning.

Despite the intensity of the planner's belief in neighborhood and public facility use, there is no evidence that these two planning concepts are as important to low income people as they are to planners. Consequently, it is fair to ask whether such concepts are as crucial to the elimination of urban poverty and deprivation as is signified by their appearance in some guided mobility plans. The answer to this question requires a brief discussion of the nature of contemporary urban poverty.

[5]Clarence A. Perry, "The Neighborhood Unit," *Regional Survey of New York and Its Environs* (New York: Committee on Regional Plan of New York and Its Environs, 1929), Vol. 7, pp. 22–140.

II

The low-income population may be divided into two major segments, which sociologists call the *working class* and the *lower class*.[6] The former consists of semiskilled and skilled blue collar workers, who hold steady jobs, and are thus able to live under stable, if not affluent, conditions. Their way of life differs in many respects from those of the middle class; for example, in the greater role of relatives in sociability and mutual aid, in the lesser concern for self-improvement and education, and in their lack of interest in the good address, cultivation and the kinds of status that are important to middle class people. Although their ways are culturally different from the dominant middle class norms, these are not pathological, for rates of crime, mental illness and other social ills are not significantly higher than in the middle class. This population, therefore, has little need for guided mobility programs.

The lower class, on the other hand, consists of people who perform the unskilled labor and service functions in the society. Many of them lack stable jobs. They are often unemployed, or forced to move from one temporary—and underpaid—job to another. Partly because of occupational instability, their lives are beset with social and emotional instability as well, and it is among them that one finds the majority of the emotional problems and social evils that are associated with the low-income population.[7]

In past generations, the American economy had considerable need for unskilled labor, and the European immigrants who performed it were able to achieve enough occupational stability to raise themselves, or their children, to working class or even middle class ways of living. Today, however, the need for unskilled labor is constantly decreasing, and will soon be minimal. Consequently, the Negro, Puerto Rican and Mexican newcomers who now constitute most of the American lower class find it very difficult to improve their condition.[8]

Guided mobility planning is essentially an attempt to help them solve their problems and to aid them in changing their lives. This makes it necessary to find out what causes their problems, what they themselves are striving for and how they can be helped to achieve their strivings.

[6]Herbert J. Gans, *The Urban Villagers* (Glencoe, Ill.: Free Press, 1962), chap. 11. See also S. M. Miller and Frank Riessman, "The Working Class Subculture: A New View," *Social Problems,* vol. 9 (1961), pp. 86–97. The nature and extent of urban poverty is described in Michael Harrington, *The Other America* (New York: Macmillan, 1962), chaps. 2, 4, 5, 7, 8.

[7]An excellent brief description of lower class culture may be found in Walter B. Miller, "Lower Class Culture as a Generating Milieu of Gang Delinquency," *Journal of Social Issues,* vol. 14 (1958), pp. 5–19. The everyday life of the lower class is pictured in Oscar Lewis, *Five Families* (New York: Basic Books, 1959), and *The Children of Sanchez* (New York: Random House, 1961). Although Lewis' books deal with the lower class of Mexico City, his portrait applies, with some exceptions, to American cities as well.

[8]For an analysis of the occupational history of the European immigrants and the more recent immigrants, see Oscar Handlin, *The Newcomers* (New York: Anchor Books, 1962).

The nature of the problem is not difficult to identify. For economic reasons, and for reasons of race as well, the contemporary lower class is frustrated— if not barred—from opportunities to hold well-paid, stable jobs, to receive a decent education, to live in good housing or to get access to a whole series of choices and privileges that the white middle class takes for granted.

In addition, some lower class people lack the motivations and skills needed to participate in contemporary society, and more important, which are necessary to accept the opportunities if and when they become available. Moreover, the apathy, despair and rejection which result from lack of access to crucial opportunities help bring about the aforementioned social and emotional difficulties.

There are a number of reasons for these reactions.[9] When men are long unemployed or underemployed, they feel useless, and eventually become marginal members of their family. This has many consequences. They may desert their families, and turn to self-destructive behavior in despair. If male instability is widespread, the woman becomes the dominant member of the family, and she may live with a number of men in the hope of finding a stable mate. The result is a family type which Walter Miller calls female-based, which is marked by free unions, illegitimate children and what middle class people consider to be broken homes.[10] Boys who grow up in such families may be deprived of needed male models, and are likely to inherit some of the feelings of uselessness and despair they see in their fathers. In addition, the children must learn at an early age how to survive in a society in which crisis is an everyday occurrence, and where violence and struggle are ever-present. Thus, they may learn how to defend themselves against enemies, and how to co-exist with an alcoholic parent, but they do not learn how to read, how to concentrate on their studies or how to relate to the teacher.[11] Those that do must defend their deviant behavior—and it is deviant in the lower class—against their peers, who, like peers in all other groups, demand that they conform to the dominant mode of adaptation. Also, many children grow up in households burdened with mental illness, and this scars their own emotional and social growth. Out of such conditions develops a lower class culture with a set of behavior patterns which is useful for the struggle to survive in a lower class milieu, but which makes it almost impossible to participate in the larger society. And since the larger society rejects the lower class individual for such behavior, he can often develop self-respect and dignity only by rejecting the larger society. He blames it for his difficulties—and with much justification—but in this process rejects

---

[9]For a more detailed analysis, see Gans, *The Urban Villagers,* ch. 12, and Institute for Urban Studies, *Social Planning: A New Role for Sociology* (Philadelphia 1962, mimeographed). See also Mobilization for Youth, Inc., *op. cit.* and Walter B. Miller, *op. cit.*

[10]Walter B. Miller, *op. cit.* This family type is particularly widespread in the Negro lower class, in which it originated during slavery.

[11]The educational and other problems of the lower class child are described in more detail in Patricia C. Sexton, *Education and Income* (New York: Viking, 1961); and Frank Riessman, *The Culturally Deprived Child* (New York: Harper, 1962).

many of its values as well, becoming apathetic, cynical and hostile even toward those that seek to help him.

This overly brief analysis is at present mostly hypothetical, for we do not yet know exactly what it is that creates the lower class way of life. We know that the nature of family relationships, the influence of peers, the kind of home training, the adaptive characteristics of lower class culture, the high prevalence of mental illness and the need to cope with one crisis after another are all important factors, but we do not yet know exactly which factors are most important, how they operate to create the way of life that they do and how they are related to the lack of opportunities that bring them about.

Similarly, we know that lower class people are striving to change their condition, but we do not know exactly for what they are striving. It is clear that they want stable jobs and higher incomes, and there is considerable evidence of an almost magical belief in education and high occupational aspirations for the children, especially among Negroes.[12] The lack of opportunity and the constant occurrence of crises frustrate most of these aspirations before they can be implemented, but they do exist, especially among the women. On the other hand, the failure of settlement houses, social workers and other helping agencies to reach the majority of the lower class population suggests that these people either cannot or do not want to accept the middle class values which these professionals preach and which are built into the welfare activities they carry out. Such programs attract the small minority desirous of, or ready for, middle class life, but they repel the rest. A number of social scientists suggest that what lower class people are striving for is the stable, family-centered life of working class culture, and at least one delinquency prevention program is based on such an assumption.[13]

These observations about the nature of lower class life have many implications for guided mobility planning. As a result of the sparsity of knowledge, much research, experiment and evaluation of experience will be necessary in order to learn what kinds of programs will be successful. It is clear that the most urgent need is to open up presently restricted opportunities, especially in the occupational sphere. The guided mobility programs which stress the creation of new jobs, the attack on racial discrimination, education and occupational training as highest priority items are thus on the right track. Even so, new ways of bringing industry and jobs to the community must be found, for conventional programs have not been sufficiently productive. Then, ways of channelling lower class people into new jobs, and keeping them at work even if their initial performance is not as good as that of other people, or of labor saving machines, must be invented. Racial barriers will also have to come down more quickly, especially in those spheres of life and activity most impor-

[12]For the most recent example of this finding, see R. Kleiner, S. Parker, and H. Taylor, "Social Status and Aspirations in Philadelphia's Negro Population" (Philadelphia: Commission on Human Relations, June 1962, mimeographed).

[13]Mobilization for Youth, Inc., *op. cit.*

tant to lower class people, so that they can begin to feel that they have some stake in society. This too is easier said than done.

Not only is desegregation difficult to implement, but the most successful programs so far have benefited middle class non-whites more than their less fortunate fellows. For lower class people, access to jobs, unions and decent low cost housing is more important, as is the assurance of fair treatment from the police, the courts, from city hall, storeowners and helping agencies. The integration of high priced suburban housing, expensive restaurants or concert halls is for *them* of much less immediate significance.

Also, methods of encouraging motivations and skills, and of maintaining aspirations in the face of frustration must be found. If the matriarchal lower class family is at fault, ways of providing boys with paternal substitutes must be developed. Where the entire lower class milieu is destructive, children may have to be removed from it, especially in their formative years. Treatments for mental illness, alcoholism and narcotics addiction that will be effective among lower class people have to be discovered, and the causes of these ills isolated so that prevention programs may be set up. Schools must be created which can involve lower class children. This means that they must teach the skills needed in a middle class society yet without the middle class symbols and other trappings that frighten or repel the lower class student.[14] Finally, it is necessary to develop urban renewal or other housing programs that will make livable dwellings available to the low income population, within its price range, and located near enough to its places of employment so as not to require unreasonable amounts of travel time and expenditures.

These program requirements demand some radical changes in our ways of doing things. For example, if lower class people are to find employment, there will need to be economic enterprises not geared solely to profit and to cost-reduction, but also to the social profits of integrating the unemployed. In short, eventually we shall have to give up the pretense that 19th century free enterprise ideology can cope with 20th century realities, and learn to replan some economic institutions to help the low-income population, just as we are now redesigning public education to teach this population's children. Likewise, if lower class people are to become part of the larger society, there must be changes in the way the police, the courts and political structures treat them. To cite just one instance, lower class people must be represented more adequately in local party politics, and their needs and demands must receive more adequate hearing at city hall than has heretofore been the case. Similarly, the professions that now seek to help lower class people will have to be altered so as to be more responsive to how lower class people define their needs, and this may mean the replacement of some professionals by skilled nonprofessionals who are more capable of achieving rapport with lower class clients. Also, urban renewal policy must concern itself less with "blight" removal, or with the use of new construction to solve the city's tax problems, and more with

---

[14]See Sexton, *op. cit.* and Riessman, *op. cit.*

improvement of the housing conditions of the slum dwellers. Changes, such as these, which require redistribution of power, income, privileges and the alteration of established social roles, are immensely difficult to bring about. Even so, they are necessary if urban poverty and deprivation are to be eliminated.[15]

III

Proper guided mobility planning must be based on methods that will achieve the intended goal. If the hypotheses about the causes of urban deprivation are correct, the basic components of guided mobility planning must be able to affect the economy, the political and social structures that shore up poverty and racial—as well as class—discrimination, the foci of lower class culture that frustrate the response to opportunities, notably the family, the peer group, the milieu in which children grow up and the helping agencies that now have difficulty in reaching lower class people, especially the school. Any programs which lack these components, and cannot bring about changes in the position of the lower class population vis-à-vis the institutions named, are unlikely to contribute significantly to the aim of guided mobility.[16]

The list of basic components does not include the two that have been especially emphasized by planners: the belief in neighborhood and the importance of public facilities. This omission is not accidental, for I do not believe that these two concepts are of high priority. Indeed, it is possible that they may divert guided mobility programs from the direction they ought to take.

By focusing programs on neighborhoods as spatial units, planners are naturally drawn to what is most visible in them, the land uses, buildings and major institutions, and their attention is diverted from what is hardest to see, the people—and social conditions—with problems. It should be clear from the foregoing analysis that the program must concentrate on the people and on the social and economic forces which foster their deprivation, rather than on neighborhood conditions which are themselves consequences of these forces.

Moreover, too much concern with neighborhoods may cause the programs to seek out the wrong people: the working class segment of the low income population rather than the lower class one. This may happen for two reasons. First, the planner often finds it difficult to distinguish between areas occupied by working class people, and those occupied by lower class people, mainly because his concept of standard housing blinds him to differences between low rent areas, usually occupied predominantly by the former, and slums, which

[15]For other programmatic statements, see Peter Marris, "A Report on Urban Renewal in the United States," and Leonard J. Duhl, "Planning and Poverty," in Leonard J. Duhl (ed.), *The Urban Condition* (New York: Basic Books, 1963), pp. 113–134, and 295–304, respectively. See also Harrington, *op. cit.*

[16]For a more detailed critical analysis of current guided mobility plans, see Gans, *Social Planning.*

house the latter.[17] Also, working and lower class people sometimes live together in the same planning area, especially if they are non-white, and a
neighborhood focus makes it difficult to reach one without the other. This is
undesirable because—as I noted earlier—the working class population does
not need guided mobility, whereas the lower class population needs it so badly
that all resources ought to be allocated to it.

Even so, these drawbacks would not be serious if neighborhood planning
could achieve the aims of guided mobility. But this is not the case, mainly
because people's lives are not significantly influenced by the physical neighborhood. The important aspects of life take place within the family, the peer group
and on the job, and the neighborhood does not seem to affect these greatly.
Moreover, although middle and working class people do sometimes participate
in neighborhood activities, this is not true of lower class people.[18] Not only do
they shy away from organizational participation generally, but because of their
great transience they do not spend much time in any one area. More important,
since life is a constant struggle for survival and an endless series of crises, lower
class people are often suspicious of their neighbors, and even more so of the
landlord, the storeowner, the police and the local politician. They harbor
similar feelings toward most other neighborhood institutions and local public
facilities.

Thus, the lower class population's involvement in the neighborhood is at
best neutral, and more often, negative. Yet even if it were more positive, the
components of neighborhood planning and the provision of the entire range
of modern public facilities can contribute relatively little to solving the problems which concern lower class people the most. To a poverty-stricken family,
the separation of car and pedestrian traffic, or the availability of park and
playground within walking distance are not very crucial; their needs are much
more basic.

This is not to reject the desirability of such planning concepts, but only to
say that given the present condition of lower class life, they are of fairly low
priority. The location and equipment of the school is much less important than
the presence of the kinds of teachers who can communicate with lower class
children, and a conventional public health facility is much less vital than an
agency that can really help a mother deserted by her husband, or a person who
must cope with mentally ill family members.

[17]Herbert J. Gans, "The Human Implications of Current Redevelopment and Relocation
Planning," *Journal of the American Institute of Planners,* vol. 24 (1959), pp. 15–25, or *Urban
Villagers,* chap. 14.
    [18]Generally speaking, middle class people participate in formal neighborhood organizations
to a much greater extent than other classes, although their social life often takes place outside
the neighborhood. Working class people are less likely to participate in formal organizations, but
most of their social activities take place close to home. For a discussion of working class attitudes
toward the neighborhood, see Marc Fried and Peggy Gleicher, "Some Sources of Residential
Satisfaction in an Urban 'Slum'," *Journal of the American Institute of Planners,* vol. 27 (1961),
pp. 305–315.

The standard neighborhood-and-facilities planning package cannot even contribute significantly to the improvement of the lower class milieu. The significant components of this milieu are other people, rather than environmental features, and until these other people are socially and economically secure enough to trust each other, the milieu is not likely to improve sufficiently to prevent the perpetuation of past deprivations on the young growing up within it.

In short, it seems clear that the kind of neighborhood scheme sought through traditional planning and zoning methods cannot be implemented among lower class people until the basic components of guided mobility programs have been effectuated. A stable, peaceful neighborhood in which there is positive feeling between neighbors assumes that people have good housing, the kind of job that frees them from worrying about where the next meal or rent money will come from, the solution of basic problems so that the landlord, the policeman or the bill collector are no longer threatening and the relief from recurring crises so that they can begin to pay some attention to the world outside the household. Similarly, only when people feel themselves to be part of the larger society, and when they have learned the skills needed to survive in it, will they be able to take part in school or community center activities, or to develop the ability to communicate with the staff of a health clinic. In short, the programs which the neighborhood planner proposes cannot come about until more basic problems have been solved; they are consequences of the elimination of urban poverty rather than devices for it.

Neighborhood planning is necessary, of course, but what is needed is of a social and political type which supports the community, state, and federal programs for the elimination of poverty. Thus, the methods required to help the low income population develop the skills and attitudes prerequisite to survival in a modern society must reach into the neighborhood and the street in order to recruit people who do not, for one reason or another, come by themselves into public facilities established for such programs. Also, local political activity must be stimulated so that low income people can use the one power they have—that of numbers and votes—to make their wishes heard at city hall and in Washington. This differs considerably from the need for "citizen participation" often called for by planners and community organization experts; that has usually been defined as citizen consideration of—and consent to—professionally developed programs, or civic activity which is decidedly non-political. The kind of local citizen participation that is needed is quite political, however, and since its aim must be to change the political status quo, it is unlikely that community organizers, who are after all employees of the existing political institution or of establishment-dominated welfare agencies, will be able to encourage such activity even if they are personally willing to do so. Hopefully, enlightened civic leaders and politicians will eventually realize that the low income population must be more adequately represented in the political process, but in all likelihood, they will resist any change in the existing political alignments until they have no other choice. Thus, the initiative for local political activity must come from the areas in which low income people live. But whoever the initiating agencies may be, these are the types of neighborhood planning that are required to do something about urban poverty.

IV

The incompatibility of traditional city planning aims and the basic components of guided mobility programming is not to be blamed on one or another set of planners, nor indeed is it a cause for blame at all. Rather, it stems from the history and nature of modern city planning, and from the basic assumptions in its approach. The description of two of these assumptions will also shed some light on the relationship between social and physical planning and their roles in the improvement of cities.

The first of these assumptions is the belief in the ability of change in the physical environment to bring about social change. Planners have traditionally acted on the assumption that the ordering of land uses, and improvements in the setting and design of buildings, highways and other physical features of the community would result in far-reaching improvements in the lives of those affected. The validity of this assumption has been seriously questioned in recent years, and indeed, the rise of what has been called social planning is one expression of this questioning.[19]

But the traditional city planning approach can also be described in another way, as being *method-oriented*. By this I mean that it has developed a repertoire of methods and techniques which have become professionally accepted, and which distinguish planning from other service-giving professions. As a result, the planner concerns himself largely with improvements in these methods. In this process, however, he loses sight of the goals which his methods are intended to achieve, or the problems they are to solve. Thus, he does not ask whether the methods achieve these goals, or whether they achieve *any* goals.

This concern with method is not limited to the planning profession; it can be found in all professions. The attempt to maintain and improve existing methods is useful if the goals are traditional ones, or if the profession deals only with routine problems. But it does not work as well when new goals are sought, and when new problems arise. As I have already noted, improvements in neighborhood planning cannot contribute significantly to the new problems of the city, or to the new goal of eliminating urban poverty.

What is needed instead is a *goal-oriented* or problem-oriented approach, which begins not with methods, but with the problems to be solved or the goals to be achieved. Once these are defined and agreed upon, the methods needed to achieve them can be determined through the use of professional insight,

[19]See, for example, Irving Rosow, "The Social Effects of the Physical Environment," *Journal of the American Institute of Planners,* vol 27 (1961), pp. 127–133.

research and experiment until the right methods, i.e., those which will solve the problem or realize the goal, are found.[20] This approach was used in the foregoing pages, in which I questioned the usefulness of traditional planning methods and proposed instead programs to cope with the problems of the lower class population—and their causes—as well as programs which would lead toward the goals this population was seeking for itself.

This approach is more difficult to implement than a method-oriented one, because it does not respect accepted methods—unless they work—and because it rejects the claims of professional traditions or professional expertise that are not supported by empirical evidence. It may require new methods and new approaches, and thus can wreak havoc with the established way of doing things. However much the goal-oriented approach may upset the profession in the short-run, in the long run it improves its efficiency and thus its expertise and status, because its methods are likely to be much more successful, thus reducing the risk of professional failure. In an effort as pioneering and difficult as guided mobility planning, a problem and goal-oriented approach is therefore absolutely essential.

The conception of method-oriented and goal-oriented planning can also aid our understanding of the relationship between physical and social planning. In the professional discussions of this relationship, the subject has frequently been posed as social planning *versus* physical planning. Although it is not difficult to understand why the subject has been framed in this competitive way, the resulting dichotomy between social and physical planning is neither meaningful nor desirable. There are several reasons for rejecting this dichotomy.

First, social planning is said to deal with the human elements in the planning process. When planners talk of the human side of renewal, or of the human factors in planning, they are suggesting by implication that physical planning is inhuman, that in its concern with land use, site design, the redevelopment of cleared land and the city tax base, it has no concern for the needs of human beings. I would not blame physical planners for objecting to this implication, and am surprised that they have not done so.

But even if this implication is inaccurate, the dichotomy has led to another, even more unfortunate implication, which has some truth to it. Every planning activity, like any other form of social change, creates net benefits for some people, and net costs for others. These may be non-material as well as material. Whether intentionally or not, physical planning has tended to provide greater benefits to those who already have considerable economic resources or political power, be they redevelopers or tenants who profit from a luxury housing

---

[20]This approach is currently receiving considerable attention in planning literature. My discussion is based on an initial formulation by Martin Meyerson, and is treated in more detail in studies conducted by him, John Dyckman, and this writer which are now being prepared for publication. For a summary statement of this approach, see Paul Davidoff and Thomas Reiner, "A Choice Theory of Planning," *Journal of the American Institute of Planners,* vol. 28 (1962), pp. 103–115.

scheme, central business district retailers who gain, or expect to gain, from the ever-increasing number of plans to "revive downtown," or the large taxpayers who are helped most when planning's main aim is to increase municipal revenues. The interest in social planning is a direct result of this distribution of benefits, for it seeks to help the people who are forced to pay net costs in the physical planning process. Too often, these are poor people, for example, residents of a renewal or highway project who suffer when adequate relocation housing is lacking. Needless to say, this political bifurcation, in which physical planning benefits the well-to-do, and social planning the less fortunate ones, is not a desirable state of affairs either for the community or for planning.

Finally, in actual everyday usage, the dichotomy refers to skills possessed by different types of planners. Physical planning is that set of methods which uses the traditional skills of the city planner and zoning official; social planning, that set favored by sociologically trained planners, by social workers and by other professionals concerned with welfare aims. Yet if the planning activities of each are examined more closely, it becomes evident that the terms social and physical are inaccurate labels. Zoning is considered a physical planning method, but an ordinance which determines who is to live with whom, and who is to work next to whom is as much social—as well as economic and political—as it is physical. So is a transportation scheme which decides who will find it easy to get in and out of the city, and who will find it difficult. Conversely, social planners who urge the construction of more low-rent housing, or argue for scattered units rather than projects, are proposing physical schemes even while they are ostensibly doing social planning. Since all planning activities affect people, they are inevitably social, and the dichotomy between physical and social methods turns out to be meaningless. Moreover, in actual planning practice, no problem can be solved by any one method, or any one skill. In most instances a whole variety of techniques is needed to achieve the goal.

The social-physical dichotomy is a logical consequence of viewing planning as method-oriented, because when methods are most important, there is apt to be competition between the people who are skilled in one method rather than another. All successful professions want to apply the methods they know best, for this permits them to maintain their power and social position most easily.

If planning is conceived as goal-oriented, however, goals become most important and methods are subordinated to the goal. In such a planning process, in which a large number of different methods are used in an integrated fashion, any single method loses its magical aura. Moreover, no goal can be defined so narrowly that it is only physical or only social. In a goal-oriented approach, then, there can be no social or physical planning. There is only *planning*, an approach which agrees upon the best goals and then finds the best methods to achieve them.

This way of defining planning has a number of implications for the future of the professions concerned with planning matters, as well as for the improvement of cities. If professionals continue to emphasize traditional method, when and where it is not applicable, they can easily lose their usefulness, and their professional prerogative for participating in programs of community better-ment.

But it is not only the methods which must be reconsidered. Even the goals which are built into these methods are turning out to be less important today. The neighborhood concept has received little support from the clients of planning; the same is true of the planner's insistence on a reduction in the journey to work, which has not been accepted by the journeying populace. Also, in an age of automation and increasing unemployment, the need for economic growth, even if it is disorderly, is becoming more vital than the ordering of growth, and the planner's desire for stability. It is, of course, still important to have efficient transportation schemes, and to locate noxious industry away from residences, but there is less noxious industry than ever before, and for those who are affluent, the inefficiency of the automobile seems to matter little, especially if it is politically feasible to subsidize the costs of going to work by car. And even the concern with land use per se is becoming less significant. In a technology of bulldozers and rapid transportation, the qualities of the natural environment and the location of land are less important —or rather, more easily dealt with by human intervention—and increasingly, land can be used for many alternatives. The question of what is the best use, given topography and location, is thus less important than who will benefit from one use as compared to another, and who will have to pay costs, and how is the public interest affected.

In short, so-called physical planning questions are receding in importance, and socio-economic and political ones are becoming more relevant. This is, of course, why the issue of social and physical planning has been discussed as social versus physical. In the long run, however, it seems clear that the future of city planning lies less in the reliance upon land use plans than in the development of a range of methods that will guarantee the improvement of those aspects of community life that are most in need of improvement.

V

One of the most important tasks in the improvement of cities is the elimina-tion of urban poverty, and of the deprivations of lower class life. Poverty is fundamentally responsible for the slums we have been unable to eradicate by attacking the buildings, and for the deprivations which ultimately bring about the familiar list of social evils. Moreover, poverty and deprivation are what make cities so ugly and depressing, and they hasten the flight of more fortunate people into the suburbs. And this in turn contributes to economic decline, the difficulties of financing municipal services, political conflict, corruption and many of the other problems of the contemporary city.

I would not want to argue that all of the city's problems can be laid at the doorstep of poverty. There are technological changes that affect its economic health, and result in the obsolescence of industrial areas and street patterns. There are political rigidities that inhibit its relations with its hinterland. And the desire of most families to raise their children in low-density surroundings suggests that suburbia is not produced solely by the flight from the city, and would exist without urban poverty. Even so, many of the suburbanites have come to hate the city because of the poverty they see there, and this in turn helps to create the hostility between city and suburb and the political conflict that frustrates schemes for metropolitan solutions.

If planners are genuinely concerned with the improvement of cities, the fight against poverty becomes a planning problem, and one that needs to be given higher priority than it has heretofore received. A beginning is being made in the guided mobility programs that are now in operation, but a much greater effort is needed, both on the local and the federal scene, before these programs can achieve their aim. If such efforts are not made, all other schemes for improving the city will surely fail.

The Dialectics of Community Control
Stanley Aronowitz

The Black movement seeks more than a piece of the white man's pie served at the white man's table. The movement today, unlike the traditional civil rights movement, is oriented toward power.

The advance from integration to Black power and community control has reversed the century-old strategy of the civil rights movement, which sought an alliance of white liberals with the Black middle class, generally under paternalistic white leadership, to achieve democratic rights for all. While the assertion of independence from white domination and the emphasis on community control represent a necessary step in the struggle for liberation, experience suggests that it is not sufficient for fundamental social change. To win its objectives, the movement for community control and Black power needs a new conception of alliances, and even a redefinition of the objectives themselves.

The replacement of the demand for equality of opportunity with that of community control reflects the failure of the struggle for integration to achieve its stated goals, despite its blessing of legal and judicial legitimacy. Though well aware of the demographic, economic and political barriers to the integration

SOURCE: Stanley Aronowitz, "The Dialectics of Community Control," *Social Policy,* 1 (May/-June 1970), 47–51. Reprinted by permission of *Social Policy,* published by International Arts and Sciences Press, Inc., 901 North Broadway, White Plains, New York 10603.

of schools, health facilities, and employment, Blacks understand the failure of integration in another dimension: racism. Whatever the causes for the failure of integration, the distress and despair at white society's determined refusal to open the doors of opportunity compelled a new strategy.

With the shift to community control, the piece-of-the-pie philosophy was not actually abandoned—rather it was reinterpreted. Black people still want to share American affluence, but are not content to receive it within the framework of white-dominated institutions. They are now asking for their share within a new context—Black control of Black communities and their institutions. But unless this struggle is broadened into a general struggle for popular, democratic control over all aspects of economic, political and social life, community control is certain to be absorbed by what Richard Cloward calls "corporate imperialism in the ghetto," a new domestic colonialism.

CONSERVATIVE AND RADICAL TENDENCIES

Inherent in the concept of community control are both conservative and radical tendencies which, in the long run, may prove irreconcilable. On one hand, the political and economic thrust of the demand remains conservative: i.e., it does not challenge the present means of allocating resources among the various elements of the political economy. To a large degree, the emphasis on community control has turned Black politics away from issues of national power and thus, in part, represents a step backwards. In struggling for a redistribution of local resources, Blacks come into conflict with white working-class and middle-class communities, rather than the national government and the corporate institutions which control it. The working assumption of much of the Black movement is that residents of white neighborhoods are their competitors for the available funds for education, health, housing and other essential services. In this paradigm, the large corporate employers and foundations appear as the allies of the Black community and the trade unions and blue-collar workers as their enemies.

On the other hand, the demand for community control raises the fundamental issue of power in a dramatic and radical fashion. The language of urban renewal legislation of the 1950s and the Economic Opportunity Act of 1964, with the terms *citizens' participation and maximum feasible participation of the poor,* promised the Black and poor communities a voice in decisions affecting their localities. But it was assumed that whatever new structures were created would be part of, and clearly subordinate within, the existing government bureaucracies. Instead, community control is challenging the prerogatives of the centralized bureaucracies to make basic policy determinations affecting local areas and represents a step in the ongoing struggle to wrest power from bureaucratic and hierarchical institutions of government and industry. It attempts to redefine the democratic process by rejecting the efficacy of representative institutions, such as the national and local legislative bodies, to reflect popular aspirations.

Community control is analogous, at least in embryo, to the demand for self-determination raised by colonial peoples in Africa, Asia and Latin America. Historically, community control has its roots in the French Revolution's ideal of mass democracy, according to which individuals delegate their prerogatives to no one, but make all essential decisions of policy themselves through popular assemblies, councils, town meetings, etc. The move toward decentralization, therefore, goes deeper than distrust of central institutions of power. Potentially, it implies an alternative model of government and social decision-making.

OBJECTIVES OF COMMUNITY CONTROL

After four years of struggle for community control and Black power, we can begin to assess both the possibilities and limitations of this approach for achieving a series of stated objectives. Generally, these objectives have been: (a) to achieve quality services under indigenous leadership within geographic communities; (b) to secure a more favorable allocation of resources by city, state and federal governments to improve service delivery systems; (c) to develop a cadre of political and social leadership within the Black community capable of reflecting the community's aspirations and helping to deliver quality services; and (d) to gain some measure of control of the ghetto economy.

There are serious limitations to the demand for community control:

1. It is based upon a narrow conception of power.
2. By limiting objectives to the local community, it fails to define, either implicitly or explicitly, the real obstacles to their achievement.
3. The goals themselves ignore the problem of national economic power.

To the extent that there is a movement for Black political power it is confined within the two-party system and defines politics as electoral politics. Working within the system, Blacks have succeeded in electing nine members of Congress, many state legislators and several hundred municipal officials. But such officials possess little genuine power, especially in the era of the military-industrial complex. The ghetto community is far from the commanding heights of national corporate power where the essential political as well as economic decisions are made.

Only the Black Panther Party and other smaller radical groups have attempted to chart the goal of Black and Third World power on a national and international canvas. These groups, however, remain on the margin of political leadership in ghetto communities and government repression may limit, if not smother, whatever influence and political outreach they do possess.

THE FALSE HOPE OF BLACK CAPITALISM

Most community control advocates accept some concept of economic self-determination. This aspiration has been expressed largely in the rejection of white-owned small businesses within the ghetto, although the alternative proposed is more Black individual or cooperative ownership of marginal businesses. Such economic development programs must rely on primary support from white-controlled corporations or government in the form of seed capital, working capital and guaranteed markets and can survive only at the mercy of white corporate finance.

The Black capitalist program is really an integration program which attempts to develop a new set of managers for white-controlled businesses in the ghetto, if control is understood in its financial meaning. Only a few of the Black economic development efforts recognize this danger, but an answer to the perplexing problem of capital formation is not easy to come by. The best that has been proposed is a system of producer consumer cooperatives or nonprofit community development corporations, neither of which can avoid the private money market or the tax system for procuring capital. The facts of national economic life, that is, the existence of central market mechanisms and capital scarcity for small business, militate against a solution to the problem within the framework of Black capitalism.

With the demands for community control of social service institutions within the ghetto, similar drawbacks emerge. White working-class and middle-class resistance to Black claims for expanded services is inevitable unless the obstacles are clearly defined and surmounted. Few community control advocates have been willing to raise the problem of national priorities, namely, that 80 percent of the federal budget, directly and indirectly, is spent on war and related activities. Nor has the tax structure of state and local government been challenged. Right now more than two-thirds of local services are provided out of nonfederal taxes. The major responsibility for schools, sanitation, health and other social expenditures rests on state and local government. The primary sources of revenue for these services are regressive excise taxes, taxes on small property and on wages or salaries. Add to this the fact that 85 percent of federal revenue is derived from the first $8,000 of income, and it becomes clear that the tax burden on working-class and middle-class people, white and Black, is so heavy that demands for increased services from any sector of the population are likely to be opposed as long as war remains the nation's major priority and large corporations which benefit from it are exempt from paying most of the costs of government and social programs.

In short, the incipient alliance of the Black poor with the large corporations and foundations against white and Black wage and salary earners is self-defeating. It does not have the social weight to win its limited objectives. More important, it puts the poor in the unseemly position of attempting to forge a coalition with their oppressors. An alternate strategy would be joint struggles of those segments of the white and Black communities who suffer equally from deteriorating services, a polluted environment and declining real wages against the corporations which manipulate the government to serve their particular interests.

LOCALISM: STRENGTHS AND WEAKNESSES

While localistic organization has prevented the development of political clout by these groups, one of the strengths of the movement for popular power has been its revival of the concept of community against the atomization and alienation of mass society. In a period of urban decay and the loosening of traditional ties of ethnicity and geography, the strong sense of solidarity engendered by welfare recipients and health rights organizations fighting to control the conditions of their own lives has provided an important antidote to the larger trends of population dispersal and consequent anomie. However, the inchoate development of community consciousness, a strength of the community control movement, has so far prevented the forging of broad alliances to achieve even the united goal of community control of specific institutions.

In New York City, where the struggle for community control has reached the highest and most intense level in the nation, the geographic community as the focus of political organization is most apparent. Not only is there little communication and a great deal of distrust among the numerous ghetto and slum communities within the city, but groups within the same neighborhood fighting for local control of different institutions are isolated from one another.

The slogan "community control" is a rubric covering many fragmented and disconnected movements. And usually it is defined differently in each case. For example, some groups seek control over the money, hiring policies and curriculum of a single school or school district. Others are content to demand any one of these prerogatives without considering their right to determine policies governing the other. Underlying the fragmentation is the proprietary aspiration of parents or health consumers who have been unable to recognize their community of interest with those functioning in another geographic area or within the same neighborhood. Contributing to this fragmentation was the way in which the community control concept was tested in New York City public schools.

THE NEW YORK CITY SCHOOL STRUGGLE

The Ford Foundation made grants to three experimental school districts in Manhattan and Brooklyn, encouraging parents and teachers to participate in the decision-making process. The central Board of Education, however, retained its control over all major areas of policy, including teacher qualifications, curriculum and allocation of educational resources. The parents and allied community groups were invited to administer schools within the district, but were forced to operate within the constraints of the guidelines astutely set up by the central bureaucracy of the Board of Education. It was community "control" defined as management. The Janus-faced policy of the central Board of Education evoked a hostile response from the community, but local groups soon discovered that they were hemmed in, not only by the Board but by the state legislature as well.

The experimental districts possessed neither the vision nor the clout to impress their demands on those who hold the real power in the schools. The requisite vision and political strength could only be obtained if the experimental districts were capable of calling upon disgruntled parents around the city to make similar demands on the Board of Education and, at the same time, to support the broadening of community power in the experimental school districts.

To a certain extent the administrative quality of the experimental districts prevented the development of a citywide strategy. Parents and teachers alike were caught in a tug-of-war with the central Board of Education and among themselves. This fight on two fronts was abetted by the spotlight of local and national publicity and thwarted any possibility of developing a citywide movement of parents, students and sympathetic teachers against the Board. Implicit in the method of struggle adopted by the experimental districts was the conflict between their need to protect their severely limited and ill-defined authority and the need to expand the fight beyond the geographic limits of the districts themselves.

From the beginning, the rules of the game were determined by the administrative hierarchy of the Board of Education, which easily convinced the teachers that their real enemy was the Black parents and the Black community in general. The leadership of the United Federation of Teachers decided that the central Board was the lesser of two evils and used the political weight of the union's 55,000 members to extract sufficient economic concessions and veto power over the decentralization plans to convince the Board that they could become a reliable reactionary mass base.

The working teachers, historically oppressed by the central Board of Education, were easily victimized by their own leadership. In the end, they won their 40 pieces of silver, but their long-standing grievances over class size and the overload of administrative responsibility, as well as chronic lack of job security, remain.

Despite some efforts toward broadening support and including teachers in a common struggle, the community control forces were unable to mount an effective counterattack. The Board of Education adroitly manipulated and divided the teachers and parents, and the Ford Foundation leadership prevented the emergence of anything more than a localistic movement for community control.

A NEW FRONT OPENS: HEALTH SERVICES

The struggle for popular control of health services is just beginning, but it may offer more promising opportunities for the development of interracial and interclass links than has the area of education. The unique feature of the deterioration of health services is that it affects large sections of the middle-class and working-class white population as well as the Black poor. Most union health insurance plans have been outstripped by the astronomical rise in costs of hospital services: coverage rarely extends to the full cost of illness. Recent increases in health insurance costs have been geared to maintain the present level of coverage rather than to broaden it. Overcrowding of hospitals is becoming endemic—even many voluntary hospitals have long patient waiting lists—as building and service funds have been restricted by the fiscal crisis of local and state governments.

There are two strategic aspects to the struggle for popular control of health institutions. First, it is becoming a fight to prevent municipal governments from turning over public property to the voluntary hospitals and to the doctors who control them. The appearance of new hospital corporations in New York and Detroit is the harbinger of a general pattern of health care. Tax monies will now be used to finance the provision of medical services by private agencies not really accountable to either the community or even the municipal government. This way of providing public service is already widespread in the transportation industry, where the creation of public corporations, sometimes called bridge, tunnel or transportation authorities, has had the effect of turning over a major public utility to the banks and to other investors. The rationale for this move is often the need for efficient and quality service at low cost. However, costs have continued to rise and services to deteriorate. There is no apparent gain in efficiency when the private sector controls essential services. The proposals for new hospital corporations are nothing more than a giveaway program.

The second aspect of popular control in the health industry is the new concept that the consumer of health services should have the power to determine the shape and content of the service delivery system. The concept of the health consumer transcends both geographic limitations and the limitations of relying entirely on the poor or the underclass for a constituency. Health movements have embraced a particular spectrum of dissatisfied persons which crosses class boundaries, although it is apparent that the poor, the working-class and lower middle-class consumers suffer disproportionately.

Once again, however, there is contention between the demand for control over a particular institution and the need for a broader concept of community control. The powers in health institutions are the doctors and the larger corporate philanthropies. Most boards of directors of community-based hospitals read like a sociological study of community power structure, for they are the very groups which hold economic, political and institutional power in most areas of community life. Unless the connection is made between control over health, education and welfare on one hand and economic and political power on the other, the contest over any individual institution remains unequal and frustrating.

BEYOND THE CORPORATE FRAMEWORK

The basic assumption behind the fragmented struggle for community control is the pluralistic model of political power, according to which control of such institutions as schools can be divorced from control in other areas of social and economic life. Most militant advocates of local control adhere to this model in assuming that it is possible actually to transform the quality of human service institutions by taking decisive power over their administration and pressuring existing government funding agencies for a reordering of fiscal priorities. They believe that the question of power can be reduced to pressure-group politics. They are ready to march, sit in and employ a wide variety of pressure tactics to achieve their aims. But they are not prepared to make a radical critique of national power, either in class or economic terms.

A radical analysis of power in America reveals the interlocking character of control over all institutions in a pyramid fashion, with the pinnacle of power in most local institutions held by the same groups of corporations and their professional servants in government or human service bureaucracies. This analysis implies the need for a generalized concept of popular control of all public institutions and the economy which can appeal not only to Black and poor but also to working-class and most middle-class people—to all who are deprived of a significant voice in the institutions which determine our lives. It requires that the movement for popular control search out societal alternatives beyond the confines of the corporate capitalist framework.

Reshaping Government in Metropolitan Areas
Committee for Economic
Development

Metropolitan areas embrace most of our greatest resources. They are centers of commerce and industry, fashion, culture, and thought. Many metropolitan areas are wealthier and more populous than most nations.

SOURCE: Committee for Economic Development, from *Reshaping Government in Metropolitan Areas,* A Statement on National Policy by the Research and Policy Committee (New York: Committee for Economic Development, 1970), pp. 9–22.

Yet metropolitan America is in trouble. In cities and suburbs alike, citizens are beset by complexities that disturb their everyday lives. They are threatened by crime in the streets, by impure air and water, by breakdowns in public transportation. They are burdened by high taxes and inflationary prices. The deprived minorities in the slums and ghettos suffer more than other citizens of metropolis, for they are more likely to be jobless or sick, badly educated or poorly housed. What is worse, they are handicapped by racial discrimination in their efforts to improve their own condition.

Vigorous leadership is essential if the plight of metropolitan Americans of all races—in cities and suburbs—is to improve. The national and state governments must develop relevant substantive programs designed to deal with a host of diverse and elusive metropolitan problems. At the same time, metropolitan areas must develop a system of government that is capable—administratively, fiscally, and politically—of translating substantive programs into action. Such a system must be geared to respond not only to problems of metropolitan-wide concern, but to those of local communities within metropolitan areas.

We do not intend in this statement to recommend substantive policies and programs to meet the many problems of metropolitan America. Proposals for dealing with some of these difficulties may be found in earlier CED statements; proposals for dealing with others will appear in statements now under way by the Research and Policy Committee. Our purpose here is to provide guidelines for redesigning the present structure and organization of government in metropolitan areas. Without a more rational, more flexible system than now exists —one that recognizes local as well as area-wide needs—new policies and programs are likely to fail.

The structure of government in metropolitan areas has a profound impact on the daily lives of metropolitan citizens. But, as this Committee has long recognized, the present arrangement of overlapping local units is not serving the people well.[1] Citizens in metropolitan areas are confronted by a confusing maze of many—possibly a dozen—jurisdictions, each with its own bureaucratic labyrinth. This baffling array of local units has made it difficult for citizens—the disadvantaged particularly—to gain access to public services and to acquire a voice in decision-making.

Clearly, a fragmented system of government works better for some than for others. In gaining access to the system, citizens with greater political influence and sophistication may succeed in bypassing bureaucratic governmental procedures. Moreover, the system generally works better for suburbanites than it does for residents of the central cities. The haphazard arrangement of local governments in metropolitan areas has created great inequalities between resources and needs. In the suburbs, the combination of superior fiscal strength and fewer problems usually yields a higher quality of public service; in the central cities the situation is reversed. But it is not entirely by chance

[1]See *Modernizing Local Government,* a Statement on National Policy by the Research and Policy Committee, Committee for Economic Development, New York, July 1966.

that such disparities have developed. One of the principal failings of a fragmented system of government is its inability to take an overview in matters of planning, transportation, and population dispersal. Zoning and other land-use control powers wielded by small suburban communities tend to exclude from the suburbs black citizens and other low-income minority groups.

Fragmented local governments reflect great variations in character and viewpoint. The fact that fragmentation persists indicates a determination among local communities to control their own affairs and preserve their own identities. While this attitude makes for greater local pride, it also results in failure of local communities to unite on matters of area-wide concern, such as environmental pollution and transportation congestion, which seriously undermine the quality of metropolitan life. The question to which this statement is addressed may be stated quite simply:

Can existing forms of government in metropolitan areas be modified to permit solution of area-wide problems and at the same time permit local communities to manage their own affairs and maintain their own identities?

Metropolitan Trends

Mounting population pressures which accelerated after World War II have sent Americans beyond their central cities in a quest for space. At the same time, there have been pressures in the opposite direction: the technological revolution in agriculture has forced residents of rural areas to abandon the farms and move in great numbers to the cities. This dual movement has intensified the problems of metropolitan areas.

The cities have suffered the most. The departure of business firms and a large proportion of the more affluent, white residents to the suburbs has severely weakened the cities' tax base. This, in turn, has made it more difficult for cities to deal with problems of race and poverty brought on by a heavy influx of poor, nonwhite residents. But the suburbs have suffered, too. The worsening condition of the cities has only speeded the outward movement, and the result has been many problems of the cities have spread beyond their borders. Suburbanites found that governmental patterns designed for rural areas were not suited to their needs. To cope with new problems, new governments were created, but they were not created with a rational view to the future. Rather, they seemed to spring up—in endless proliferation. These new governments, tacked on to one another around the central city, have formed the crazy-quilt that is metropolitan America today.

The U.S. Bureau of the Budget defines a metropolitan area as "an integrated economic and social unit with a recognized large population nucleus." These units are called "standard metropolitan statistical areas" (SMSA's), defined by the Budget Bureau as normally consisting of one or more entire counties, primarily nonagricultural and closely related to and including a central city, or cities, of 50,000 or more. Nearly two-thirds of the U.S. population is concentrated today in 233 metropolitan areas compared with only 55 per cent in 1940. Until the mid-1960's a majority of the residents of metropolitan areas lived in central cities; now the preponderance has shifted to the suburbs. (See Figure One.)

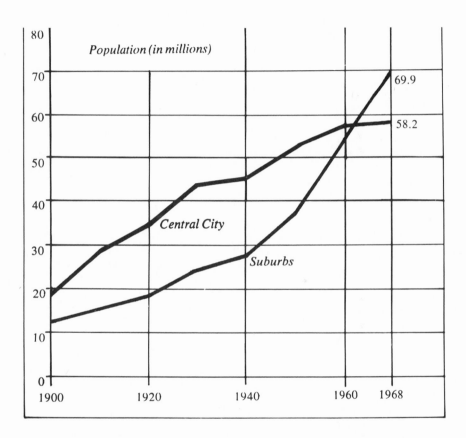

Figure 1.   U.S. Central City and Suburban Population, 1900–1968
SOURCE: U.S. Bureau of the Census.

Growth is still generally toward metropolitan areas. Between 1960 and 1966 their population increased 11 per cent compared to 6 per cent for nonmetropolitan areas. By 1985 it is projected that more than 70 per cent of the population will live in metropolitan areas. The metropolitan areas of the Northeast represent the largest concentration of metropolitan population in the United States: they account for 79 per cent of the region's total population. The metropolitan areas of the West account for 72 per cent of the region's total population and are the fastest growing. Metropolitan population concentration in the North Central region is 60 per cent; in the South, 48 per cent.

There are metropolitan areas in 47 of the 50 states. Alaska, Vermont, and Wyoming have no population now defined as metropolitan. Eight states have at least 80 per cent of their population in metropolitan areas. These are led by Massachusetts with 97 per cent and California with 90 per cent. However, 28 states have less than 50 per cent of their population in metropolitan areas.

At last count, there were 455 metropolitan counties. Nearly half of the nation's metropolitan areas consist of a single county. Fifteen metropolitan areas consist of five counties or more.

In 1967 the nation's metropolitan areas were served by 20,703 local governments, or about one-fourth of all the local governments in the United States. The average is 91 local governments per metropolitan area—46 per metropolitan county. But these averages cover great extremes. The Chicago metropolitan area, for example, has 1,113 local governments (186 per county); the Philadelphia area has 871 (109 per county); the Pittsburgh area has 704 (176 per county); and the New York area has 551 (110 per county). At the other extreme there are 20 metropolitan areas with less than 10 local governments each.

In both population and physical size most local governments in metropolitan areas are extremely small. For example, two-thirds of the municipalities (usually cities, boroughs, villages, or towns) have a population of less than 5,000, and about half cover less than a single square mile of land area. Fewer than 200 municipalities cover as much as 25 square miles.

Most metropolitan residents are served by at least four separate local governments—a county, a municipality or a township, a school district, and one or more special districts whose functions range from garbage collection to mosquito control. Some, of course, are served by many more. The residents of Blue Island, Illinois, must contend with 13 separate, independent local governments.

STEPS TOWARD REFORM

In *Modernizing Local Government,* this Committee underscored the need for local government reform as follows:

The bewildering multiplicity of small, piecemeal, duplicative, overlapping local juris-dictions cannot cope with the staggering difficulties encountered in managing modern urban affairs. The fiscal effects of duplicative suburban separatism create great difficulty in provision of costly central city services benefiting the whole urbanized area. If local governments are to function effectively in metropolitan areas, they must have sufficient size and authority to plan, administer, and provide significant financial support for solutions to area-wide problems. [2]

[2] *Modernizing Local Government, op. cit.,* p. 44.

To this end we recommended reducing through consolidation the number of conflicting jurisdictions and competing tax units. We also proposed that county governments—because they are less limited in area, population, and fiscal resources—be utilized where possible as the primary basis for consolidation.

Aware of the need for change, enlightened business and civic leaders in metropolitan areas have spearheaded campaigns to replace small-scale, overlapping local governments with consolidated, federated, or other forms of metropolitan government. These campaigns have stressed the fact that the economic and social interdependence of metropolitan areas has created problems which can only be solved on an area-wide basis.

CENTRALIZATION VS. DECENTRALIZATION

Steps in the direction of area-wide government are not surprising when considered in their historical context. For nearly two centuries, American government has become increasingly centralized. Cities have expanded their boundaries by annexation. States have assumed new functions or have taken more responsibility for old ones. The national government has broadened its role in domestic affairs. Traditionally, much support for centralization has been based on the assumption that it leads to better, more responsive government and more humane social policies.

It may seem paradoxical, therefore, that today's growing support for decentralization should rest upon the same assumption. Much of the popular discussion of decentralization centers on current demands of black citizens for control over those institutions which most affect their lives, and for a stronger voice in the political process. The dialogue over black community control has focused public attention on many legitimate grievances of black citizens. The issue of decentralization, however, is not limited to the black community. White citizens, too, are impelled toward decentralized government (witness the suburban village) by some of the same factors that are motivating blacks: a desire for greater separatism and a stronger sense of local pride and community identity. Indeed, decentralization goes beyond questions of black and white. Its advocates see it as a means of humanizing government, giving the voter greater access to public services, more control over the bureaucracy which manages his affairs, and a more important role in decisions in which he has a stake.

The case for decentralization, however, cannot ignore the economic, technological, and social arguments which favor a centralized system. Small-unit governments are poorly equipped to take advantage of economies of scale and technological innovations; hence, they often find it more difficult to respond to the growing and disparate needs of their citizens. Proponents of centralization argue that the interests of the disadvantaged are best served by a larger rather than a smaller unit of government. They point to the economic weakness of the ghetto, the historic conservatism of America's small communities, and the growing dependence on the federal government for social progress.

It is clear from the foregoing that what is needed is a system of government that adequately recognizes *both* forces, centralization and decentralization. Such a system must permit a genuine sharing of power over functions between a larger unit and a smaller unit. It must recognize a larger unit to permit economies of scale, area-wide planning, and equities in finance. It must recognize a smaller unit to permit the exercise of local power over matters which affect the lives of local citizens.

* * *

SUMMARY OF RECOMMENDATIONS

All metropolitan areas are affected to a greater or lesser extent by the conflicting forces of centralization and decentralization. The interdependence of activities within metropolitan areas requires area-wide institutions for some functions or parts of functions of government. Just as clear is the need for units of government small enough to enable the recipients of government services to have some voice and control over their quality and quantity.

However, no two metropolitan areas are alike. Each has its own history and life style, and its own economic base. Both demographically and geographically, each differs from the other. For this reason, our proposals will not apply alike to all metropolitan areas. Each must examine its own capacity to govern and determine what particular organization suits it best.

It has been argued that the present governmental system already possesses the necessary combination of smallness and bigness. Small government already exists, at least in suburbia, and when area-wide action is needed, special districts may be created for the purpose. Further, the present system could govern effectively, it is often claimed, if only it had enough money.

None of these justifications for the present system is satisfactory. Uncoordinated area-wide special districts, fragmented by function, are no better than governments fragmented geographically. They do not permit a genuine regional approach to problems that are genuinely regional; nor do they create a system of decision-making and power-sharing capable of dealing with political conflicts. The state and federal aid solution within the present system has already been tried and so far has been found wanting.[3] Aid is badly allocated. Often it is wasted or assigned without proper priorities.

[3]See *A Fiscal Program for a Balanced Federalism,* a Statement on National Policy by the Research and Policy Committee, Committee for Economic Development, New York, June 1967.

A TWO-LEVEL GOVERNMENTAL SYSTEM

In principle a governmental system for America's metropolitan areas must recognize the need for both a community level and a metropolitan level of government. There are many different governmental arrangements which will meet this need. As long as legitimate demands for centralization and decentralization are met, the specific arrangements may vary to fit the economic, cultural, and political characteristics of each area. Some may require greater emphasis on consolidation of local units; others may require greater emphasis on creating units which will enhance community participation.

Therefore, in the following proposals to achieve the dual advantages of a combined community-metropolitan governmental system, we would expect variations in application. In some areas a comprehensive solution may be feasible at an early date. In other areas achievement of an effective two-level system may require several steps over a period of time.

To gain the advantages of both centralization and decentralization, we recommend as an ultimate solution a governmental system of two levels. Some functions should be assigned in their entirety to the area-wide government, others to the local level, but most will be assigned in part to each level. More important than the division of functions is the *sharing of power*. Local communities will be assigned some power over functions placed at the area-wide level of government. Further, state and federal governments must be involved in most functions. This two-level system will not provide neatness and symmetry, but effectiveness, responsiveness, and adequate resources.

In those situations where the metropolitan area is contained within one county, a reconstituted county government should be used as the basic framework for a new area-wide government. This may, but need not, include consolidation of a large dominant central city with the county government in which it is located. If there are two or more sizable cities in the county, consolidation may not be appropriate. Counties in some states already have very wide powers. An indispensable requirement is the restructuring of such counties with a suitable legislative organ, a strong chief executive, and modern management.

In cases where the metropolitan area spreads over several counties or towns, a new jurisdiction should be created which embraces all of its territory. Although a federation of existing counties and towns might be considerably easier to implement, it is clear that rapid metropolitan growth makes a stronger jurisdiction considerably more appropriate, especially for purposes of long-range planning.

In addition to an area-wide level, modern metropolitan government should contain a community-level government system comprised of "community districts." These units might consist of existing local governments with functions readjusted to the two-level system, together with new districts in areas where no local unit exists. The new community districts should not be imposed from without, but created through local initiative by the simplest possible methods.

A state boundary commission or similar body might be established to begin the process of delineating new districts. Citizen groups which seek community-district status might first make their appeal to this body if it is established.

In some cities there are areas which already possess strong community identity and these could become the new community districts. But in many cities, particularly the big cities, the sense of community is diminishing. Isolation and alienation, on the other hand, are increasing. Once the smaller political units are created—units with genuine power—a stronger sense of community is bound to emerge. In the suburbs, existing municipalities are likely to be retained as the community districts. Except in the most recently settled suburbs, these municipalities tend not only to represent "natural areas," but also to have well-developed community identities. Thus, local communities in both cities and suburbs can be guaranteed full participation within the metropolitan system.

DETERMINING SIZE

A major difficulty in establishing community districts will be determining their size. Although much of the literature on government organization places heavy emphasis on appropriate size of minor jurisdictions, the fact is there is little hard economic evidence of what the optimum size should be. Therefore, how a community perceives its identity becomes important as well as the number of people it contains.

States should establish suggested, but not mandatory, criteria to guide the actual determination of community boundaries. The states should, in addition, set down requirements which will guarantee the representativeness of the government established. Although the community districts should be allowed to determine their form of government—council, strong executive, commission, or some other form—the basic requirement of one-man, one-vote should be met.

State governments should assist the organization of community districts by enacting enabling legislation to permit the creation of a two-level form of metropolitan government and by establishing a procedure through which community districts may be created. Great flexibility as to size and governmental organization should be permitted.

The states should also prescribe guidelines for determining size and representation of the area-wide government. The practice exists in some metropolitan areas of representing community units—towns and villages—on an area-wide governing council. However, this form of representation rarely produces an area-wide point of view but rather a bargaining process through which the various smaller units try to protect their parochial interests. Therefore, we suggest that delegates to the area-wide government represent legislative districts on a one-man, one-vote basis instead of representing the community districts as such.

It is important to underline the full significance of the changes advocated here. City boundaries would become less important than they now are. There would be a boundary surrounding each metropolitan area as well as boundaries surrounding community districts within each metropolitan area.

FINANCING THE SYSTEM: STATE AND FEDERAL HELP

Reorganization of government in metropolitan areas will make it possible to increase over-all fiscal resources. America's wealth is concentrated largely in its metropolitan areas and metropolitan-wide government is advocated, in part, so this resource base may be preserved and improved. The existing system of overlapping local governments results in a poor match between needs and resources and perpetuates waste, inefficiency, and confusion.

Although the establishment of metropolitan-wide government will make possible a greater local fiscal contribution, it will by no means eliminate the need for substantial state and federal aid. There is urgent need for a greater and more equitable state aid contribution and more attention by the states to the adequacy of their local governmental systems. The states have responsibilities for their local governmental systems. They should adapt their aid systems to the facts of metropolitanism and adjust the boundaries of local governments to fit current realities.

The states have the power to assume functions that are now performed locally, but few have assumed them. In some states, highways and welfare have become a major state responsibility, and a few municipal higher educational institutions have been taken over by the states. But there has been no major reshuffling of responsibilities to ease local fiscal burdens.

The response of the federal government to local fiscal problems has been more positive. The federal aid system, for example, through such programs as urban renewal, aid to education, and the anti-poverty program, is adjusting its assistance programs to the problems of the cities. It is possible that by giving more attention to the flow of aid the federal government will be able to help fill the gap left by the state aid system.

Both state and federal aid systems should be restructured in order to put resources where they are most needed. Equally important, state and federal aid should be used to stimulate government reorganization. The use of aid for this purpose has a precedent in its use in promoting school consolidation by the states. Therefore, we recommend that state and federal aid should be used as an incentive to promote the kind of restructured government outlined in this statement.

An Urban Strategy

Bernard Weissbourd
and Herbert Channick

Our efforts to deal with the race crisis and the urban crisis have failed to achieve any great measure of success because we have not been willing to commit an adequate portion of our national resources to these efforts, and what we have committed has been used in a scattered and patchwork fashion rather than as part of an over-all strategy. We are still unable to answer the most essential questions. If the funds now being spent in Vietnam were to become available, what priority should be established among housing, education, job training, income subsidy, transportation, and social services? Should the primary emphasis be on rebuilding the ghetto or on attempting to achieve real integration? Or should we try to progress simultaneously on both fronts? We cannot answer these and similar questions as long as there is no national agreement on goals or on strategy.

Prophecies about the development of black cities encircled by white suburbs are in the process of being fulfilled. Washington and Newark now have Negro majorities. According to Census Bureau estimates, eleven more major cities, including Chicago, Philadelphia, and Detroit, will have joined this category by 1984. In the next ten years, total Negro population in metropolitan areas may increase from sixteen million to twenty-two million. Of this six million increase, 5,400,000 will be in the central cities, already nearly twenty per cent Negro, rather than in the suburbs where Negro population is insignificant. As a consequence, if present trends are allowed to continue, 1978 will find more than seventeen million persons living in black ghettos where twelve million now live. Meanwhile, the flight of whites to the suburbs will continue: some twenty-five million new white suburban residents will further aggravate the already alarming rate of urban sprawl. Finding homes in the suburbs for 5,400,000 Negroes is necessary merely to hold the line in the ghettos, but if we are to make any real progress in rebuilding the ghetto, we must accommodate considerably more than that number of Negroes outside the central cities during the next decade.

A color-blind society should be our ultimate goal, and it is neither unrealistic nor unattainable. We recognize the important role the black-power move-

SOURCE: Bernard Weissbourd and Herbert Channick, "An Urban Strategy," *The Center Magazine,* 1 (September 1968), 56–65. Reprinted by permission from the September 1968 issue of *The Center Magazine,* a publication of The Center for the Study of Democratic Institutions in Santa Barbara, California.

ment plays in raising the self-esteem of many American Negroes and making them aware of their strength and their ability to control their own destiny. But we do not agree with that part of the black-power movement which is striving for a separatist solution to our problems. A separatist solution in our view is an admission of defeat for our most basic beliefs. We do not believe that most Negroes will turn to separatism unless they finally become convinced that there is no good faith in the white response to their economic and social demands. This has not yet happened. A survey in *Fortune* found that only five per cent of Negroes are opposed to any kind of integration and ninety-three per cent want desegregation in schools, jobs, and neighborhoods.

The strategy we propose is aimed at the elimination of the ghetto and the creation of a desegregated society. Desegregation, as we use the term, does not require that every street or apartment building have Negro residents in precise proportion to the total population. Obviously, economic status, distance from work, arbitrary personal preferences (including those based on race), and many other factors will continue to play their roles in where and how people choose to live. Desegregation does require, however, that Negroes have the same opportunities as whites to make choices.

If some Negroes choose to live in separate communities as white ethnic groups have done, as long as the decision is theirs we have a condition of desegregation. Desegregation is, therefore, different from integration, for it includes separate Negro and white neighborhoods as well as mixed ones. That this distinction is significant is shown by the same *Fortune* survey, which says that while ninety-three per cent of Negroes want desegregation, only twelve per cent want total integration. Desegregation preserves the same potential for varying degrees of integration and pluralism as exists in white society. Desegregation does, however, require elimination of the ghetto as we now know it, for it has become a prison that bars interaction between Negro and white societies. It limits the ability of Negroes to gain control over their lives and enormously increases the difficulties of improving their employment, educational, and housing opportunities.

The essential elements of our strategy are these:

[1] A massive ten-year program of development of new towns in outlying areas to accommodate the projected Negro and white population growth.

[2] The construction in these new towns of some additional 350,000 subsidized housing units each year for ten years, which will allow the ultimate replacement of urban substandard housing and create a temporary housing surplus.

[3] The withdrawal of public expenditures for housing subsidies, sewer, water, roads, and mass transportation from ordinary subdivision development and their rechanneling into new towns, thus virtually eliminating the competition of segregated housing development.

Accommodating the increased Negro population in outlying areas is required to keep the ghettos from getting larger. The housing surplus is necessary to "loosen up" the housing pattern so that normal market forces can begin to work in favor of desegregation. The new-town concept lends itself admirably to dealing with the critical problems of our urban areas as well as with the race crisis. The withdrawal of public expenditures from other areas will allow the population growth to be channeled into the desegregated communities that our program will create.

The pursuit of this strategy for five years can reduce the size of the ghetto by somewhat more than half. It is possible that population movements by then will lead on to complete elimination of the ghetto and to desegregation with less governmental participation. If not, the program can be carried on for another five years until the ghetto as we know it has ceased to exist.

THE ARITHMETIC OF DESEGREGATION

Desegregation requires more than changes in social conditions and attitudes. It requires a process of population movement that recognizes the fact that twelve per cent of our metropolitan-area population is now Negro. Arithmetic cannot make the process work, but it can illuminate the dimensions of the problem and illustrate how the process can begin. The arithmetic here deals with an extreme case both in percentages of Negro population and in terms of eliminating the ghetto entirely. If we can deal with this extreme case we can deal with any lesser situation.

Assume that the population of a hypothetical metropolitan area is one million, of which 750,000 are white and 250,000 are Negro. If the Negroes are living in a ghetto and we want to desegregate and permit them to live anywhere, we should build enough surplus housing units in outlying areas to accommodate a fourth of this ghetto population and three times as many white people. Thus, if we have

GHETTO	METROPOLITAN WHITE	OUTLYING AREA SURPLUS
250,000 N	750,000 W	250,000

and if we want to achieve the one-fourth, three-fourths proportion in the population of the outlying area, the following movements occur:

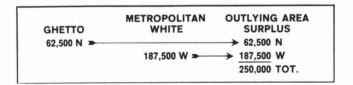

GHETTO	METROPOLITAN WHITE	OUTLYING AREA SURPLUS
62,500 N ➤		➤ 62,500 N
	187,500 W ➤	➤ 187,500 W
		250,000 TOT.

The vacancies resulting from the metropolitan white movement to outlying areas make possible a second movement of 187,500 Negroes from the ghetto into metropolitan white areas. The result then is:

	GHETTO	METROPOLITAN WHITE	OUTLYING AREA SURPLUS
	250,000 N	750,000 W	
(1)	−62,500 N		62,500 N
(2)		−187,500 W	187,500 W
		562,500 W	
(3)	−187,500 N	187,500 N	
	0 N	750,000 TOT.	250,000 TOT.

The ghetto has been eliminated, the outlying area population is now twenty-five per cent Negro, and what had been metropolitan white is now twenty-five per cent Negro.

Although so far this is just an exercise in arithmetic, it suggests that it is possible to eliminate the ghetto in any metropolitan area by building the proper housing surplus. We hypothesized here a metropolitan area in which the Negro population is twenty-five per cent of the total because no metropolitan area other than New Orleans (which is twenty-six per cent Negro) has a greater Negro population than that. Even in Washington, although the city itself is sixty-six per cent Negro, the metropolitan-area percentage of Negroes is less than twenty-five per cent.

On a national scale, as we have indicated, the projected population growth for the next decade is going to require housing for approximately twenty-five million more people in our metropolitan areas. But if we are to replace the substandard housing in the urban areas and provide an escape from the ghetto, we will have to provide accommodations for an additional twelve million persons. Thirty-seven million people living in outlying communities would need approximately 10,500,000 housing units or 1,050,000 units per year for ten years. This is well within the capacity of the building industry. Of these, 700,000 will be required each year to satisfy normal growth and should need no government subsidy; the other 350,000 units will create the surplus that can break through the ghetto pattern and ultimately eliminate urban substandard housing. (The 3,500,000 new surplus housing units that we recommend be built over a ten-year period are less than the number called for by either the National Commission on Civil Disorders or by President Johnson, but by building fewer units in the right places a better result can be achieved than by building a larger number of units without a coördinated strategy.)

If the Negro population of the outlying communities turns out to be around twenty-five per cent, as we would expect, 9,200,000 Negroes will have found housing outside the central city. This figure surpasses the projected growth of the Negro population by more than three million and would reduce the ghetto population by more than a fourth.

The arithmetic reveals another significant fact. Having built surplus housing units for some twelve million people—of whom 3,200,000 are Negro—we find we have room in the outlying communities for 8,800,000 more white people. Now, if 8,800,000 white people move into new communities from older residential neighborhoods in the city and from older suburbs (a movement that is already taking place), a substantial vacancy will have been created in some of these areas. This is a strong economic incentive for landlords to encourage Negroes to move into these residential neighborhoods. If this comes about, in effect the ghetto will have been entirely eliminated and the whole metropolitan area will have been desegregated.

This is powerful arithmetic. It demonstrates that it is actually possible within ten years to eliminate the ghettos. By intervening in the natural real-estate market in one place only, that is, in the outlying areas, we can liberate the market from its past constraints and bring about desegregation throughout the metropolitan area.

Our calculations are on a national basis, but the problems, of course, must be solved city by city. The accompanying charts show possible population movements during a five-year first phase for two large cities in the United States with high percentages of Negro population. The charts show that, in these cases, if we build sufficient outlying housing to accommodate Negro and white population growth and sufficient surplus housing to allow an initial movement of one-eighth the ghetto population and three-and-a-half times as many persons from white city neighborhoods and suburbs, more than fifty per cent of the ghetto can be eliminated in the first five years.*

A five-year program that would result in an exodus of half the ghetto residents is an appropriate first phase. Not all of them will wish to move, and not all Negro housing is substandard. We can be reasonably certain, however, that at least half will prefer better housing accommodations at lower cost in environments where their children can be educated in integrated schools and in locations where employment opportunities are available. For those who choose to stay, the premium rents of today, which reflect an artificial scarcity caused by segregation, should begin to disappear. Moreover, while we have said that the movement of whites from older suburbs and city residential neighborhoods to outlying areas is already occurring, part of it is the result of the pressure of "block-busting" as the ghetto expands outward. Once this pressure is relieved the white movement may slow down.

*Population statistics in the text and charts are based generally on the Bureau of the Census Series "B" and Series "C" projections. The percentage of Negro residents in suburbs and white city neighborhoods in 1975, as shown on the charts, should be regarded as incremental since the relatively small number of Negroes now residing in these areas is not taken into account. The Bureau of the Census has projections at both higher and lower growth rates than those used here but the principles illustrated are valid unless Negro migration to the cities increases beyond any expectation.

In short, in five years, at the halfway point, the program we have outlined can be evaluated and the actual movements during that period can be measured. Then either the full program can be continued for another five years or there can be a reduction in the rate of building in outlying areas and a start toward eliminating the substandard ghetto housing that has been abandoned and in its place the reconstruction of desegregated communities. Vacancies cannot be permitted to increase to a point where the effect on the neighborhood is negative, so that landlords begin to neglect their property and the neighborhood begins to deteriorate. Where this problem seems to be arising, the rate of new construction can be adjusted until a level of vacancy is restored sufficient to encourage movement into, but not so high as to create problems for, the neighborhood.

It is possible to subsidize enough of the surplus housing units by rent supplements or otherwise so that the proportion of Negroes in the outlying areas is about equal to the proportion of Negroes in the entire metropolitan region. Since there are more than twice as many whites as Negroes in the poverty group and more than twice as many white substandard housing units as Negro, the subsidies will be of as much importance to poor urban whites as to Negroes.

NEW TOWNS

The arithmetic shows that desegregation can be achieved by building 350,000 surplus housing units a year. We propose that these units be built as part of new towns with populations of 50,000 to 100,000 each.

There has been enough experience in Europe as well as in the United States to prove that new towns built according to regional plans and linked to the central city and to each other by mass transportation are important in improving the quality of the urban environment and in solving the problems of suburban sprawl. Although actual development of the new towns can and should be by private enterprise, legislative action by federal, state, and local governments is needed to insure that the new-town program can cope with the transportation, land use, pollution, public utility, and other problems of the metropolis as well as with the race problem. The fact is that the urban crisis and the race crisis today both point toward the same solution.

Substantial bipartisan support for a new-town program already exists. In a previous publication, it was pointed out that the present pattern of metropolitan growth is not an inevitable one, but is, at least in part, the unintended result of a whole array of federal and state programs involved in subsidizing housing and land development.* Federal subsidies for homes for middle-income families in the suburbs and for public housing and apartments in the city have

---

*"Segregation, Subsidies, and Megalopolis," by Bernard Weissbourd, Center for the Study of Democratic Institutions, 1964.

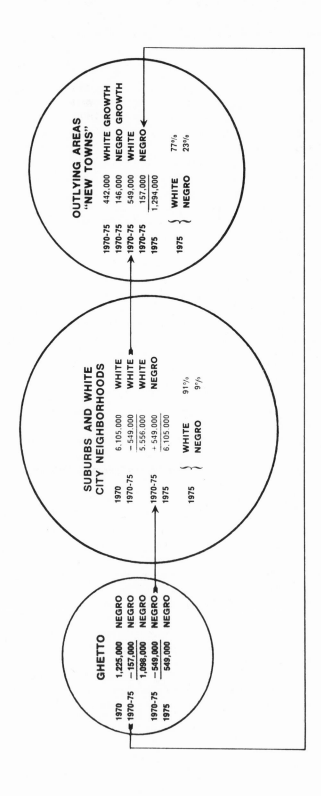

CHICAGO: POPULATION MOVEMENTS, 1970-1975

GHETTO

1970	1,225,000	NEGRO
1970-75	− 157,000	NEGRO
	1,098,000	NEGRO
1970-75	− 549,000	NEGRO
1975	549,000	NEGRO

SUBURBS AND WHITE CITY NEIGHBORHOODS

1970	6,105,000	WHITE
1970-75	− 549,000	WHITE
	5,556,000	WHITE
1970-75	+ 549,000	NEGRO
1975	6,105,000	

| 1975 | WHITE | 91% |
| | NEGRO | 9% |

OUTLYING AREAS "NEW TOWNS"

1970-75	442,000	WHITE GROWTH
1970-75	146,000	NEGRO GROWTH
1970-75	549,000	WHITE
1970-75	157,000	NEGRO
1975	1,294,000	

| 1975 | WHITE | 77% |
| | NEGRO | 23% |

helped to increase the degree of segregation in the United States since World War II. These subsidies, together with the expenditure of public funds for expressways, roads, sewers, and water, have made possible the suburban-tract development of the last twenty years. Without intending to, we have used public funds to finance the white exodus from the cities. We have created powerful tools to encourage land development and home production and their side effects have merely intensified the race crisis and the urban crisis. However, these tools can now be used to reshape and desegregate the urban environment. By focusing federal and state help on a new-town program and by creating a housing surplus, we not only can achieve desegregated new towns but can release the normal economic forces in the housing market to bring about desegregation in the cities as well.

A large-scale new-town program requires an essentially negative approach to ordinary subdivision development. It is necessary to withdraw federal subsidies from suburban-tract development outside of the scope of the program and from high-income residential areas in the city. If the financing made available by the federal savings and loan associations, the F.H.A., and the V.A. are directed solely to new towns constructed in outlying areas, pursuant to regional open-space and transportation plans, and if the major insurance companies can be persuaded to coöperate with such a program, the funds heretofore available for segregated new construction would virtually dry up. The resulting structure of real-estate development would be one in which desegregated new towns are the predominant aspect of housing growth in the nineteen seventies as the segregated suburban tract development was the predominant aspect of such growth in the fifties and sixties.

Decisions about the expenditure of other public funds can also control land use. Federal and state agencies responsible for roads, sewers, water, and mass transportation have, in the past, generally made their plans and put through their programs independently. If these were to be carried out by one agency in each region working with the federal government, the benefits could be withheld from regions that did not have a plan calling for desegregated new-town development.

Federal legislation already exists providing for loans to state or local agencies to acquire land for new towns, using the power of eminent domain if necessary. The state agency can then sell individual tracts of land to builders who would be required to adhere to the plans of the agency. This procedure has been followed in urban renewal. However, whereas urban-renewal land is sold to the builder at a discount, it is possible for new-town land to be sold at a profit, since it would be in areas of rapid population growth and competing land would have been taken off the market by the location of road, sewer, and water facilities. The historical pattern has been for private real-estate investors to reap the benefits of increased land values that flow inevitably from the extension of public utilities or from the construction of major facilities such as bridges, airports, and subway lines, but there is no reason why the government should not begin to reap such benefits on behalf of the public. If public funds for land development and housing are used only for desegregated new towns, only the very wealthy will be able to build white enclaves. As a result, virtually all new housing would be desegregated.

Decisions about the amount of subsidized housing and about the kind of new towns to be developed ought to be made locally by metropolitan authorities in each region. It is vital for the communities from which the new-town population will come to be represented on these authorities. It is conceivable that an authority in a particular region may elect to build some desegregated towns, and perhaps some that are all-Negro. While we are opposed to the latter idea, the wishes of Negro communities may require some experimentation in this direction.

New towns afford an opportunity to bring together ghetto residents with available jobs in industries that have demonstrated a preference for one-story plants in outlying areas. At the same time, these industries provide an economic base for the new towns.

Today, every morning, an enormous two-way movement takes place on the expressways of our metropolitan areas. White-collar workers travel in their automobiles and on buses and rapid-transit lines to the central city, while blue-collar workers travel in car pools to outlying areas where their jobs are increasingly located. The failure to match available jobs with available personnel is in large part due to this movement of new jobs into the suburbs and out of large central cities where unemployment, underemployment, and poverty are greatest. Since 1954, new factory and commercial building has increasingly concentrated in the ring about the metropolitan areas, as has, also, a relatively large proportion of community building such as schools and hospitals. New York City, for example, has lost about 100,000 manufacturing jobs to the outlying areas during the last seven years.

Although many of these jobs outside the city are within the capabilities of the ghetto residents, most of them are too difficult to get to. The median income of non-white households in the central cities is little more than half that of white central-city households, and so the cost of commuting to a suburban job imposes a much greater burden on ghetto residents than that of the suburban commuter into the city. Ghetto families are generally dependent on public transportation, and this, even when it exists, is expensive and often circuitous.

There have been some suggestions that industry be brought into the ghetto. I.B.M., for instance, is locating a plant for production of computer cable in the Bedford-Stuyvesant section of Brooklyn that will employ three hundred local residents. Such a program is desirable but self-limiting. Only those industries which can be set up in multi-story structures can be successfully located in New York's Harlem or Chicago's West Side, and they are few in number. The typical one-story industrial plant employs too few persons per acre to justify its being located in most ghettos and provides too few jobs for the housing that it would displace.

One way of bringing central-city workers and outlying jobs together is through mass transportation. This deserves high priority in any event, because an efficient mass-transportation system is a necessary part of a coördinated new-town and regional plan. But mass transportation does not work in areas of low density. Ordinary subdivision development cannot be satisfactorily served by mass transportation; it requires one or more automobiles per family. It works well only in highly concentrated areas where trip origins and destinations are clustered. One of the strongest arguments for a new-town program is that it would involve a mass-transportation system linking the new towns to each other and to the central city. But more important, the need for transportation would be lessened to the extent that people who work in the new towns can live there and people who work in the central business district can live in the city. The savings in transportation may be a significant factor in the total cost of the program.

The new-town program will create some 350,000 new jobs in the construction industry and possibly an additional 350,000 jobs in service and material-supply industries. Many of these can be filled by Negroes. Construction skills can be learned in the traditional apprentice method, and the apprentice is paid while learning. There is also a certain amount of unskilled labor required in the construction industry. A job-training program in the construction industry, therefore, is an important tool in the strategy of Negro employment.

The new town also offers the opportunity to integrate schools. Educators and sociologists have known for years that what children learn from their peers in the classroom may be as important as what they learn from their teachers. There can be no doubt that regular informal contact between Negro children whose parents have moved from the ghetto and middle-class white children is one of the most effective techniques for furthering the development of both the ex-ghetto Negro child and the white child who has been living in the artificial, segregated world of the suburbs.

Although the new town will be desegregated, it is not necessary, as we have said, that every street and every neighborhood should reflect the population pattern of the total community. But if the new town is of appropriate size, schools and other public facilities will be integrated. The Chicago suburb of Evanston offers a hopeful forecast. It has a population of approximately 80,000 and some twenty per cent of its schoolchildren are Negro. Despite the fact that the housing is largely segregated, considerable success has been achieved in integrating the school system. This is attributable in good part to the intelligent direction of the school administration, but it may also be said that it was easier to achieve integration in a community of 80,000—the approximate size of a new town—than in the neighboring city of Chicago with its ghetto of nearly one million Negroes.

The undeniable fact today is that it is no longer possible to provide housing for the growing Negro population in the confines of the central city except by forcing more and more whites to leave. Sufficient land is not available, and almost all of the new housing in the ghetto, whether public housing or urban renewal, has created fewer units than were demolished. It is hard to equal the high densities of our overcrowded ghettos except by building high-rise apartments—very high indeed. The use of new towns in England to accommodate "over-spill" or to "decant" the urban population has been very successful, and the English have wisely built their new towns before demolishing the slums from which the new-town residents would come. They have, therefore, avoided the problem that has beset our own public-housing and urban-renewal programs, which have demolished more housing units than they created, thereby forcing people out of one slum area only to cause a new one to come into existence.

We are not proposing that the new towns in this country encircle the central city as do London's, or that new towns of a million population should not be attempted as well as the smaller new towns discussed here. The important point is to build enough new-town housing to create a surplus of housing in the inner city. Then we can begin to deal with the inner-city problems without displacing people who otherwise have no place to go.

New towns can accommodate neighborhoods of different economic status, although the difficulty of mixing housing for different economic classes should not be underestimated. One of the important conclusions of a recent conference on central-city renewal by the Urban Land Institute was that "no special hindrance exists to racial integration when persons and families share the same economic status. . . . However, it has been shown that economically disparate groups do not make congenial neighbors. Families at one end of the economic strata or the other usually move out, leaving behind an economically homogeneous neighborhood." We should expect a tendency toward neighborhoods differentiated by income level and thus differing degrees of integration (until the income gap between whites and Negroes narrows).

As Wolf Von Eckardt points out, new towns would conserve precious open countryside. Our present rate of urbanization is thirty acres per hundred people. Thirty-five million people would therefore use 10.5 million acres. Even low-density new towns like Reston and Columbia in the United States and Tapiola in Finland, despite their abundant green spaces, use only about ten acres for a hundred people. Three hundred fifty new towns of comparable density would consume only a total of 3.5 million acres—a two-thirds saving. But the new towns in a program such as we have described would be of greater density, since they would include many apartments as well as town houses and single-family houses. The Swedish new towns demonstrate that higher density is not incompatible with good planning, including abundant open space and recreational facilities. It is in our power, therefore, to conserve seven million acres of countryside for better health and greater enjoyment not only of the new-town residents but of all the people in our metropolitan areas.

A new-town program costs the least of any program for dealing with the problem. By building on outlying land we are using the cheapest land. By concentrating development, the costs of utilities and roads are decreased. Moreover, since we are working with market factors and in the direction of normal population growth, the economic forces of the marketplace add to,

POPULATION MOVEMENTS, 1970-1975

WASHINGTON:

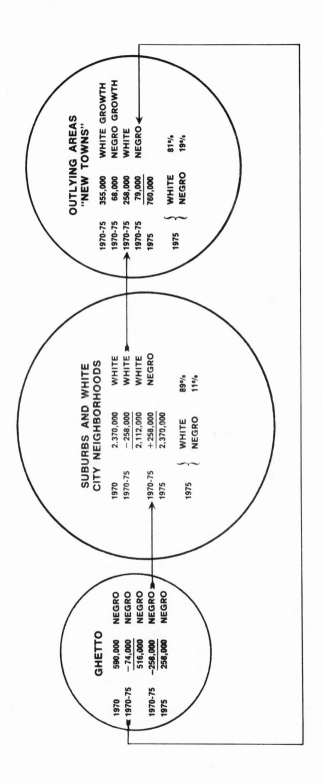

GHETTO

1970	590,000	NEGRO
1970-75	−74,000	NEGRO
	516,000	NEGRO
1970-75	−258,000	NEGRO
1975	258,000	NEGRO

SUBURBS AND WHITE
CITY NEIGHBORHOODS

1970	2,370,000	WHITE
1970-75	−258,000	WHITE
	2,112,000	WHITE
1970-75	+258,000	NEGRO
1975	2,370,000	

1975	WHITE	89%
	NEGRO	11%

OUTLYING AREAS
"NEW TOWNS"

1970-75	355,000	WHITE GROWTH
1970-75	68,000	NEGRO GROWTH
1970-75	258,000	WHITE
1970-75	79,000	NEGRO
1975	760,000	

1975	WHITE	81%
	NEGRO	19%

rather than conflict with, the subsidized effort. For example, decent older housing will become available to lower-income persons and this will help to eliminate the irrationality of constructing expensive public housing on valuable inner-city land.

A new town is a new place and a new frontier. It is a place to make a new beginning. We already have enough experience to know that desegregation is more apt to be successful in new developments than in old and particularly so where the housing offered is regarded as a bargain. However, it is necessary to be hardheaded about the fact that whites at the present time are not likely to accept a desegregated situation if the proportion of the Negro residents to the whole exceeds a breaking point which can only be pragmatically determined in each area. It is also important that the whites be given reason to believe that the population mix will remain relatively stable. It is clear that the proportion of Negroes to whites in the new towns will reflect the extent to which governmental subsidies are employed (only thirty-eight per cent of Negro families have incomes over $7,000 a year while fifty-nine per cent of white families do). Governmental subsidies can be used, therefore, to determine generally the economic and racial composition of the new towns.

With the passage of time and the lessening of economic differences, whites will, we believe, be willing to remain in communities that have a higher proportion of Negro occupancy than may be acceptable today. If we are successful in building a significant number of substantially desegregated new towns, perhaps even the suburbs will, in time, follow the example.

The scope of the new-town program is not, as we have already seen, limited to the urban housing situation. It will have positive effects on the transportation system, on employment, on education, on land conservation. It could alter the way of life of millions of Americans, for it has the potentiality of making a real breakthrough in the unreal isolation of middle- and upper-class whites from the Negro and white residents of the city slum and ghetto areas. What could emerge are communities imbued with a sense of common participation and common purpose rather than communities divided by anger, fear, and distrust.

There are those who argue that diminishing the size of the ghetto is of such overriding importance as a national goal that its accomplishment should not be hindered by the need to gain political support for a new-town program. They say that we should build sufficient subsidized housing in outlying areas to accommodate Negro population growth and ghetto residents in ordinary subdivision development and without regard to new towns. If, in fact, the result is a more or less segregated black and white development in outlying areas, at least the size of the ghetto has been reduced. Moreover, by building sufficient surplus housing units a certain amount of desegregation could be achieved in older city and white suburban neighborhoods. We are not willing to settle for this. Respect for future generations demands that we attempt to improve the urban environment by regional planning and new-town construction which, at the same time, gives us the opportunity to achieve desegregation, improved employment opportunities for ghetto residents, and integrated education.

THE EFFECT ON THE METROPOLIS

We have proposed that new towns be built in outlying areas in accordance with a regional plan that would govern open space, transportation, and public utilities, and on a sufficient scale to create the housing surplus that is needed to bring about the necessary population movements for desegregation. What about the other parts of the region?

If we look at the region from the point of view of a business executive with responsibility for locating a new office or industrial facility, we will see that its economic strength lies in its dual nature as a labor market and as a market for goods and services. Because of this strength, metropolitan-area growth can be expected to continue, and it is better strategy to attempt to control and direct it than to try to develop entirely new cities in remote locations.

At the heart of almost every metropolitan region in the United States there is a central business district containing office buildings, department stores, theaters, and, if the region is large enough, a luxury-apartment area. The district also usually houses the cultural facilities of the region, such as museums and art galleries. It is the center of the local transportation network. Its access to the white-collar labor pool of the region as well as the proximity to those with whom a given company does business are primarily responsible for its continuing economic strength. The "downtown shopping district," which stagnated during the period of suburban development in the fifties, has revived as a further reflection of the vigor of the central business district.

The business community has long recognized its stake in the central city —a stake that runs into billions of dollars—and such things as the formation of the Urban Coalition suggest that business is now preparing to take the lead in programs designed to deal effectively with the race and urban crises. But the suburbs also have an enormous stake in the central city. The suburbs and the city are one economic unit, and the prosperity of the former is dependent on the health of the latter. Thus, despite the fact that most of the political opposition to programs concerned with central-city problems now comes from suburban residents, ultimately their interests require an understanding that the problems are mutual.

If the new federal anti-discrimination laws are vigorously enforced, they should result in some Negroes with incomes comparable to suburban residents moving into the outer ring. However, this is not likely to be significant in any near future, since for every fifteen white families able to afford suburban housing there is only one Negro family. Construction of low-income housing in the suburbs prior to making significant progress in desegregation either in new towns or elsewhere is also unlikely, for suburban residents see low-income housing as a threat to property values and to a way of life that most of them find very satisfactory.

On the other hand, anti-discrimination legislation can prove very effective in the white neighborhoods of the city and older suburbs, for there are housing accommodations in these areas that Negroes can afford. If vacancies are created by a housing surplus, if enforcement of the anti-discrimination laws is coupled with effective use of the rent-supplement program and a real rehabilitation program, and if these programs can be made to work together before decay sets in, we should be able to progress toward stable, desegregated neighborhoods in this inner part of the region. The condition of a residential neighborhood does not necessarily depend on the chronological age of the housing; there are houses in Europe four hundred years old and more that have been rehabilitated many times.

The inner city usually contains obsolescent industrial land now used for things like coal and lumber yards and railroad yards that no longer need to be centrally located. This land should be used to further the goals of the desegregation program. To the extent that industries able to provide significant employment for ghetto residents can be induced to locate here, this should be done. The Brooklyn Navy Yard is an example of land of this type. In some instances the land will also be suitable for construction of integrated apartment units serving white-collar workers in the central business district. However, the short-term goal of providing jobs for ghetto residents (black and white) should predominate.

The final result of a successful new-town program on the scale we have described will be the disappearance of the urban ghetto. In the interim, at least during the first five years, emphasis in the ghetto itself should not be on new building programs that displace more persons than they accommodate, but on programs that seek to improve the quality of education, to reduce unemployment, and to give ghetto residents a voice in the public decisions that affect their lives. What should be built in the ghetto are medical facilities, schools, libraries, neighborhood centers, and adult job-training facilities. Ghetto housing can be substantially improved by short-term rehabilitation. In Chicago, for example, a foundation with experience in rehabilitation and a local community organization are jointly sponsoring a short-term rehabilitation program designed to bring substandard housing up to code requirements in the least possible time. They have estimated that typical slum housing in Chicago can be made decent, safe, and sanitary at a cost of $500 to $700 per unit as compared to $10,000 to $15,000 per unit for permanent rehabilitation.

More important, the creation of a housing surplus will have an immediate impact on overcrowding in the ghetto. For the first time, the poor will have the power to make a real choice as to where they will live and in what type of accommodation. With overcrowding ended, ghetto rents will decrease and the artificially high value of slum buildings will disappear. Thus, the cost of acquiring slum properties will be lower when the time comes to begin reconstruction of the ghetto itself as the last stage in the program.

Ten years may be too short a time to expect the changes we have called for. Every program requires lead time. But one in five Americans moves every year, and one need only look at recent history to recognize how rapidly change is taking place in the United States. In the past ten years we have seen open country turn into subdivisions and many all-white neighborhoods become all-Negro. The changes we propose can occur as quickly. We must, of course, be wary of side effects. Uncontrolled urban sprawl was an unforeseen and unintended consequence of various federal programs; the mechanization of agriculture and the consequent migration of rural Negroes to Northern cities was, in part, a side effect of federal programs designed to aid the farmer. This sort of thing can happen in a new-town program.

We have said that our failure to cope with our urban and racial problems has been because we have lacked a strategy. The strategy we have proposed can, in fact, eliminate the ghetto, achieve desegregation, bring ghetto workers and industrial jobs together, achieve integrated education and a more efficient transportation system—in sum, create a better urban environment. Undoubtedly, other strategies can accomplish some of these goals. We know of no other strategy, however, that can accomplish all of them.

SELECTED
URBAN STATISTICS

TABLE 1. URBAN AND RURAL POPULATION, 1790 TO 1970

	Urban	Rural	Percent change from preceding census		Percent of total population	
			Urban	Rural	Urban	Rural
UNITED STATES						
Current urban definition						
1970	149,324,930	53,886,996	19.2	−0.3	73.5	26.5
1960	125,268,750	54,054,425	29.3	−0.8	69.9	30.1
1950	96,846,817	54,478,981	. . .	. . .	64.0	36.0
Previous urban definition						
1960	113,056,353	66,266,822	25.4	8.3	63.0	37.0
1950	90,128,194	61,197,604	20.6	6.5	59.6	40.4
1940	74,705,338	57,459,231	8.0	6.3	56.5	43.5
1930	69,160,599	54,042,025	27.5	4.4	56.1	43.9
1920	54,253,282	51,768,255	29.0	3.2	51.2	48.8
1910	42,064,001	50,164,495	39.2	9.1	45.6	54.4
1900	30,214,832	45,997,336	36.7	12.5	39.6	60.4
1890	22,106,265	40,873,501	56.5	13.4	35.1	64.9
1880	14,129,735	36,059,474	42.7	25.8	28.2	71.8
1870	9,902,361	28,656,010	59.3	13.6	25.7	74.3
1860	6,216,518	25,226,803	75.4	28.4	19.8	80.2
1850	3,543,716	19,648,160	92.1	29.1	15.3	84.7
1840	1,845,055	15,224,398	63.7	29.7	10.8	89.2
1830	1,127,247	11,738,773	62.6	31.2	8.8	91.2
1820	693,255	8,945,198	31.9	33.2	7.2	92.8
1810	525,459	6,714,422	63.0	34.7	7.3	92.7
1800	322,371	4,986,112	59.9	33.8	6.1	93.9
1790	201,655	3,727,559	. . .	. . .	5.1	94.9

SOURCE: United States Department of Commerce, Bureau of the Census, 1970 Census of Population, vol. 1, *Characteristics of the Population,* "Number of Inhabitants, United States Summary," PC (1) -A1, Table 18.

TABLE 2. TWENTY LARGEST CITIES IN 1970: POPULATION CHANGE, 1920 TO 1970, RACIAL COMPOSITION 1960 AND 1970, AND DENSITY 1970 (IN THOUSANDS)

City	Total Population						Racial Composition			Density 1970
							White	Negro		
	1970	Percent Change 1960-70	1960	1950	1940	1920	Change 1960-70 (Percent)	Percent of total population 1970	Percent of total population 1960	Population per square mile
1. New York	7,895	1.5	7,782	7,892	7,455	5,620	−9.3	21.2	14.0	26,343
2. Chicago	3,367	−5.2	3,550	3,621	3,397	2,702	−18.6	32.7	22.9	15,126
3. Los Angeles	2,816	13.6	2,479	1,970	1,504	577	5.4	17.9	13.5	6,079
4. Philadelphia	1,949	−2.7	2,003	2,071	1,931	1,824	−12.9	33.6	26.4	15,164
5. Detroit	1,511	−9.5	1,670	1,850	1,623	994	−29.1	43.7	28.9	10,953
6. Houston	1,233	31.4	938	596	385	138	25.5	25.7	22.9	2,841
7. Baltimore	906	−3.5	939	950	859	734	−21.4	46.4	34.7	11,568
8. Dallas	844	24.2	680	434	295	159	14.2	24.9	19.0	3,179
9. Washington	757	−1.0	764	802	663	438	−39.4	71.1	53.9	12,361
10. Cleveland	751	−14.3	876	915	878	797	−26.5	38.3	28.6	9,893
11. Indianapolis	745	56.3	476	427	387	314	7.4	19.0	20.6	1,963
12. Milwaukee	717	−3.3	741	637	587	457	−10.4	14.7	8.4	7,548
13. San Francisco	716	−3.3	740	775	635	507	−15.0	13.4	10.0	15,764
14. San Diego	697	21.6	573	334	203	74	17.2	7.6	6.0	2,199
15. San Antonio	654	11.3	588	408	254	161	9.8	7.6	7.1	3,555
16. Boston	641	−8.1	697	801	771	748	−12.4	16.3	9.1	13,936
17. Memphis	624	25.3	498	396	293	162	21.2	38.9	37.0	2,868
18. St. Louis	622	−17.0	750	857	816	773	−31.6	40.9	28.6	10,167
19. New Orleans	593	−5.4	628	570	495	387	−17.6	45.0	37.2	3,011
20. Phoenix	582	32.4	439	107	65	29	31.2	4.8	4.8	2,346

SOURCE: United States Department of Commerce, Bureau of the Census, *The Statistical Abstract of the United States, 1971*, Section 33, "Standard Metropolitan Statistical Areas with 200,000 Population or More"; United States Department of Commerce, Bureau of the Census, 1970 Census of Population, vol. 1, *Characteristics of the Population*, "Number of Inhabitants, United States Summary," PC (1)-A1, Tables 28 and 31.

TABLE 3. DISTRIBUTION OF SMSA POPULATION BETWEEN CENTRAL CITIES AND
OUTSIDE CENTRAL CITY, AND THE NATION, 1900 TO 1970
(IN PERCENT)

	National Population Within SMSA	SMSA Population Within the Central City	SMSA Population Outside the Central City
1970[1]	68.6	45.8	54.2
1960[2]	62.3	51.4	48.2
1950	59.0	58.7	41.3
1940	55.1	62.7	37.3
1930	54.3	64.6	35.4
1920	49.6	66.0	34.0
1910	43.8	64.6	35.4
1900	41.3	62.2	37.8

[1]Percentages for 1970 are based on SMSA and central city boundaries as defined in 1970.
[2]Percentages for 1960 and earlier years are based on SMSA and central city boundaries as defined in 1960.

SOURCE: United States Department of Commerce, Bureau of the Census, *The Statistical Abstract of the United States, 1971,* Section 33, "Standard Metropolitan Statistical Areas with 200,000 Population or More", Table 14, p. 16; U.S. Department of Commerce, Bureau of the Census, 1960 Census of Population, vol. 3, *Standard Metropolitan Statistical Areas,* PC (3)-ID, Table 1.

TABLE 4. SMSA POPULATION AND POPULATION CHANGE WITH RACIAL CHANGE BY SIZE CLASS, 1970 AND 1960

Size Class of SMSA in 1970	Population (In thousands)		Percent change in population 1960-1970	Proportion population change accounted for by increase outside central city	Change by Race, 1960-70 (In thousands)				Percent Negro Population			
					Inside Cent. City		Outside Cent. City		Inside Cent. City		Outside Cent. City	
	1970	1960			White	Negro	White	Negro	1970	1960	1970	1960
Total	139,374	119,581	16.6	.84	−607	3,234	5,301	820	20.6	16.3	4.8	4.8
2,000,000 or more population	52,181	46,591	12.0	1.08	−2,489	1,755	5,262	547	28.2	20.3	5.1	4.0
1,000,000 to 1,999,999	28,433	22,467	26.6	.83	322	637	4,645	182	19.5	15.4	4.0	4.1
500,000 to 999,999	21,935	18,589	18.0	.78	273	417	2,564	33	18.4	15.7	3.8	4.5
250,000 to 499,999	19,761	16,992	16.3	.71	488	238	1,779	69	14.8	13.1	5.8	6.2
Less than 250,000	17,065	14,943	14.2	.50	826	186	1,051	−11	11.3	10.5	6.0	7.2

SOURCE: Executive Office of the President—Domestic Council, *Report on National Growth 1972* (Washington, D.C.: G.P.O., 1972), Tables 9 and 11; 1970 Census of Population and Housing. *General Demographic Trends for Metropolitan Areas, 1960 to 1970, United States Summary.* PHC (2)-1, Table 9.

TABLE 5. SUMMARY OF POPULATION CHANGES FOR CENTRAL CITIES BY SIZE CLASS, INCLUDING AND EXCLUDING ANNEXATIONS, 1960–1970

Central cities by size	Total population 1970	Population Change, 1960–1970			Percent Change	
		Including annexations	Due to annexations	Excluding annexations	Including annexations	Excluding annexations
Less than 100,000	10,141,890	780,205	832,915	−52,710	8.3	−0.6
100,000 population or more	53,682,590	3,088,107	2,711,858	376,249	6.1	0.7
100,000 to 249,999	11,483,502	1,154,822	1,012,474	142,348	11.2	1.4
250,000 to 749,999	20,197,844	1,613,033	1,637,494	24,461	8.7	−0.1
750,000 or more	22,001,244	320,252	61,890	258,362	1.5	1.2

SOURCE: Report on National Growth (Washington, D.C.: G.P.O., 1972), Table 10.

682

TABLE 6. LOCAL GOVERNMENTS, BY NUMBER AND TYPE WITHIN AND OUTSIDE SMSAs, 1967

Type of local government	United States	Within SMSAs	Outside SMSAs	Percent in SMSAs
Total	81,248	20,703	60,545	25.5
School districts	21,782	5,018	16,764	23.0
Other	59,466	15,685	43,781	26.4
Counties	3,049	404	2,645	13.3
Municipalities	18,048	4,977	13,071	27.6
Townships	17,105	3,255	13,850	19.0
Special districts[1]	21,264	7,049	14,215	33.1
Dependent school systems[2]	1,608	511	1,097	31.8

[1]Largest examples include fire, natural resources, water supply, sewerage, school buildings, and housing and urban renewal districts.
[2]Not included in count of governments.

SOURCE: U.S. Department of Commerce, Bureau of the Census, Census of Governments, 1967, vol. 5, *Local Governments in Metropolitan Areas,* p. 1.

TABLE 7. NEGRO POPULATION AND ESTIMATED NET OUT-MIGRATION OF NEGROES FROM THE SOUTH: 1940 TO 1970 (IN THOUSANDS)

	Population	Out-migration[1]
1940	9,905	1,599
1950	10,222	1,473
1960	11,312	1,474
1970	11,970	—

[1]That is, 1940–1950, 1950–1960, 1960–1970.

SOURCE: U.S. Department of Commerce, Bureau of the Census, *Current Population Reports,* "The Social and Economic Status of Negroes in the United States, 1970," P-23, No. 38, July 1971, Table 5.

TABLE 8. SELECTED CHARACTERISTICS OF THE ADULT NEGRO POPULATION BY MIGRATION STATUS. FEBRUARY 1967

Subject	Rural population of rural origin	Rural-urban migrants[1] (urban population of rural origin)	Urban population of urban origin
Population, 17 years and over (thousands)[2]	2,389	2,056	7,040
Families (thousands)	836	874	2,649
Percent male head	81	74	69
Unrelated individuals (thousands)	194	329	863
Percent high school graduates	15.9	25.9	38.7
Median years of school completed	8.0	8.8	10.9
Median family income, 1966	$2,778	$5,116	$5,105
Percent population below the low income level	57.7	26.6	26.9
Percent families receiving any public assistance income, 1966	19.9	17.3	15.6

[1]Persons who have never lived more than 50 miles from their 1967 address.
[2]Population 17 years old and over by 1967 residence and residence at age 16 or earlier.

SOURCE: U.S. Department of Commerce, Bureau of the Census, *Current Population Reports,* "The Social and Economic Status of Negroes in the United States, 1970," P-23, no. 38, July 1971, Table 15.

TABLE 9. SELECTED SOCIAL AND ECONOMIC CHARACTERISTICS OF PERSONS BY CENTRAL CITY, SUBURBAN, AND METROPOLITAN AREAS

Selected Characteristics		Metropolitan Areas		Non-metro-politan areas
	Total	Inside central city	Outside central city	
EDUCATIONAL ATTAINMENT OF PERSONS 25 TO 29 YEARS, 1970				
Percent with 4 Years of High School or More				
Total	78.2	74.7	80.8	69.6
White	80.3	77.5	82.0	72.4
Negro	61.3	62.5	55.3	41.3
LABOR FORCE STATUS, 1970 (Nos. in 000s)				
Persons 16 years and over	89,919	41,367	48,552	47,445
In civilian labor force	54,157	24,832	29,325	27,536
Employed	51,729	23,638	28,092	26,241
Unemployed	2,428	1,195	1,233	1,294
Percent unemployed	4.5	4.8	4.2	4.7
Not in civilian labor force	35,762	16,535	19,227	19,909
In Armed Forces	754	224	530	407
LABOR FORCE PARTICIPATION RATES, 1970				
Male				
Total, 16 years and over	78.6	76.9	79.9	75.9
White	78.9	76.8	80.3	76.6
Negro	77.9	78.2	76.6	68.2
Female				
Total, 16 years and over	43.9	45.6	42.4	41.7
White	42.8	44.1	41.9	41.7
Negro	52.4	51.9	54.2	42.5
MEAN ANNUAL INCOME, 1969				
All races	$11,506	$10,450	$12,348	$8,872
White	11,958	11,124	12,516	9,185
Negro	7,725	7,575	8,291	4,972
Negro, as a % of white	64.6	68.1	66.2	54.1
% DISTRIBUTION OF PERSONS BELOW POVERTY LEVEL, 1969				
All races	9.5	13.4	6.3	17.1
White	7.3	10.2	5.4	13.5
Negro	24.4	24.7	23.2	41.4

FAMILY CHARACTERISTICS, 1969
Average Size

All races	3.6	3.5	3.7	3.6
White	3.5	3.3	3.7	3.5
Negro	4.2	4.1	4.4	4.7
Type (by parent)				
Husband-Wife	86	82	90	88
Other male head	3	3	2	2
Female head	11	15	8	10
POPULATION DISTRIBUTION BY MEDIAN AGE, 1969	28.4	30.0	27.2	28.0

SOURCE: U.S. Department of Commerce, Bureau of the Census, *Current Population Reports,* "Trends in Social and Economic Conditions in Metropolitan and Nonmetropolitan Areas," P-23, No. 33, September 3, 1970, Tables 9, 10, 12, and 13; and "Social and Economic Characteristics of the Population in Metropolitan and Nonmetropolitan Areas: 1970 and 1960," P-23, No. 37, June 24, 1971, Tables B, C, and D.

TABLE 10. EMPLOYMENT PATTERN FOR FIVE LARGE METROPOLITAN AREAS, 1951–1965

	Number of new jobs		
	City	Suburbs	Metropolitan areas
Baltimore	1,450	86,086	87,536
New York	127,753	387,873	515,626
Philadelphia	−49,461	215,296	165,835
St. Louis	−61,800	141,911	80,111
San Francisco	9,346	185,742	195,089

SOURCE: Report of the National Commission on Urban Problems, *Building the American City* (Washington, D.C.: G.P.O, 1969), Table 18.

TABLE 11. SELECTED CHARACTERISTICS OF THE TWENTY LARGEST SMSAs

SMSA by Rank, 1970	Population		Population Central City Percent of SMSA	Personal Income 1969		Physicians per 100,000 Population 1970
	Total 1970 (In thousands)	Change 1960–70 (Percent)		Per Capita	Ave. Annual Rate of Growth, 1959–69	
United States	203,166	13.3	45.5	$3,688	6.88	148.3
1. New York, N.Y.	11,529	7.8	68.2	5,055	6.33	279.4
2. Los Angeles-Long Beach, Calif.	7,032	16.4	45.1	4,728	6.81	202.0
3. Chicago, Ill.	6,979	12.2	48.2	4,678	6.20	169.7
4. Philadelphia, Pa.-N.J.	4,818	10.9	40.4	4,028	6.01	201.5
5. Detroit, Mich.	4,200	11.6	36.0	4,677	7.44	138.6
6. San Francisco-Oakland, Calif.	3,110	17.4	34.6	3,126	7.47	147.9
7. Washington, D.C.-Md.-Va.	2,861	38.6	26.4	4,359	8.48	196.2
8. Boston, Mass.[1]	2,754	6.1	23.3	4,281*	6.62*	262.4*
9. Pittsburgh, Pa.	2,401	−0.2	60.1	3,807	4.88	148.5
10. St Louis, Mo.-Ill.	2,363	12.3	26.3	3,993	6.15	155.4
11. Baltimore, Md.	2,071	14.8	43.7	3,856	6.95	231.7
12. Cleveland, Ohio	2,064	8.1	36.4	4,393	6.00	201.0
13. Houston, Tex.	1,985	40.0	62.1	3,674	8.22	152.2
14. Newark, N.J.	1,857	9.9	20.6	4,755	6.62	191.5
15. Minneapolis-St. Paul, Minn.	1,814	22.4	41.0	4,419	7.57	170.9
16. Dallas, Tex.	1,556	39.0	54.3	4,052	8.59	155.7
17. Seattle-Everett, Wash.	1,422	28.4	61.8	4,463	7.82	202.8
18. Anaheim-Santa Ana-Garden Grove, Cal.	1,420	101.8	31.4	4,141	12.01	155.4
19. Milwaukee, Wisc.	1,404	9.8	51.1	4,215	5.74	148.7
20. Atlanta, Ga.	1,390	36.7	35.7	3,993	9.31	161.6

*Data refers to the larger Boston SEA (State Economic Area), rather than the Boston SMSA.

SOURCE: United States Department of Commerce, Bureau of the Census, *The Statistical Abstract of the United States, 1971,* Section 33, "Standard Metropolitan Statistical Areas with 200,000 Population or More."

Housing Units in One-Unit Structures 1970 (Percent)	Local Governments, 1967		Public Assistance February 1971			Crime Rate per 100,000 Population 1970
	Property Taxes per Capita	General expenditures per capita	Total payments (In thousands)	Families with Dependent children Total no. of recipients	Aver. payment per family	Total
69.4	$129	$247	$807,369	9,648,400	$187	2,741
28.3	454	454	104,489	1,001,106	272	5,220
60.1	209	356	65,907	623,489	210	5,064
46.6	153	241	33,141	379,203	245	2,789
72.5	114	223	31,412	332,433	261	2,079
70.5	150	292	20,080	189,164	235	5,149
58.5	242	400	24,013	232,766	179	5,329
54.0	127	309	6,569	89,844	199	4,111
43.7	217	318	19,350*	165,691*	262*	3,098*
70.9	106	204	10,928	112,293	240	2,030
66.0	128	212	8,296	137,232	155	3,556
83.8	132	259	8,079	129,745	165	4,370
58.8	170	242	8,437	110,969	197	3,083
73.9	123	196	3,337	59,880	126	3,593
47.5	212	307	10,718	140,520	258	3,480
63.3	176	293	7,082	70,514	256	3,246
70.4	121	187	2,986	53,265	120	4,139
70.6	114	264	5,504	58,327	221	4,133
68.2	193	302	4,590	56,319	178	3,587
55.0	182	297	4,855	49,879	220	1,999
77.6	112	214	3,129	66,048	102	3,568

**TABLE 12. POPULATION AND PUBLIC ASSISTANCE PROPORTIONS FOR SELECTED
MAJOR CITY-COUNTIES**

	City proportion of statewide totals of:		
City	*Population* *(1965)*	*All public* *assistance* *recipients* *(June 1966)*	*AFDC* *recipients* *only* *(June 1966)*
New York City	44.2	70.2	71.7
Philadelphia	17.8	29.6	32.8
Baltimore	26.8	66.4	71.2
Boston	13.6	32.0	38.4
San Francisco	3.9	4.9	4.6
St. Louis	15.5	25.5	37.1
Denver	25.1	34.5	43.2

SOURCE: Report of the National Commission on Urban Problems, *Building the American City*
(Washington, D.C: G.P.O., 1969), Table 9.

TABLE 13. PERSONS BELOW THE LOW-INCOME LEVEL IN 1970, BY SEX AND ETHNIC ORIGIN OF HEAD, MARCH 1971 (IN THOUSANDS)

Number below the low-income level and sex of head	Total population			Spanish Origin		
	All races[1]	White[2]	Negro	Total[3]	Mexican	Puerto Rican
All persons	25,522	17,480	7,650	2,177	1,407	424
In families with male head and male unrelated individuals	14,310	10,667	3,362	1,430	1,003	207
In families with female head and female unrelated individuals	11,212	6,813	4,288	746	404	218
Percent Below Low-Income Level						
All persons	12.6	9.9	33.6	24.3	28.0	29.2
In families with male head and male unrelated individuals	8.3	6.8	21.7	19.2	22.9	20.9
In families with female head and female unrelated individuals	38.4	31.5	59.0	50.0	62.4	47.5

[1]Includes person of "other races," not shown separately.
[2]Includes almost all persons reporting Spanish origin.
[3]Includes persons of Central or South American, Cuban, and other Spanish origin, not shown separately.

NOTE: The low-income concept used here, formerly called the poverty level, classifies families and unrelated individuals as being above or below the low-income level, using cutoffs adjusted to take account of such factors as family size, sex and age of family head, number of children, and farm-nonfarm residence. In 1970 the low-income thresholds ranged from about $1,950 for an unrelated individual to $6,470 for a family of seven or more persons. The threshold for a nonfarm family of four was $3,968.

SOURCE: U.S. Department of Commerce, Bureau of the Census, *Current Population Reports*, "Selected Characteristics of Persons and Families of Mexican, Puerto Rican, and Other Spanish Origin: March 1971," P-20, No. 224, October 1971, Table 5.

TABLE 14. SUBEMPLOYMENT RATE AND UNEMPLOYMENT RATE IN GHETTO AREAS, 1966 (IN PERCENT)

	Unemployment	Subemployment
Boston	6.9	24
Cleveland	15.6	49
New Orleans	10.0	45
New York:		
Harlem	8.1	29
East Harlem	9.0	33
Bedford-Stuyvesant	6.2	28
Philadelphia	11.0	34
Phoenix	13.2	42
St. Louis	12.9	39
San Antonio	8.1	47
San Francisco	11.1	25

NOTE: The subemployment index covers an entire employment hardship area and takes into account not only the traditionally "unemployed" (those actively seeking work but unable to find it) and the working poor (heads of households earning less than $60 a week and individuals over 65 earning less than $56 a week); but also those working part time but seeking full-time jobs; half the number of nonparticipants in the male age group 20-64 who are not in the labor force; and a "conservative and careful considered estimate of the male 'undercount' group."

SOURCE: Report of the National Commission on Urban Problems, *Building the American City* (Washington, D.C.: G.P.O., 1969), Table 21.

TABLE 15. PERCENTAGE OF NONWHITE OCCUPIED HOUSING UNITS DEEMED IN VIOLATION OF LOCAL HOUSING CODE BY VIRTUE OF CENSUS CLASSIFICATION. FOURTEEN LARGE U.S. CITIES, 1960

	Percent
New York	42
Chicago	43
Los Angeles	18
Philadelphia	32
Detroit	30
Baltimore	32
Houston	37
Cleveland	34
Washington, D.C.	21
St Louis	52
San Francisco	34
Dallas	46
New Orleans	57
Pittsburgh	59

NOTE: Dilapidated, deteriorating, or sound but lacking certain plumbing facilities. These classifications do *not* cover all housing code violations.

SOURCE: Report of the National Commission on Urban Problems, *Building the American City* (Washington, D.C.: G.P.O.), Table 8.

TABLE 16. VICTIMS AND ASSAILANTS BY TYPE OF CRIME IN SEVENTEEN CITIES, 1967

Subject and race	Type of crime				
	Homicide	Aggravated assault	Rape	Armed robbery	Unarmed robbery
Total crimes	3,274	75,198	7,908	54,942	51,255
Negro victims	70	68	60	40	38
With Negro assailants	66	66	60	38	37
With white assailants	4	2	0	2	1
White victims	31	32	41	60	62
With Negro assailants	7	8	11	47	44
With white assailants	24	24	30	13	18

NOTE: The seventeen cities included are: Atlanta, Boston, Chicago, Cleveland, Dallas, Denver, Detroit, Los Angeles, Miami, Minneapolis, New Orleans, New York City, Philadelphia, St. Louis, San Francisco, Seattle, Washington, D.C.

SOURCE: U.S. Department of Commerce, Bureau of the Census, *Current Population Reports,* "The Social and Economic Status of Negroes in the United States, 1970," P-23, No. 38, July 1971, Table 84.

TABLE 17. MUNICIPAL GOVERNMENT REVENUE BY SOURCE, 1957 TO 1966–1967 (IN MILLIONS OF DOLLARS)

Item	1966–67 Census of Governments	1962 Census of Governments	1957 Census of Governments	Percent Increase 1962 to 1966–67	Percent Increase 1957 to 1962
REVENUE					
REVENUE, TOTAL	24,096	16,794	12,047	43	39
GENERAL REVENUE	19,283	13,127	9,285	47	41
INTERGOVERNMENTAL REVENUE	5,081	2,668	1,756	90	52
FROM STATE GOVERNMENT ONLY	4,001	2,128	1,489	88	43
GENERAL REVENUE FROM OWN SOURCES	14,202	10,459	7,529	36	39
TAXES	10,507	7,940	5,908	32	34
PROPERTY	7,351	5,812	4,297	26	35
SALES AND GROSS RECEIPTS	1,645	1,302	934	26	40
GENERAL	977	866	602	13	44
SELECTIVE	669	437	332	53	32
OTHER	1,511	824	676	83	22
CHARGES AND MISCELLANEOUS	3,695	2,519	1,621	47	55
UTILITY REVENUE	4,043	3,136	2,378	29	32
LIQUOR STORES REVENUE	97	77	60	26	28
INSURANCE TRUST REVENUE	672	454	323	48	41

SOURCE: U.S. Department of Commerce, Bureau of the Census, *1967 Census of Governments*, Vol. 4, *Government Finance*. No. 4, "Finances of Municipal and Township Governments," Table 1.

TABLE 18. MUNICIPAL GOVERNMENT EXPENDITURE BY FUNCTION, 1958 TO 1968–1969

Function	Total expenditures (In billions) 1958	Total expenditures (In billions) 1968–1969	Percent of total expenditure 1958	Percent of total expenditure 1968–1969	Percent increase from 1958 to 1968–1969
Education	1.6	4.0	16	18	150
Police protection	1.1	2.6	10	11	140
Highways	1.5	2.3	14	9	53
Public welfare	0.5	2.1	5	9	320
Fire protection	0.8	1.6	7	6	100
Hospitals	0.7	1.3	2	5	86
Sewerage	1.2	2.4	7	10	100
Parks and recreation	0.5	1.1	5	4	120
Housing and urban development	0.5	1.0	5	4	100
Other	2.0	6.1	29	26	140
Total general expenditure	10.4	24.5	100	100	136

SOURCE: International City Management Association, *The Municipal Yearbook, 1972* (Washington, D.C., 1972), Table 1/2.

TABLE 19. LEVELS OF PER CAPITA FINANCE IN SMSAs BY SIZE Group, 1966–1967

SMSA size group (1966 population)	Average per capita amount Total revenue[1]	Average per capita amount General revenue[1]	Average per capita amount Direct expenditure	Average per capita amount Total debt
1,000,000 or more	$409.94	$367.41	$417.31	$539.30
500,000 to 999,999	320.48	286.49	335.32	458.10
300,000 to 499,999	304.21	275.23	317.72	405.80
200,000 to 299,999	292.77	267.03	303.83	364.74
100,000 to 199,999	273.77	249.57	286.49	362.27
50,000 to 99,999	258.85	235.78	268.99	320.01

[1]Excluding interlocal revenue.

SOURCE: U.S. Department of Commerce, Bureau of the Census, *1967 Census of Governments,* vol. 5, *Local Government in Metropolitan Areas, p. 7.*

SELECTED
BIBLIOGRAPHY OF
URBAN STATISTICS

International City Management Association. *The Municipal Yearbook.* Washington, D.C.

United States Department of Labor, Bureau of Labor Statistics: various

United States Department of Commerce, Bureau of the Census:
Census of Business
Census of County Business Patterns
Census of Governments
Census of Housing
    vol. I   *Housing Characteristics for States, Cities, and Counties*
            Series HC (1)
            Chap. A. *General Housing Characteristics* Series HC (1)-A
            Chap. B. *Detailed Housing Characteristics* Series HC (1)-B
    vol. II   *Metropolitan Housing Characteristics* Series HC (2)
    vol. III *Block Statistics* Series HC (3)
    vol. IV *Components of Inventory Changes*
    vol. V   *Residential Finance*
    vol. VI *Estimates of "Substandard" Housing*
    vol. VII *Subject Reports*

Census of Population:
    vol. I   *Characteristics of the Population* Series PC (1)
            Chap. A. *Number of Inhabitants* Series PC (1)-A
            Chap. B. *General Population Characteristics* Series PC (1)-B
            Chap. C. *General Social and Economic Characteristics* Series PC (1)-C
            Chap. D. *Detailed Characteristics* Series PC (1)-D
    vol. II   *Subject Reports* Series PC (2)

vol. III   *Selected Area Reports*   Series PC (3)

Census of Population and Housing:
    vol. I   *Census Tract Reports*   Series PHC (1)
    vol. II   *General Demographic Trends for Metropolitan Areas, 1960
              to 1970*   Series PHC (2)
    vol. III   *Employment Profile of Selected Low-Income Areas*   Series
              PHC (3)

County and City Data Book

Current Population Reports, Series:
    P-20   *Population Characteristics*
    P-23   *Special Studies*
    P-25   *Population Estimates*
    P-28   *Special Censuses*
    P-60   *Consumer Income*

Statistical Abstract of the United States
Directory of Federal Statistics for Local Areas, A Guide to Sources
Directory of Federal Statistics for States, A Guide to Sources
Directory of Non-federal Statistics for States and Local Areas